MYTHOLOGY

MYTHS, LEGENDS, & FANTASIES

MYTHOLOGY

MYTHS, LEGENDS, & FANTASIES

Grange
BOOKS

CONTRIBUTORS

Greg Bailey is a reader in Sanskrit at La Trobe University in Melbourne, Australia. Greg has published books and articles on Hindu mythology, Buddhism, and contemporary Australian mythology. He teaches Sanskrit, Indian, and Religious Studies at La Trobe University, and is presently completing the translation of a mythological text about the elephant-headed god, Ganesha.

Michael Carden completed his Ph.D. in Biblical Studies at the University of Queensland in 2002. His dissertation examined interpretations of the story of Sodom and Gomorrah in Judaism, Christianity, and Islam. He has taught in the areas of biblical studies, comparative religion, and religion and contemporary studies in the Religion Department at the University of Queensland. In 1999, he introduced a course on Religion and Sexuality, the only course of its kind in Australia. He is contributing two chapters—on Genesis and on the Twelve Minor Prophets—for the Bible in Translesbigay Perspective, an international project to be published in 2005. Outside of academia, he has had a long involvement in community work on sexuality, HIV/AIDS, and social justice issues.

Dr. Philip Clarke has an academic background in biology, geography, and anthropology. After studying at the University of Adelaide in Australia, he started working in the Aboriginal ethnographical collections at the South Australian Museum in 1982. Dr. Clarke's research interests back then were chiefly Aboriginal use of plants as foods, medicines, and materials for making artifacts. This eventually broadened out to Aboriginal perception and use of the land, with a particular focus on the cultural geography of southern Australia. This research produced a number of publications on Aboriginal mythology. From the early 1990s, Dr. Clarke has mainly worked in central and northern Australia, investigating Aboriginal links to the land. A major project at the South Australian Museum was the repatriation of Aboriginal men's secret sacred objects back to senior cultural custodians. During 1998–2000 his major task was curating the Australian Aboriginal Cultures Gallery Project. Dr. Clarke is presently the Head of Anthropology and Manager of Sciences at the South Australian Museum.

Dr. Elizabeth Dimock is a Research Associate in the African Research Institute at La Trobe University, Melbourne, Australia. She has lived and worked in Africa, and her research interests have been concerned with colonial histories of Africa and African women's history. More recently she has been involved with the history of African communities in Victoria, Australia, and settlement problems faced by Africans after migration.

Christine El Mahdy is an Egyptologist. She became fascinated with the subject at the age of seven, and was reading hieroglyphs before she was nine. Today she is the Professor of Egyptian Studies at the British Centre for Egyptian Studies, a distance learning provider, which she founded in 2000. She has written and broadcast material on ancient Egypt for more than 30 years, as well as lecturing widely. Over the years she has made more than a hundred visits to Egypt, taking many people to sites rarely seen. Previous books include *Exploring the World of the Pharaohs; Mummies, Myth and Magic;* and *Tutankhamen, Life and Death of the Boy-King.* She lives in Hampshire, England, with her twin daughters Nadine and Yasmine.

Denise Imwold is a writer and editor from Sydney, Australia, who has also worked for many years as a bookseller. She studied literature and anthropology at Macquarie University, where she received a Bachelor of Arts, as well as a Postgraduate Diploma in Editing and Publishing. Denise has contributed to a wide range of publications in fields such as travel, literature, sport, gardening, health, and spirituality. Currently she is writing her first novel, which draws inspiration from Irish mythology and history. Her interests include reading, walking, animals, and traveling, and she finds special joy in visiting sacred places.

Deanna Paniataaq Kingston is half King Island Inupiaq Eskimo and an Assistant Professor of Anthropology at Oregon State University, U.S.A. She conducts research with the King Island Native Community and teaches about Native North Americans, natural resources, and oral traditions. Her primary interests are in folklore, songs, dances, oral traditions, ethnohistory, and visual anthropology. Dr. Kingston earned her Ph.D. in Anthropology from the University of Alaska Fairbanks in 1999. Her dissertation is entitled "Returning: Twentieth Century Performances of the King Island Wolf Dance." She currently lives in Corvallis, Oregon, U.S.A., with her son and husband.

Dr. 'Okusitino Mahina holds a Ph.D. in Pacific History from the Australian National University located in Canberra, Australia. His doctoral thesis examined the formal and functional relationships between oral and written history. Dr. Mahina has taught at both 'Atenisi University in Tonga and Massey University, Albany Campus, Auckland, New Zealand. He currently teaches Pacific political economy and Pacific arts in the Department of Anthropology at the University of Auckland, New Zealand, and has been published in each of these fascinating fields. Dr. Mahina has also published poetry, mainly in the Tongan language. His areas of research interests include time and space, culture and history, language and art, and political economy and development.

Hugo McCann was born in Ireland in 1937. He was educated in Belfast and Tasmania, after immigrating to Australia. He taught in high schools in Ireland in the sixties and, in the next two decades, taught literature for children and general literature to education students. At the same time, he taught philosophy to teachers. Hugo has been a lecturer in drama in Australia and worked in theater in Ireland. He is now retired and living in Tasmania.

Dr. Alice Mills is an associate professor of literature and children's literature at the University of Ballarat located in the Australian state of Victoria. One of the many interesting subjects that she teaches is Myth and Mythmaking. She began learning Latin when she was just 11 years old, then classical Greek when she was 12, and has had a lifelong interest in the mythical stories and characters that underlie contemporary Western culture. Dr. Mills has published many scholarly articles on the topics of children's literature and fantasy, and has edited several anthologies of children's literature including the Random House *Treasury of Children's Literature.* She is also a Jungian psychotherapist and she brings Jung's ideas about the human psyche to bear on her understanding of the ancient myths of Greece and Rome.

Antone Minard received his Ph.D. in the subject of Folklore and Mythology from the University of California, Los Angeles, in 2002, with an emphasis on folkloric material as it appears in the literature of medieval Europe. He has also done research into ethnicity and identity, especially his own family's experiences as Italian-Americans. As Stott Fellow at the University of Wales's Centre for Advanced Welsh and Celtic Studies in Aberystwyth, Wales (from January 2001), he is engaged in preparations for an Atlas of Celtic Studies, a multidisciplinary resource designed as an introduction to Celtic Studies with data from archaeology, history, linguistics, and literature.

Dr. Peter Orton was born in Leicester, England, and completed his Ph.D. thesis at the University of Exeter on the transmission of Old English verse-texts. He taught at University College, Dublin, for several years, following a series of temporary appointments at the University of Leeds, during which he first began to study Old Norse. He now lectures in Old English, Old Icelandic, and the history of English at the University of London. Special research interests of his are the Old English elegies, on which he has been extensively published, and the meter and style of Germanic alliterative verse. He is also particularly interested in the possible correlations between Old Norse and Old English mythological, poetic, and epigraphical traditions.

Simon Roberts was born in Hobart, Tasmania (Australia), in 1964. His interest in mythology was ignited when, as a child, his father read him the Greek myths and brought them to life. More recently he fell in love with the Icelandic sagas and developed an avid interest in the mythology of northern Europe. He worked as an Air Traffic Controller for six years before graduating with a Bachelor of Law in 1995. He currently works for the Tasmanian Department of Police and Public Safety. Simon has previously written entries for *Trees and Shrubs* (Global Book Publishing, 2000). A keen traveler, Simon has recently settled back in Tasmania about a hundred meters from the hospital in which he was born.

Mark Anthony Rolo is a member of the Bad River Band of Ojibwe in Wisconsin, U.S.A. He holds a bachelor's degree from the University of Minnesota-Twin Cities. He has reported on Native American affairs and arts for numerous publications, and is the former Washington D.C. correspondent for *Indian Country Today.* Mark also served as executive director of the Native American Journalists Association. He edited *The American Indian and the Media— Second Edition,* which is a resource guide for journalists covering Native American issues. Mark has also written and produced work for the theatrical stage. He continues to write plays and articles about Native American communities.

Dr. Paul Rule completed an honors degree in history at the University of Melbourne located in Victoria, Australia, and a doctorate in Asian Studies at the Australian National University in Canberra. Until 2002 he was the Senior Lecturer in History at La Trobe University in Melbourne, and formerly he was Director of the Religious Studies program at that same university. He taught courses on Chinese and Aboriginal religions, religious theory, and modern Catholicism. Paul's research and publications include *K'ung-tzu or Confucius? The Jesuit Interpretation of Confucianism* as well as books and articles on Christianity in China, other Chinese religions, Australian Aboriginal religion, and peace and justice issues. He has been Editor for the Australian Association for the Study of Religions and a member of the Australian Catholic Social Justice Council. At present he spends part of each year at the Ricci Institute for Chinese–Western Cultural History at the University of San Francisco as EDS–Stewart Distinguished Fellow working on a history of the Chinese Rites Controversy.

Rudolf Simek was born in Austria in 1954. He completed his Ph.D. in Vienna in 1980, a Masters in Theology in 1981, and a PhilHabil in 1990. His main fields of research are pre-Christian Germanic religion, Viking Age Culture, and Medieval Scandinavian nonfictional prose literature. Rudolf has worked at numerous universities in Europe and internationally and has had guest professorships and academic exchanges with educational institutions in Bergen, Catania, Cagliari, Kracòw, Durham, Krems, Reykjavík, and Rome. As well as lecturing around the world, Rudolf has had research stays in cities as far afield as London, Reykjavík, and Sydney. He is currently the Head of the German Department at the University of Bonn.

Dr. Elisabeth Stuchbury spent three years in the northwestern region of the Himalayas. The resulting anthropological fieldwork, which took place in a small Tibetan hermitage, was the basis for her extensive academic research. She received a Ph.D. from the research School of Pacific and Asian Studies at the Australian National University located in Canberra, and continued her research with a Post-Doctoral Fellowship from the Australian Research Council. She has taught in several different universities throughout Australia and has presented the results of her research internationally in lectures and publications. During her time in the northwestern part of the Himalayas, Elisabeth also began her engagement with the practice of Vajrayana Buddhism. She has recently left the academy, continuing her work in a more expansive environment. Chögyal Namkhai Norbu, a renowned Dzogchen master of the Tibetan tradition and Professor Emeritus from the University of Naples, Italy, continues to inspire and guide her. She has a prominent position within his international following.

Rawiri Taonui is of Maori descent from the tribes of Nga Puhinuitonu, Ngati Maniapoto, Te Aupouri, and Te Rarawa. He lectures at the Department of History, University of Auckland, Aotearoa–New Zealand and teaches in the areas of Maori Oral Tradition, the Treaty of Waitangi, Indigenous Issues, and Human Rights. He has also taught in Maori Studies and Pacific Studies. Rawiri's research covers oral tradition; the politics of treaties and settlements with indigenous peoples in Aotearoa–New Zealand, Canada, and Australia; and human rights. He has written extensively for magazines and newspapers including *The New Zealand Herald*. In 2001 he received the internationally recognized Qantas Media Award for the "Best New Zealand Columnist on the Human Condition." He has recently finished writing and co-producing the documentary series *Hawaiki*, which traces the origins of the Maori and Polynesian peoples.

Geo Athena Trevarthen completed her M.Sc. (Magna Cum Laude) in 1997, focusing on Old Irish texts, and received her interdisciplinary Ph.D. in July, 2003. Her research focus is Pagan Celtic religion and mythology, including its shamanistic elements and underlying cosmology. She also has a thorough knowledge of Welsh mythological sources and recently led a retreat at Glastonbury with a focus on Arthurian mythology. She has developed and currently teaches a course on Pagan Celtic religion for Edinburgh University's Open Studies, and tutors for the Celtic Civilisation course in Celtic and Scottish Studies. As well, Geo has developed a website for general readers, www.celticshamanism.com, which also features much of her own artwork. She lives in Edinburgh, Scotland.

Ramona Louise Wheeler is a science fiction writer, whose stories appear regularly in the premier SF magazine in the world, *Analog*. Her best-known works, the *Ray and Rokey* series, are collected in two volumes: *Have Starship, Will Travel* and *Starship For Hire*. Ramona Wheeler's essays on Egyptian religion and literature, as well as comparative mythology, began appearing online in 1995. These writings were subsequently published as *Walk Like An Egyptian, A Modern Guide To The Religion And Philosophy Of Ancient Egypt*. A third edition will include the only full translation of the ancient Egyptian calendar and horoscope available in an English-language print edition. Ramona has owned and operated Tokapu Graphics since 1976, producing promotional publications for local music bands. She lives in Massachusetts, U.S.A.

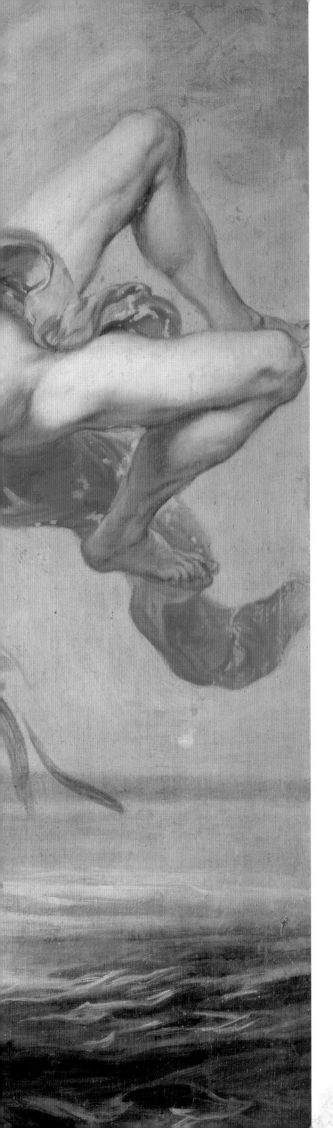

CONTENTS

WHAT IS MYTHOLOGY?

All myths are stories of a special kind. They are not realistic tales—not stories of people doing ordinary things in an ordinary world. Instead, they tend to be about extraordinary characters in a world that is not our ordinary waking reality, a world that is sometimes full of magic and sometimes full of gods and goddesses, where the earth can be alive and animals can talk. Most myths are stories set in a time that cannot be measured by the clock, or a time before clock time began; when great suffering and pleasure can last for eons. They are like fairy tales that tend to begin "Once upon a time," except that most fairy tales have a happy ending and many of the world's myths end in tragedy.

Myths are significant stories for their culture, and their significance sometimes resonates over millennia and far beyond their original culture. Myths permeate every culture, and are borrowed, retold, and live again in fresh imaginings. They are the stories of cultural beginnings, of

Therefore, even the lover of myth is in a sense a philosopher; for myth is composed of wonders.

ARISTOTLE (384–322 B.C.)

how people's lives and ways of thinking came to be shaped, and they still help to shape the way that many people understand themselves and the world.

THE PURPOSE OF MYTHS

Some myths are explanatory, posing and offering the answers to questions that puzzle the philosophers. What is the beginning of life? How did human beings come to exist? What happens after death? Are there gods and goddesses, and if so, what are they like and how should humans behave toward them? How will the world end? What is the best way to die? Such questions cannot be answered from a purely rational framework, and the greatest philosophers have sometimes resorted to the language of myth to treat such issues.

Some myths are etiological, explaining the range of phenomena in the world. Why is this mountain shaped the way it is? Who or what hollowed out this waterhole? How did this river come to rise in just this spot? What is the cause of eclipses? What do the constellations represent? Many etiological myths offer answers that science casts aside, as science has its own rational explanations for celestial visitors like comets and eclipses, phenomena of the weather, geological formations, and the like, but these myths still offer a truth of the imagination, if not the scientific truth that can be weighed and calculated and predicted.

Some myths legitimate a particular people or a ruling family, and they are among the most changeable of myths, as ruling dynasties change and as empires grow and fall. Rulers in cultures

Right *Storyteller with Villagers* by
Giacomo Mantegazza (1853–1920).
Traveling storytellers would captivate
the crowd in each new village with
tales of divine realms and heroic
quests, sometimes entwining local
lore in the myths from other places.

friendly to myth are often legitimated by direct descent from a god. Myths give the peoples of the world reasons for ritual, and enforce certain social behaviors with promises of divine favor and real threats of divine punishment. Especially in tribal cultures, myths are potent means of socializing children into the ways of the people. Myths lay down the many important rules, for instance, for the right behavior toward animals that are hunted, or set up the precedent for a people's system of law. There is no area of traditional life unaffected by myth.

The writers of most myths are anonymous, as many tales go back before the invention of writing, and few can be traced back to an original teller of the tale. In times before literacy was widespread, in the days before the printing press, such tales were told and retold countless times. Some cultures valued the precise words of their myths as sacred texts given to them by the gods, and they sought to transmit their myths in exactly the same way, by a strenuous program in which the myth-tellers were trained in word-for-word memorization. Other cultures enjoyed varying the elements of the story, so that each time the myth was retold, it would be slightly different, with its listeners enjoying the variations as part of the pleasure of hearing this particular version of the traditional tale. There is rarely just one correct version of Greek and Roman or Arthurian myths, for instance.

With the introduction of the printing press, myths were collected and written down in fixed form, and this helped the fixing of myths in one version, rather than their endless variation in spoken form. But words are not the only medium in which myths have been transmitted. Myths can be told via sacred artworks or carvings on rocks, via special dances or music, and ritual enactment. The magnificent images in this book represent the visual component of many myths in their own cultural setting (and in those of the other cultures that have subsequently taken them up). For some myths, the words only gesture toward the totality of an evocation of a myth in such forms as chanting, drumming, body decoration, and dance. It was through such bodily participation, using all the senses, that those celebrating a specific myth moved toward the experience of mythic time and space.

As well as evoking mythic space, beyond the space of ordinary waking reality, many myths point to a real and specific location in a mythic time. Here, on this rock, was where the hero rescued the maiden. This very mountain was once a giant. This volcano housed the monster, its lava heaving and surging with the creature's efforts to free itself. This wood or this icy expanse housed a supernatural being that was perilous for human beings to meet. Such stories can offer a deep satisfaction to listeners who are familiar with the landscape so infused with mythic power. For such myths, the supernatural is evident everywhere around, and what happened in mythic time and space resonates with the here and now.

Above *Montezuma Sighting the Comet* by Diego Duran (1537–1588). In 1519 the Aztec ruler Montezuma saw a comet and believed it foretold the return of the much-loved god Quetzalcoatl. Later that year the Spanish conqueror Hernando Cortés arrived in Mexico, and the Aztecs mistook him for Quetzalcoatl.

Right **The Hindu god Krishna surrounded by his milk carriers.** In his youth, Krishna—the eighth incarnation of the god Vishnu—fell in love with the milkmaid Radha. This perfect spiritual love is represented in the Raas Lila dances, and symbolizes the union of masculinity and femininity, as well as humanity and deity.

UNDERSTANDING MYTHS

There have been a great many attempts to explain myths in rational terms. Perhaps some of the heroes of mythology commemorate the distant, distorted memory of human beings who once lived. If so, the historical explanation does not explain just why the particular myths developed in the way that they did, just why these characters and no others grew into figures of myth. Certainly some myths glorify a kingdom or city, give divine sanction to conquest and colonization, but this does not explain why such myths can outlast the kingdom or the empire by millennia. There is something powerful about myths that transcends both reason and the boundaries of a culture.

Perhaps the truth is that all peoples have a thirst for insights into the mysteries of life, from the origin of consciousness to the end of the world. Myths tend to have an enduring power because they do not limit the world to statistically verifiable facts and figures, because they people the familiar world with wonder and marvel, and because they intersect humanity with the world of the animals and that of the gods. To explore the world of myth is to find a range of beliefs about the world from the stoic to the pessimistic, from the tragic to the comic— but never the neutral. Some myths set out to celebrate the trickster, others the hero; all stretch our ways of perceiving the world, and have the power to lift us away from our mental habits. In a world full of fear, loneliness, and alienation, myths can console with stories of a more heroic, more chivalrous time, one when it was a lot easier to determine the difference between good and evil in the hearts of human beings, and when animals and people were the same kind of

being and could talk together quite easily. Myths have always spoken to people's longing for meaning, a longing that is especially poignant, perhaps, in what seems to be an increasingly secular Western society.

JUNGIAN THEORY OF MYTH

Carl Jung speaks of the psychological truths of myth, which he claims to be universal and necessary for the health of the human psyche. We need the stories of myth, he claims, to make sense of the confusion of our society and our own psyches. Myths voice the truths of our unconscious selves, and he believes the gods, goddesses, and heroes of myth embody aspects of creativity, cleverness, grief, joy, aggression, and ecstasy. The monsters of myth are really monsters of

Above **Ram mask, Baoulé culture.** From the Ivory Coast in western Africa, the Baoulé are famous for their remarkable masks. Many were used in sacred ceremonies designed to appeal to gods such as Gu and Alouroua for help with rainfall and fertility.

The fascinating myths in this collection are all stories from times past, whether collected last century or recorded thousands of years ago. The creation of new myths became less possible when the printing press came into popular use, with its ability to fix one form of a story as the correct version. With the advent of radio, film, television, and video came more fixed-form stories that discouraged the art of telling and retelling traditional stories over and over again. The Internet has reversed this trend, and myth may once again flourish in chat rooms and e-mail transmissions, on a scale far beyond that of the ancients. How could such new myths be recognized? Would it take a time-scale of centuries to determine which stories, if any, lasted and gained the cultural resonance of ancient myths? Perhaps some potentially powerful myths can be detected in the process of development even now.

Even in the most secular of centuries, ancient mythic patterns have recurred. The belief that some hold in the survival of Elvis looks back to the Near Eastern myths of a dying vegetation god who comes back to life each spring, and to the myths of European nations that say their national hero is not dead, but merely in seclusion until he is needed again. The surge of grief at the death of Princess Diana resonates with the surge of grief across the world at the untimely death of the Norse god Baldr. The Gaia hypothesis revives the ancient mythic idea of a living earth goddess, whose wrath has been slowly aroused by human beings' increasing mistreatment of her. The most popular work of fiction in the twentieth century, J.R.R. Tolkien's *The Lord of the Rings*, takes up many different elements of Germanic and Finnish mythology and reshapes them, imagining them afresh to reexamine ideas of the hero and the quest. Perhaps in another millennium, hobbits and the "One Ring" will be part of traditional myth, along with that mythical figure Elvis and that lost Princess Diana. Myths are not only ancient tales of wonder and glory, but they are all around us, in the making.

the mind; the tragedies and triumphs of myth reflect upon the ways in which we seem to be tossed to and fro psychologically by forces that are beyond our control. Human beings are myth-makers by nature, always curious, always psychologically living out the patterns of myth or being lived out by them. In psychological terms, according to this theory, we are always in one mythic pattern or another, and our freedom of choice as conscious human beings is the freedom to dance rather than stumble our way through the greatest story in the world—life.

Below *The Werewolf* by Lucas Cranach the Elder (1472–1553). The werewolf is one of the most well-known and feared mythological creatures in the world. It is prominent in the stories of Europe, and an ancient Greek tale tells of Zeus transforming King Lycaon into a wolf. This Greek myth inspired the word "lycanthrope"—meaning a person who can change into a wolf—as *lykos* is Greek for "wolf" and *anthropos* means "man."

Left **Basilisk.** Renowned for its ability to kill with just one look, the basilisk (also known as the cockatrice) is represented as a large snakelike creature. It is often seen in old European tales, and has once again come to the fore in popular culture with its appearance in J.K. Rowlings's book *Harry Potter and the Chamber of Secrets*.

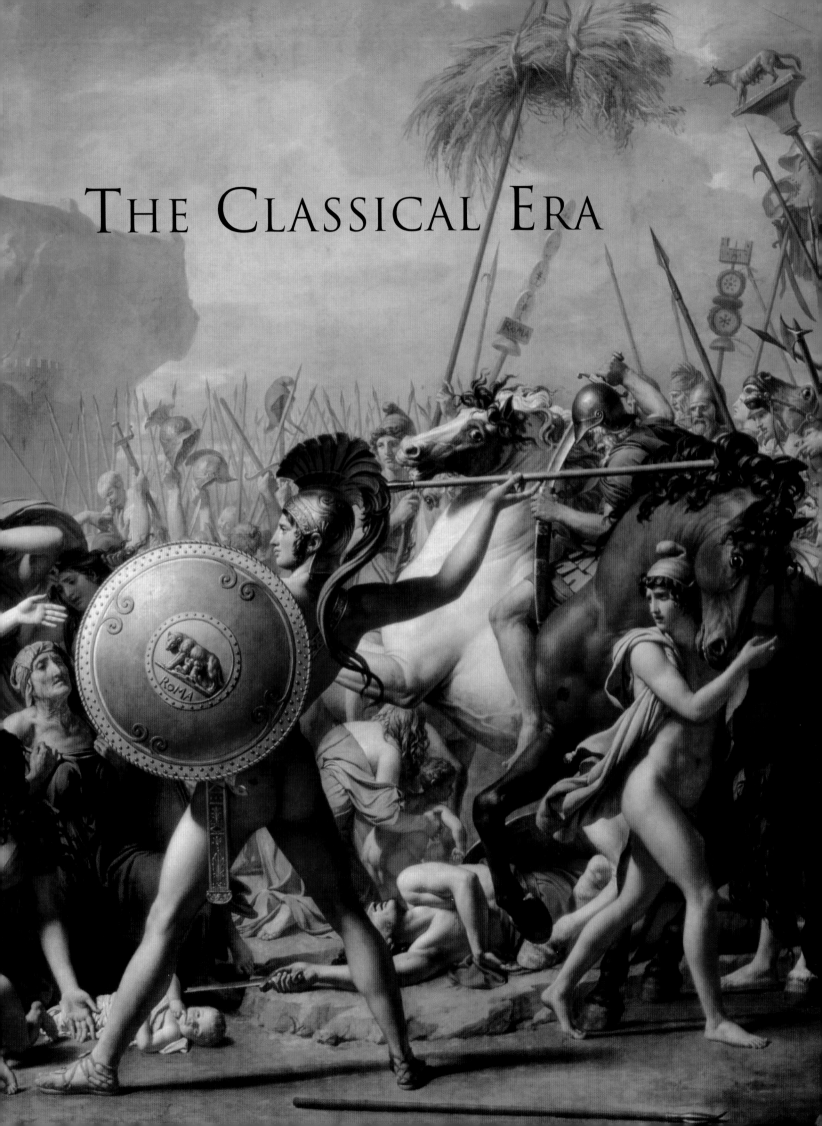

THE CLASSICAL ERA

GREEK AND ROMAN MYTHOLOGY

Below *Zeus and Hera* by Ambrogio Figino (*c.* 1550–*c.* 1595). The goddess Hera was honored by the Greeks as the goddess of women, marriage, and childbirth. However, Zeus's wandering eye meant Hera spent much of her time plotting revenge against his lovers.

When Westerners think of myth, they think in terms of Greek and Roman myths. For Western culture, Greek and Roman myths are the foundation of myth, with their well-worked-out stories of gods and heroes, wars to fight and monsters to defeat, and families suffering their way through the workings of a curse. No other myth system is so familiar, or permeates Western culture so thoroughly. The Greeks produced the most culturally resilient myths that the world has known, partly because their myths concern the middle of things rather than their beginnings or endings. Their myths do not focus primarily on how things came into being. Hephaestus (Vulcan) invents individual items for the first time, but most Greek and Roman myth takes place well after the world has come into being, and the gods and their antagonists are already in place. Greek and Roman myth is equally unconcerned with endings, with questions of how the world ends or what happens after death. There are stories of heroes descending into the underworld for brief visits, but only the philosophers spent much time speaking about the fate of the soul. Greek and Roman myth focuses on the here and now of life for the gods feasting and quarreling on Olympus, for heroes seeking immortal fame, for both gods and mortals wanting revenge. Its themes are divine and human hopes and pains, disappointments, and tricks and transformations. These myths are not often set in sacred space, but take place among fallible characters—the gods being as fallible, temperamental, irascible, and prone to tantrums as any human being. Such stories transcend cultural boundaries.

The Gods

The gods of Greek myth, and of Roman retellings of Greek myths, are much closer to human beings than the gods of most other mythologies. They endlessly interact with human beings. In Greek and Roman daily life, any girl out on her own fetching water or visiting a temple, any ship on a voyage over the wine-dark sea, any trader wanting to make a profit, anyone wanting to gain revenge or to win love, was aware of the gods' powers to change a human life. Anyone wanting to know about the future relied on the gods' priests and priestesses to transmit their words of truth. In the myths, the gods regularly took on the disguise of human bodies to tease and test human beings. This meant that one of the gods might at any time substitute for a member of your family, your neighbor, the person you worked for. A prime directive of Greek myth was to honor and be generous to strangers, for no one could be

certain just who was human and who might be a god in disguise. The gods took many other nonhuman forms, especially when they came to Earth in search of desirable human beings to rape or take as lovers, and they also took the form of ideas, inspirations, moments of particular clarity, or confusion. When Ares (Mars) walked on the battlefield, battle frenzy, terror, and fear accompanied him. When Athene (Minerva) accompanied her favorite hero, Odysseus (Ulysses), she whispered bright ideas to him, so that the hero's ingenious mind became indistinguishable from the cleverness of the goddess. When Eros (Cupid) struck someone with his arrow, the overwhelming desire and love that he inflicted was felt both as falling in love and as an affliction sent by the god. Aphrodite (Venus) made her favorites gleam and glow with beauty. Hera (Juno) clothed her favorites with stately majesty. Human beings' glory was the glory of the gods, for who could tell the inspiration of the gods from that of the humans that they befriended, harassed, and molested?

These gods were not moral beings. The gods of Greece and Rome were neither good nor bad. They are best described as being more like energies, whose use could be judged right or wrong, fair or unfair by humans, but they used their powers without being bound by any system of morality. The only thing that they insisted upon was proper respect from mortals. Many of the myths of Greece concern people who claimed to be equal to the gods or had the insolence to set themselves up as

greater than the gods. Such claims attracted instant retribution. The gods did not always punish murderers, but they always punished those who dared to act insolently toward them.

The gods of the Greeks are the most human of the gods of myth, but with powers that often destroyed the humans with whom they mixed. To take a god as one's lover often led to suffering and death. To resist a god's attentions, however, guaranteed an unpleasant fate. These gods also had favorites. Aphrodite favored Paris, the Trojan prince who gave her the apple destined for the fairest of the goddesses. Artemis (Diana) favored those who loved the hunt and vowed themselves to chastity. Zeus (Jupiter) took an interest in the rulers of the world, and wars that involved the whole of the known world. Ares loved battle, and Athene loved subtlety of mind. Hermes (Mercury) could not resist a clever liar and thief.

Greek myth is as alive and changeable as fairy tales. Retellings of fairy tales frequently put forward very different details to the story, especially its ending. In Greek and Roman times, different

Top left **Zeus flanked by soldiers while being nursed.** While the nymphs nursed Zeus, it is said that the Curetes danced about, clashing their spears and shields to hide the child's cries from Cronus. The Curetes were believed to be semidivine counterparts of Cretan youths who performed ritual dances to honor Zeus.

Left *Eros* by Praxiteles (*c.* 400 B.C.–*c.* 330 B.C.). Over time, there came to be many different traditions and perceptions of the god of love. The Greeks named him Eros, referring to love of a sexual kind, while the Romans called him Amor, meaning love, or Cupid, meaning desire.

NAMING THE GODS

NAME IN GREEK MYTHOLOGY	NAME IN ROMAN MYTHOLOGY
AIAS	AJAX
APHRODITE	VENUS
ARTEMIS	DIANA
ASCLEPIUS	AESCULAPIUS
ATHENE	MINERVA
CRONUS	SATURNUS
DEMETER	CERES
DIONYSUS	BACCHUS
EOS	AURORA
EROS	CUPID
HADES	PLUTO
HECABE	HECUBA
HELIUS	SOL
HEPHAESTUS	VULCAN
HERA	JUNO
HERACLES	HERCULES
HERMES	MERCURY
HESTIA	VESTA
HYPNUS	SOMNUS
NYX	NOX
ODYSSEUS	ULYSSES
OURANUS	URANUS
PERSEPHONE	PROSERPINA
POLYDEUCES	POLLUX
POSEIDON	NEPTUNE
RHEA	CYBELE
ZEUS	JUPITER

versions of the myths kept arising. Greek drama transfigured the heroes and gods from noble to villainous, from scandalous to blameless. Genealogers reconfigured family trees to suit the local nobility for whom they worked. As a result of this, there is very rarely one, and only one, right version of a Greek or Roman myth.

The Myths of Heroes

The myths of the Greek and Roman heroes merge into history. Many myth systems set their myths in sacred time, a dream time, or a time outside human chronology. For the ancient Greeks, the myths of the fathers of the gods were longer ago, but still in time that could be measured in years. The hero myths were believed to be history of just a few generations ago, when the Trojans and Greeks fought over Helen of Troy, or a couple of generations before that, when Heracles (Hercules) walked the earth and the Argonauts went in quest of the Golden Fleece. For modern scholars, these myths merge into history in a different way, by reflecting such events as the collapse of the Minoan empire or the development of trading routes north of the Black Sea. The myths were also a source of local prestige and every town and city wanted to claim that one of the heroes was born or buried there. There are discrepancies between different lists of the Argonauts, fostering the claims of different city-states to have sent a hero

on the quest for the Golden Fleece. There were only 50 places available on the Argo, but in the story of the Trojan War, the number of ships sent by the Greeks was easily expanded to fit in new claimants. In this way, modifying the myths remade local history.

Greek myths also merge into everyday geography. Many of the details of the myths are quite specific about the mountain path where a monster used to lurk, or the temple where a god raped a girl, or the route taken by a ship keeping close to land. These locatable details merge into mythic space, which cannot be reconciled with the details of the atlas. In the story of Odysseus's return, for instance, the journey of his son Telemachus can be mapped accurately to show where Mycenae and Pylos are located, but it is a fruitless endeavor to try to locate the island of the Sirens or the land of the Lotus-Eaters from Odysseus's travels. Even Odysseus's Ithaca, described in loving detail by the Greek poet Homer, cannot be mapped with confidence on the island now called Ithaca. Mount Olympus stands in Greece, but in our everyday reality it does not house the gods of Greek and Roman myth. They live on in the mythic geography of the imagination.

Perhaps the stories of Greek gods and heroes live on also in everyday psychology. Carl Jung argues that the Greek myths (like all others) tell truths about the human psyche, especially those overpowering impulses and uncontrollable behaviors that affect groups rather than individuals. Jungians would see

the god Ares in action as nations go to war, Hermes playing the trickster in every business that tries to lie and deceive its way through financial difficulties, Dionysian energies at work at rave parties, Aphrodite's glamor evident in each new film starlet's box office appeal, and the hero's descent to the underworld in every bout of depression. To this way of thinking, the Greek gods do not live on Mount Olympus, but their stories can be read afresh in every news broadcast or newspaper headline. Greek myths are more often than not remarkably specific in their location, but for the Jungians, their psychological truths transcend the millennia and are still being acted out today by people all over the world.

Thus have the gods spun the thread for wretched mortals: that they live in grief while they themselves are without cares

HOMER (800 B.C.–700 B.C.), *THE ILIAD*

The Romans were not great inventors of myths like the Greeks. They were great empire builders, and in the course of exploring, conquering, and administering nations, they assimilated each nation's myths. Where a similarity could be found between gods, for instance, this was interpreted as signifying the same god under different titles. Thus the Greek goddess Athene was assimilated into the Etruscan and Roman goddess Minerva. In the following collection of myths, the Greek names of gods and humans are given first and then the Roman equivalent, except for the two sections on Myths of the Romans and the Roman tale of Aeneas, which put forward the Roman names first.

Above *The Rape of Helen* by Gavin Hamilton (1723–1798). Although some authors refer to the "rape" or "abduction" of Helen, other scholars are not so convinced. Many believe that Helen chose to go with Paris of her own accord because she fell in love with him.

IDENTIFYING THE GODS

When they are not in disguise, each of the Greek and Roman gods can be recognized by their body features or their special emblems. These emblems may be weapons or they may be animals and birds that are always associated with them. Zeus (Jupiter), for example, wields the thunderbolt as his weapon, and his bird is the eagle. Athene (Minerva) is associated with the owl, while Aphrodite (Venus) is associated with the dove and Hera (Juno) with the peacock. As messenger for the gods, Hermes (Mercury) has small wings at each ankle and a winged cap. He carries the caduceus, a staff whose handle is made up of intertwined snakes.

The emblem of Cronus (Saturnus) is the sickle with which he mutilated his father, but since he is often confused with Chronos, the god of time, he is sometimes represented as an old man with an hourglass. If that is the case, the artist has introduced emblems of time that should in fact belong to Chronos.

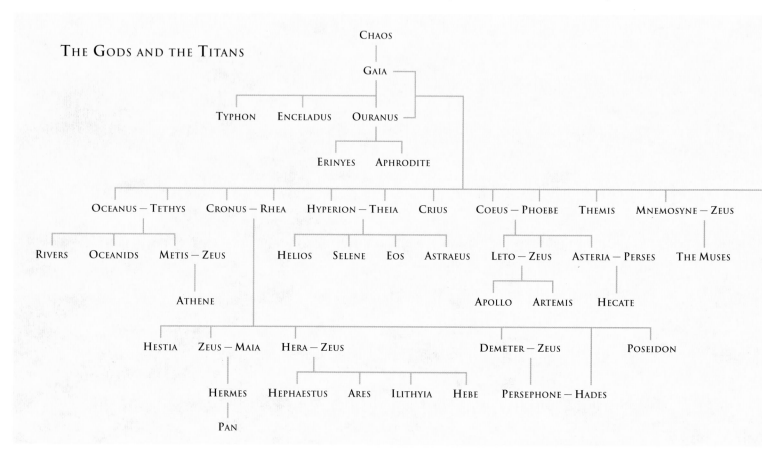

Right *Zeus and the Eagle* by the Naukratis Painter *c.* 575 B.C. In some tales, Zeus is simply accompanied by an eagle, his special emblem, whereas in other tales, he is actually transformed into the bird itself.

THE FATHERS OF THE GODS

There is no all-powerful, all-wise, and totally good father god in Greek myth. Instead, the story of the gods of Olympus is a complicated tale of crime, conspiracy, mutilation, and murder. One god after another claimed sovereign power, but their hold on kingship was shaky. Pictures and sculptures often show the gods sitting in confident majesty, but the myths tell a different tale.

How it all began was really never quite clear. Was there a gigantic egg, perhaps, from which hatched Eros (Cupid), the god of love? Did everything start off as a giant chaos of water and mud, fire and air, from which Earth slowly came into being? Was Chaos a god, whose wife was Nyx (Nox), the goddess of night? And did their son Erebus overthrow Chaos before he was overthrown in turn by his children Aether and Hemera, Light and Day? Or perhaps was the goddess of Earth, Gaia (or Ge) there from the very beginning, giving birth to the seas, the mountains, and the sky?

Gaia and Ouranus

The ancient Greeks thought of the earth-mother goddess Gaia as a gentle giver of life and nourisher of all her children. And she had a multitude of children. From the union of Gaia and her son, the sky god Ouranus (Uranus), were born a family of gods who were called the Titans. Oceanus was the Titan god of the great oceanic river that forever circles the world, and Tethys was his sister and wife. The Titan Hyperion was the first sun god, and his sister-wife was Theia. Coeus and Phoebe the moon goddess, Cronus (identified by the Romans with

THE GODS AND THE TITANS

CHAOS

GAIA

TYPHON ENCELADUS OURANUS

ERINYES APHRODITE

OCEANUS — TETHYS   CRONUS — RHEA   HYPERION — THEIA   CRIUS   COEUS — PHOEBE   THEMIS   MNEMOSYNE — ZEUS

RIVERS   OCEANIDS   METIS — ZEUS   HELIOS   SELENE   EOS   ASTRAEUS   LETO — ZEUS   ASTERIA — PERSES   THE MUSES

ATHENE

APOLLO   ARTEMIS   HECATE

HESTIA   ZEUS — MAIA   HERA — ZEUS   DEMETER — ZEUS   POSEIDON

HERMES   HEPHAESTUS   ARES   ILITHYIA   HEBE   PERSEPHONE — HADES

PAN

their god Saturnus) and Rhea (identified with the goddess Cybele), Crius, Japetus, Themis (the goddess of justice), and Mnemosyne (the goddess of memory), made up the rest of the 12 Titans. Gaia also gave birth to the Hundred-Handed Giants and to the Cyclopes, giants who each had a single eye in the middle of his forehead. Gaia had many grandchildren, including the three Fates, and the nine Muses, and the two young Titans Prometheus and Epimetheus.

Ouranus did not allow his children to see the light of day, because he was afraid of their power. Perhaps he was mindful of his family history, the overthrow of Chaos by his son Erebus, and then of Erebus by his children. Even though Ouranus ruled all the wide heavens, his sons and daughters were forced to stay underground, chained in the black cavern of Tartarus. Gaia became angry with her husband, and encouraged her children to conspire against him. Her youngest child, Cronus (Saturnus), made himself ruler of the world when he attacked and castrated Ouranus with a sickle. He threw Ouranus's severed genitals into the ocean, and where they fell the sea foamed up and gave birth to Aphrodite (Venus), the beautiful goddess of sexual

desire and love. Drops of Ouranus's blood fell to the ground and from them were born the Erinyes, Furies who torment the minds of criminals.

How Zeus Overthrew His Father

Cronus was as fearful a king as his father, Ouranus, and for better reason. Cronus's mother Gaia had once prophesied that one of his children would grow up to overthrow him, or perhaps the words were uttered as a curse from his mutilated father's mouth. Cronus and Rhea had three male children, Poseidon (Neptune), Hades (Pluto), and Zeus (Jupiter), and three female children, Hestia (Vesta), Hera (Juno), and Demeter (Ceres).

As soon as each baby was born, Cronus swallowed it whole, and there it stayed in his stomach helplessly. Rhea was determined to stop her husband from eating his children, but she was afraid of his great strength. She needed to overthrow him not by force but by trickery.

When she was about to give birth to her youngest child, Zeus, she hid a large stone in her bed, and when Cronus demanded the child, she offered him the stone instead. Cronus must have gulped the stone down, because he did not notice the trick, and Rhea hid her newborn son in a cave. The goat Amaltheia supplied him with milk to drink, and he was fed honey by the bees. Rhea asked some minor deities, the Curetes, to keep her child safe, and when he cried, they made a loud noise with their spears and shields so that Cronus would not hear the baby.

As soon as the child Zeus was strong enough, he forced his father to vomit up all the babies that he had swallowed, then threw him underground to Tartarus again. Some myths say that Cronus was not imprisoned in the depths of Tartarus but lives on in Elysium. The fields of Elysium are the place where the fortunate dead, those who have pleased the gods,

Left **The birth of Aphrodite.** The goddess of love, beauty, and sexual ecstasy, Aphrodite was born from the *aphros* (Greek for "sea foam") that was churned up where Cronus cast the severed genitals of his father, Ouranus, into the ocean. Some myths say Aphrodite was carried by the sea to Cyprus, others say to Cythera.

Above *Cronus Devouring His Son* by Peter Paul Rubens (1577–1640). Cronus was always shown carrying the sickle with which he castrated his father. He swallowed his children whole as soon as each was born.

JAPETUS — CLYMENE   CYCLOPES   HECATONCHEIRES
(HUNDRED-HANDED GIANTS)

PROMETHEUS   EPIMETHEUS — PANDORA

War With the Titans and Other Troubles

But before the troubles of the human race began, Zeus had to deal with his brothers and sisters. He married his sister Hera, gave dominion over the hearth to Hestia, and put Demeter in charge of the crops and the world's fertility. Zeus and his brothers divided up the kingship of the world, with Poseidon taking charge of the oceans and Zeus, as oldest brother, becoming king of the gods. It is because Rhea's other children were all born again from their father's belly that Zeus is considered to be both the youngest and the oldest of her sons. Hades was given the underworld to rule, and he was not satisfied with his share. That is why Hades so rarely appears in Greek myth, for he usually keeps his distance from the other gods who, in turn, do not care to visit Hades' realm. Instead, most of the greater gods of Greek myth have their palaces on Mount Olympus (an actual mountain in Thessaly).

Only four of Gaia's other children accepted Zeus as ruler of the gods. The rest went to war with the gods of Olympus, and they seemed likely to win by sheer numbers. Zeus remembered the Hundred-Handed Giants and the Cyclopes, who were still chained down in Tartarus. He offered them freedom on the condition that the Hundred-Handed Giants would fight alongside the gods of Olympus, and the Cyclopes would forge a weapon that no god, no Titan, and no monster could withstand. Zeus soon gained his weapon, the jagged thunderbolt, but even with its help he took 10 years to bring the war to an end and cast the rebels into Tartarus.

The war against the Titans was over, but Gaia was angry with Zeus for seizing power from the rest of her children. She gave birth to the hundred-headed giants Typhon (Typhoeus) and Enceladus, who could breathe fire and pile mountain upon mountain. The gods of Olympus were terrified at the sight of these giants and started to run away to Egypt, disguising themselves as animals. To escape Typhon's attention, Hades put on a helmet of invisibility, made for him by the Cyclopes. The giant Typhon took Dionysus (Bacchus) by surprise on the banks of the Nile, and the god jumped into the river, transforming himself immediately into a creature that was part-goat and part-fish; the constellation of Capricorn commemorates this event. Aphrodite and Eros disguised themselves as fish, a transformation which

Above *Enceladus Buried Underneath Mount Etna* by Bernard Picart (1673–1733). Giants differed from mortals mostly in their size rather than in their appearance, but some giants were much larger than the rest. The hundred-headed, fire-breathing giant Enceladus was so enormous that he had to be buried underneath Mount Etna in order to be subdued.

enjoy a most happy existence. Nothing about his treatment of his children would have pleased the next generation of gods, but although Cronus was the worst of fathers to his own children, he was a generous ruler over humankind. The age of Cronus is called the Age of Gold, when the earth provided food without the need for labor, and murder was unknown to humans who lived peacefully together. As soon as Cronus was cast down from his throne by his son, the Age of Silver began, and the seasons came into being. Then came the Age of Bronze, an age of war, and finally the Age of Iron, an age of toil and injustice, crime and punishment. This is the age which all of humankind is still suffering through.

It is not possible either to trick or escape the mind of Zeus.

HESIOD (C. EIGHTH CENTURY B.C.), THEOGONY

Opposite page *Four Ages of Life* by Pietro da Cortona (1596–1664). The Age of Gold was a tranquil era devoted to peaceful existence.

THE GAIA HYPOTHESIS

The idea that Earth is a living goddess has long been rejected by science, and played no part in the development of the earth sciences, biology, or meteorology. In 1979, however, James Lovelock published *Gaia: A New Look at Life on Earth*, a book in which he argues for something like the idea of a nurturing earth goddess. He puts forward the Gaia hypothesis that all that is alive on Earth can be understood as one organism. Just as human beings regulate their own body temperature, for example, the planet

Earth seems to regulate its temperature to exactly the range needed for life to survive. The Gaia hypothesis talks of a planet that is friendly to the life on its surface, just like the Greek goddess Gaia, the mother and nurturer of all life.

Right **Goddess of Earth.** Gaia, once thought of as the source of all the gods in Greece, later fell from favor. She is often depicted suckling her children, and is shown here with the mother goddess Thalassa.

is commemorated in the constellation of Pisces. Even Zeus, king of the gods, disguised himself as a ram. Zeus alone found the courage to return and fight each of the giants with his new weapon, the thunderbolt. The struggle was fierce and, even when the giants were defeated, Enceladus kept on breathing fire, writhing in his prison under Mount Etna. That is why Etna is such an active volcano; each time the giant tries to break free, the earth shakes, and each time he breathes fire, lava spouts into the air.

The Children of Zeus

Zeus was married to Hera, goddess of marriage, and their sons were the god of war, Ares (Mars) and the blacksmith god Hephaestus (Vulcan); but he fathered many other children, who, if their mother was a goddess, were born gods and goddesses. Apollo, the sun god, and Artemis (Diana), the moon goddess and huntress, were the children of Zeus and Leto. Hera was so jealous that she did not allow Leto to stay anywhere on solid earth when it was time for her to give birth. Only the floating island of Ortygia gave her sanctuary, and as a reward, it became fixed with pillars of adamant. Hermes (Mercury) was the son of Zeus and the minor goddess Maia, and the maiden Persephone (Proserpina) was the daughter of Zeus and Demeter.

Zeus's first wife was the goddess of wise prudence, the Titan Metis, daughter of Oceanus and Tethys. Gaia prophesied that, like his father and grandfather, Zeus would be overthrown by a son. She said that Metis was destined to give birth first to a strong-minded daughter and then to a son who would be the next ruler of gods and men. Zeus

found a way to avoid this prophecy: he promptly swallowed the pregnant Metis, as his father Cronus had swallowed his children, so that she would have only the one child, a daughter. Metis's daughter grew within the body of her father until one day his head started to ache unbearably, so badly that he ordered Hephaestus to take an ax and split his brains open. Out sprang his daughter, the goddess Athene (Minerva), already dressed in full armor and ready for battle.

Even though Athene was born as a fully grown warrior goddess, she was not about to challenge her father or try to rescue her mother in the same way that Cronus had challenged Ouranus and Zeus had rescued his brothers and sisters from the stomach of his father. When Zeus had swallowed Metis, he was incorporating prudence and wisdom into his life, and this put an end to the cycle of resentment and anger that had brought about the overthrow of his father and grandfather and generations before them. Athene was Zeus's favorite daughter and was always loyal to her father. She was the goddess of craft and craftiness, cleverness and ingenuity, and she enjoyed the trick that her father had played on the Fates. With the birth of Athene, a pattern of murderous hate and fear between parent and child in the family of the Olympian gods comes to an end.

Opposite page **Detail from *Zeus Launching His Thunderbolts* by Giulio Romano (c. 1499–1546).** As well as being the ruler of the gods, Zeus was believed to be the weather god. He controlled thunder, rain, and lightning. He used thunderbolts as his main weapons of war.

Left **Warrior goddess.** The goddess Athene, daughter of Zeus, was renowned for her clever strategies and practical wisdom. She was the goddess of war, industry, craft, and justice.

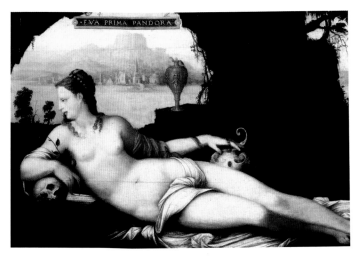

Left *Eva Prima Pandora (Eve, the First Pandora)* by Jean Cousin, the Father, (c. 1490–c. 1560). Hephaestus created Pandora, and the gods endowed her with many gifts. Among them were the gift of beauty from Aphrodite and the gift of music from Apollo.

so many fireplaces that the gods could never put them all out. Prometheus had given humankind one of the greatest gifts of civilization.

Pandora

Zeus was furious, but he decided not to use the thunderbolt to gain his revenge. Instead, he played a trick of his own on the Titans and humankind. He was wary of trying to trick the clever Prometheus, but he was quite confident that his brother, at least, could be easily fooled, for Epimetheus, the one who looked backward, was not the cleverest of Titans. Zeus asked Hephaestus (Vulcan), the blacksmith god, to make a beautiful woman out of clay, and he named her Pandora (a name that means "full of all gifts"). Zeus put in Pandora's arms a large box that was closed and sealed, and told his son Hermes (Mercury) to take her to Epimetheus as a bride, a present from the gods.

Prometheus warned his brother to be very wary of any gifts coming from Zeus, who had no reason to be friendly, but Epimetheus saw how beautiful Pandora was and decided to marry her. Hermes had told her never to open the box, and for days and weeks she tried not to think about it, but every day

she felt more curious about its contents. Surely there must be something very precious in there, she thought, and it was unfair of the gods to give her something and then forbid her to enjoy it. In the end she broke the seals and opened the box. Out flew all the diseases, sorrows, and disasters that afflict humankind. Pandora tried to close the box, but more and more troubles surged out, covering the whole Earth. The only thing that she was able to keep hold of was Hope.

One version of the story of Pandora tries to excuse the behavior of the gods. If, in fact, Hope was in the bottom of the box, surely the rest of its contents must have been equally delightful. In this version, the box was really brimful of good things, the gods' gifts from Olympus, and all of them except Hope are lost to us through the curiosity of a foolish woman.

This story of how evil came into the world (or goodness was lost) through a woman's folly is reminiscent of the biblical story of how Eve was tempted to eat the apple, which brought death into the world along with other woes. Some theologians have argued that the myth of Pandora is a faint reflection of biblical truth. Secular critics of myth often classify all stories that blame women for the introduction of evil into the world as a product of a patriarchal society. Where men are in power, who better to blame for evil than women?

Above *Pandora Opens the Box* by Walter Crane (1845–1915). In one version of this myth, Pandora released all types of disasters on humankind. In another, the box was full of her wedding presents— gifts and blessings given to her by the gods.

VIRGO AND LIBRA

The Age of Gold was the first age of the world, without hardship or toil for those who dwelt on Earth, and was without crime. The most recent age of the world, full of troubles and evils, is called the Age of Iron, but perhaps it would be better to call it the Second Age of Gold, for many of its troubles began when gold first tempted humankind to wickedness and war. Through the Ages of Gold, Silver, and Bronze, Astraea, the goddess of justice, still remained on Earth, but when the Age of Iron began, she found she could stay here no longer. Now she shines down from the sky as the constellation Virgo, the virgin. Astraea once carried a pair of scales with which she weighed up the rights and wrongs of any dispute. Now Astraea's scales shine close by Virgo, as the constellation Libra.

Opposite page **The chariot of Mercury and Virgo.** Astraea, which means "the star maiden," was the last deity to leave Earth. She and her scales became constellations.

The Punishment of Prometheus

Humankind was now punished with the contents of Pandora's box, and the next target for Zeus's revenge was Prometheus. Not only had the Titan disobeyed Zeus, stealing fire for humankind, but he was also keeping a dangerous secret. He had heard a prophecy that the goddess Thetis would give birth to a son destined to overthrow his father. Zeus knew part of the prophecy, but not the name of the goddess.

Above **Deucalion and Flood by J. Briot (c. 1610).** Some believe that Zeus's main reason for wanting to destroy humankind was because he was alarmed that so many gods continued to have children with the mortals, making humans more powerful.

Below **Zeus throwing a thunderbolt.** Zeus's name is from an Indo-European word meaning "to shine." He was the god of the sky and all its phenomena.

TALES OF ZEUS

After the horrors of Lycaon's banquet, Zeus (Jupiter) decided that the whole of humankind deserved to die. The other gods thought anxiously about their temples and their festivals. Who would make sure that the sweet smells of sacrifice would continue to rise up to Mount Olympus if there were no more human beings? Who would be left to worship the gods? Zeus promised that the human race would not die out completely. He would find a way for a new breed of humans to come into being, people who would be properly respectful of the gods and careful to observe every festival with its proper rituals.

Zeus stood on Mount Olympus with the thunderbolt in his hand, choosing his first target. He was just about to hurl the thunderbolt into the marketplace of the closest city when he remembered a prophecy that the world was doomed to end in fire. Carefully, he laid aside his weapon, for he wished to cleanse the world, not to destroy it utterly. "Let the waters carry my revenge and then subside," he decreed, "so that life can return once more."

As he spoke, the winds began to blow up a tempest. The South Wind gathered black storm clouds that poured their rain down onto the land. The crops were washed away; this year, all of humankind would go hungry. But Zeus was not satisfied with this revenge. He wanted not just to hurt the troublesome human race, but to drown almost all of them.

He called to his brother Poseidon (Neptune), lord of the sea. Poseidon commanded all the rivers and streams of the world to flood, and then he struck the surface of the earth with his trident. Poseidon is sometimes known as the Earth Shaker, and on this day he shook the earth until it cracked open, letting the sea flood in. Gigantic waves smashed across the land. Cities were washed away. No temple, no palace, could stand against the roaring tide. There was no more boundary between earth and water, nowhere to take refuge on solid land, and when people tried to outride the storm by taking refuge in ships, they ended up starving to death on the ocean.

Deucalion and Pyrrha

Almost every human being was now dead. Only two people, Deucalion and Pyrrha, were still alive, afloat on the ocean in a small boat, and Zeus knew that if the human race were to survive, he would have to let these two live. Deucalion was the son of Prometheus and Pyrrha the daughter of Epimetheus, but they were neither disobedient nor stupid. In fact they were the best of humans, and always quick to honor the gods. They would make the best possible parents for the new race of human beings.

Little by little, the ocean grew calm and the highest peaks of mountains began to appear. As the flood receded, the two summits of Mount Parnassus, which before and since the flood reared high enough into the heavens to pierce the clouds, now pierced the surface of the ocean, and the little boat stuck between them. The first thing that Deucalion and Pyrrha did was to give thanks to the gods of Mount Parnassus and pray for their help, as they watched the waters diminish and the mountain grow tall again.

From their vantage point high on the mountain, Deucalion and Pyrrha could see far across the countryside. They watched as the rivers began to flow once more within their banks and the trees shook mud off their leaves. They could now see the ruined temple of Themis, but no other signs that humans had

ever lived on Earth. Quickly, they walked down to the River Cephisus and sprinkled drops of its water onto their wet clothes and wet hair, as a mark of respect for the goddess. Then they knelt down close to the temple, praying that Themis would help them rescue the entire human race from extinction.

Themis is a gentle goddess who is remarkably skilled at foretelling the future. She announced to Deucalion and Pyrrha, "You must walk away from the temple, veiling your heads and loosening your garments, throwing behind you the bones of your mother." Pyrrha was totally

Zeus is the air,
Zeus the earth, Zeus all things
and what transcends them all.

AESCHYLUS (525 B.C.–456 B.C.),
FRAGMENTS

appalled at the thought of digging up the grave of her mother and throwing away her bones, but then she remembered that oracles usually spoke in riddles. Together with Deucalion, she puzzled over the goddess's command. "The oracle would never tell us to do anything that would offend the gods," said Deucalion. "The mother that she speaks of, must mean the great mother of all, Gaia the earth goddess, and the mother's bones must be the stones in the ground."

Neither Deucalion nor Pyrrha was confident that this was what the oracle meant, but they could think

Below **Poseidon on his chariot.** Poseidon, the god of the sea, lived in the ocean and drove a chariot pulled by horses. One of his emblems was a trident, with which he would strike the ground to cause tidal waves and earthquakes.

of no better interpretation of her words. With their heads veiled and their garments loosened, they picked up stones from the muddy ground and began to walk away from the temple. At every step they threw a stone or two behind them. Each stone, as it fell back into the mud, started to change shape and grow larger. They began to look like roughly carved marble statues, then like statues as big as life, and finally they grew warm and started to breathe. Each stone that Pyrrha threw behind her turned into a woman, and each stone that Deucalion threw behind him turned into a man. This is why the peoples of Earth are strong and tough, because their origin was the strong, tough stones of Parnassus.

Zeus and Io

Io was the daughter of the river god Inachus, and she became a priestess of Hera (Juno). Hera is the goddess of marriage, and she had much to complain about in the behavior of her royal husband Zeus. It was beyond forgiveness when Zeus fell in love with Io and tried to persuade her to lie down with him in the secret woodlands of Lerna. Io was horrified by the idea, and ran away as quickly as she could, but Zeus spread rain clouds over the countryside so that it became as dark as night, and she could not see where she was going. When she stopped running, he took her virginity by force.

Hera looked out from the Olympian palace and noticed a patch of darkness in Argus while the rest of the world was in bright sunshine. This had to be one of Zeus's tricks, she thought, and she hurried down to Earth and ordered the sun to disperse the clouds.

Opposite page *The God Hermes Plays Flute to Argus While Io Disguised as a Cow Watches* by Jacopo Amiconi (Amigoni) (1682–1752).

In the sunshine, she could see no sign of any woman or nymph. There in the fields was a beautiful white heifer, with her husband standing beside it. The cow's eyes looked almost human to her, and the goddess began to wonder if this might be her rival, metamorphosed into animal disguise to fool her. "Give me this beautiful creature as a present," she asked Zeus, and as he could think of no good excuse to refuse her, he gave her the heifer.

Hera became convinced that the heifer was her missing priestess, Io, and she thought that Zeus might try to steal her back again, and so she gave the creature to Argus to guard by night and day. Argus had a hundred eyes, and he was never completely awake and never wholly asleep. His eyes took it in turns to sleep, so that some of them were constantly on guard, and the eyes in the back of his head meant that no one could possibly creep up on him from behind to surprise him.

Io hated her new body. She hated eating grass and lying in the open on the hard ground. She stood by the banks of the River Inachus and tried to explain to the river god who she was, but she could not speak human words. Then she wrote her name in the mud using her hoof, and the river god wept for the fate of his dear daughter.

Zeus watched from a distance, longing to rescue Io from the troubles that he himself had brought upon her. He sent his son Hermes (Mercury), the trickster, to kill Argus of the hundred eyes. Hermes

Left **After the flood.** Some say that Zeus had no intention of allowing Deucalion and Pyrrha to live to repopulate the earth. Instead, they say Prometheus warned his son and daughter-in-law to build a boat so as to thwart Zeus's intentions.

HEPHAESTUS'S LIMP

Once Zeus (Jupiter) had become king of the gods, there were no more killings of gods by gods, but they were still capable of injuring one another. The blacksmith god, Hephaestus (Vulcan), walked with a limp, which was caused by either his father, Zeus, or his mother, Hera (Juno), depending on which version of the story is accepted. In one version, when Hephaestus was born, his mother thought he was the ugliest of babies and threw him out of the palace and down the side of Mount Olympus. His legs were permanently broken and twisted in the fall. In the other version, Hephaestus was an ugly baby but his mother did not reject him. He grew up without ever being injured until he was foolish enough to become involved in an argument between Hera and Zeus. When he agreed with his mother, his father threw him down the mountain.

Left *Hephaestus at Forge* by Peter Paul Rubens (1577–1640). Hephaestus, the god of the forge, was the patron of craftsmen.

Above **Constellation of Ursa Major.** Callisto, from "Kalliste," meaning "most beautiful," was eventually joined by her son, whose constellation is said to guard her. Hera saw to it that Callisto could never rest—she is doomed to revolve ceaselessly around the North Star.

Below *The Goddess Hera Receives Head of Argus from Hermes and Places Eyes in Tail of Peacock* by Jacopo Amiconi (Amigoni) (1682–1752). Argus has been described as a man, a giant, and a monster. He had many eyes that were placed in the tail of Hera's sacred bird, the peacock.

did not try to outfight Argus, but walked up playing the flute, and sat close by him playing sweet tunes until the hundred eyes all closed. As soon as Argus was asleep, Hermes cut off his head. Hera took those hundred eyes of her faithful servant and placed them on the tail feathers of her bird, the peacock. This is how the male peacock was given its splendid and uniquely patterned plumage.

Hera was already angry with Zeus for betraying his marriage bed, and angry with Io for abandoning her vows as priestess (no matter that she had been raped by the god). Now she was even angrier, after the killing of Argus, and she made up her mind to torment Io. She sent a gadfly, the kind that bites at cattle in the hot weather, and it drove Io across country after country without rest. She visited the shores of a sea that was named in her honor, the Ionian Sea. She swam across the straits that join the Black Sea and the Mediterranean, and that is why they are called the Bosphorus, a word which in Greek means "the straits of the cow." She struggled up the slopes of Mount Caucasus, where she met Prometheus, chained to his rock. She traveled as far as the Nile, where the poor heifer fell to her knees and prayed to Zeus for help.

Zeus promised Hera by the waters of the Styx that he would be a better husband to her, if only she would let Io take human form again. An oath that invokes the River Styx is binding on anyone, god or mortal. Hera decided to let go of her anger and jealousy, and Io became human once more. Now she is a goddess in her own right, worshipped in Egypt, and her son by Zeus is called Epaphus.

Callisto

Callisto was a companion of Artemis (Diana) the huntress, and along with all the other virgins who attended upon Artemis, she had vowed never to take a sexual interest in any male, whether man or faun, satyr or god. Zeus saw her and desired her passionately, and because he knew that she would never accept a male lover, he disguised himself as Artemis. Callisto was deceived by this disguise until he forced himself upon her, and she was unable to defend herself from him. She tried to keep her rape secret, but it soon became very difficult to hide the fact that she was pregnant. On a hot day, Artemis called all her companions to bathe with her in a cool stream. Callisto undressed with everyone else, and at once the goddess noticed her swelling body and ordered her to go away, never again to be her companion in the hunt.

This banishment was punishment enough for trying to conceal what had happened from the virgin goddess, but Callisto had to face the angry Hera as well. Hera found out that Callisto had given birth to Zeus's son, Arcas, and came down from Olympus to destroy her rival. She grasped Callisto's hair and pulled it hard. Then the jealous goddess transformed Callisto from human form into the frightening shape of a bear, with a huge snout and dangerous teeth, with powerful legs and claws that could rip a man to shreds. Callisto was appalled at the loss of all her past happiness, and her sufferings increased even more when she found that she was now terrified of hunters and dogs.

For 15 years Callisto suffered life as a great bear, until one day her son Arcas was hunting in the forest. He did not know what had happened to his mother, and so, when he spotted the bear, he was terrified for his life. Callisto recognized her son at once and tried to speak to him, but all that came out

of her mouth was a frightening growl. Arcas then took his hunting spear and readied his arm to kill the bear as she stood close by, neither attacking him nor defending herself. His aim could not miss.

At the very moment when Arcas thrust the spear toward the bear's heart, Zeus grasped his hand and held him back from the crime of killing his own mother. Then the god carried them both into the sky where he transformed her into the Great Bear constellation, known as Ursa Major, and her son into the Little Bear constellation, Ursa Minor.

Who would not love,
if loving she might be
Changed like Callisto to
a star in heaven?

HENRY WADSWORTH LONGFELLOW
(1807–1882), "BIRDS OF PASSAGE"

Hera became even more furious than before. Not only could her rival boast of a son fathered by Zeus, but Callisto was now also shining gloriously in the night sky. In her anger and frustration, Hera turned for assistance to the Titans Oceanus and Tethys, asking them to find a way to prevent the Great Bear from ever dipping below the horizon into the ocean that rings the world. The Titans agreed to Hera's request, which is why, in the night sky of the Northern Hemisphere, the distinctive constellation of Ursa Major never entirely dips below the horizon.

Above *Arcas and Callisto* by Jean-Francois Millet (1814–1875). There are differing accounts as to when Arcas was transformed into the Little Bear constellation. At some stage during his life he succeeded his uncle, Nyctimus, to the throne and became king of Arcadia. He taught his people the arts of breadmaking, weaving, and the cultivation of crops.

TALES OF APOLLO

Apollo was the son of Zeus (Jupiter) and Leto, and one of the 12 gods who lived on Mount Olympus. In many myths, he is the god of the sun, but there is also another Greek sun god, Helius, as well as the Titan sun god Hyperion (who lost his powers when Zeus became king of the gods). Apollo first showed his powers when he was only four days old. One of the children of Mother Earth was the great serpent Pytho, as big as a hillside. Pytho was the serpent who harassed Leto when she was trying to find somewhere to give birth to Apollo and his sister Artemis (Diana). The baby Apollo asked for weapons to avenge the treatment of his mother, and Hephaestus (Vulcan) gave him a bow and arrows.

Apollo overcame the serpent on Mount Parnassus, letting fly a thousand of his new arrows until the poison bled from the snake through a thousand wounds. Then he set up a festival of athletic games, called the Pythian games after the serpent Pytho, so that his victory would never be forgotten. Every athlete who triumphed at these games was rewarded with a wreath of oak or beech leaves. Later in Greek and Roman history, victors were rewarded with laurel wreaths, and the story of Apollo and Daphne explains how the laurel tree (daphnē in Greek) came into being.

Apollo and Daphne

Like most love stories, the tale of Apollo and Daphne begins with the god of love, Eros (Cupid). Eros had his own bow and arrows, but he wanted to try out the much bigger bow of Apollo. He had just managed to bend the bow, ready to loose an arrow, when Apollo caught him and said, "What use is a warrior's bow to you? Your task is to use your dainty bow and arrows to wound the heart, while the great bow belongs to me when I hunt my enemies, like the huge serpent Pytho that I killed even though it stretched over a whole hill. Stay within your own province, Eros, and do not intrude into mine." It was a rash comment. Eros was determined to show Apollo who was master, and he flew high into the air and shot two arrows. One wounded Daphne, a nymph of the woodlands, daughter of the river god Peneus, and the other found its mark in Apollo's heart. But they were not both arrows of love. Apollo burned with desire for the nymph Daphne, but Eros had wounded her with a blunt-tipped arrow, the kind that deters the heart from love.

Daphne immediately decided that she wanted nothing to do with men or male gods, sexual desire, or marriage. Apollo used all his arts to woo her, but she ran away whenever she saw him. At first he pretended to be a mortal man, and then he revealed himself as Apollo, god of oracular wisdom, god of music, god of the sun, god of medicine. Nothing that he said made any difference. Daphne ran away again, and Apollo could think of no better tactic than to run after her. She was spurred on by fear and he by desire. On they ran, until the nymph could feel Apollo's breath as he gasped for air just behind her, and she could hardly keep on her feet for weariness.

Now she was running downhill toward the River Peneus, and she called out, "Help me, father! If you have any powers as a river god, use them now to save me from Apollo. He loves my beauty, he says. Father, destroy my body and keep me safe for ever!" Then she stopped, unable to run another step, and as she stood on the riverbank, her feet were held fast in the wet soil. Her body became thinner and her skin grew a layer of bark. Her arms became branches, her fingers became leaves; she had changed into the first laurel tree.

Apollo could not forget the nymph, and promised that he would always wear a wreath of her laurel leaves. Every athlete who won at the games would wear a laurel wreath in memory of Daphne, and the prize for the best poet would always be a laurel wreath.

Till Daphne,
desperate with pursuit
Of his imperious love,
At her own prayer transformed,
took root,
A laurel in the grove.

WILLIAM WORDSWORTH (1770–1850),
"THE RUSSIAN FUGITIVE"

Apollo and Phaethon

Phaethon was the son of Apollo and Clymene, but he was born months after she had been left by the sun god. Phaethon boasted that he was the child of a god, but no one believed him. "No one knows who your father is," he was told, "but if he is really a god, surely he will give you some proof of it, and you can take your rightful place on Olympus with the rest of the gods." Everyone laughed at the idea, until Phaethon could no longer bear their mockery.

Left **Apollo crowned with laurels.** The emblems of Apollo were the lyre, the bow, and the tripod. There were many animals sacred to Apollo including the wolf, the swan, the hawk, the raven, the snake, and the mouse.

Opposite page *Apollo and Daphne* by Antonio Pollaiuolo (1432–1498) and Piero Pollaiuolo (1443–1496). When his beloved Daphne was transformed into a laurel tree, Apollo resolved that a garland of laurel leaves should decorate his lyre, his quiver, his own head, and the heads of his minstrels in Daphne's honor.

Below **Daphne.** Daphne was not the only maiden in distress rescued by the River Peneus. Known also by its Arcadian name, the River Ladon, the Peneus also rescued the nymph Syrinx when she was transformed into a reed while fleeing from Pan.

He ran home and entreated his mother to give him
some proof that he really was the sun god's child,
and she faithfully swore that she had told him the
truth. "If you do not believe me," she said, "you
can easily walk to the edge of the world where the
chariot of the sun rises every morning. That is where
his palace is built, and you can ask Apollo himself
if he is your father."

Phaethon set off at once, and within a few days
he had reached the palace of the sun, bright and
glistening with gold and ivory. There sat Apollo in
glory among the Seasons and Hours, the Days and
Months and Years. Apollo noticed the young man
standing on the threshold and recognized him. "You
are welcome, my dear son," the god said, but this
alone was not enough to satisfy Phaethon. He asked
for clear evidence that he was in truth the son of
Apollo, evidence that would convince all the mockers
and doubters back home.

PHAETHON'S REQUEST

Apollo promised to grant any request that would
help Phaethon prove his parentage. He promised by
the waters of Styx, and that is an oath that neither
gods nor men can break. As soon as he heard the
sacred oath, Phaethon asked to be allowed to drive
the chariot of the sun for one course across the
heavens, from morning to evening of a single day.
Apollo was appalled at Phaethon's request, for the
horses of the sun would endure no hands on the
reins but his own, not even the mighty hands of
father Zeus. Only the sun god himself could drive
this chariot, and sometimes even he was terrified
at the heights of noon, and how now and then the
horses nearly dragged the chariot astray in their
hurry to get home at dusk. The father begged his
son repeatedly to ask for something else, from all the
treasures of the world; anything that Phaethon cared
to ask for would be his.

Tartarus, where Hades (Pluto) and Persephone (Proserpina) blinked their unaccustomed eyes in the glare of noon. The seas began to boil wildly, and Poseidon (Neptune) and Gaia appealed to Zeus to save them. Life on Earth was in danger of absolute destruction, and a cry went up to Olympus from every nymph and satyr, every river god and every human being, begging the king of the gods to save them from the sun.

Zeus threw a thunderbolt across the sky toward the hurtling chariot and struck the charioteer, setting him on fire and hurling him down to the ground. The chariot was wrecked

Above *Apollo and Phaethon* by Giovanni Mannozzi (1592–1636). There is speculation as to the origins of the god Apollo. In earlier times Apollo and Helius had been regarded as two separate deities, but in later tales Apollo seems to have taken over the functions of the ancient sun god, including the parentage of Phaethon.

But Phaethon would not listen. He was afire with longing to drive the chariot of the sun, and could hardly wait until morning. The dawn began to brighten the sky with her rosy fingers, and the night stars faded. Up sprang the horses, but Phaethon could not hold them on their proper course. How far away it looked now, the path that the horses should be treading toward noon and on to evening. As his fingers dropped the reins, the sun raced a zigzag path across the sky, sometimes little and pale and far away, and then scorchingly close to the earth. The boy looked down from the sky in panic, longing to be back on firm ground, but as he looked, he could see the forests bursting into flames, then the cities burning, until the whole world seemed to be on fire.

That was the time when the Ethiopians' skin darkened, to save them from being burned alive by the sun, and deserts spread across all of North Africa. The earth cracked open as far as the chasms of

and the horses ran home to their stable in terror. Leaving a trail of fire, Phaethon fell like a shooting star into the waters of the River Eridanus, and the nymphs of Italy found his scorched body. There in Italy he is buried, far away from his native Argos.

His mother and his sisters, the Heliades, daughters of the sun, found his grave and wept for him without pause, for four days and four nights. Eventually the girls' bodies began to change to trembling poplars. Clymene tried to stop the metamorphosis, pulling down their branches and tearing the bark from their trunks. The trees wept sap which dried in the sun to become

Left **Apollo and his bow.** Apollo was also called "the lord of the silver bow." Apollo had the god Hephaestus fashion him his own bow and arrows. It is said that once forged, Apollo declared these weapons sacred to him.

CYGNUS THE SWAN

The river god Eridanus, into whose waters Phaethon fell, became a constellation in the

heavens, now called simply the River. Cygnus was a friend of Phaethon who was also later transformed into a constellation. He mourned for his dead friend until his skin grew feathers and his feet became webbed, his face grew a beak, his neck lengthened and curved elegantly, and his arms turned to white wings. This is how the first swan came into being, and because he hated the flames that had killed his friend Phaethon, he chooses to live in rivers and keeps dipping his head below the water where the sun's heat cannot reach him.

Left *Cygnus Transformed into a Swan and Phaethon's Sisters into Poplars* by Bernard Picart (1673–1733). The tears of Phaethon's sisters continue to fall as drops of amber.

amber. This is where amber is said to originate: it is the tears shed by the sun god's children.

Niobe and Tityus

Niobe was the daughter of Tantalus and Dione, and she married Amphion, king of Thebes. Queen Niobe gave birth to six sons and six daughters, though some say that she had seven sons and seven daughters. Niobe was foolish enough to mock Leto, who had once been the lover of Zeus and had given birth to only two children, the gods Apollo and Artemis (Diana). Leto complained to her children about the intolerable remarks that the insolent mortal woman had dared to make against her. At once Apollo and Artemis took their bows and arrows, with which they bring a gentle death to

those mortals who die from diseases. They shot down all of Niobe's children in the royal palace, and her husband subsequently killed himself with grief.

As a result, there was no one left alive to help Niobe bury the dead, and she was too distressed to do anything but sit and weep. As she sat still, for day after day, her body turned to stone, but even the stone wept with grief. It can still be seen somewhere in the mountains of Greece, with a stream of tears endlessly coursing down its face.

Leto asked for the help of her children again when she was attacked by the giant Tityus—son of the earth goddess Gaia—who had tried to rape her. Once more they took up their bows, killing the giant and sending him down to the underworld where he is even to this day tormented for his crime. His enormous body is secured down on the ground, covering as much area as that of a small town, and his punishment is the same suffering that Prometheus once endured, only twice as bad. While Prometheus was mutilated night after night by a vulture pecking at his liver, he was at least left alone during the day for his body to regenerate. Tityus is savaged by two vultures, pecking at his liver night after night and day after day, without any respite.

Coronis and Asclepius

The raven is a bird with black feathers, but there was a time when all ravens were as white as swans. This story explains how the raven's once fair plumage turned from white to black.

GOD PRAYER CHART

WHICH GOD	COULD BE PRAYED TO FOR:
APOLLO	MODERATION IN ALL THINGS; ORDERLINESS; ORACULAR ADVICE ABOUT THE FUTURE
ARES (MARS)	THE ONSET OF WAR; SATISFACTION OF AGGRESSIVE IMPULSES
DIONYSUS (BACCHUS)	FREEDOM FROM SOCIAL EXPECTATIONS; ECSTATIC UNION WITH THE GOD
EROS (CUPID)	WINNING THE LOVE OF THE BELOVED
HADES (PLUTO)	DEATH TO ONE'S ENEMIES
HEPHAESTUS (VULCAN)	SKILL AT MAKING MACHINERY AND WORKING AT THE FORGE
HERMES (MERCURY)	PROSPERITY AS A TRADER OR MERCHANT
PAN	SUCCESS FOR HUNTERS IN FINDING THEIR QUARRY
POSEIDON (NEPTUNE)	SAFE JOURNEY BY SEA
ZEUS (JUPITER)	SUCCESS IN BUILDING AN EMPIRE; FIRM RULE AND CONTROL

Coronis was Apollo's beloved, but she also secretly shared her bed with a young man from Thessaly. She was careful to hide what she was doing from gods and mortals alike, but she did not think of hiding from the birds of the air. A white raven saw her and her Thessalian lover together and flew as fast as it could to take the news to Apollo. He was beside himself with anger, and taking up his bow and arrows, he shot his beloved Coronis in the heart. Before she died, she said to him, "Apollo, I was foolish but you were far too hasty in punishing me. I am carrying your child, and in killing me you have killed him too."

Apollo was angry with himself for acting so impetuously, and angry with the bird that had brought him the bad news. He turned the raven's beautiful white feathers to black as a punishment. Apollo is a great healer as well as an expert killer, but he could do nothing to bring Coronis back to life. All that he could achieve was to remove the unborn child from the dead mother's womb and take him to the cave of the Centaur, Cheiron, who was also a great healer, asking him to take great care of the child until he was a fully grown man. The Centaur did as he was asked.

The Centaur's daughter, Ocyrhoe, was able to prophesy the future, and when she saw the baby, she said, "This child will become the greatest healer among humankind. He will even surpass his father, the god Apollo, for he will be able to bring the dead back to life, but he will use his healing powers too often and displease the ruler of the underworld. Then he will die and be reborn." This was all that the gods allowed her to say.

Apollo's son was called Asclepius (Aesculapius) and, just as Ocyrhoe had prophesied, he became the greatest of healers. Hades started to fear that no more of the dead would come to his realm, and asked Zeus to put an end to Asclepius's miracles. Zeus struck Asclepius dead with his thunderbolt, but he was made a god and worshipped in temples where the sick came to find the answer to their diseases in a dream.

Admetus and Alcestis

When Zeus killed Asclepius with a thunderbolt, his father Apollo took revenge by killing the Cyclopes who had long ago made the thunderbolt as a weapon for Zeus. Now it was Zeus's turn to take revenge on his son, Apollo. He ordered the sun god to serve a mortal king for a year. Apollo chose to serve Admetus, king of Thessaly, as a shepherd.

Apollo grew fond of his master and helped him to win Alcestis, daughter of Pelias, as his wife. Pelias had decreed that she would marry only the man who could drive a chariot drawn by lions and wild boars;

Left **Asclepius the healer.** Asclepius, the god of medicine and healing, was schooled in the use of drugs, love potions, and incantations. It is said that Athene gave him two vials of Gorgon's blood, one drawn from the veins on the right side and the other from the left. One vial could be used to destroy life, while the other could restore it.

Below **Admetus and his carriage drawn by a boar and a lion.** Admetus showed Apollo such kind hospitality that the god was only too happy to return the favor. As well as taming the wild beasts to help Admetus win Alcestis, Apollo caused all his cows to have twins so that his wealth would increase.

THE NINE MUSES

Apollo's companions were the nine muses who inspire all artists and scientists. They were the children of Zeus and Mnemosyne, the goddess of memory. Calliope is the muse of epic poetry, Clio the muse of history, Erato the muse of love song, Euterpe the muse of lyric poetry, Melpomene the muse of tragedy, Polymnia (sometimes called Polyhymnia) the muse of sacred song, Thalia the muse of comedy, Terpsichore the muse of the dance, and Urania the muse of astronomy. They could be found on the slopes of Mount Parnassus where the Castalian spring rises near Apollo's oracle of Delphi, or alternatively on Mount Helicon.

Above *Muses* attributed to Francesco Primaticcio (1504– 1570). The name "Muses" denotes "memory" or "a reminder," since, with no books, poets had to rely on their memories.

it was easy for Apollo to help Admetus tame the wild beasts. Admetus and Alcestis lived happily together until the king became so unwell that he was on the point of dying. Apollo once again served his master to the best of his divine ability, going to the Fates to ask them to spare his life. But the Fates had already ordained his death, and the most that they were willing to do for Apollo was to allow Admetus to live as long as he could manage to persuade some other mortal to die in his place.

Admetus was sure that someone in his kingdom would die for him, but his people all refused. He turned to his old parents, but they said that the few years left to them were too precious to throw away. The only person willing to die for him was his adored wife, Alcestis. Admetus was torn between joy that he would be allowed to live and shame and grief that his life was saved at the expense of his wife's death.

She grew sick as fast as he grew well, until she was lying on her bed very close to death. As Alcestis lay dying, Heracles (Hercules) arrived to visit his friend Admetus. The king tried to hide the truth, but Heracles soon found out why everyone was in tears and promised to help. That night, he waited at the doorway of Alcestis's bedroom until he spotted Death coming to take her to the underworld. Heracles seized Death and forced him to leave empty-handed, and Alcestis came back to health again.

ORACLES

The word "oracle" refers to both what the gods say and where it is said. An oracle in Greek myth can be a prophecy, or it can be the sacred spot where visitors come to ask the gods for advice. Such prophecies shaped many of the stories in Greek myth, for both gods and humans wanted to know the future. When an oracle foretold disaster, both gods and humans took action to prevent this unwelcome future. Oracles were almost infallible, and those who tried to avert their prophetic words most often brought upon themselves the very doom that they were trying to avoid. Oedipus and his parents, for example, acted in ways that seemingly guaranteed that the oracle could not be fulfilled, but those actions led directly to the very fate predicted by the oracle. Zeus (Jupiter) was more successful at averting those oracles prophesying that a son would surpass his father, but at a cost. In the case of Metis, he ate his sexual partner to prevent her from bearing him a son, and in the case of Thetis, he did not act upon his desire for her and he married her to someone else. Zeus's success in averting the prophecy of Thetis was clever, however, the oracle was still fulfilled when Thetis's son surpassed his mortal father; the god's success in thwarting the prophecy of Metis was much more unusual. This is a rare example of an oracle not being fulfilled at all. In general, though oracles were spoken in the name of many of the Greek gods, what they really stated were the decrees of the Fates, and the Fates were ancient powers that ruled even the gods.

Oracles were not only common in the myths but a fact of life in ancient Greece and Rome. People went to the oracles and consulted the gods there, for over 1,000 years. There are archaeological records of many votive offerings by grateful clients of the oracles, and a Roman visitor speaks of 3,000 statues at Delphi, all given in thanks to the oracle over the centuries. The oracles' prophecies must have been helpful and accurate on enough occasions for people to keep coming back to ask for more advice. Rulers of Greek city-states consulted an oracle when making decisions as important as whether to wage war, whom to make an alliance with, or where to found a new colony. At least one Roman emperor is also believed to have consulted a Greek oracle.

Both in myth and in everyday life, oracles were notorious for their ambiguity. The oracle given to Deucalion and Pyrrha, for example, told them to throw the bones of their mother behind them, a command which turned out to refer to rocks, the bones of Mother Earth, rather than to the literal bones of a dead human mother. Heracles was told that he could be killed only by a dead man, a condition that seemed impossible until he was

Left **Detail from a mosaic floor of a figure carrying an offering**. Gifts, often of fruit, from supplicants were common as offerings accompanying requests for advice from oracles.

Below **Ministers of the Fates**. The oracles were the ministers of the Fates who handed down the decrees of these ancient powers. In this painting, Admetus and Alcestis consult an oracle seeking advice on how to prevent Alcestis's death.

Above **The Oracle at Dodona**. Zeus's oracle at Dodona was the oldest oracle in Greece. The prophecies from the Fates were delivered from the rustlings of the sacred oak, which is shown here as having human form.

Right **Detail from a vase fragment showing Apollo at Delphi**. Apollo, the ruler of Delphi, is said by some to have set up the oracle there. Supplicants would make a regular pilgrimage to Delphi to consult him. This was once said to be the site of a shrine first of all to Gaia, and then later shared by Poseidon.

Opposite page *The Sibyl* by Domenico Zampieri Domenichino (1581–1641). Sibyls, prophets who were said to be under the influence of Apollo, possessed the power of prophecy or divination without it being requested of them. They simply foretold the future.

poisoned by the blood of a long-dead enemy. Cynics argue that the oracles were deliberately couched in ambiguous language so that the words could be twisted to correspond to one of several futures. If someone asked, "Who will win the war?" the oracle might reply symbolically, or phrase the answer in such a way that both sides could argue that it favored them in battle. Then, whichever side actually won, the oracle could claim prior knowledge of its success. The first Greek historian, Herodotus, tells of King Croesus's visit to the oracle at Delphi, where he asked whether he should make war against the Persians. The oracle replied that if he crossed the River Halys, a mighty empire would be lost, and Croesus took the answer to predict his success. When he was vanquished, the oracle was reinterpreted to predict the loss of his own mighty empire. Most of the other historical evidence (as distinct from the evidence from myth), however, is much less slippery, as the oracle gives advice on how to honor gods or whether it would be good to institute a new law.

How the Gods Spoke

The most famous of Greek oracles were those of Zeus at Dodona and Apollo at Delphi. In Dodona, in the north of Greece, the words of Zeus were heard in the rustling of the leaves of a sacred oak tree. The priests and priestesses of the shrine interpreted the rustling noises to the petitioner. Originally there were three priestesses, who always slept on the ground and went barefoot, and never washed their feet, to keep as close contact to the sacred oak's way of life as they could. Later in this oracle's history there were priests as well as priestesses, and they, too, went barefoot and slept on the ground. Prophecies were also derived at this oracle from the casting of lots, from birdsong, and in an elaborate ceremony involving a cauldron and a statue. The statue of a boy held a whip with three chains that could move if the wind blew it. When it moved, the buttons on the chains hit the cauldron and made a ringing sound. It was this sound that was believed to convey the words of the king of the gods.

The Oracle at Dodona

The oracle at Dodona was established, so the myth goes, when two black pigeons flew from the Egyptian city of Thebes, where a temple of Zeus already existed. One pigeon went to Ammon in Libya and the other to Dodona. Both started speaking in human words when they arrived, commanding the people to establish an oracle of Zeus at that spot. The Greek historian Herodotus interprets this story as reflecting a historical truth, that an Egyptian woman was captured and sold as a slave in Ammon and another in Dodona, and that these women were priestesses of the temple of Zeus in Thebes who eventually set up similar oracles in Ammon and Dodona. They were represented in the myth as pigeons because the Greeks could not understand their language and thought they sounded like birds.

The Oracle of Apollo at Delphi

The oracle of Apollo at Delphi was the greatest of Greek oracles, and its buildings can still be visited on Mount Parnassus. These buildings are the latest in a series of temples, each replacing the last as it was destroyed in an earthquake. A huge stone still stands in the temple, known as the Omphalos stone, the

navel of the world. In some accounts, Apollo set up the oracle at Delphi, but his fight with the giant serpent Pytho on Mount Parnassus has also been interpreted as an allegorical account of the invading race of Dorian Greeks conquering the older Pythian oracle, replacing its female deity with an Olympian male. Those who heard the voice of the god were always female and were each called Pythia. Some (more or less) historical accounts of the oracle are unexciting, with the Pythia of the moment behaving like a professional, calmly transmitting the god's message. More thrilling are those accounts that describe the Pythia as sitting on a tripod above a fissure or cave, an opening in the ground inside the temple, where she chewed laurel leaves and inhaled volcanic gases from Mount Parnassus. In these versions, it was in a prophetic trance that she spoke the words given to her by the god. The words came out sounding like incoherent babble, and it was the priests' business to interpret and transmit the message to the petitioner. Nowadays there is no sign of a cave emitting volcanic gases on the slopes of Mount Parnassus, but this is a geologically active part of Greece and it is not impossible that such a cave did exist but has been destroyed in one of the region's earthquakes.

While the Pythia was unique to Delphi, the Sibyls were female prophets who spoke Apollo's words in many regions of the world, including Babylon, Egypt, and Libya. The Sibyl of Cumae was given the

> *The word*
> *by seers or sibyls told,*
> *In groves of oak, or fanes of gold,*
> *Still floats upon the morning wind,*
> *Still whispers to the willing mind.*
>
> RALPH WALDO EMERSON (1803–1882),
> "THE PROBLEM"

gift of very long life by Apollo, when she allowed him to become her lover. She scooped up a handful of sand and asked the god for as many years' life as there were grains of sand in her handful, but just like Eos's lover, Tithonus, she forgot to ask for long-lasting youth as well. She shriveled with age until she became so tiny that she was kept in a bottle. There she kept whispering, over and over again, how much she longed for the death that the god had denied her.

It was common for prophets to be disbelieved, mocked, or reviled for the messages they brought from the gods. The blind seer, Teiresias, offered the gods' unwelcome truth to Oedipus and Creon, and his fate was to be ignored or accused of conspiracy, rather than respected and believed. The seer Cassandra of Troy heard directly from Apollo what was to happen to her city and herself in the future, but her fate was always to be disbelieved. Seers tell the truth in Greek myth, but their words rarely bring a story to a happy ending.

On many occasions, a god appeared directly to a favored human being and spoke clear words of advice or command, but more usually, the god came in disguise as a stranger, acquaintance, relative, or friend. No one could be altogether sure, then, that the passing stranger was really just a human being and not a god come to set a test with a fearful penalty for failure. The strong reverence for guests in Greek myth derives from this sense that a god might be wronged whenever a human stranger was maltreated. Some gods sent messages in dreams, and it took great skill to determine which dreams were false and which spoke a divine truth. Some gods sent portents in the form of birds in flight. Sometimes the entrails of sacrificed animals were read to provide a prophecy, or seers practiced foretelling the future in bowls of water, a skill known as scrying. In Pharae, the oracular advice of Hermes (Mercury) was transmitted in the first words that the petitioner heard while walking out of the marketplace (an appropriate place to seek help from Hermes, god of merchants). Zeus's anger was manifested in bad weather. When a thunderstorm raged, his displeasure was very clear.

THOSE WHOM THE GODS LOVE, DIE YOUNG

The twin brothers Agamedes and Trophonius built a stone threshold for the temple at Delphi. Apollo was pleased with their work, and his oracle told the brothers that they should live life to the fullest for the next week. Then, on the seventh day, they would be given their heart's desire. On the sixth night they could hardly sleep for excitement, but eventually they fell asleep, and in the morning they were found dead in their beds.

The same gift was given to Cleobis and Biton, sons of Hera's (Juno's) priestess at Argos. One of the rites of Hera involved a chariot drawn by white oxen. The day of the festival dawned, but the oxen were missing. Cleobis and Biton pulled the chariot a long and sweaty distance to the temple. The priestess prayed that Hera would give these dutiful young men the best gift that the gods could give to mortals. In the morning, they were found dead.

Left and Right **Cleobis and Biton.** The Greek gods believed that death was the best thing that could happen to mortals because it released them from their human life that was so full of suffering.

EROS AND PSYCHE

The Greeks usually imagined their god of love, Eros, in the shape of a boy with wings, his weapons a bow and arrows. Renamed Cupid by the Romans, he steadily grew smaller over the centuries until by the time of Renaissance art, he became a chubby-cheeked infant who hardly seemed strong enough to bend his bow and loose his arrows. In the story of Eros and Psyche told by the Roman writer Apuleius, however, the god takes the shape of a young man, though not yet old enough to be quite independent of his mother Aphrodite (Venus).

The gods of Olympus were always quick to punish the arrogance of any mortal who dared to claim equality with a god. Tales of human folly and arrogance almost always ended badly for the human being concerned, but the myth of Eros and Psyche is an exception to this norm, though the foolish princess

Psyche had to endure struggles and suffering before she finally reached her happy ending.

Perhaps her story ends well because it was not Psyche herself who dared to compare her beauty with that of a goddess, but her proud parents, who

Above **Eros.** Eros used to be seen as one of the creative powers of nature who was born at the beginning of time with Chaos.

BEAUTY AND THE BEAST

The fairy tale of *Beauty and the Beast* was strongly influenced by the myth of Eros and Psyche. Both are stories of love being tested by outward show. Beauty and Psyche both fail the test at first, as Beauty does not learn to love the Beast until he lies dying, while Psyche believes her sisters' story that her husband is a murderous monster. Where Beauty is literally confronted with a Beast, however, it is only in Psyche's imagination that Eros is anything but a most desirable god in the shape of a man. In the fairy tale both Beauty and the Beast have something to learn before they can fully love one another. In the myth, there are numerous ordeals for Psyche but not for Eros, who manages to stay hidden at his mother's house while his beloved is suffering. Perhaps this helps to explain why Eros is so often depicted as a little boy who never grows up.

Left **The god Eros.** Eros is often portrayed as a wild and mischievous god who did what he wanted without regard for former commitments or any consideration for the future welfare of those he targeted.

Below *Psyche Showing Her Sisters Her Gifts from Eros* by Jean-Honore Fragonard (1732–1806). After Psyche's sisters learned of her husband's true identity and that he had abandoned Psyche, they climbed the mountain in their wedding gowns and leaped off, hoping to be swept away by the west wind. Instead, they plummeted to their deaths.

claimed that their youngest daughter was more beautiful than the goddess of love, Aphrodite. Worse still, all the people of Greece and the lands around began to visit Psyche's palace to worship her, while the temples of Aphrodite stayed empty. The goddess begged her son, Eros, to punish the girl by wounding her heart with his arrow, so that she would fall in love with some miserable wretch of a man and make an unhappy marriage. In the meantime, Psyche became sad because people were treating her like a goddess and no one was bold enough to love her as a woman and try to marry her. Both of her older sisters married, but Psyche stayed at home, unhappy and lonely.

The king became worried as time passed and no one came courting his youngest daughter. In the end, he asked the oracle of Apollo where a husband might be found for his lonely child. The oracle's reply was terrifying. Psyche must be dressed as a bride and taken to the top of a steep mountain. Her husband would be no mortal man but a poisonous monster, a creature powerful enough to frighten even the greatest of the gods, Zeus (Jupiter) himself.

Psyche and her parents walked to the top of the mountain in tears, as though they were going to her funeral instead of her marriage. Everyone knew that she was being punished by Aphrodite, but there was

nothing that they could do to calm the offended goddess. They had to walk away from Psyche while she waited fearfully at the mountain top for the monster to arrive.

She tensed her body, expecting an attack, but instead, a soft wind blew at her garments until she was swept off her feet and carried gently down to the foot of the mountain. There she saw a marvelous palace, so magnificent that she guessed at once that it belonged to one of the gods. The whole palace seemed to be empty, but she could hear kind voices, and invisible hands fetched food and drink and played sweet music for her. There was no sign of any monster, and she went to bed wondering who her husband would be. In the middle of the night she was woken by someone—a person, not a monster—climbing into the bed. It was her new husband, but she could not see him in the darkness. He left while it was still dark, and every night he came back to her bed in the darkness and left again before daybreak. Psyche was falling in love with someone that she had never seen.

Psyche Loses Her Husband

One night, he warned Psyche that her sisters were about to climb the mountain in search of her, dead or alive. He begged her not to pay any attention to them, but when Psyche heard her sisters calling and weeping, she could not help asking the wind to blow them gently down to her palace. The two sisters grew jealous when they saw all of Psyche's jewels and rich clothes and all the treasures of her palace, and the next day they came back to find out if there was any way that they could hurt Psyche and spoil her marriage. "What is your husband like?" they kept asking, and eventually Psyche had to admit that she had never seen him. "He is a monster," they told her, "and that is why he has never had the courage to show you his face. Now you are

Celestial Cupid
her fam'd son advanc't,
Holds his dear Psyche
sweet intranc't
After her wandring
labours long

JOHN MILTON
(1608–1674), "COMUS"

pregnant, and everyone knows that a monster's favorite food is a pregnant woman. He is just waiting for your baby to grow big inside you, and then he will feast on both of you together. You must kill him before he kills you; use a lamp to see by, and cut off his head with a knife!"

Psyche believed everything that her sisters told her. She found a lamp and a knife and hid them both beside the bed. That night, after her husband had fallen asleep, she lit the lamp and saw his body for the first time. There beside her lay the god of love in the shape of a man, but more handsome than any mortal could be. Close to his hand were his bow and arrows, and Psyche scratched herself on an arrow as she bent closer to kiss him. The wound from the arrow ensured that she would love Eros for the rest of her life.

Psyche was just about to kiss the god when the lamp in her hand tipped forward and a drop of burning oil fell onto his shoulder and woke him. Eros sprang up from the bed and started to fly away, but Psyche clung onto him for a few moments, so that he carried her out of the palace and onto the mountainside. She could hold him no longer, and fell to the ground. Eros told her that he must return to his mother so that his shoulder would heal from its burn. Aphrodite would be furious when she found out that instead of tormenting Psyche, he had fallen in love with her and married her. If only the foolish girl had kept silent about him, her baby would have been born a god, but now she would be lucky to stay alive long enough for her baby to be born, for he could not protect her against Aphrodite's anger. Then he flew away into the night.

Psyche's Tasks

Psyche felt so miserable and so frightened of Aphrodite that she tried to drown herself in a river, but the river god recognized her as the bride of Eros and would not let her die. Then she asked Hera (Juno), the goddess of married love, for help and Demeter (Ceres), who knew the pain of losing her daughter Persephone, but neither of these goddesses was willing to offend Aphrodite by helping Psyche.

Left *Psyche Carried off by Zephyrus* by Egisto Ferroni (1835–1912). The divine personification of the west wind, Zephyrus was known by the Romans as Favonius. Represented as a young man with wings, he glided through the air bringing freshness and bountiful rain.

Below *Psyche Abandoned* by Augustin Pajou (1730–1809). The jealous and spiteful nature of her sisters weighed heavily on Psyche. She lost faith in her lover and had to pay a heavy price for her doubt.

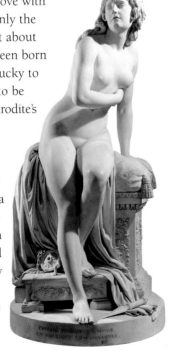

THE MISSING HALF

The philosopher Plato explained the nature of love by telling a myth about the first human beings, who were circular creatures each with two faces on a single neck, four legs, and four arms. They traveled by rolling their bodies along the ground. Zeus (Jupiter) grew angry with these early humans when they challenged the rule of the gods, and sliced each of them in half, leaving humankind with only one face, two arms, and two legs. Zeus threatened that, if ever there were any more serious trouble from humankind, he would cut everyone in half again. Then, with one leg and one arm each, reduced to hopping everywhere, people would finally learn how to treat the gods with respect. According to this myth, we are all halves of lost wholes, each longing and searching for its missing half. Love, according to this myth, is the desire and pursuit of the whole.

In the end, Aphrodite found Psyche and began to punish her at once with a flogging. Then she decided to torment the poor girl with tasks that could not be accomplished, so that she would have endless excuses to beat her again. First, Aphrodite took handfuls of all the grains and beans and poppy seed and mixed them together. Then she threw them on the hearth and demanded that Psyche separate them again before nightfall. If she failed, she would be whipped. Psyche started to sort out a little pile of millet seeds but after a few minutes she realized that she would never sort all the seeds by evening. She began to cry, but then noticed an ant running as fast as it could across the hearth, calling out to all the other ants in the palace, "The bride of Eros is here, and needs our help." Immediately all the ants in the goddess's palace raced to the seeds and began to carry them into separate piles. By evening, the task was done.

"You must have had some help, you sly creature," the goddess complained, "but do not think you can escape my anger so easily. Tomorrow I want you to go to the field where the golden sheep are grazing, and fetch me a handful of their shining wool." This task sounded easy, but in the morning, as Psyche walked toward the field, she could see that all the sheep had long, sharp horns. She had to cross a little stream to reach the sheep, and as she stood there hesitating, a reed from the stream said to her, "Psyche, if you cross over the water now, you are going to your death. The sheep will use their horns on you, and if that does not kill you, their teeth are also poisonous. But these sheep are only dangerous in the daytime, when their golden fleeces grow burning hot in the sun and enrage them. Wait until the evening, when they will be calm and peaceful. Then you will be able to walk among them safely and gather all the wool that has been caught on thorns and briars."

That night, Aphrodite was even more angry with Psyche. "Surely some mischievous god has been helping you," she scolded, and Psyche remembered how Pan's beloved Syrinx had been transformed into a reed. Perhaps it had been the great god Pan who had helped her, in the guise of a reed. Aphrodite was quick to devise a new ordeal for Psyche. "Your next task will be harder to find help for, because even the gods are in awe of the river of death. You must go to the River Styx and bring me back some water from

its source, high in the mountains, where it falls down a cliff before pouring down into the underworld. I want water from the middle of the river, not just from its edge."

Psyche understood all too well that the goddess intended to kill her, when she came to the cliff and the waterfall and saw that dragons guarded both banks of the dark river. She started to think again about killing herself, but the eagle of Zeus noticed her just as she was about to run toward the dragons

Above *Psyche in the Underworld* by Ernest Hillemacher (1818–1887). Psyche collected water from the River Styx.

Opposite page *Psyche at the Throne of Aphrodite* by Edward Hale (1852–1924). Psyche pleaded for clemency from Aphrodite.

53

Above *Psyche Receiving the Casket Back from Persephone* by Sir Edward Burne-Jones (1833–1898). Eros swooped down to rescue his beloved Psyche. He carried her to Olympus where she was made immortal. In due course, she bore Eros a daughter called Volupta (Pleasure).

in despair, and flew down to help her. He recalled the time that Eros had helped him, when Zeus had ordered him to abduct the beautiful boy Ganymede and carry him to Olympus to be the gods' cupbearer. The huge eagle snatched the jug from Psyche's hand and carried it to the middle of the river, then brought it back full of dark water.

Descent to the Underworld

Aphrodite was angrier still. Surely all the gods were conspiring to thwart her, but she could think of one task that would bring Psyche to her death, no matter who tried to help her. The rule of the underworld, for the Greeks as for the peoples of Mesopotamia, was that anyone living could go there but none

could return. She ordered Psyche to go down to the underworld to visit its queen, Persephone (Proserpina) and ask her to give Aphrodite some of her beauty.

Once again Psyche thought of killing herself, for that would be her speediest way to the underworld; she could see no prospect of going there and coming back alive. She began to climb the steps of a high tower, getting ready to jump to her death, when the tower started to speak to her. "Psyche, do not be so quick to despair. You can go down to the underworld alive and come back alive, if you do what I say. You must take two barley cakes and two coins, because Charon, the ferryman over the River Styx, takes no one across without payment, and the three-headed dog, Cerberus, will tear to pieces anyone

who tries to pass without feeding him. You must ignore anyone who asks you for help, you must eat nothing but bread and drink nothing but water, and even if you are offered a throne to sit on, you must sit on the ground. If you do all of these things, Persephone will give you a box of beauty and you will be able to come back to the world of the living, feeding Cerberus the second barley cake and giving Charon the second coin. Remember that you must not open the box; it is not wise to uncover the secrets of the underworld."

Psyche ran down the road that led to the underworld, and soon found Charon with his ferry. On the way a man was struggling to load a donkey with wood, and asked Psyche to help him tie the load on securely, but she remembered the tower's advice and ran past him. While Charon was rowing her across the Styx, she saw an old man drowning and heard him call out to her, but she sat still in the boat and did nothing to help. On and on she went, and Aphrodite sent more and more poor victims to tempt her into helping them, but even when Psyche saw dying children, she remembered to ignore them. They were only phantoms, sent by the goddess to entice Psyche into letting go of the barley cakes that she held in her hand. At last she saw Cerberus standing in the roadway, snarling at her from each of his three mouths, and she threw him one of the cakes. Now she was close to the palace of Persephone and Hades, and the goddess was waiting to give her the box of beauty.

But there was one more test. The tower had warned Psyche not to open the box, but as she walked back to the upper world, feeding the second barley cake

to Cerberus and giving Charon the second coin, she kept imagining being with Eros once again, and longed to take just a little of Persephone's beauty for herself. She opened the box and found that it was empty, except for the air of the underworld. As she breathed it in deeply, she fell to the ground, dying.

Just in time, Eros flew down and blew the lethal air away. His wounded shoulder had healed and he was ready to defy his mother and make sure that Psyche became a goddess and his unborn child a god. He carried Psyche to Olympus where Zeus gave her ambrosia, the luscious food of the gods that makes the person eating it immortal. Like her husband, Psyche now had wings, but hers were like the wings of a butterfly rather than the feathered wings of Eros. As a caterpillar leaves its familiar earthbound life and later emerges as an air-traveling butterfly, so Psyche left her life as a princess among human beings and she became one of the goddesses of Olympus.

Left **Winged Eros and his lyre.** Far from being the monster Psyche had expected, Eros was kind and patient, fetching food and drink for Psyche, and playing music for her on his lyre.

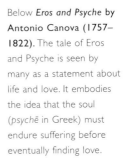

Below *Eros and Psyche* by **Antonio Canova (1757–1822).** The tale of Eros and Psyche is seen by many as a statement about life and love. It embodies the idea that the soul (*psychē* in Greek) must endure suffering before eventually finding love.

Above *Aphrodite and Hermes* by Filipepi Botticelli (1445–1510). Some have said that Aphrodite was originally a Middle Eastern goddess, similar to the Mesopotamian Ishtar, the goddess of love and fertility, and the Syro-Palestinian goddess Ashtart.

TALES OF APHRODITE

Aphrodite (Venus), the goddess of sexual desire, was born from the foam of the sea. She stepped out of a seashell and first set foot on land in Cyprus or else in the island of Cythera. She was sometimes celebrated as a goddess of orderly affection and community, like Hestia (Vesta), goddess of the hearth, or Hera (Juno), goddess of marriage, but the love that she inspired was most often urgent and unrestrained, beyond reason and common sense. She was the goddess of infatuation and sexual obsession, of desire that leads its sufferer to sacrifice everything in order to obtain the beloved, but when she was thought of as a sea-born goddess, sailors prayed to her for calm waters and safe passage. Like most of the other Olympians, Aphrodite was a combination of opposites, but the best-known stories about Aphrodite all focus on passion beyond control.

Aphrodite and Ares

The god of war, Ares (Mars) was the son of Zeus (Jupiter) and Hera, and he was usually to be found on the battlefield. Not many of the other gods of Olympus enjoyed his company, for he had a fierce temper and thought that violence was a good answer to most problems. One of the Olympians, however, not only liked him but enjoyed a passionate love affair with him. Aphrodite was as capable as Ares of being carried away by her passions, regardless of her husband Hephaestus (Vulcan). She even managed to persuade Hephaestus that he was the father of her four children, Phobos (meaning "fear" in Greek), Deimos (meaning "terror"), Eros (Cupid), the god of love, and Harmonia, the harmonious one; but they were really her children by her lover, Ares.

One morning Aphrodite visited Ares' palace overnight and stayed too long in his bed in the morning. The sun god caught sight of them together. He was quick to tell tales to Hephaestus, who usually said very little but felt so angry at the news that he let all the gods of Olympus know that he was planning revenge. All that day he hammered at a bronze net, whose meshes were fine enough to surround any prey closely but strong enough to be unbreakable. When Aphrodite came back to the palace that she shared with Hephaestus, he pretended that he was going to the island of Lemnos, but he went no

or woman or immortal nymph when she was planning to overpower a god or mortal with sexual desire. As soon as her victims laid eyes on those wearing the golden belt, they would become overwhelmed with sexual desire, unable to control themselves or weigh up the consequences of their passion. Aphrodite, golden goddess of desire, was the cause of many wars.

She even overpowered the mind of Zeus with sexual desire so many times that he finally decided to pay her back with her own technique for trouble. He made her fall deeply in love with a mortal man, Anchises, who was the king of the Dardanians. Zeus's enchantment lasted only one night, and in the morning Aphrodite made Anchises promise that he would never tell anyone that he had shared a bed with her.

Anchises was terrified when he realized that he had made love with a goddess, for he knew all the stories of mortals who had been killed because they had come too close to one of the gods. Aphrodite reassured him that she would never hurt him; after all, she said, she was now pregnant with his son, Aeneas. Anchises soon forgot both his terror and his promise. A few days later, he was drinking with his friends, and they were talking about women as men do when they drink.

"That woman serving the wine," said one of the men, "I would rather sleep with her than with golden Aphrodite. Don't

Above **Aphrodite and Ares.** Aphrodite's husband, Hephaestus, used his expert skills to make her lavish jewelry. The girdle Aphrodite wore around her waist, her weapon that made her irresistible, was made by her husband. He fashioned the belt with finely wrought gold and wove magic into it.

farther than the palace stables. There he hid, while Aphrodite sent word to her lover that it would be safe for him to spend the night with her in her marriage bed. Ares arrived and climbed onto the bed with the goddess, but as soon as they lay down, the bronze net fell onto them. They could not escape, however much they twisted and turned.

Hephaestus called all the other gods to come and see the fine fish that he had caught with his new net. The goddesses stayed away, but in crowded the laughing gods. Instead of sympathizing with the wronged husband, they kept telling Ares what a lucky god he was, and asking if they could change places with him. In the end, Poseidon (Neptune) persuaded Hephaestus to let the lovers go. Ares swaggered off to his latest war, but Aphrodite fled to the island of Paphos until her long-suffering husband forgave her.

Aphrodite and Anchises

Aphrodite's girdle, the golden belt that she wore around her waist, was the weapon that she used against gods and mortals alike. She would lend this golden girdle to some man

Left **Aphrodite.** Over time, Aphrodite developed as a symbol of pure love, in particular wedded love, as opposed to sensual lust. While the perception of the goddess changed, many of her emblems remained constant, including the swan, the dolphin, and the dove.

The planet Mars is named after the Roman god of war, Mars, the equivalent of the Greek god Ares. The god's name lives on in the English language, not only in the name of this planet, but also in the terminology of war, with "martial" and "court-martial." The planet has a reddish color, which was easily associated with the blood shed in battle. Astronomers have named the two small moons of Mars after the sons that Aphrodite (Venus) bore Ares—Phobos and Deimos. Ares was not well liked among the gods of Olympus, but the planet Mars boasts a Mount Olympus of its own, the largest volcano found in our solar system.

Left **The planet Mars.** Ares (Mars) had a reputation for violence. The month of March, named for him, was a time when wars were often started or renewed.

aware that incest was forbidden, and was afraid of the Erinyes, the Furies who come from the under-world to torment criminals with their guilt. But when her mother, Cenchreis, was away celebrating the nine-day festival of Demeter (Ceres), Myrrha gave in to her desires and visited her father's bed-room in secret, in the darkness, pretending to be a serving girl who had fallen in love with the king. She became pregnant on that first night, and came back to his bed the next night, and the next, until he became curious to see her. He brought in a lamp and, to his horror, discovered that the woman in his bed was his daughter.

Cinyras was so distraught and disgusted that he drew his sword and went to kill her. Myrrha fled through the darkness, escaping from the palace and skulking across Arabia as a fugitive. For nine months she hid herself while her womb grew big with the unborn child. Then she began to pray, not knowing which god might listen to her. "If there are any gods who heed those who are truly sorry, I beg them to

Opposite page *Aphrodite and Anchises* by Benjamin Haydon (1786–1846). There are various accounts of the punishment that Anchises suffered as a result of his boasting. Some say he was paralyzed or killed, while others say that he was struck blind by Zeus's thunderbolt.

Right *Aphrodite and Adonis* by Vecellio Tiziano (1487–1576). Aphrodite was completely enamored of Adonis and wanted him with her as much as possible. The infatuation was caused by a wound the goddess received while playing with her son, Eros.

you agree, Anchises?" Anchises had just enough sense not to offend the goddess by agreeing, but he could not help saying that he was particularly well equipped to judge between the woman and the goddess, for he had shared his bed with both. Zeus heard the boast and instantly threw a thunderbolt at him, but Aphrodite held her golden girdle out to protect Anchises. He did not die from the attack, but was paralyzed, and he had to lie in his bed for the rest of his life with no beautiful goddess to console him.

Aphrodite and Adonis

The story of Aphrodite and Adonis begins badly, with a daughter overcome by sexual desire for her own father. It may well have been Aphrodite who inspired Princess Myrrha with her passion for her father, King Cinyras of the Arabian realm of Panchaia. Myrrha struggled with her feelings, well

Above *The Death of Adonis* attributed to Martin de Vos (1596–1678). In one version of the myth, Adonis's tragic death is considered to have been foreshadowed by his birth. The story of his birth has it that after Myrrha was transformed into a tree, a wild boar opened the trunk with its tusks and set the child free.

hear me. I deserve punishment, and I know that I pollute the world of mortal men and women by my mere existence. If I go down to the underworld, I will pollute the world of the dead. Change me, I beg, so that I become neither a living nor a dead human being, so that the pollution ends with me alone, and let the punishment affect me but not the child in my womb who has done no wrong."

The goddess Gaia, bountiful Mother Earth, heard this prayer and held Myrrha's feet fast to the ground. Her toes grew into long roots, traveling deep into the dark earth to support her body, which was gradually lengthening and transforming into the trunk of a tall tree. Her soft skin hardened to bark, and all her human flesh became tree, but she was

still able to weep tears of aromatic sap. This is how myrrh first came into the world.

Myrrha's child Adonis was born from the trunk of the myrrh tree. He grew up to be the handsomest of men, and Aphrodite herself was overwhelmed with desire for him. She wanted nothing but his company, and fretted when they were apart even for a moment. Adonis loved to hunt, and to please him, Aphrodite also took up the hunt, but she wanted to seek out only small creatures without sharp teeth or horns or claws. She entreated Adonis to run no risks, to stay at her side and enjoy her love rather than spend his time hunting savage prey, wild boars or lions or bears.

Adonis seemed to listen and agree, and she felt safe enough to leave him on his own for a day while

she traveled to her beloved island, Cyprus. As soon as her chariot took to the skies, borne by its team of swans, he took up his spear and called his hounds to the hunt. He did not mean to seek out a wild boar, but when the hounds tracked one down by scent, he did not retreat. He cast a spear which wounded the boar on the side. However, the wound was not deep, and the boar easily brushed the spear away. Now Adonis was weaponless, and the boar rushed at him and drove its tusks deep into his groin. He fell to the ground, dying.

Aphrodite heard Adonis cry out and looked down from the sky to see him bleeding to death. She wept and tore at her hair, but she could not persuade the Fates to avert his death. She knelt beside him and touched the blood-soaked earth. "I shall remember you, Adonis," she said, "and so shall all the world. From your blood will grow a flower, quick to blossom in the spring and all too quick to die." The blood of Adonis became the anemone, a flower that no sooner blooms than its petals fall away in the wind.

Hermaphroditus and Salmacis

Some of the nymphs in Greek myth are dryads, each belonging to a particular tree and living and dying with the lifespan of their tree. Others are oreads, nymphs of the mountains, and still others are naiads, nymphs of rivers, streams, and pools. Naiads are at their strongest when nearest to their waters. Salmacis was a naiad, one who treasured her pool so much that she chose to stay close by it rather than joining the other nymphs as Artemis's companion in the hunt.

Hermaphroditus was the son of Aphrodite and Hermes (Mercury) and his name is derived from both his parents, while his alluringly good looks came from his

mother. Hermes was a great traveler, and so too was his son. One day on his travels, Hermaphroditus met Salmacis beside her pool of water. As soon as she saw him, she could not restrain herself from saying, "Are you mortal or god? Surely you are Eros, Aphrodite's son, come to Earth to strike me with a golden arrow. I am so deeply wounded with love that I entreat you to make me your wife, or if you are already married, to take me for your lover."

Hermaphroditus was more than surprised. He was Aphrodite's child, but he knew nothing of passionate desire, and he certainly did not want to marry this nymph. She wrapped her arms around him, and he awkwardly shook them off. She tried to kiss him, and he backed away. "Go away," he shouted, "or do I have to run away myself?"

Salmacis pretended to leave, but she was unable to go far from him. She hid behind a bush, still keeping him in sight while he sat on the ground, resting. Then he decided to bathe in the pool, for the day was hot. He took off his clothes and Salmacis felt her desire flame up, looking at his naked body. As soon as he dived into her pool, she cried out, "He is mine!" and immediately jumped in after him, holding him, kissing him, clinging to him, pressing her body to his, refusing to let him go. "May we always be together," she prayed, and the gods listened to her prayer. The two bodies, so tightly intertwined, began to dissolve together into one body, neither wholly male nor wholly female. What climbed out of Salmacis's pool was neither a man nor a woman but the first hermaphrodite.

Above *Adonis Resting after a Hunt* by Nicolas Cousteau (1658–1733). Adonis is thought to have been originally an Asiatic deity of nature. He was also identified with the Near Eastern god Tammuz.

Below *Ceiling with Hermaphroditus and Salmacis* by Ubaldo Buonvicini (eighteeenth century). Hermaphroditus, shocked at what he had become, prayed to his parents. As a result, Aphrodite and Hermes caused the pool to have a similar effect on all men who bathed in it.

Above **Arachne spinning wool.** Arachne thought that nothing could represent the gods better than to weave the stories of them and their lustful behavior into her cloth. When she proved herself to be equal in skill to Athene, the goddess flew into a jealous rage.

TALES OF OTHER GODDESSES

Greek myths abound in strong women such as Medea, Antigone, Alcestis, and Penelope. These women had some strong role models among the Olympian goddesses. Hera (Juno), the goddess of marriage, frequently defied Zeus (Jupiter), causing trouble for the many mortal women whom he made pregnant, and for their children. Athene (Minerva) was the goddess of the domestic crafts such as

weaving, and she was also a skilled warrior and a friend of heroes such as Perseus. She invented the first ship and chariot. Artemis (Diana) was the goddess of the hunt and also of wild animals, and she was quick to punish any man who intruded on her privacy. Demeter (Ceres) was a gentler goddess, except when her daughter Persephone (Proserpina) was lost to her; then she was as vengeful as any of the other Olympians. Of the Olympian goddesses, only Hestia (Vesta) was completely dedicated to domesticity; peaceful and determined to avoid conflict. The only myth about Hestia is the one that tells the story of the time that Poseidon (Neptune) and Hermes (Mercury) both came wooing her. She was so reluctant to be the cause of conflict between the two that she vowed to stay a virgin forever. It is the other Olympian goddesses, with their enemies and their favorites, who provide rich material for stories.

Athene and Arachne

Like the other gods of Olympus, Athene did not tolerate any insolence on the part of human beings. Of all the Olympians, it was Athene who most appreciated and encouraged the cleverness of human beings, but when her student Arachne boasted that Athene's hands were no more clever than her own hands at weaving, the goddess could hardly believe her ears. Athene visited Arachne in the disguise of an old woman, urging her to talk about her weaving skills to find out just how far her boasts would go. Arachne now claimed to have taught herself all the tricks of weaving and started to boast again that she would beat Athene at any weaving competition. Athene revealed herself as a goddess, casting off her disguise, but Arachne would not apologize or admit that she had told a lie. Instead, she sat down at her loom, picked up the shuttle and started to weave stories of gods and mortals into the cloth.

Athene did the same, the cloth on her loom telling the story of the contest between herself and Poseidon over who was to be the god of a Greek city, which at that point was without a name. On her cloth, Athene depicted the citizens of this nameless city crowded together in the citadel, looking at what the gods were offering them, and deciding which of the two to vote for. As her bid for the citizens' votes, Athene had created the first olive tree for the city, while Poseidon had offered a miraculous spring of water on the rocky heights of its acropolis. All the men were looking with interest at the water, recognizing how useful it would be in times of siege, and all the women were praising the olive tree, noting its many uses in the household. There was one more woman than man in the picture, as in the competition itself. Athene did not bother to show her victory, for everyone knew that she had won by a single vote, and the city was called Athens in her honor.

Arachne was too much carried away with pride and insolence to heed the warning implied by the goddess's weaving, the demonstration that Athene always wins. She took it as a challenge rather than

a threat, and responded by weaving into her cloth the many stories of the gods' deceptions, showing how they changed shape to seduce mortal women.

When the tapestries were finished, no one could decide whose cloth was the finer. Athene tore up the girl's weaving and started to beat her with the wooden shuttle. In desperation, Arachne took hold of a rope and tied it around her neck, then looked around for a roof beam to hang herself from. "Hang yourself all you like," said Athene, "you will never die from it, nor will your children, nor the children of your children. You will suffer for your insolent folly for the rest of your life." She struck Arachne once again and as a result the girl's body began to grow smaller and smaller until her head seemed to almost disappear. No ears, no hair, no nose, nothing but stomach and legs, Arachne was

Left **Athene in armor.** As a goddess of war, Athene is represented in full armor with a helmet, spear, and shield. Over her breast she is often seen wearing the "aegis," a breastplate made of goatskin with tassels. The Gorgon's head is painted on the aegis, or sometimes on her shield.

Below *Arachne* by Walter Crane (1845–1915). Just as Arachne condemned herself to hang, so did Athene. The goddess transformed the girl into a spider so that she may hang on a thread and spin forever. The spider retained Arachne's skill as a weaver.

GODDESS PRAYER CHART

WHICH GODDESS	COULD BE PRAYED TO FOR:
APHRODITE (VENUS)	IRRESISTIBLE GOOD LOOKS
ARTEMIS (DIANA)	EASY CHILDBIRTH; SUCCESS IN RUNNING
ATHENE (MINERVA)	CLEVER STRATEGIES; DOMESTIC SKILLS; PRACTICAL WISDOM
DEMETER (CERES)	FERTILITY
HECATE	WEALTH; MAGICAL POWERS
HERA (JUNO)	FAITHFULNESS IN MARRIAGE
HESTIA (VESTA)	PROTECTION AT THE HOME AND HEARTH
MUSES	INSPIRATION IN POETRY AND MUSIC

Above *Actaeon Metamorphosing into a Deer* by Francesco Albani (1578–1660). Another version of the Actaeon myth is that he offended Artemis by claiming to be a more skillful hunter. Yet another version is that Artemis destroyed him because he wanted to marry Semele.

Right *Eos* by Jean-Simon Berthelemy (1743–1811). Eos had countless love affairs with mortals and gods. As well as the four winds and the stars, she gave birth to Emathion, who became king of Arabia, and Memnon, who died in combat with Achilles.

transforming into a spider, and her many eight-legged descendants can still be seen in the corners of the ceiling spinning their intricate webs of the finest gossamer thread.

Artemis and Actaeon

Artemis was a virgin goddess who did not enjoy the company of men. She and her many virgin companions, nymphs of the trees, mountains, and streams, lived together in the woodlands, and their favorite sport was the hunting of wild animals. When they were hot and weary from the hunt, they would cool off by bathing together in a pool in the valley of Gargaphie.

One hot day a huntsman became lost in the woods. Actaeon was a prince, grandson of Cadmus who founded the city of Thebes, but his royal blood did not deter the goddess from taking a savage vengeance when he wandered into Gargaphie. Artemis was being washed in the cool waters by one of her nymphs, while another tied up the goddess's hair and a third waited beside the pool with her cloak and sandals. The rest of Artemis's companions were washing themselves clean from the dust of their morning hunt. All were as naked as the goddess.

The nymphs shrieked with dismay and anger when they noticed that a man was looking at them in all their nakedness. Artemis stood up, her cheeks red with anger, as her companions hurried to cover her with their own bodies. Her bow and arrows had been put aside, to protect them from being splashed while the goddess was bathing. Now she longed to have them in her hands, so that she could shoot the intruder dead at once.

There were other ways, though, for a god to punish a human being. Artemis scooped up water from the pool and threw it in Actaeon's face and hair, saying, "Now you can tell all the world, if you are able, just what it was like to see the goddess of the hunt without her clothes on." Where the water fell on his forehead, horns began to sprout. He fell toward the ground with arms outstretched to break his fall, but instead of human hands, sharp little hooves landed on the ground, and at the same time his arms began lengthening into slender legs to match his new hind legs. He had become a stag.

As a man, Actaeon had been frightened of the goddess and her nymphs, but as a stag he became terrified of everything. He ran and wept, not knowing where to turn for help. Suddenly he heard the yelps of hunting hounds. His own dogs had caught his scent and they were eagerly rushing toward him. "Melampus," he tried to call out, "Ichnobates, Dromas, Laelaps, I am your master, Actaeon," but he could say nothing. The dogs leapt up at him, tearing at his flesh and pulling him down. Some of them looked around, puzzled that their master was not with them to urge them on. Then Actaeon's friends ran up, shouting for him to join them at the kill as he lay there bleeding before them. No one realized until too late that the magnificent stag whose antlers they were taking home as a trophy was their friend and leader, the prince of Thebes.

Eos and Her Lovers

Eos (Aurora), daughter of the Titans Hyperion and Theia, was the goddess of the dawn. Poets praised her rosy fingers that colored the sky in readiness for the sun god's chariot to set out on its daily path. Eos gave birth to the four winds, the North Wind Boreas, the East Wind Eurus, the West Wind Zephyrus, and the South Wind Notus, with Astraeus (whose name in Greek means "starry") as their father.

Eos looked down every morning on the world of mortals, and she took particular notice of handsome young men. Her first lover was Ares, but the goddess

Below *Death of Actaeon* by **Francesco Parmigianino (Parmigiano) (1503–1540).** The Centaur Cheiron created a statue of Actaeon to soothe his dogs afterward.

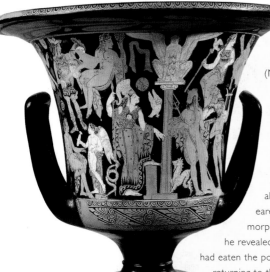

ATHENE'S OWL

There are many different kinds of owl. Athene's (Minerva's) owl is the Little Owl, and it is so strongly associated with the goddess that the scientific name for this owl is *Athene noctua*. Athene was the patron goddess of Athens, and the coinage of Athens in classical times used to be stamped with the picture of a Little Owl. Athene herself is described as having "owl eyes" as a mark of wisdom and perceptiveness. Not all owls are birds of wisdom, however. The Short-eared Owl was once a man, Ascalaphus, meta-morphosed by Demeter (Ceres) to punish him when he revealed that her daughter Persephone (Proserpina) had eaten the pomegranate seeds that kept her from wholly returning to the upper world.

Left **Athene, Poseidon, and other gods.** The sea eagle, the cock, the serpent, and the olive tree were sacred to Athene, but above all she was most identified with the owl.

Below *Cephalus and Procris* by Jean-Honore Fragonard (1732–1806). Thinking he was hunting an animal, Cephalus hurled his spear and killed his unfortunate wife. The grieving husband was subsequently charged with murder and sentenced by an Athenian court to a lifetime of exile.

Aphrodite (Venus) became very jealous because she regarded Ares as hers, and she punished Eos with an insatiable hunger for young men. Clitus was one man whom Eos saw and desired, and she carried him away to her palace for a while. Clitus enjoyed his time with the goddess, but Cephalus was less fortunate. He was the son of Hermes and Herse, happily married to the princess of Athens, Procris. Cephalus was out hunting when Eos noticed him and began to long for his love. She told him that his wife was unfaithful to him, and then, to prove what she was saying, she sent him to Procris in disguise to tempt her with rich gifts; Procris quickly agreed to share her bed with the stranger, and then Cephalus revealed who he was. Procris ran away to Crete in

shame, and Artemis allowed her to become one of her companions in the hunt even though she was certainly not a virgin. The goddess even gave her a spear that always found its target, and a dog that ran as fast as the wind. Procris's husband joined Eos for a while as her lover, but eventually he returned to the world of mortals.

He was out hunting once more when he met a strange woman. It was his wife, Procris, but he did not recognize her. He saw her dog running as swiftly as the wind, and her spear hitting its target each time it was cast, and longed to own both of them. Cephalus offered to share his bed with the woman if only she would give him her dog and spear. Procris laughed and told him who she was. Cephalus went red with shame, and begged for her forgiveness. "Let us forgive each other," she replied, "for we have each betrayed the other equally." Cephalus and Procris were reconciled, and for a time they lived together happily.

But Procris was a jealous woman, and when she heard that her husband kept calling for "Aura" when he was out hunting, she thought he was summoning some nymph to make love to. All that he was doing, though, was to summon the breeze, "aura" in Greek, to cool him down. Procris hid in the bushes to catch her husband in the act, and as Cephalus ran past with his hounds, she made a rustling noise. He thought that some wild animal was hidden there, and threw the spear that could never miss its mark. It found its way to Procris's heart. Cephalus had killed his wife

endlessly, but he could never shed his
human years to regain his youth.

Selene and Endymion

Selene was the daughter of the
Titans Hyperion and Theia, and
was the goddess of the moon.
Sometimes she is identified
with Artemis, the virgin
huntress and sister of the
sun god Apollo, but
unlike Artemis, Selene
clearly enjoyed the
company of men and
was no virgin. One
night she looked down
from the sky and saw a
very handsome young
man asleep in a cave.
He was Endymion, the
son of Zeus and the
nymph Calyce, and
Selene took him as her
lover. They are said to
have had 50 children, a
story that suggests that he
lived many years in her
company, but he is also said
to lie in perpetual sleep, never
ageing from the handsome young
man that she first fell in love with.
Was his sleep a punishment, brought
upon him by the king of the gods, Zeus,
because the mortal's
beauty might have
tempted his wife Hera, or
was it an offering from the
love-struck Selene, wanting
to keep him forever young
and beautiful? Did Endymion
ask to remain in ageless sleep
so that he could avoid old
age, or was it the goddess's
way of restraining her lover
from making passionate
love? After giving birth to
50 children, perhaps she
was quite simply too tired of
becoming pregnant over and
over again. Whatever the
truth, Endymion is said to
be still sleeping with the
moon continuing to shine
lovingly down upon him.

with her own spear. Some say that this was Artemis's
revenge on both husband and wife for bartering her
gifts in order to buy sexual favors.

Tithonus was another of the lovers of Eos. He was
young and desirable, and Eos was so pleased with
him that she asked Zeus to grant him immortality.
Zeus agreed, but as the years went by, Eos's immortal
lover began to look older, then to become less supple
and energetic, and then to become very thin and
frail. The goddess had forgotten to ask Zeus to give
her beloved Tithonus eternal youth. She entreated
Zeus to restore Tithonus's youth, but the only gift he
would now give was to change the aged man into a
cicada. This was a mocking gift, for cicadas renew
their bodies every year by shedding their outward
husks. Tithonus could renew his cicada form

Above **The goddess Persephone.** Persephone and her mother, Demeter, were celebrated in many rites, notably the Eleusian Mysteries and the Thesmophoria. In these rituals, Persephone's name was not uttered, she was instead referred to simply as "Kore" (maiden).

Opposite page **Demeter.** The great earth goddess was particularly revered by women, for example at the festival of the Thesmophoria, which was a ceremony for women who prayed for fertility for themselves and their city.

Right *The Abduction of Persephone* by **Gian Bernini (1598–1680).** Some versions of the myth have Zeus ignorant of Hades' intentions, while others do not. Some say that Hades fell in love with Persephone and sought permission from Zeus to marry her. Zeus said nothing. If he gave his consent, Demeter would be heartbroken, but to withhold it would offend his brother.

PERSEPHONE

Demeter (Ceres) is one of the goddesses of ancient Greece of whom little is told. She was the goddess of the crops, especially the grain harvest, and was responsible for the fertility of the world. She played little part in the battles of mortal men or the sexual entanglements of the gods of Olympus.

The daughter of Demeter and Zeus (Jupiter) was called Persephone (Proserpina) and she grew up to become a beautiful maiden who enjoyed gathering flowers—though she outshone any flower in beauty. The Greeks thought of her as perfection in a young girl, and she is sometimes named simply Kore, maiden. One day she was picking flowers, some say in Crete, or else in the fields of Sicily near Enna, when the black horses of Hades (Pluto), the god of the underworld, hurtled out of the ground pulling the chariot in which Hades himself was standing. He had decided that Persephone was to be his queen, and without a word he pulled her into the chariot and urged his horses to race down to the depths of the earth again, to the world of the dead. Some say that Hades had been wounded by the arrows of the mischief-making Eros (Cupid), son of golden Aphrodite (Venus), seeking to put all the gods of Olympus under the control of his mother and himself.

No one could tell Demeter where her daughter had vanished to—no one, that is, who was prepared to tell her. All-seeing Zeus was well aware of what had happened, but even though Persephone was his own daughter, he did nothing to help her. Zeus did not want to offend his brother, who was angry enough with him already. Hades always resented the division of the world among the three brothers Zeus, Poseidon, and himself, after the overthrow of Cronus (Saturnus). Poseidon (Neptune) enjoyed his sea kingdom and Zeus was lord of all the world, but Hades had to live underground and his subjects were the dead. If Zeus were to make a ruling that Persephone must be returned to her grieving mother, Hades' resentment might turn to uncontrollable anger.

*And I will sing
how sad Proserpina
Unto a grave and gloomy
Lord was wed*

OSCAR WILDE (1854–1900),
"THE GARDEN OF EROS"

The Wanderings of Demeter

Demeter wandered the world searching for her lost daughter. While she was searching, she set aside her duties as goddess of the harvest and fertility. The crops failed. The people began to starve. There were no births anywhere in the world, among the birds or the fish, the insects, the animals, or the human beings. Fewer and fewer people came to the temples to worship the gods and there were fewer animals to give in sacrifice to the gods. Perhaps it was the dwindling number of sacrifices that eventually forced Zeus to help Demeter, as much as the sufferings of the human beings calling out to the gods of Olympus for help.

But before Zeus was ready to tell Demeter that her daughter was now queen of the underworld, before the harvests totally failed, before people's cries to the gods became so loud that someone had to listen, Demeter found her way to the royal household of King Celeus in Eleusis. A baby prince, Demophoon, had just been born, and she was employed as a nursemaid. No one recognized the woman weeping for her lost daughter as the great goddess Demeter. Each night, secretly, she would touch the baby's skin with ambrosia, the food of the gods, and then put him into the middle of the fire for a few moments. When she lifted him out, he was unharmed. One day a frightened servant told the queen that the nursemaid was torturing the baby. The next night the queen rushed into the kitchen and found the nursemaid once more calmly putting the baby into the fire. The poor mother shrieked and pulled him out, but the flames had not hurt him at all. He even seemed to glow with good health. Demeter sighed at the folly of human beings. She revealed herself as a goddess and explained that if only she had been left alone, she would have given the baby the gift of immortality in the flames.

The Return of Persephone

Demeter wandered on, once again searching for her daughter. Now the crops failed entirely and everything that lived was suffering along with the

goddess. It began to seem as though the whole world was dying. At last Zeus decided that Demeter's grief must be healed and her daughter given back, or else all that lived on Earth would perish and the gods would receive no more sweet-smelling sacrifices to enjoy. Reluctantly, he sent the messenger of the gods, Hermes (Mercury), to tell Demeter the story of how the earth had opened and the black horses and chariot of Hades had emerged, how the god had driven onto the spring meadow, had leaned out from his seat and put his huge arm around the maiden's waist and pulled her to him. The horses

Above *Demeter Mourning for Persephone* by Evelyn De Morgan (1855–1919). In some versions of the myth, it was not Zeus, but the sun god Helius who revealed the truth to the grieving Demeter.

Right **Persephone and a pomegranate.** Persephone came to be represented in two different ways. As a beautiful young virgin, she usually had a cornucopia and a sheaf of wheat, but as the queen of the underworld, she often held a torch or a pomegranate in her hand, symbolizing death and rebirth.

being from ever returning to the world of mortals. Persephone did not eat much—only a few seeds from a pomegranate—but this would be enough to keep her in the underworld of her uncle and bridegroom, Hades.

Zeus was faced with a problem. He had to give Persephone back to her mother, or else the world would come to an end with no harvests and no mothers giving birth ever again. At the same time, he needed to placate his brother Hades, who already felt that all the other gods had pleasures that he could never share. Zeus ruled that Persephone could return to her mother, so that the crops could come to harvest once more, so that babies could once more be born and there would still be people in the world to give sacrifices to the gods. But Persephone would also have to go back down to Hades' kingdom each year, for just as many months as the number of pomegranate seeds that she had eaten.

Rape or Renewal

The number of seeds varies in different retellings of the story of Persephone. Sometimes it is three, or four, or even six. This reflects the climate of the region where the story is being told, and how short the growing season is there; for the story of Persephone is a myth that explains how the seasons came into being and why the crops sprout from the soil after a period each year when nothing seems to grow. In the northern regions, the myth of Persephone is an explanation for winter. When Persephone goes down to Hades' kingdom, winter arrives, and when she returns, so too does the spring. The story of Persephone is usually understood as explaining the seasons of winter and spring, but in warmer climates, it is in the scorching summer that nothing grows. Here the myth speaks to its listeners about the ending of the hot season and the coming of the cool months when everything revives again. Where the icy winter or scorching summer is short, Persephone is said to eat only a few seeds from the pomegranate,

had plunged back into the darkness, the chariot and Hades and Persephone all disappearing into the ground, which closed up behind them. This was why Demeter had found no trace of her daughter anywhere on Earth.

Hermes promised Demeter that her daughter would be returned to the bright upper world, to feel the sun and enjoy the fresh air, if only Demeter would agree to look after the harvest again and allow new life to be born on Earth. He added, as an afterthought, that Persephone would, of course, be free so long as she had not eaten any of the foods of the underworld.

Hermes is a trickster god, and perhaps he already knew perfectly well that Persephone had eaten some of the food of the underworld. After all, it had been weeks and months since she had disappeared, and even gods need to eat now and then. Centuries later, in medieval stories, the warning was often given that if anyone were to be kidnapped by the fairy folk, they should not eat or drink anything, however fine the feast and however hungry and thirsty they became, for a single taste would keep a human

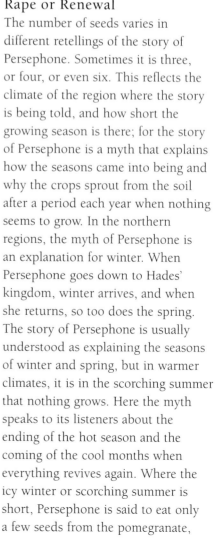

THE MYSTERIES OF ELEUSIS

The mysteries of Eleusis are one of the best-kept secrets of ancient Greece. Demeter (Ceres) found kindness when her wanderings led her to Eleusis, where she was employed as the prince's nursemaid, and when she had regained her daughter, she thanked the people of Eleusis who had given her food and shelter by telling them how she wished to be worshipped. No one knows for certain all that happened in the rituals of Eleusis, but they were based on the story of Persephone's (Proserpina's) descent into the world of the dead and her yearly return to the world of the living. The mysteries offered the promise of a life

to come that was much more appealing than Hades' (Pluto's) gray kingdom where the dead simply endured and existed, or else suffered for the evils they had committed while alive. This promised life after death was not available to all, but only to those who were initiated into the mysteries. For centuries the mysteries continued to be celebrated, and for centuries no one did more than hint at what really happened there.

Below **Eleusian Mysteries.** The three stages of induction were initiation *(meusis)*, perfection *(teleth)*, and beholding *(epopteia)*.

and where the harsh months are long, she is said to eat more seeds.

This, then, is an etiological myth, one of those myths that gives an answer to a question that perplexed the science of the time—why do the seasons exist and why are there times in the year when nothing grows? Persephone is a distant cousin of the Mesopotamian goddess Inanna, who also went down to the world of the dead and came back. Inanna was a strong-willed goddess who knew quite well how to look after herself. Persephone, in contrast, was something of a victim, needing to be rescued by her mother who did not know how to help her daughter except by threatening the whole world with extinction, no longer doing her duty as goddess of the crops and goddess of fertility.

Or was it quite so simple? Was Persephone really a victim of rape, as so many poets and painters have depicted her? In some lesser known myths, Persephone seems to be quite happy to be queen of the underworld, and very ready to protect it from invaders. When two mortal heroes, Theseus and his

Thou makest me remember where and what Proserpina that moment was when lost Her mother her, and she herself the Spring.

DANTE ALIGHIERI (1265–1321), *THE DIVINE COMEDY,* "PURGATORIO," CANTO XXVIII

friend Peirithous, drank too much and dared one another to go down to the underworld and bring back Persephone as their prize, she set out to trap them with a table covered with good food and tempting wine, and two golden thrones. Clearly Theseus and Peirithous had learned nothing from the story of Persephone and the pomegranate seeds, because they sat down on the golden seats and began enjoying the food and drink. Suddenly they noticed that they were stuck to their seats. Theseus was eventually rescued when Heracles (Hercules) came down to Hades' realm in quest of the three-headed dog, Cerberus. Heracles tore him from the throne, but he left most of his skin behind. Neither Hades nor Persephone could do anything to prevent Heracles, son of Zeus, from carrying off either Cerberus or Theseus, but at least Hades' queen had the satisfaction of keeping Peirithous stuck to his golden chair forever.

So perhaps Persephone was not such an unwilling bride. European art has depicted her as the victim, taken by surprise, dragged down to a dark kingdom full of horrors; but perhaps she came to love her new husband, her new realm of death, and her new powers. Although at every new growing season she returned to her mother, perhaps she was not altogether sorry to go down once again to her kingdom, her husband, and her darkness. After all, it is out of darkness that the new life of spring emerges, out of the dark soil that the spring bulbs send their green shoots, and out of the hidden womb that the babies push their way. The story of Persephone is usually told from the point of view of her desperate mother, Demeter; but what would Persephone say?

FLOWER AND PLANT MYTHS

There are many Greek myths about the origin of various trees, flowers, and other plants. Most involve the metamorphosis of a human being into a form of vegetation; occasionally a nymph like Daphne is also transformed into a plant. These metamorphoses are irreversible. It is very rare in Greek myth for metamorphosis into a plant to function as a reward, as in the story of Baucis and Philemon. Much more often, the creation of a new plant is the occasion for bitter-sweet celebration. Even the gods, in Greek myth, cannot restore a mortal life once lost, but sometimes, as a last resort, they commemorate their beloved friends and lovers forever in the form of some new plant.

Sometimes transformations of people into plants occur as a punishment, even a self-imposed punishment, as in the case of Narcissus. In his case, the misguided human being wasted his precious life, which could not be restored to

him. The narcissus flower, which grows anew each year, mocks at his foolishness at the same time as it commemorates his beauty.

Echo and Narcissus

Narcissus was the son of a naiad, Liriope, and a river god, Cephisus, the god of the same river where Deucalion and Pyrrha purified themselves before becoming the parents of a new human race after the flood. At Narcissus's birth, Teiresias the soothsayer prophesied that he would live long, provided that he never came to know himself. No one knew what this prophecy meant, but it became clear all too late, when he was just between boyhood and manhood.

Narcissus was the most handsome of young men, and many felt the stirrings of sexual desire for him, but he responded to no one's advances. He kept aloof, preferring to hunt wild animals than to enjoy the company of humans or nymphs. One day the nymph

Above *Echo and Narcissus* by John Waterhouse (1849–1917). Another version of this myth sees Echo as the object of the god Pan's unrequited love. Pan cursed her with the power of repetition. The shepherd people grew so infuriated at her habit that they tore her to pieces, scattering her body all over Earth. This is why Echo's voice can still be heard everywhere.

Left **Dish depicting the story of Narcissus from the workshop of Francesco Durantino (sixteenth century).** Narcissus found it impossible to look away from his own reflection. From his name comes the word "narcissism," meaning "self-love."

"You can still chatter," Hera told her, "but nothing you say will be your own."

Echo longed to tell Narcissus how much she loved him, but she had to keep silent until she could echo someone else, hoping that they would voice her desires for her. Narcissus heard a rustling among the trees and called out, "Is someone in the bushes?" Echo answered, "In the bushes." He said, "Come out and let me see you," and she replied, "Let me see you." Then she came out into the open, boldly walked up to him and wrapped her arms around him. For a moment Narcissus was too surprised to do anything, but the next moment he pushed her away, saying, "Keep your hands off me! You disgust me! Never, ever, touch me like that!" All that poor Echo could say was, "Touch me like that."

Echo pined away for love of Narcissus. She stopped eating, she hid away from all the other nymphs, and eventually her body simply disappeared. All that was left of her was the voice that still repeats the last thing that someone has said. Narcissus just did not care about the miseries of Echo, or of the hundred others whose love he had rejected. One day, someone who sighed for Narcissus grew angry and prayed to the gods that the sulky boy would fall in love and be treated as badly as he had treated others.

Echo met him, and fell in love with him on the spot. She was a nymph then, and had been cursed with the habit of saying nothing new, but only repeating the last part of whatever someone else said in her hearing. This curse was laid on her by Hera (Juno), queen of the gods, because the chatterbox Echo had diverted her too often from noticing her wayward husband enjoying himself with the other nymphs.

One day Narcissus went out hunting, as usual, and began to feel thirsty in the heat of noon. He found a pool and knelt down to drink, but he caught sight of his own reflection in the still waters and fell instantly in love. He tried to convince himself that the face he saw in the pool was that of someone else, someone who kept mocking him by duplicating all his actions. Narcissus would put out his hand to touch the beloved boy in the water, and the boy would put out his hand in response, but instead of warm fingers, all he could feel was the water. He tried to kiss his beloved, but though the face in the water drew close, it was only water that met his lips. Narcissus could not eat, he could not sleep, and he could not leave the pool. He knew that he was in love with his own reflection, but his heart ignored anything that he told himself. He wished to separate himself from himself, so that he could love himself as he longed to do. Narcissus pined away as Echo had done, until he was on the point of death.

Then Echo came back to the pool, listening to her beloved Narcissus for the last time. "I am so miserable," he groaned, and Echo replied, "I am so miserable." Narcissus moaned, "My love is futile," and Echo responded, "My love is futile." He had no more strength to speak, and soon he was dead. The nymphs wept over his wasted body and prepared it for the funeral rites, but when they were ready, the body was no longer there. It had become a pale yellow and white flower with trumpet-shaped petals, that blooms in early spring. That is how the first narcissus came into being.

Apollo and Hyacinthus

Those mortal men and women whom the gods desire usually die young, sometimes because they reject a god's advances and sometimes because another jealous god decides to punish them. Hyacinthus died because two gods fell in love with him at the same time. He was the son of King Amyclas and Queen Diomede, and became famous throughout Laconia for his beauty. Apollo fell in love with him, and so did the god of the west wind, Zephyrus. One hot summer's day, Hyacinthus and Apollo were playing a game of quoits, when Zephyrus interfered with the game. He blew at the quoit that Apollo was throwing, so fiercely that it hurtled toward Hyacinthus. The quoit struck him on the head so hard that he died. Apollo wept over the body of the beautiful boy, and changed the blood that soaked the ground into a flower, the hyacinth. On its petals can be seen the letters "AI," which in Greek are the sound of lamentation. When the boy Hyacinthus died, the god could not bring him back to life as a human being, but the hyacinth plant dies

THE FIRST CYPRESS TREE

The cypress tree was once a beautiful young man, Cyparissus, who was loved by Apollo. Cyparissus loved his pet stag to the point of obsession, and wanted to do nothing except care for this animal. He did not go hunting with the other young men, he did not go chasing after women, nor did he pay any attention to Apollo. One day he accidentally stabbed his beloved stag with his javelin, and then he pined away with grief. "If you love me," he sobbed to Apollo, "grant that I may mourn for my stag forever." The god granted his unusual prayer, and Cyparissus changed from human shape into a cypress tree, the tree of mourning.

Right *Cyparissus* by Burney (1823). In some stories, Cyparissus was a Cretan youth who found himself fighting off Apollo's advances. As the young man tried to flee, he was turned into a cypress tree.

down in each scorchingly hot summer, as though it had been killed by the sun, and then revives again in the spring of the following year.

Apollo and Clytie

Aphrodite (Venus) decided that Apollo had been prying into her affairs too much. It was Apollo who had told her husband, Hephaestus (Vulcan), about her love for Ares (Mars), and as a punishment she told her son, Eros (Cupid), to shoot an arrow of love into the sun god. After being struck by Eros's arrow, Apollo immediately fell in love with Leucothoe, princess of Persia, and disguised himself as her mother. Then he ordered the servants to leave the room and revealed himself to Leucothoe as a god. What else could she possibly do except submit and weep?

Leucothoe's sister, Clytie, desired Apollo just as passionately, but the sun god was only interested in his beloved Leucothoe. That night, as soon as she realized that Apollo cared nothing for her, Clytie ran to her father, King Orchamus, in a jealous rage and told him that Leucothoe had a secret lover. The king sentenced Leucothoe to be buried alive immediately under a huge pile of sand. The following morning, Apollo looked down from his chariot and saw what had happened. He scattered the sand, but it was already too late. Leucothoe

Left *Apollo and Hyacinthus* by Cellini Benvenuto (1500–1571). Apollo was distraught at the death of Hyacinthus. The god decreed that Hyacinthus be honored in an annual festival, called the Hyacinthia, held over three days during July at Amyclae.

lay crushed and dead. All that the god could do was to transform her lifeless body into a new plant, the frankincense tree whose sap was burned for its aromatic smoke in his temples.

Clytie had daydreamed of Apollo falling in love with her now that her sister and rival was dead, but he hated her for what she had done. Clytie could not eat or drink, she could not sleep, and all she could do was to weep all night and sit in the sunlight all day, turning her head to keep looking toward Apollo in his chariot. After nine days, her legs grew into roots and her thin body metamorphosed into a tall, thin stalk, while her head became a golden flower. She had become the first sunflower, a plant whose flowers follow the steps of the sun.

Baucis and Philemon

The gods often liked to disguise themselves as human beings, to investigate crimes, give advice to heroes, and test people's devotion to them. One day Zeus (Jupiter) and his son Hermes (Mercury) came down to Earth, to Phrygia, disguised as ordinary people, and started to ask for a place to stay the night. It was the duty of every Greek to offer hospitality to strangers, but the two gods tried many houses until they found one that would let them in. It was the poorest of houses, built of mud, thatch, and reeds, and was beginning to collapse back into the swamp in which it stood. An elderly couple opened the door to their home and immediately invited the gods to come in, while at the same time apologizing for their poverty. The old woman, Baucis, took down a piece of the long-hoarded fletch of bacon that had been hanging from the ceiling, and cut off a generous portion for her stew. The old man, Philemon, used all his firewood to build up the fire, and then went into his garden and started picking all the vegetables and fruit that he could find, to add to the stew. Then the couple gave the gods water to wash in, and

put their much-mended festival cloths onto their only couch, in the hope that their unexpected guests would feel welcome.

The table was shaky, the couch was dilapidated, and their festival cloths were worn, but Baucis set about wiping the table with mint and putting out all the food in the house—eggs, fruit, cheese, and fresh vegetables, and then the bacon and vegetable stew. She brought out the wine and watered it well, and when all had been eaten, she then offered the gods nuts and berries, dates and apples, and honey just taken from the hive. She was concerned that her guests would still be hungry and thirsty at the end of the meal, but there was nothing more in the house that she could give them. Then she noticed that the wine pitcher was somehow still full, even though Philemon had refilled the guests' cups several times already. She fell onto her knees, and Philemon knelt beside her, praying that their divine visitors would accept such a humble meal.

Philemon had a sudden idea. The goose that guarded their cottage, warning them of the arrival of visitors with its incessant cackling, could be killed and cooked in honor of these exalted dinner guests. Philemon then went out to catch the bird, but old age slowed him, and the goose quickly ran indoors and took refuge on the lap of the great Zeus himself. "Do not kill your faithful guard," said the god, "and do not stay here any longer. We intend to take vengeance on all those people who turned us away and violated the law of hospitality to strangers, but

you deserve to live. Climb up the mountain with us, and do not look back until you are at the top."

It took Baucis and Philemon a long time to climb the mountain, and when they finally reached the top and looked back, they saw that the whole country-side was flooded. Only their little cottage in the marshes still stood, but it was no longer a cottage. Instead of mud and reedy thatch, it had become a marble temple with a roof of gold. Zeus offered Baucis and Philemon any gift that they desired. "Let us serve you," they replied, "as priest and priestess of your temple. Then, when it is time for us to die,

grant that we die in the same instant, so that neither of us has to grieve for the loss of the other." Zeus was very happy to grant both their wishes.

For years afterward the old couple lived on as priest and priestess of Zeus, until one day they were standing in front of the marble temple and found that they could no longer walk. Their four legs had become firmly rooted to the ground, and their bodies started growing leaves. Zeus had granted their special wish, that they should leave their human life together, and they continued to live on as intertwining trees in front of the temple.

Above *Clytie Transformed into a Sunflower* by **Charles de Lafosse (1636–1716).** A different version of the legend reveals Clytie as one of Apollo's former lovers. Devastated that she had been abandoned, Clytie revealed the god's identity to her rival's father—with disastrous results.

Above *Landscape with Hermes and Apollo as a Shepherd* by Claude Lorrain (1600–1682). Although he was the god of prophecy, healing, and music, Apollo was the protector of flocks and herds. He was often referred to as Lycius, the wolf god.

HERMES AND OTHER MUSICIANS

Hermes (Mercury) was the son of Zeus (Jupiter) and the nymph Maia. He was one of the two messengers of the gods; the other was Iris, goddess of the rainbow that joins sky to earth. Hermes and Athene (Minerva) were the two Olympians who best loved humankind, enjoying rather than resenting their trickery. Like Athene, Hermes was calculating and clever, and he was worshipped as the god of all those who buy and trade, the god of thieves, and the god who presides over mining what lies hidden beneath the earth. Hermes was also the god of roads and travelers; if something valuable or unusual was picked up on the roadway, it was called a gift from Hermes. Hermes was also responsible for looking after land boundaries, and he showed the newly dead the way to the underworld.

being done, but a nymph at the entrance to the cave told them that she was looking after an extraordinarily clever and talented baby called Hermes, who had invented the first musical instrument from the shell of a tortoise and the guts of a cow, and was playing it to help his mother go to sleep.

The satyrs pricked up their hairy ears when they heard the word "cow," and then they noticed two cow skins stretched out in front of the cave, in the process of becoming leather. "Apollo, here is the thief," they shouted, and very soon Apollo joined them, ready to punish the criminal. He marched into the cave and woke Hermes' mother, Maia, demanding the return of his cows. "My son is a mere baby," said Maia, and showed Apollo the little child who was doing his best to seem asleep. "He was born only three days ago—how could he have walked that distance and driven a whole herd of cows back here?"

But the hides outside the cave were definitely those of Apollo's cows, and the god was determined to have the culprit punished. He seized the baby in his arms and carried him up to Olympus, to the throne of Zeus. It was there that Hermes finally admitted that he was the thief, and agreed to hand back the herd—all 18 of them. "But there were 20 cows in the herd," complained Apollo, "and I want all 20 of them back."

"Brother," said Hermes, looking up sweetly into his half-brother's face, "you saw the two hides outside the cave. Those two cows were the ones I cut up and sacrificed to the 12 gods of Olympus." Zeus and Apollo were both taken aback. They knew of only 11 Olympian gods: Who was the twelfth, and how did the baby know so much about the pantheon? Hermes pretended to be embarrassed as he explained to them that he was the new twelfth god of Mount Olympus, but he was feeling secretly triumphant.

Even when he was a baby, Hermes could outwit his half-brother Apollo almost without effort. He could hardly walk, but he managed to wander far away from his mother, getting halfway across Greece. As Hermes looked down from the top of a hill, he discovered Apollo tending a herd of cows. Hermes' first thought was to steal the cows. Noticing that their hoof marks showed which way they were walking, he deceived Apollo by making shoes for the cows from tree bark and putting them on back to front, so that the tracks led one way while the cows were walking in the opposite direction.

Apollo could see no trace of his cattle, and no sign of where they had disappeared to. There were plenty of fresh hoofprints leading into the field, but none going out. He searched the world from his sun chariot, but even from the sky he could see no sign of the cows anywhere. In the end Apollo offered a reward for his lost herd, and the satyrs, who were followers of Pan, started to search for them in hidden places.

Some of the satyrs went looking in Arcadia, and there they heard a very strange sound coming from a cave. It was the first music ever to be played. They could not see how it was

Ah, leave the hills of Arcady, Thy satyrs and their wanton play, This modern world hath need of thee.

OSCAR WILDE (1854–1900), "PAN: DOUBLE VILLANELLE"

Apollo and Marsyas

Apollo remembered the story that the satyrs had told him, about the strange noise coming out of Hermes' cave, and he asked to see the new instrument. With its cow-gut strings stretched over its tortoise shell, it was the first lyre, and Hermes plucked the strings skillfully and sang a lyric poem that he had just composed in honor of

Above **Musical competition.** Not content to be pronounced the winner of the competition over Marsyas, Apollo flayed his opponent alive. For a very long time Apollo refused to allow the flute to be played in his presence, but he finally allowed one to be played at Delphi on special occasions.

Right *Arion Preserved by a Dolphin* by Bernard Picart (1673–1733). The myth of Arion was based on an historical figure Arion, the likely son of Cycleus of Methymna in Lesbos. This Greek poet and singer is said to have invented the dithyramb—a choral song or poem of wild character and irregular form.

the great sun god. Apollo was so delighted with the music and the words that he forgave the child. He was even willing to leave the cows with Hermes if only he could have the lyre. Hermes was happy to agree, and at once he began inventing another musical instrument. This time, he made a pipe from some reeds. Again Apollo asked for the instrument, offering his shepherd's staff in return. If Hermes took the staff, he would become the god of all who herded cattle or sheep or goats. Hermes was already very skilled at bargaining. He said that the staff was not enough; he wanted the art of augury as well.

Apollo hesitated at this candid and self-assured suggestion. He wanted to become the god of music, to excel with the lyre, but he was lord of Delphi and was reluctant to give his oracle over to Hermes, however sweet the pipe.

"I will teach you how to prophesy from pebbles," he proposed, and that was good enough for Hermes. The new god not only practiced the art of auguring from pebbles in water, but he also invented the game of knucklebones and a technique for telling the future from the bones. Zeus was pleased with his astonishingly clever little son, and made him the gods' herald, the first negotiator and smooth-tongued diplomat in the world.

Hermes was not the only god ingenious enough to invent a new musical instrument. The flute was invented by Athene, but when she puffed out her cheeks as she played it, the other gods laughed at her. It was the satyr Marsyas who took up the flute and practiced until he played to perfection. He was so proud of his flute playing that he challenged Apollo to a musical competition, the

PAN AND PANIC

The word *pan* means "everything" in Greek, but the god Pan was not one to claim supreme power. He did not care to live in Olympus, preferring a simpler life in the Arcadian countryside where he helped herdsmen and hunters and the keepers of bees. Yet Pan can be a terrifying god. The word "panic" derives from Pan, referring to the sudden terror that is inflicted on those who intrude into solitary places, when the god does not wish to be disturbed (especially when he is enjoying an afternoon sleep).

Above **Detail of wall showing Pan playing pipes by Franz von Stuck (1863–1928).** Pan passed the time by either playing his pipes or resting. Pan liked to have a sleep in the middle of the day and would frighten anyone foolish enough to disturb his slumber. Knowing this, shepherds did not play on their pipes at midday.

flute against the lyre. The nine Muses were the judges, and Marsyas was the loser. Apollo flayed him to death for his insolence in challenging a god.

Pan and Syrinx

Syrinx was one of the dryads of Arcadia. She was an eager companion of Artemis (Diana) in the hunt, and like Artemis she had vowed herself to chastity. She dressed like Artemis and was armed just like her, except that the goddess carried a golden bow and the nymph carried a bow made of horn.

One day the god Pan met Syrinx as she was returning from the hunt. Instantly he felt an overwhelming attraction toward her, and he put out his hand to stroke her. She recoiled, then fled, and he chased after her on his fast goat hooves. As she ran, Syrinx prayed to any god who was listening, to help her escape, and when she saw the River Ladon in her way, she begged the river god for aid. Pan had almost caught up with her, reaching out his arms to grasp her waist, but as he embraced her, he found in his arms only a bundle of reeds. Syrinx had become the reeds that grow in shallow waters and marshlands. Pan sat disconsolately by the river, looking at the reeds and longing for the nymph. As he sat there, he heard the thin music that reeds make when the breeze plays through them. He broke off reeds of different lengths and tied them together, making the first panpipes. From then on, the panpipes were called *syrinx* in Greek.

Some say that it was the god Pan who invented the first musical instrument in the form of the panpipes. Hermes' pipe, the one that he traded with Apollo in exchange for the art of prophecy and lordship over herdsmen, was only a copy of Pan's pipes, which he had left behind one day in the fields.

Pan himself,
The simple shepherd's
awe-inspiring god!

WILLIAM WORDSWORTH (1770–1850),
THE EXCURSION, BOOK IV

Arion

Arion was the son of Poseidon (Neptune) and the nymph Oneaia. He lived in Corinth, and the ruler of Corinth, the tyrant Periander, loved to hear him sing and play on the lyre. Arion went to Sicily to compete in a musical competition and won. He gained not only the victor's wreath to bring back to Corinth, but also money and other gifts from those who had heard him play the lyre so well.

He boarded a ship with all his treasures, but the sailors did not intend to take him home to Corinth. When the ship was far from land, they stood around him and explained politely that he would have to die, because they could not risk stealing his treasure and letting him live. Arion begged for one last favor, to sing a final song.

He stood at the very front of the ship, singing in praise of the gods, then leapt overboard. The sailors looked over the side and could not see him. He had saved them the trouble of killing him, or so it seemed.

But Arion was not dead. A school of dolphins had heard his wonderful singing and swam all around him, nudging him until he climbed onto the back of the largest of them. Then they all went speeding through the water, overtaking the ship on its way to Corinth. Arion arrived days before the ship, and the dolphin made sure that everyone had time to witness his arrival, plunging through the sea like a prancing horse. Arion told his story to the tyrant Periander, who waited for the ship to arrive and then sent for the sailors. "Where is my dear Arion?" he asked them. "He is still in Sicily," they replied, "and he asked us to tell you that his beautiful songs are so well liked there that he intends never to leave the

Above **Orpheus.** Many believe that Orpheus was a more ancient poet than Homer. He is credited as the author of many poems, hymns, prayers, and mystical books. Orpheus is also said to be the founder of a religious sect who called themselves the Orphics.

place." Periander then confronted the men with the living Arion, and passed a sentence of death on them.

Arion lived a long and happy life, and according to some stories, the gods placed the Lyra constellation in the sky at his death to commemorate his truly wonderful talent with the lyre.

Orpheus

Orpheus was the finest musician who ever lived. When he made music, everyone and everything listened. People fell silent, animals clustered around him, and even the trees drooped their branches so that they could hear with every leaf. Playing the lute, he could enchant even the wildest of beasts—hungry lions and tigers—and he could charm the fish out of the sea with his singing. It was the Iron Age of

humankind, and evil ways tempted everyone alive; but when Orpheus played, people's hearts grew calm, and when he sang, their hearts filled with joy.

Orpheus traveled with Jason and the Argonauts, but his greatest adventure was one that he had to face without help. The story of Orpheus and Eurydice begins in happiness, with a wedding. The marriage feast of Orpheus and his bride Eurydice was nearing its end, and some of the guests had drunk too much wine. Aristaeus was so drunk that he forgot all the respect due both to his host and to a married woman. While Orpheus was busy with his other guests, Aristaeus began to attack the bride, trying to rape her. Eurydice fled into the garden and, as she ran, a poisonous snake bit her on the foot. Within a moment she was dead.

Orpheus laid aside his lute and could think of no reason why he should ever sing again. He could not bear to stay at home, so full of memories of his lost Eurydice, and so he began wandering the world. Wherever he wandered, though, he could not escape his thoughts, and his longing for his dead bride. In the end he remembered the myth of Persephone, the maiden who had been raped and abducted from the upper world, whose mother had grieved so strongly that Zeus was moved to allow the girl to return to the world of life. Surely Persephone would understand his grief, if he could only go down to the underworld and sing to her. Perhaps, like the goddess Persephone, his beloved Eurydice would be allowed to return from the realm of death. Since his magnificent song could enchant every creature on earth, Orpheus was willing to risk his life on the chance that he could also enchant the god and goddess of the world below.

ORPHEUS IN THE UNDERWORLD

It was easy enough for him to find his way down to the palace of Hades, easy to pay the ferryman with a song and charm the three-headed dog Cerberus to sleep. It was not easy to sing before Hades and Persephone, for all his hopes lay in this moment. He felt the pain in his heart and sang to Persephone about her longing for the daylight and the heart beating with life. He felt his longing for the bride he had lost on their wedding day and sang to Hades about his loneliness, condemned to a world of shades. He sang to both god and goddess about the heart glowing with love, melting away all pain and isolation and loneliness.

The shades of the dead had long forgotten the pains and pleasures of life, but now they crowded close around, like birds huddling together in the winter for warmth. When Orpheus sang, the Furies,

THE BIRTH OF PAN

Pan was the son of Hermes, but no one except Hermes knows for sure who his mother was. Some say that she was a nymph, and some that she was Penelope, wife of the hero Odysseus (Ulysses), and others wonder whether she might have been the goat Amaltheia. Pan was born half-goat, half-man, with little goat horns and a tail, a goat beard and sturdy little goat legs. Hermes took his son to Olympus where the gods all laughed at him, but later he was a true friend to Athene, helping her people, the Athenians, to win the battle of Marathon by making the Persian invaders panic.

Below **Pan** from the *Book of Hours* (mid-sixteenth century). Pan was a peculiar and sometimes frightening-looking god. Later, the medieval image of the Devil was derived from his strange appearance.

the pitiless voices of tormenting guilt, learned how to weep, and the tortures of the wicked came to a pause. His marvelous song moved the goddess Persephone to take pity on him, and she thereby decreed that he could take Eurydice back to the world of the living. The only condition was that he must walk ahead, without turning around, keeping silent, until they reached the upper air. Orpheus caught one glimpse of his dead wife among the clustered shades, and then turned to walk the long path back to the world of the living.

Left **Orpheus and Cerberus.** The father of Orpheus by some accounts was Oeagrus, the king of Thrace, but by others, it was Apollo. When Apollo gave Orpheus the seven-stringed lyre, it is said that Orpheus added another two strings in memory of the Nine Muses, one of whom was his mother, Calliope. The gentle music he played and the beauty of his voice were enough to soothe savage beasts.

Above **Orpheus and Eurydice.** When Orpheus returned to Thrace without his beloved wife, he resolved to spurn the love of all women. While this is seen as the reason behind his murder by the Maenads, some authors believe that each of the raging women wanted Orpheus for herself and tore him apart in the ensuing struggle.

Right **Death of Orpheus.** The Muses were overwhelmed with grief over the loss of Orpheus. They gathered the pieces of his body and buried them at Mount Olympus. It is said that the nightingales there sing more beautifully than anywhere in the world.

As he walked, he began to doubt Persephone's warning. Was Eurydice really there, following him, or was this merely a malicious trick on Persephone's part? Surely, if Eurydice was walking close behind him, he would be able to hear something, some footfall, some sound of her breathing, but all remained silent. He kept on walking until light began to glimmer ahead, where the long path climbed to the upper world. With only a few steps to go, he could no longer bear the silence and the uncertainty, and quickly turned to look back. There was his beloved wife Eurydice, tears streaming down her cheeks, with a wind of death blowing her away from him. She held out her arms to him, and he reached out for her, but already she was far away, silently calling out to him with her eyes. Orpheus would have gone back into death's kingdom for his bride, but Charon the ferryman would not let him pass.

FINAL DAYS

He wandered the world restlessly until his death. In Thrace he met the Maenads, the wild followers of Dionysus, who attacked him with spears and stones, and when these weapons refused to hurt the marvelous musician, they wrenched his body apart. He may have intruded unknowingly upon their sacred rituals in honor of the god, or else they were taking vengeance for his rejection of women. Since the double loss of his wife, he had not been able to consider marrying again. The Maenads tore off his head, and it kept singing as it floated down the River Hebrus, and across the Mediterranean to the island of Lesbos. There it was buried with proper funeral rites, and the shade of Orpheus traveled the familiar route down to the underworld, where he could at last be together again with his bride Eurydice.

MYTHS OF TRANSFORMATION

Metamorphosis was one of the favorite themes of Greek myth. The gods changed themselves into many forms when in pursuit of new sexual partners, and they liked to take on the forms of human beings when speaking to their favorites. When Athene (Minerva) helped Odysseus (Ulysses), for instance, she often took the form of a surprisingly helpful stranger. Some of the lesser gods had a small repertoire of shapes that they could assume, but a god like Zeus (Jupiter) could choose any form that he wanted. In contrast, human beings were at the mercy of gods who chose to transform them, and this transformation was rarely of benefit to the one who endured it.

Midas and the Golden Touch
One day the old satyr Silenus, the unruly companion of the god Dionysus (Bacchus), drank too much wine, as usual, and was taken captive by some Phrygians working in the fields. He offered no resistance, and so they tied him up with chains made from flowers and led him to their king. When King Midas saw the satyr tottering toward him, garlanded with flowers around his neck, wrists, and hooves, he instantly recognized him as Silenus, and celebrated his arrival with a festival, including plenty of watered wine. Then he gave the satyr back to Dionysus, who offered the king in return anything he could wish for. "I wish that all I touch would turn to gold," Midas eagerly replied. "Are you quite sure?" asked Dionysus, and Midas assured him that the touch of gold was exactly what he wanted.

Midas was delighted to find that the god had granted his wish. He touched a flower, and it became solid gold. He picked up a pebble, and it shone golden. He ran his hands up the sides of trees, and they became a golden avenue fit to welcome a god. Midas imagined transforming his whole palace into gold, wearing cloth of gold, and heaping up gold treasures for himself. His dream of golden glory lasted until his mealtime. Out came the bread and the roasted meat, piled high on his plate, but when he tried to break off a piece of bread, it all turned to gold, and when he speared a piece of meat on his golden dagger, it turned to gold as soon as his lips touched it. He lifted his cup to his mouth, and the wine turned to molten gold. Midas was beginning to starve amid splendor. He did not dare to touch his wife or children, and he bitterly regretted the wish that he had made.

King Midas prayed to Dionysus, humbly acknowledging how foolish he had been, and the god was willing to take back his gift. "Go to the River Pactolus where it rises in the mountain," he said to Midas, "and dip your whole body into it,

Left **Sleeping Silenus.** Silenus, teacher and companion of Dionysus, was almost always in a state of drunkenness. He was considered to be very wise and if captured by mortals, could reveal a great number of secrets.

Below *King Midas* by Nicholas Tournier (1590–1638). Although Dionysus warned Midas about the danger of his wish for "the golden touch," Midas would not listen. In some myths, he even accidentally killed his daughter by turning her to gold when he touched her.

part in a competition to determine who was the better musician, and Apollo proved overwhelmingly superior, Midas dared to disagree with the verdict. In his opinion, the peasant song that Pan played on his pipes outshone anything that Apollo could produce on his lyre.

Apollo punished Midas for both his presumption and his poor taste in music, by transforming his ears into the ears of an ass, while the rest of him stayed just as it was. Midas was ashamed and embarrassed, and tried very hard to keep his new ears a secret by wrapping a huge turban around them. He deceived everyone except his barber. When he realized that the barber had noticed his enormous gray ears, Midas swore him to secrecy. The barber longed to tell someone, anyone, this choice piece of gossip. If only he could speak to someone about it!

The barber could not bear to remain silent, but he wanted to keep his oath to the king. He went out into the fields and dug a little hole. He put his mouth close to the earth that he had dug out of the hole, and he whispered to it, "King Midas has ass's ears!" Then he filled in the hole and went away,

Above *The Judgment of Midas* by Domenico Zampieri Domenichino (1581–1641). Midas, who was a follower of Pan, was punished by Apollo by having his ears changed to ass's ears. Midas was so embarrassed by the gossip of his people, he ran away from Phrygia forever.

so that the clean water can wash away the power of gold." Midas did as he had been told, and from then on, flecks of gold could be found in the Pactolus River.

Midas and the Ass's Ears

It is never safe for a mortal to intervene in a dispute among the gods, as Troy found out when Paris judged which of the goddesses was the fairest, and Teiresias found out when he adjudicated between Zeus and Hera (Juno). When Pan and Apollo took

feeling much better. The earth sprouted reeds, and when they were fully grown, they sighed in the wind, "King Midas has ass's ears." Someone heard, and ran to tell someone else, until the whole of Phrygia was full of gossip and laughter.

Tereus and Philomela

Tereus, the son of Ares (Mars), was a king of Thrace, and he married Procne, the daughter of King Pandion of Athens. Their son was called Itys. When Itys was five years old, Procne asked her husband to invite her sister, Philomela, for a visit. Tereus went to Athens to escort Philomela back to Thrace, and as soon as he saw her, he lusted after her. He urged her to go with him, telling her how ardently his wife desired her company, but it was his own ardor that made his words so urgent. Philomela was overjoyed at his invitation, and she set off for Thrace in his ship. All went well on the voyage, under the eyes of the sailors, but when they reached the coast of Thrace, the king invited her into his chariot and, instead of making for the city, drove her to a hunting lodge long abandoned in the forest. There he raped her.

As soon as she could speak, Philomela hurled reproaches at Tereus, evil king, evil husband, evil brother-in-law. She threatened to accuse him before his wife and his people, and to entreat King Pandion of Athens to take revenge for her rape. She also promised that she would accuse him before the gods if he kept her imprisoned in the forest. Her speech was bold, but she did not have the strength to resist Tereus when he seized her again, tying her arms behind her back. Fearful of what she might say, he cut off her tongue with his sword and left her imprisoned in the hunting lodge, keeping her alive for his sexual pleasure but making sure that she could not escape. He went home to his wife and told her that Philomela had died on the journey, weeping as he spoke. "Tereus, you are the best of men," said his weeping wife, and Tereus secretly gloated while he was pretending to lament.

Philomela recovered from her wound and longed to tell the world what had been done to her. She had been silenced, but her hands could still weave a story. There was a loom and spun thread in the hunting lodge, and she spent her long days weaving a white cloth with the story of her rape set out in red. Then she persuaded a servant, with gestures and tears, to take the cloth to the king's wife, as a gift.

Procne looked at the scene woven in red and understood her sister's message.

She was too angry to weep, instantly casting her mind around for a means of revenge. It happened to be the time of the Bacchic festival, when women left their cities dressed in fawn skins, garlanded with vine leaves, and carrying spears. After some time, Procne pretended to be overcome with Bacchic ecstasy and ran to the hunting lodge where she found her sister. Procne dressed Philomela in festival costume and covered her poor face with vine leaves and ivy, so that she would not be recognized. Then the two sisters ran back to the palace to take their revenge.

Procne wanted to hurt Tereus as badly as he had hurt Philomela. She told Tereus that she wanted to practice a ritual of her own country, where the wife, not the servants, cooked and served a meal to her husband. When he agreed, she took her small son into the kitchen and forced herself to kill him. Then the sisters cut up his body and cooked the pieces, boiling some and roasting others. Tereus enjoyed his meal, and when he had finished, he called for his son. "Itys," he called, "come here to your father." "He is already here," replied Procne, and Tereus looked around the room for him. Out sprang

Left **The sisters' revenge.** Procne and Philomela plotted a dreadful revenge on Tereus, killing Itys, his son. Exacting revenge on one family member by harming or killing an innocent relative rather than the wrongdoer was common practice in Greek myth.

Below *Tereus Confronted with the Head of His Son Itys, Whose Flesh He Has Just Devoured* by Peter Paul Rubens (1577–1640). As in a number of myths, revenge was made complete with the presentation of the child's severed head to his father. In Greek myths, taking revenge was more acceptable for men than for women.

Opposite page *Pyramus and Thisbe* by Lucas Cranach the Elder (1472–1553). Pyramus, believing Thisbe to be dead, was overcome with grief and stabbed himself with his sword. Thisbe asked him to wait for her and then plunged the sword into her heart. So, they died together. William Shakespeare's play *Romeo and Juliet* is said to have been based on the story of Pyramus and Thisbe.

Philomela, smeared with the boy's blood, panting with her eagerness to accuse the king but unable to speak. She was carrying the head of Itys, and pointing to the meat.

Tereus howled with fury and ran after the sisters, ready to impale them both on his sword. The gods intervened, changing Tereus to the bird called a hoopoe, with a great beak like a sword and a crest of feathers like a crown. They changed Procne to a swallow, her feathers red as if stained with blood, and voiceless Philomela they changed to the sweetest singer among the birds, the nightingale. From that day the nightingale has sung "Tereu! Tereu!" accusing the king with every note that she utters.

As at the name
of Thisbe oped his lids
The dying Pyramus, and gazed upon her,
What time the mulberry became vermilion

DANTE ALIGHIERI (1265–1321), *THE DIVINE COMEDY,*
"PURGATORIO," CANTO XXVII

Pyramus and Thisbe

Pyramus and Thisbe were neighbors in the city of Babylon, and the houses that they lived in were separated only by a wall. They fell in love and wished to marry, but their parents refused to allow this. Some old disagreement between the neighboring families had festered into a feud. Pyramus and Thisbe could not talk to one another in public, but they found a little hole in the wall and whispered words of love through it, Pyramus telling Thisbe how much he longed for her, Thisbe telling Pyramus how she longed to be closer to him. They often talked to the wall, reproaching it for not opening wider

for them, so that they could reach through to one another. They used to kiss the wall each night, because their lips could come no closer than this.

One day, they whispered to each other that they could no longer endure being separated. They decided to run away that night, and planned to meet under the mulberry tree that grew by the tomb of Ninus. Thisbe was the first to creep outdoors, at midnight, and she sat under the mulberry tree, waiting for Pyramus. As she waited, a lioness came to drink at a stream that flowed past the tree. Thisbe crept away fearfully into a cave, and the lioness paid her little attention. She had come to drink after making a kill. Thisbe had dropped her veil, and the lioness played with it, tearing at it and staining it with blood from her earlier kill, before she ambled off into the night.

By the time Pyramus arrived, it was dawn. There was light enough for him to see the lioness's paw prints, and the bloodstained veil that he recognized as Thisbe's. In despair, certain that she was dead, he killed himself with his sword. His blood spurted onto the mulberries, which at that time were white. Thisbe now felt brave enough to creep out of her cave and look for Pyramus. She came back to the mulberry tree and saw her dear Pyramus lying there in his blood. Thisbe lifted up his head, and he opened his eyes for the last time to see her beloved face. Then he died, and Thisbe cried out her futile reproaches to the deceiving veil and the lioness. Words gave her heart no ease, and she ended by picking up the sword stained with Pyramus's blood and using it to stab herself through the heart. Her blood, like that of Pyramus, spurted onto the berries. Since the death of Pyramus and Thisbe, all mulberries have been colored a deep blood-red.

THE PERFECT WIFE

Pygmalion was a sculptor who looked in vain for a woman to suit him as a marriage partner. He was a hater of women, finding some fault in all of them, but he carved an ivory statue of his ideal woman, as true to life as he could make it. So realistic was it that he fell in love with his own creation, naming it Galatea, kissing and stroking it, and he longed for the ivory to turn into human flesh. He prayed to the goddess Aphrodite (Venus), and she granted his prayer. That night Pygmalion kissed the statue, and as he did, the ivory became a human woman. He had found his perfect wife.

Left **Pygmalion.** Aphrodite brought the statue of Galatea to life because she thought it looked like herself. Pygmalion and Galatea happily paid homage to Aphrodite for the rest of their lives.

Right **Dionysus with satyrs and Maenads.** Dionysus is the god of wine, intoxication, and creative ecstasy. Orgies held in his honor began in Rome around 200 B.C. These parties were outlawed by the Roman Senate in 186 B.C.

TALES OF DIONYSUS

The Greeks talked about Dionysus (Bacchus) as though he were the newest of the gods, arriving as an adult from Asia long after Zeus (Jupiter) and the rest of his family had established themselves on Mount Olympus. Archaeological evidence indicates, however, that he was one of the oldest of the Greek gods, and that it was really the Olympian gods who were the newcomers. According to myth, he was a son of Zeus, born long after Artemis (Diana) and Apollo, Athene (Minerva) and Hermes (Mercury). Zeus disguised himself as a mortal man in order to seduce Semele, the daughter of King Cadmus of Thebes. His jealous wife, Hera (Juno), found out as usual what her husband was up to, and took a nasty revenge. She too disguised herself as a human being, this time as Semele's old nurse. She told the girl that her lover was hiding his true identity. If he truly

loved her, he would show her who he really was. Semele was six months pregnant with her lover's child— surely he could not refuse her now.

That night, Semele asked Zeus for a gift, to prove that he loved her, and he promised to give her whatever she asked for, sealing his promise with an unbreakable oath by the River Styx. "I want to see you as you really are," she said, and the king of the gods was dismayed, for no mortal can look on Zeus in his glory and live. He tried to persuade her to change her mind, to ask for jewels or a palace of her own or a kingdom for her son to rule, but she kept saying the same words, until he was forced to yield to her.

Zeus discarded his human disguise and showed himself in his splendor, intolerably bright to mortal eyes. Semele was burned to ashes, but Hermes was hovering close by, ready to rescue the unborn child. He seized the child from her womb and sewed him into Zeus's thigh, where he grew for the next three months. Then Hermes helped Zeus cut himself open again and delivered the baby. That is why Dionysus is called the twice-born god.

Hera was still angry, and ordered the Titans to capture the baby and kill him. They tore him into tiny pieces and boiled them in a cauldron. From his blood sprang up the first pomegranate tree. Zeus's mother Rhea noticed what the Titans were doing with her grandson, and put together all the scraps of flesh so that Dionysus could live once more. After surviving this dismemberment, Dionysus might well have been called the thrice-born god!

Below *God Zeus and Goddess Semele Dying from his Love* by Luca Ferrari (1671–1753). The Orphic version of this myth sees Dionysus originally as the child of Zeus and Persephone. The child, then named Zagreus, was devoured by the Titans, but Zeus saved his heart and served it to Semele in a drink, causing her to fall pregnant. When the child was born, Zeus named him Dionysus.

The God of Wine

In order to hide the baby from Hera, Hermes metamorphosed him into a baby goat and asked the nymphs of Mount Nysa to care for him. They hid him in a cave and fed him on milk and honey and, as a reward, Zeus placed the nymphs among the stars as the Hyades. When Dionysus was a little older, he was turned back again into the form of a god. He then began experimenting with the juice of the grapes that grow on Mount Nysa and had soon invented wine. Ivy and grape vines were always associated with the god of wine; he and his followers each carried a staff called the thyrsus, entwined with ivy and tipped with a pinecone.

Dionysus never settled on Mount Olympus. He traveled the world with his riotous, hard-drinking, and lecherous companions, the goat-legged, goat-horned satyrs, and his especial friend, Silenus.

Silenus was the son of Hermes and the oldest of the satyrs, with a bald head and a bulging stomach, and he was perpetually drunk. Dionysus was also accompanied by women who left their ordinary everyday lives to worship him far away from houses and cultivated fields, dressing like the god in fawn skins and praising him in song and dance. They were known as Maenads, Bacchae, or Bacchantes. Some Bacchae followed Dionysus for a lifetime, others for only a few days. Respectable Greek men living in the cities liked to imagine that all sorts of orgies were going on somewhere in the wilds, with wine, half-naked women, sexual promiscuity, and feasts on raw meat torn from living animals, but there are also stories of these women peacefully singing in praise of the god, with songs that could charm savage beasts to tameness.

Above **Dionysus.** Like other gods, Dionysus had a number of icons attributed to him. These include his drinking cup, an ivy wreath, grape vines, and the thyrsus. Some accounts describe the thyrsus as being a long fennel stalk topped with ivy leaves.

Left **Dionysus and Silenus.** Silenus was the faithful tutor and companion of Dionysus. In his consistently drunken state, Silenus was often seen being propped up by satyrs, or being carried by a donkey.

Above *Pentheus and Dionysus* by J. Briot (c. 1610). Pentheus opposed the cult of Dionysus. After the king discovered that the Theban women had gone out to worship Dionysus on the mountain, Pentheus retaliated and imprisoned Dionysus and the women. Later, he found that the walls of the jail that held them crumbled of their own accord and they were set free.

Right *Pentheus Torn Apart by Maenads* by Berlin Painter (c. 500 B.C.– 460 B.C.). The Maenads, also known as Bacchantes or "Frenzied Ones," sometimes painted or tattooed their faces and arms to disguise themselves. They were endowed with great physical strength, which enabled them to tear apart wild beasts. Pentheus was no match for them.

Dionysus and his followers traveled to Egypt and across North Africa to Libya, revealing the secrets of winemaking everywhere they went. They reached India, with some difficulties along the way. At the River Euphrates, a local king tried to stop their progress, but Dionysus killed the king and then sent ivy and grapevines twining across the river until they were strong enough to serve as a bridge. Everywhere that people welcomed Dionysus, they experienced not only revelry but also good government, for he founded cities and restored order, but where he was opposed, he brought riot, madness, and death.

Lycurgus, the Thracian king of the Edonians, sent his army to stop these dangerous foreigners from invading his land. He captured all of Dionysus's followers, but the god escaped by jumping into the sea. Perhaps Dionysus and his satyrs put up little resistance because they were exhausted from their drinking the night before. His grandmother, Rhea, was ready once more to help, this time by taking vengeance on the king. She drove Lycurgus mad, and he started to hallucinate that he was pruning a grapevine. When he struck with his ax, it was no grapevine that he severed, but the neck of his own son, Dryas. Then he kept on cutting at the vine, or so he believed, but it was hands and feet that he was really pruning from his dead son's body. This deed so horrified the gods that they cursed the land of Thrace. Nothing would grow there, they decreed,

Bacchus, that first from out the purple grape Crush'd the sweet poison of misused wine.

JOHN MILTON (1608–1674), "COMUS"

until the criminal was punished. The Edonians did not want the blood-guilt of killing him themselves, and so they took him to a mountain where he was killed by wild horses.

Pentheus and the Bacchae

Pentheus was the king of Thebes and the nephew of Semele. When Dionysus arrived in Thebes, disguised as a mortal man, Pentheus thought that this fellow claiming godhead could only be an imposter, and his band of Bacchae could bring only trouble into the city. The king found it impossible to believe that Dionysus, the son of his own aunt, could be a god, for surely, he thought, all the gods had existed long before people came into the world. Even when the blind seer Teiresias told him that Dionysus was telling the truth, Pentheus refused to accept him as a god. He found it ridiculous that Theban women had gone out to worship this charlatan, and told Cadmus and the seer Teiresias how idiotic they were when they dressed themselves in fawn skins and took up the thyrsus, ready to join the Bacchae outside the city. He did not laugh, though, when he found that his own mother, Agave, had gone to join the Bacchae on the mountainside.

Dionysus stood in front of Pentheus, daring him to keep on disbelieving despite the consequences, but all that Pentheus could see was some ridiculously dressed troublemaker.

Even when Dionysus caused an earthquake to shake the palace walls, Pentheus would not believe. The god was determined to be honored in his own city, and to make sure that his mother, Semele, also received due honor. He put the idea into the king's head that Agave was disgracing herself and the royal house with scandalous orgies on the mountainside, along with the other women of Thebes. "It would

be sensible," Dionysus suggested, "for you to spy out what exactly they are up to, and you will have to dress as a woman to escape their notice. Everyone knows that they will tear apart any man who intrudes on their antics." Pentheus was now deeply under the god's influence, and he agreed to the whole plan. Dionysus dressed him as a woman and sent him on his way by night to spy on the so-called orgies of the Bacchantes.

The god then made the women of Thebes hallucinate as though they were drunk or drugged. They spotted Pentheus as he crept up the hill that night in his woman's clothing, but what they thought they saw was a mountain lion. They were fearless, intoxicated with the god's presence, and they took hold of Pentheus's body and tore it to pieces, believing that they were killing a wild animal. Agave tore off the head and proudly led the parade

DIONYSUS AS HUSBAND

Despite his reputation for orgies, Dionysus (Bacchus) was the only one of the gods except, perhaps, for the equally unlikely god of love, Eros (Cupid), to be totally faithful in marriage. He found Ariadne weeping on the island of Naxos, where Theseus had abandoned her. Dionysus married Ariadne and they had many children. She was made a goddess at their marriage, and Zeus (Jupiter) took the crown that she was wearing and set it in the sky as the Corona Borealis constellation.

Above *Dionysus and Ariadne* by Vecellio Tiziano (1487–1576). Ariadne was propelled into Dionysus's world of endless celebration.

back to Thebes, to show the men just how capable and strong the women had been. When Agave reached the palace, Dionysus lifted his hallucination from her mind and she saw what she had done. In her arms was no lion head, but the severed head of her own son, Pentheus. Agave cried out with grief and horror. Thebes had learned all too well that Dionysus was indeed a god.

Above **The triumph of Dionysus.** In many tales, as in the story of the sailors, Dionysus was associated with lions, panthers, lynxes, and tigers. He, too, is often dressed in the skin of a wild animal, with his head crowned with a wreath of ivy or vine leaves.

Dionysus and the Sailors

A Lydian ship was sailing for the island of Delos, when it ran short of fresh water. They were passing the island of Chios, and so they rowed to the shore and went looking for a spring. The captain went one way and his men went another. The captain found a stream and called his sailors to join him, but when they arrived, they brought with them a stranger. In both face and dress this person could have been either a young man or a young woman, but when he began to speak, there was no doubt that he was a man, or rather a boy. They had found him asleep in a field, and he was still half-asleep, smelling of the wine that he had been drinking.

The captain looked at the boy with awe, for he was as beautiful as any of the immortal gods, and his clothes were finer than any woven by mortals on a loom. He must be a god, the captain thought, and he started to pray, asking for forgiveness and help with their voyage. The sailors thought that this was ridiculous behavior. To them the boy was no more than a captive, a lucky find that they could put up for sale as a slave. They would not listen to the captain when he forbade them to take the god on board. "A curse will fall on the ship and all of you," the captain began to say, but one of his men hit him in the stomach to keep him quiet. Then the crew set sail for Delos again, threatening to throw their captain overboard if he tried to stop them.

Dionysus woke up properly when the ship was out at sea, and asked where he was and where they were taking him. The sailors all put on friendly faces and swore that they would take him anywhere he wanted to go, but they had no intention of keeping their sacred oath. The captain refused to help in any way with the ship's voyage, fearing what would happen when the beautiful boy decided to punish his captors.

Before he showed himself to be a god, Dionysus tested the sailors, giving them one last chance to change their minds. He wept and begged them to pity him, saying that he was only a child and had done them no injury. They paid no attention to any of this, and just sailed on. Then the ship suddenly stopped dead in the water, even though some of the sailors were rowing and a breeze was filling the sails. The oars became too bulky and heavy to move through the water, for ivy twined thickly around them, and more ivy weighed down the sails. The boy seemed no longer a boy, but a grown man adorned with a wreath of vine leaves and grapes. It seemed as though he were surrounded by panthers and tigers and lynxes, all lying at his feet.

The sailors took fright and jumped overboard, and as they hit the water, their bodies changed, their skin grew dark, and their backs arched, their arms disappeared and their feet stretched out into the shape of a curved tail. They were now dolphins instead of men. Only the god-fearing captain lived on as a human being to tell his story.

Come, thou monarch of the vine, Plumpy Bacchus with pink eyne!

WILLIAM SHAKESPEARE (1564–1616), *ANTONY AND CLEOPATRA*

Left **Io and Isis.** Io was forced to wander the land in the form of a white heifer. It was only when she reached Egypt that Zeus finally interceded and restored her to her natural form. Although she is shown here being received by the goddess Isis, the Egyptians worship Io and Isis as one and the same.

THE HOUSE OF CADMUS

The tale of Dionysus (Bacchus) about his mother, Semele, and his father, Zeus (Jupiter), and the death of his cousin, Pentheus, comes in the middle of a series of tales about the kingdom of Thebes and the shifts in fortune within the house of Cadmus that ruled it. Like many Greek myths, the story of the house of Cadmus goes back many generations, with the gods moving in and out of the tale. Many of the Greek myths about a family's fortunes, such as the stories about the house of Tantalus, begin with horror and end with almost everyone dead. The stories about the house of Cadmus are different, because after each catastrophe, things seem hopeful for a while, until the next disaster. The house of Cadmus always seems to gain a little breathing space before its next ordeal.

The Daughters of Danaus

The story goes back as far as Io's troubles with Zeus, when she wandered the earth in the form of a cow and eventually became a goddess. The son of Zeus and Io was called Epaphos, and he married the nymph, Memphis. Their daughter was called Libya,

and she became the lover of the god Poseidon (Neptune), giving birth to twin boys, Belus and Agenor. Then Belus became the father of two boys, Danaus and Aegyptus. Many of these names relate to territories in North Africa: Egypt, Libya, and the Egyptian city of Memphis. Clearly, after Io's wanderings, the family flourished royally, and by the time Danaus and Aegyptus were born, Belus had two kingdoms at his disposal—Egypt, which he gave to Aegyptus, and Libya, which he gave to Danaus.

Things were not quite as harmonious as this, however, because Belus did not want to divide his kingdom. Indeed, his first idea was not to divide his kingdom into two parts, Libya and Egypt, but to arrange for his twin sons to share the rule of the whole, taking it in turns to be king. The twins balked at the idea, each suspicious that the other intended to oust him. Danaus married and fathered 50 daughters, while Aegyptus married and fathered 50 sons. It seemed obvious to Aegyptus that the way to trust and peace was to pair all these sons and daughters in marriage. The daughters of Danaus did not like the idea at all. If they married,

Below **Dionysus.** The festival of Dionysus is celebrated over two days, 16–17 March. The Greek god is equated with the Roman god Bacchus, and with the Italian god, Liber.

95

Above *The Rape of Europa* by Francesco Zuccarelli (1702–1788). Zeus and Europa became lovers, and as a result of their union, Europa bore three sons. In exchange for these children, Zeus gave Europa three gifts: Talus, a bronze man who guarded her island; a dog that never missed its prey; and a spear that never missed its mark.

they would lose their property rights to their husbands, so that Aegyptus and his sons would be the only winners.

Then Danaus began to suspect that the sons of Aegyptus might be planning to kill their brides as soon as they were married, to make absolutely sure that the kingdom of Libya would pass to their family. When an oracle confirmed his suspicions, he did not know how to resist the 50 strong warrior sons of his twin brother and enemy, about to arrive for their weddings. He prayed to Athene (Minerva) for help, and she advised that he and his daughters should flee from their home immediately. They sailed

> *Jupiter himself was turned into a satyr, a shepherd, a bull, a swan, a golden shower, and what not for love.*
>
> ROBERT BURTON (1577–1640),
> "ANATOMY OF MELANCHOLY"

to Argos as suppliants in a ship that Athene had helped Danaus to build. There they begged King Pelasgus to save them from the sons of Aegyptus, who would no doubt be on their heels.

Pelasgus was reluctant to help, not wishing to bring trouble on his own people by helping strangers. The Danaids, the daughters of Danaus, were desperate for his help, and they threatened to hang themselves in the temples of Argos if he tried to turn them away. Such an act would have polluted the land and infuriated the gods. Pelasgus had no choice but to help the women, and he promised that he would not let the sons of Aegyptus marry them by force.

THE SIEGE

Soon the 50 sons of Aegyptus were besieging King Pelasgus's city, and very soon after that, the city ran out of water. The people of Argos would die of thirst if they did not surrender or hand over the Danaids. "You must marry your cousins," Danaus told his daughters, "but let it be a fake marriage. They were planning to kill you once the marriages were celebrated; learn from your delightful bridegrooms how to conduct yourselves as married women. Here are some knives—use them well tonight."

The Danaids agreed to their father's plan, and the 50 sons of Aegyptus came into the city ready to celebrate their marriages. The women gritted their teeth as they kissed their new husbands, and once each pair was in bed and the man was falling asleep, the bride took out her hidden knife and slit his throat. So died 49 of the sons of Aegyptus. The fiftieth son was a kind and honorable man, called Lynceus, and he was married to the gentlest and kindest of the Danaids, Hypermnestra. She could not bring herself to kill him, just as he had resolved that he would never kill his new wife.

Eventually Danaus became king of Argos, and later still, Lynceus and Hypermnestra succeeded him as rulers of Argos. The other 49 daughters were polluted by blood-guilt, and though Hermes (Mercury) eventually purified them for the remainder of their lives on earth, they received an everlasting punishment when they died and went to the kingdom of Hades (Pluto). There they were forced to draw water in sieves, so that their task could never be completed. In the world of the living, however, it seemed as though family troubles had worked themselves through to a happy ending.

Zeus and Europa

The Danaids' grandfather, Belus, had a brother called Agenor, who was also the son of Poseidon, the god of the oceans. Agenor was king of Phoenicia and his children were not prone to quarreling or plotting against each other. Trouble came to them through Europa, Agenor's beautiful daughter. So remarkably beautiful was she, that she caught the eye of Zeus himself. Europa was never far from her brothers, and Zeus decided to pursue her with cunning as well as brute force. He ordered his son, Hermes, to drive all King Agenor's cattle down to the fields that bordered the sea. Then Zeus transformed himself into a bull, the most magnificent of animals, huge but seemingly gentle.

Europa could not resist patting the bull's head, then stroking his neck, hanging garlands on him, and feeding him with flowers. Finally, when he knelt down before her, she climbed onto his back. Zeus stood up and began to pace across the meadow toward the sea, then gently waded into the water, deeper and deeper, until he was swimming far out to sea. By the time Europa noticed, it was too late for her to escape. Zeus swam on with the speed of a god until he reached the island of Crete. There he took the form of an eagle, the bird of Zeus, and took the girl's virginity by force. She gave birth to three children from this rape, Minos, Sarpedon, and Rhadamanthus. The continent of Europe was named after her, while the constellation Taurus

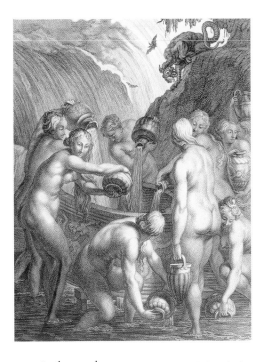

Above *Danaids Punished* **by Bernard Picart (1673– 1733).** The 49 Danaids who killed their husbands escaped punishment during their lifetime; their father eventually found them new husbands by offering them as prizes in a footrace. Punishment after death, however, was another story.

THE NAME "PALLAS ATHENE"

Athene (Minerva) was a prudent goddess, a trait inherited from her mother, Metis (meaning "prudence" in Greek), but early in her life she once acted without thinking and regretted the outcome forever. She and her mortal friend Pallas were playing together, trying out their strength as warriors by casting spears at each other. Pallas protected himself with a shield, but the goddess's strength was too much for him and she struck him a killing blow with her spear. Athene bitterly regretted his death, and in his memory, she called herself from then on Pallas Athene, to remind herself in future to be more mindful of the difference between mortal men's puny powers and the immortal strength of a goddess.

Left *Pallas Athene,* **Fontainebleau School (sixteenth century).** Though famous for her armor, Athene was more than just the goddess of war. She was also the goddess of wisdom, the arts, industry, and skill.

Right **Cadmus, founder of Thebes.** The oracle at Delphi directed Cadmus to embrace his destiny as the founder of a city. Overcoming dangers and difficulties, Cadmus was joined by five others in the building of the city of Thebes. These were Echion, Udaeus, Chthonius, Hyperenor, and Pelorus.

commemorates Zeus's disguise as the bull. Europa's son, Minos, became king of Crete, and it now seemed for a while that this branch of the family had found its way to happiness.

Cadmus and the Founding of Thebes

Europa's family were left on the shore, watching helplessly as the bull carried her far out to sea. Her father, Agenor, ordered his sons Cadmus, Phoenix, Cilix, Thasus, and Phineus (the same man who was later harassed by Harpies), to scatter across the world in search of their sister, and not to return without her. Not knowing which direction to choose, Cadmus went first to Rhodes, then to Thera, but he could find no trace of Europa. In the end he consulted the oracle at Delphi, and was given some

Below *Cadmus Sowing the Dragon's Teeth* by Peter Paul Rubens (1577–1640). When Cadmus sowed the teeth of the dead serpent into the earth, a crop of armed warriors emerged. The five who survived to help him build the city of Thebes are known as the "spartoi" or "sown men."

enigmatic advice: "Abandon your quest for your sister. Find a milk-white cow that has never been put to the plow, and let her roam freely. Follow her until she falls to the ground, and that is the place where you must build a city." Cadmus could not understand why the oracle told him to abandon his search for Europa. He had no intention, however, of ignoring the god's advice, and so he wandered the lower slopes of Mount Parnassus until he found a milk-white heifer that had never been put to the plow. He came close and she ran away. He followed and she trotted onward, until finally, she fell to the ground in exhaustion. On this spot, Cadmus knew, was the place to build his new city.

Cadmus was well aware of the right way to found a city. The first thing to do was to sacrifice to the gods, and the white cow seemed just the right animal to offer them. A sacrifice needed not only a fine animal but also fire and water. Cadmus sent his men upstream in search of a spring, so that he could honor the gods with the first and freshest outpourings from the earth. They followed a stream back toward its source, into a cave where a monstrous serpent was waiting to attack them. The stream belonged to the god of war, Ares (Mars), and he was not at all willing to let strangers wander in and take its water without asking.

The serpent reared up and struck out with its fangs, again and again, until Cadmus's men were all dead. Then Cadmus himself went into the cave to find out why they were taking so long to fetch the water. Luckily, he was still wearing his armor and carrying his spear and shield. It took all of Cadmus's agility and strength to kill Ares' snake, and this killing offended the god of war still more. "Agenor's son has killed my snake," Ares' harsh voice rang out, "and I demand compensation. Turn to snake, Cadmus, and take over the guarding of my cave

Cadmus glanced down at his body, expectin he would never see it again in human form, bu the goddess Athene whispered in his ear, "No ti for that! Go to the dead snake and pull out its t as fast as you can, then sow them in the field." Cadmus recognized the goddess's voice. He did understand what she was telling him to do, but was quick to obey. The goddess helped him bre apart the serpent's jaw, showering the ground w

falling teeth. Everywhere a tooth fell, it sank into the ground and the earth began to bulge. By the time he finished, the mounds of earth were breaking apart and out of them were stepping warriors in full armor. It was a whole army, and they were all threatening Cadmus. He prayed to Athene for help, and heard her whisper in his ear, "All you need to do is to throw a rock toward them."

The warriors did not notice the rock until it hit one of them, and then they started to blame one another. One of them hit the man next to him, then a couple more hit him, and soon the whole army was fighting itself with spear and sword. Cadmus watched as one after another, the men fell down dead. There were only five men left standing when Athene called out, "Stop!" Once they realized that a goddess was helping Cadmus, these five men agreed to help him build the city as the oracle had prophesied. This was how the city of Thebes was founded.

Above *Cadmus and the Dragon* by Francesco Zuccarelli (1702–1788). Cadmus first tried to crush the serpent with a huge stone, but it made no impression. Eventually he killed it with his spear. Some say that the serpent was the offspring of Ares.

THE ROYAL HOUSE OF THEBES

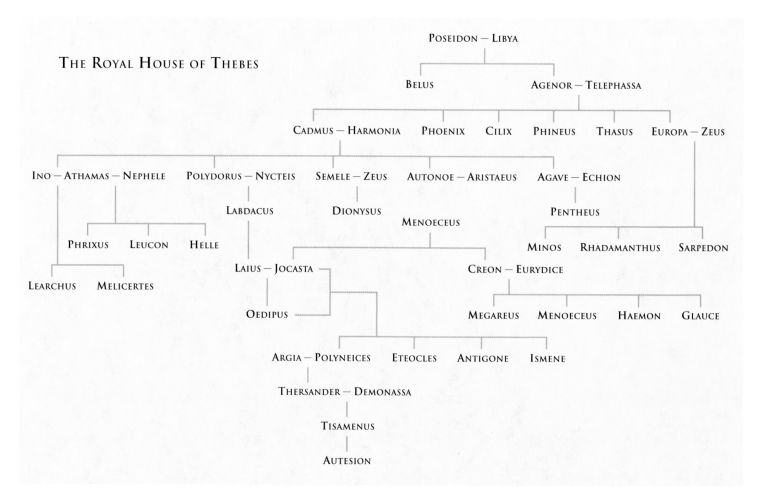

Disasters for the House of Cadmus

At first all went well in Thebes. Cadmus served Ares for eight years as a punishment for killing his serpent, and then married Harmonia, the daughter of Ares and Aphrodite (Venus). All the gods of Olympus came to the wedding, and it seemed as if the house of Cadmus would now flourish in harmony, befriended by all Olympus. Harmonia was given wonderful wedding presents by the gods. Aphrodite presented her with a golden necklace made by Hephaestus (Vulcan), which gave its wearer a beauty that no man could resist. Athene gave her a golden robe that invested her with the dignity of a ruler. Hermes gave her a lyre, and Demeter (Ceres) gave the gift of fertility by frolicking in the fields with her new lover, Jasion. Some of the wedding guests thought that Demeter's behavior was scandalous, but it did lead to plentiful harvests in the fields and a wealth of children for Theban families. The king and queen had four daughters, Autonoe, Agave, Ino, and Semele, and one son, Polydorus. Then the troubles began again.

Autonoe's son was that same Actaeon whom Artemis (Diana) turned into a stag when he came upon her bathing naked after the hunt. Semele was the woman who demanded that her mysterious lover reveal his true identity, and was burned to ashes when Zeus was forced to show himself as a god in divine glory. Then came more troubles when Cadmus handed over the kingship of Thebes to Agave's son Pentheus. The new king sneered at the twice-born son of Semele, Dionysus, and the god drove Agave mad, so that she tore off her own son's head, believing that he was a lion. Cadmus was prudent enough to worship Dionysus as soon as he appeared in Thebes, and so there was no reason for the god to punish him. But Cadmus remembered Ares' anger when he had killed the serpent long ago, and kept wondering if all the disasters that his children and grandson endured could be traced back to that well-meant intrusion into Ares' cave for water. Cadmus offered himself up to Dionysus as a willing victim, and his wife Harmonia did so too, in order to put an end to the miseries befalling their house. The god transformed them into snakes. And so, years after Cadmus's fight with the serpent, Ares' curse had come true, but not in anger. When Cadmus and Harmonia died in their snake form, Zeus sent them to the Elysian Fields to live forever among the blessed dead.

Right **Cadmus, Harmonia, and Apollo.** The gods left the comfort of their home on Mount Olympus to attend the wedding of Cadmus and Harmonia. As a wedding present, the gods gave Harmonia a robe, and a necklace specially wrought for the occasion by Hephaestus.

THE HOUSE OF OEDIPUS

After the founding of Thebes by Cadmus, and after the follies of Pentheus in not accepting Dionysus (Bacchus) as a god, the troubles of Cadmus's family were still not ended. Pentheus was succeeded as king by his son, then his grandson, and it seemed as if the gods were no longer paying attention to this royal house. But then came the turn of Laius to become king, and a fresh brew of troubles began. Laius married Jocasta, and when they had no children, he asked the oracle of Delphi for advice. The oracle responded with a message that, for once, seemed unambiguous. Laius's son would kill his father.

Laius was beside himself with grief and anxiety when he heard this, and his worries grew when he returned to Thebes and found that Jocasta was pregnant. The royal pair decided that if this child were a boy, he would have to die, to avert the oracle. However, oracles are impossible for human beings to circumvent. The king and queen did not want the blood-guilt of killing their child, or of ordering him to be killed, and when a son was indeed born to Jocasta, they ordered him to be taken to Mount Cithaeron and exposed to the elements. Everyone believed that this meant certain death, but there was always the remote possibility that such a child might be rescued and adopted by someone else. Thus there was no actual blood-guilt for the miserable parents.

The unlikely happened. The baby was taken to Mount Cithaeron to die, but first his ankles were pierced through with iron rods. That is how he

Left **Consulting an oracle.** The priestess sat on a tripod, which was positioned above a fissure in the floor of the temple. Strange, hallucinating vapors rose up from the floor, and in a state of trance, the priestess would mumble her answer.

Below *The Finding of Oedipus,* French School (seventeenth century). Overwhelmed with pity for the baby, the herdsman did not abandon Oedipus, but instead gave him to the care of a Corinthian peasant. Oedipus was saved from dying from exposure on the hillside.

himself might all have been averted. But the oracle chose to tell Oedipus about his future, not his past. He would be the most accursed of mortals, he was told. He would marry his own mother and kill his own father.

The Oracle Comes True

Oedipus was distraught. He swore to himself that he would never return to Corinth. If he kept away, he would be in no danger of marrying Merope or killing Polybus. All might yet be well. He was hurrying down the road to a place where three roads met, a place of ill luck sacred to the goddess Hecate. Coming toward him was a chariot, and the driver and the passenger rudely demanded that he step aside and let them pass. Oedipus

Above **Detail from a crater showing Oedipus and the Sphinx, attributed to the Painter of the Birth of Dionysus.** The Greek Sphinx was an evil creature of death, destruction, and general misfortune. She struck fear into the hearts of everyone except Oedipus, who managed to outwit the beast.

received his name, Oedipus, which in Greek means "swollen foot." The Theban shepherd who took him to the mountain did not abandon him there, but gave him to a Corinthian shepherd, who took him to his king and queen, Polybus and Merope. This pair were longing for a baby to adopt, since they could not bring one into the world themselves. Merope treated the child as her own, and in a little while everyone seemed to have forgotten that he was not the royal heir of Corinth by blood.

It was not until he was nearly grown up that Oedipus heard the story that he was not the true son of Merope and Polybus, and when he asked the king and queen for the truth of the matter, they swore that he was their son by blood. But then he heard another rumor that he was an adopted child, and he determined to find out the truth. If he could not be sure who among mortals was speaking the truth, surely the oracle of Apollo at Delphi would not lie. It was a long journey from Corinth to Delphi, and when he arrived, the oracle did not even answer his question. If only it had told him what he asked, the miseries that befell his family and

Right *Sibyl* by Lorenzo Ghiberti (1378–1455). "Sibyl" was the name given to those prophetesses who prophesied while in a state of ecstasy inspired by the god Apollo. Two of the most famous Greek Sibyls are the Cumaean Sibyl and the Erythaean Sibyl.

was not about to yield to rudeness. He stood in the middle of the road, refusing to budge. The driver swore at him, and then the passenger, an elderly man, struck out at him with a staff. Oedipus struck back, and killed the passenger, the driver, and all their companions except one, a man who ran away.

Oedipus walked on, a long and weary journey, until he was close to the city of Thebes. The people that he met on the road were full of the city's bad news. Its king, Laius, had just been killed by some villains, while he was far away on a journey, and a monster, the Sphinx, was attacking and killing everyone who tried to get in and out of the city. Queen Jocasta had promised that whoever killed the Sphinx would become king of Thebes and gain her as his wife.

The Sphinx was a monster with the head and upper body of a woman and the lower body of a lion, and she liked to play with her victims. She offered not to kill and eat them, if they could answer a riddle. The road past Mount Phicion, where the Sphinx waited for her next victim, was covered with bones of men who had failed to find the right answer. Oedipus decided that he would try his wits with the monster, and walked along the road that passed by Mount Phicion. There the Sphinx was waiting for him, and once he was in earshot, she asked, "What goes on four feet in the morning, then two at noon, then three in the evening?" Oedipus did not panic, like those who had left their bones on the hillside. He thought for a moment and answered, "A human being, for people go on four feet when they are babies, then on two feet as adults, and then, when they are old and infirm, they use a walking stick as a third foot to balance them." This was the correct answer. Enraged, the Sphinx threw herself down the mountainside and died on the rocks below. Oedipus had won for himself the kingship of Thebes and its queen for his wife.

Oedipus the King

All went well for King Oedipus for a while, and his mother-wife Jocasta gave birth to four children by her son-husband, two sons, Polyneices and Eteocles, and two daughters, Antigone and Ismene. Oedipus was loved by his people, and regarded as the wisest of rulers. Years passed, and then a plague came to Thebes, making the whole countryside barren. Crops failed, and there were no new births of children or animals. Such a disaster

meant that the gods were displeased with the city; someone must be polluting Thebes by their presence. Oedipus sent a servant to the oracle at Delphi to ask for its advice. When the servant returned, he brought the answer that it was the murderer of Laius who was at fault. The city would not be healed until the murderer was punished.

Oedipus turned to the blind Teiresias to help find the murderer, for he was famous throughout Greece for his supreme skills as a prophet. Teiresias refused to help him, saying that he would not bring pain on the king, but Oedipus insisted, anxious to fulfill his duty as a king and punish the murderer of Laius.

THE OEDIPUS COMPLEX

Sigmund Freud developed a theory about the early life of children in which they find and organize satisfaction in a variety of ways. In what Freud called the Oedipus complex, a boy chooses an object of satisfaction based on his mother, who has satisfied such basic needs as feeding and nurturing. This love of the mother brings him into rivalry with his father. Girls have to overcome their initial attachment to the mother to form an affectionate relationship with their father, and then relate to the mother as a rival. Freud believed that the myth of Oedipus, as dramatized by Sophocles, held the key to this organization of sexual difference and satisfaction. For Sigmund Freud, this powerful Greek myth spoke one of the most formative truths of the human unconscious mind.

Right **Oedipus kills his father.** Unaware that King Laius, who was one of the travelers in a group Oedipus met on the road, was really his father, Oedipus killed him after a heated argument.

Above *Oedipus* by Ernest Hillemacher (1818–1887). Overcome with the horror of his crimes, Oedipus punished himself by stabbing his eyes until he was blind. That way he was unable to look at the misery he had caused.

Eventually Teiresias revealed that the murderer was Oedipus himself. Oedipus was a wise king, but when he heard this revelation, he could not accept the gods' truth. He cast around for someone to blame. Teiresias must have lied, Oedipus reassured himself, and Jocasta's brother Creon must have conspired with him because he wanted the kingship for himself.

Still the king fretted over the oracle, for the plague still tormented the land, the animals, and the people of Thebes. He decided to investigate the murder of Laius to the best of his ability. The only

thing of which he could be certain was that the murderer was not himself, for everyone knew that Laius had been killed by a group of rogues, while the murders that Oedipus had committed near Delphi, he had done without help. He tried talking his thoughts over with Jocasta, but what she said did not comfort him at all. She wanted to reassure him by telling him of an oracle that she and her previous husband, Laius, had thwarted years ago. The oracle had said that Laius's son would kill his father, yet the child had been exposed on the mountain and died.

It was some completely unrelated villains who had lain in wait at the intersection of three roads near Delphi and ambushed Laius's chariot.

OEDIPUS DISCOVERS THE TRUTH

Oedipus could hardly bear to listen to this. It was at the intersection of three roads near Delphi that he had killed the elderly man and his servants. He began to dread the unfolding of the truth, but he knew that for the sake of his people, he must not stop investigating who had killed Laius. Now he sent for the herdsman who had exposed the baby and who, it turned out, was also the man who had run away from the fight where Laius had died. Oedipus was horrified when the servant admitted that it was just one man who had killed the king of Thebes, and that the story about a crowd of villains was only an exaggeration to excuse his cowardice in running away. Oedipus heard all this with difficulty, and his wife begged him to stop the investigation then and there. Then she ran out of the room, as she realized that he was on the point of discovering all the truth. The servant admitted that the baby he had been ordered to expose on Mount Cithaeron had been taken by a Corinthian shepherd to be adopted by Merope and Polybus. Oedipus could not escape the chain of evidence. It was he, Oedipus, who had killed his father and married his mother, while trying so hard to avoid any contact with them. It was he, Oedipus, who had brought plague on his people. His sons and daughters were the product of incest. His mother-wife—and there he stopped thinking and ran after her—Jocasta had killed herself, hanging herself by a rope from the roof beam of the royal bedroom.

Oedipus vowed that he would never again look on the miseries of his family, his wretched wife and children. He took up the brooches from Jocasta's garments and stabbed his eyes blind. "Bring up my children well," he implored Jocasta's brother Creon, "for you must be regent in Thebes until my sons are old enough to take the throne. Let me be led to Mount Cithaeron, where I should have died as a baby, and perhaps the gods will finally be willing to take my life now." Creon agreed to all of this, and the great King Oedipus left his kingdom, the most wretched of men.

Oedipus at Colonus

Oedipus did not die quickly after he had blinded himself and stumbled out of Thebes. He lived for many years, treated by the kings of neighboring city-states with a mixture of honor and dread. Here was a most unfortunate man, one whose deeds had broken the laws of gods and men, guilty and yet blameless for what he did. No one wanted to call down the wrath of the gods for sheltering someone so accursed; no one wanted to be the gods' target

Below *Antigone from "Antigone" by Sophocles* by Marie Stillman (1844–1927). Antigone was determined that the body of her brother would be treated with respect. Defying the king's orders, she secretly performed a ceremonial burial by sprinkling dust on him. Some versions of the story say she burned his body on a funeral pyre.

for not protecting a suppliant. When he was close to death, Oedipus was summoned by Apollo to Athens, where the just and merciful King Theseus ruled. Just outside the city, at Colonus, the blind man entered the sanctuary of the Erinyes, the Furies, whose secret place all other people feared to enter. Finally, Oedipus found peace of heart in the sacred grove dedicated to those dreaded beings whose task is to punish the minds of the guilty. He had transcended human shame and guilt, and was now favored by the gods. Oedipus was said to be buried in the sanctuary

For the gods, though slow to see, see well, whenever a man casting aside worship turns folly.

SOPHOCLES (C. 496 B.C.–C. 406 B.C.), *OEDIPUS COLONUS*

at Colonus, but the only person to know his final fate was King Theseus. The Athenians believed that his bones were buried there, or that he had descended to the underworld from Colonus. His body had the power to protect the place of his death, and the Athenians long prided themselves on being the one state to welcome Oedipus on his sorrowful wanderings.

The Sons and Daughters of Oedipus

Once again, things went well for a while. Creon ruled well and justly until Eteocles and Polyneices

came of age. They agreed to share the kingship in alternating years, one year for Polyneices and the next for Eteocles. Polyneices ruled well for his first year, and then handed over the kingship to his brother, but at the end of the next year Eteocles would not relinquish the crown. Polyneices was forced into exile, where he found allies in the exiled Tydeus of Calydon and King Adrastos of Argos. They assembled a mighty army of Argives, divided into seven smaller armies under seven commanders, to attack the seven gates of Thebes.

Creon advised Eteocles not to attempt full-scale battle but to send out seven champions to fight in single combat at the seven gates, against the seven battle leaders of Polyneices's army. Polyneices himself did not die there, but the six other commanders did. One of them, an Argive called Capaneus, was killed by Zeus (Jupiter) himself. Capaneus was an insolent fellow, who swore that he would win through even if Zeus were to try to stop him. He brought a ladder to climb the wall surrounding Thebes, and he was just about to jump into the city when Zeus's thunderbolt knocked him back to the ground and killed him. Now Polyneices's Argive army retreated a little way, and a general battle began. Eteocles called out in a loud voice, "Men of Argos, do not die for a cause which is not yours! Let the issue be decided in single combat between Polyneices and myself." Polyneices was eager for the fight, and the two brothers fought until both were streaked with blood and sweat. The end came quickly, Polyneices stabbed through the stomach by Eteocles, Eteocles mortally wounded by Polyneices. They fell dead almost in one another's arms.

CREON AS KING

The armies disbanded; the war was over. The new king of Thebes would be Creon, Jocasta's brother. His first decree as king was that Eteocles should be buried as befitted a king of Thebes, but that the rebel Polyneices should be left in the dust as food for the dogs. Creon's second decree as king was that anyone caught trying to bury Polyneices would be put to death. So began the next round of troubles for the children of Oedipus.

One of Oedipus's daughters, Ismene, was a pliant young woman who wanted nothing more than to live a quiet life, and she was determined to obey the new king, Creon, and leave her brother to rot outside the walls of Thebes. His other daughter, Antigone, was as firm-minded as her father-brother Oedipus. She planned to bury her brother, if only symbolically, by scattering a little dust over his corpse. She made her way out that night, and succeeded in reaching the body and pouring a handful of dust over it, but the next day the furious king ordered the body to be brushed clean again. Anyone who disobeyed and was caught would die a very unpleasant death. Again Antigone went out, took up a handful of dust, and sprinkled it on the body. This time she was caught.

Above **Burial denied.** King Creon forbade the proper burial of the rebels. He commanded that the bodies be left on the battlefield as dog's fodder. This decree was offensive to his people and the gods.

Below **Antigone, Eteocles, and a woman carrying a hydria to the tomb of Oedipus.** When he died, Oedipus was finally at peace. Some myths say that his daughters remained faithful to him throughout his wanderings.

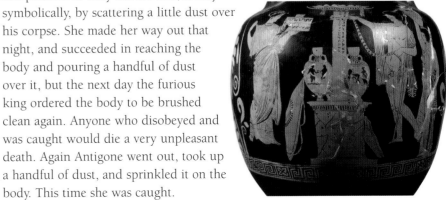

Creon found himself in a painful position. Antigone was only doing her duty by her dead brother, and every Greek could sympathize with a sister wanting to help her beloved brother to go to the underworld, rather than have him linger as an uneasy ghost. Yet she had disobeyed the first edict of the king of Thebes by giving succor to someone who had invaded the kingdom with an army. As a king, Creon felt that he could not yield his authority to a girl. As a father, he had a still more difficult decision to make. Antigone was soon to be married to his own son, Haemon. It would have been possible to forgive her, Creon thought, if only the wretched girl would promise not to try to bury her brother a third time; but Antigone would not consider such a promise. Instead, she swore that she would keep on trying to bury her brother properly until Creon had her executed.

In exasperation, the king ordered her to be buried alive. As so often in Greek myth, he was trying to avoid the blood-guilt of actually ordering her to be killed, in the knowledge that lack of air or starvation would soon enough kill her for him. Antigone went to her death in triumph, knowing that what she had done would please the gods. Haemon pleaded with her to change her mind, and then, when she would not listen, secretly joined her in her prison.

ANTIGONE'S DEATH

While Antigone was still on her way to her place of entombment, the blind prophet Teiresias came to give Creon a last chance to change his mind. Teiresias told the king that what he was doing offended the gods and would mean the ruin of his family line. Creon blustered and then suddenly gave in, ordering his men to run after the guards who had been leading Antigone to her death,

and countermand his order. It was too late. There in the burial chamber, she had already hanged herself, and when Creon himself arrived, his son Haemon despairingly committed suicide next to his beloved Antigone. The king knew that his own wife would be the next to kill herself out of grief for her dead son.

This is how the line of Cadmus came to an end. Perhaps Ismene lived on, perhaps she married and had children, but those of Oedipus's children who most resembled him, his stubborn sons and daughter Antigone, were all dead. Jocasta's bloodline was coming to an end as well, with the deaths of Creon's wife and son. The long-drawn-out story of Oedipus and his children is characterized by themes of obstinacy, defiance, and readiness to face death. The larger sequence of myths about the house of Cadmus lurches between times of good rule, prosperity, orderliness, and quiet, and times of trouble that strained sufferers beyond the limits of their humanity. But what else could Antigone have done, and still been true to herself? What else could Oedipus have done, or his parents, other than trying to avert the prophecy? Their tragedy was inescapable, and yet it was also the opportunity for Oedipus, tormented seeker after truth, and Antigone, dauntless honorer of the gods' law, to achieve heights of heroism to which none of the Greek warriors came close.

GANYMEDE

Ganymede, the son of King Tros of Troy, was an exceptionally handsome young man. Zeus (Jupiter) found him desirable, and changed himself into the form of an eagle to abduct him from Troy. He snatched Ganymede into the air with his claws and carried him to Olympus, much to the annoyance of his wife Hera (Juno). Annoying Hera further, Zeus made Ganymede cupbearer to the gods, a task which had previously been carried out by Hebe, the daughter of Zeus and Hera. Zeus went further still, commemorating his love for Ganymede in the constellation Aquarius, the waterbearer.

Left *Ganymede* by Benvenuto Cellini (1500– 1571). Zeus's liaison with Ganymede saw Zeus infatuated and Hera outraged once more. The affair is believed by some to be a religious justification for homosexuality within the Greek culture.

the tower, Acrisius did not find out about Danae's son Perseus until he was four years old. Perseus grew up to be an active child, making so much noise that he could be heard even through the tower walls, and that was how Danae's secret became known. Acrisius was beside himself with anger and perplexity. How had any lover found his way to Danae? And how could he destroy Perseus without incurring blood-guilt? Acrisius ordered a large wooden chest to be built, and the mother and baby to be put inside it. Then it was cast adrift on the sea, where the king hoped that the pair would die.

Almost all oracles come true, however hard people fight against them. Perseus and Danae survived their time in the wooden chest, which was caught in a net by a fisherman near the island of Seriphus. The fisherman, Dictys, took the child and his mother to the court of King Polydectes, who was very much attracted to Danae. For years he courted her, but she kept refusing him, saying that she was devoted only to her son. One day the king invited Danae to a feast along with Perseus, who was by now a young man. All the guests ate and drank well. Polydectes asked each man present to give him a horse, pretending that he needed them for his courtship of a distant princess. Perhaps the wine went to Perseus's head, for after admitting that he had no horse to give, he found himself promising that he

Above *Danae* by **Francesco Primaticcio (1504–1570).** Not even an impermeable brass tower could dampen Zeus's desires. By transforming himself into a shower of gold pouring down into Danae's lap, he fathers Perseus.

Left *Danae and the Brazen Tower* by **Sir Edward Burne-Jones (1833–1898).** Hoping to change his fate, the king imprisoned his daughter Danae. In some stories the prison is described as a bronze tower, while in others, it is an underground chamber.

PERSEUS

Acrisius was the king of Argos, and his life was made miserable by an oracle, which prophesied that his grandson, the child of his daughter Danae, would kill him. In order to thwart this prophecy, he kept his daughter indoors, virtually in prison, shut up in a tower of brass. This was no obstacle to the king of the gods, Zeus (Jupiter), who manifested in Danae's lap in a shower of gold. Soon she became pregnant by the god, but because she was hidden in

Right *Medusa* by Glen Vause. Some people believe that the mythological beheading of the Gorgon Medusa symbolizes the domination of patriarchal society. "Medusa," which means "sovereign female wisdom," had been silenced, and her powers had been brought under the control of the male order.

Below *Study for Perseus and the Graiae* by Sir Edward Burne-Jones (1833–1898). The three Graiae or "gray ones" were sisters. They were guardians of the Gorgons. Gray-haired from birth, the siblings were Deino ("dread"), Enyo ("horror"), and Pemphredo ("alarm").

would do anything to please the king. He would even kill the monster Medusa. That was just what Polydectes had been hoping to hear, to give him an excuse to get rid of the inconvenient young man, and instead of treating it as the wine talking, he promptly accepted Perseus's kind offer.

Athene (Minerva) and Hermes (Mercury) liked young Perseus, and were waiting for him next morning with good advice and gifts. Athene gave him the equipment he needed to fight Medusa—a bag, a shield burnished as bright as any mirror, and a helmet that had once belonged to Hades (Pluto), the god of the underworld. This helmet made its wearer invisible. Hermes gave him a curved sword like a sickle and a pair of sandals with wings, rather like his own ankle wings. Athene told him to try out his wings by flying to the kingdom of Night, to the home of the Graiae, the only ones who knew just where to find Medusa.

The Graiae were three ancient deities who shared a single eye that they took in and out of their empty eye sockets, and a single tooth that they took in and out of their gummy mouths. Perseus was ready to fight them, but Athene urged him to use cleverness, not force. He waited just by the entrance to their cave with Hades' helmet on his head, to make him invisible, but the Graiae could feel that someone was there. "Give me the eye, sister," insisted one of them, and blindly stretched out her hand. The one with the eye reluctantly eased it out and for a moment, all three Graiae were blind. In darted Perseus, grabbing the eye out of her hand. Then he waited for one of the panic-stricken goddesses to take out their one tooth, to pass it to the next, and immediately grabbed it as well. Once they were at his mercy, he told them that he would give them back their precious tooth and eye only on one condition: that they would tell him where to find Medusa. The Graiae had no choice but to mutter the directions that he asked for. In some accounts he gave the eye and tooth back to the sisters, but some say that he threw them into the depths of a lake, leaving the Graiae in despair.

Medusa

Medusa was one of the three Gorgon sisters. They were the daughters of a sea god, and lived far from the lands of mortal men and women on an island in the remotest ocean. Two of these Gorgons, Euryale and Stheno, were immortal, but their sister Medusa could be killed. In some versions of the story, however, Medusa was not the immortals' sister by birth, but a mortal woman who had been punished by Athene for intruding on her mysteries, or

else for making love with Poseidon (Neptune) in the virgin goddess's temple. Athene did not take away Medusa's beauty, but turned her hair to a wild tangle of snakes and condemned her to lurk in the darkness, unable ever to be intimate with a man. Anyone who looked at her with love in his eyes would instantly turn to stone. In many accounts and many works of art, Medusa is represented as hideously ugly, with a fat tongue protruding from her mouth, but she is sometimes portrayed as a serenely beautiful woman whose snakes are regal ornaments on her head, rather than loathsome disfigurements.

Perseus used the helmet of invisibility to make his way into the cave where the Gorgons were sleeping, and he used the mirrorlike shield to look for Medusa indirectly, staring at her reflection as he came closer and drew his sickle sword. The Gorgon's snaky hair writhed, sensing danger, but she could see nothing to strike at. Out of nowhere flashed the sword, and cut off her head. Even in death, the terrible head had the power to turn to stone anyone who looked directly at it. Perseus thrust the bleeding thing into his bag and flew away. He needed all the swiftness and agility of his winged sandals to outfly the other Gorgons, but eventually they were left behind, thrashing about and wailing in the darkness.

As soon as he had cut off Medusa's head, out of her severed neck sprang the winged horse, Pegasus, and a fully grown human warrior, Chrysaor, her children by Poseidon. Medusa's blood dripped from the bag as Perseus flew onward over the deserts of Libya, and each drop turned into a different kind of snake. Eventually the hero became tired and wanted to rest, but when he tried to land in northwest Africa, the Titan Atlas pushed him back into the sky, because an oracle had once told him that he would be robbed by a son of Zeus. When Atlas would not let him land, Perseus pulled the head out of the bag, and the gigantic Titan was robbed of life and turned into an even more gigantic mountain range, the Atlas Mountains that to this day hold up the sky with their summits.

Below **Perseus and Medusa.** The Greek Medusa is an import from Libya where she was worshipped by the Libyan Amazons as their Serpent Goddess. Originally symbolizing wisdom, female mysteries, and the cycles of nature, she was eventually made instead into an evil monster.

Left **Gorgon.** The Gorgons' powers were greatly respected. The Gorgon mask symbolized fierce strength and power. These masks were often used in temples and sanctuaries and even in battle on the armor of the warriors.

AN OATH BY THE WATERS OF STYX

Styx was one of the six rivers of the underworld, and an oath by the waters of Styx was the most binding oath that a god could take. When an oath was sworn in Olympus by the Styx, the goddess of the rainbow, Iris, sped to the river to fetch its water in a golden cup. Those who drank the water and swore a false oath were punished with a year of sickness and silence, starved of nectar and ambrosia, and were then banished from Olympus for another nine years.

Opposite page **Crossing the Styx** by Joachim Patenir (Patinir) (c. 1485–c. 1524). The Styx is said to wind around Hades nine times. The other rivers of Hades are Acheron, Cocytus, Phlegethon, Lethe, and Aornis.

Andromeda and the Monster

Perseus flew on, delighting in the speed with which he could travel to the farthest north and then the south. As he flew across the sea to the coast of Ethiopia, he saw a huge rock on the beach with a naked young woman chained to it. She had been struggling, for her arms and legs were bruised from the chains, but now she was rigid with terror, looking out to sea where a monstrous serpent was riding the waves toward her.

The woman in chains was Andromeda, daughter of King Cepheus and Queen Cassiopeia. This queen was as foolish as Niobe, daring to set herself up as equal to the gods in beauty and, as with Niobe, her boasting ended in tears. Cassiopeia claimed that she was more beautiful than any of the sea nymphs, more beautiful than Hera (Juno) herself, and the sea god Poseidon retaliated by laying the country waste with floods of water and sending a sea serpent to attack the people. Cepheus consulted the oracle of Zeus to find out how to save his country from flood and monster, and was told that only the willing sacrifice of his own daughter would placate the god of the sea. That morning, the wretched parents had walked in tearful procession to the sacrificial rock to chain down their weeping daughter, just as Psyche's parents wept when taking her to a marriage with death.

Perseus flung himself downward, sickle sword in his hand, and tore gashes in the serpent's coils until it died. Then he slashed Andromeda's chains apart and carried her back to her parents, though he longed to keep her in his arms. What could the king do but consent to Perseus's marriage with his daughter, even though she had already been promised to her uncle, Phineus?

Andromeda did not want to marry her uncle, but he very much wanted to marry her, and at the wedding feast he and his men started to cause trouble. Perseus knew just how to silence their angry tongues; he took the dripping head of the Gorgon out of its bag, and as Phineus and his men looked at it, they turned to stone. Some say that Cassiopeia also objected to her daughter's marriage, and like Phineus, was turned to stone. It seems more likely, though, that she was overjoyed with her daughter's rescue, for Poseidon eventually forgave her and commemorated her in the night sky as a constellation, close to the constellation Cepheus that commemorated her husband. Poseidon's sea monster can also be found in the sky as the constellation Cetus. Perseus and Andromeda were also given constellations as a memorial at their death, with the star Algol representing the head of Medusa in Perseus's hand.

LATER YEARS

It was many years before Perseus and Andromeda grew old and died. Before they could settle to a happy marriage, Perseus had affairs to resolve with two kings. First he took vengeance on Polydectes, the king who had tried to send him to his death. He flew back to Polydectes' palace and told the king that he had killed Medusa, as promised, but Polydectes accused him of idle boasting. The king summoned all his people to the marketplace, to put the liar to public shame. No one would believe Perseus's claim, except for his mother, Danae, and the fisherman, Dictys, who had rescued both of them from the sea. "Cover your eyes," Perseus told Danae and Dictys, and then he pulled Medusa's head once more from the bag and held it up high,

Below **Perseus and Andromeda** by **Pierre Puget (1620–1694).** Perseus swooped down from the sky to rescue Andromeda from the sea monster. Some say his winged sandals were a gift from Hermes, while other accounts name the Graiae as the gift-bearers.

so that everyone could see. In that instant, the marketplace became full of stone statues instead of living people.

After that mass extermination, Athene decided that the head of Medusa was too potent for any mortal to use as a weapon, and she took it for herself. It adorns her aegis, the goatskin that she wears when she goes armed into battle. Perseus gave back the helmet of invisibility and the winged sandals, but he still had one task to accomplish, seeking out and forgiving King Acrisius who had forced Danae into the tower and then sent mother and son out onto the sea in a wooden chest to die. Acrisius was hiding in the city of Larissa, assuming that Perseus was coming to kill

*The Gorgon's head
its leaden eyeballs rolled,
And writhed its snaky horrors
through the shield*

OSCAR WILDE (1854–1900),
"CHARMIDES"

him. Even when he discovered that the head of Medusa was no longer in Perseus's bag, he found it hard to believe that his life was not in danger. Perseus suggested a ritual of reconciliation, and then joined in an athletics contest being held in Larissa. He entered the discus competition, and when he hurled the discus, it somehow flew the wrong way and hit Acrisius on the foot. The king was an old man by then, and the pain and shock killed him. The oracle had come true, and he had died by the hands of his own grandson. Was it an accident, though, with the discus just happening to slip sideways as Perseus threw it, or did it fly true to his feelings, if not his conscious intent?

Above **The wounded Chimaera.** The Chimaera, offspring of Typhon and Echidna, was a ferocious fire-breathing monster. It was believed that the Chimaera represented a volcanic mountain of the same name in Lycia, the peak of which was the home to lions, the middle part was where goats resided, and the foot was the home of serpents.

Opposite page *Mount Helicon with God Pegasus and Centaur Cheiron and Fountain Hippocrene with Zodiac Sign Sagittarius by Giovanni Falconetto (1458–1534).* Mount Helicon was part of a range of mountains in western Boeotia, not far from the Gulf of Corinth. Both the Hippocrene and Aganippe springs began here, and it was the abode of the god Apollo, leader of the muses.

Right **Poseidon.** Poseidon was the god of the sea and earthquakes, and was associated with dolphins, horses, and bulls. In art, Poseidon was usually represented as a tall, bearded, powerfully built man in the prime of his life. It is often difficult to distinguish his figure from that of Zeus.

TALES OF REVENGE

Both gods and humans frequently sought revenge in Greek myth. Taking revenge was a normal and acceptable action for a man in Greek myth, but not for a woman. In the story of Jason and Medea, for instance, Medea was regarded with a mixture of sympathy and horror for her extensive revenge on Jason and all close to him. For men in Greek myth, standards were different. If a king was overthrown or killed, for example, it was expected that his son or grandson would eventually seek revenge on the usurper. The gods also took revenge, avenging insults to themselves by killing the insolent human being responsible, and sometimes extending their vengeance to a family, however innocent its other members may have been (as in the story of Niobe and her children). The stories of Bellerophon and Orion tell of heroes, those favored by the gods, who became impertinent and presumed the gods' good will, and thus became the objects of divine revenge.

Bellerophon

No one knows the true name of the man called Bellerophon, who was the son of Poseidon (Neptune) and the sea goddess Eurynome. "Bellerophon," meaning "slayer of Belleros" in Greek, was his nickname, and the story goes that he murdered a Corinthian man called Belleros and fled to Tiryns, to the court of Proetus. Proetus was the brother of Acrisius, who was the father of Danae and brother of Perseus's grandfather. The twin brothers had quarreled even before they were born, and they had fought over the kingship of Argos, but by the time Bellerophon arrived seeking sanctuary, that quarrel at least had been resolved. The kingdom was split, and Proetus ruled over his share from the city of Tiryns.

It was not King Proetus but his wife, Stheneboia, who quarreled with the newcomer, Bellerophon. He suffered a fate like that of the biblical Joseph or Theseus's son Hippolytus, as Stheneboia became infatuated with him and tried to seduce him. When he refused her, she could not restrain her

Oh for a beaker full of the warm South, Full of the true, the blushful Hippocrene! With beaded bubbles winking at the brim, And purple-stainèd mouth.

JOHN KEATS (1795–1821), "ODE TO A NIGHTINGALE"

feelings, but they had changed from longing to fury. She forced herself to weep and then ran to her husband to show him her tears, crying out that Bellerophon had tried to seduce her. Bellerophon protested, but in the uproar, no one paid him any attention beyond throwing him into a dungeon.

Proetus did not want to be directly involved in the death of this wicked young man, because Bellerophon had come to Tiryns seeking sanctuary, and the gods looked sternly on anyone who violated sanctuary by killing the suppliant. So the king sent Bellerophon to his wife's father, Jobates, in Lycia, carrying a wax tablet bearing the message that Bellerophon had tried to seduce Stheneboia and must be put to death for it. Either Bellerophon was a remarkably honorable messenger or he was unable to read. Without reading its contents, he brought the tablet to Jobates, who was reluctant to acquire blood-guilt by killing a guest. Jobates came up with what he thought was a very clever solution. He would send Bellerophon to his death against the monster that was troubling his kingdom, rather than simply kill him on the spot.

BELLEROPHON AND THE CHIMAERA

Jobates sent Bellerophon to kill the Chimaera, a horrifying monster that breathed fire. The first third of its body was that of a lion, the middle was a goat, and instead of back legs it had the coils of a serpent. Some say that the Chimaera had the heads of a lion, goat, and serpent, with the goat's head coming out of the middle of its back and the serpent's head attached to the end of its tail.

Athene (Minerva) and Poseidon favored Bellerophon, and suggested to him that he travel to the fountain of Peirene in Corinth. There he saw a wonderful winged horse, stooping to drink. This was Pegasus, the son of Poseidon and Medusa, born from her dead body after Perseus had put an end to her. Pegasus usually lived on Mount Helicon with the Muses. A spring emerged at the spot where he struck the ground with his hoof, and it was named the Hippocrene spring (Hippocrene meaning "horse fountain" in Greek), much invoked by later poets seeking inspiration. Today, though, the gods had inspired the winged horse to leave his mountain spring and fly

to the citadel of Corinth, where Bellerophon was waiting with a golden bridle, the gift of Athene.

Soon the winged horse was tamed, all the more easily because Bellerophon was his half-brother. Pegasus learned to trust his rider enough to face the fiery breath of the monstrous Chimaera with him. They swooped around the monster faster than it could twist and turn its unwieldy body, and Bellerophon aimed and shot the lion, goat, and serpent parts of the monster's body full of his arrows. Then he used his spear for the first time. He had tipped it with lead, and when he plunged it down the Chimaera's lion throat, the monster's flames melted the lead. That is how the creature killed itself, seared to death by the hot lead that its own fire had made into a lethal weapon.

Then Jobates sent Bellerophon to war against the Amazons and their allies, the Solymians, and again the hero won with the help of Pegasus. Jobates was becoming afraid of the young man who seemed to be invincible, and organized an ambush to greet him on his return, but again Bellerophon was triumphant. Confronted with armed men, he prayed to his father Poseidon, who sent a torrent of water to drown his enemies on the Xanthian plain. It was only when the Xanthian women came out naked that Bellerophon called back the flood; he was always very shy in the company of seductive women.

IN THE COMPANY OF THE GODS

After Bellerophon killed the Chimaera, Jobates knew that he was assisted by the gods, and made the sensible decision to welcome him back. He sought out the truth of what had happened at Tiryns, and discovered that Bellerophon was totally innocent of seduction there. Then he offered the young man his daughter in marriage, and made him the heir to Lycia. Bellerophon became foolishly proud because of all his good fortune, and dreamed of flying to Olympus, like a god, with the help of Pegasus. He mounted the winged horse and began the flight upward, but Zeus (Jupiter) sent a gadfly to attack Pegasus, who reared up until Bellerophon dropped to the ground. In his fall, he hurt his legs and lost the sight of both eyes, and he lived on in great misery until his death. Pegasus, however, was welcomed into the company of the gods where he sometimes hauls thunderbolts for the king of the gods and sometimes carries Eos (Aurora), goddess of the dawn.

Orion the Hunter

Orion was the son of Poseidon and Euryale. He was a famous hunter, and when he visited the island of Chios, he fell in love with Merope, the daughter of Oenopion, who was the son of the god Dionysus (Bacchus) and his wife Ariadne. Like many other rulers in Greek myth, Oenopion felt threatened by a visiting hero and planned to kill him off by sending him out on a dangerous quest. The king promised that he would give his daughter to Orion if the hunter would free the island from all the wild animals that plagued it. Day after day, Orion piled up the skins of slaughtered animals in the palace, but Oenopion kept telling him that there were still more creatures lurking in caves and among the rocks. He did not want to keep his promise; monstrous though it sounds, he was overcome with desire for his own daughter.

One night, Orion drank too much and could not restrain himself from raping the unfortunate Merope. The next day, Oenopion pretended that he knew nothing of his daughter's rape, but he called on his father Dionysus for revenge, and the god provided him with more strong wine. Oenopion (whose name in Greek means "plenty of wine") insisted on filling Orion's cup time and time again with the strong wine that had not been watered down. After a very short time Orion collapsed into a heap on the floor, drunk and completely helpless. Oenopion quickly came forward and gouged out both of his eyes and threw him out of the palace. Orion stumbled blindly to the shore of Chios, praying to the gods for help.

Opposite page *Bellerophon Riding Pegasus Fighting the Chimaera* by Peter Paul Rubens (1577–1640). The winged horse Pegasus roamed the sky and land and refused to let any man approach him. It is said that Bellerophon enlisted the help of the seer Polyeidus, who advised him to spend the night on Athene's altar, whereupon he was rewarded with a dream in which Athene offered him the magic bridle.

Left **Bellerophon on Pegasus.** Before the lovely Medusa was transformed into a Gorgon, Poseidon had seduced the young maiden. It was not until after she had been killed and her head cut off that the offspring of this union were born—Chrysaor and the winged horse, Pegasus.

Right *Orion Killed by Scorpion* by Burney (1816). There are many different accounts of the death of Orion. While the tale of the scorpion is widely known, another version is that Orion was in amorous pursuit of the Pleiades, the daughters of Atlas, and that Zeus placed all of them in the sky as stars. This is why the Orion constellation appears to be hunting the Pleiades in the night sky.

The gods helped him by sending a prophecy that he could regain his sight if he traveled far to the east and looked—if eye sockets can be said to look—toward the point where the chariot of the sun first rises above the horizon. Orion groped along the shore until he laid hands on a boat, and rowed it out into the Mediterranean, to the utmost east, where the goddess of the dawn, Eos of the rosy fingers, prepares the night sky for the horses of the sun. There he regained his sight, and the goddess fell in love with him.

For a while Orion stayed with Eos as her lover, but he ached for vengeance, and soon returned to Chios looking for Oenopion. The king was nowhere to be found (in fact he was hiding in a secret room underground), and Orion kept traveling, determined to track him down. Meanwhile Apollo was planning vengeance on Orion himself, for he was not pleased that Eos had taken him as her lover on Delos, the island sacrosanct to Apollo himself. Apollo's concern was not only for the violation of his island, but also for the chastity of his sister Artemis (Diana). He had heard that Orion had joined Artemis's band of hunters, from which men had always

Below *Acis and Galatea* by I. Briot (c. 1610). The giant Polyphemus, like the other Cyclopes, was said to draw sustenance from the flocks of sheep he kept, as well as the occasional human. Like all the gods of woods and fields, Polyphemus filled his lonely hours and days by playing music.

previously been barred, and he started to wonder whether she might be planning to abandon her vows of chastity and take the mortal as her husband. Nor did Apollo like Orion's foolish boast that he would free the whole world of wild animals. It is always a mistake for a mortal man to pretend to have the powers of a god.

Apollo went to Gaia, the goddess of earth, and informed her that Orion had threatened to kill off every animal in the world. Gaia wasted no time in sending a huge scorpion to kill the hunter before he destroyed any more of her children. Orion could not kill the scorpion, and dived into the sea to escape. Apollo then begged his sister Artemis to shoot the swimming man, claiming that he was a wretch who had just tried to seduce one of her nymphs. Artemis could not make out the swimmer's identity, but she sent an arrow through his brains. Then she discovered that her brother's story was a lie, and that she had shot her own dear companion in the hunt. She begged Asclepius (Aesculapius) to bring the dead man back to life. It was then that Zeus destroyed Asclepius for interfering with Death's proper prey. Artemis could not restore Orion to life, but he is commemorated in one of the most easily recognizable star patterns in the northern sky, the Orion nebula, with three stars representing his sword belt, while the scorpion forever shines close by as the constellation Scorpio.

Acis and Galatea

Galatea was a nereid, a nymph of the sea, who loved Acis, the son of Faunus and Symaithis, and he loved her in return. The Cyclops Polyphemus, son of Poseidon (the same one-eyed giant who eventually met a sorry fate at the hands of Odysseus) also longed for Galatea, and followed her around the countryside. Galatea shrank from Polyphemus, but nothing that she said or did could discourage him from pursuing her. Polyphemus tried his hardest to please her. He worried about his clothes, tried to smile whenever he thought she might be looking, and even trimmed his beard and washed his face.

One day Polyphemus had the idea of pleasing his beloved Galatea by serenading her. He made a colossal pipe of a hundred reeds and blew it so loudly that it could be heard several mountains away. He bellowed a love song, piling together all the images

of love that he could think of. Galatea was an unplucked rose, he sang, a bud yet to spread its petals, as sweet as honey, as intoxicating as unwatered wine, lovely as the morning, but as elusive as the wild deer, and as cold as ice. "If only," he roared, "you would melt in my arms, my dear." Then he played his pipe for a while before bellowing out the whole song again.

Meanwhile Galatea was lying on the Sicilian shore in the arms of her lover, Acis, laughing at the giant's love song. She laughed too much to notice that Polyphemus had stopped singing. Suddenly he was standing over her, shouting with anger instead of love. "No more kissing and fondling for you!" he yelled, and Galatea rushed into the water to hide. Acis tried to follow, but the giant grabbed at the hillside and threw most of it at him. Acis fell down under an avalanche of rocks, crushed to death.

Galatea did not have the power to bring her lover back to life as a man, but she could at least transform his blood into water. Faster and deeper the new stream flowed to the sea, and then the hillside that Polyphemus had torn apart began to gush with springwater that mingled with Acis's blood. In a few moments, a river was formed, and out of its depths rose Acis, transformed into a new river god. As a god, Acis could still be the lover of the sea nymph Galatea, and they clung together as closely as the fresh waters of the River Acis, perpetually intermingling with the sea.

Above *Coastal Landscape with Acis and Galatea* by Gellée Claude (1600–1682). While most versions of the myth tell of the love and sorry fate of Acis and Galatea, there is another account that has a completely different outcome. In this version, Polyphemus wins the heart of the nymph and she bears him three children—Galus, Celtus, and Illyrius.

Above **Heracles holding his club.** Heracles was worshipped throughout the Mediterranean world. Every town, city, and village wanted to be associated with him in some way, and often added some act or exploit to the legend of Heracles, which would identify him with their people.

HERACLES

Heracles (Hercules) was the son of Alcmene and Zeus (Jupiter). Alcmene's story begins with Perseus and Andromeda, whose children ruled over golden Mycenae, Tiryns, and Midea in Argos. Electryon ruled in Mycenae, and his rule was threatened by Taphian raiders who stole his cattle and killed seven of his sons. Electryon's nephew, Amphitryon, found the cattle safe in the fields of the king of Elis, and bought them back from him. When Electryon found out that his own cattle had to be paid for again, he

quarreled furiously with his nephew. Amphitryon threw his stick at one of the cows and it hit and killed his uncle by accident, or so he claimed in his defense. He was judged to be polluted by the killing, and his punishment was to be banished from Argos and prevented from having sexual relations with his new wife, Electryon's daughter Alcmene, until he had avenged the deaths of his uncle's seven sons.

Alcmene and Amphitryon traveled to Thebes, where Creon was king. There the uncle-killer was cleansed of his pollution, and he soon avenged his cousins' death by going to war with the Taphians and conquering them. One night, while her husband was on the road home to Thebes from this war, Alcmene lay in bed worrying about him, hoping that he would come home safe and unwounded. In walked someone who certainly looked just like Amphitryon and sounded like him, full of news about the war, but he was really Zeus in disguise. He was carrying a finely carved golden beaker as well as a magnificent golden necklace, gifts for the bride from the gods. That night, Alcmene conceived a son by Zeus. The next night, her real husband returned home from his war and shared her bed for the first time, and she conceived a second son. Nine months later, she gave birth to twin sons, Heracles, son of Zeus, and Iphicles, son of Amphitryon.

A day before Alcmene was due to give birth, Zeus had been boasting to the other gods that the child about to be born, a descendant of Perseus, would rule all the other descendants of Perseus. Hera (Juno) was already angry with Alcmene for sharing her bed with Zeus, and these boastful comments drove her to vengeful action. She went to Argos, where the wife of

King Sthenelus (another of Perseus's sons) was also pregnant but not yet due to give birth. Hera hastened her labor, so that her son was born prematurely, and prolonged Alcmene's labor, so that Heracles came into the world later than Zeus had intended. Now Zeus's prediction would have to be applied to little Eurystheus instead of little Heracles. It would be Eurystheus instead of Heracles who would become king of Mycenae and Tiryns in Argos, and the son of Zeus would be forced to serve the son of Sthenelus until he had accomplished 12 mighty labors.

The Childhood of Heracles

Alcmene left her newborn sons alone for a few moments in their cradle. When she came back, she saw two snakes poised to sink their fangs into the children's faces. Alcmene ran over, ready to put her body in between the snakes and her sons to protect them, but before she could reach the cradle, the baby Heracles had taken hold of the snakes, one in each hand, and was strangling them to death. This was the first of many occasions when Hera tried to have Heracles killed, and when he won glory from her actions. The name Heracles means "glory of Hera" in Greek, and it seems an inappropriate name for the hero because of Hera's enmity toward him. Some think that originally, Heracles was the son of Hera and Zeus, and the stories of her anger were later inventions. But perhaps the "glory" in his name can be understood as the glory that Hera evoked, time and time again, by providing him with so many monsters to overcome.

As a child, Heracles had an ungovernable temper. He had many tutors, and while he enjoyed learning the arts of war, he would not put up with the tutor who tried to teach him how to read and write. One day he attacked this teacher, Linus, with the nearest weapon to hand, the chair that he was sitting on. When he heard about this outburst of temper, Heracles' stepfather, Amphitryon, thought that it would do the boy good to spend time on the mountains herding sheep. Heracles soon heard from the other shepherds about a lion that was attacking the sheep on Mount Cithaeron and Mount Helicon. He provided himself with a club and a massive wild olive tree that he pulled out of the ground, and easily killed the lion. Perhaps this lion was the one that provided the lion skin that Heracles is usually shown wearing, draped around his neck, with its head showing on top of his own head.

Heracles' next heroic deed was to help Creon, the king of Thebes. Like Athens in the time of King Minos of Crete, Thebes was a defeated kingdom owing tribute to its conqueror, the king of Orchomenus. Heracles met the men from Orchomenus who were coming to collect the tribute and picked a quarrel with them, then defeated them all and cut off their ears and noses, saying, "Take these bits of your bodies back to your king. That is all the tribute he will be getting out of Thebes." In response, the people of Orchomenus gathered an army to enforce the tribute, but Heracles overcame them with absolute ease. King Creon proposed a marriage between the hero and his only daughter, Megara, and, when Heracles agreed, offered him the kingship of Thebes as well. All seemed to be going well for the young hero, but Hera's vengeance was about to unleash itself.

Zeus had boasted that the next descendant of Perseus to be born would rule the others, and now Eurystheus, the king of Tiryns and Mycenae, had demanded that Heracles should perform and finish 12 labors for him, as a servant of the king.

The First Labor

The first task that Eurystheus gave Heracles was to destroy the Nemean lion, a creature that could not be killed by club, sword, spear, or arrow. The lion may have been brought to Nemea by Hera, or it may have been the one that Selene, the moon goddess, gave birth to and threw down to Earth. Heracles soon discovered that his weapons were useless against the lion, for all the good that they did was to force it to retreat into its den. He decided that the only way to kill the lion was to move in closely, risking its teeth and claws, so that he could wrestle it to death. Into the narrow opening of the den he

Hercules was the strongest man on earth and he had the supreme self-confidence magnificent physical strength gives. He considered himself on an equality with the gods.

EDITH HAMILTON (1867–1963), MYTHOLOGY

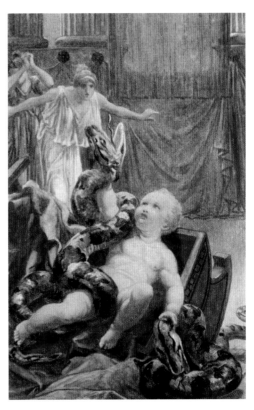

Left **Head of Heracles.** Heracles was the symbol of strength, energy, and heroism. The stories of his valor, spirit, generosity, and pity for the weak saw Heracles become the most famous and popular of all Greek heroes.

Above *Infant Heracles* by **Innes Fripp.** Many believe that it was his stepfather, Amphitryon, not Hera, who placed the snakes in Heracles' cradle. It is thought that he wanted to settle, once and for all, which of the boys was really his own son, and which was the son of Zeus.

crept—not the best way to start a wrestling match—and as the lion leaped at him, Heracles caught hold of its front legs with one huge hand and its back legs with another, forcing its body backward until he broke its spine. This lion is another possible contender for providing the massive skin and head that Heracles usually wore over his head and shoulders. He carried the carcass back to Mycenae and threw it down at Eurystheus's feet. The king was both disgusted and frightened, and immediately commanded Heracles never again to bring his trophies back into the city, but he changed his mind with the labors still to come, demanding to see with his own eyes evidence that Heracles had really done as he had been ordered. Zeus commemorated this first labor of Heracles by putting the lion in the sky as the constellation of Leo.

The Second Labor

Eurystheus now sent Heracles on a more tricky mission, to kill the Hydra of Lerna. Lerna is a swampy area on the sea coast, full of streams that sometimes open into bottomless depths. There lived the Hydra, a water snake whose breath was poisonous. Heracles knew that she had many heads, at least nine and possibly a hundred. Few had seen the Hydra and lived to tell their story, and with each story the number of her heads increased. All but one of these heads was mortal, and if Heracles wanted to kill the Hydra, he would have to find a way to cut off the immortal head. Otherwise, she would simply grow twice as many new heads to replace those that he cut off.

Heracles took his nephew, Iolaus, son of his twin brother Iphicles, as a helper. Iolaus busied himself building a huge fire, while Heracles started to attack the Hydra. Down in one of the deep pools of Lerna lived a huge crab, one of Hera's creatures, which helped the Hydra by biting Heracles' foot. He turned his attention to the crab and killed it; this is the crab that shines in the night sky as the constellation Cancer. Then Heracles fought on. Each time he lopped off one of the Hydra's heads, he called to Iolaus to cauterize the bleeding neck in order to slow down its regrowth. Eventually, he fought his way to the immortal head and chopped it off. The whole body of the Hydra collapsed in a dramatic turn of events, and Heracles proceeded to return to Mycenae

Opposite page *God Heracles Kills Hydra of Lerna* by Giovanni Falconetto (1458–1534). The Hydra was half-sister to the Nemean lion. Heracles buried the head beside the road from Lerna to Elaeus.

in triumph, after dipping his arrows in the poisoned blood of the vanquished Hydra. Eurystheus complained that Heracles had not carried out this labor by himself, but Heracles paid no attention to this. He was well aware that Eurystheus hoped that he would die during one of these labors. The king was terrified of Heracles, expecting that he would finish his 12 labors by killing the man who had imposed them on him. Eurystheus was so frightened that he took to hiding underground in a huge bronze jar whenever Heracles was in his palace.

The Third Labor

Now Eurystheus changed his mind about banning Heracles' trophies from his city. He hankered after the hind of Ceryneia, a young deer that Artemis (Diana) cherished. She had given it golden antlers, and Eurystheus longed to have the hind for himself. It seems an easy enough task to catch a young deer, but this hind had the intelligence of a goddess. She was once the Titan Taygete, and had been metamorphosed into a deer to protect her from the amorous advances of Zeus. When Heracles came hunting for her, she led him to the ends of the Earth. First she ran through Arcadia, in northern Greece, then farther north to the land of the Hyperboreans, the northernmost land which human beings inhabit. There he finally caught the deer, put her over his shoulder, and started to carry her back to Mycenae. Artemis came hunting for Heracles, ready to take revenge for the murder of her companion, but he showed her that the deer was not dead and explained that he was only carrying out the decree of their father, Zeus. Artemis accepted this explanation, and stored up her anger against Eurystheus instead.

The Fourth Labor

The next labor that Eurystheus demanded from Heracles was to fetch him the boar of Erymanthus. The hind had been much too easy a prey, the king thought. It would be far riskier for Heracles to catch a savage wild pig alive, and then

Above **Sagittarius.** Each of the 12 signs of the zodiac symbolizes a myth, legend, or constellation. The Centaur Cheiron, known as the constellation Sagittarius, was wounded in battle by mistake. It seems that he was wounded in one of two ways—by either dropping a poisoned arrow on his own foot, or by his friend Heracles accidentally shooting him.

Right **Heracles and the Erymanthian Boar** by **Giambologna (1529–1608).** The great Heracles captured the wild boar quickly and easily. Heracles waited outside its lair and shouted loudly until it came rushing out into the snow, whereupon Heracles cast his net over it.

transport it across Greece. Eurystheus did not consider that Heracles would run any risks in going to the region of Erymanthus, because the Centaurs who lived there were friendly to human beings. But it was the Centaurs who caused Heracles the most grief in this labor. It was easy enough for him to catch the boar and take it back to Mycenae, and it was not the fight with the boar that littered the countryside with dead Centaurs. The trouble started when Heracles visited the cave of Pholus and was welcomed with a banquet.

The Centaur tried to provide food and drink suitable for a human guest, and opened a jar of wine that Dionysus (Bacchus) had given him. This was the first time that any Centaur drank wine, and it went straight to his head. Then the other Centaurs smelled the wine, galloped up, and started drinking. Soon the banquet turned to a brawl, and Heracles started to shoot down those who were attacking him. His arrows were tipped with the Hydra's poison, and killed most of the drunkards, but he also wounded the Centaur Cheiron by mistake. Cheiron was the wisest of the Centaurs, and a great healer, and he had been granted immortality by the

gods. He could not die, but he could do nothing to cure the wound that Heracles had inflicted. Cheiron did eventually die, centuries later, bargaining his life for Prometheus's freedom, but when Heracles abandoned Erymanthus with the boar, it seemed as though the Centaur was doomed to an eternity of pain. When Cheiron did finally die, he was commemorated in the starry heavens as the constellation Sagittarius.

The Fifth Labor

The next labor of Heracles concerned the Birds of Lake Stymphalus. Stymphalus was more of a swamp than a lake, and its host of birds were creatures of Ares (Mars), the god of war. They were part-human creatures with the claws of birds and the heads of women, and their favorite food was human flesh. Instead of shooting arrows, they shot their feathers, which were sharp enough to slice open a human hand, and they rampaged among the people of Arcadia, wantonly destroying their farmlands and killing anyone who tried to stop them. Heracles was only required to drive these birds away from the lake, not to kill them, and this task was the easiest of his labors. All he needed to do was to alarm them with the sound of a bronze rattle, and they flew off to the Black Sea to torment people there.

The Sixth Labor

Eurystheus was now so frightened of Heracles that he could not control his bowels when the hero was in the palace. Perhaps it was this embarrassment that gave him the idea of the next labor, cleansing the stables of Augeias. King Augeias of Elis had herds of cattle whose dung had piled up in the stables for years, and Eurystheus required Heracles to clean it up in a single day. If he failed, he was to stay there

for the rest of his life as a stablehand and dung raker. Augeias was so confident of the task's impossibility that he promised to give Heracles a tenth of his herds, if the stables were cleaned in one day. Heracles could wield a rake as forcefully as he wielded sword or club, but even he could not rake the stables clean in a day. He looked around and noticed that the palace had been built between two rivers. A couple of trenches would be enough to lead the waters into the stables. Within a day, the rivers were running in their new course, straight through the stables, and all the dung had been washed away. The king tried to

wriggle out of his promise, refusing to give Heracles a tenth of his cattle, arguing that it was the rivers, not the man, that accomplished the task. Heracles went back to Mycenae, nursing a grievance against Augeias. Eurystheus jumped at the chance to postpone the day when Heracles would be a free man again, and he too claimed that this was not to be counted as a genuine labor.

The Seventh Labor

After the Augeian stables were cleansed, Eurystheus cast about Greece to find another peril for Heracles

Above *Heracles and the Stymphalian Birds* by Albrecht Durer (1471–1528). Heracles shook the bronze rattle so violently that the huge, pestilent birds took off in fright. The hero was then able to shoot a great number of them with his arrows. The rattle had been forged by Hephaestus and given to Heracles by Athene.

Above *Heracles and the Cretan Bull* by Alexander de La Borde (1813). Heracles had no trouble capturing the Cretan bull. King Minos is believed to have even offered to help the hero with his task as he was so eager to rid the island of the animal. It was not only an embarrassment to him, but it was wreaking havoc and destroying all the crops on the land.

Right *Theseus Abducting Antiope* attributed to Myson (c. 480 B.C.). Heracles was sent to fetch the girdle of Queen Hippolyta in order to bring it back for Admete, the daughter of Eurystheus. The belt was a gift from the queen's father, Ares. The plan was running smoothly until Hera stepped in, resulting in the death of the queen and the abduction of Antiope.

from the sea and which King Minos had failed to sacrifice. The god punished the king firstly by making his queen become infatuated with the bull, and then, after the Minotaur had been conceived, by driving the bull completely mad. Heracles was by this time an expert at dealing with wild animals, and he managed to subdue the bull with his club and take it across the sea to mainland Greece, where Theseus eventually killed it.

The Ninth Labor

Eurystheus decided that it was not profitable to keep sending Heracles after wild animals, for he always managed to dispose of them without effort. The gods seemed not to care, either, when their creatures were killed or tamed by this son of Zeus. If wild animals could not kill Heracles, the king thought, perhaps wild women could. He asked for the girdle of Queen Hippolyta of the Amazons, the belt that she wore around her waist to tie up her garments for battle. The Amazons were a race of women who sent all their boy children out for adoption, and only tolerated the company of men for the purpose of becoming pregnant. They cut off their right breasts, so that they could use their bows with complete freedom.

Heracles took several other heroes with him on this expedition, including Theseus. At first the Amazons were friendly, and it seemed that he might acquire the girdle simply by asking, but Hera made sure that there would be trouble, spreading a rumor that he was there to kidnap the queen. A fight broke out, and in the melee, Heracles killed Hippolyta. That was the fight in which Theseus abducted Antiope, who became the mother of Hippolytus. The quest for the girdle of Hippolyta brought glory to neither man.

to face. He decided upon the mares of Diomedes, the king of Thrace. Diomedes was the son of Ares, and had inherited his father's bloodthirsty nature. His mares were meat-eaters, and like the gruesome, part-human birds of the Stymphalian lake, their favorite food was human flesh. Along the way to Thrace, Heracles decided to visit his friend Admetus, and it was then that he rescued Alcestis from the death that she had invited upon herself.

Then he traveled on to Thrace, to the palace of Diomedes. The king was always happy to see strangers at his door, fresh food for his horses, but this time it was Heracles who marched the king over to his stables and left him to the teeth of his mares. Then, when their stomachs were full of food and they were less savage, Heracles led them in a line, bridled and roped together, to Mycenae, to give Eurystheus a problem of his own. Eurystheus liked the mares, however, and their offspring could still be found in the kingdom of Mycenae until the period of Alexander the Great.

The Eighth Labor

It was at this time that Jason and the Argonauts set off on in quest of the Golden Fleece, and since Eurystheus could not instantly think up another labor, Heracles joined the Argonauts for a short time, until the death of Hylas. Then he returned to Thebes, sure that the king had something nasty in store for him. This time, he was ordered to fetch the bull of Minos, the same bull which Poseidon (Neptune) had sent

The Tenth Labor

Eurystheus sent Heracles farther and farther abroad for each successive labor. When the king asked for the cattle of Geryoneus, Heracles had to travel to the utmost west, crossing the wide stream of

Opposite page *Diomedes Devoured by His Horses* by Gustave Moreau (1826–1898). Some say that Heracles just fought the grooms and took the horses.

Above *Heracles Slaying Cacus* by Hendrik Goltzius (1558–1617). Heracles was hailed as hero once more when he defeated Cacus. The giant and thief, surrounded by the skulls and bones of his victims, was crushed to death by Heracles. One version has it that Cacus's own sister fell in love with Heracles and she told him where her brother could be found.

Right *Heracles Wrestling Antaeus* by Euphronios (fl. c. 520 B.C.–500 B.C.). Heracles almost met his match in the giant Antaeus. Shrewd as well as strong, Heracles overcame the giant. Afterward it was said that he subdued all of Libya and put it under cultivation.

Oceanus to the island of Erytheia. There a two-headed dog, kin to Cerberus and the Hydra, guarded the cattle of Geryoneus, the grandson of Medusa and son of the warrior Chrysaor. Geryoneus had two legs just like other people, but from the waist up, his body branched out into three trunks, with six arms and three heads. Eurystheus ordered Heracles to overcome this monster of a man, take the cattle, and bring them to Mycenae.

In order to get to the island, Heracles needed to find a ship. He went to Pylos, but its ruler, Neleus, barred the city gates against him. The gods of Olympus took an interest in this conflict, and some went down to fight alongside Neleus, others to support Heracles. On the side of Heracles were his father, Zeus, and his half-sister, Athene (Minerva). Against him were Hera, of course, and Ares, Apollo, Hades (Pluto) the god of the underworld, and Poseidon. Heracles struck out at the immortal gods and wounded Ares in the thigh, Hades in the shoulder, and Hera in the breast. Not even the gods could save Neleus and his sons (all except Nestor, who was away from home) from death at Heracles' hand.

5. Tartess

6. Erytheia

Journeying on to the west, Heracles passed through the north of Libya, and there he met Antaeus, a belligerent giant who insisted on challenging him to a wrestling match. Antaeus was the son of Gaia and Poseidon, and whenever he touched the ground, he was filled with the strength of a god. In the past, Antaeus had always won the wrestling matches that he forced on strangers, and he had decorated his father's temple with the smashed skulls of his many victims. Heracles was a very skilled and strong wrestler, and kept throwing Antaeus to the ground. Any other wrestler would have suffered broken bones, at the very least, but Antaeus just kept on lumbering back to his feet and attacking Heracles again and again, gaining fresh strength with every fall. Heracles could hardly believe that a mere giant was in danger of beating him, when he had just sent some of the immortal gods scurrying back beaten to Olympus. He was very nearly overpowered by Antaeus during the wrestling, but eventually he made the connection that Antaeus's strength seemed to leave him when his feet left the ground. Then Heracles stopped using his wrestling throws, and tried holding Antaeus up off the ground at the full stretch of his arms. The giant grew feebler and feebler while he was held aloft, and so Heracles easily broke his neck and killed him.

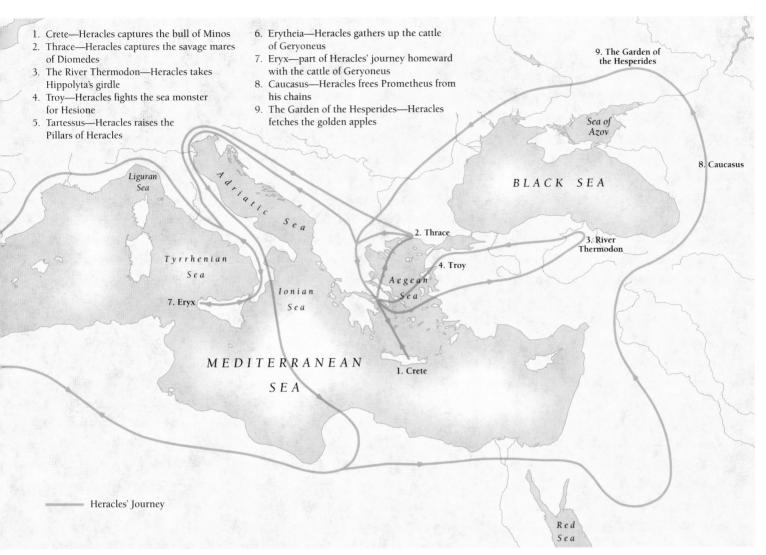

1. Crete—Heracles captures the bull of Minos
2. Thrace—Heracles captures the savage mares of Diomedes
3. The River Thermodon—Heracles takes Hippolyta's girdle
4. Troy—Heracles fights the sea monster for Hesione
5. Tartessus—Heracles raises the Pillars of Heracles
6. Erytheia—Heracles gathers up the cattle of Geryoneus
7. Eryx—part of Heracles' journey homeward with the cattle of Geryoneus
8. Caucasus—Heracles frees Prometheus from his chains
9. The Garden of the Hesperides—Heracles fetches the golden apples

9. The Garden of the Hesperides

8. Caucasus

Sea of Azov

BLACK SEA

Liguran Sea

Adriatic Sea

2. Thrace

3. River Thermodon

Tyrrhenian Sea

4. Troy

Ionian Sea

Aegean Sea

7. Eryx

MEDITERRANEAN

SEA

1. Crete

Red Sea

—— Heracles' Journey

Heracles then passed the narrow waters of the Mediterranean, where Africa almost meets Europe, and there he raised the Pillars of Heracles. On he went to the island of Erytheia, where he killed first the two-headed dog and then the three-headed owner of the cattle. It was easy to win the cattle by force, but considerably less easy to bring them back to Mycenae. Along the way Heracles encountered another three-headed creature, Cacus, who could breathe fire. Cacus was the son of Hephaestus (Vulcan), but he possessed the cunning of Hermes (Mercury). When Cacus he decided to steal some of Heracles' cattle, he pulled them backward by their tails so that their footprints all pointed in the direction from which they had been taken. Heracles was completely fooled by this detraction, but he heard the mooing and bellowing of the stolen beasts and came running to the cave where Cacus had hidden them. Heracles tore open the cave and crushed Cacus to death in a wrestling hold. As he drove the cattle onward, Hera sent a gadfly to annoy them, and they scattered across Greece. It took Heracles months to gather the cattle together again.

Above **Heracles' journey.** Over the centuries, many historians have put forward their own versions of the labors, and their own maps of the route they believe Heracles followed. This version was compiled by Apollodorus in the third century B.C.

Left *The Giant Antaeus* by **Gustave Dore (1832–1883).** The giant Antaeus derived his amazing strength from contact with the earth. By breaking that contact, Heracles was able to overpower him. Some say he did this by breaking Antaeus's neck, others that he crushed Antaeus's bones until he suffocated.

129

Then, as he was driving them toward Mycenae, he met another giant, Alcyoneus of Corinth. This giant happened to be a stronger opponent than either Cacus or Antaeus, and he hurled an enormous rock at Heracles, completely decimating 12 chariots that were clustered round, full of startled onlookers. Then the giant picked up the rock again and threw it at Heracles, who thumped it back toward him with his club, crushing Alcyoneus to death. This was the last obstacle that Hera put in Heracles' way during this labor. He was able to bring the cattle to Mycenae with no more trouble, and there they were promptly sacrificed to Hera by Eurystheus.

The Eleventh Labor

The king next came up with a labor that he considered totally impossible to achieve. Eurystheus told Heracles to fetch him the golden apples of the Hesperides. No one knew where the Hesperides might be—that is, no one mortal. But Heracles was a favored son of Zeus, and perhaps his half-sister Athene whispered to him the idea that he should ask for directions from the Fates. These three ancient goddesses are usually busy spinning and weaving the threads of human lives, but they set aside their tasks for a moment to speak to the hero. "We have been here almost since the beginning," they said, "but even we do not know where the island of the Hesperides might be. Only a sea god would be sure to know where such an island might lie. Find Nereus, the old man of the sea," they advised Heracles, "and hold him tightly until he gives you directions."

Nereus was a shape-shifter, and he did not want to talk to Heracles. First he shifted shape to a fire that burned, then to a sea serpent that tried to slide through his fingers, then to water that almost slipped away into the sea. But Heracles held fast, and Nereus eventually took on his own form as a sea god, and told him which way to journey, first on land and then by sea. It was on this journey that Heracles came to Mount Caucasus and heard the sorrowful story of Prometheus. For once, the hero could make life better rather than spread violent death. When he heard that Prometheus could only be freed if some immortal would agree to die in his place, he remembered the wound he had given the Centaur Cheiron, and that is how Prometheus became unbound.

Heracles now had to travel by ship, or rather by cup, for the sun god Helius (Sol) provided him with a huge golden cup, the one in which the sun traveled across the ocean each night from farthest west to farthest east, ready to rise the next dawn. Heracles sailed the cup from east to farthest west, getting ever closer to the remote island of the Hesperides with its tree of golden apples guarded by serpents. This tree was a wedding gift from Gaia, the earth goddess, to Hera, and so Heracles risked enraging an already angry goddess by taking her apples. He looked around for help, and found it in the giant Atlas, a Titan from the time before Zeus ruled the gods. Atlas had been one of those who rebelled against the new king of the

Below *Heracles and Atlas* by Walter Crane (1845–1915). Heracles used the sun god's huge golden cup to see him safely across the ocean. Helius provided him with the cup after Heracles, overcome by the immense heat, threatened the sun with his arrows. Helius gave him the cup, either to appease him, or in admiration of his boldness.

gods, and Zeus had punished him by forcing him to carry the weight of the heavens on his shoulders. When Heracles came asking for help, Atlas could not believe his luck. At last someone else might be tricked into holding up the skies. "You have to take the weight for only an hour or two," he assured Heracles. "As soon as I have brought back the apples for you, of course I will take up my burden again." Atlas did steal the apples from Hera's tree, and he did bring them back to Heracles, but then he refused to bend his back and take up the weight of the heavens again. "My shoulders are hurting," Heracles complained, "and I need a cushion. Take the heavens back for just a moment, while I make myself comfortable." When the Titan agreed, Heracles eased himself out from under the sky and walked off, leaving Atlas trapped under his burden. So he remained, until the day that Perseus flew by and turned the giant to stone.

> *Cerberus, monster cruel and uncouth,*
> *With his three gullets like a dog is barking*
> *Over the people that are there submerged.*
>
> DANTE ALIGHIERI (1265–1321), *THE DIVINE COMEDY,*
> "INFERNO," CANTO VI

The Twelfth Labor

Heracles had survived even this task. Eurystheus had been confident that Hera would be so angry with him that he would not survive. What worse labor could he devise, that would certainly mean the death of Heracles? "The death of Heracles…" thought the king. "A visit to the place of death would be just what I am looking for." And so he told his cousin to bring up from the underworld the three-headed dog, Cerberus. Only Persephone (Proserpina) had so far come back from Hades' kingdom to the world of the living, and only with difficulty, even though she was a goddess. What chance did Heracles have?

It turned out that he had all the skills needed to force his way down to the underworld and back to the world of life. He had no coin to buy his passage across the Styx, but Charon was too terrified of his mortal strength to refuse to ferry him over. Cerberus saw him coming, and fled to the side of his master, Hades. Heracles found Theseus and Peirithous stuck fast to thrones that their own folly had brought them to, and pulled Theseus free by force. He met the ghost of Meleager, who begged Heracles to marry his sister Deianeira. He even met the ghost of Medusa and

somehow outfaced her stony stare. Then Heracles arrived at the throne room of Hades and Persephone, daughter of Zeus and Demeter (Ceres). Like Athene, Persephone was Heracles' half-sister, and she wanted both to please her father by helping the hero, and also to rid the underworld of its invincible visitor as soon as possible. Persephone told Heracles that he could take Cerberus up to the world of the living, if he could do so with his bare hands. No sword or spear or club had any power in the underworld; Heracles would have to try his wrestling tricks on the three-headed dog.

Despite his three heads, Cerberus was no match for Heracles, and soon he was dragged up into the light. He growled and snarled his way to Mycenae, where Eurystheus fled into his bronze jar once more, cursing himself for ever asking for death's dog. Cerberus did not stay long in the upper world. Once Eurystheus had seen him, and acknowledged that the 12 labors had been properly accomplished, Heracles freed him, and he raced back to his customary darkness.

After the Labors

Heracles conducted his own Trojan war, a generation before the war over Helen. The king of Troy at that time was Laomedon, and when Apollo and Poseidon had worked for him for a whole year for wages, the foolish king cheated them of their pay, a team of horses that Zeus had given him. Perhaps he was emboldened by seeing the immortal gods reduced to serving as mere shepherd and laborer, but he failed to consider how they would behave once their term of service was completed. As soon as their contract had ended, Apollo proceeded to fire plague arrows into Troy, and the sea god sent a sea monster to torment the coast. The oracle told Laomedon that the only way to appease the angry gods was to allow the terrifying sea serpent to take his daughter, Hesione.

Below *Heracles in the Garden of the Hesperides* by William Hunt (1827–1910). Some say there were not only serpents guarding the apple grove, but also three sweetly singing nymphs as well— Aegle, Erytheia, and Hespera—the Hesperides, whom it is said were the daughters of Atlas.

Left *Heracles Bringing Cerberus to Eurystheus,* Greek School (sixth century B.C.). Heracles again showed his amazing strength by subduing the monster-dog Cerberus. It is said that when Cerberus faced the light of the living world for the first time, foam fell from his jaws onto the ground. From his spittle sprang wolfsbane, a poisonous plant, which, it was claimed, flourished ever after in that region.

Hearing of the king's promise that he would give his horses to anyone who rescued his daughter, Heracles went out onto the beach to fight the monster. It came at him with a gaping mouth and swallowed him. Heracles stayed in its stomach for three days, but then he cut his way free, killing the monster. Laomedon promptly refused to give him the reward, and Heracles rampaged through the city of Troy, killing at will. Laomedon died at the hands of Heracles, and so did all his sons except the youngest, Priam, who became the next king of Troy. Heracles married Hesione to his comrade, Telamon, and she became queen of Salamis.

Heracles had not seen much of his wife, Megara, during his labors, but they had managed to have three sons (some accounts say eight). While he was away in the underworld, taming Cerberus, many people assumed that he was dead and would never return. Lycus, the son of Poseidon, killed Creon and became tyrant of Thebes. The tyrant Lycus was so confident of Heracles' death that he began to persecute Megara and old Amphitryon, Heracles' stepfather, who had been living in the Theban palace for years. Heracles' family believed that they would all be killed, but he hurried back to them just in time. He found Lycus and his supporters in the palace, and instantly began to shoot his poison-tipped arrows at them. Those who were not shot dead, he clubbed to death. Then Hera struck madness into him. He hallucinated that the children clinging to him were the sons of his enemy, Eurystheus, and he killed his wife and all his children before falling into a stuporous sleep.

Above *Heracles and Omphale* by Santi di Tito (1536–1603). While in Queen Omphale's servitude, Heracles performed many deeds and defeated many of her enemies. Some historians say that before she freed Heracles, they married and had a son called Lamus.

THE OLYMPIC GAMES

Heracles (Hercules) was believed to be the founder of the Olympic Games, at the city of Olympia. Previously there had been a festival at Olympia in honor of Zeus (Jupiter), but Heracles organized an athletics competition and a truce, which all the Greek cities agreed to honor while the games were in progress. Like the modern Olympic Games, these games were held once every four years. At their peak, they included running, chariot racing, boxing, wrestling, and the pentathlon (running, jumping, discus, javelin, and wrestling). Heracles competed in the first games, and won every contest.

Right **Heracles.** Before the Olympic Games were founded by Heracles, a festival of games held in honor of Hera, called the Heraean Games, had been founded by Pelops, the husband of Hippodameia.

When he woke, he had forgotten everything that he had done in the palace. As soon as Heracles remembered what had happened, all Thebes rang with his cries of grief, guilt, and horror. What he had done to his wife and children was dreadful, but it was an act of madness sent by the goddess. The next dreadful thing that he did had no such excuse. He went to Oichalia to compete in an archery contest. The winner's prize was to be the daughter of King Eurytus, Iole, but when Heracles won the competition, the king withheld the prize. Heracles lashed out and killed two of King Eurytus's sons, and he forced the king to give Iole to him in marriage. So far, the gods considered Heracles to be in the right, but when King Eurytus's son Iphitus came to Heracles' city of Tiryns, the hero welcomed him as a guest, then threw him to his death from a tower. Such a betrayal of hospitality called out for punishment from the gods; it

Left *Struggle for the Delphic Tripod* by Roulez (1854). Some believe that Heracles went to the oracle at Delphi for help. He was consumed with guilt and remorse over his actions, and he was desperate to be purified. However, when the priestess refused to speak to him, Heracles became angry and seized the tripod.

was as though Heracles was somehow seeking to be punished for his tragic fit of madness before.

Then he directly offended one of the gods, going to Apollo's shrine at Delphi and stealing the tripod on which the Pythia used to sit to give her oracles. Heracles was helped by his half-sister Athene, and the two of them got a long way down the road before Apollo caught up with them, accompanied by his sister Artemis. The four children of Zeus confronted one another, and were just about to start fighting when Zeus himself intervened, sending down a thunderbolt to force them apart. The tripod went back to Delphi, and Heracles was punished for all his previous wild behavior by going back into service, this time as a slave. Hermes sold Heracles in the common market, and he became the property of Queen Omphale.

Omphale was the queen of Lydia, and the Greeks liked to imagine her court as the height of decadence. There women played the men and men played the women. Omphale entertained herself by dressing her new slave in women's clothing, while she draped herself in the lion skin and tried to lift his club. As a slave, Heracles was assigned women's work and he promptly set to the task of spinning.

Blood and Death

Once his term of slavery was over, Heracles went in search of a new wife. He remembered that Meleager had spoken of his sister Deianeira in the underworld, asking Heracles to marry her, and now he wanted to find out why Meleager had said that Heracles was

HALCYON DAYS

King Ceyx and Queen Alcyone of Trachis had a very happy marriage, but the queen unfortunately had an inordinate fear of storms that the winds blew up at sea. When her husband decided to consult the oracle at Delphi, she knew that he would be forced to go by sea, because the land road was completely blocked by their enemies. Alcyone prayed to Hera (Juno) for his safe return, but all that the goddess could grant was that he would always love and cherish Alcyone best of all women. Ceyx died in a storm at sea, and poor Alcyone discovered his body, washed up on the coast of Trachis. The gods transformed this faithful husband and wife into a pair of halcyon birds, kingfishers that build their nest in the ocean during seven days of calm in the stormy winter. Such days of calm in a stormy winter season are still called halcyon days.

THE MILKY WAY

Though Hera (Juno) is always described as hating Heracles (Hercules), she was once deceived into nurturing him like a mother. While she was asleep, the trickster god Hermes (Mercury) carried the baby Heracles to Olympus and put his mouth near her breast. The goddess instinctively began to suckle him, until he bit her breast so hard that she woke and threw him off. Heracles was not harmed at all by this, but Hera's milk continued to spurt out, jetting far into the sky to form the Milky Way.

Right *The Birth of the Milky Way by Peter Paul Rubens (1577–1640).* In another version, Athene deceived Hera into nursing the baby Heracles.

the only man in the world who was suitable to be her husband. Heracles made the long journey to Calydon, where Deianeira lived in the palace of her father, Oeneus, and discovered that she was being courted by the river god Achelous, a deity who enjoyed shifting his shape to that of bull and snake. Deianeira did not want a husband such as this, and welcomed Heracles as a rescuer. As so often before, Heracles used his skills as a wrestler to overcome the river god. He snapped off Achelous's horn when the river god turned into a bull, and that was the end of the fight. The horn became the miraculous horn of plenty, the cornucopia, that always spills over with food.

Heracles had won both the horn of plenty and Deianeira as his wife, but as usual, he attracted trouble on the way home. He was about to cross the River Lycormus when the Centaur Nessus came up to him, saying that he was the ferryman, and that it was his responsibility to carry them across the river

Right **Detail from a crater showing Heracles fighting Achelous.** Some claim that Achelous begged Heracles to give him back his horn, and in its place gave him the horn of Amaltheia. Amaltheia was, depending on the myth, either a nymph or a goat who had been Zeus's nurse.

on his back. "First," he said to Heracles, "let the bride sit on my back, and when she is safely across, I will come back for you." Heracles lifted Deianeira onto the Centaur's back, and off they went into the surging river. When they were nearly at the other side, Nessus started to pull Deianeira toward him, threatening to rape her, and she screamed to her husband for help. Heracles took up his bow and shot the Centaur. Nessus took a few moments to die, and with his last breath, he kept trying to injure Heracles, "Deianeira," he whispered, "my blood is worth keeping. It has the power to restore your husband's love if he ever loses interest in you." Deianeira collected his blood, keeping it hidden from her husband, and on they went to the city of Trachis.

Heracles now went on another campaign, fighting yet another war, and he brought back a captive, Iole the daughter of Eurytus. Deianeira became overwhelmingly jealous of Iole and decided to make use of Nessus's magic blood to win back her husband. She gave him a magnificent robe, smeared on the inside with the Centaur's blood. But instead of restoring love, the blood burned flesh to the bone, for the arrow that had killed Nessus had been tipped with the caustic poison of the Hydra. Heracles was

not able take off his robe, because the blood stuck to his body, and he immediately knew that he would soon die. At this moment, he remembered an oracle, which had told him that he would never be killed by anyone living. Now the oracle had been fulfilled. Heracles ordered a pyre to be built on Mount Oeta, and was transported there to die. No one would step forward to light the pyre, as he was still alive, and he was forced to wait until a stranger, a man called Philoctetes, came by and agreed to help relieve him from his agony. As a reward for lighting the pyre,

Heracles gave this man his great bow, and Philoctetes took it with him to the Trojan war.

Heracles did not die in the funeral pyre. He became a god in the flames, and Athene came down for him in her chariot, to take him to Olympus. Now, at last, Hera forgave him, and he took his place with Apollo and Artemis, Hermes and Athene, all children of Zeus. Deianeira killed herself when she found out that the robe was killing her husband, and in Olympus Heracles made his third and final marriage, to the goddess Hebe, daughter of Zeus and Hera.

Above *The Apotheosis of Heracles* by Francois Lemoyne (1688–1737), showing a detail of the gods on Mount Olympus. At last Heracles achieved the immortality he had won with his 12 labors. Reconciled with Hera, the goddess permitted Heracles to marry her daughter Hebe.

JASON AND THE ARGONAUTS

The story of Jason begins with Ixion, the prince of the Lapiths, who wanted to seduce the queen of the gods. Zeus (Jupiter) was well aware of his intentions and shaped a phantom Hera (Juno) out of a cloud, naming her Nephele. Ixion seduced Nephele, believing that he was sharing a bed with the great goddess, and Zeus punished him for his presumption by first whipping him, and then binding him to a wheel of fire that whirled forever through the sky without a pause. Hera was grateful to Nephele, and married her to King Athamas of Boeotia. They had two sons, Phrixus and Leucon, and a daughter, Helle.

After some years of marriage, Athamas's attentions strayed to Ino, the daughter of Cadmus, and she became his lover; some say that he abandoned the goddess and married the mortal woman in her place. Athamas and Ino had two children, Learchus and Melicertes. Nephele turned to Hera for recourse, and the goddess swore eternal enmity to Athamas and his family. Ino was well aware of what was going on, and plotted to take revenge on Nephele's children. She did not dare to injure Nephele directly, because she knew that the cloud-woman was Hera's favorite. In the spring, Ino persuaded the women of Boeotia to cook the seeds of grain before planting them. No grains sprouted and there was no harvest. Then, as Ino had hoped, the king sent messengers to the oracle at Delphi to find out how to bring fertility back to the land. Ino bribed Athamas's messengers to suppress the oracle's answer, and to tell the king instead that he must sacrifice his and Nephele's son, Phrixus.

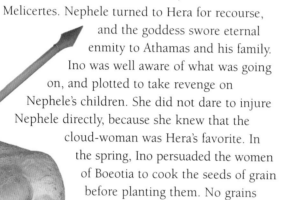

Athamas took Phrixus to a mountaintop and reluctantly prepared to slit his throat. Just in time, Heracles (Hercules) came by, and he was appalled to see a father getting ready to kill his own son. "The gods abhor human sacrifice," said Heracles, and took the knife out of Athamas's hand. Then Zeus sent a miraculous ram flying down from Olympus, a creature with wings and a golden fleece. Phrixus

leaped onto its woolly back, and his sister Helle climbed on behind him. The ram flew for Colchis, but its journey was long and Helle grew weary. She fell into the straits now called the Dardanelles, which the Greeks named the Hellespont after Helle. Phrixus clung to the ram's fleece and arrived safely at Colchis, a land far to the east, where the sun rose each morning. He sacrificed the ram, and its golden fleece was placed in the sacred grove of Ares, god of war. This ram was commemorated by the gods in the heavens in the form of the constellation Aries.

Ino's deceitfulness became clear when the messengers confessed that she had bribed them to give a false report of what the oracle had said. Nephele was furious, and appealed to Hera for revenge. The goddess drove Athamas mad, so that he shot his son Learchus, one of Ino's children, believing that he was shooting a stag. Then Athamas tore apart the boy's body while it was still warm and bleeding. He looked around for Ino and her remaining son, Melicertes, but madness clouded his vision. He grabbed hold of a goat and started to whip it, believing that he was punishing Ino. She jumped into the sea with her son and drowned. Ino and Melicertes were turned into deities by Zeus, as usual going against his wife's wishes. The family of Athamas was almost obliterated in a single day, and his remaining son, Leucon, died shortly afterward.

Athamas lost the kingship of Boeotia and was exiled because of the horror of what he had done. He asked the oracle at Delphi where he should live, and the Pythia told him to settle down in the place

where his dinner was provided by wild beasts. He wandered through Greece until he came to wild countryside in Thessaly where he noticed a pack of wolves attacking a flock of sheep. The wolves ran off, leaving the dead sheep for Athamas to cook and eat. Athamas obeyed the oracle and founded a city there, marrying again and starting another family.

Jason

Aeson, king of Iolcus in Thessaly, was the grandson of Athamas's brother, and Aeson's son was Jason. When Jason was a child, Aeson was dethroned by his half-brother, Pelias, and at once he sent his son away in secret to keep him safe. On Mount Pelion, Jason was educated by the Centaur Cheiron, wisest of his kind, and he was favored by the goddess Hera. One day he was out hunting, and he met an old woman by a river in flood. Without hesitating, he offered to carry the woman over the river on his back. The weight on Jason's back was far more than that of a human body, and he staggered as he waded

across the current, but he managed to get both of them safely across. Once across the river, she revealed that she was the goddess Hera, and from that moment he was her particular favorite. Jason lost a sandal in the water while carrying Hera across, but he kept walking downriver until he reached the coast, dusty and footsore.

On the beach, Pelias was making a sacrifice to the sea god Poseidon (Neptune), and he was horrified to see this man with one sandal limping past, because he had been given a prophecy that a man with one sandal would bring about his death. He ordered Jason to come closer and asked him, "If an oracle had named someone as the man who would kill you, what would you do?" Jason replied, "I would send him to fetch the Golden Fleece, knowing that it is guarded by a serpent and that he will probably die in the attempt." Pelias nodded his head and was about to tell Jason that he had passed sentence upon himself, but first he asked the stranger's name. When the king discovered that

Still what a royal aspect he retains! That Jason is, who by his heart and cunning The Colchians of the Ram made destitute.

DANTE ALIGHIERI (1265–1321), THE DIVINE COMEDY, "INFERNO," CANTO XVIII

Above **Detail from a vase showing Phrixus escaping on a ram (c. 460 B.C.).** Once in Colchis, Phrixus married Chalciope, the daughter of King Aietes. When he eventually died, Phrixus was denied a proper burial, so his ghost haunted Pelias (who had dethroned King Aeson), demanding proper burial rites as well as the return of the Golden Fleece.

137

THE ARGO AS A SHIP OF WAR

Like the fighting ships of Greek history, the 50-oared penteconters, the great ship Argo was built long and narrow so that it could ram enemy ships, either directly attacking to sink another ship or sailing alongside and breaking off the enemy ship's oars. The Argo's fighters also served as oarsmen; Heracles (Hercules) rowed so long and hard that he broke one of the oars. Orpheus the musician played the flute to help the oarsmen keep time. The Argo was a ship of shallow draft, so that the Argonauts could carry it overland. Ships like this were not built to withstand savage storms out at sea, and it is for this reason that voyagers in Greek myth rarely ventured too far from a coastline.

Right *The Argonauts' Ship Argo* by Lorenzo Costa (1459–1535). When the Argonauts made a sacrifice to Apollo before they left, Idmon, the seer, predicted from the coils of smoke that he was fated to die on the voyage.

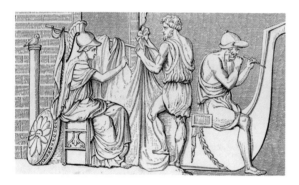

Above **Building the Argo.** Athene and Apollo were said to be protectors of both the Argo and the Argonauts. On their departure, the crew made sacrifices to Apollo, who was known as the god of embarkations.

the man with one sandal was the only son of his half-brother Aeson, he congratulated himself doubly on getting rid of a man who would probably have tried to kill him and regain the kingdom for his ousted father. "Jason," he said, "it will serve the kingdom well if you go in quest of the Golden Fleece, for the ghost of Phrixus is calling to me in my dreams, asking to be brought home along with the fleece. If you succeed in this quest, I shall renounce my kingship in your favor."

Jason knew that he could not achieve the quest for the Golden Fleece without some help. The forthcoming journey would be arduous, going up into the Black Sea and beyond, and then he would have to confront or outwit King Aietes, who was the son of the sun god Helius (Sol) and likely to enjoy the god's protection. Jason decided to assemble a band of

heroes to go with him, and they were known as the Argonauts (meaning "those who sailed in the Argo") after the name of his ship, the Argo (meaning "swift"). The goddess Athene (Minerva) helped with the building of the ship, and because its prow was made of oak wood from Zeus's sacred grove at Dodona, the great ship Argo could prophesy in human words. The Argo was built for sailing, and it could also be rowed when the winds were not favorable. It had

The Voyage of the Argo

The Argonauts experienced many adventures on their way to Colchis. First they visited Lemnos, an island where the women did not enjoy the company of men. The Lemnian men brought women from beyond the island to provide them with children, and the Lemnian women did not tolerate this arrangement either. They killed all the men on the island, all the foreign women, and all the male children, including the newborn babies. The sole survivor of this terrible massacre was the Lemnian king, Thoas, whose daughter Hypsipyle enclosed him in a chest and then sent it out to sea. She subsequently became queen of this nation of women. The Argonauts were forced to land here because of a storm and the Lemnian women tried to prevent them from setting foot on the island. Jason was already skilled at charming women, and he managed to charm Queen Hypsipyle into letting the Argonauts disembark. She did not tell Jason the truth about the absence of men on the island; instead, she talked vaguely about the women forcing the men to leave. The Argonauts intended to stay for just a few days, but days stretched to years, while Jason and Hypsipyle delighted in one another's company. She became pregnant, and gave birth to twin sons, Euneus and Thoas, and the other women

Above *Heracles and the Argonauts* attributed to the Niobid Painter (475 B.C.–450 B.C.). As well as Heracles, among the men who joined the Argonauts was Acastus, the only son of Pelias. It is not clear whether he defied his father out of sympathy for Jason, or for the love of adventure and glory.

seats for 50 rowers, and Jason sent heralds through all of Greece inviting heroes to join his crew.

All the famous men of Greece answered his call, including Heracles and Orpheus the musician. Castor and Polydeuces (Pollux) also became Argonauts, and so did Augeias of the filthy stables that were cleansed by Heracles. Zetes and Calais, sons of the wind, joined the voyage, as did Meleager and Atalanta, Theseus and Peirithous, and a host of many others.

Above *Hylas and the Nymphs* by John Waterhouse (1849–1917). It is said that Heracles was wild with grief at the loss of his beloved companion Hylas. Heracles searched everywhere, and made the local people promise to keep looking for the boy. For centuries after, it became an annual tradition to wander the countryside calling out Hylas's name.

of Lemnos also took the opportunity to replenish the island's population. The Argonauts might have stayed there for the rest of their lives, forgetting their quest, but Heracles, who had remained on the shore guarding the Argo, stormed into the royal palace one day demanding that they leave. The Argonauts sailed on in their ship to the next adventure of the journey, leaving behind a new generation of male babies, and from that time on, Lemnos was no longer an island solely populated by man-hating women.

It is young Hylas, that false runaway
Who with a Naiad now would make his bed
Forgetting Herakles

OSCAR WILDE (1854–1900), "CHARMIDES"

KING CYZICUS

Before traveling out of the Mediterranean and into the Black Sea, the Argonauts visited the Arcton Peninsula, a region dominated by Mount Dindymon. The king of this region, Cyzicus, welcomed the visitors, and warned them not to climb the mountain, a warning that made the Argonauts all the more eager to explore. Six-armed giants, children of the earth goddess Gaia, lived on this mountain, and began attacking the Argonauts when they went

THERE'S MANY A SLIP...

Anchaeus was the helmsman of the Argonauts. He was the king of Tegea, and a seer told him that he would not live long enough to drink the juice of his own vines. Anchaeus hoped to prove the oracle wrong, and when he returned from the quest for the Golden Fleece, as soon as the first crop was harvested, he squeezed the juice of the grapes into a cup, and put it to his lips. The seer warned him again: "There's many a slip 'twixt the cup and the lip." Anchaeus was about to drink when suddenly someone called out that a wild boar was ravaging his vineyard. Out he ran, grabbing his spear and shield, but the boar was too strong for him. In a moment, he lay dead. The seer had spoken the truth.

earth-giants, and now she sent bad weather that kept the Argo in the harbor for many days. Eventually the Argonauts' soothsayer, Mopsus, learned from a bird's song that they would be able to leave only if they propitiated the goddess. Argus, the man who built the Argo, carved a fine statue of Rhea, and then the winds blew fair and they sailed on.

THE LOSS OF HYLAS

At the next stop, Hylas became lost. He was Heracles' friend and lover, a beautiful young man. When he went to collect water, the naiads of the pool saw how handsome he was and longed to kiss and fondle him. They stretched out their arms and pulled him down into the water, drowning him. None of the Argonauts could find any trace of him, except for a water jug lying beside the pool. Heracles searched again and again for Hylas, until eventually Jason and the Argonauts sailed on without him. Some say that the Argo's speaking oak told Jason to leave Heracles behind, because he was too heavy for the ship. In the end, Heracles went back to Thebes to continue with his labors.

POLYDEUCES THE BOXER

The next hero to find an adventure was Polydeuces, the great boxer. On the island of Bebrycus lived King Amycus, a man who believed that he was the greatest of boxers. He used to force all visiting men to box with him and had so far killed every opponent, not only because he was a huge, heavily muscled man, but also because his boxing gloves had steel spikes concealed in them. This time he challenged the Argonauts, who sent Polydeuces out as their champion. Polydeuces did not flinch when he saw the spiky boxing gloves, because he knew that he would be much faster on his feet than the rather too solid king. Amycus never even had a chance to land

climbing, but Heracles and the other heroes had no trouble in killing them all. Then the Argonauts went back to their ship and set sail, but the winds were against them, and in the night they were driven back toward the island. King Cyzicus thought that he was under attack from enemies, and took his soldiers to the coast to fight off the invaders. The Argonauts fought back, and by morning the king was dead along with many of his soldiers. The ancient mother goddess Rhea (Cybele) had been angered when Cyzicus killed a lion sacred to her, and the unfavorable winds that led to Cyzicus's death were sent by her. She was also angered by the Argonauts' killing of the

Above **Mopsus the soothsayer.** Mopsus was a warrior seer from Thessaly, although he won more fame for his prophetic powers than his combat abilities. Mopsus could read the future in the flight of birds, an art he learned from Apollo.

Above *Phineus Is Delivered from the Harpies by Calais and Zetes* by Bernard Picart (1673–1733). Some say Phineus was blinded not by Zeus, but by Poseidon. The sooth-sayer was apparently being too helpful when he assisted Phrixus in find-ing his way to Colchis.

Above right *The Argonauts Pass the Symplegades,* French School (nine-teenth century). The Symplegades were also known as "The Clashing Rocks," as they were said to clash together when driven by the wind.

a blow with his gloves. In less than a minute after the start of the match, Polydeuces knocked King Amycus down, fracturing his skull and killing him.

PHINEUS AND THE ARGONAUTS

Then the Argo went on into the Bosphorus, where they landed in Thrace and met a blind seer called Phineus. He had been so successful as a soothsayer that Zeus had punished him with blindness, and a band of Harpies arrived to harass him whenever he tried to eat, squabbling, shrieking, and befouling his food. These Harpies had the bodies and heads of women, but the wings and claws of carrion-eating birds. Phineus was starving to death in the middle of a prosperous country, his tables laden with food. He appealed to the Argonauts for help, and Calais and Zetes, sons of Boreas, offered to drive the Harpies away. As sons of the North Wind, they could fly, and

as soon as they were sure that no god would be offended by what they planned to do, they soared into the air and plummeted down on the Harpies. Many of the creatures died, and the rest retreated far to the south, never to trouble Phineus again.

Phineus was most grateful for all the help that the Argonauts had given him, and in return he told Jason the secret of safe passage through the Symplegades, clashing rocks that had always previously exacted the toll of a life when anyone tried to pass through them. The rocks took a toll even on the doves of Zeus when they carried ambrosia to Olympus; out of a flock, one always died. Although the Argo was the fastest of ships, the rocks would still close in on her if the gods did not favor Jason's voyage. Phineus gave Jason a caged dove, and told him to set the bird free when he drew close to the rocks. If the bird flew through and lived, it would be a good omen, and the Argo should be able to get through safely as well, but if the bird died, Jason should give up the quest. The ship set sail for the huge, sheer-sided rocks, and the Argonauts could see them lean toward each other and then surge apart. The dove scudded through, and the rocks clashed shut as it passed, catching only a few tail feathers. Then the Argo scudded through, and the rocks caught just the tip of her wooden stern. Some say that Athene lent a hand to hold the rocks apart for the ship that she had helped to build. From that moment, the Symplegades no longer had the power to clash together. The Argonauts were now on the last stage of their journey, up the Black Sea to Mount Caucasus, and then up the River Phasis.

JASON AND MEDEA

Once the Argo was through the clashing rocks, the Argonauts found themselves in a world of more marvels. First, they saw bright Apollo, the sun god, walking toward the east just before sunrise, and turned their eyes away in dread. Then they sailed by the land of the Amazons and came to the island of Ares, which had recently been populated by the birds that Heracles had expelled from Lake Stymphalus in one of his labors. The Argonauts had been forewarned about their feathers that were sharp enough to cut like knives, and as the Argo drew closer to the island, half the rowers stayed at their oars while the others held up their shields as a wall against the birds. They hit their spears on the underneath of the shields, making such a din that the birds were afraid to attack.

Further Travels of the Argo

Farther into the Black Sea went the ship, and now the Argonauts could see Mount Caucasus in the distance, and they heard the cries of Prometheus, tortured daily by beak and claw. Heracles would soon arrive to end his centuries of pain, but the Argonauts did not want to offend Zeus (Jupiter) by interfering, and sailed past, up the River Phasis. At last they arrived in the harbor of Aia, and went to the palace of King Aietes. The king was not welcoming, intent that his visitors should not gain the Golden Fleece. Phrixus had died childless after marrying Aietes' daughter, and Aietes would not give the fleece back to anyone akin to Athamas's family. After all, the last thing that Athamas had done to his son Phrixus was to try to cut his throat. If the fleece belonged to anyone, Aietes believed, it was to the king who had taken Phrixus into his family.

THE THREE TESTS

"You can have the fleece," Aietes mocked Jason, "if you can pass three tests. First, equal me at the task of plowing. Then take the fleece from its guardian serpent, and finally sow the teeth of a dragon and kill the warriors who will spring up from your sowing." Phrixus had placed the fleece in the sacred grove of Ares where it was guarded by a gigantic serpent, and the king was confident that anyone who tried to retrieve it would die either by venom or asphyxiation, so that the other two tasks were little more than ornamental flourishes. He did not realize that his daughter Medea was falling in love with Jason as he spoke. Hera (Juno) had asked Aphrodite (Venus) to inspire Medea with an irresistible passion for Jason, so that he could win the Golden Fleece, and Eros (Cupid) flew unseen into the palace, drew his bow, and pierced Medea's heart. As her father named the three tasks, Medea was already planning how to help Jason achieve them.

First came the plowing match. Poseidon (Neptune) had given King Aietes two fire-breathing bulls made of bronze, and an iron plow that never rusted. Aietes plowed a deep furrow, and then dared Jason to take hold of the plow. While the king was busy in the field, his daughter Medea secretly gave Jason some magical ointment that would protect his skin from the heat of the bulls' bodies and breath. With her help, he was easily able to plow his own deep furrow, and so he passed the first test.

Jason requested that King Aietes let him complete his second task unobserved, because Medea had whispered to him that she would help him if no one was watching. At midnight he walked quietly toward

Above *Jason Taming the Bulls of Aietes* by Jean Francois de Troy (1679–1752). Jason was well able to accomplish the first task, having enlisted the help of Medea. Some say that the magic drug she gave him was from a plant that had grown out of the blood of Prometheus as it dripped from the eagle's talons.

Above **The Argo.** The Argo was built by Argus, the son of Arestor, and was subsequently named after him. With the help of Athene, Argus built the largest and most elaborate ship of his time.

Above **Engagement of Jason and Medea.** It is said that Aphrodite was concerned that Medea would be torn between filial duty and her love for Jason. The goddess appeared to her in the form of Circe to persuade her to follow her heart, even if it meant betraying her father.

Opposite page **Medea and the Fleece.** Medea, meaning "cunning" or "knowing," was a priestess of the underworld goddess Hecate. Lulling the serpent to sleep was an easy task for Medea, who was well acquainted with magical herbs and potions, and could work miracles for both good and evil.

Right *Jason and the Golden Fleece* by Erasmus Quellinus (1607–1678). Jason was finally able to take possession of the Golden Fleece. The famous ram who saved Phrixus was said to have been an offspring of Poseidon and Theophane. It was blessed with intelligence and reason, and was able to speak, as well as fly.

the sacred grove of Ares, and, as he had hoped, there was the princess waiting for him. She asked him to swear to take her to Greece with him, marry her, and always remain faithful to her. Once he had murmured his vows, she crept over to where the serpent was coiled around one of Ares' sacred trees, with the fleece hanging beside its head. As she moved closer, she began to sing and hum a magical charm of sleep, and the serpent's head drooped. She dripped a sleep potion into its eyes and it fell deeply asleep. Jason took the fleece and left without disturbing the serpent's sleep. Now he owed his life twice over to the magic-maker Medea.

Medea was a priestess of the goddess Hecate, who was a triple goddess, manifesting as maiden, mother, and crone. In some accounts of Hecate, the triple goddess was made up of Persephone (Proserpina) as maiden, Demeter (Ceres) as mother, and Hecate as crone. In these accounts Hecate was a fearsome goddess of witchcraft and death, but when she was understood as the full triple goddess, she had powers over life as well as death. Hecate was the goddess of the crossroads, the place where decisions must be made and where one can look back into the past and forward into the future. The coming of Jason was a crossroads in Medea's life, and it was Hecate's magic that Medea used to betray her father's treasure into the hands of her new lover.

For Jason's final task, he needed no help from Medea. He took the dragon's teeth and sowed them in the field where he and the king had plowed their furrows. Jason knew exactly what to do with the warriors who had erupted from the ground, as Cadmus had previously faced a very similar problem in Thebes. He hurled a rock right into the middle of the crowd of armed men, and at once they all started pushing each other around, each one blaming the next for trying to attack him with the rock. Very soon they were all dead.

THE SACRED OAK

Erysichthon was a foolish man who continued to cut down an oak tree after he saw blood oozing from his first cut. His servants gave him fair warning that the oak was sacred to Demeter (Ceres), but he did not pay any attention. Demeter sent a fearful punishment, instructing Famine to stay close to him, day and night, so that he could never fill his stomach. He gorged himself until he had spent all his wealth on food, yet still he was starving. Then he sold his daughter as a slave to buy food. Poseidon (Neptune) took pity on her and changed her into a fisherman, and so she escaped. Time and time again Erysichthon sold her and then retrieved her, but the food that he bought could never satisfy his stomach's demands. In the end he started consuming his own body, and so he died. That is how the goddess of all growing things took her revenge.

Above *Erysichthon Punished* by I Matheus (c. 1610). The blood from the oak tree is said to be that of the Dryad or tree nymph.

Above right *Medea and Pelias* by I. Briot (c. 1610). In another version of this story, Jason returned home to find that King Pelias, who thought that Jason had perished, had killed Jason's father and younger brother. Jason's mother, as a result, had committed suicide.

Right *Medea's Flight to Corinth with Jason* by the Policoro Painter (fifth century). Some say that Medea's half-brother Apsyrtus was not a child, but a grown man. When Medea learned of his deal with Jason to leave her behind in return for being allowed to keep the Golden Fleece, she convinced Jason to kill him.

FLIGHT FROM COLCHIS

Now Jason and the Argonauts fled from Colchis, with the Golden Fleece and Princess Medea, who snatched up her baby half-brother Apsyrtus from his cradle as she ran. The king of Colchis and his navy followed them, ready for a sea battle, and Medea could see that the Argo would be attacked and sunk if she did not act. She sacrificed her brother to the goddess Hecate, slicing up his small body and throwing the pieces into the sea. Jason joined in the murder, desperate to delay the enemy. Aietes yelled for his men to stop, to jump into the water, and retrieve the body of his son. By the time all the pieces had been recovered, the Argo was safely away.

Jason and Medea had committed a crime that only Hecate as crone goddess would countenance. Their existence was now an offense to all the other gods, polluted as they were by murder. The Argo's oracular oak wood prophesied that they would reach home again only if Jason and Medea went to the island of Hecate's daughter Circe, who had the power to cleanse them of their crime. Circe performed the ritual of purification, but she did not welcome Medea into her house, because the princess was still guilty of betraying her father.

Onward the Argo sailed, past the rocks where the Sirens sang their lethal song, as they would sing two generations later to Odysseus (Ulysses) and his men. The Argonauts sailed safely past, because the musician Orpheus sang one of his lovely songs so loudly that the Sirens could not be heard. They went past the islands that Odysseus would visit on his way home from Troy, and Jason married Medea on the island of the Phaeacians. Orpheus sang the wedding song, and the Golden Fleece was the blanket for their bed.

A storm drove them to the country of Libya, and a huge wave carried the Argo a long way inland, leaving the ship aground in the desert. Here Jason had a prophetic vision of the three daughters of Libya, who told him that he and his men must carry the Argo across the desert, as their mother had carried them in the womb. After 12 days of trudging across the sandy, rocky desert, the Argonauts came to the site of another of Heracles' labors, where the apples of the Hesperides—Aegle, Erytheia, and Hespera— had grown. Heracles had been there only the day before their arrival, and the most keen-sighted of the Argonauts, Lynceus, swore that he could just make out the figure of Heracles walking away, slowly receding into the distance.

The Argonauts found their way to a salt lake, but they could find no outlet to the sea. Then Jason remembered that the

Pythian oracle had advised him to take two tripods on the voyage. He offered one of them to the local god, not knowing what name to invoke. Poseidon's son, the half-man, half-dolphin Triton, rose from the lake in response, gave a lump of earth to one of the Argonauts, a man called Euphemus, and then helped them pull the ship to the open sea.

The Argo then traveled across the Mediterranean to Crete. The island was guarded by a metal creature called Talus, made by Hephaestus, which sleeplessly walked around the shores, circling the island three times a day. Talus's only weakness was a vein that ran the length of his body, and Medea bewitched him so that he tripped and fell, tearing open this vein. Ichor, the fluid that runs in the veins of the gods, spurted out of his body, and so he died. Onward sailed the Argo, calling in at many other islands on the way. The gods sent a dream to Euphemus, reminding him of the clod of earth that the Triton had given him. In his dream, he held it close to his heart, where it changed into the form of a nymph. "I am the daughter of the Triton and the goddess Libya," she told him, "and I want to live in the sea." When he woke, Euphemus threw the clod of earth into the sea, and up rose a new island, the volcanic isle of Thera.

Medea among the Greeks

Jason returned with his new bride to Iolcus, where he found his father, Aeson, close to death. Medea was glad to use her magical powers for life rather than death. She ordered servants to cut up the body of Aeson and boil the pieces in her magic cauldron. Soon the body took shape again, as a young man. Pelias, the king who had sent Jason on the quest for the Golden Fleece, was also ageing, and eager to be transformed back into a young man by Medea. She ordered his daughters to cut up his body and boil it in a cauldron, but without her magic, he remained dead. So the oracle was fulfilled, that his death would come about through the man with one sandal.

Jason knew that it was for the love of him that Medea had organized the killing of Pelias, and so he went willingly into exile with her to Corinth. There he beached the ship Argo, dedicating it to Poseidon in gratitude for a safe voyage. For a while Medea and Jason lived together happily, but Jason became restless, stirred up by ambition and perhaps by love. He decided to set aside his marriage with Medea on the pretext that she was a foreigner, and wed instead

When the first Ship sailed for the Golden Fleece— ARGO—exalted for that daring feat To fix in heaven her shape distinct with stars.

WILLIAM WORDSWORTH (1770–1850), *MEMORIALS OF A TOUR ON THE CONTINENT*

Princess Glauce, daughter of King Creon of Corinth. On Creon's death, Jason could become king. When Medea found out what he had planned, she was overcome with anguish. For this man she had betrayed her father, killed her brother, caused the death of a king, and gained a reputation as an evil witch, and now he was proposing to send her into fresh exile from the exile she already endured for his sake. First she wept, then she argued the injustice of what he was doing, and then she spoke sweetly to him. "Let me give a bridal gift to Glauce," she said, "and rather than showing my unwelcome face to her,

Below *Orpheus Plays Harp* by T.H. Robinson.
Orpheus played his harp and sang loudly so the Argonauts would not hear the deadly songs of the Sirens. Some say the Sirens were originally the nymph companions of Persephone. When the goddess was snatched away by Hades, the nymphs prayed for wings so that they could search the seas for her. Their wish was granted, and they became half-maiden and half-bird.

let me send my children with the gifts." Jason agreed, and Medea piled their arms full of finely woven cloth. It was a wedding robe, enchanted so that it would burn its wearer, and with it came a golden diadem, which would sear the forehead of its wearer to the bone. Glauce and her father died in torment, and in the outcry and confusion, Medea also killed her children. She did all of these things to put Jason through as much misery as she suffered through him, and the cost of her children's lives did not seem such a high price to pay.

Any other woman behaving like this might expect the wrath of the gods to fall upon her, but for Medea, granddaughter of Helius (Sol) and priestess of Hecate, the gods sent a chariot drawn by dragons so that she could escape. She fled to Athens and married Aegeus, and remained living there until Theseus arrived and cast her out when she tried to have him poisoned. Next she traveled to the country of Persia,

becoming the goddess of the Medes, a people named after her. Jason lived on in wretched obscurity, hated by the gods because he had broken his oath to Medea. Years later, when he was sitting on the shore in the shadow of his beloved ship, the Argo, a piece of its oracular oak wood fell on his head and killed him. The great ship was not guilty of murder, and to commemorate its amazing voyage, the constellation Argo was placed in the night sky.

Of all the heroes of Greek myth, Jason was the one who owed most to a woman. It was Medea who provided the magic ointment that saved him from being burned alive by the bulls. It was Medea who enchanted the serpent into sleeping, so that he could steal the Golden Fleece. It was Medea who slaughtered her own brother to delay the pursuing navy, and it was also she who brought about the catastrophe that ended Jason's hopes of starting a new life, with a new bride. Jason was never a hero in his own quest.

MELEAGER AND ATALANTA

Meleager was the son of Queen Althaia of Calydon, but his father was Ares, the god of war, and not Althaia's husband, King Oineus. At Meleager's birth, the three Fates appeared in Althaia's bedroom. The youngest, Clotho, who spins the thread of mortal life, prophesied that the baby boy would become a man of courage and noble deeds. The grown woman, Lachesis, who weaves the cloth of human life, prophesied that he would be a hero of great renown. The oldest of the Fates, Atropos, who cuts off the thread of life, looked at the fire, where a log was burning, and prophesied that he would live until the log was totally burned. Althaia jumped out of bed and pulled the log out of the fire. Then she hid it in the palace, hoping that it would never be found again.

Meleager grew up to be devoted to the hunt. When he was a young man, a wild boar came to Calydon. It was sent by Artemis (Diana), the goddess of the hunt, angry because King Oineus had forgotten to honor her with sacrifice. No one could catch or kill the boar, and Meleager decided to summon all the hunters of Greece to the Calydonian hunt. Many heroes joined the quest for the boar. Heracles (Hercules) did not come, because he was busy with his labors, but Jason joined in, along with Theseus and some of the Argonauts. The huntress Atalanta also came to Calydon, and caused much disagreement among the huntsmen, who did not want any women on this quest. Meleager insisted that Atalanta should be allowed to hunt, for the arrow of the love god had pierced his heart as soon as he first saw her.

When Atalanta was born, her father was disappointed that she was not a boy, and ordered her to be exposed on the nearest mountain. She was saved from death by a mother bear that suckled her, and then she was found by hunters and reared among them. Atalanta grew up to be a magnificent runner, and she vowed that she would marry only the man who could outrun her in a race. The conditions of the race were difficult, for she gave herself the right to kill any man who failed. Many men were tempted by her beauty, and they all died with her arrow in their heart.

There was no time for Meleager to challenge her to a footrace, but he made sure that he was close to her for the six days of the hunt. At last the two of them killed the boar together, Atalanta shooting it with an arrow and Meleager slitting its throat. Then it was time for the banquet, along with the presentation of the boar's head and skin to the victor. Meleager should by rights have kept these prizes, as he struck the blow that actually killed the boar, but he offered them to Atalanta. Feasting turned to furious debate among the hunters, then to fighting,

Left **Hunting the Calydon boar.** Meleager joined the Argonauts in the search for the Golden Fleece. When he set sail, his uncle, Lacoon, had to accompany the celebrated warrior because he was too young to be on his own.

Below *The Three Fates* by Sebastiano Mazzoni (1611–1678). In some stories, the Fates appear to carry out the will of the gods, while in others, it is the gods who bow to the will of the Fates.

GEMINI

The twin brothers Castor and Polydeuces (Pollux) were sons of Leda. Polydeuces was the child of Zeus (Jupiter) and Castor the child of the mortal king, Tyndareus of Sparta. When Castor died, Polydeuces prayed to his father, Zeus, begging that he might also die, even though he had been born immortal. He had no wish to outlive his mortal brother. Zeus offered Polydeuces eternal life among the Olympians, but Polydeuces would not accept this gift unless Castor could share it. In the end, Zeus decreed that the twins should share both immortality and death, alternating their places in the underworld and among the gods on Olympus. He marked their brotherly love for one another with the two brightest stars in the constellation of Gemini, the Twins.

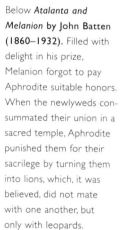

Left **Dioscuri (Castor and Polydeuces).** The heavenly twins were known as Dioscuri, which means "sons of Zeus." When they became stars, they also became the guardian of seafarers.

Below *Atalanta and Melanion* by John Batten (1860–1932). Filled with delight in his prize, Melanion forgot to pay Aphrodite suitable honors. When the newlyweds consummated their union in a sacred temple, Aphrodite punished them for their sacrilege by turning them into lions, which, it was believed, did not mate with one another, but only with leopards.

and Meleager ended by killing his uncles, who were also Althaia's brothers.

The palace was full of turmoil. Althaia crouched down on the floor in grief and anger, praying to Hades (Pluto) and Persephone (Proserpina) that her son might join them in the underworld as soon as possible. Then she went to her bedroom, where she had hidden the log from her fire in a chest of finely woven clothes. Althaia took out the charred log and thrust it into the flames. Meleager felt the fire attack his limbs, then climb up toward his heart, and then he died, killed by his distraught mother.

Atalanta and the Apples

After the disastrous end to the Calydonian hunt, more suitors challenged Atalanta to a footrace and died as a result. No man alive could run as fast as this favorite of the goddess Artemis. Her cousin Melanion fell in love with her, and thought carefully

about the race that he would have to run in order to claim her. She could be won only through trickery, he concluded, and he prayed to the goddess of sexual desire, Aphrodite (Venus), for help. The goddess was very impatient with Atalanta's attitude toward her admirers, and came down from Mount Olympus to give Melanion three golden apples, irresistibly beautiful fruit that she had begged from Dionysus (Bacchus). "Use them wisely," she told Melanion, "and Atalanta will be yours."

The day of the footrace came, and Melanion made ready at the starting line, carrying the apples in his hands. Atalanta was about to mock him, to ask if he thought that holding weights in his hands would make him run faster, but then she saw the apples more closely, and their golden sheen captivated her. Once the race was over and Melanion dead, she thought, the beautiful fruit would be hers, and she promised herself that she would run her fastest for the sake of these golden marvels.

The race began, and Atalanta was already ahead of Melanion, when he threw one of the apples past her, away from the racetrack. She left the track, unable to help herself, chasing the apple and scooping it up into her hand. Then she hurtled back in pursuit of Melanion, and quickly overtook him again. He threw the second apple, and despite herself, she followed it away from the racetrack until she had it safely in her hand. Now Melanion was ahead once more, and the race was nearly over, but even so, she was fast enough to catch and kill him—but there went the third apple, and Atalanta's feet followed it off the track as though she were running for her life. Now she was back again, running faster than she had ever run before, but Melanion was already at the finishing line—the race was over and the bride had been won.

THESEUS BECOMES A HERO

There are two stories about the birth of Theseus. In one, he was the son of the sea god Poseidon (Neptune); in the other, he was the son of a mortal man, King Aegeus. In the first version, Athene (Minerva) sent a dream to the unmarried princess of Troezen, Aethra. Athene said that Aethra must visit her temple and make a sacrifice there to the ghost of a charioteer buried close by. Aethra went to the temple the next day and there she met Poseidon, waiting to take her virginity by force. Nine months later, she gave birth to his son, Theseus, who grew up in Troezen as heir to the kingdom. It was most unusual for the virgin goddess Athene to approve of anyone, even another Olympian, engaging in sexual activity within her temple, yet this time she not only approved, but even sent the girl to her attacker. It was more important to her for Theseus to be born than for her temple to keep its virginal purity.

In the other version, Aethra gave her virginity to King Aegeus of Athens, with the encouragement of her father. After two childless marriages, Aegeus longed for a son, and asked the oracle at Delphi how he could become a father. The oracle told him, "Do not open your wine skin until you get

back to Athens." Aegeus did not understand the veiled meaning of these words and, rather than returning to Athens by the direct road, he visited the king of Troezen, Pittheus, who was an expert at deciphering the meaning of oracles. Pittheus understood at once that the oracle had been telling Aegeus to stay chaste until he was back in Athens, because the first time he had sexual relations with a woman, he would father a son. The king of Troezen did not explain this, because he wanted his daughter Aethra to be the mother of Aegeus's son who would become Aegeus's heir as king of Athens. That night, he persuaded his daughter to share her bed with the guest, and in the morning, before leaving for home, Aegeus asked her

MEDEA'S MAGIC

Medea was expert at the use of magical herbs. When she prepared the poisoned cup for Theseus, she put some wolfsbane into it. This noxious plant came into being when Heracles dragged the three-headed dog, Cerberus, up from the realm of the dead. Cerberus was foaming at the mouth as he tried to escape, and drops of this foam fell to the ground, becoming the poisonous wolfsbane. Much earlier in her story, the ointment that she gave to Jason, to protect him from being burned to death, was made from the Caucasian crocus, sprung from the blood that flowed from Prometheus's liver as Zeus's (Jupiter's) bird ripped at it daily.

Right *Jason and Medea* by John Waterhouse (1849–1917). Some say that as well as using her magic to help Jason, the sorceress Medea also cured Heracles of the madness that caused him to murder his children.

Below *Theseus Finding His Father's Sword* by Giovanni Ghisolfi (1632–1683). When Theseus grew to manhood, he traveled to Delphi to offer, as was the custom, the first clippings of his hair to Apollo. It was on his return home that his mother told him the story of Aegeus and took him to the rock under which the sword and sandals were hidden.

to ride a little way out of the city in his chariot. He found a place where there was a deep hollow in the road, and there he put his sandals and sword. Then he rolled a huge rock over them with a great effort, until it sat snugly in the hollow. "Aethra," he said, "only a hero will be able to shift this rock and find my sword and sandals. I doubt that you are pregnant with my child, but if you do give birth to a son of mine, take him here and let him try his strength against the rock. If he can move it away, let him come to Athens carrying the sword and wearing the sandals so that I can recognize him and make him heir to the kingdom. It would not be safe for him to come to Athens before then, in case one of my unpleasant nephews tried to assassinate him." Then Aegeus left, standing barefoot in his chariot.

Nine months later, Aethra gave birth to Theseus, and he grew up at the court of King Pittheus. When he was seven years old, Heracles (Hercules) came visiting, in the course of his 12 labors, and threw off his fearsome lion skin so that he could be

From Themistocles began the saying, "He is a second Hercules."

PLUTARCH (C.46–C.120),
LIFE OF THESEUS

more comfortable at the welcoming banquet. All the other children at court panicked at the sight of the lion skin on the floor, looking just like a live lion; but Theseus seized an ax and ran up to the creature, ready to kill it, before he realized that it was only an empty skin. This was his first heroic deed, but he was not yet strong enough to lift the rock and take his father's sword.

Dangers on the Road

When Theseus was no longer a child, his mother took him to the place where Aegeus had buried the sandals and sword under the rock. The young man

effortlessly pushed the rock out of the hollow and uncovered his father's tokens of recognition. He put on the sandals and, with sword in hand, started the long walk to Athens. The road was beset with murderers, as he knew, and he could have chosen a safer route by sea, but he wanted to prove himself a hero. Theseus admired Heracles and wanted to win the same kind of glory; as well as this, he wanted to meet his father in Athens, not as an unknown young man but as an established hero.

THESEUS AND PERIPHETES

Soon after he set out, he met Periphetes, the crippled son of the lame god Hephaestus (Vulcan), who used to lurk in the undergrowth beside the road and assault passersby with a large bronze club. Because he took people by surprise, Periphetes had killed and robbed many travelers, but Theseus was on the lookout for trouble. When Periphetes jumped out onto the road behind him, Theseus turned, took hold of him, and threw him to the ground. Then the murderer was battered to death with his own club. Theseus took this massive club with him, perhaps in deliberate imitation of Heracles, and it was to kill many more men on his travels.

SINIS THE PINE-BENDER

Farther along the road to Athens was a pine forest, the haunt of a murderer called Sinis, the son of Poseidon. Whenever Sinis captured a traveler, he used to bend two pine trees together and tie his victim to both of them; he even forced the poor wretch to help bend the trees. Then Sinis would release the pine trees and the victim would be torn apart. Theseus allowed Sinis to take him into the forest, and even helped him choose two sturdy pine trees and bend them together, but then it was Theseus who tied Sinis to the trees, paying no attention to his screams for mercy, and let them spring apart again. So died the pine-bender, torn apart as he had torn apart so many others.

SCIRON THE MURDERER

The road then passed along the very steep slope of a mountain with a cliff to one side and, on the other side, a precipitous drop to the sea. Any travelers who fell from the path or tried to wade around the foot of the mountain, were eaten by a turtle one of the

Above *Theseus's Adventures by the Dinos Painter* (c. 425 B.C.). Theseus wanted to be known as a great hero like Hercules, so he traveled to Athens along a road haunted by scoundrels, murderers, and savage animals. Among the many villains and beasts he met along the way was the Crommyonian Sow, a fierce creature that had killed many travelers.

servants of Hades (Pluto). A rascal called Sciron took full advantage of the narrow mountain path. He used to sit on a rock in the middle of the road and demand that every traveler wash his feet, as a toll. As soon as his victims knelt down, Sciron would kick them over the mountainside and into the sea, where the turtle was waiting to devour them. Theseus came up to Sciron's rock and gave it a mighty kick, so that it toppled into the sea. Sciron tumbled with it, straight into the mouth of the waiting turtle, and did not even have time to scream as he fell.

> *I know, indeed,*
> *the evil of that I purpose;*
> *but my inclination gets the*
> *better of my judgment.*
>
> EURIPIDES (484 B.C.–406 B.C.),
> *MEDEA*

CERCYON AND PROCRUSTES

Closer to Athens, near Eleusis, there lived a wrestler called Cercyon. He forced all passersby to wrestle with him, and all of them lost both the competition and their lives. Theseus was far more skilled as a wrestler, and he killed Cercyon by hurling him against the ground and smashing his bones. A little way down the road lived Sinis's father Procrustes, another murderer, who used to offer travelers a bed for the night. He had two beds, one was a very long one and the other was very short. He measured tall people on the short bed, and sliced off the overhanging parts. Similarly, he measured short people on the long bed and then stretched them to fit. All who suffered this kind of rough measurement died.

Theseus forced Procrustes onto his short bed and measured and pruned him until he died.

By the time Theseus reached Athens, every Athenian had heard about the new hero who had made the road safe for travelers, but no one knew that he was the son of Aegeus and heir to the throne—no one except the king's wife, Medea. This was the same Medea who had helped Jason win the Golden Fleece. Now, as queen of Athens, she wanted her son, Medus, to be the heir to the ageing king's throne. Using her magic, she persuaded Aegeus to poison the new champion with wine at his welcoming banquet. All that Theseus could think about was the moment when his father would recognize him. He took the wine cup from Aegeus and offered him the sword in return. The king suddenly recognized the weapon that he had hidden so long ago in Troezen. He knocked the cup out of Theseus's hand and cried out, "Seize that wicked woman, my wife!" Medea could not hide her guilt, and was banished from Athens with her son Medus, while Theseus was welcomed afresh with honor as the king's son and heir.

Theseus, the New Heir

Not everyone welcomed the new heir. Aegeus had a brother, Pallas, who had 50 sons. For years they had expected to rule the kingdom between them when Aegeus died, and now they planned to ambush Theseus and kill him. Luck ran Theseus's way, for he discovered this plan and killed most of the 50 sons of Pallas. After this, Aegeus wanted his newfound son to stay in Athens and not risk his life on any more adventures. After all, he told Theseus, the killing of so many rogues while he was on his way to Athens had established his reputation as a hero. He had no need at all to prove himself any further. But Theseus fretted at court, as though he were in a gilded prison. At the first chance, he crept out of the royal palace to seek another adventure.

Heracles had brought a fire-breathing bull to Marathon, as part of his labors, and it was

Below **Detail from a calyx-crater showing Theseus and Procrustes by the Dinos Painter (c. 425 B.C.).** The scoundrel Procrustes was also known as either Damastas or Polypemon. He was quickly given the nickname of "Procrustes," which means "the stretcher."

The Rape of Helen

Theseus had a friend, Peirithous, the king of the Lapiths, who was a son of Zeus (Jupiter). Each of the friends was a bad influence on the other. They told each other that sons of gods deserved the very finest of women in their beds, and that they would settle for no less than daughters of Zeus. They had heard of a daughter of Zeus, Helen of Sparta, who was rumored to be the most beautiful of girls, and they planned to abduct her and force her into marriage, casting lots to decide who was to be the lucky man. It did not bother them that she was still a child. Theseus won, and with Peirithous's help, he abducted Helen, offending the gods by seizing her in the temple of the virgin goddess Artemis (Diana). He took her to his mother, Aethra, for safe keeping after marrying her by force. Helen's brothers, Castor and Polydeuces (Pollux), came to free her, and took Aethra back to Sparta as a slave. When Helen was stolen away again, years later, by Paris of Troy, Theseus's mother went to Troy with her, still as a slave. Theseus did himself no credit

Left *Helen of Troy* by Dante Gabriel Rossetti (1828–1882). It is believed that Theseus sent the beautiful Helen to be with his mother because he was so worried about the consequences of his marriage. The Athenians were displeased with his actions, afraid that they would be attacked by Sparta in retaliation for the abduction.

Below **Detail showing Heracles and Greek heroes by the Niobid Painter (c. 475 B.C.– 450 B.C.).** When Theseus and Peirithous ventured into the underworld, they accepted the offer to be seated. Unbeknown to them, they sat down on the Chairs of Forgetfulness. At once their bodies became one with the chairs and the men lost all memory of who they were and why they were there. Heracles eventually rescued Theseus, but could not help Peirithous.

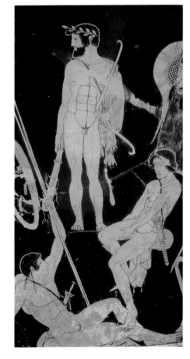

now rampaging in the plain and terrorizing the villagers. As soon as Theseus heard of this problem, he found his way secretly out of Athens and went to Marathon. Long before he could see the bull, he heard its roars, but they did not frighten him at all. What Heracles had achieved before him, he promised himself, he would be able to equal. Theseus walked fearlessly up to the bull, knowing exactly what to do. With one hand, he grabbed hold of one of its horns, and with the other, he grasped its nostrils; then he pulled its head sideways and down, so that the bull fell to its knees. Then he tied a rope around its neck, and the bull did not dare to give any more trouble as it walked behind him all the way to Athens.

by this adventure, and brought years of suffering and humiliation upon his mother. Peirithous and Theseus learned nothing from this, because their next unsuccessful plan was to carry off another daughter of Zeus, Persephone (Proserpina), from the underworld. This attempt ended with the two men stuck to thrones in the underworld, from which Heracles rescued Theseus, but Peirithous was left there forever. Theseus had longed to equal Heracles' feats, and so far he had proved himself a hero in his dealings with wicked men, but in his dealings with women, he was proving himself to be a scoundrel.

Right *Fall of Icarus* by
Thomas Fedrianus.
Icarus's father, Daedalus,
was famous for his cre-
ative devices. The Athenian
craftsman, whose name
means "the ingenious,"
was said to have invented
masts and sails, glue, and a
number of carpentry tools
such as the ax, the auger,
and the plumb line.

THE MYTHS OF CRETE

The Greek myths of Crete speak
of a kingdom contemporary
with the royal families of
Thebes and Athens, superior
in might to any realm on
the mainland of Greece.
Archaeological evidence
suggests that these myths
of Crete look back to a
realm that existed well
before Thebes, Mycenae,
or Athens became powerful
cities. The civilization of
Crete, called Minoan after the
mythic King Minos, lasted for
about 1,500 years but went into
decline after the volcanic eruption
of Thera in about 1450 B.C. The
Cretans worshipped a mother goddess,
and surviving pottery shows young men performing
a gymnastic dance with a bull, perhaps in celebration
of the goddess. Memories of this bull dance, distorted
over generations, may have contributed to the story
of the Cretan Minotaur.

Minos and the Minotaur

Minos was one of the three sons of Zeus (Jupiter) and
Europa. He became the king of Crete, after a struggle
for power with his brothers. "Send me a bull from
the sea," Minos prayed to Poseidon
(Neptune), "to confirm that the
kingship is rightfully mine."
A magnificent white bull swam
to the Cretan shore, and there
Minos should have sacrificed it in
honor of the sea god, but he admired the
bull so much that he could not bear to have it killed.
Instead, he kept it among his herds, sacrificing an
inferior animal in its place and hoping that Poseidon
would not notice the difference.

Poseidon was not fooled, and he swiftly took
revenge. Minos's queen Pasiphae
also noticed the magnificence of
the white bull. Now Poseidon
asked Aphrodite (Venus),
the goddess of desire, to
inflame Pasiphae with
lust for the animal, and
she became obsessed
with the idea of having
sexual intercourse
with it. She ran the

*Sing to me of
the Labyrinth in which the twi-
formed bull was stalled!*

OSCAR WILDE (1854–1900),
"THE SPHINX"

risk of being trampled to death
if she approached the bull
unprotected, and she turned
to the great Greek inventor
Daedalus for a solution. He
built her a wooden cow in
which she could conceal
herself, something like
a miniature version of
the Trojan horse, and
the bull was deceived
by this. Pasiphae became
pregnant with the bull's
offspring, and nine months
later she gave birth to a
child, Asterius. His name in
Greek means "starry," but he
was born with the head and
upper torso of a bull and the lower
body of a man, and he was most
commonly known by his nickname, the
Minotaur (meaning in Greek, "the bull of Minos").
Minos felt ashamed and disgraced by the monstrous
birth, and wanted to hide the Minotaur from view.
He asked Daedalus to build a labyrinth at Knossos,
a huge underground maze with a locked door as its
sole entrance and exit. There, he hoped, the Minotaur
would live out his days in secrecy. In the meantime,
Pasiphae recovered from the mad longing with which
Aphrodite had afflicted her, and she became her
husband's faithful wife once more. Pasiphae and
Minos went on to have many children,
including two daughters, Ariadne
and Phaedra, and a son, called
Androgeus. Androgeus visited
Athens to take part in athletic
games, all of which he won, but
the Athenian king, Aegeus, started to
suspect that this Cretan champion was not only an
athlete but a supporter of the rebels who were
causing trouble in his kingdom. On the way home,
Androgeus was ambushed and killed by Aegeus's
men. That crime was the starting point for a war
between Athens and Crete, which ended in the
defeat of the Athenians. Their punishment was to
provide a tribute once every nine years, made up
of seven young men and seven young women. Everyone knew that these young Athenians were doomed
to be eaten by the Minotaur.

Daedalus and Icarus

After Daedalus had built the intricate maze of the
Cretan labyrinth, Minos imprisoned him together
with his son, Icarus, in a tower. He wanted the

Below **Minotaur.** The story
of the Minotaur may have
been associated with, or
indeed have evolved from,
certain ancient rituals. It
was not uncommon for
the priest or priest-king of
Knossos to wear an animal
head mask similar to the
Minotaur during particular
ceremonies.

Minotaur's existence to be kept secret, even though he was aware that everyone was gossiping about it, but his most compelling reason to keep the secret was to stop the spread of scandal about his wife, Pasiphae, and the bull. The tower was high and Minos had Daedalus and his son imprisoned at the top, with the stair under heavy guard. He was confident that neither of them could escape, and so he did not bother with shackles.

Daedalus looked around the room for something to work with, to devise a way to escape. He had some wax tablets with him, and the corners of the room were littered with leaves and feathers blown in through the window. No one had cleaned the tower since it had been built. Daedalus collected the feathers and made two pairs of wings from them, sticking them together with wax. He put on the larger pair and gave the others to Icarus. "Be careful," he urged his son. "You must follow me closely. Do not fly too close to the sea, because you will drown if your feathers become wet; do not fly too close to the sun, because you will fall to your death if the wax gets too hot and melts."

Father and son flew out of the tower window, and the Cretans who saw them thought that they were immortal gods. They flew on past many of the Greek islands, and Icarus grew bored with the slow, steady pace that his father was setting, and the unvarying height at which they were flying. Surely, he told himself, his father would not notice if he tried just a

Above **Daedalus and Pasiphae.** Pasiphae, like her sister Circe, was skilled in the use of herbs, charms, and spells. A lesser known version of the myth of Daedalus is that it was Pasiphae who freed the father and son from their prison. Daedalus escaped with Icarus in a boat propelled by a sail that he had just invented.

157

little maneuvering with those splendid wings. Soon Icarus was swooping and somersaulting through the sky, always gaining height until he flew too close to the sun. The wax very quickly melted and he fell into the sea and drowned. When his father looked back, all that he could see was a collection of feathers floating on the surface of the sea. That is how the greatest of inventors, Daedalus, helped his son Icarus to both freedom and death.

Years later, Minos tried to force Daedalus back to Crete. He did not know where the inventor might have gone, and devised a plan to find him that was worthy of Daedalus himself. Minos offered a reward to anyone who could pass a thread through a spiraling conch shell, from opening to tip. He believed that only Daedalus would be clever enough to work out this puzzle, and so it turned out. Daedalus bored a hole at the tip of the shell and smeared it with honey. Then he tied a thread to a large ant, which he stood at the shell's opening. The ant found its way to the honey, pulling the thread along behind it. The king of Sicily took the reward, and soon revealed to Minos that the problem had, in fact, been solved by his guest, the great inventor. Minos came in search of Daedalus, but the Sicilian king's daughters did not want to lose their beloved guest, and so they lured Minos into a bath where they murdered him. Daedalus's final invention for Minos was a pipe that came out of the roof just above the bath where Minos was, down which the princesses poured scalding water until the Cretan king died.

Above **Detail from an oil flask showing Ariadne and Theseus** (c. 460 B.C.). The piety of Theseus was certainly rewarded. Before leaving for Crete, Theseus made vows and a sacrifice, and was told by a priestess to pay particular homage to Aphrodite. By keeping in favor with the goddess of love, he secured a wife, Ariadne, and his safety.

Theseus and Ariadne

When he entered Athens as a hero, Theseus knew nothing of the hostages that were sent to Crete to die, but soon he noticed that everyone in the city was more anxious than usual, and saw the palace being readied for some sorrowful ritual. When he learned the story, he was determined to help, if only by volunteering to be one of the hostages this time. Aegeus was desperate to convince him not to go, but

Theseus announced his decision in the market-place, and once it became public, the king was forced to send him to Crete. "Trouble yourself no more," said Theseus. "I promise to bring all these hostages back in triumph, along with the head of the Minotaur." So convincing did he sound that Aegeus gave him some white sails for the ship's return voyage. Previously, the ship traveling between Athens and Crete with its death-bound cargo carried black sails to signify death and sorrow. Now, Aegeus dared to hope that he would see the ship return with white sails of happiness.

On the voyage, Theseus told the ship's captain to make sure that he and his men stayed in Crete over-night, ready to spread sail at any time. The ship arrived at the Cretan harbor, and King Minos came down to inspect the hostages, along with his wife and his daughter Ariadne. The princess fell in love with Theseus as soon as she saw him, and as they went in slow procession back toward the palace, she snatched her chance to whisper to him, "The Minotaur is my half-brother, but if you will marry me, I will help you to kill him." Theseus nodded in satisfaction; luck, as usual, was running his way, or was this the work of golden Aphrodite, the goddess of desire, to whom he had made a sacrifice just before leaving Athens?

THROUGH THE LABYRINTH

Ariadne devised a way for Theseus to track his path through the black maze of the labyrinth, so that he could find his way out again if he managed to kill the Minotaur. She gave him a ball of thread, telling him to tie the end to the door. The thread would unwind as he walked into the maze, and to find his

Left *Ariadne and Theseus* by Jean-Baptiste Regnault (1754–1829). Overcome with passion for the handsome Theseus, Ariadne was determined to see him safely through the maze. It is believed that she went to Daedalus, the designer of the labyrinth, and begged him to help her rescue Theseus. It was the inventor's suggestion to use the ball of thread.

Below **Theseus slaying the Minotaur.** According to most authors, the Minotaur devoured the victims who were offered up to it in the maze. Others maintain, however, that the poor wretches simply wandered about the labyrinth until they eventually starved to death.

way out, all that he needed to do was to follow the thread and let it lead him back again. In the evening, the hostages were taken to the doorway, and thrust, one after another, into the darkness that smelt of slaughter. Theseus managed to tie Ariadne's thread to the door as soon as it clanged shut. He told the Athenians to stay there, without wandering away and losing themselves, while he went into the maze to find the monster and kill it. He was weaponless, of course, and groped forward in the dark, pausing to listen at every turn of the maze. Eventually he heard the Minotaur, who was waiting patiently for the first victim to start panicking and screaming. Theseus fought his hardest fight there in the darkness, with his bare hands, against an enemy

with lethally sharp horns, but the Minotaur had grown complacent on his limited diet of terrified Athenians and misjudged his opponent. In the end Theseus threw him to the ground, then twisted his head by the horns until his neck was broken.

Ariadne stole the key to the labyrinth and was waiting at its open door with the Athenian hostages when Theseus returned, clutching at her thread. They ran to the harbor and jumped into the ship, which set sail at once for Athens. The captain and crew had not wasted their time

while waiting in the harbor. They had punched holes into most of the Cretan ships in the darkness, and there were few left that were seaworthy. Someone sounded the alarm, and the Cretans rushed to their ships to prevent Theseus from leaving, but in the confusion, only a couple of the Cretan ships got close to the Athenian ship, and they could not prevent it from slipping away.

The voyage home was leisurely, and after a few days, Theseus and Ariadne arrived at the island of Naxos. Ariadne soon fell asleep on the shore, and Theseus crept back on board and sailed on. No one knows why he deserted her. Was he already regretting his promise to marry her? Was he instructed by Dionysus (Bacchus), who was planning to wed Ariadne himself? Or was he tired of her after a couple of nights' pleasure, and already pursuing some other woman? Whatever the reason, Ariadne's alarm and misery when she awoke did not last long. She prayed to the gods for help, and at once Dionysus appeared with his wild companions, ready to marry her on the spot. The crown that Ariadne wore for this marriage was later placed in the skies as the Corona Borealis.

Theseus sailed on to Athens without her. Somehow, in the tumult of their adventures, he forgot to order the sails

Opposite page **Dionysus and Ariadne** by Nicola Carta (nineteenth century). Why Theseus abandoned Ariadne is uncertain. Whatever the reason was, Ariadne found happiness afterward with Dionysus .

to be changed from black to white. Aegeus was looking out from the Acropolis, the high rock with precipitous sides, for the first glimpse of Theseus's ship. Seeing the black sails, he believed that his son was dead, and threw himself from the Acropolis to his death. It is from the death of Aegeus that the Aegean Sea derived its name.

KING OF ATHENS

Theseus then became king of Athens and ruled long and, for the most part, wisely. One of his less wise decisions was to marry the Amazon Hippolyta, the same woman whose girdle Heracles (Hercules) took as one of his labors; other versions of the story speak not of Hippolyta but of her sister, Antiope. Whoever the Amazon was, Theseus abducted her and brought her to Athens where she later gave birth to his son, Hippolytus. Hippolyta's sisters traveled to Athens and attacked the city, but with no success. They had the misfortune to kill Antiope (or was it Hippolyta?) with an arrow during the fighting.

Theseus's next wife was an equally reckless choice. Phaedra was the daughter of Minos and Pasiphae and the sister of Ariadne, whom Theseus had abandoned on Naxos. When Theseus brought her to Athens, she became infatuated with Hippolytus, who was not at all infatuated with her. Aphrodite brought this love-madness on Phaedra because she was offended by Hippolytus, who had vowed himself to chastity as a devotee of the virgin goddess Artemis (Diana), and scorned the goddess of sexual desire. Phaedra fell ill with longing. Eventually her nurse found out her secret desire and approached Hippolytus, who was

Left *Theseus Leaves Ariadne* by Innes Fripp. After abandoning Ariadne on the island of Naxos, Theseus sailed on to Delos where he dedicated a statue of the goddess Aphrodite to the temple of Apollo. While on Delos, he and his companions celebrated his slaying of the Minotaur in Crete, by taking part in dancing and festivities.

Below *Phaedra and Hippolytus* by Baron Pierre-Narcisse Guerin (1774–1833). Phaedra bore Theseus two sons, Demophon and Acamas, and then fell passionately in love with Hippolytus, her stepson. It is said that she went to great lengths to be near him. She even built a great temple to Aphrodite, which over-looked the gymnasium where the young man exercised each day.

THE WATERS OF LETHE

Lethe was one of the rivers of the under-world along with Styx (across which the dead were ferried by Charon), Acheron, Cocytus, and Phlegethon, the river of fire. The waters of Lethe gave their drinker the gift of forgetfulness, and apart from those tormented for their crimes, all the dead drank from Lethe. They could regain their memories only temporarily when some hero descended to the underworld and gave them blood to drink. The philosopher Plato speculates that souls are reborn after

death, and that rather than drinking Lethe waters soon after death, they are given Lethe's gift of oblivion just before their next birth. This is why people have no memories of their past lives.

Above *The Waters of Lethe by the Plains of Elysium* by John Stanhope (1829–1908). The souls of the dead drank from the River Lethe not only to forget their former life, but also to forget the horrific images of death and the underworld.

Right *The Death of Hippolytus* by Peter Paul Rubens (1577–1640). According to some tales, Hippolytus was revived by Asclepius. However, since it was against the law to return to life, Artemis changed Hippolytus's appearance and took him with her to Italy, where he was honored as the minor deity, Virbius.

with any woman, but most especially his father's wife. Phaedra was now terrified that Hippolytus would tell Theseus about her guilty desire for him, and in desperation she hanged herself, leaving behind a wax tablet containing an accusation against Hippolytus, claiming that he had tried to rape her. Theseus believed his wife and sentenced his son to exile. Poseidon had long ago given Theseus the gift of three wishes, and now Theseus wished for his son to die. As Hippolytus drove his chariot along the coast, away from Athens, Poseidon shook the earth and sent a bull from the sea. Completely out of control, the horses galloped along the beach, and dragged Hippolytus along until he died. Some say that the constellation of the Charioteer represents Hippolytus. The goddess Artemis appeared to Theseus, revealing the truth, that Hippolytus was innocent. If gods had been allowed to weep, she would have wept for her beloved friend's death. Theseus performed no further deeds of note before his death. With his accomplishments, he had freed the world from many wicked men, but his life had been filled with troubles that were largely of his making, especially his rash and foolish dealings with women.

THE HOUSE OF TANTALUS

The Trojan War, the last great assembly of heroes in Greek myth, had many causes. There were the present grievances that brought the Greek fleet to Troy; there were causes going back a generation; and there were causes going back to humankind's earliest days, when gods and men mingled more freely. The causes of the Trojan War can be traced back as far as Tantalus, a son of the Titans from before the wars that left Zeus (Jupiter) as the new king of the gods. Tantalus was king of Paphlagonia and had three children, Pelops, Niobe, and Broteas, all of whom offended the gods. Niobe was the woman who considered herself superior to a goddess in her wealth of children, and ended up turned to stone. Broteas came to an even worse fate, and Pelops's behavior redoubled the offense that Tantalus gave to the gods.

The troubles began when Tantalus abused the trust that Zeus had shown him. He was a frequent guest at banquets on Mount Olympus, and enjoyed the sweet taste of ambrosia a little too much. He stole some of the food of the gods and took it back to share with his human friends. This was an unwise act, which Zeus might have ignored out of friendship, but when Tantalus invited the gods to a feast at his palace and cooked up the body of his son Pelops for them, he committed a crime against the laws of gods and men alike, and his monstrous act could not be ignored. No one knows for certain whether he made this monstrous feast in the hope of pleasing the immortal gods, or whether he was testing the limits of Zeus's knowledge. The strange meat appalled the gods, who instantly recognized it as human flesh and refused to eat it—all except Demeter (Ceres) who was still grieving for her lost daughter, Persephone (Prosperpina) and, as a consequence, absentmindedly ate Pelops's left shoulder.

Zeus struck Tantalus down with his thunderbolt, and punished him after his death by hanging his body in a fruit tree that dipped over a stream. Tantalus thirsted for the water, which flowed almost within his grasp, but when he bent down to drink, it would recede out of hands' reach. He hungered for the fruit, which was bountiful, but when he reached out for it, the branches always swayed out of his grasp. Tantalus was forever frustrated, and his fate is still commemorated in the English language in the word "tantalize."

Immersed in the fountain,
Tantalus tastes not
The water that wastes not!

HENRY WADSWORTH LONGFELLOW (1807–1882),
BIRDS OF PASSAGE

Above *Tantalus's Torment* by Bernard Picart (1673– 1733). Some say that Tantalus was tormented even further by having a huge stone perched over his head, ready to fall.

Below **Detail from a cup showing a banquet scene (c. 500 B.C.).** Banquets at Mount Olympus offered nectar and ambrosia. These were said to possess life-giving properties.

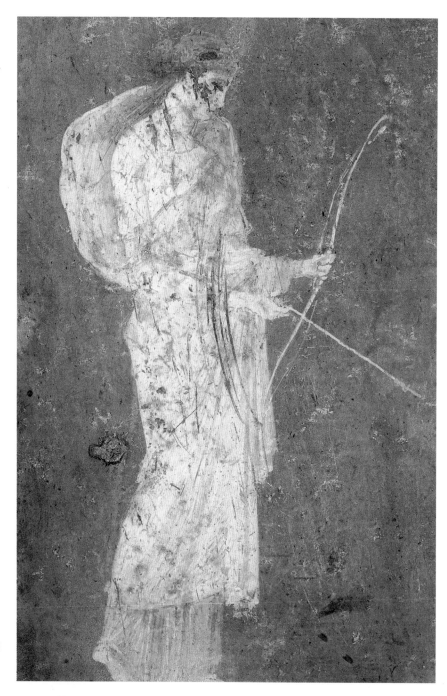

hunter, and he followed his father's example in defying the gods. He refused to honor Artemis (Diana), the goddess of the hunt, and as punishment she drove him mad. He came to believe that he was invincible against fire, and jumped onto a burning pyre to prove it. The flames consumed him, reinforcing the fearful lesson of Tantalus's death, that the gods will destroy those who offend them. Yet even with these two examples before him, and his own death and remaking to reinforce the message, Pelops did no better than either his father or his brother.

A Curse on the House of Pelops

Pelops lost his kingdom to barbarians, and looked for a new kingdom to conquer in Greece. He also looked for a wife, and chose Princess Hippodameia, the daughter of King Oenomaus of Arcadia. Oenomaus was reluctant for his daughter to marry, perhaps because he himself secretly lusted after her, and he set up a chariot race in which every suitor must compete against the king. The prize would be Hippodameia, and the cost of failure would be death. The king was prepared to give these suitors a generous start, and even allowed his daughter to ride in their chariots, but he was confident of victory, because his horses were the gift of Ares (Mars) and ran swifter than the wind.

Oenomaus had already killed at least 12 suitors, nailing their heads above his palace gates, and he was hoping to pile up enough skulls to build a temple in mockery of the immortal gods. Pelops prayed to Poseidon for help, and the god provided him with winged horses and a winged chariot that could ride over the ocean without breaking the surface of the water. Pelops should have trusted the god's gifts, but when he arrived at Oenomaus's palace and saw the rotting heads above the gates, he began to doubt. He spoke to the king's chariot driver,

Zeus ordered Hermes (Mercury) to collect all the pieces of the murdered child's body and cook them again in the cauldron. Then the king of the gods used his divine powers to restore Pelops, but his shoulder was missing. Demeter fashioned a new shoulder for him out of ivory, and he became the next king of Paphlagonia. His restored body was so beautiful that Poseidon (Neptune) fell in love with him, taking him to Olympus as his cupbearer. Tantalus's other son, Broteas, was a great sea. As he sank to his death, the wretched Myrtilus cursed Pelops and every member of his house.

Pelops conquered most of the southern part of Greece, renaming it the Peloponnese. He built a great kingdom and for the most part ruled wisely, but he also cut up the body of a rival king, Stymphalus of Arcadia, and scattered the pieces so that no one, not even a god, could reassemble them. Pelops and Hippodameia had numerous children, including Pittheus of Troezen, the twins Atreus and Thyestes, and Sciron the murderer whom Theseus slew. Pelops had another son, Chrysippus, whose mother was the nymph Astyoche. King Laius of Thebes visited Pelops and became besotted with Chrysippus, abducting him in his chariot and taking him back to Thebes by force. Hippodameia had long been jealous of Pelops's affection for Chrysippus, fearing that the illegitimate son would be named heir to the kingdom in preference to her own children. She was so intensely jealous that she pursued Chrysippus to Thebes, where she found him in Laius's bed and stabbed him to death. Chrysippus just managed to name his murderess before he died, and Hippodameia fled from Thebes and then killed herself. This was the first unfortunate consequence of Myrtilus's curse on the house of Pelops.

Left *Pelops and Hippodameia* by Burney. Myrtilus paid dearly for betraying his king. It is thought that as Oenomaus lay dying, he cursed the charioteer for his treachery and prayed that Pelops, too, would die a painful death.

Myrtilus the son of Hermes, promising him anything he wished if the man would betray his master. Myrtilus asked for half the kingdom, and the privilege of sharing Hippodameia's bed on the marriage night, and Pelops hastily agreed.

Myrtilus took out the lynch pins that held the wheels to the axles of Oenomaus's chariot, and replaced them with pins made of wax. The king gave Pelops the usual start, and then ordered Myrtilus to drive his chariot faster than the wind, while he readied his spear to kill Pelops. But as the chariot raced faster and faster, the wax melted and the wheels suddenly fell away from the chariot. The chariot crashed, and Oenomaus was killed in the wreckage. Then Pelops married Hippodameia, and as part of the marriage celebration, he drove their winged chariot over the sea, in the company of the traitor Myrtilus. Hippodameia became thirsty, and so Pelops landed his horses on an island and went in search of water. When he returned, Hippodameia was in tears, and recounted to him how the driver had tried to rape her. "That is not true," interrupted Myrtilus. "You yourself promised that I could enjoy your bride on her wedding night, and I was only taking what was mine." Pelops said nothing, and on they drove until they neared Euboea. Suddenly Pelops kicked Myrtilus out of the chariot into the

EUREKA!

Archimedes was a figure in Greek history rather than myth, a brilliant mathematician who invented machinery still in use today. One of his discoveries was the law of displacement. The king of Syracuse thought that someone might have made his new crown out of alloy, rather than pure gold,

and ordered Archimedes to find out without damaging the crown. The story goes that Archimedes got into his bathtub to think about it, and noticed water overflowing onto the floor. "Eureka! (I have found it!)" he cried, bursting out of the bathroom and running down the street naked. He realized that the volume of water displaced by his body equaled the volume of his body. Now he could work out the volume of the crown by putting it into a full basin of water, and then weigh it against a pure gold ingot of the same volume. If they matched, the crown was pure gold too. The "Eureka!" story is only doubtfully historical, but it has become one of the inspiring myths of Western science.

Above *Archimedes* by Giuseppe Nogari (1699–1763). The Greek mathematician, physicist, and inventor was thought to have lived between 287 B.C. and 212 B.C. He was credited with discovering the principles of the lever and specific gravity.

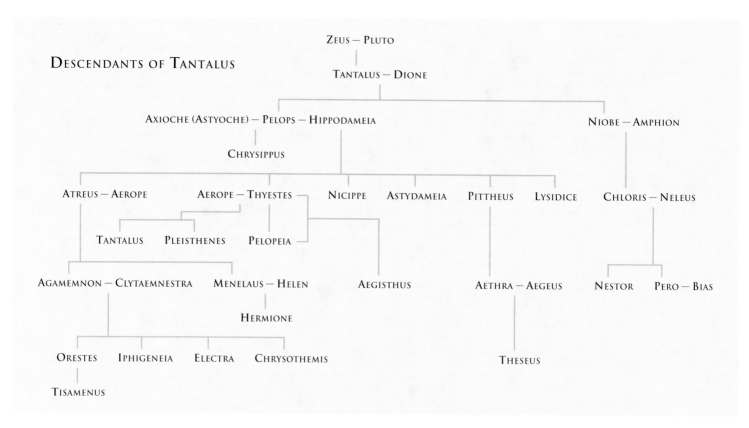

DESCENDANTS OF TANTALUS

ZEUS — PLUTO

TANTALUS — DIONE

AXIOCHE (ASTYOCHE) — PELOPS — HIPPODAMEIA   NIOBE — AMPHION

CHRYSIPPUS

ATREUS — AEROPE   AEROPE — THYESTES   NICIPPE   ASTYDAMEIA   PITTHEUS   LYSIDICE   CHLORIS — NELEUS

TANTALUS   PLEISTHENES   PELOPEIA

AGAMEMNON — CLYTAEMNESTRA   MENELAUS — HELEN   AEGISTHUS   AETHRA — AEGEUS   NESTOR   PERO — BIAS

HERMIONE

ORESTES   IPHIGENEIA   ELECTRA   CHRYSOTHEMIS   THESEUS

TISAMENUS

A Curse on the House of Atreus

Pelops gave a flock of fine sheep to his sons, Atreus
and Thyestes, anticipating that joint ownership of
the flock would teach them how to live together
peacefully, but they soon quarreled over it. The fault
lay with Hermes, who wanted to avenge the death of
his son Myrtilus and sent a lamb with a golden fleece
to join the flock. Atreus had promised to sacrifice the
best of his sheep to the goddess Artemis, but he could
not bear to give up this new treasure. He killed the
lamb but kept its golden fleece, having it stuffed to
resemble a living lamb. His brother Thyestes became
extremely envious, coveting the golden lamb. When
Atreus's wife, Aerope, made a sexual advance toward
him, Thyestes said to her, "I will do anything you
want, if only you will give me back the golden lamb.
After all, it really belongs to me, because it belonged
to my half of the flock in the first place."
Aerope opened the chest in which the
golden lamb was stored, and secretly
gave it to her new lover.

The king of Mycenae died, leaving
no heir, and the people of Mycenae sent
a herald to the oracle to ask who should
be their next king. "The one with the
golden lamb," the oracle replied, and
as soon as the herald returned, Atreus
claimed the throne. "Do you agree that
the man with the golden lamb should
be king?" Thyestes asked his brother,
and when Atreus agreed, he produced

the golden lamb and claimed the throne for himself.
Now it was Zeus's turn to interfere with the brothers'
lives. He wanted Atreus, not Thyestes, to rule over
Mycenae, and he sent Hermes down to the city to
ask Thyestes whether he would be prepared to give
up his claim to the throne if the sun started to move
backward in the sky. Thyestes thought that this was
utterly impossible, and blithely agreed. Zeus then
turned the horses of the sun back in their tracks, and
Thyestes was forced to renounce the kingship of
Mycenae, going into exile.

ATREUS'S REVENGE

Atreus now knew that his wife had been his brother's
lover, but he pretended to forgive them both, even
when Aerope gave birth to Thyestes' twin sons,
Pleisthenes and Tantalus. Aerope and Atreus had two
sons, Agamemnon and Menelaus, and a daughter, and
Atreus also had a son, Pleisthenes, by a previous
marriage. The curse against the house of Pelops came
into play once more when Atreus sent murderers to
kill Pleisthenes the son of Thyestes, and they killed
Pleisthenes the son of Atreus by mistake. Then Atreus
again offered Thyestes his forgiveness, and half the
kingdom along with it, and Thyestes was foolish
enough to believe him. He came back to Mycenae

Below **Hermes.** Hermes
was heartbroken over the
death of his son Myrtilus.
He placed him in the sky
as the constellation Auriga,
the Charioteer. At Olympia,
charioteers made sacrifices
to Myrtilus (whose ghost
haunted the stadium) so
he would not frighten the
horses or harm the drivers.

Opposite page **Detail from a tapestry showing Hector, Menelaus,
Agamemnon, and Achilles.** For the most part, Agamemnon and
Menelaus were known as the Atreidae, "the sons of Atreus."
However, some say they were sons of Atreus's son Pleisthenes.

with Aerope's baby sons, Pleisthenes and Tantalus, and three more, older children whose mother was a nymph. Atreus invited him to a feast of reconciliation, and made elaborate preparations for the banquet. He killed the three older sons of Thyestes, cutting them into small pieces, and then he added the flesh of the two babies and cooked it all up in a huge pie. The pie was served to the guest of honor, Thyestes, who ate his fill. At that point, Atreus signaled for a servant to carry in a dish piled with the children's severed hands, feet, and heads. Horrified and grief-stricken, Thyestes vomited up what he had eaten, and then laid a curse on his brother's house.

Thyestes consulted the oracle at Delphi to find out how best to take his revenge on Atreus, and was told that he must father a child by his own daughter. He felt so much hatred toward Atreus that he did not hesitate to seek out his daughter Pelopeia, a priestess of Athene, and rape her, hiding behind a mask so that she would not recognize him. He dropped his sword as he fled, and Pelopeia kept it as the only clue to his identity. She was already pregnant when Atreus came courting her, having had his first wife, Aerope, thrown

Say what meant the woes
By Tantalus entailed upon his race,
And the dark sorrows of the
line of Thebes?

WILLIAM WORDSWORTH (1770–1850),
THE EXCURSION

into the sea to her death. Pelopeia married Atreus but the child that she gave birth to, eight months after the wedding, was Thyestes' son. She named the baby Aegisthus and then tried to kill him by leaving him exposed on a mountainside, but Atreus believed that Pelopeia was suffering the aftereffects of giving birth, and sent servants to the mountain to rescue the child. Aegisthus was treated as Atreus's true son, and was proclaimed the rightful heir to Mycenae.

So far so bad, but this was not the worst. Atreus's true sons, Agamemnon and Menelaus, captured Thyestes and brought him back to Mycenae. Atreus ordered his so-called son, Aegisthus, to kill Thyestes in his dungeon, even though he was only seven years old. Thyestes easily overpowered the boy, wrenching his sword from his hand, and was about to kill him when he suddenly recognized the weapon. It was the same sword that Thyestes himself had lost when he raped his daughter. "I will spare your life if you swear to do three things that I command," he told the boy. "First, bring your father's wife here in secret." Aegisthus kept his word, and brought Pelopeia into the dungeon. She was overjoyed to see her father again—that is, until Thyestes revealed that he was the owner of Aegisthus's sword, and the man who had raped her. Pelopeia was so horrified that she thrust the sword into her heart, dying in front of her rapist-father and son-brother. Then Thyestes ordered his son Aegisthus to show Atreus the bloody sword and tell him that Thyestes was dead, as ordered. Once this was done, Thyestes finally explained to Aegisthus who he was, and told the boy to kill King Atreus for him. Aegisthus took Atreus by surprise as he sat celebrating his brother's murder. On the death of King Atreus, Thyestes once more became king of Mycenae, with Aegisthus as his heir. And still the curses on the house of Pelops and the house of Atreus had not been completely fulfilled.

Below **The Delphic Oracle.** The Delphic Oracle featured in countless myths and legends. While it had a reputation of being reliable, this was perhaps because of the ambiguous wording used by the priests. Sometimes the advice was cryptic, sometimes clear but misleading, and sometimes clear but seemingly unreasonable.

SIBILE DELPHICEN

THE START OF THE TROJAN WAR

When Thyestes murdered his brother Atreus and claimed the kingship of Mycenae, Atreus's sons Agamemnon and Menelaus fled for their lives to Sparta. King Tyndareus of Sparta eventually helped them to overthrow Thyestes, and the kingship passed to Atreus's older son, Agamemnon. Thyestes and Aegisthus were now the ones that had to flee for their lives. Agamemnon proved to be a great general and leader of men, and soon the kings of many Greek kingdoms paid him tribute.

He killed his cousin, the second Tantalus, and married his widow, Clytaemnestra, as a spoil of war. Clytaemnestra was the twin sister of Helen, soon to be called Helen of Troy. Their mother was the beautiful Leda, queen of Sparta, one of the many mortal women that Zeus (Jupiter) found desirable. While Leda was walking by the river Eurotas, Zeus transformed himself into a magnificent swan and raped her in that form. She gave birth to four children: Helen, Clytaemnestra, Castor, and Polydeuces (Pollux). Some say that Helen and the two boys were hatched from a single egg, as children of Zeus; others say that Helen and Polydeuces were children of Zeus, and Clytaemnestra and Castor were children of King Tyndareus of Sparta. Clytaemnestra, all agree, was entirely of mortal birth.

Clytaemnestra's twin brothers, Castor and Polydeuces (also known as the Dioscuri, meaning the sons of Zeus) marched to the rescue of Clytaemnestra when they learned that Agamemnon had taken her by force, but Agamemnon appealed to her father Tyndareus and gained his consent to the marriage. Then Menelaus asked Tyndareus for the hand of Leda's other daughter, Helen. When she was a child, she had already been abducted and forcibly married by Theseus, and when she was of an age to be properly married, she was so beautiful that her many suitors seemed likely to start a war over her. Tyndareus wanted to marry Helen to Menelaus and hand over the kingship of Sparta to him, but he did not know how to prevent violence from the other suitors. He asked the wise Odysseus (Ulysses), king of Ithaca, who had come to Sparta with all the other suitors, though well aware that as a poor king of a rocky island, he had few prospects. Odysseus said, "I will help you, if you will help me in turn. I wish to marry Penelope, daughter of Icarius, and

Left **Leda and the swan.** According to some writers, Leda was completely overcome with shame when she learned that her daughter Helen had eloped with Paris. She was so distressed that she eventually hanged herself.

Above **Helen and Menelaus.** It is not really known whether Helen chose Menelaus herself. Regardless of her wishes, the gods had devised their own plan for Helen and Menelaus's future.

Left **Agamemnon and Clytaemnestra.** The brothers of Clytaemnestra were alarmed to find that she and Agamemnon were together. Not only had Agamemnon killed her husband, but he had snatched Clytaemnestra's child from her breast and murdered it.

Above *The Feast of Peleus* by Sir Edward Burne-Jones (1833–1898). Eris, who attended the feast of Peleus, was the goddess of discord. She was known to stir up strife by inciting jealousy and creating hatred. She is said to have given birth to abstract divinities such as Hunger, Pain, and Oblivion.

need someone powerful to speak for me." When Tyndareus agreed to this, Odysseus advised him to make all of Helen's suitors swear an oath that they would accept her chosen husband and aid him against anyone who tried to injure their marriage. That is why so many Greek rulers came to Menelaus's aid when Helen was lost to him.

Agamemnon and Clytaemnestra had four children, a son Orestes, and three daughters, Electra, Chrysothemis, and Iphigeneia; Menelaus and Helen had four children, three sons and a daughter, Hermione. Both married couples seemed to be settling into prosperous, happy lives, but the curse against the house of Atreus had not died, and the goddess Aphrodite (Venus) was also angry with Tyndareus for neglecting to worship her. She made up her mind to punish Clytaemnestra and Helen for their father's offense. With trouble brewing, neither the royal family of Mycenae nor their kin in Sparta had any chance of a strife-free marriage.

The Apple of Discord

It was the goddess of Strife, Eris, who had started the chain of events that led to the abduction of Helen and Clytaemnestra's murder of her husband. Many years earlier and far away from Mycenae or Sparta,

Was this the face that launch'd a thousand ships, And burnt the topless towers of Ilium? Sweet Helen, make me immortal with a kiss!

CHRISTOPHER MARLOWE (1564–1593), *FAUSTUS*

Eris had attended the wedding between Peleus and the sea goddess Thetis, the same goddess whom Zeus had longed for, and whose son was destined to surpass his father. Zeus arranged the marriage of Peleus and Thetis to avert war in the heavens, but Eris slyly set in motion the trouble that would lead to the greatest war among men in Greek myth, the Trojan War. She threw down on the banquet table a golden apple that was inscribed with the words, "For the fairest," and laughed spitefully as the goddesses wrangled over it. Hera (Juno), Athene (Minerva), and Aphrodite were each convinced it belonged to her, and when none of the gods could stop the quarrel, Zeus sent them to a human judge, Prince Paris of Troy.

Paris was the son of King Priam and Queen Hecabe (Hecuba) of Troy. Before his birth, Hecabe dreamed that she gave birth to a firebrand that set fire to the whole of Troy. The seer Aesacus interpreted the dream as saying that the son in her womb would destroy the kingdom, and told her to expose the child on the mountainside, to stop the dream from coming true. The baby Paris was exposed on Mount Ida, but a she-bear suckled him and then he was adopted by shepherds. Only the chief herdsman of Troy, Agelaus, knew the truth of his parentage. Paris

Aphrodite's victory would mean the destruction of Troy.

Paris went from Mount Ida to Troy to compete in some athletic games, and he won every event that he entered. The princes of Troy, Priam's other sons, became angry and talked of killing this fellow who put them all to shame. Then Agelaus cried out, "This is your brother, Paris." Hecabe and Priam were delighted, even when an oracle warned them that they must kill him at once, or else Troy would be destroyed. When Priam had agreed, years ago, to expose his baby son on the mountainside, that decision had aged him and given him years of regret. Now, whatever message of doom the oracle spoke, he refused to kill his son a second time. "I would rather see Troy burn," he said, prophesying his city's doom as accurately as any oracle.

Preparing for War

Paris forgot about Oenone entirely and became obsessed with the idea of winning the most beautiful woman in the world—and who could this be but

Below *The Judgment of Paris* by Jacques David (1748–1825). Paris could not resist the thought of having the love of the most beautiful woman in the world. Aphrodite honored her promise by protecting him and enabling the prince to abduct the lovely Helen.

fell in love with the naiad Oenone, famous for her healing skills, and lived the carefree life of a shepherd on Ida. Perhaps Zeus chose him to act as judge because he was such a simple, carefree young man, or perhaps the king of the gods had already decided upon a war that would consume the youth of Greece and Troy for the next 10 years. It would be easy for Zeus to use the contest among the goddesses to induce Paris to abduct Helen, and so cause the Trojan War.

The three goddesses came down to Mount Ida, with Hermes (Mercury), who was the messenger of the gods, to tell Paris what Zeus wanted him to do. Paris did not know which way to turn. Whichever one of the goddesses he chose, he would make two powerful enemies. He begged them to accept his decision without taking offense, and then requested that the goddesses stand in front of him, naked. As he hesitated, Hera said, "Choose me, shepherd, and I will make you ruler of all Asia, and give you all the wealth that you desire." Athene of the flashing eyes quickly added, "Choose me, and I will give you wisdom and prudence, and you will win every battle." Aphrodite waited until last, and murmured, "Choose me, and I will give you the most beautiful woman in the world." Paris was intoxicated with this promise, and gave the apple to Aphrodite, goddess of sexual desire. Hera and Athene had promised Paris that they would not take offense, but inwardly they seethed with fury, and promised themselves that

Right **Agamemnon preparing to leave for Troy.** With the Greek fleet assembled ready to sail, it is said that Agamemnon himself caused the delay in departure. He boasted of having slain a stag with skill greater than that of the goddess Artemis (Diana).

Below *Odysseus Trying to Tempt Achilles, Disguised as a Girl, Away from the Court of Lycomedes* by Alessandro Tiarini (1577–1668). Once discovered, Achilles was eager for battle. He was a strong and swift fighter who instilled terror into the hearts of the enemy. He was made admiral of the fleet when he was only 15 years old.

Helen, the daughter of Zeus and Leda and the wife of King Menelaus of Sparta? He told his family that he was going in search of Hesione, the woman taken by Heracles a generation earlier, but he was really planning to visit Sparta and somehow entice Helen onto his ship. He sailed to Greece and visited Menelaus's palace, where he was treated with the hospitality appropriate for a prince of Troy. After a few days, Menelaus sailed away to Crete, leaving his wife to accommodate their guest. Aphrodite took all of Helen's powers of reason and self-restraint away and in their place put an overwhelming passion for Paris, so that by the time that Menelaus returned, guest and wife had succumbed to temptation and gone off together to Troy.

When Menelaus learned that his wife had gone off with Paris, willingly or under duress, he turned to his brother for help. Agamemnon first asked the king of Troy to return Helen, and when Priam refused, he

sent messengers to all the kingdoms of Greece to remind Helen's suitors of their oath. He summoned them to gather their soldiers and provide ships for an expedition to Troy to fetch Helen home. Almost everyone obeyed, but at least two people were opposed to this expedition. The young prince of Ithaca, Odysseus, wanted to stay at home like a sensible man with his wife Penelope and his newborn son Telemachus. When Agamemnon and Menelaus came to Ithaca to summon him and his men to war, Odysseus pretended to be mad, yoking a donkey and an ox to the plow and then sowing the land with salt instead of seed. The kings knew of Odysseus's reputation for craftiness, and tested just how mad he was by putting the baby Telemachus on the ground in front of the plow blade. Odysseus stopped his plowing, and admitted that he was sane enough to go to Troy with the rest.

The young Achilles, the son of Pelias and Thetis, would gladly have gone to the war, but his mother wanted to keep him safely at home, and dressed him in girl's clothes to fool the messenger, Odysseus. He was aware of her trick, and played a trick of his own in return, piling up in the palace such presents as girls tend to like, fine garments and jewels, and among them a spear and a shield. He had already ordered his men to clash their spears on their shields and sound the war trumpet outside the palace; as soon as Achilles heard the noise, he grasped the spear and shield and ran outside. Thetis wept bitterly, because an oracle had told her that Achilles would enjoy a long life only if he stayed at home. She knew

full well that his career at Troy would be violent, glorious, and short.

The Greek fleet assembled at Aulis. Then the curse on the house of Atreus manifested again, with unfavorable winds that trapped the fleet in the harbor. The men began to talk of abandoning the war, for the gods were clearly against them. The seer Calchas told the king that the only way to placate the gods was for him to sacrifice his daughter Iphigeneia to the goddess Artemis (Diana). Agamemnon sent for Clytaemnestra and Iphigeneia, saying that he wanted to marry his daughter to the young hero Achilles. He offended Achilles with this fabrication, and did worse than this when he carried out the sacrifice of his own daughter, slitting her throat. Some say that as his knife started to bite, Artemis replaced the girl with a young deer, but in most versions of the myth, Agamemnon actually killed his daughter. His wife Clytaemnestra returned to Mycenae, planning to take vengeance when he came home from Troy. The winds blew fair, the fleet set sail, and the war was about to begin.

Left **The sacrifice of Iphigeneia.** Accounts disagree as to what actually happened to Iphigeneia. One version recounts that, having been rescued by Artemis at the last moment, she was then transported to Tauris. Iphigeneia's duty as a priestess in the temple was to prepare all strangers who inadvertently came to Tauris so they could be human sacrifices for Artemis.

GREEK BURIAL RITES

It was very important in classical Greek belief for correct funeral rites to be held for the dead. This meant either cremation or burial, with a coin placed in the dead person's mouth to pay the ferryman Charon to ferry the dead soul over the River Styx to the underworld. Those left unburied, or without a coin, were forever stranded on this side of the River Styx and came back to haunt the living. Similarly, those who died by drowning, and whose bodies were never recovered, stayed on this side of the Styx as uneasy ghosts. The fate of those who were given a proper funeral was not much more cheerful, as they became gray, twittering shades in the realm of Hades, but at least they were where they properly belonged.

Above *Charon's Boat* by James Gillray (1757–1815). Charon, the immortal son of Erebus (Darkness) and Nyx (Night), was usually portrayed as a squalid, bad-tempered old man.

Above **Fighting in the Trojan War.** It did not take the Greeks long to work out that the wealthy and strong-walled city of Troy would never fall as long as it could count on aid and supplies from nearby cities. As a result, the Greeks set about destroying the surrounding allies one by one.

THE TROJAN WAR

The war lasted 10 years, as all the seers had predicted. The Greek ships were hauled ashore, close enough to Troy for the Greek troops to drive their chariots for a day's fighting in front of the walls of the city, and for the Trojan troops to drive their chariots over to threaten the ships with fire. Many of the warriors fought heroically, many men died of wounds and many of disease, but for over nine years the Greeks could not storm the gates of Troy and the Trojans could not drive them away. The gods of Olympus took an interest in the war, for some of the warriors were their children or grandchildren. Ares (Mars) and Apollo took the side of the Trojans, along with Aphrodite (Venus), who did not prove to be much of a fighter in battle, while Athene (Minerva) favored the Greeks, especially the crafty Odysseus (Ulysses). Hera (Juno) and Poseidon (Neptune) also favored the Greeks over the Trojans, and Zeus (Jupiter) kept the war going evenly for the 10 years that it was destined to endure.

The day shall come,
that great avenging day
Which Troy's proud glories
in the dust shall lay

ALEXANDER POPE (1688–1744),
THE ILIAD OF HOMER

In the tenth year, the soothsayer Calchas, who had been a Trojan and had left the city of Troy when he foresaw its fall, wanted his daughter Briseis to join him in the army of the Greeks. He asked King Agamemnon to send envoys to King Priam of Troy, to ask for Briseis to be sent to her father. With Priam's consent, Briseis came to the Greeks, and soon she shared the bed of Achilles. Then Chryses, a priest of Apollo, came to ask for his daughter back from Agamemnon, who had captured her and kept her as a concubine. When the king refused his request, Apollo sent disease upon the Greeks until she was finally surrendered. Then Agamemnon demanded Briseis from Achilles as her replacement in his bed. Achilles was obliged to obey his leader, but he nursed his resentment and refused to keep fighting.

With their best warrior unwilling to fight, the Greeks proposed a general truce for the two armies while Helen's lover, Paris, and her injured husband, Menelaus, fought for her in single combat. Paris was an expert archer but not so skilled at fighting hand-to-hand, and Menelaus was winning the fight when Aphrodite wrapped Paris in a mist, so that Menelaus could not see him to strike at him. The goddess whisked him back to the city, to the arms of Helen. Then the champion of the Trojans, Prince Hector, challenged Achilles to single combat, but Achilles still refused to fight. The Greeks chose Aias (Ajax) as their next best champion and he fought Hector for hours, without either gaining the advantage. They left off their fight when it was too dark to see one another. The Trojans agreed to observe a truce while the Greeks went onto the battlefield to bury their dead, but as soon as this was over, the Trojans came forward to attack again and drove the Greeks almost to their ships. Another day's fighting like this, and the Trojans would win the war.

The Greeks were on the verge of mass panic. Achilles was now threatening to take his soldiers and sail home with them. Then the resourceful King Odysseus came up with a crafty plan. He and his friend Diomedes crept out from the Greek tents and raided the tents where the allies of the Trojans were

Right **Briseis being taken away.** After Agamemnon ordered Briseis to be taken away from him, Achilles and his troops could not be persuaded to fight again. Only after the death of Achilles' friend Patroclus did the hero take up arms again, and Agamemnon restored Briseis to him once more.

sleeping. They killed one of Troy's allies, King Rhesus, and stole his horses. An oracle had prophesied that Troy would never fall if these horses ate Trojan food and drank from the River Scamander that flows close by the city of Troy. They had still not done so, and when the Trojans found them gone, they lost heart and retreated from all the territory that they had gained the day before.

To and fro the battle surged the next day, with Hera favoring the Greeks, then Zeus helping the Trojans until they reached the Greek ships and began to set them on fire. Then Achilles relented. He still would not fight, but he sent his friend and lover Patroclus out to battle in his place. Patroclus wore Achilles' armor and drove Achilles' chariot onto the battleground. The Trojans retreated, fooled into thinking that Achilles had returned. The ships were saved, and Patroclus led a charge against

the walls of Troy. Apollo intervened, striking Patroclus and bewildering his brains, and then Hector of Troy had no trouble in killing him. Achilles forgot his hurt pride and resentment in grief for his beloved friend, and solemnly promised that he would avenge Patroclus on Hector's dead body.

Above *Achilles Contemplating the Body of Patroclus* by **Giulio Romano (1492–1546)**. Achilles refused to bury the body of Patroclus, or even to eat until he had exacted his revenge.

THE ORIGIN OF DEW

Memnon, son of the dawn goddess Eos (Aurora) and Tithonus, was killed by Achilles at Troy. Eos sent Memnon's brothers, the four winds, to carry his body away. In her grief, she wept all night for her dead son, and her tears can still be seen every new morning in the form of dewdrops. There is an enormous statue in Egypt that the ancient Greeks (but not the Egyptians) called the statue of Memnon. The Greeks claimed that every morning the enormous statue uttered a musical sound as Memnon greeted his immortal mother, the dawn. The statue still stands, but it no longer sings at dawn.

Left **Eos carrying the body of Memnon.** Drops of blood are said to have fallen from Memnon's body, becoming a river known as the Paphlagonia, whose waters flowed each year on the anniversary of Memnon's death.

Above *Thetis Giving Achilles His Arms* by Giulio Romano (1492–1546). Hephaestus fashioned a new set of arms for Achilles as a favor for his mother, Thetis. When Hephaestus was just a child, he was thrown out of heaven by Hera, and it was Thetis and her sister nereids who found and cared for him.

Right **Battle between Achilles and Hector.** Hector was a noble character in Greek literature—honorable, compassionate, and courageous. Although he did not approve of the war and he knew he was destined to die if he joined it, he still fought valiantly.

The Death of Hector

Achilles was now impatient to get back to the battle-field, but his armor had been taken by Hector from Patroclus's body. Achilles' mother, Thetis, brought him a new set of arms forged by Hephaestus (Vulcan). Wearing his new arms and carrying his splendid new shield, Achilles drove the Trojans to the River Scamander, and beyond it to the walls of Troy. All the Trojans were afraid to face Achilles in his wrath—all, that is, except Hector. He adequately prepared himself to fight Achilles in single combat, as he had long wished to do. Hector's father, King Priam, and his mother, Queen Hecabe (Hecuba) wept with fear that their beloved son might die. Hector's wife Andromache wept too, holding out his small son Astyanax to say goodbye to his father. As a last goodbye, Priam, Hecabe, Andromache, and the

baby boy watched from the top of the wall as Hector marched on through the great gate of Troy.

Hector—wearing Achilles' own armor that he had taken from Patroclus—at first stood his ground, until Achilles came close, and then he shuddered with fear and ran away. He ran three times around the city, trying to retreat through one of its gates, but Achilles was too close on his heels. In the end Hector turned to face his enemy and Achilles stabbed him through the neck. Hector begged that the Trojans might ransom his body so that it could receive a proper burial, but Achilles refused. He pierced Hector's ankles behind the anklebone and threaded leather thongs through each foot, then tied these straps to his chariot and drove three times around Troy before dragging the body back to his tent. All Troy feared that the death of Hector meant the city's imminent fall.

Achilles inflicted further violence on Hector's body, dragging it three times around Patroclus's tomb every day. The gods abhorred this outrageous behavior and took pity on Hector, whose shade could not find its way to the underworld without a proper burial. Apollo kept the body from decay and Zeus sent his messenger, Hermes (Mercury) to help King Priam visit Achilles' tent secretly by night and ransom his beloved son. Achilles agreed to exchange the body for its weight in gold, and the Trojans piled up all the gold that they could find on one side of a huge pair of scales, while the body rested on the other scale. Princess Polyxena, one of the daughters of Priam and Hecabe, came forward with her golden bracelets to add to the pile, and Achilles fell in love with her on sight; but he did not love her enough to abandon the war for her sake.

Even though Hector was dead, there were still many warriors in Troy, and new allies came to help the Trojans. Among these was Penthesileia, the Amazon. She was the warrior who killed Theseus's wife, Antiope, so that she could not have been young at the time of the Trojan war, a generation later. She arrived during the funeral of Hector and went

out to battle after the 11 days of mourning. Achilles killed her during that battle, a deed that he regretted when he saw, too late, that his enemy was, in fact, a beautiful woman. Shortly after came another ally from far away, Memnon of Ethiopia. Zeus weighed the fates of Achilles and Memnon in his scales, and the fate of Memnon proved the heavier. Soon he lay dead, pierced by Achilles' spear.

The Death of Achilles

Achilles seemed to be invincible in his wrath at the killing of his friend Patroclus. Now he drove the Trojans into the city and followed them through the Scaian gate. It seemed as though the Trojan war would be over by the end of the day, with the Greeks ready to pour through the gate after him. But Achilles was struck on the heel with an arrow that Prince Paris shot at him, helped by Apollo. It seemed not much of a wound, but it proved deadly, for his heel was the only vulnerable part of his body. His mother, Thetis, knew from an oracle that her son would surpass his father, and she wanted to protect Achilles, as a baby, from the dangers in battle that she guessed he would face as a man. She dipped the baby in the River Styx, holding him by the heel, and the waters rendered his whole body invulnerable, all but the heel (this story is the origin of the name "Achilles tendon" given to a tendon at the back of the ankle, which athletes are prone to injure).

It was this one weak spot that Paris struck, and then the rest of Achilles' body lost its god-given

Left **Detail from a shield showing Achilles and Penthesileia fighting.** The Amazon queen was no match for Achilles. It is said that the god Ares was so enraged by the death of his daughter that he was about to kill Achilles when Zeus intervened.

Below *Thetis Immerses Son Achilles in Water of River Styx* by Antoine Borel (1743–1810). It is said that Thetis had tried to save Achilles from his fate by placing him in flames when he was a baby (to burn away his mortality) and then rubbing him with ambrosia. She was unable to perform the entire rite and so it was unsuccessful.

Above *The Death of Achilles* by Peter Paul Rubens (1577–1640). It is said that the mournful wailing of Achilles' mother Thetis, the nereids, and the Muses was so frightful that the Greeks fled to their ships in terror.

protection. Paris shot a second arrow and Achilles fell dead, struck to the heart. It was now the Greeks' turn to retreat, carrying Achilles' corpse back to his tent. The goddess Thetis came to the tent to mourn for her son, along with the nine Muses and the nereids, sea-nymph daughters of Nereus. Achilles went down to the underworld where Odysseus met him years later, while journeying home from Troy.

There the great Achilles told Odysseus that he would rather be the least of living men, a poor slave, than the greatest of the shades of the dead, a king in the underworld. He was the greatest of Greek warriors of his generation, yet his final judgment on himself was that he had wasted his life on war and its glories.

Achilles' death led to another death among the Greeks, as Odysseus and Aias (Ajax) competed for the armor that Hephaestus had given Achilles. Odysseus was judged the braver warrior and was awarded the armor. Aias planned murderous revenge on all the Greeks. That night, Athene maddened Aias, so that he mistook cattle and sheep for Greek warriors, tying them up, taunting them, and then killing them. In the morning he realized how ludicrous his behavior had been, and in shame and misery, he killed himself.

Bereft of Achilles, the Greeks now looked for help to prophecies, to discover if there might be some condition set by the gods that they must fulfill in order to conquer Troy. They found three prophecies: they must fetch Achilles' son Neoptolemus to the war, Philoctetes must use his bow in the fighting, and the Palladium must be stolen from Troy. To fulfill these prophecies, the Greeks turned to the crafty Odysseus, who had a well-deserved fame for eloquence and was much favored by Athene.

It was easy enough for Odysseus to sail to Scyros and fetch Neoptolemus, but Philoctetes was much more difficult to persuade. When Heracles lay dying on his funeral pyre, it was to Philoctetes that he gave his bow. Philoctetes set sail for Troy with the other Greek heroes, but he was wounded long before they came to Troy with a snake bite that did not heal. It discharged pus and gave off such an intolerable stench that the other warriors abandoned him on the island of Lemnos. Now Odysseus had to try to win him over to the Greek cause again. Odysseus tried all his tools of flattery and cajolery, but Philoctetes was not moved. It was not until Heracles appeared and told him to go to Troy that he agreed to leave Lemnos. The doctors among the Greek army healed his wound, and he bent Heracles' bow against Paris and shot him dead.

The Fall of Troy

Odysseus then turned his mind to stealing the Palladium. This was a statue of Pallas, Athene's friend whom she had killed as a child, and it was said to have fallen from heaven. Athene favored the Greeks in the Trojan War, but the presence of the Palladium in Troy, with all its implied personal meaning, held her back from destroying the city. It would not be easy to steal the statue; not only did Odysseus have to enter a city at war, but he also had to take the genuine Palladium. The Trojans had made many replicas of the statue, knowing that it was crucial to the survival of their kingdom.

Odysseus disguised himself as a beggar and found his way to Helen's bedroom in Priam's palace. Now that Paris was dead, Priam had married her to another of his sons, Deiphobus, but she was longing to leave Troy. Helen was the only person whom Odysseus could not deceive, and she saw through his beggar's disguise. She was eager to help him, explaining where the statues were kept and how to tell the real one from all the copies—it would be the smallest one. Odysseus crept out of Troy and back in again, with Diomedes. They entered the palace through its drain, and brought the Palladium out the same way. Troy had lost its protection.

Left *Diomedes stealing the Palladium* by the Diomed Painter (fifth century B.C.). The Palladium was said to have protective powers. Some say "palladia" was the name given to objects that were not made by human hands, but fell from heaven instead.

Below **Detail from an oil flask showing the dispute over the arms of Achilles (fifth century B.C.).** When Aias (Ajax) killed himself in shame, he used a sword that Hector had presented to him in admiration of his skill after their combat.

179

THE WOODEN HORSE

Now Athene helped Odysseus devise a brilliant stratagem—the building of the wooden horse. This was a huge creature, hollow on the inside and able to conceal 30 warriors. It towered higher than the great Scaian gate of Troy, so that the Trojans would have to destroy part of the gate if they decided to take the horse into the city. The Greeks carved an inscription on the side of the horse, saying that it was their gift to Athene in recompense for the theft of the Palladium. Then they made ostentatious preparations to leave the coast of Troy, setting fire to their tents. When the Greeks had gone, the Trojans came out cautiously at first, then running and shouting for joy because their enemies had abandoned the war and no more men need die. Only two people in the whole of Troy thought otherwise. Cassandra, the daughter of Priam and Hecabe, had

been given prophetic powers by the sun god Apollo when he was wooing her, and when she refused him, he cursed her, saying "You will always foretell truly, but no one will ever believe you." Now Cassandra ran to and fro urging the Trojans not to trust the Greeks, especially when they were offering gifts. No one bothered to listen.

Laocoon, who was the priest of both Apollo and Poseidon, urged the same caution as Cassandra. Sensing that the horse contained many armed men, Laocoon tried to probe it with his spear. Two huge snakes suddenly appeared and came out of the sea, coiling their heavy weight around Laocoon and his two sons, pulling them into deep water and then drowning them, before slithering toward a statue of Athene in the Trojan citadel. The Trojans should have been appalled at these omens, and alerted to the ensuing danger. Athene no

Right Men pulling the Trojan Horse by a rope. The wooden horse was too large to fit through the city gates, so the Trojans broke them down. Building the horse so large was a deliberate act by the Greeks to lend more support to their story that the horse was to stay outside the walls as a sacrifice to Athene.

plan. She called out in different voices to the warriors inside the horse, sounding like each of their wives in turn. She fooled everyone except Odysseus, who recognized Helen's strategy, and Neoptolemus, who did not yet have a wife. Odysseus held the trapdoor shut, whispering to his friends that their wives could not all suddenly be in Troy, and they felt ashamed of themselves for succumbing to Helen's trick. She kept calling out seductively, but no one was now tempted to jump down into her arms. Why she did this, no one can be sure. Was it a last attempt by Aphrodite to save the Trojans, whose cause she favored? Or was Helen a woman of moods, fickle as the wind, first betraying her husband, then her new home, then trying to betray the Greeks again?

THE END OF THE HOUSE OF TROY

Helen left and very soon the Trojans were all asleep. Odysseus opened the trapdoor and the Greek warriors leaped out of the wooden horse into the city, ready to slaughter their defenseless Trojan enemies. They proceeded to set fire to houses and herd women together to take home as slaves. The fires sent a signal to the Greek ships, which hurried back to shore. Agamemnon and the rest of the army ran to the Scaian gate and joined in the killing. Achilles' son Neoptolemus turned his sword against old King Priam who had taken refuge at the altar of Zeus. He also killed Hector's baby son Astyanax, to make sure that the boy would not grow up to kill him in turn. Andromache was taken captive, as she

Left *The Construction of the Wooden Horse of Troy* by Giulio Romano (1492–1546). According to the poet Tryphidorus (fifth century A.D.), the wooden horse was white, with a purple-colored mane and a gold fringe. Its eyes were green beryl and purple amethyst, and it even had ivory teeth. The harness was inlaid with bronze and ivory, and was also purple.

longer favored them at all, and neither Apollo nor Poseidon protected their priest. Some god drove the Trojans to their doom, so that they paid no attention to these warnings. They pulled the wooden horse into the city, breaking down the great gate to let it in, and then they feasted late into the night.

Inside the horse, Odysseus waited with the best of the Greek warriors. While the Trojans were still feasting, Helen approached the horse with her new husband Deiphobus, and she nearly ruined Odysseus's

had foreseen on that fateful day when she watched her husband die outside the walls of Troy. Old Hecabe did her best to strike back against the Greeks until she died. Then her shade

ORIGIN OF THE TROJAN HORSE

The Greeks and Trojans did not ride warhorses into battle; prolonged hand-to-hand combat from horseback depended on the invention of the stirrup, which would be introduced into Greece centuries after the classical period. The poor fought on foot, while the rich and powerful had horse-drawn chariots. Each chariot would house a warrior and a driver, and on the battle-field the warrior would either fight from the chariot or jump down to fight hand-to-hand. The Trojan Horse was not, then, a gigantic

representation of a warhorse such as the knights of King Arthur might have used. It probably derives from siege engines such as the ancient Greeks used, movable towers full of armed men.

Right **Detail from an amphora showing the Trojan Horse (seventh century B.C.).** As the Trojan Horse was described as towering over the city walls, some people believe that the story could be a representation of the use of scaling ladders.

Right *Menelaus Spares Helen* by H. J. Ford. When Menelaus charged forth to confront his wife, it is said that he had every intention of killing her. First he killed her husband, Deiphobus, but once his eyes rested on Helen, he forgot his anger and embraced her.

Below *The Sacrifice of Polyxena* by Giovanni Pittoni (1687–1767). The sacrifice of Polyxena on Achilles' grave was no coincidence. The ghost of Achilles appeared to his son Neoptolemus and demanded that she be slain on his tomb so that they might be united after death.

became a dog-spirit, a follower of Hecate. Polyxena, whom Achilles had loved, was sacrificed on his tomb. Cassandra was taken by Agamemnon as spoils of war. The royal house of Troy was destroyed.

Menelaus ran to find Helen. Some say that she melted away in front of his eyes, for this was only a phantom Helen, and that he regained his true and loyal Helen in Egypt, where she had taken refuge for the 10 years of the Trojan war. Others say that the true Helen had lived in Troy, married first to Paris, then to Deiphobus, and now she expected Menelaus to kill her. She said nothing in her defense. The only thing that she did was to uncover her breasts. Menelaus remembered his passionate love for his beautiful wife, and it was as though the war had never happened. Aphrodite smiled to see the husband and wife in each other's arms. For this couple, there were no more trials to come. However, for the rest of the Greeks, with the exception of the wise and prudent Nestor, returning to Greece proved difficult and sometimes deadly.

Left *Sacrifice of Iphigeneia* by Giambattista Tiepolo (1696–1770). Clytaemnestra had to endure the death of two of her children by the hand of her second husband, Agamemnon. The first daughter—the child of her first husband Tantalus—was murdered when Agamemnon took Clytaemnestra as his wife, and now Clytaemnestra had been tricked into sending Iphigeneia to her death.

THE HOUSE OF AGAMEMNON

One of the spoils of war for Agamemnon as leader of the Greeks was his pick of the women of Troy. He chose Cassandra, the daughter of Priam and Hecabe (Hecuba), even though she kept prophesying doom to him and all his house. He took this as the ravings of a woman demented by the deaths of all her family, and paid it little attention. At home in Mycenae, his wife, Clytaemnestra, was waiting with their children, Orestes, Electra, and Chrysothemis. Another daughter, Iphigeneia, had been sacrificed by Agamemnon to gain a fair wind for his fleet to reach Troy. During the 10 years of the Trojan War, Clytaemnestra had taken her husband's half-brother Aegisthus as her lover. Both of them brooded over past injuries, Clytaemnestra over her innocent daughter's death, Aegisthus over wrongs going back to the time of Tantalus.

There was a prophecy that Agamemnon could be killed neither on land nor in water, neither naked nor clothed, neither inside nor outside the house, a prophecy which seemed to promise him immunity from violent death. Clytaemnestra and Aegisthus had 10 years to work out just how the prophecy could be fulfilled. When Agamemnon returned, the queen had a purple carpet ready for him to walk upon, when he dismounted from his chariot. This act would displease the gods, as the privilege of purple cloth belonged only to them. Agamemnon arrived, with Cassandra beside him in his chariot, and demurred only for a moment when he saw the carpet. Then Clytaemnestra ushered him to the bathhouse to take a bath before his welcome feast. Cassandra was left in the courtyard, prophesying her own death and his, but her listeners had nothing to offer her except pity.

From inside the bathhouse came shouting, then silence. Agamemnon had been killed in accordance with the prophecy. The bathhouse was built onto the side of the palace, so that it was neither inside nor outside. Clytaemnestra waited until Agamemnon had one foot in the bath water and the other on the ground, then she threw a net over him. After he was captured in the net, Aegisthus ran in with an ax and they both hacked at him until he died. Clytaemnestra announced that she and Aegisthus were now joint rulers of Mycenae, and no one ventured to say otherwise. The unfortunate Cassandra was led away to her death, since Clytaemnestra blamed her for

Below **The death of Agamemnon.** Clytaemnestra, whether considered strong and fearless or a monster, felt she was completely justified in killing her husband. In fact, she claimed the day as a monthly festival.

HERO AND LEANDER

goddess of desire, yet her parents wanted her to stay chaste. She lived in a tower on the sea coast, and every night she lit a lamp in a high window to guide Leander to her tower. He swam the Hellespont to spend the night with his beloved Hero, enjoying the rituals of Aphrodite's worship, then swam back again before daybreak. They kept their passion secret, knowing that Hero's parents would disapprove. One stormy winter night, the wind blew out Hero's lamp. Leander lost his way and drowned. The next morning his body was washed up beside Hero's tower, and she threw herself down to die beside her lover.

Hero was a beautiful young woman who lived in Sestus, and Leander was a handsome young man who lived in Abydus. These cities faced one another across the straits of the Hellespont (now called the Dardanelles). Hero was a priestess of Aphrodite (Venus),

Above **The head of Hero.** As with many tragic love stories, Hero could not face the world without her lover, Leander. Their story was told by Musaeus, who was said to have been either one of the sons or one of the teachers of Orpheus.

becoming Agamemnon's partner in bed, without any regard for the fact that she had been taken by force.

Vengeance Comes to Clytaemnestra and Aegisthus

Orestes grew up a long way from Mycenae, with King Strophius of Crisa. His older sister, Electra, made sure that he left the city immediately after Agamemnon's murder, so that he would be safe from Clytaemnestra and Aegisthus, who were bound to fear that he might avenge his father's death upon them. At Crisa, Orestes found a faithful friend in the king's son, Pylades. Electra stayed at the court in Mycenae, hating her mother and her mother's consort, Aegisthus. Chrysothemis also stayed at court. She had been too young at the time of Agamemnon's murder to remember anything about it, and like Oedipus's daughter Ismene, she was a peacemaker, always trying to reconcile her angry sister Electra to their mother.

Clytaemnestra and Aegisthus expected Orestes to come back for his revenge when he was old enough. Aegisthus was a fearful man, and he even feared that Electra might marry someone who would try to avenge Agamemnon's death. He and Clytaemnestra therefore forced her to marry a peasant who could never raise an army against Mycenae. It would have been simpler to kill the daughter as they had already killed the father, but they kept her alive, not wishing to offend the gods any more than they had already

Death is not the worst evil, but rather when we wish to die and cannot.

SOPHOCLES (C.496 B.C.–406 B.C.), *ELECTRA*

done. Electra kept denouncing her mother and Aegisthus, and secretly corresponded with Orestes in Crisa. The desperate longing that he would return was all that kept her alive.

ORESTES' DILEMMA

When Orestes was old enough to take his revenge, he went to the oracle at Delphi to ask if he should perpetuate the troubles of his family by killing his mother and Aegisthus. He was in mental anguish, facing a terrible prospect as either the man who refused to avenge his father's murder or the man who murdered his own mother. The oracle told him that unless he took revenge, he would be afflicted with leprosy and barred from all the temples of the gods. He was instructed not to raise an army but to take revenge by guile. He should cut off a lock of his hair and place it on Agamemnon's tomb as soon as he arrived in Mycenae. The oracle warned him, however, that the Erinyes, the Furies who torment the minds of criminals, would set upon him if he murdered his mother. Apollo gave Orestes a bow, to drive the Erinyes away temporarily at least, and promised his protection if Orestes returned to Delphi after heeding his advice. In the end, he decided to follow the advice of the Pythian oracle and kill Clytaemnestra.

Pylades accompanied Orestes to the tomb of Agamemnon, and joined him in prayer to Hermes (Mercury), the god of cunning lies. Then Orestes cut off a lock of his hair and put it on the tomb. In a little while, some slaves came to the tomb to pour libations to the ghost of Agamemnon. Clytaemnestra had sent them after suffering a nightmare in which she gave birth to a snake that she put to her breast. As she was suckling it, the snake bit her nipple and drew blood. The soothsayers interpreted this dream not with its true meaning, that her son Orestes had come back with the intention of killing her, but as an omen that the ghost of Agamemnon needed placating. Clytaemnestra sent the slave women to ask Agamemnon's shade to pardon her, but Electra went with them, and her prayers were for vengeance, not forgiveness.

Electra saw the lock of hair on the tomb and recognized it as Orestes' offering to his father, but she was afraid to hope. Soon he came out of hiding and put his arms around his beloved sister, proving that he was really her brother by showing her the garment in which he had been wrapped when he escaped from Mycenae as a child. Electra and Orestes prayed to Zeus (Jupiter) that their revenge might not end with their own deaths, and then Electra went back to the palace, trying to act as if nothing unusual had occurred. Orestes stayed behind for a short while and then walked over to the palace in order to seek an audience with the queen.

Clytaemnestra came out to talk to the stranger. Orestes made up an elaborate lie, saying that he had heard from someone else of the death of Orestes. Clytaemnestra was delighted to hear this news and invited Orestes inside, sending for Aegisthus so that he could rejoice with her. As Aegisthus entered the palace, so too did Pylades, holding an urn that, he said, held the ashes of the dead Orestes. Aegisthus came closer to look at this evidence of his enemy's death, and Orestes slit his throat from behind. Then Clytaemnestra at last recognized her son, and begged for mercy as his mother. She opened her robe and showed him her breast, but he would neither look nor listen. He lifted up an ax and cut off her head.

Vengeance Comes to Orestes

On the same day that he killed his mother, Orestes was tracked down by the Erinyes—Alecto, Megaera, and Tisiphone. These three females with the heads of dogs and serpents for hair, with bat wings and blood-red eyes, were immortal inhabitants of the underworld, existing long before the Olympian gods. They avenged wrongs done by child to parent or host to guest, bad treatment of suppliants or murder, with ceaseless mental torments. Their victims soon died under this savage and constant punishment. These incarnations of a guilty conscience were much dreaded, and when people spoke of them, they were named not the Erinyes (Furies), but the Eumenides (the kindly ones). Changing their names, however, did nothing to change their nature.

Orestes fell sick, under constant attack from the Erinyes whom he alone could see and hear. He lay on his bed, slowly starving himself to death. Then Clytaemnestra's father, Tyndareus, arrived from Sparta, to charge Orestes before the nobles of Mycenae with the crime of killing his mother. Menelaus and Helen arrived for a remarkably ill-timed visit, and they were not welcomed either by Electra or by Tyndareus. "Why," Tyndareus asked, "did Orestes not simply banish his mother? Since he killed her, he must be punished as befits a matricide, by stoning to death. Electra deserves that death too, because she urged her brother on."

The trial finished with the judges' decision that Orestes and Electra should not be stoned to death, but should be allowed the dignity of killing themselves. Pylades now took action. He had fallen in love with Electra and hoped to marry her, and could not bear to lose both her and his beloved friend, Orestes. He planned to kill himself along with them, but first he decided to kill Helen, as the origin of all the troubles that had befallen the house of Agamemnon from the killing of Iphigeneia onward. Orestes and Pylades attacked Helen and could easily have killed her, but Zeus raised his daughter to Olympus, finally freeing her from all the perplexities and assaults of mortal life.

Above **A mask of Agamemnon.** According to the great poet Homer (c. 750 B.C.), Agamemnon was known not only for his dignity and majesty, but for his eyes and head that closely resembled those of the god Zeus.

Left **Orestes and Electra.** Orestes was deeply troubled by the knowledge that, as a good son, he should avenge the death of his father. There was no such doubt, however, from Electra, who was convinced it was his filial duty.

185

Left **Orestes and Pylades in Tauris.** Apollo, who had advised Orestes to kill his mother in the first place, now offered him peace of mind. The god told the young man that he would regain his sanity if he traveled to Tauris to retrieve the wooden statue of Artemis and bring it back to Attica.

While Orestes and Pylades were assaulting Helen, Electra was abducting Helen's daughter Hermione as hostage. Menelaus stormed into the room, and death was imminent for Orestes at the hands of Menelaus and for Hermione at the hands of Electra. Suddenly Apollo appeared, halting the violence. He told Menelaus that Helen had gone to Olympus and that he should now return to Sparta and marry again. He told the king to wed Hermione to Orestes, while not promising that Orestes would ever recover his peace of mind. When Apollo spoke, humans obeyed. The people of Mycenae buried their dead, and Orestes married Hermione. Still the Erinyes tormented his mind. Apollo's intervention had prevented slaughter, but it did not to cure the voices that berated Orestes.

THE SECOND TRIAL

Orestes wandered across Greece, tormented by the Erinyes, moving in and out of sanity. He finally came to Athens, pursued by Tyndareus, who still wanted him to die as a punishment for killing Clytaemnestra. Athene (Minerva) called together the Athenian judges, and a second trial began, with Apollo defending Orestes and the Erinyes prosecuting him. Nobody disputed the facts of what happened, and the trial arguments centered on whether it was more important to honor one's father or one's mother, or whether, in this case, Orestes had been correct in killing his mother to avenge his father. The judges were deadlocked, equal numbers voting both ways. Athene used her casting vote in favor of Orestes.

The Erinyes were furious with the outcome of Orestes' trial, and threatened to blight Athens. Athene offered them a shrine, on condition that they dealt kindly with her people, and the Erinyes consented to be worshipped at the side of the citadel of Athens, the Areopagus. Orestes was now legally free from blood-guilt, and one version of his story ends here, with Pylades marrying Electra. In another version, the Erinyes still tormented him. He finally found peace of mind when he followed Apollo's instructions and sailed to Tauris, where his sister Iphigeneia was still alive. In this version of her story, she had been miraculously rescued from Agamemnon's knife by Artemis (Diana), and lived on through the Trojan War, Agamemnon's return, and Orestes' revenge, far away on the island of Tauris. She helped Orestes and Pylades escape from Tauris, with the help of Poseidon, and eventually married Pylades. With this happy ending, Orestes' sanity was forever restored, and he lived long with his wife Hermione, ruling both Mycenae and Sparta. For other accursed families in Greek myth, the curse ended only with the death of the whole family. For the house of Tantalus, after generations of bloodshed, Athene and Apollo found a way to appease the pangs of conscience, to honor the law, and to counter the curse. Orestes' trial marks a crucial change in ideas of civilization from the rule of vengeance to the rule of law.

Above **Iphigeneia.** According to some stories, Iphigeneia, having been reunited with her brother and sister, ended her days serving as a priestess in a temple in Brauron, where the wooden statue of Artemis that Orestes retrieved from the island of Tauris was then kept.

Opposite page **Orestes and Iphigeneia.** Some say Iphigeneia, Orestes, and Pylades escaped from the island in Orestes' ship.

ODYSSEUS AND OTHER TRICKSTERS

Like most other myth systems, Greek myth abounded in trickster figures. Inuit, Norse, Native American, and African myth, for example, were equally full of trickster figures, but their tricksters were usually from the supernatural world. In Greek myth, both gods and humans played the trickster role. Among the gods, Hermes (Mercury) was the preeminent trickster, always playing tricks on Apollo almost from birth. From the stories of the fathers of the gods, with Rhea tricking her husband into swallowing a stone, to the stories of the Titans Prometheus and Epimetheus, Greek myth valued cleverness rather more than brute strength. Among humans, Odysseus (Ulysses) was the master trickster of Greek myth, with his wife Penelope playing the trickster at home as he did on his long voyage to return home to her,

but many other heroes—even the powerful Heracles (Hercules), who was not renowned for his intelligence—displayed trickster elements in times of need.

Autolycus and Sisyphus

Odysseus was the most resourceful, wily, and ingenious of men, and it is not surprising that he was a descendant of Hermes. Odysseus's mother, Anticleia, was the daughter of the king of thieves, Autolycus, who was the son of Hermes. His father gave Autolycus the talent of altering the appearance of any animal, and this helped him to acquire a very fine herd of cattle from his neighbors. He kept stealing cows from King Sisyphus of Ephyra, changing them from brown to white, from horned to hornless, from old to young, from female to male. Sisyphus knew that someone was taking his cows, and he noticed that Autolycus's herd kept increasing at the same rate as his own herd was decreasing, yet the cows were

188

clearly different. Sisyphus believed that Autolycus was the thief responsible, but saw no way to prove this.

One day Sisyphus had an inspiration. He decided to carve the letters SIS on the hooves of all his cows, and the next morning, he found these hoofprints going from his herd to Autolycus's fields. Autolycus vigorously denied that he had stolen the cows. "It is all your doing," he accused Sisyphus. "Your men took my cows to your fields and carved letters on their hooves, so that you could steal them from me."

Sisyphus won this battle of wits, but he was the loser in his clash with Zeus (Jupiter). It happened when Zeus fell in love with Aegina, who was the daughter of the river god Asopus. The river god looked everywhere for his missing daughter, and Sisyphus was impetuous enough to betray Zeus's secret. Asopus rushed out to rescue Aegina and found Zeus in her arms, with his thunderbolts hanging from a tree. Zeus could think of nothing better than to turn himself into a rock until Asopus had run past. Then he took back his Olympian shape, retrieved his weapons and threw a thunderbolt at the river god. Asopus walked with a limp after that attack.

Sisyphus was condemned to eternal punishment in the underworld as a result of this indiscretion. Zeus asked Hades (Pluto) to deliver the king to his realm, but when Hades came for him, Sisyphus refused to go. First he said that it was the task of Hermes, not Hades, to lead souls to the underworld, and then he said that it was not his time to die. Finally Sisyphus asked Hades how he planned to drag him down to the underworld. "With these new inventions of Hephaestus (Vulcan)—handcuffs," answered Hades. "Show me how they work," asked Sisyphus, and very soon Hades was handcuffed to the wall.

For a whole month Sisyphus kept Hades captive. No one could die, and Ares (Mars) lost all patience with the man who was taking all the fun out of his battles. He threatened to dismember Sisyphus, and in the end, reluctantly, the king released Hades and accompanied him on the dismal road to the underworld. Next he tried his golden words on Persephone (Proserpina), who allowed him to go home because he had not yet been buried. But this was his last escape. Hermes came for him the next day, and this time he died and was buried, and Charon ferried his shade over the River Styx. Sisyphus was punished by

being forced to push a large rock uphill—a rock just like the one into which Zeus had transformed himself. He kept pushing the rock to the top of the hill, and then it would roll back over his body and down to the bottom again. Then he had to roll the stone up again, and again, and again, forever.

Autolycus's daughter Anticleia married King Laertes of Ithaca, a small rocky island. Their son, Odysseus, grew up as clever as his grandfather, but not quite clever enough to slip out of his duty to fight in the Trojan War. It would be 10 years before the war ended, and 20 years before his wife Penelope and son Telemachus saw him again.

Odysseus and the Cyclops

Odysseus set sail from Troy at the same time as all the other surviving Greek warriors, but none of them took as long to return home as he did. The winds and seas were against him from the start. In stormy weather, his ships struggled across the sea to the land of the Lotus-Eaters. These people led a blissful life, doing nothing at all except eating, drinking, and sleeping. The lotus fruit gave them forgetfulness, so that they neither grieved nor worried, giving no thought to either their future or their past. Odysseus sent some of his men inland to find water, and the Lotus-Eaters offered these sailors their fruit. When the men did not return, Odysseus himself went to

Above **Sisyphus.** It is thought that Sisyphus was given eternal punishment for two reasons. One, because of the crimes he committed, and the other, to safeguard others. By keeping him busy, the gods were confident that he would have neither the time nor the opportunity to cause more trouble.

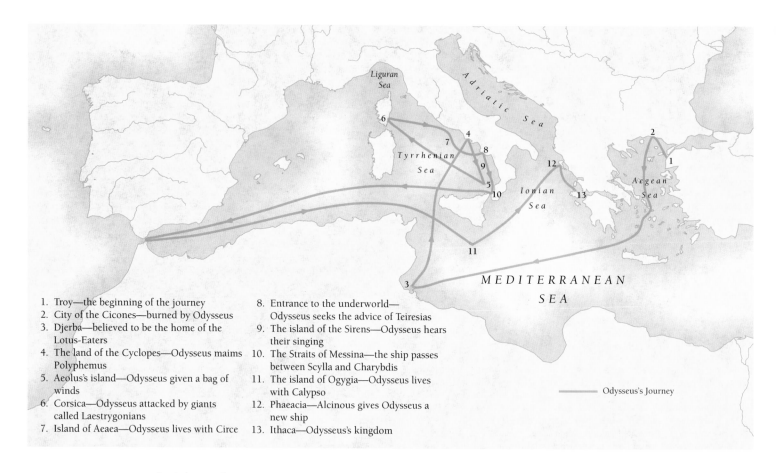

Above **The journey of Odysseus.** Historians put forward many differing accounts of where the adventures of Odysseus really took place. Many locations exist only in myth. This map is just one of the possible reconstructions of his journey.

1. Troy—the beginning of the journey
2. City of the Cicones—burned by Odysseus
3. Djerba—believed to be the home of the Lotus-Eaters
4. The land of the Cyclopes—Odysseus maims Polyphemus
5. Aeolus's island—Odysseus given a bag of winds
6. Corsica—Odysseus attacked by giants called Laestrygonians
7. Island of Aeaea—Odysseus lives with Circe
8. Entrance to the underworld—Odysseus seeks the advice of Teiresias
9. The island of the Sirens—Odysseus hears their singing
10. The Straits of Messina—the ship passes between Scylla and Charybdis
11. The island of Ogygia—Odysseus lives with Calypso
12. Phaeacia—Alcinous gives Odysseus a new ship
13. Ithaca—Odysseus's kingdom

—— Odysseus's Journey

find them. They were sitting on the ground, munching on lotus, smiling and thinking of nothing. Odysseus had to send more sailors to carry them back to the ships, and then he sailed away at once, before anyone else could be tempted.

The next land that they sighted was a fertile island, full of freshwater streams, and here they caught and killed a few goats to add to their provisions. Odysseus and his men went to explore the neighboring mainland, where they came upon a large

HERA'S PUNISHMENT

time, however, when Hera and the other Olympians became so vexed with Zeus that they bound him with leather thongs while he slept, so that he could not move. The goddess Thetis freed Zeus, and he was so annoyed with his wife as leader of the rebels that he hung her from the heights of Olympus, chaining her hands to the roof beam of their palace and hanging anvils as weights on her ankles. He only released her when all the gods promised never again to attack him.

Hera (Juno) and Zeus (Jupiter) were a quarrelsome pair, but their quarrels were usually acted out below Olympus in their dealings with human beings. There was a

Left **Zeus and Hera.** The ancient peoples attributed the storms in the skies to the many quarrels of Zeus and his queen. Hera allowed Aeolus, the keeper of the winds, to release them at her command.

cave with a huge stone beside its opening. The cave was clearly someone's home, with a fireplace and sections fenced off to keep goats and sheep. There were lambs and kids at the back of the cave, but the owner of the cave was not there. Odysseus and his men helped themselves to some cheese that they found in the cave. They could find no wine, but Odysseus had brought plenty of wine for their expedition, and he planned to share it with the cave owner in exchange for his hospitality.

The ground shook with the weight of the cave owner as he came home. He was a Cyclops, a descendant of the giants with one eye in the center of their foreheads who had fought alongside Zeus against the Titans. The whole island was inhabited by Cyclopes, most of whom were quite sociable, but this Cyclops, Polyphemus, had become something of a hermit after his unsuccessful wooing of Galatea. He ate raw meat, while the other Cyclopes ate cooked meat, as civilized people do. Polyphemus drove his flock of sheep into the cave and closed its entrance with the stone. Then he caught sight of Odysseus and the sailors. The giant wasted little time on conversation. He grabbed hold of a sailor and tore him apart, stuffing the pieces down his throat. Then he reached for a second man, to complete his meal. The others could do nothing but cower against the cave wall, watching the Cyclops fall asleep after his meal, and waiting for more death in the morning.

TRICKING THE CYCLOPS

In the morning, the Cyclops consumed more men and drove his flock out, shutting the cave again with its stone. By that time Odysseus had thought of a plan. He took the Cyclop's huge staff and sharpened one end with his sword, then hardened it in the fire. That night, after Polyphemus had returned and killed two more men, Odysseus said to him, "Cyclops, what good is meat without wine? We have plenty of good

wine that we would like to share with you. If you would like to know my name, I am called 'No One'." The Cyclops appeared somewhat surprised that his captives were proving such well-behaved guests, but he could see no good reason to refuse their kind offer of wine. Odysseus poured him a giant bowlful of wine that was unmixed with water, then another and another, until Polyphemus was so drunk that he collapsed into unconsciousness.

Above **Odysseus and Polyphemus the Cyclops.** Polyphemus, the chief of the Cyclopes, had been warned about Odysseus. Telemus, a seer, had told Polyphemus that one day a man named Odysseus would pierce his eye with a stick.

191

Odysseus heated the end of the staff in the fire, then he and his men carried it over to the snoring Cyclops and rammed it into his eye. Polyphemus clutched at his charred eye socket and screamed with shock and pain. The other Cyclopes came along to find out what was causing all this noise. "Who is hurting you?" they shouted through the stone door, and all that Polyphemus could reply was, "No One," until they went away again. He groped for his enemies to kill them, but they easily slipped away. They were still trapped, though. Sooner or later, he promised himself, he would catch them and eat them all.

Polyphemus now rolled the stone sideways, making a small opening to let his sheep out. As each sheep went through, the Cyclops felt along its back to make sure that no man was trying to escape that way. Odysseus whispered to his men to hang on the underside of the fleeces, so that the giant would not notice them as the sheep carried them outside. Odysseus himself clung onto a massive ram that was the last to leave, and then, safely outside, they ran for their ship.

Odysseus ordered his men to row the ship out to sea, and as soon as he thought he was far enough away, he could not resist taunting Polyphemus, who came running to and fro on the beach, trying to catch them. "I am Odysseus, sacker of cities," he boasted. Polyphemus picked up a huge stone and hurled it in the direction of the sound. It splashed

short of the ship, but the sailors rowed their hardest to get away before the next rock hit them. Polyphemus prayed to his father Poseidon (Neptune) for revenge, and for the remainder of his journey home, Odysseus was hindered by all the bad weather that Poseidon could manage to throw his way.

The Sirens

On one of the islands that Odysseus had to pass by, lived the Sirens. They were women down to the waist, and had huge wings, feathered legs, and claws. Their song promised fulfillment of each man's innermost desire, tempting sailors to their deaths. The island was littered with the bones of eaten men. Odysseus had been forewarned of the danger, and he gave all his sailors pieces of wax to put in their ears, so that they could not hear the Sirens singing. But Odysseus was insatiably curious, and he wanted to hear this irresistible song. He ordered his men to bind him to the ship's mast and not release him while they were within earshot of the island, however much he commanded and begged. Other men might have been tempted with songs of love, but for Odysseus, the Sirens sang of knowledge and wisdom. He strained at his bonds and tried to persuade the crew to release him, but they kept him tied up until they were safely past the island. That is how Odysseus became the only man to hear the Sirens' song and survive.

Our Sirens,
in those dulcet clarions,
As primal splendour that
which is reflected.

DANTE ALIGHIERI (1265–1321),
THE DIVINE COMEDY, "PARADISO,"
CANTO XII

Below **Odysseus and the Sirens.** According to some classical writers, the Sirens were doomed to die when any mortal heard their song and actually resisted them. It is said that after Odysseus had done so, the Sirens flung themselves into the sea and became rocks.

ODYSSEUS'S RETURN

One of the islands that Odysseus (Ulysses) visited was ruled by Aeolus, who had control over the winds. He gave Odysseus a leather bag that contained the winds, all except the West Wind that would blow them safely home to Ithaca. But Odysseus's men thought that Aeolus had given him some secret treasure that he would not share out with them, and while he was asleep, they cut the bag open. Out rushed the winds, and the ships were carried back to Aeolus's island. This time Aeolus refused to help, recognizing that at least one god was hindering Odysseus's return. Soon after this Odysseus lost all but one of his ships when they came to the lands of the Laestrygonians, giants and cannibals much like the Cyclops. Most of his men were now dead.

The winds blew his remaining ship to another pleasant-looking island, ruled over by Circe. Some say that she was the daughter of Helius (Sol), others that she was Hecate's child. She had the power to turn human beings into animals, and most of the animals on her island had once been human. Some of Odysseus's men came to her palace, seeking her help, and she sat them at her table, feeding them generously before waving her wand in their direction and turning them into pigs. Only one man escaped to tell the others. Odysseus set off to the rescue, and Hermes (Mercury) met him on the way, showing him an insignificant plant called moly, that would protect him against Circe's magic.

Odysseus sat at Circe's table and ate her food, hoping that he was not eating human flesh. Then Circe waved her wand and tried to transform him into an animal, but the moly protected him. She was quick to recognize that a god had helped him, and so without further ado invited him into her bed. Odysseus agreed to this, on condition that she transform all the animals back into men again. Odysseus stayed with Circe long enough to father three children.

When he started to long for home again, Circe told him what he must do next. In order to reach Ithaca, he must go down to the underworld as a living man, and ask the seer Teiresias for his advice. Circe gave him directions to the underworld and explained how to restore the voices of the dead for a few moments, by giving them the rich blood of freshly

Above **Landscape with Odysseus and the Laestrygonians.** The crew were delighted to meet the daughter of the king of the Laestrygonians when they first arrived on the island. Their delight soon turned to horror, however, when upon being presented to the king, he promptly ate one of the sailors. The men tried to escape, but most were speared like fish and eaten.

Left **Odysseus's companions being changed into pigs.** Circe was happy enough to transform the swine back into sailors when she became the lover of Odysseus. However, it is said that when she changed the crew back into human form, she made them taller and more handsome than they had been before.

Left column captions:

Right **Odysseus arriving on Calypso's island.** The nymph Calypso was the daughter of the Titan Atlas. Her island was described as somewhat of an oasis. It was shrouded by poplars and cypresses, and abounded in vines that were laden with grapes.

Below *Odysseus at the Court of Alcinous, King of the Phaeacians* by Francesco Hayez (1791–1882). King Alcinous had for many years offered his assistance to shipwrecked sailors, despite the warning from Poseidon that this sort of generosity would be punished. Poseidon kept his word following the rescue of Odysseus. He turned the ship to stone and blocked the Phaeacian harbor with a mountain.

slaughtered sheep to drink. All the shades would cluster around, eager to taste the blood, and he would have to drive off the rest to allow Teiresias to drink and speak. Odysseus found his way to the entrance to the underworld and slaughtered the sheep that Circe gave him. Among the shades that crowded close were his mother Anticleia and the great warrior Achilles. Odysseus made sure that Teiresias had room to reach the blood, and after drinking, the seer spoke. He warned Odysseus to keep his men under control when they reached the island of the Sun, or the god would become their enemy. Odysseus would have trouble in Ithaca, too, and even when safely home, he would still not have ended his travels. Eventually he would have to go voyaging again, with an oar over his shoulder, until he came to a region where oars were unknown. Only then could he finally appease the wrath of Poseidon (Neptune), and go home for good.

Losses and Gains

Odysseus passed through many more ordeals on his voyage, until he had lost all his men and his remaining ship. Six men died when the ship passed between Scylla and Charybdis. Scylla was a sea monster with

six heads, each of which devoured one of Odysseus's crew while they were avoiding the whirlpool of Charybdis. The rest of his crew died as a punishment for killing and eating the cattle of the Sun on the island of Thrinacie, while Odysseus was asleep. Zeus (Jupiter) sent a storm that swamped the ship, and only Odysseus survived, clinging to the broken mast

until he was washed ashore on the island of Ogygia, where the nymph Calypso lived. She kept Odysseus there as her lover for seven years, offering him immortality, yet every day he looked toward Ithaca and wept. Eventually Zeus sent Hermes to order Calypso to release him. Odysseus built a raft and, after this was wrecked in one more attempt on his life by Poseidon, he swam through stormy seas to an island inhabited by Phaeacians.

King Alcinous and Queen Arete ruled this island, and their daughter was Princess Nausicaa. Athene (Minerva) sent a dream to Nausicaa, suggesting that she should go to the beach to wash clothes. Here she found Odysseus, naked and in need, and brought him back to her parents' palace. The king and queen would gladly have married their daughter to the stranger, who captivated them with his stories of cleverness and bravery, but Odysseus wished only to return home. They gave him the richest of gifts and sent him on his way home in one of their ships. The ship reached the harbor of Ithaca while he was asleep, and he was left on shore with all the presents stacked beside him. Poseidon took a final revenge on the helpful sailors by turning ship and crew to stone, but not until they had brought Odysseus home at last.

Troubles in Ithaca

Odysseus was now back on his beloved island, but there were more troubles to face. Seventeen years after he had left for Troy, a host of suitors came to woo his wife Penelope, refusing to believe that he was still alive. They feasted daily at his palace, eating his provisions and drinking his wine. Penelope kept putting off making a decision, for she was certain that Odysseus would come home one day. She could not refuse them directly, for she had little support. Odysseus's father Laertes was too old to fight, and his son Telemachus was unable to dispose of the suitors on his own. But Penelope was as much of a trickster as her husband. She told the suitors that she was weaving a shroud in preparation for the burial of Laertes. Every day for three years, she would work on the shroud, and every night she would undo her day's work. Eventually one of her

ANTS INTO MEN

The realm of Aegina was ruled over by King Aeacus, the son of Zeus (Jupiter) and the nymph Aegina. A plague afflicted the kingdom, brought upon it by Hera (Juno), furious at her husband's affair with the nymph, and even angrier that the kingdom was named after her rival. All the animals died, then the farmers, then the city folk, until there were too few of the living to bury all the dead.

Aeacus prayed to his father, Zeus, for help. Then he noticed a long line of ants climbing an oak tree sacred to Zeus, each hauling a huge load of food. "Father," the king prayed to Zeus, "give me as many citizens for my empty city as I see ants climbing your tree." That night, all the ants were transformed into people, who were called the Myrmidons (a Greek word meaning "the ant-people").

serving women informed the suitors of this trick. Now she had to finish her weaving. She told the suitors that she would choose someone to marry, now that Telemachus was a man, as Odysseus had counseled her long ago.

Telemachus had grown up during his father's long absence, and Athene now inspired him to go overseas in search of his father. Telemachus was in danger from the suitors, who would not hesitate to kill the heir to Ithaca in secret. Athene thought it best to send Telemachus to visit Odysseus's old companions from the Trojan War, Menelaus and Helen in Sparta and Nestor in Pylos. He found no trace of his father on this journey, but came home loaded with presents, and with the friendship of some of the most powerful men in Greece.

ODYSSEUS THE BEGGAR

When Odysseus awoke on the Ithacan beach, Athene disguised him as an old beggar so that he could find out how matters stood in his kingdom without being recognized. He found refuge with his swineherd, one of the servants who was still loyal to him (though he did not recognize his master). Then Telemachus arrived back from his voyage, and Odysseus revealed

Below **Telemachus on Calypso's island.** Athene appeared to Telemachus in the form of Mentor, his tutor. In this disguise, she was not only able to educate him, but to inspire him with the boldness of spirit that he needed to travel the world in search of his father, Odysseus—a search that took him to Calypso's island.

Above *Telemachus, Son of Odysseus* by Alessandro Ciccarelli. Telemachus was just an infant when Odysseus left to fight in the Trojan War. Returning home to Ithaca, Odysseus found Telemachus a mature and courageous man, ready to fight beside his father.

Right *Penelope* by J. Cavalier (1849). Penelope and Odysseus had many happy years together until the hero, by then an old man, was unintentionally killed by Telegonius, his son by Circe. The family traveled to Circe's island to bury Odysseus. Penelope eventually married her stepson.

himself to his son. They began to plot their revenge on the suitors with Athene's help. As a first step, Odysseus went to the palace as a beggar. Outside the palace, on the dung heap, lay an old dog. This was Argus, Odysseus's faithful dog that had been neglected and left to die on the dung heap. Argus immediately recognized his master and had the strength to lift his head in greeting, but he could do no more. He felt the joy of knowing that his master had returned, and then his head sank down again and he died.

In the palace, Odysseus tested the limits of the suitors' insolence, allowing them to mock him and even throw furniture at him. Penelope reproached the suitors for behaving so badly toward a guest and suppliant, an act that the gods would be sure to punish. Her prophetic words made little difference to their insolent behavior. Later that night, Penelope decided to question the old beggar, who promised her that Odysseus was on his way home. She wept to hear news of her husband and offered him a bed for the night, ordering Eurycleia, the family's old nursemaid, to wash his feet. Eurycleia washed his feet and legs and suddenly cried out, seeing a long scar on his thigh which Odysseus had acquired as a boy while out hunting. Odysseus held her by the throat, whispering that she must keep silent.

Athene inspired Penelope with the clever idea of challenging the suitors to an archery competition. Penelope decided that she must choose one of these disagreeable men, if only to allow Telemachus to keep some of his father's rich estate, and she told them that whoever could string Odysseus's great bow and shoot an arrow through the rings of his 12 axes, could have her as reluctant bride. None of the suitors could string the bow. Telemachus ordered the bow to be given to the beggar, and he effortlessly strung it and shot an arrow through all the axes. Then he turned the arrows on the suitors. Telemachus had hidden all the weapons in the palace, and the father and son, together with their loyal swineherd and cowherd, slew these wretched men until piles of dead bodies littered the palace floor.

Then Odysseus spoke to his wife, Penelope, telling her who he was. Penelope was as subtle-minded as her husband and needed some proof, something that only Odysseus and she knew about. So she said to him, "Let me fetch the bed out of our bedroom and set it up for you in another room," knowing that her husband had fashioned one of the bedposts out of a living tree, growing in the middle of the house. Odysseus was outraged at the thought that someone had cut the bedpost so that the bed could be moved. When Penelope heard what he said, she knew that he really was her beloved husband. Her years of waiting and grieving were over at last.

The people of Ithaca discovered the next day that all the suitors, princes, and lords of the island and nearby lands had died at the hands of Odysseus, Telemachus, and their two loyal servants. Some of the Ithacans recognized that a god was helping Odysseus, and acknowledged that the suitors deserved death because of their bad behavior in Odysseus's palace. Others armed themselves to

take revenge, and so the goddess Athene intervened once more to bring about peace for her much-beloved hero Odysseus and his constant wife.

Dante's Odysseus

Teiresias prophesied that this was not the conclusion of Odysseus's journeyings, but this is where Homer's epic poem, *The Odyssey*, leaves him. In the millennia since Homer's poem, numerous other writers have provided sequels to this intriguing story. In the twelfth century, the Italian poet Dante wrote of Odysseus and Diomedes in his "Inferno," (part of *The Divine Comedy*) which is a visionary poem setting out his own descent into a (Christian) underworld. Dante's Odysseus burned in endless torment because of his theft of the Palladium and the deception that he practiced with the Trojan Horse. Odysseus related his final voyage to Dante, endlessly driven on by the desire for knowledge. Neither old age nor love of his wife and son could ever hold this Odysseus at home, and he died at sea, while continuing to stretch the limits of human questioning and questing.

Above *Goddess Athene Disguises Odysseus as a Beggar* by Giuseppe Bottani (1717–1784). The goddess Athene admired the ingenuity and cunning of men such as Odysseus, which is why she continued to help him. She disguised him as a beggar to keep him safe from the wrath of Penelope's suitors.

Left **Odysseus greets his faithful dog.** Odysseus was forced to take harsh action in order to assume control of his household once more. He killed not only all of the suitors, but also many of his servants who had helped the suitors in his absence.

197

THE TALE OF AENEAS

Aeneas was the son of Venus (Aphrodite) and Anchises, and became king of the Dardanians. After Achilles raided his cattle, he fought in the Trojan War alongside the Trojans. His mother often helped him; though she could not fight alongside him, she was quick to rescue him from trouble. Neptune (Poseidon) and Apollo also protected him, because all the gods knew that he must survive the war to found a new kingdom. Only Juno (Hera) dared to show him ill will, still brooding over the past, when Paris gave the apple to Venus, and resenting the future, when Aeneas's descendants were destined to overthrow her city of Carthage. The other gods sent omens and visions to help Aeneas survive the fall of Troy, promising that he would rule a new kingdom in Italy. As the Greeks sacked Troy, Aeneas escaped, piously rescuing his household gods and carrying his old father over his shoulder. He held the hand of his small son, Ascanius, and his wife, Creusa, followed, but she became lost and could not be found again.

Aeneas set sail with a small fleet of refugees, first for Thrace, then for Crete, and then for Italy. Along the way he visited the island where the Harpies took refuge when the Argonauts drove them away from Phineus, and like Phineus, he had his food befouled by their droppings. His people attacked the Harpies unsuccessfully, drawing down a curse from the Harpy Celaeno, who prophesied that they would eat their tables in severe hunger before building the walls of their new city, as punishment for this attack. Aeneas found Andromache living happily in Epirus with a new Trojan husband, Helenus, now that her enslaver Neoptolemus was dead. They were building a new city modeled on Troy, with a miniature Scaian gate and a little stream for Scamander. But it was not Aeneas's destiny to stay there.

Helenus advised him how to pass safely by the twin dangers of Scylla and Charybdis. The little fleet sailed past Etna in eruption, and rescued a Greek sailor left behind by Odysseus in his flight from the Cyclops's cave three months earlier. They sailed on to Sicily, where Anchises died, and then toward Italy. They would have arrived there without incident, if Juno had not intervened. She

Below *Aeneas and Anchises* by Pietro Bernini (1562–1629). Aeneas, a good and faithful son to his father, carried Anchises for two reasons: because his father was old and because he was lame. Anchises had been crippled by a thunderbolt sent by Zeus when he revealed the name of Aeneas's mother, Venus (Aphrodite).

asked Aeolus, guardian of the winds, to send out a storm. Out went the East and South Winds, then the South-West Wind, damaging Aeneas's ships. The refugees were all in danger of drowning, but Neptune ordered Aeolus to call back his winds, and the weary Trojans found shelter in a Libyan harbor.

The next day, with Venus's guidance, Aeneas found his way to the city of Carthage, still under construction. It was ruled by Queen Dido, a widow who had fled from her brother's persecution in Tyre. Dido welcomed the Trojans, offering them help with their onward journey or a new home in Carthage. That evening, at the welcoming feast, Venus's son Cupid (Eros) disguised himself as Ascanius and inspired in Dido a passionate love for Aeneas. She began to think of marrying him, and prayed to all the gods for their support, especially to Juno, the goddess of marriage. Juno was anxious that Carthage,

Left *Dido with Aeneas Recounting the Misfortunes of Troy* by Baron Pierre Guerin (1774–1833). Many scholars believe that Aeneas was as eagerly in love with Dido as she was with him. In fact, Aeneas was so infatuated that he forgot about his destiny in Italy. Mercury (Hermes) was twice sent to remind him, and it was with great regret that Aeneas had to leave.

not Rome, should fulfill the prophecies of a new empire, and she granted Dido's prayer. Out hunting the next day, the Tyrians and Trojans were scattered in a violent storm, and Dido and Aeneas found themselves sheltering together in a cave. Here they married with Juno as celebrant and the heavens as witness—a ceremony that Aeneas found it easy to repudiate when Jupiter (Zeus) recalled him to his destiny and ordered him to leave Dido. She wept, then reproached, then cursed him, and finally, as the Trojans rowed hastily out to sea, stabbed herself to death with the sword that he had left behind.

Descent to the Underworld

The winds did not favor a voyage to Italy, and Aeneas ordered his fleet to sail to Sicily once more, to the place where his father had died a year earlier. He held elaborate funeral games, where the men

HOUSEHOLD GODS

The Romans worshipped household gods called the Penates and Lares. The Penates were two household gods of the storeroom, where provisions were kept. The amount of stores amassed in this room told the Romans whether the Penates were favoring them. The Lares were the spirits of dead ancestors who brought good luck to the living, if properly honored, with one main Lar for each family. They were offered food every morning and on special occasions such as birthdays, sacrifices were made to them. The Romans feared the Lares' opposites, the Larvae and Lemures, malevolent ghosts of dead criminals, suicides, and the like, who appeared in terrifying shapes at night and could drive people mad.

Left **The Altar of Lares.** The Lares were sometimes worshipped as fertility spirits who brought the family prosperity. A Lar was often represented as a youth with a drinking horn and cup—both symbols of fertility.

Ancient Italy

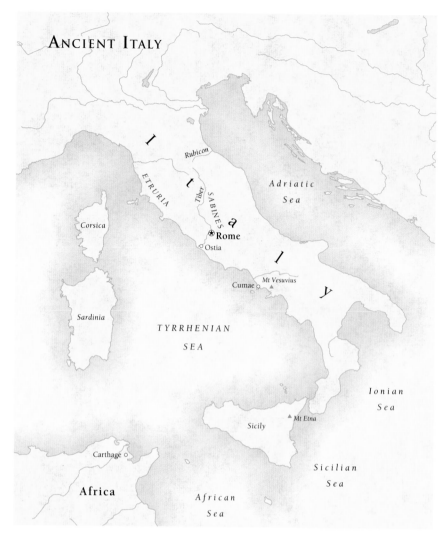

Only one man died on the short voyage to Italy, Palinurus the helmsman, who was overpowered by Somnus (Hypnus), god of sleep, and fell into the sea. The ships arrived safely at Cumae where Apollo's Sibyl lived, giving out her prophecies in a huge, dark cave. She informed the Trojans that they would arrive safely in their destined country, but then they would be afflicted with war. Aeneas asked the Sibyl to help him go down to the underworld as a living man, to revisit his beloved father. "Easy is the descent," replied the Sibyl, "for the door stands open at Avernus, but it is a hard task to return. You must go into the forest and find a golden bough, sacred to the goddess Juno. Only those chosen by fate can take the bough, and once it has been broken off, the tree grows another golden bough ready for another hero. If you can find the golden bough and break it off, this is a sign that you will be allowed both to go and return."

THE JOURNEY

Venus's doves led Aeneas into the forest, flying a short way, then stopping to feed, then flying again,

competed at rowing, running, boxing, and archery. Meanwhile the Trojan women bewailed the death of Anchises, and Juno sent Iris, the messenger of the gods, disguised as one of these women, to create fresh difficulties for Aeneas. She reminded the women of their weary years of wandering, and suggested that Sicily would be a good place to build a new city. In the end she persuaded them to set fire to the ships, to force Aeneas to stay there. Jupiter promptly sent heavy rain to douse the fires, but four ships had been destroyed, and the remaining ships could not carry all the Trojans. Anchises' shade appeared to Aeneas, advising him to leave behind all those too old to fight, too tired from the voyage, or too reluctant to go on. They could found their own city of Acesta in Sicily, while the best and strongest went on to Italy.

Right **Aeneas and the Sibyl in the Underworld** by Jan Brueghel the Elder (1568–1625). The Cumaean Sibyl was one of the most famous of all prophetesses. Remembered for her descent to the underworld to guide Aeneas, she was also known as an author. Over her thousands of years of life, she wrote down many of her riddling prophecies.

JANUS AND THE GATE OF PEACE

Janus was the Roman god of openings and thresholds of all kinds. He was represented as having two faces looking in opposite directions. In terms of place, he was the god of doorways and crossroads, and the sources of rivers and streams were sacred to him. He was also a god of travelers, those who cross boundaries by land and sea. In terms of time, he was the god of dusk and dawn, the thresholds between night and day, and of the transition from month to month and year to year. The first month of the year, January, is named after this god. In Rome the gates of his shrine were opened when war was declared, and shut in time of peace (a very rare event in Roman history).

Right **Double-headed Janus.** Janus was also the god of beginnings. The Romans believed that all beginnings were crucial to the success of any venture, regarding them as portals to the future. Janus's blessing was sought at the beginning of each day, month, and year.

until they came to the golden bough, shining like bright-leaved mistletoe on a tree in winter. Aeneas easily broke off the bough and went into the dark gorge of Avernus with the Sibyl, after making sacrifices to Hecate, Proserpina (Persephone) and Pluto (Hades), to Nox (Nyx) and Gaia, the goddesses of Night and Earth. They passed Disease and Old Age, Famine and Fear and Penury, War and Death, Sleep and Dreams, and the Furies. They met the monsters of Greek myth, the Centaurs, the Gorgons and Harpies, the Chimaera and the Hydra, but these were only phantoms and had no power to hurt. Aeneas walked on in the constant gray dusk of the underworld to the rivers of Acheron and Cocytus, to the ferry over the Styx and its aged ferryman Charon. He saw the shades of the dead clustering around the ferry as thickly as autumn leaves, and he saw Charon taking on board the shades of those properly buried and turning away the unburied. He saw his missing helmsman, Palinurus, who said that his body could be found in the foam, just off the coast of Italy. Palinurus begged Aeneas to spread earth over his body so that he could pass over the Styx, but the gods did not permit it. Charon tried to forbid Aeneas from crossing the Styx,

but the golden bough allowed him free passage. As the living man stepped into the boat, its planks groaned under the weight and took in water.

On the other side of the River Styx, Cerberus was barking, but the Sibyl gave him a poppy cake that sent him to sleep. Aeneas went on, hearing the laments of babies who died almost as soon as they were born, then the laments of those judged guilty and executed, though they were innocent. He saw the shades of suicides, longing for the life that they had thrown away, and of those who died for love. Dido wandered here, like the moon half-visible through cloud, and when she saw Aeneas, her face set in a grim glare

Below *Dido's Suicide* by Liberale da Verona (c. 1445–1529). The heartbroken queen of Carthage ordered a pyre to be raised so that she could destroy everything that reminded her of Aeneas. Rather than be without him, she stabbed herself with a sword he had given her, and threw herself into the flames.

Above *The Vision of Aeneas in the Elysian Fields* by Sebastiano Conca (1680–1764). Even after he died, Anchises continued to help his son. His ghost told Aeneas to visit him in the underworld, where he would find out what the future held. Anchises pointed out the souls that were to later win honor in the new empire Aeneas was destined to found.

phantom body. Anchises gave his son a reassuring prophetic account of the future rulers of the Italian kingdom that was to be founded by Aeneas.

THE RETURN

Then Aeneas returned to the upper world through the gates of ivory, through which false dreams travel each night. His fleet set sail again and passed safely by Circe's island, arriving at the mouth of the River Tiber. The land here was ruled by King Latinus, whose daughter Lavinia was courted by many men. Turnus was the man that her parents wanted her to marry, but the omens were unfavorable, pointing instead to a marriage with some foreigner who would go on to establish an empire.

Aeneas and his men were now eating their first meal on land, piling fruit and vegetables on wheat cakes that they had placed on the ground. Then they ate the cakes, and in doing so fulfilled the Harpy's curse, that they would eat their own tables. Now they could begin building the walls of their new city, while negotiating for the land with King Latinus. Recognizing that this was the prophesied stranger, Latinus was happy for Aeneas to marry his daughter and establish a new city, but Turnus declared war on Aeneas. This war was short and bloody, and concluded in the Trojans' victory. Aeneas lived on as ruler of the new city for only three years, but his son Ascanius ruled Alba Longa for the next 30 years, and some 300 years later the great city of Rome itself would be founded there by his descendants, Romulus and Remus.

and then she turned away. He entreated her to stay and make peace with him, but in vain.

Then he met other famous shades of the dead from the Trojan War and before, some eager to speak with him, others shrinking away as if he might give them a second death. He saw the great wall of Dis with Phlegethon as its fiery moat and a Fury as its guardian. Since he was not a wicked man, Aeneas was not allowed to pass beyond this wall and only heard about the torments of the damned from the Sibyl. She hurried him onward to the Elysian Fields where he at last met his dead father and tried to embrace him, but his arms kept slipping through the

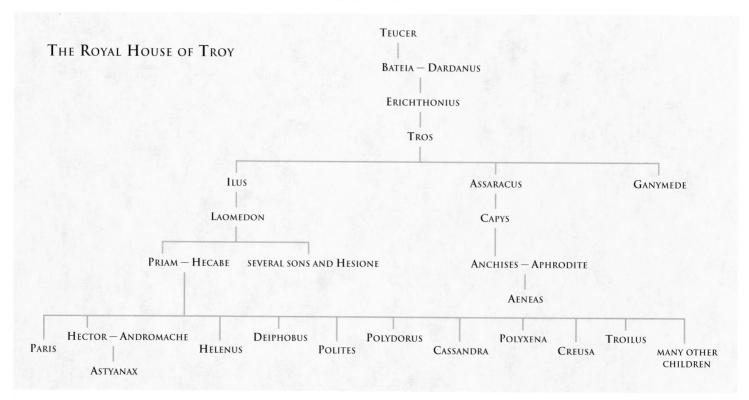

THE ROYAL HOUSE OF TROY

TEUCER

BATEIA — DARDANUS

ERICHTHONIUS

TROS

ILUS   ASSARACUS   GANYMEDE

LAOMEDON   CAPYS

PRIAM — HECABE   SEVERAL SONS AND HESIONE   ANCHISES — APHRODITE

AENEAS

PARIS   HECTOR — ANDROMACHE   HELENUS   DEIPHOBUS   POLITES   POLYDORUS   CASSANDRA   POLYXENA   CREUSA   TROILUS   MANY OTHER CHILDREN

ASTYANAX

MYTHS OF ROME

As a founding myth for a nation and an empire, the story of Aeneas led back not to a warrior god nor to the king of the gods, but to the frivolous, laughter-loving goddess of sexual desire. Such a genealogy was perhaps seen as inadequate by the Romans, who prided themselves on the spread of empire, the rule of law, and good government, none of which was a quality that Venus (Aphrodite) cherished. The second founding myth of Rome offered a different divine origin for the nation, deriving it from Mars (Ares), the god of war, a deity regarded much more favorably by the Romans than the Greeks.

Romulus and Remus

Rhea Silvia was the daughter of King Numitor. When Amulius took the throne from Numitor, he killed the king's son and forced Rhea Silvia to become a Vestal Virgin (priestess of Hestia), so that she would have no husband, sons, or grandsons who might avenge Numitor's overthrow. One day, she was fetching water from the spring in the sacred grove of Mars when the god himself came down from the sky and raped her. Rhea Silvia did her best to conceal her pregnancy, and nine months later, gave birth to twin boys, Romulus and Remus. Amulius did not believe her story about the god, and threw her into the Tiber where the river god Tiberinus saved her life, married her, and transformed her into a goddess.

Amulius ordered the twin babies to be put in a wooden chest and thrown into the river (as in Greek myth, this was to avoid blood-guilt). The Tiber carried them to the Palatine hill where the box opened and they were left stranded under a fig tree. There a she-wolf found them. She had just given birth to cubs of her own, and she was willing to suckle these crying man-cubs as well. The king's swineherd saw this amazing sight, and knew that a god was favoring Rhea Silvia's children. He took the children to his wife, whose own baby had recently been stillborn, and the couple brought up the twin boys as their own sons.

Romulus and Remus grew up with their father's warlike nature, dispensing rough justice to wrong-doers, loving to hunt, and enjoying a good quarrel. One day, when the boys had grown to young men, the herdsmen of Numitor quarreled with the herdsmen of Amulius, while

Above *Romulus and Remus, Legendary Founders of Rome, Suckled by the She-wolf* by Giuseppi Cesari (1568–1640). Romulus and Remus, stranded and left for dead, were not destined to die on the hillside. Instead they were found and cared for by a she-wolf and a wood-pecker. Both of these animals were sacred to the father of the twins, Mars.

Left **The god of the River Tiber with the she-wolf and the twins.** Tiberinus, the god of the River Tiber, was particularly revered in Rome because he rescued its founders. He is often shown holding the Horn of Plenty, to symbolize the fertile power of the water.

Opposite page *Rape of Sabine Women* by Giovanni-Antonio Sodoma (1477–1549). Though they were abducted and forced to marry the Romans, the Sabine women eventually resigned themselves to their new lives. Their intervention not only stopped the killing, but also brought the two tribes together. The Confederation was governed by both King Romulus and the Sabine king, Titus Tatius.

Romulus was away. Quarrel turned to fight, and Remus was captured and taken to Numitor. Romulus was keen to counterattack and free his brother, but his foster father now revealed the truth of who the twins were. Romulus and he planned not just to rescue Remus, but to regain the kingdom that had been taken from their grandfather, Numitor. At the same time, Numitor was working out the truth of who the twins were, by questioning his captive, Remus. Soon the twins were together once more, ready to mount an attack on King Amulius with Numitor's support. The attack succeeded, Amulius was killed, and Numitor was restored to his kingship.

There are many different versions of the quarrel that destroyed brotherly love between Romulus and Remus. Numitor gave them permission to build a new city, and some say that they quarreled over which hill the city should be built upon. When the omens favored Romulus, he began by digging a trench around the boundaries of the new city, ordering his men to kill anyone who came in without permission. Remus taunted his brother, saying that the trench was far too narrow. "Any enemy will be able to jump over this ditch, just like this," he said, as he jumped across it. Immediately one of the workmen killed him with a spade for entering without permission. Other versions say that Romulus himself killed his brother, saying, "So perish all invaders!" The founding myth of Rome, then, derived its imperial glory not only from the god of war but from brother killing brother. Rome was founded on a crime; but unlike the Greek myths of cursed ruling families, where a curse works its way through generations, this Roman myth ends

with the death of Remus. Romulus became the first king of Rome, and was finally deified as the god Quirinus.

The Rape of the Sabine Women

Romulus was the first king of Rome, but almost all his subjects were men. He badly needed to attract women to the city, and sent messengers to many nearby cities to arrange marriages, but without success, since this new city had a bad reputation for lawlessness. The Romans began to urge war, but Romulus devised a less bloody solution to their problem. He invited the citizens of all neighboring states to attend a festival in Rome, and crowds of people came, mainly from the Sabine state. All the visitors were waiting for the chariot race to begin, when Romulus signaled his men to take hold of every woman in the audience and carry her off. The male visitors were not prepared for a fight, and went home angrily, planning a raid on Rome to fetch their women back and teach the lawless Romans a lesson in hospitality. They hoped that the gods, too, would take revenge, for it was an offense against the gods to violate friendship toward a guest.

Romulus forced the women to marry Roman men, and gave them all Roman citizenship. He believed that they would become reconciled to their marriages if only they stayed in Rome until their first children were born, but the Sabines and the men of the other nearby city-states did not wait that long before raising armies against Rome. Three times Romulus defeated an army and made generous terms with a city-state, but when the Sabines sent their army against Rome and attacked its citadel, the Roman commander's daughter Tarpeia betrayed the city to them. The Sabines had caught her outside the citadel and asked what price she would ask to betray Rome. She looked at the jewelry on the king's arms and said, "I will betray my people for the things that you wear on your arms." That night she opened the gate and asked for her reward. The Sabines gave her what they wore on their arms—shields, not jewels—until

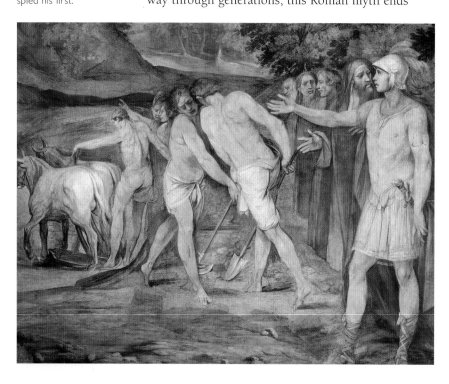

Below *Romulus Marking Out with Furrows the Plans for the Foundation of Rome* by Giuseppe Cesari (1568–1640). When Romulus was declared the official founder of the city, his twin brother was outraged. Relying on augury, they argued over which omen should be recognized. Remus spotted six vultures, whereas Romulus spied twelve. Remus felt he should win regardless of number, because he spied his first.

they crushed her to death. Then they threw her body from the top of the citadel's rock, which was known from then on as the Tarpeian Rock. The Sabines took the citadel and then attacked Rome. In the middle of the battle, the Sabine women ran out onto the battlefield, shouting out that they wanted neither their fathers nor their husbands to die. Hearing this, the Sabines made peace with the Romans. The influence of the new city-state was growing.

The Sibylline Books

The Sibylline books consisted of prophecies that one of the Greek sibyls was supposed to have uttered, and that were brought from Greece to Cumae in Italy. The myth of the Sibylline books tells of the Cumaean Sibyl taking the books to Tarquin the Proud, the last king of Rome, and offering them to him for a price. What she offered was nine books of prophecies, and when he refused to pay the price, she burned three of the books. Tarquin still refused to buy the prophecies, and she went away to burn another three of the books. This tactic worked, as he became afraid that he would lose the whole set of prophecies, and he

THE PROBLEM WITH TWINS

The birth of twins was considered so portentous in Greek myth that it was explained supernaturally. Only one of the twins could live as a normal mortal. The other twin must be the child of a god. The myths of Castor and Pollux (Polydeuces), Clytaemnestra and Helen, and Hercules (Heracles) and Iphicles all follow this pattern. There are traces of such a pattern, too, in the story of Romulus and Remus. The twins could not coexist as joint rulers of Rome, and only Romulus achieved apotheosis, by taking his place as a god with his divine father, while Remus died and was buried as a mortal man.

Above **The Dioscuri (Twins Castor and Pollux).** When Castor was killed, Pollux also wanted to die, but he could not, because he was the son of Zeus. Zeus let him share his immortality with Castor, splitting their time between the upper and lower worlds.

205

agreed to buy the remaining three, even though the asking price was exactly the same for three as for the original nine. In 83 B.C. the Sibylline books were destroyed, and the Romans collected as many similar prophetic utterances as they could from Greece and Asia Minor, with the specific aim of using them for the interpretation of portents. The prophecies were used to interpret such worrying events as earthquakes, plagues, and the arrival of comets. In the early fifth century A.D., this second collection of Sibylline prophecies was also destroyed.

How Horatius Kept the Bridge

When the last king of Rome, Tarquin the Proud, had been overthrown, he gathered an army of Etruscans to force his way back into power. He persuaded King Lars Porsena of Clusium to help him, and their army laid siege to Rome. The city had one particularly weak point, however, which was a wooden bridge over the Tiber, and if Tarquin's forces captured this bridge, it would certainly mean that Rome could be starved into submission.

The battle began across the Tiber from Rome, and the Etruscans were winning. The Roman line broke, and the soldiers ran back across the bridge with the Etruscans racing after them. Horatius, the commander of the soldiers who were guarding the bridge, knew that in minutes the bridge would fall if his men gave way to panic like the rest of the soldiers. He ordered his soldiers to destroy the bridge, while Horatius himself stood at the far side, ready to defend it single-handedly against all the enemy forces.

The Etruscans were amazed at this man's courage, and the Romans were ashamed by it. Two of Horatius's companions, Spurius and Titus, ran forward to join him, and the three Roman soldiers defeated every

Below *Horatius Cocles Defending the Bridge* by Charles Le Brun (1619–1690). Horatius was greatly rewarded for the way in which he put his own life at risk. As well as land, he also received the honor of having a statue of himself erected in the place of Assembly, the Comitium.

Etruscan who tried to cross the bridge. The other Romans were chopping away the supports of the bridge, and now they called the three men to come back quickly, before it was too late. Spurius and Titus ran back, but Horatius stayed on the enemy side of the Tiber, holding back the Etruscans until the bridge finally collapsed. Horatius prayed to the river god Tiberinus and jumped into the river, wearing the full weight of his armor. The god must have helped him to swim across, and he was welcomed as a hero by the Romans and given as much land as he could plow around in a day.

The Story of Camillus

When Rome was still a small city-state at war with its neighbors, the Etruscans, the Romans besieged the Etruscan city of Veii. Like Troy, it took 10 years to be conquered. In the tenth year, the Roman commander, Camillus, ordered a tunnel to be dug under the city walls, and the Romans overpowered the Etruscans both inside and outside their city. Camillus gave his men permission to rampage through the city but not to injure the temples of the gods. He was particularly concerned not to do any violence to the temple of Juno (Hera), the patron goddess of Veii. He even asked the goddess for permission to take her statue to Rome. The statue nodded and said that she was willing to move, and the Romans took this as a great sign of divine favor.

The next Etruscan city that Camillus besieged was Falerii, and it was here that the schoolmaster betrayed his city to the Romans by taking all his pupils to Camillus's tent and offering them up as hostages. Camillus was too honorable to accept this gift, and ordered the boys to whip their teacher all the way back to Falerii. The Etruscans were so impressed by their enemy's just and honorable code of war that they decided to make peace with him.

The Geese That Saved Rome

Rome now attracted enemies from much farther away. The Gauls of northern Europe invaded Italy and came as far as Rome. They had a huge army and the Romans could not withstand them. It seemed highly likely that Rome would fall. People either fled from the city or assembled on the steep citadel of Rome, the Capitoline hill, fearfully waiting for the invaders to arrive. The Gauls found no resistance as they continued on their rampage, burning and looting and then setting fire to the buildings of Rome. Then they assembled at the foot of the Capitoline hill, looking for an undefended way to climb it and destroy the city entirely. After days of searching, they found a way up the steep rock, and that night, they quietly started to climb up.

On the citadel lived a flock of geese sacred to the goddess Juno. The Romans were all asleep but the geese heard the small sounds of men struggling up the rock and panting for breath. The birds attacked the Gauls, hissing and cackling and beating at the men with their wings. Their noise woke up the Romans, who hurried over to throw the invaders down to their deaths. The geese had saved Rome, and from then on, no goose was sacrificed on the altar of Juno. They had won the right to live out their days as honored guardians of the city.

Left *Horatius Cocles* by Pietro Perugino (c. 1445–1523). The name "Cocles," meaning "one-eyed," came to be identified with Horatius because of his single-mindedness and determination. In historical times, there was a statue of a one-eyed figure that stood at the head of a wooden bridge near Rome.

APOTHEOSIS

Apotheosis is the transformation of a mortal into a god. In Greek myth it occurs at the moment of death for Heracles (Hercules). Some mortal men and women beloved by the Greek gods were transformed into deities; Psyche, for instance, achieved apotheosis after enduring Venus's (Aphrodite's) trials, and Ariadne was transformed into a goddess when she married Bacchus (Dionysus). In Greek and Roman history, there were some rulers who were said to have achieved apotheosis as gods. After the death of Alexander the Great, rulers of his empire were worshipped as gods while alive. Julius Caesar was worshipped after death as the divine Julius, and so, too, were a good many Roman emperors and also some empresses.

Above **Apotheosis of the god Heracles.** The Athenians were the first to worship Heracles as a god, although he was soon honored throughout the Mediterranean world. As his popularity grew, so did the tales of his great feats and exploits.

ENDURING TALES

The Greeks and Romans were not particularly interested either in tales of the beginning of things, or in speculating on the end of the world or life after death. The principal Greek myth about the ending of a world concerns a civilization that preceded the stories of the heroes, nine thousand years before the civilization of classical Greece, and this story can be found only in the writings of the philosopher Plato. The myth of Atlantis was not a widely spread traditional myth, rather a literary artifact, which has enjoyed much wider currency in modern Europe than it ever did in classical Greece or Rome.

Right **Thera**. According to one story, the island known as Thera developed from a clod of Libyan earth. The god of Lake Tritonis gave it to the Argonaut Euphemus who, following the orders of the god, threw it into the sea. Thera later became part of the Atlantis myth.

Lost Atlantis

According to two of Plato's dialogues, the Critias and Timaeus, Atlantis was an island bigger than Libya and Asia combined. It lay beyond the Pillars of Heracles (Hercules) out in the Atlantic Ocean, closest to Spain. The patron god of the island was Poseidon (Neptune), and he and a mortal woman, Cleito, were the ancestors of its ruling family. Its first ruler was called Atlas, and from his name derived the island's name, Atlantis, and the name of the ocean surrounding it. The island of Atlantis abounded in fertile land, and was full of fruit trees. From underground came the precious metal orichalcum. The main city was a marvel of architecture and sculpture, with wonderfully ornamented palaces and a magnificent temple to Poseidon. Atlantis was well governed, with all of its people knowing their duties to the state and obedient to its laws, which Poseidon had laid down.

For generations, all went well in Atlantis. The Atlanteans obeyed the laws and worshipped Poseidon, and although their island was full of riches, they did not value gold and other treasures over-highly. In the end, though, they became decadent and corrupt, no longer obeying the laws of Poseidon and not content to stay within the boundaries of the realm that Poseidon had allotted them. They built a great empire, sub-duing North Africa from the Pillars of Heracles in the west to Egypt in the east, and all the southern part of Europe except for Greece. When they invaded Greece, the Athenians led a Greek army against them. Little by little, the Atlanteans defeated each city-state until only Athens was left unconquered. Thus it was the Athenians alone who eventually defeated the people of Atlantis and freed all the other regions from their tyranny. Soon after this episode the earth became disturbed with earth-quake and flood. In one day and one night the whole Athenian army was swallowed up in a mighty earthquake, and the city of Atlantis sank into the depths of the sea. According to Plato, the sea was still disturbed by the fall of Atlantis less than 200 years before he wrote these dialogues, with a shoal of mud preventing ships from passing through.

Over the years, many have tried to locate lost Atlantis as an actual physical island, and there are two main competing theories as to its whereabouts. Some think that the myth speaks of a huge eruption that occurred within historical time on the volcanic island of Thera. This massive eruption seems likely to have destroyed the pre-classical Minoan civilization existing on Crete. Others take literally Plato's state-ments about the geographical location of Atlantis, and seek for the island's remains in the Atlantic Ocean, perhaps in the vicinity of

THE DEATH OF PAN

Some time in the first century A.D., a ship was sailing past the island of Paxi and a sailor heard a huge voice crying out, "The great god Pan is dead," followed by cries of lamentation. But was this really a voice from the heavens announcing the death of the god? Some scholars of myth believe that the sailor heard the sounds of lamentation from the yearly festival of the god Tammuz ("Dumuzi" in Sumerian myth) who died and was resurrected, as one of his titles was "pan-megas" meaning "all-great." The sailor misunderstood the use of "pan" here as referring to the god Pan. Certainly the worship of Pan, and of the other gods of the Greek pantheon, was not dead by the first century A.D.

Left *Pan* by Adolf Martial Thabard (1831–1905). As well as the god of shepherds and flocks, Pan was also believed to be the god of fertility and male sexuality. Even though Pan was reported to be dead in the first century A.D., shrines, altars, trees, mountains, and even caves that were sacred to Pan were still visited and honored over a century later.

the Azores. Plato's dialogue, the Timaeus, also speaks of a succession of civilizations that are each in turn destroyed by either flood or fire, and this idea also resonates with Mesoamerican myth. The debate continues as to whether Atlantis is an imaginary place in myth or something whose physical remains may one day be recovered by archaeologists.

The End of Greek Myth

In A.D. 312, the Roman Emperor Constantine converted to Christianity, which soon became the state religion. The Emperor Julian's attempt to revive the worship of the Greco-Roman gods as the state religion in A.D. 360 was a failure. The oracles fell into disuse, the temples were abandoned, and the festivals were forgotten. What was never totally forgotten, however, even in the Dark Ages of western history, were the myths of Greece and Rome. When Byzantium fell in the fifteenth century, many of its scholars fled to Italy. The influx of classical literature and learning inspired the art, literature, and science of the Renaissance.

The myths of Greece and Rome have provided subject matter for artists from Leonardo da Vinci to Picasso, and from the Romans on, countries aspiring to literary greatness have measured their achievements against the Greeks' tellings of their myths.

Composers, too, have looked to Greek myth for inspiration, as in the operas dealing with Orpheus and Eurydice, Helen of Troy, and Clytaemnestra's children. Philosophers like Nietzsche have drawn on Greek myth, and psychoanalytic theory has named issues in human development like the Oedipus complex and ailments of the psyche like narcissism after characters in Greek myth. The myths remain potent sources for television series and films, from *Xena* to Disney's *Hercules*. Greek myth still lives, and continues to shape our lives and our understanding of ourselves.

Above **Minoan fleet (c. 1500 B.C.).** After the first Minoan civilization was destroyed, a new Minoan race began, said to be the children of the Argonauts and the women of Lemnos.

Below **Minoan river landscape.** The disappearance of the first Minoan civilization may have inspired the Atlantis myth.

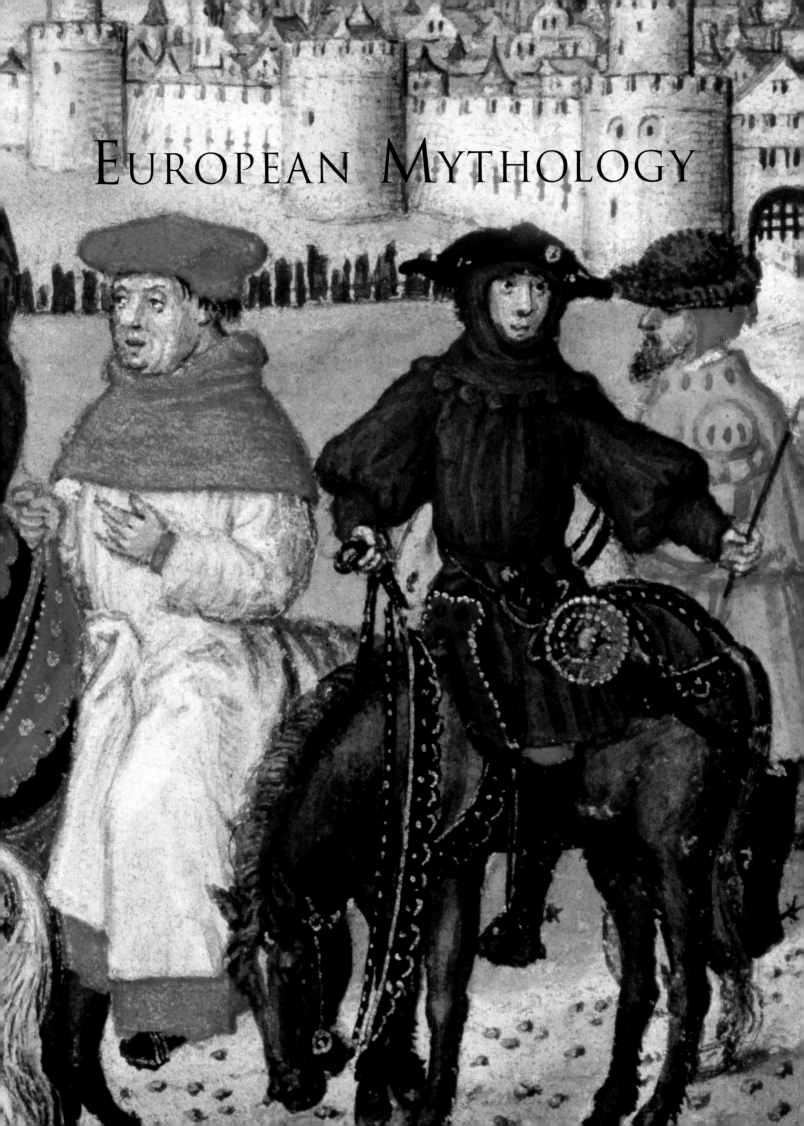

EUROPEAN MYTHOLOGY

CELTIC AND IRISH MYTHOLOGY

Above *Ossian's Lament* by K. Kisfaludy (1788–1830). This painting was inspired by *The Tale of Ossian* from the third century A.D. These stories by the warrior and poet Oisin recount the exploits of his father, Finn MacCool, and the Fianna.

Right **Statue of a god with a lyre, from Paule Saint Symphorien, France.** One of the typical features of all Celtic peoples is their love of music, and people skilled in song and verse were highly valued.

Celtic-speaking peoples have ranged over much of Europe and Asia Minor over a period of more than 3,000 years—from 1400 B.C. to the present. By the sixth century B.C. they had spread from their probable homeland in what is now western and central Germany, across much of western and northern Europe and over into the United Kingdom and Ireland. By the end of the millennium, they had moved as far east as the Black Sea, the Ukraine, and western Turkey. Although of the same race, the Celts were made up of individual tribal groups and were not politically united.

The various language groups give us an outline of the different Celtic tribes, and the recorded Celtic languages may be divided into two categories: continental Celtic and insular Celtic. Continental Celtic, in possibly three or four different forms, was spoken by Celtic tribes across Europe: in central, north, and northwestern Iberia (now Spain and Portugal); in Gaul (France); in the valley of the Po, south of the Alps; and a possible fourth in the middle Danube valley.

Insular Celtic has been spoken in Britain, Ireland, and Brittany until the present. This language divides into two main branches: the Celtic that forms Welsh, Cornish, and Breton; and the Celtic spoken in Ireland, Scotland (highlands and islands), and the Isle of Man, off the English coast.

The Celts did not leave written records, unlike other ancient cultures such as the Egyptians or Greeks; instead, they preferred and valued an oral tradition of storytelling, and this has had an impact on how we form an understanding of them and their beliefs. What does exist of Celtic origin is largely restricted to Celtic inscriptions, coins, and place names, which can offer only a limited insight into their values and beliefs. In particular, little remains of the myths of the continental Celts, who most greatly felt the force of the Roman Empire. The insular Celtic myths are more intact, precisely because the Celtic culture remained alive to be recorded. Indeed, from Ireland, Scotland, and Wales, we have a rich store of related and interconnected myths and legends.

However, the majority of our knowledge of the ancient Celts comes from non-Celts, those conquering peoples who came into contact with the Celts as a consequence of either war or religion. These ancient writers, among whom are military opponents such as Julius Caesar (100–44 B.C.), left many records, much of which can be useful in drawing a fairly detailed picture of these long-ago people. Caesar noted that the Celts were brave in battle, some fighting naked, while the Greek Diodorus Siculus (*c.* 90–21 B.C.) gave the following description: "The Celts were tall of body, with rippling muscles, and white of skin, and their hair blond." The women "are not only like

IMPORTANT FEASTS OF THE CELTIC YEAR

The Celts celebrated four lunar festivals that marked important passages in the year.

Samhain, November 1, Celtic New Year. Samhain, or "end of summer," coincides with Halloween and the slaughter of stock before winter. Rituals are conducted in honor of the the dead as well as to seek protection from them over the harsh months of winter.

Imbolc, February 1, Brigid's Feast. Little is known about Imbolc, however, it probably included rituals that centered on the ewes coming into milk, heralding the arrival of spring. This later became St. Brigid's festival.

Beltane, May 1, Belinus, the God of Fire. This feast included rituals such as the driving of animals, especially cows, between two fires, suggesting it may have been connected with purification and rebirth rituals. Its timing marks the beginning of summer.

Lughnasa, August 1, Anticipation of the Harvest. The Lughnasa feast in Ireland was a harvest feast, and the rituals appear to have centered on the marriage between the earth goddess and the sun god Lugh. Many contests of skill and strength took place and betrothals were made at this time.

the men in their great stature but they are a match for them in courage as well."

Taken together, these early writings suggest a society that was essentially tribal, each tribe being led by a chief or king. The society was divided into nobles (who had horses), druids (priests), bards who told memorable tales, commoners or freemen, and slaves. Women, at least the aristocratic ones, seem to have played an active part in society. While the tribes were fiercely independent, to the degree where it appears that much of their time was spent in battle with each other, a number of common features can be discerned. Chief among them is a great love of story, decoration, and of music. In these areas their talented bards excelled, creating a universe of mighty warriors, powerful gods, headstrong women, shape-changers, wailing banshees, and leprechauns.

CELTIC BELIEFS AND RITUALS

Though the names of deities appear in the surviving myths, we know few details about the actual forms of worship followed. The druids were wise men and philosophers, extremely learned, who also divined future events from a variety of sources. Animals were sacrificed throughout Celtic regions, as was done elsewhere in the world. Human sacrifice is thought to be a part of their rituals, which is supported by the recovery of bodies of executed people from European and insular bogs. European archaeological evidence, as well as Irish and Welsh myths, indicate headhunting in war, where victims were decapitated and the heads kept as trophies and parts of shrines.

Of Celtic origin is the terrible wicker man—a huge construction of woven branches in the form of a human being, which contained prisoners who were then burnt alive. Julius Caesar wrote of this practice, as did others, though their comments were often only hearsay. Not much is really known, and hints about it in the myths may be more symbolic than actual.

Left *Human Sacrifice* by Stephen Reid (1873–1948). A Celtic mother sacrifices her child under the watchful eye of a druid, trusting that the gods will bestow milk and corn in exchange. Celtic sacrifice has caused much debate, though human remains seem to support the idea. The Lindow Man, recovered from a bog, from the second century B.C., was killed in a three-step process: strangled, hit on the head, then throat cut. This may have been ritual sacrifice or execution.

THE CELTIC COSMOS

Celtic peoples over time and place appear to have had many gods, and there is evidence for over 360 names of gods across the Celtic world, but only around 20 or so appear more than once. These include names like: Lugos, Cernunnos, Esus, Sequana, Brigantia, Epona, and Matrona. However, as many Celtic gods had a variety of names, many of the gods may be one and the same. Our knowledge is sometimes sketchy: duties for the male gods included war, oratory, and the youthful savior. Female roles were related to the earth and fertility, and included the earth mother, as well as goddesses of springs, lands, and the tree fruit. These deities existed side by side with people and were very real. It was not a case of the gods being worshipped so much as that they were present and had to be respected.

Only two gods can be identified almost everywhere: the god Lugos (Irish Lugh, Welsh Llew), whose name we find from Germany to Spain and probably even further east, and the mother goddess Matrona (the Welsh Modron). She is also known as Noreia, Sequana, Brigantia, and, probably, also Eriu and Boand.

The Otherworld

The Celtic-speaking peoples appear to share a common view that there are several layers to reality: the ordinary world, and another reality where other beings exist that might easily erupt into everyday life. It is possible to cross from the ordinary world into the Otherworld, a feature seen in both Irish and Welsh myths, such as in legends of the hunt, where creatures and gods move freely from that world to this. The Otherworld could be a place where the dead live well, enjoying feasting and music, and where warriors live to fight again, or it could be a dark, somber, and dangerous place, especially for a human who visits it before death. Celtic stories often take great pleasure in this shifting reality, using animals and birds to indicate the supernatural.

The Celts and the Natural World

The Celts observed nature closely. Water was vital and there were specific springs, lakes, rivers, and bogs that were considered sacred. Animals such as horses, bulls, boars, and stags were worshipped variously for their speed, ferocity, fertility, courage, and beauty. The Celtic god, Cernunnos, is frequently pictured as having stag antlers. When they hunted, the Celts appear to have respected their prey, and the death of such animals required acts of propitiation.

The flights of birds were read by Celts and their druids to divine possible futures, and were also seen as an allegory of the human soul. Ravens and doves were listened to as voices telling of coming events. Water birds linked sky and water. In Welsh stories, the birds of the goddess Rhiannon lull the sick to sleep. Crows and ravens—considered scavengers—were associated with impending death.

In Celtic myths there is no impenetrable frontier between the human and the animal worlds. There is also a belief in the ability of humans to shape-change, or be transformed, into animals, and many Irish and Welsh myths involve people being transformed into animals, or animals dispensing wisdom to humans. Magic and shape-changing, often as much as bravery and valor, affect the outcome of Celtic stories.

Gods and Goddesses of the Insular Celts

The two branches of insular Celts—those peoples from Wales, Cornwall, and Brittany; and those from Ireland, Scotland, and the Isle of Man—believed that the gods and goddesses all descended from a mother goddess called Don in Welsh and Danu in Irish. The descendants were thus called the Children of Don in Wales and the Children of Danu (Tuatha De Danaan) in Ireland. Among the Children of Don were the sons Amaethon, god of agriculture; Gwydion, god of the arts; and Nudd. The only daughter was Arianrhod who, with Gwydion as the father, gives birth to Llew (Irish Lugh), known as "the Bright One."

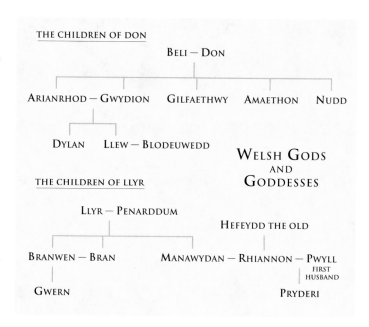

WELSH GODS AND GODDESSES

THE CHILDREN OF DON

BELI — DON

ARIANRHOD — GWYDION   GILFAETHWY   AMAETHON   NUDD

DYLAN   LLEW — BLODEUWEDD

THE CHILDREN OF LLYR

LLYR — PENARDDUM

HEFEYDD THE OLD

BRANWEN — BRAN   MANAWYDAN — RHIANNON — PWYLL
FIRST HUSBAND

GWERN   PRYDERI

Below **Mater (mother goddess), Gallo-Roman statuette, Alésia, France.** Many of the Celtic female deities were worshipped as mother goddesses, strong figures that were linked to areas such as fertility, fire, inspiration, and healing. They were also often active in war and could take the form of ravens, the sign of coming death.

In Welsh myth there are also the gods, possibly connected with the goddess Don, that are the descendants of the god Llyr, god of the sea and king of the ancient Britons. Llyr has two sons, Bran and Manawydan, as well as a daughter Branwen. These two male gods appear in Irish myth as Bron and the more familiar Manannan Mac Lir. While there are similarities between them, there is much that differs, and they are involved in different exploits.

WELSH MYTH

Existing Celtic myths come predominantly from Wales and Ireland. These oral stories were collected and written down in the Middle Ages by writers who were deeply influenced by Christianity. Hence, apart from the long delay in time, there is also the bias of the writers themselves to bear in mind.

Many of the Welsh myths come from a collection of stories known as the *Mabinogion*, which was given its name by Lady Charlotte Guest who translated what are essentially Welsh medieval stories between 1838 and 1849. These medieval tales come from two main sources, themselves collections of earlier stories: the *Red Book of Hergest,* a fourteenth-century manuscript kept at Jesus College, Oxford, in England; and the *White Book of Rhydderch,* an incomplete set of the tales, also from the fourteenth century. The stories were probably first drawn up in their present shape toward the end of the twelfth century, but the stories are of much greater antiquity, some belonging even to the time of Celtic paganism and to the period of unity between Wales and Brittany.

Lady Charlotte Guest's *Mabinogion* contains eleven tales in all, though the term applies really to just the first four, which recount the tales of the children of the Welsh gods Don and Llyr. The title derives from the Welsh word *mab* meaning "youth," and the tales of the gods' youthful exploits may have been be intended as instructive.

Early Sources of the Arthurian Legends

The second part of the *Mabinogion* includes four tales that feature King Arthur, and while they reveal more about medieval themes and concerns than they do pagan Celtic beliefs, they do shed some light on the ancient Celtic origins of those stories. These tales are also related to the well-known story of Tristan and Iseult, which connects Wales, Cornwall, Brittany, and Ireland, the remaining medieval sites of the Celtic speaking world. Tristan and Iseult is one of the great Celtic love stories, and it has parallels with Irish stories such as that of Deirdre and Naoise.

Above *Tristan Abducting Queen Iseult,* from *Le Roman de Tristan,* fifteenth-century manuscript. A love potion, intended for Iseult and her betrothed, King Mark, sets this tale on its tragic course when it is accidentally drunk by Iseult and Tristan. They separate, Tristan heading to France and marrying, but his heart remains faithful. Finally, he is fatally wounded and calls for Iseult. She comes but Tristan's jealous wife tells him otherwise. He dies grief-stricken, as does Iseult when she arrives. They are buried together and two trees grow from their graves, their branches forever intertwined.

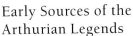

Left *Four Episodes in the Life of Tristan,* from *Le Roman de Tristan,* fifteenth-century manuscript. Though the tale is perhaps best known through the medieval Arthurian tales, it still retains some traces of its Celtic past, such as the use of a magic love potion. It may have its roots in the real-life figure of Drustan, son of Cunomorus, whose name is recorded on the famous "Tristan Stone," a sixth-century grave marker in Cornwall, England.

PWYLL IN THE OTHERWORLD

In Episode One of the story of Pwyll, told in the first book of the *Mabinogion*, Pwyll, Lord of Arberth and Prince of Dyfed, meets Arawn, Lord of Annwn (the Otherworld) one day when Pwyll was out hunting stags. Pwyll is about to take Arawn's kill when he is surrounded by Arawn's shining white hunting dogs with red ears—colors typical of Otherworld beings. Pwyll can redeem himself only by changing places with Arawn for a year, at the end of which he must fight and kill Arawn's Otherword enemy, Hofgun, if he is to return to his world. Arawn warns Pwyll to strike Hofgun only once because, if Hofgun is struck twice, he will recover and become stronger. Pwyll keeps his pledge and, at the appointed time, meets Hofgun. He deals Hofgun a mighty blow, and Hofgun pleads for Pwyll to finish the job. Pwyll resists and thus defeats Hofgun. Pwyll returns home, and from that time on is called Lord of the Otherworld. When he dies his son, Pryderi, maintains the family friendship with King Arawn of the Otherworld.

Pwyll and the Goddess Rhiannon

The second part of the story relates Pwyll's meeting with the goddess Rhiannon. While at the magical meeting place for his court, the Mound of Arberth, Pwyll spies a beautiful young woman dressed all in shining gold and riding a shining white horse. Pwyll is entranced and rides after her, but though her horse seems to move at a leisurely pace, and though Pwyll urges his horse forward, he cannot catch up with her. Pwyll calls to the shining woman who reveals herself as Rhiannon. The pair swear their love but she is betrothed to Gwawl. Only through trickery is Pwyll able to win her hand.

In the third year of her marriage to Pwyll, Rhiannon gives birth to a son, Pryderi, who is surrounded by supernatural mystery. When he reaches his first birthday he is stolen while his watchwomen are asleep. To avert blame, the women accuse Rhiannon of his murder.

The story then moves from the castle of Arberth to the house of Teynrnon Twyl Liant, Lord of Gwent Is-Coed. Teynrnon has determined to find out why, on every May eve, his mare has a foal, usually a fabulous colt, which disappears. Hiding in wait, he sees a giant claw seize the foal and drag it away. He hacks off the claw and finds a baby boy. Teynrnon and his wife decide to foster the child, who develops at such speed that after three years the boy is given the foal saved on the night he arrived. His foster parents note a strong resemblance to Pwyll and realize that the boy must really be Pryderi. The boy is then returned, to the great joy of Pwyll and Rhiannon.

GODDESSES OF THE HORSE

Horses were very important to the Celts, both practically and symbolically, who used them for riding from around 800 B.C. They also used horses to pull wagons and, more importantly perhaps, to pull their two-horse war chariots into battle against the Romans. The horse was revered for its beauty, speed, bravery, and sexual vigor. The nobles of Celtic society were linked with the horse, and legends suggest that kings were ritually wed to Epona, the greatest of the horse deities. Worshipped throughout Gaul, Epona was later adopted by the Roman cavalry. The Welsh goddess Rhiannon and the Irish Macha may also be some kind of horse goddesses.

Right **Epona, limestone statue, Alésia, France.** Epona is usually shown riding sidesaddle, and it was said that she rode with the soul of the dead on its final journey. The horn of plenty often accompanies her, symbolizing abundance.

BRANWEN AND BRAN

Matholwch, the King of Ireland, seeks the hand of the lovely Welsh Branwen, daughter of Llyr, king of Briton. Her brother Bran agrees, and the wedding takes place at his court. However, Efnisien, a half-brother on her mother's side, objects to the marriage and during the wedding festivities, mutilates Matholwch's horses while they are stabled at the court. Bran attempts to appease Matholwch by presenting him with various gifts, the greatest of which is a magic cauldron that was made in Ireland. Its power is such that it can revive dead warriors, though without the power of speech.

Matholwch accepts the offer, and he and Branwen sail to Ireland, but he resents his treatment in Wales and he treats his new queen like a servant, making her work in the kitchens where she is roughly treated by the butcher.

In desperation, Branwen trains a starling to carry a message back to Bran, who immediately sets out to attack Ireland and avenge his sister. An enormous man, he wades across the Irish Sea, appearing to the Irish as a mountain coming toward them. The Irish position themselves behind an impassable river and destroy the bridge. Bran, however, lies down across the river and his army advance to the other side, soon defeating Matholwch's army.

Peace follows, but it doesn't last. When fighting breaks out again, once more partly due to the actions of Efnisien, Bran is wounded by a poisoned spear and only seven of his men survive. He commands the men, who include Pryderi of Dyfed and Manawydan, his brother, to cut off his head and carry it around the country, before burying it in London at the White Mount, facing east, guarding against foreign invasion of Britain. The journey to London is a wondrous saga in itself, taking 87 years. The head remains alive and telling of wonders, until its final interment.

Meanwhile, Branwen dies of a broken heart at Aber Alaw, lamenting that through her, the two great islands are at odds with each other.

Left **Celtic stone head, from Dorset, England.** The head was regarded by the Celts as the center of spiritual power, and images of the head in art had a protective function. In the story of Branwen and Bran, the wounded leader puts his people first, instructing that his head be cut off and buried facing France. As long as it remains there, Britain will be safe from attack.

MANAWYDAN AP LLYR AND THE ENCHANTING OF DYFED

The third book of the *Mabinogion* is set after Pwyll's death. When Pryderi and Manawydan return from burying Bran's head in London, Manawydan marries Pwyll's widow, Rhiannon. With Pryderi and his wife Cigfa, Rhiannon and Manawydan go to Gorsedd Arberth in Dyfed. Although unharmed themselves because they are on the magic Mound of Arberth, the four see Dyfed fall under enchantment: all the inhabitants and houses vanish, and the countryside is covered in a magical mist.

With nothing left in Dyfed, the four are forced to head to England where Manawydan and Pryderi set up as skilled craftsmen making saddles and shoes. Wherever they go, the skills of Manawydan incite the envy and malice of the local craftsmen, so the four

And by force of strength, fierceness, and by the magic of Gwydion, Pryderi was slain.

LADY CHARLOTTE GUEST (1812–1895)
THE *MABINOGION*

return to Dyfed where they make a living by hunting. On one hunting expedition, Manawydan and Pryderi encounter a huge boar, dazzling white (a sure sign that it comes from the Otherworld).

The boar lures their dogs toward a strange castle. Despite Manawydan's warnings, Pryderi follows the dogs to the castle. He sees a golden bowl and touches it, then becomes fixed to the spot and is struck dumb. Rhiannon follows Pryderi and she also suffers a similar fate.

Manawydan and Cigfa, bereft of their families, and without hunting dogs, turn to wheat growing. The crops flourish, but just before harvest two fields are destroyed by armies of mice. Manawydan lies in wait for them when they come to waste the third field. All but one, a pregnant mouse, escapes. Manawydan sets about hanging this mouse, despite the pleas of passersby. Finally a bishop interrupts the proceedings and tries to redeem the mouse.

Manawydan has recognized the bishop as a fellow magician, and refuses to yield until Rhiannon and Pryderi are restored and the 700 farmsteads of Dyfed are released from the enchantment. The bishop then reveals himself to be Llwyd. He claims that he cast the spell over Dyfed to avenge the wrong done by Pwyll to Gwawl, Rhiannon's first suitor, when Pwyll married Rhiannon and took her from him.

The pregnant mouse is really Llwyd's wife. She and her women were transformed into mice and sent to destroy Manawydan's wheat. Manawydan's magic proves stronger, however; Dyfed is restored, and the mice return to human form.

MATH AND HIS TWO NEPHEWS

The convoluted story of Math Ap Mathonwy, Lord of Gwynedd in the North, forms the fourth book of the *Mabinogion*. As with many of these tales, it involves deception and magic, and slips easily back and forth between this and the Otherworld; it is a magical tale, in which the wrong are punished, but only just.

When Math, a magician, is not out surveying his lands or at war, he has to set his feet in the lap of a virgin. His two nephews, sons of the goddess Don, Gilfaethwy and Gwydion, desire the virgin footholder, whose name is Goewin.

The brothers, who have been trained in the art of magic by Math himself, plan to distract their uncle by starting a war with Pryderi, Lord of Dyfed in the South. Gwydion tricks Pryderi out of his magic white pigs and, as planned, war breaks out between the towns Gwynedd and Dyfed. While Math is at war,

Below *Rabbits, Hare, Boar, and Mouse* from *Bestiary*, manuscript, *c.* A.D. 1300. As with objects with magical properties, animals in the Celtic world were often more than what they at first seemed. In the hunt, they can be understood as symbolizing the search for wisdom, particularly in their capacity to connect with the Otherworld.

The Birth of Llew Llaw Gyffes, the Bright One

Arianrhod, the sister of Gwydion and Gilfaethwy, applies to Math for the vacant position of virgin footholder. She fails the purity test, however, giving birth to two sons when she steps over Math's magic staff. Arianrhod curses the second boy three times: he shall have no name unless she agrees to name him; he will bear no arms unless she gives them to him; and he shall have no mortal wife.

Gwydion takes pity on the boy—some stories suggest he is the boy's father—and, disguising himself and the boy as cobblers, Gwydion tricks Arianrhod into giving the cursed son a name: Llew Llaw Gyffes ("the bright one of the skillful hand"). He next tricks her into arming him, then Math and Gwydion conjure a wife for Llew—a beautiful, mystical creature created from flowers of meadowsweet, broom, and oak. She is called Blodeuwedd ("woman made from flowers").

Despite his beginnings, Llew is charmed. He cannot be killed inside or outside of doors, not on land or water, neither clothed or unclothed. Only a spear made at a time when work is forbidden can kill him.

The Faithless Wife

Blodeuwedd, born without roots, is faithless. She takes Gronw Pebyr as her lover and they plot to kill Llew. Blodeuwedd first finds out how the spear can be made and contrives to have Llew reveal how he may be killed. When Llew shows her, the hidden Gronw spears him. Llew is transformed into an eagle and flies into an oak tree.

Here Gwydion finds him and entices him through song back to earth where he restores Llew to human form. Blodeuwedd, in contrast, is turned into an owl, shunned by other birds and forced to hunt by night.

the brothers rape Goewin, then return to the battle-field. Gwydion next kills Pryderi, by using his magic.

When Math returns, his anger at discovering their treatment of Goewin leads him to punish the two brothers. For three consecutive years he turns them into pairs of animals: a stag and a hind; a boar and a sow; a wolf and a she-wolf, forcing them to take on their nature. The brothers alternate between male and female each time, and every year they produce an animal offspring. At the end of this time, Math forgives the brothers and restores them and the off-spring to human form, but they retain animal names.

Left **Blodeuwedd and Gronw Pebyr** *by Ernest Wallcousins*. Though the wife of Llew, Blodeuwedd asks Gronw Pebyr into her home, forming the classic Welsh three-sided affair. The two plot to kill Llew but this is not easy: some versions say Llew can only be killed at twilight, draped in a fish net, with one foot on a cauldron of water and the other on a goat, and only with a specially made spear.

Below **Boar-shaped votive figure, first century B.C.** Like many animals in Celtic mythology, the boar can act as an agent of the Otherworld. As befits an animals of great strength, dreams that feature boars are usually connected with warriors. In some tales, boars can be eaten, to be magically reborn.

CULHWCH'S IMPOSSIBLE TASKS

One of the most popular tales from the *Mabinogion* concerns Culhwch and Olwen. Culhwch is of royal blood, indeed he is the cousin of Arthur. His birth is unusual: before he was born, his mother, Golenddyd, developed a violent antipathy to pigs. While passing a herd of pigs she is frightened by them and gives birth to a child whom she abandons. A swineherd later restores him to his parents.

Golenddyd dies and her husband Cilydd remarries. The new wife has a daughter whom she wishes Culhwch to marry. But he demurs, claiming that he is too young. The queen curses Culhwch, proclaiming that the only woman he will ever marry is Olwen, daughter of Ysbaddeden, the Chief Giant. On hearing her name, Culhwch falls passionately in love with her.

Culhwch decides to ask Arthur for help in finding this maiden. He leaves in great splendor, fully armed with battle ax, golden sword, and a hatchet that "can make the air bleed." He has an ivory horn, two gray hounds, and is mounted on a great horse.

When Culhwch reaches Arthur's court the gate-keeper attempts to stop his entry. Culhwch threatens to utter three shouts that will make women barren and the pregnant abort. He duly passes and meets Arthur, who is persuaded to help him in his search for Olwen. Scouts search for a year, with no luck. Eventually, they assemble a team of the best knights, each blessed with remarkable traits. They include Kay, whose sword gives wounds no doctor can heal;

Bedwyr, the swiftest of all knights, and Gwalchmai, who never returned from a quest with it unfulfilled. After more searching, Olwen is finally found.

She returns Culhwch's love but explains that her father Ysbaddeden is fated to die when she marries. Olwen advises Culhwch to accept without complaint any demands that Ysbaddeden may make of him.

Culhwch approaches the Chief Giant and is given a long series of "impossible tasks." The most daunting of these is the recovery of the scissors, razor, and comb from between the ears of the great destructive boar Twrch Trwyth. However, Culhwch accepts all the tasks willingly.

Culhwch and Arthur further enlist the help of Mabon, the hunter who has been kept prisoner in a castle after being stolen from his mother, Modron. By the time he is freed, he is called "the young," although he is the oldest of all creatures.

Mabon, Culhwch, and the knights are helped by magical animals: the Eagle of Gwernabwy, the Blackbird of Kilgory, the Stag of Rhedynvre, the Salmon of Llyn Law, and other enchanted beasts. One of Arthur's men, Gwrhyr, can speak to each in its own language. After a long pursuit through South Wales, Cornwall, and Ireland, in which the evil boar lays waste to much of the land, and with Mabon's help, Twrch Trwyth is finally overcome and driven into the sea. The razor, scissors, and comb are delivered and Culhwch and Olwen finally marry.

IRISH CELTS AND THE TUATHA DE DANAAN

It is not known when the Celts came into Ireland. Although they have beliefs in common with other Celtic peoples, and their mythology has various similarities with Welsh myths, there are also many variations. Many of the myths come from manuscripts transcribed by monks in the twelfth century, such as the *Book of Leinster* (A.D. 1150), although various myths are mentioned in an eighth-century manuscript known as the *Book of Dun Cow* (supposedly because the fabric it is written on actually came from St. Ciaran's cow). The myths themselves are surely much older.

The story of the Tuatha De Danaan is the foundation myth of Irish lore. Meaning "the tribe or children of the goddess Danu," the Tuatha were a beautiful, golden-haired, godlike race—people of the light—who came down to earth from the heavens on a cloud. Their horses were sleek and fleet-footed, decorated in gold and silver. They were said to be descendants of the great mother goddess Danu (also known as Anu or Aine), whose two chief consorts were Echdae, the sky horse, and Manannan, a god of the sea.

There were three levels in Tuatha society, each having different functions: the chiefs (*tuatach*), the gods (*de*), and the gifted people (*dan*), which included healers, artists, and druids.

THE DAGDA

The Dagda, which means "the good god," was the son of the goddess Danu and a major personage of the Tuatha De Danaan. A great and benign patriarch, he was the Lord of Perfect Knowledge. He is associated with feasting and sexuality—important attributes of a chieftain. He was romantically linked with the gentle Boann, goddess of the sacred River Boyne in Ireland, as well as the fiery war goddess Morrigan, who he coupled with each year at Samhain.

There are three magical objects associated with the Dagda: an enchanted club that had powers of both destruction and restoration; a harp that could play wonderful melodies by itself; and a cauldron that produced a never-ending supply of food, and was so large that it needed a chariot to transport it.

In the second of the Tuatha De Danaan's three earthly battles, it is told how the Fomorians, enemies of the Tuatha De Danaan, forced the Dagda to consume a gigantic bowl of porridge, threatening to kill him if he did not finish it. The porridge was enough to feed an army, and even contained live sheep and goats—not even Dagda's cauldron could contain it. But his legendary appetite was so gargantuan that not only did he eat the entire meal, he made love with a young woman afterward.

When the Tuatha were forced underground by the Milesians, the Dagda settled his people into *sidhe*, or "fairy mounds." As befitting a god of his stature, his home became the large burial mound at Newgrange in the Boyne Valley. At the winter solstice, a beam of light shines through the main passage of the tomb.

> *I hope to make the old stories as familiar to Irishmen at any rate as are the stories of King Arthur and his Knights to all readers of books.*
>
> W.B. YEATS (1865–1939)

Above **Exterior of the megalithic passage tomb, c. 3000 B.C., Newgrange, County Meath, Ireland.** This mound is said to be one of four underground palaces of the Dagda, mighty ruler of the Tuatha. An all-powerful figure, his titles include Earth God, God of Magic, and High Druid. At the same time, however, he is often shown as a rotund figure dressed in a short tunic that exposes his buttocks.

Right **Head of a female deity, first century A.D., France.** This bronze figure is thought to be Brigid, a Celtic goddess now mixed with the story of St. Brigid. The goddess's name means "fiery arrow," and her cult is associated with fire.

Below **The Fort of Dun Aengus on the Isle of Inishmore.** Dating from the first to the fifth century A.D., this fort is said to have been built by the Fir Bolg. The stones at the front are part of a defensive ring, intended to slow down and hamper attackers once they were in slingshot range.

NUADA AND THE FIRST BATTLE OF MAG TUIREADH

The Tuatha fought three major battles during their time above the ground. The first was the Battle of Mag Tuireadh (also known as Moytura, the plain of the towers), fought against the Fir Bolg for control of Ireland, and is said to have taken place in today's Connemara region of County Galway. The Fir Bolg, or "bag men," were slaves that had come from Greece and who were forced to carry bags of soil. The bags were made into boats that brought them to Ireland. These people were dullwitted and no match for their brilliant rivals, the Tuatha De Danaan, who quickly forced them into retreat.

Nuada was the Tuatha De Danaan king who led the battle against the Fir Bolg. Though owner of a magic sword, Nuada's arm was severed during the battle and the kingship went to Bres. This was in keeping with Tuatha law, which stated that a king must have no physical flaws. But Bres was an unpopular monarch, partly due to the fact that he had Fomorian blood, and also because he demanded heavy taxes and was not very sympathetic to bards and harpers.

Bres did not stay ruler for very long, however. Nuada enlisted the help of Dian Cecht, the god of healing, who fashioned an arm out of silver for the king, thus restoring him to health and to the throne. He was given the name Nuada Airget-Lam, or "Nuada of the silver arm." Dian Cecht's skills in herbal medicine also helped many warriors wounded in the battle. After the Fir Bolg were defeated, the Tuatha banished them to the Aran Islands off Galway.

LUGH AND THE SECOND BATTLE OF THE MAG TUIREADH

In this second battle, so central to Irish mythology, the Tuatha De Danaan struggled yet again for control of the land, this time against the fearsome forces of the Fomorians. The Fomorians are often depicted as one-legged, one-armed, ugly sea monsters, and they were indeed malicious and grotesque.

The ruler of the Fomorians was Balor, a repulsive Cyclops with an evil eye whose mere look would kill anyone who gazed upon him—a fate which befell Nuada, the Tuatha king. When Nuada died, the leadership fell to the celebrated Lugh.

Lugh, the Bright One, was a sun god lauded for his many talents. He was a craftsman, musician, poet, sorcerer, and warrior. He was also, it turned out, the grandson of the evil Fomorian Balor. Before Lugh's birth it had been prophesied that Balor would be killed by his grandson. Balor tried to get rid of Lugh, without success, however, because the sun god was protected by powerful magic.

After Nuada's death, Lugh took it upon himself to slay the evil-eyed monster. As Balor was falling asleep,

Lugh attacked him with a stone from an enchanted slingshot, shooting it with such force that it drove the monster's eye out of the back of his head, thus turning his evil gaze toward his own army. Balor was killed, and the Fomorians returned to the sea. Lugh was given the title Lugh Lamfhada ("Lugh of the long arm"), and the summer harvest festival Lughnasa (August 1) is named in his honor.

Morrigan, the war and fertility goddess, assisted the Tuatha De Danaan in their battles against both the Fir Bolg and the Fomorians, taking up arms, or transforming herself into a raven or crow to startle the enemy.

DEFEAT OF THE TUATHA DE DANAAN

The third and final battle of the Tuatha was heralded by the arrival of the Milesians on the southwest coast of Ireland on the feast of Beltane in 1000 B.C. Also known as the Sons of Mil, they came from Spain, and were said to be the descendants of the biblical Noah and ancestors of the present-day Irish. They are also attributed with naming the country Eriu.

When the Tuatha De Danaan saw the Milesians approaching the coastline of Ireland, they sent a magic wind in an attempt to drive them away. However, the Milesians had their own vital magic, in the form of the poet Amhairghin, who calmed the wind with his chanting so that the invaders were able to land. He sang:

I am an estuary into the sea.
I am a wave of the ocean.
I am the sound of the sea.
I am a powerful ox.
I am a hawk on a cliff.
I am a dewdrop in the sun.

BRIGID: GODDESS AND SAINT

Brigid (or Brigit), meaning "greatness," was the daughter of the Dagda, the good god of the Tuatha De Danaan. She was also the wife of Bres, who ruled over the Tuatha De Danaan after Nuada's injury. Because Brigid's virtues and skills were so many and varied (she was the patron of poetry, fertility, healing, and childbirth), it is thought that she may even be an aspect of the Great Mother deity Danu. Her dedicated festival is Imbolc, the lambing time when ewes' milk comes in, signifying nourishment and the end of winter.

With the arrival of Christianity, many qualities of the goddess were attributed to St. Brigid who, along with St. Patrick and St. Kevin, is one of Ireland's best-loved saints. St. Brigid founded a convent in Kildare in the sixth century A.D., and was renowned for her hospitality and great kindness to the poor. Her feast day on the Christian calendar is February 1, which coincides with Imbolc. Both Celtic goddess and Christian saint are associated with purification by fire, and are the keepers of the flame.

Above *A Banshee from Dictionnaire Infernal by C. de Plancy (1794–1881).* The banshee, as a portent of coming death, has a long history in Irish folklore. In an eighth-century poem, the goddess Morrigan is depicted washing the entrails of the soon-to-be dead. It is believed that if a banshee is caught, she will divulge the name of the doomed person.

Right *Cuchulainn Carries Ferdiad Across the River* by Ernest Wallcousins. According to legend, the valiant Ferdiad was forced by Medb to wage battle with his foster-brother Cuchulainn. For three days they fought until the magic spear of Cuchulainn ended the battle. Grief-stricken, he carried his friend back to the Ulster camp rather than leave him with Medb.

At the battle of Teltown in County Meath, the Milesians defeated the Tuatha De Danaan with their great iron weapons. Not intending to go down without a fight, however, the Tuatha cast a spell, destroying the Milesians' crops. The Milesians were so impressed by the Tuatha's magical prowess, however, that they came to an arrangement. They allowed the people of Danu to go beneath the earth and occupy the hillocks and mounds (*sidhe*). Other Tuatha migrated to Tir Na Nog, the land of eternal youth.

Still others were changed into banshee (the *bean sidhe* or "woman of the fairies"). The banshee can manifest itself as a fair young maiden or as an old hag—both having long flowing tresses and eyes red from crying. The appearance of the banshee is always a frightening occurrence, as it takes place just before someone's death, accompanied by lamenting and wailing in a strange language.

The talented and handsome sun god Lugh went underground and became a craftsman, and was called "little stooping Lugh," or Luchorpain. His companions became known as leprechauns and are depicted in popular folklore as tricksters, shoemakers, and the keepers of hidden treasure and pots of gold.

And so the powerful and magnificent Tuatha De Danaan became the fairy folk of Irish mythology, occasionally making brief sojourns above ground at such times when the veil between the Otherworld and the ordinary world was lifted, such as at Samhain and Beltane.

CUCHULAINN: HERO AND WARRIOR

Cuchulainn is perhaps the best-known and loved of all the ancient Irish heroes. Belonging to the Ulster Cycle of stories, Cuchulainn is the archetypal Celtic tribal leader. He was conceived from an Otherworldly affair between the sun god Lugh and Dechtire, said to be the daughter of the druid Cathbad or of the chieftain Conchobar. At Cuchulainn's birth, it was predicted that his life would not be long.

From the time he was a small child, Cuchulainn was charismatic, handsome, and courageous. He was first given the name of Setanta, meaning small, but he became known as Cuchulainn (Hound of Culann) after he killed the vicious dog belonging to Culann, the local smith, at the tender age of seven. He then took over the duty of guarding Culann's property.

Cuchulainn was sent to learn military skills under the tutelage of Scathach, the famed warrior woman on the Isle of Skye. And Scathach was an extremely generous mentor. Not only did she give Cuchulainn the *gae bolga,* an enchanted javelin, she also sent her daughter Uathach to train him in the art of love.

When Cuchulainn went into battle, his mind and body would undergo a dramatic transformation that was known as "battle frenzy" or "warp spasm." His limbs contorted, his face became like a bright red

Right *Macha Curses all Ulstermen* by **Stephen Reid (1873–1948).** Macha embodied the apparent opposites of earth mother and slaughterer of men. She was one of the three war goddesses, and warriors drew their inspiration from this formidable creature.

bowl, one eye was sucked back into his head while the other protruded, and a fountain of red-black blood came out of his head. When he was in this altered state, he was unable to tell friend from enemy and his battle cry was so shrill and discordant it would send people mad. Only by being dipped three times into a vat of water could he be calmed.

Lover and Father

As well as having a reputation as a fierce warrior, Cuchulainn was known to have an extremely powerful effect on women. Emer, the woman who would become his long-suffering and jealous wife, would only marry him if he first proved himself as a warrior, and could perform certain superhuman tasks, such as stay awake for an entire year. Cuchulainn succeeded, won the heart of Emer, and was married.

When Cuchulainn was apprenticed to Scathach, she enlisted his help in fighting her rival Aoife, a fierce warrior from the land of shadows. Cuchulainn conquered Aoife as well as her heart, and when he left her she discovered herself pregnant. About 15 years later, a fiery-tempered youth named Connla arrived in Ulster and challenged Cuchulainn to a fight. After Cuchulainn killed the boy with his javelin, he noticed that Connla was wearing the gold ring that he had given Aoife years before, and realized, too late, that Connla was his son.

Cuchulainn also fell in love with Fand, the beautiful fairy woman who was married to Manannan Mac Lir. When Emer and Mac Lir discovered the infidelity, they arranged for a druid to wave a magical cloak between the pair so that they would never see each other again. Cuchulainn was heart-broken, but Emer had the druid give Cuchulainn a potion of forgetfulness that destroyed all memory of Fand.

Right *Macha Curses all Ulstermen* by **Stephen Reid (1873–1948).** Macha embodied the apparent opposites of earth mother and slaughterer of men. She was one of the three war goddesses, and warriors drew their inspiration from this formidable creature.

WARRIOR GODDESSES

The three Celtic warrior goddesses—Badb, Macha, and Morrigan—are all aspects of the triple goddess "The Morrigana" (the great queens). These goddesses of both war and regeneration are inextricably linked to the Cuchulainn story.

Badb appears either as a wild, red-haired woman or as a crow. In either guise, she is a harbinger of death, and a terrifying presence on the battlefield.

Macha is the archetypal fertility goddess and sorceress. Her mortal husband Crunnchu made a bet that his pregnant wife could win a race against the Ulster king's horses. The effort of winning the race brought on the birth of the twins, and she cursed all Ulstermen: at their time of greatest need they would suffer labor pains. Their need arose during the Cattle Raid of Cooley, leaving Cuchulainn to fight alone.

Morrigan is the supreme sex and fertility goddess and oracle, and is strongly identified with the land. Because Cuchulainn rejected her amorous advances, she did not assist him in his final battle; rather she transformed herself into a crow and flew onto his shoulder at the time of his death.

The Cattle Raid of Cooley

Considered the grandest epic poem in the Irish language, The Cattle Raid of Cooley (*Tain Bo Cuailnge*) was written in the eighth century A.D. It tells the story of the greedy and manipulative goddess and warrior-queen Medb (Maeve) of Connacht and the heroic death of Cuchulainn against cowardly forces. Medb was obsessed with the desire to own the brown bull of Cooley, in order to upstage her husband Ailill, the owner of the great white-horned bull.

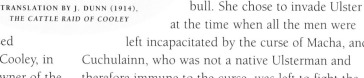

Dismay of battle riseth
For there was never found
One like unto Cuchulainn

TRANSLATION BY J. DUNN (1914),
THE CATTLE RAID OF COOLEY

Below *Finn Encounters Otherworldly Creatures* by Stephen Reid (1873–1948). Many of the exploits of the great warrior Finn are concerned with the Otherworld, and involve magic. A giant of a man, it is said that he built the Giant's Causeway as stepping stones to get to Scotland.

The brown bull was owned by the Ulster chieftain Daire, and Medb, who was famous for her powers of seduction, "extended him the friendship of her upper thighs" (so the epic goes) in exchange for the beast. Daire refused, and Medb summoned an army to help her steal the bull. She chose to invade Ulster at the time when all the men were left incapacitated by the curse of Macha, and Cuchulainn, who was not a native Ulsterman and therefore immune to the curse, was left to fight the mighty Medb single-handed.

Going into his battle frenzy, he was able to repel Medb's forces for some time until a fatal wound to the stomach finally overcame him. Cuchulainn fastened himself to a pillar stone so that he could remain upright and continue fighting. His death was signaled by crows landing on his shoulder.

FINN MACCOOL

The equally popular tale of Finn MacCool (Finn Mac Cumhaill) is part of the Fenian Cycle of myths that tells of the adventures of Finn and his son Oisin. (It is sometimes referred to as the Ossianic Cycle.) Finn was a great military leader, visionary, and poet but, unlike Cuchulainn, he was a wandering hero rather than a tribal leader. His father was the warrior Cumhaill and his mother, "Murna of the white neck," was a descendant of the godlike race, the Tuatha De Danaan.

Demne (which was the name Finn was first given as an infant) was sent away to be fostered by two wise warrior women to hide him from the man who murdered his father. Like Cuchulainn and other mythical heroes, Demne was a very gifted child, with a great understanding of the natural world. He was renamed Finn, meaning "fair" or "shining."

The Salmon of Knowledge

When Finn was a bit older, he was sent to continue his education with Finegas, a noted bard and wise man. For seven years, Finegas would go every day and patiently sit by the River Boyne, waiting for a certain salmon to appear. It was said that the person who caught and ate this special fish (who was known as Fintan) would receive the gift of second sight, and "nothing would remain unknown to him."

One day, a jubilant Finegas caught the salmon, a large orange and gold creature, and told his young apprentice to cook it while he went to collect more wood for the fire. Finegas gave strict instructions for Finn not to eat any of the fish because Finegas wanted the gifts all for himself.

Finn accidentally burned his thumb on the salmon and, in a reflex action, immediately put the thumb in his mouth, tasting the oil of the fish. The teacher was disappointed but philosophical, realizing that it must have been the young boy's destiny to eat of the salmon. From that time on, Finn would only have to put his thumb in his mouth to receive the wisdom. With this knowledge, Finn was now ready to fulfill his destiny and he set off to find the Fianna.

The Fianna

The Fianna was an elite band of mighty warriors that supported and protected the High King at the royal seat of Tara. Every year at Samhain (November 1), the underworld demon Aillen Mac Midna would wreak havoc on Tara, putting everyone to sleep with his enchanted music, then burning down the palace. The High King, Cormac MacAirt, was so tired of this annual occurrence that he asked for helpers to try to rid the palace of the demon. Finn MacCool accepted the challenge, but requested the leadership of the Fianna, the king's warriors, in return for killing the demon. Because Finn had magical weapons, he was able to resist the enchanted music, and beheaded Aillen with his spear. Cormac MacAirt granted Finn his wish, as agreed.

Under Finn's expert guidance, the Fianna grew in strength and excellence. His requirements were very stringent, and he demanded a high level of physical prowess, honor, chivalry, and literacy. It is thought that some aspects of the King Arthur and the Knights of the Round Table legend have been patterned on the Fianna. The modern-day Irish political party known as "Fianna Fail" has taken its name in honor of its ancient predecessor.

Sabd and Oisin

One day when Finn was out hunting, he came across a gentle doe. Finn's hounds did not attack her; rather they played with her very affectionately and Finn was rather bemused to find the doe following him home.

The next morning the doe had vanished and a beautiful maiden

greeted Finn instead. The young woman, called Sadb (Sava), was the granddaughter of the god Dagda, and she had been changed into a doe by an evil wizard. Finn's kindness and healing touch had transformed her back into her human state.

They fell in love, and lived together for many happy months. However, Finn was eventually called away on Fianna business, and when he returned a week later, Sadb had disappeared, lured away by the sorcerer.

After a long, fruitless search, Finn eventually gave up. Several years later, when hunting around Ben Bulben in County Sligo, he came across a strange little boy who had a tuft of deer hair on his forehead. Finn recognized the boy as his son. He named him Oisin ("little fawn") and the boy grew up to be a Fianna warrior and poet.

Above *Finn MacCool Aids the Fianna* by Stephen Reid (1873–1948). The Fianna was a military elite founded around 300 B.C., responsible for guarding the king. Before Finn was leader, they were unruly; he introduced a code of honor and made them into champions of the people.

Left *The Druid Warns Medb about Cuchulainn* by Stephen Reid (1873–1948). Medb used all her skills and magic to kill Cuchulainn. According to legend her own demise came at the hands of King Conchobar's son Furbaide, who hit her with a piece of cheese, flung with such force that it killed her.

TRAGIC LOVE STORIES

Among the saddest tales in Irish mythology are those of Deirdre of the Sorrows and of Diarmuid and Grainne. They share several common traits: both have strong magical components; they both tell of a love triangle between a beautiful woman and two men (one young and the other much older); and in both, the woman actively pursues the younger man, a noted characteristic of Celtic tales. But most of all, the stories are about the fragility of the human heart when denied true love, and the endurance of love beyond the grave.

Deirdre of the Sorrows

Written versions of the story date back to the ninth century. It is part of the Ulster Cycle and, as in the great Cuchulainn legend, it begins with a bleak prophecy from Cathbad, King Conchobar's chief druid. Before Deirdre was born, Cathbad predicted that she would be a great beauty, but would bring destruction to the king and to all of Ulster.

When the Ulstermen heard this prediction, they wanted the child destroyed at birth. But King Conchobar decided to let her live, raising Deirdre in a remote castle under his watchful eye, and planning to marry her as soon as she came of age.

When Deirdre grew up, she had a dream that she would fall in love with a man with hair as black as raven's wings and pale skin with rosy cheeks. She soon learned of a handsome, talented, young warrior known as Naoise who had those attributes. From her castle keep, she heard a man singing and was captivated by his voice. When she discovered that the singer was Naoise, she immediately decided that she would marry him.

DRUIDS

Druids were an intrinsic part of the religion, politics, and myths of Celtic Ireland. They were believed to have been descended from the Tuatha De Danaan, and therefore were afforded godlike status.

The responsibilities of the druid were many and varied. Depending on the situation, they could be called upon to act as priest, bard, healer, sorcerer, oracle, or sage, and serve as mediator between the physical world and the spirit realm. King Conchobar's druid, Cathbad, was skilled as a prophet, and the Tuatha sun god, Lugh, enlisted the help of a militaristic druid to defeat the Fomorians. As the holders of ancient lore, and the teachers of noblemen and bards, they controlled knowledge in the tribe.

Ceremonies were held in places of great natural beauty and energy (such as on the Hill of Tara) or in secluded groves. Druids had the power to cause storms or earthquakes and could predict the future, but they could not change the course of fate. To train as a druid was not to be taken lightly—it took 20 years to qualify.

Above *An Arch Druid* from *Costume of the British Isles* by Meyrich and Smith (1821). Mystery surrounded the druids and still does. The early Christians did their best to destroy their knowledge and power and, as the druids passed on their lore by word of mouth, little information survives that is not secondhand.

Although Naoise was captivated by Deirdre's wondrous charms, he was frightened off by the prophecies. His brothers Ainle and Ardan tried to dissuade him from Deirdre, but to no avail—she was a woman obsessed. Eventually Naoise and Deirdre married, and the couple, along with Ainle and Ardan, fled across the sea to Alba, now Scotland.

Because Naoise and his brothers were such excellent warriors, the Ulstermen convinced the king to grant them a pardon. Conchobar agreed, and the brothers were summoned back to Ireland. The night before their journey, Deirdre received a message in a dream that Conchobar's offer of peace was a false one, and pleaded with Naoise not to return. However, Naoise and his brothers chose to ignore her, and all three of them were killed on their return.

Deirdre became Conchobar's prisoner, and she never smiled again. One year later, while Deirdre and Conchobar were traveling in an open carriage, they passed by Naoise's tomb. Deirdre was inconsolable at the sight of it and, rather than continue her hateful life, she threw herself out of the carriage, smashing her head on a rock and killing herself. Two yew trees grew on that very spot, their branches becoming intertwined for eternity.

Diarmuid and Grainne

Grainne, the striking and spirited daughter of the High King Cormac MacAirt, was promised to the ageing leader of the Fianna warriors, Finn MacCool. At the couple's engagement feast, Grainne set eyes on Diarmuid, a young Fianna officer, and fell instantly and tragically in love.

Diarmuid's loyalties were with the Fianna, and he initially rejected Grainne's advances. Eventually he succumbed to her seductive powers, and the pair eloped. Finn was furious to have been so betrayed, and relentlessly pursued the lovers for many years. Several times when the Fianna were close to catching them, Diarmuid and Grainne were assisted in their flight by Aengus, a god of love and Diarmuid's foster father. He gave them a cloak of invisibility so they could avoid being caught by Finn, and Finn never saw them when he was chasing them.

Finn finally gave up the chase, and accepted the loss of Grainne. Diarmuid and Grainne made a home, but Diarmuid came to miss his friends from the Fianna. So, when Finn invited Diarmuid to join him in a boar hunt at Ben Bulben, as an apparent token of good will and forgiveness, Diarmuid accepted, even though he had been warned in his youth that

he would be killed by a boar. The prophecy proved true: Diarmuid was mortally wounded by the boar, and when Finn came across the dying man, he refused him a drink of water, even though he knew that, as he had the power of healing, it would have saved Diarmuid's life.

Grainne was heartbroken to have lost her true soul mate. But the magical Aengus came to their assistance again. He transported Diarmuid's body to an enchanted spot in the River Boyne, and there the unhappy lovers could communicate with one another.

Left **Stone votive offering, Alésia, France.** Although Celtic life revolved around the tribe, Irish tales are full of deeds by individuals, often in the name of love.

Below *A Farmer Rescues His Wife from Fairies* by Henry J. Ford (1860– 1941). The fairies of the Tuatha live in a blessed land, but do visit the world of mortals; they have been known to take humans back with them .

Right *St. Brendan the Navigator, c. A.D. 486–575.* This fifteenth-century woodcut is from *The Marvellous Adventures of St. Brendan and his Monks,* 1499, and legend puts St. Brendan in his seventies at the time of this voyage. The travelers encounter much on their trip including a siren and a whale with fire.

Below *Sailing with St. Brendan the Navigator,* manuscript, c. A.D. 1200. The story of St. Brendan harks back to that of Bran, which pre-dates the arrival of Christianity in Ireland. His story begins when a lady from mysterious lands appears in his yard though the ramparts are locked.

FANTASTIC VOYAGES

There is a genre in Irish mythology known as the imram story, which tells of perilous sea voyages to the mysterious "blessed islands," or to "phantom islands," thought to be located in the Atlantic Ocean west of Ireland. The tales of Bran and Mael Duin were subsumed into the Christian adventure of St. Brendan the Navigator, while the legend of Oisin, perhaps one of the most captivating of all, has inspired several plays, films, and poems.

The Voyage of Bran

One day Bran encountered a stunning, seductive woman who presented him with a silver bough laden with magnificent white blossoms. The woman told of her Otherworld home, the "island of women" (Tir Inna mBan), which was described as a true paradise:

endless food, endless love, a never-ending summer, and eternal youth.

Bran recruited a crew of 26 men and headed west in search of this enchanted isle. When he crossed a crystal bridge and arrived on the island, he found it was all that he had hoped it would be and much more; he became the lover of the beautiful goddess. There was only one catch: the goddess had put a spell on the men and warned that they could never return home.

For a year, everyone was happy. Then some of the men began to miss Ireland and their families, and persuaded Bran to take them back. When their ship was approaching Irish soil, the men on the boat began to wave eagerly, but no one on shore recognized them. In his excitement to be home, one man jumped ashore, and as soon as his feet touched the land, he crumbled into a pile of ashes. Bran and his remaining crew turned and headed west, never to return.

Mael Duin and the Amazing Islands

Mael Duin was the son of Ailill, a warrior who was brutally killed in battle. As soon as he was old enough, Mael Duin swore to avenge the untimely death of his father. A druid warned him that he would have to travel to an island far across the sea if he wanted to find the murderer.

The druid also warned him to carry only 18 men on the boat, and not a single person more, otherwise misfortune would occur. Mael Duin duly obeyed the druid's instructions. But just as he was departing, his three foster brothers climbed on board, determined to make the voyage.

After several days, the men neared the island home of Ailill's killer. But a ferocious storm blew the boat off its course and into the enchanted waters of the Otherworld, where they encountered many weird places and saw many wonderful creatures.

On one island there was a palace filled with food, drink, and precious jewels. One brother stole a necklace there, and was promptly destroyed by a giant magic cat. The second brother landed on the

island of his father's murderers. With all resentment and malice gone from his heart, Mael Duin made friends with the people there who, in turn, hailed him as an explorer and hero.

Oisin and the Land of Eternal Youth

Niamh of the Golden Hair was a lovely fairy woman and daughter of the sea god Manannan Mac Lir. She had heard good stories of the poet and warrior Oisin (son of Finn MacCool) and was drawn to earth to seek him out for her husband.

Niamh found Oisin hunting near misty Lough Leane, one of the lakes of Killarney. She enticed him into the lake, which was a portal into the Otherworld known as Tir Na Nog, "the land of eternal youth." Tir Na Nog was indeed a paradise: breathtakingly beautiful, alive with birds, color, and music, and where love was always fresh and new. Its inhabitants were blessed with eternal youth, oblivious to such concepts as time, rules, or work. The days fled, and Oisin led a blissful life with Niamh.

But as humans do, he became homesick—for his father, for the Fianna, and for Ireland—and told Niamh he wanted to go home. Niamh gave him a handsome white horse and told him he could return to Ireland, but under no circumstances should he get off the horse and set foot on the soil.

When Oisin arrived in Ireland, he discovered that 300 years had passed. Everyone he knew had departed, but what was even worse, all the old ways and beliefs had disappeared, and even the legendary deeds of Finn MacCool had become just a distant memory. Thus dispirited, he forgot Niamh's warning and dismounted. Immediately he became a withered, blind, and decrepit old man.

Some versions of the story say that St. Patrick found Oisin and took care of him, encouraging him to tell the stories of Finn and the days of old, which were recorded for posterity.

Isle of Weeping where he was forced to remain for all eternity crying. Then they visited the Isle of Women, where they were lured by dreams of immortality and love. Mael Duin enjoyed his stay there for a while, but eventually decided to head home. On the return journey, the last brother set foot on the Isle of Mirth where he still lives with the laughing folk to this day.

With the loss of his foster brothers, Mael Duin was back on course, and eventually came to the

Left *The Journey* by Stephen Reid (1873–1948). Niamh of the Golden Hair takes Oisin to her father's land. According to some versions of this story, the lovely Niamh had been watching Oisin for some time before approaching him. When they arrived at her land, she waved her hand and the mist parted to reveal a shining castle.

Above **Votive ship from Broighter, Derry, first century B.C.** This model represents a real ship, intended for the high seas. It was probably a votive offering, possibly to Manannan Mac Lir, King of the Sea, to ensure a safe voyage. He used mist to shroud his land and he gave the Tuatha the gift of invisibility and sanctuary in the underground mounds.

GERMANIC AND NORSE MYTHOLOGY

Below *Representation of the Valkyrie* from *The Ring Cycle* by Richard Wagner (1813–1883). Germanic mythological figures are perhaps best known to us today through much later works such as Wagner's operas, with the swooping Valkyries, or via Tolkein's stories. Early compilations of the oral traditions reveal a complex world of gods, giants, and heroes, pitted against each other and against the elements.

This section covers the mythologies and religious perceptions of the various Germanic tribes that emerged from the dark of prehistory in Northern Europe during the early Iron Age, that is, sometime before 500 B.C. The origins of these tribes is still a matter of scholarly discussion, but there were well-defined groups among them by the time they came into their first contact with the Roman Empire in the last centuries B.C. Among these tribes were the Angles, Saxons, Jutes, Danes, and Swedes in the north, the Franks in the northwest, the Suebi in the southwest, the Vandals in the northeast, and the

Lo now, Allfather, wouldst thou have me toil for ever, nor win the wages due?

ANON. VÖLSUNGA SAGA C. 1300

Goths in the east. They spoke different languages to each other and the tribes were not always a single group—each could be made up of smaller tribes.

The Alemanni, for example, probably belonged to, or broke away from, the Suebi, and their language, Alemanic, is the dialect of High German that is spoken in Swabia (from Suebi), which is Germany today.

During the course of the first millennium A.D., and especially as the Roman Empire weakened, the Germanic tribes—many of whom remained semi-nomadic—spread and settled large parts of Europe.

The Goths, who were divided into the Ostrogoths and Visigoths, moved south following the attacks of the Huns, eventually moving into Spain. The Franks moved into Gaul (France) and the Vandals moved south and west into Spain and then Africa, from where they sent an army to sack Rome in A.D. 455. The Saxons moved south and along the coast of Gaul, and eventually into Britannia (England). The Lombards, also from the north, moved through Hungary and Austria, and the Alemanni and Burgundians settled areas of central Europe. Thus, the Germanic peoples were spread from Iceland and Britain to Spain and west to the Black Sea.

Broadly speaking, the Germanic peoples were pagans who worshipped many gods, though little is known of their religion. Naturally, migrating over such an extensive area, their religions developed differently, depending on local experiences and also as a result of exposure to foreign influences (mainly pagan Roman and Christian, but also Slavonic and Celtic). Consequently, there does not appear to be a unified Germanic mythology. Except for a number of runic inscriptions or pictures on stones, writing as a means of recording historical events had not been developed. Their myths were instead passed down by oral tradition, especially by poets and minstrels, or *skalds* as they were known in the Scandinavian countries. Therefore, Germanic mythology, to a large degree, was recorded by others.

CHRISTIANITY AND ITS IMPACT

Christianity came to the various tribes at different times. By the time information about their beliefs was recorded, much had been lost as the tribes had dispersed or moved to new lands. The mostly Christian writers worked with fragments and local memory, and with a Christian interpretation that did not wish to show paganism in a favorable light.

While the Goths were already Christians in the fourth century A.D., the Germanic tribes to the very north remained somewhat isolated from the developments in central Europe, and retained more of their original mythology than elsewhere. The Old Norse peoples, today's Scandinavians—the countries of Denmark, Sweden, Norway, and Iceland—only converted to Christianity in the course of the tenth and eleventh centuries, with paganism being alive and well in Sweden as late as A.D. 1100.

This uneven development of the tribes, combined with varying contact with the other groups, means that the sources available for the myths are also very uneven in their quality and distribution. The richest sources of the traditions are preserved in the Norse corpus of works, especially in Icelandic works from the thirteenth century known as the poetic *Edda,* and the slightly later prose *Edda* written by Snorri Sturluson (1179–1241).

This Norse corpus of mythology is more uniform and extensive than that of both central and eastern Germany. Previously, most Scandinavians, like all the Germanic peoples, were polytheistic pagans who worshipped a variety of gods and goddesses, many of whom were familiar to all other Germanic tribes under different names. The best known of the Norse deities were Odin, Thor, Freyr, Freyia, and Niord; but although we know their names, as elsewhere, we have very little reliable information about how they were worshipped. Archaeological evidence of pagan activity exists, but much of it is very uncertain in its implications. Scandinavian place names sometimes

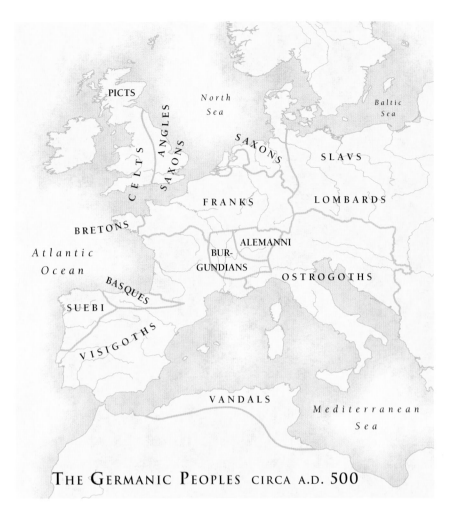

THE GERMANIC PEOPLES CIRCA A.D. 500

incorporate the names of pagan gods or goddesses, indicating their worship in parts of Scandinavia; but they tell us virtually nothing about pagan practices and rituals in any detail.

Later, from the thirteenth century onward, the Icelandic sagas in the two *Edda* contain retrospective accounts of pagan activity, but the late date of these sources—getting on for 300 years or so after Iceland's conversion to Christianity around A.D. 1000—means that their evidence cannot be relied upon too heavily. They bear the stamp of typical Icelandic storytelling through their medieval Christian authors, and these sources may give a picture of pagan mythology that is rather too systematic and learned, the stories reflecting literary rather than religious qualities. There is some evidence—including allusions in the preserved poems of pagan Norse poets of the ninth and tenth centuries, pictorial sources such as stone engravings and, very rarely, old runic inscriptions—that corroborate these medieval Icelandic stories, but some care is required when assessing their validity as sources for the wider Germanic pagan mythology.

Above **Principal Germanic peoples.** Incursions against the Romans by the Goths, Saxons, Franks, and others had been occurring since the third century A.D. This took on greater urgency with the arrivals of the Asiatic Huns around A.D. 350. By the fall of the Roman Empire 100 years later, various distinct Germanic empires had established themselves across Europe.

Left *The Gods of Northern Europe* from *Historia Gentibus Septentrionalibus* by Olaus Magnus (1490–1557). The three gods shown here are Frigg, the wife of Odin; Thor, their son; and Odin. Many of the different Germanic tribes believed in the same gods, despite their differences in geography and language.

SOURCES OF MYTH AND HISTORY

Most of the specific information scholars possess about Old Norse pagan mythology derives from a relatively small number of written sources. One is the collection of heroic and mythological poems that are known as the poetic *Edda*. This was compiled from various sources by unknown writers, probably sometime during the early thirteenth century. The second source is the prose *Edda*, written by the Icelandic politician Snorri Sturluson (1179–1241), a little after the poetic *Edda* was completed. Sturluson lived an adventurous life as a political leader, gaining great wealth and influence. His prose *Edda* is a guide to the conventions of traditional Icelandic poetic composition, written for the benefit of aspiring poets. Of its four parts, the two most important sources of mythological information and narratives are *Skaldskaparmal* (poetic diction) and *Gylfaginning*. In *Gylfaginning* a fictional king, Gylfi, goes in disguise to Asgard, the city of the gods, to find out about the gods and to learn all of their wisdom. Odin comes to King Gylfi in three guises and tells the history of the stories of the gods. Snorri Sturluson clearly drew heavily on the poetic *Edda* for some of the myths he records in his prose *Edda*.

Only occasionally are we given brief glimpses of Germanic mythological tales outside Scandinavia, but here too we must be aware that they were normally either written down by Roman authors with only limited knowledge of conditions in the Germanic areas, or else by Germanic authors who had converted to Christianity.

Tacitus

One of the most ancient references to Germanic myths is given by the Roman historian Gaius Cornelius Tacitus (who lived approximately A.D. 56–120). He wrote a brief ethnography of the Germanic peoples living outside the Roman Empire at that time, called *Germania*. The problem of recording another culture with only limited knowledge can be seen in his discussion of various goddesses.

In Chapter 9 of *Germania*, for example, Tacitus concludes that the Suebi venerated a goddess who was similar to the Egyptian goddess Isis because ships appeared to be a part of the ritual. This goddess is more likely Nehalennia, who was intensely venerated, especially by the Frisians in the third century (living mostly on the Frisian islands off the northwestern coast of Germany). Nehalennia is named on votive stones as far afield as Cologne, in western Germany. Some of the inscriptions explicitly mention her assistance in trading voyages, which depict her as a goddess of seafaring Frisian merchants. The Suebi lived far from the coast, and probably would have had very little to do with a goddess related to seafaring.

Tacitus, however, provided much other useful information, and this mention of the goddess, even if misleading, is valuable for its rarity.

GERMANIC CREATION MYTHS

One of the oldest references to Germanic myths is given by Tacitus. In his *Germania*, he mentions that in "ancient songs" the Germanic tribes celebrate the origin of mankind as going back to a certain "Tuisto, a god born from the earth, and his son Mannus, as the forefathers and founders of the nation. To Mannus they assign three sons, after whose names so many people are called: the Ingaevones, dwelling next to the ocean; the Herminones, in the middle country; and all the rest, Instaevones." That is, these three sons were seen as the forefathers of the principal Germanic peoples, living in the east, center, and west of northern Europe.

Although these mythical Germanic forebears are referred to only in Tacitus, the name "Mannus" clearly refers to Germanic "man." The Norse creation myth, as presented through sources like the two *Edda*, is different, though there are some similar concepts.

Right **Mannus, the First German King**, from *The Origin of the First Twelve Old Kings and Princes of the German Nation*, *1543*. According to the writings of Tacitus, Mannus is the father of the three German tribes: the Ingaevones, the Herminones, and the Instaevones. In popular oral tradition, the god Heimdall created the three classes of society after spending one night each with three different couples. The children borne from this union were slave, freeman, and noble.

Below **Yggdrasill, the Mundane Tree or World Tree.** The great tree of the world extends through all levels of the universe: the heavens, earth, and underworld. The Bifrost Bridge, which humans see as a rainbow, links the real and supernatural worlds. Near the roots of the tree dwell the *norns*—fate.

Old Norse Tales of the Cosmos

Unlike the myth of Tuisto and the first father of the middle Germanic tribes, as given by Tacitus, the origins of the cosmos, according to Norse stories, were supposed to lie in obscure but dynamic interactions between water, ice, and fire. A number of distinct subworlds were the result, many of them inhabited by specific types of being. The Norse sources do not, it is true, present an entirely consistent or systematic vision of the universe's structure, but some aspects of it are fairly clear. Midgard, conceived as a central landmass surrounded by sea, is where the gods and humankind live. Within it lies Asgard, the city of the gods, presided over by Odin, the lord of all the gods. Underneath it is the world of the dead, which is ruled by the goddess Hel. The giants have their own world, located rather vaguely on the fringes of the cosmos, perhaps beyond the encircling sea. Finally, dwarves live in the rocks and caves below the earth. All the various subworlds in the Norse myths are dominated by the world tree Yggdrasill, which towers over all while its roots are buried in each of the three worlds—Asgard, Midgard, and the Underworld.

As the various Old Norse myths explain it, the earliest of all living creatures were the giants. All beings came from the "protogiant" Ymir, who had a son, Buri, begotten by Ymir's two legs with each other, who in turn had a son called Burr. This son conceived three sons with a giantess, namely the gods Odin, Víli, and Vé. The gods evolved from them, and created the first man and woman from two logs that they found washed up on the shores of Midgard.

The body parts of the dead protogiant Ymir were used as the basis for the principal features of the universe: his blood became the sea, his cranium the round vault of the sky, his brains the clouds, and his bones the rocks.

Despite the difference in their names, the three descendants of the protogiant Ymir—Odin, Víli and Vé—appear to be the forefathers of the main tribes across the Germanic lands, as described in the Tuisto myth. This suggests common origins of the myth, especially as Odin is widely named as a mythical ancestor of the western Germanic tribes and of royal houses from Scandinavia to Britain and Lombardia. In the case of the three "peoples" Tacitus mentions, it may be possible to see links here, too. The ancestors of the Ingaevones may be identified in Scandinavian tradition as Yngvi, a name that is assigned to the god Freyr, who was the protector of the Swedish royal dynasty of the Ynglings.

Two Families of Gods

In this world created out of Ymir, there were two distinct families of gods, the Vanir and the Aesir. In the long-ago history of the universe they had fought each other, but by the time in which most of the myths are set their differences are forgotten and they live harmoniously together in the realm of Asgard. The chief members of the Vanir are Niord and his children—the goddess Freyia and her twin brother Freyr. All the Vanir are closely associated, in both religion and myth, with love, fertility, and material wealth. All the other most prominent deities—Odin, Thor, and Tyr—are Aesir, though the distinction between the two races is rarely noted in the sources.

Below *Hel, Daughter of Loki and Goddess of the Underworld* by Johannes Gehrts (1855–1921). It is said that Hel was born after Loki ate the heart of a giant witch known as Angerbotha. Hel was cast into the lowest level by Odin, to emerge again only at the final battle. Her hall was Elvidnir, or Misery, and her realm, Niflheim (Hel).

OF GODS AND GIANTS

The gods and the giants are traditional enemies, and many of the myths tell of skirmishes between them. Thor, with his hammer, is a warrior god, the enemy most feared by the giants. The myths state that one day this enmity will boil over into a final war, known as the Ragnarok. The whole universe will be destroyed in this war, along with most of its inhabitants. However, the sources hint at a new dawn: a few gods and men will survive and together they will begin the work of rebuilding and repopulating a better and more peaceful world.

A Giant Builder

The following story comes from that part of Snorri Sturluson's prose *Edda* called *Gylfaginning*, which refers to the tales told to King Gylfi on his visit to the city of Asgard. It illustrates the dishonesty of the gods in their dealings with the giants, and some see this moral flaw in divine society as leading ultimately to the gods' destruction at the Ragnarok.

The myth is set in an early part of the mythical past, after the gods have established Midgard, and built there the great hall Valhalla. A builder visits them and offers to make them a fortification that will be proof against attack by mountain giants and frost giants, even if they force entry into Midgard itself. As payment, he asks for the goddess Freyia as his wife, as well as the sun and the moon.

The gods accept, on the condition that he completes the work within a single winter without help from any man; otherwise he forfeits all payment. The builder agrees, but asks that his stallion Svadilfoeri be allowed to help him, and this is granted on the advice of the mischievous god Loki. The agreement is sealed with solemn oaths on both sides. The builder begins the work. Svadilfoeri, who works during the night hauling stones, has twice the builder's strength, and by the time summer approaches it looks as though the work will be finished on time. The gods now wake up to the terrifying prospect of losing not only Freyia, but also the sources of all light in the world. They

blame Loki for his bad advice and force him to devise a way of preventing the builder from finishing the job on schedule. Loki's solution to the problem is simple: he transforms himself into a mare. That very evening, as the stallion begins its work, he entices it away. The two horses disport themselves in the wood all night, and work on the fortifications is held up. The builder, faced with the loss of his fee, goes into a rage so terrifying that the gods realize that he is not really a man but a mountain giant. Forgetting their agreement, they summon Thor, who raises his hammer, Miollnir, and shatters the giant's skull. Thus the story ends, though there is an epilogue: Loki, in the form of a mare, has mated with the stallion and gives birth to a remarkable foal with eight legs, which grows up to be Sleipnir, the best of all horses and the chosen mount of Odin.

ODIN, RULER OF THE GODS

The god Odin was by far the most widely known of the Germanic gods in the first millennium A.D. Known to the Anglo-Saxons as Woden, to the Alamanic and Saxon tribes as Wodan, and to the Langobards as Godan, he was seen as the mythical ancestor of many of the Germanic tribes as well as several Anglo-Saxon royal families of

Above **Thor's hammer Miollnir, amulet, tenth century A.D., Sweden.** Associated with a thunderbolt, Thor's hammer was used to defend the gods and their world. It always returns to his hand after being thrown. This amulet would have been worn as a protective charm and is decorated with the staring eyes of Thor.

Right ***Thor Fights the Jotunes* by Martes Winge (1825–1896).** Thor leads the fight against the giants, (the Jotunes or Jotun). The sound of thunder accompanies his chariot, which is drawn by magical goats. His power is aided by his Girdle of Strength and he often wears iron gauntlets at his wrists, which enable him to wield his hammer.

the early Middle Ages. Much earlier, however, he was seen in general as a god of healing, magic, runes, and knowledge, as well as the god of death, war, and fate. However, his followers were also well aware of the ambiguities of this multifunctional god, as they knew that in battle he could give victory as well as death to those who were dedicated to his worship.

ODIN AND THE RUNES

An Icelandic poem, the *Hávamál,* which in its preserved written form was only compiled in the twelfth century, along with the prose *Edda* from the thirteenth century, gives us a poetic but remarkably powerful version of how the god Odin became the first to obtain knowledge of the runes, that is, of the power and uses of writing. In both works,

Odin himself talks, declaring how he won the runes by hanging "on the wind-swept tree, for nine nights in all, wounded by a spear and dedicated to Odin, given myself to myself." As a result of this nine-day fast, he gained insight into the nature of the runes.

This scene, known as Odin's self-sacrifice, has similarities, even if only superficial, to Christ's sacrifice through both the hanging from a tree and the wounding by a spear. Some say it suggests a very early adoption of the central Christian myth by the ancient Scandinavians, possibly by way of the British Isles. Similar forms of self-sacrifice, however, are also found in the initiation rites of numerous archaic cultures, and its origins may more accurately be seen in the context of shamanistic initiation rites into the knowledge of poetry and magic.

Above **Viking picture stone from Gotland, Sweden, eighth century** A.D. This stone features the god Odin (Wodan) on his horse Sleipnir, assisted by Valkyries. The greatest of all horses, Sleipnir has eight legs, and it is he who bears the valiant dead to Valhalla.

Left **Rune stone, Uppsala, eleventh century** A.D., **by Gamla Torget.** Germanic mythology invested great value in writing, which was in the form of runes. This knowledge was not gained without suffering, however. Odin, the father of the gods, underwent nine days of fasting and pain in order to gain understanding.

POETIC MEAD: THE ORIGIN OF POETIC INSPIRATION

This myth comes from the part of Snorri Sturluson's prose *Edda* called the *Skaldskaparmal* and is very complex, with several episodes together forming a cycle (that is, several tales together forming a complete narrative about a person or event). The myth tells of poetry as a product of divine inspiration, and gives us an idea of the value placed upon poetry and the prestige of poets in the Scandinavian world.

Following an early war between the Aesir and the Vanir, a truce is declared, symbolized by both sides spitting into a vat. The gods make a man, Kvasir, out of the accumulated spittle. Kvasir was born fully grown, omniscient, and filled with the knowledge of both the Aesir and Vanir.

In Midgard, where mankind dwell, Kvasir became renowned for his ability to answer any question, no matter how learned the questioner. Those in need of advice knew they had only to send for him, and he would come. On one such trip he meets two dwarfs, Fialar and Galar, who invite him to a meal deep within their caves. There, they murder him and drain off his blood into two crocks and a kettle. They mix it with honey to produce a mead that turns anyone who drinks it into a poet or scholar.

The dwarves tell the gods that Kvasir has died, after choking on his own great learning because he could find no one who was able to compete with him in knowledge.

The two dwarves next invite Gilling, a giant, and his wife to their dwelling. They take Gilling rowing, but their boat strikes a rock and capsizes. Unable to swim, Gilling drowns, though the dwarves were able to right the boat and return home to tell the giantess of her husband's death. The dwarf Fialar asks her if it would ease her grief to look out to sea in the direction of the drowning, but this is a

Left *The giant Baugi, persuaded by Odin, drills into his brother Suttung's chamber.* This illustration shows the giant Baugi making a hole into the cave where the mead is hidden. The drill has magical powers, getting longer and longer the more it is used. No depth is too great for it.

trick: as she passes out through the doorway, Galar kills her by dropping a millstone on her. When the giants' son, Suttung, learns of what has happened, he seizes the two dwarfs and maroons them on an island that is covered at high tide. They beg for mercy, offering Suttung the mead as compensation for his parents' death. Suttung agrees, takes the precious mead, and hides it inside a mountain called Hnitbiorg, setting his daughter Gunnlod to guard it.

Odin's Search for the Mead

The story now turns to Odin's efforts to obtain the mead from Suttung. Dressed as a farm hand, Odin sets out on his mission. One day, Odin comes across nine serfs mowing hay. He carries a whetstone as part of his normal equipment, and he sharpens the serfs' scythes with it. The serfs are so impressed by the result that they offer to buy the whetstone from Odin, which he agrees to on condition that the price is right. He then throws the whetstone up into the air and in their eagerness the serfs all struggle for it; in the melee they all manage to cut one another's throats with their scythes.

Odin takes lodging with a giant called Baugi, who is Suttung's brother; but Odin conceals his true identity, giving his name as Bolverk. The nine serfs had worked for Baugi, who now faces the task of finding new workers to mow his hay. Odin offers to do the work of all nine men in return for one drink of Suttung's mead. Baugi is doubtful if his brother will surrender any of the mead, but agrees to help Odin to get hold of it once the work is done. Odin completes the mowing, and he and Baugi approach Suttung, but he refuses to part with any of the mead. Odin produces a drill called Rati and tells Baugi to bore a hole through Hnitbiorg to get at the mead. Baugi deliberately drills short of the cave where the mead is kept, but Odin forces him to extend the hole as far as the cave.

After changing himself into a serpent, Odin slithers through the hole. Baugi, in a last attempt to thwart him, stabs with the drill at the snake's tail as it disappears, but misses. Once inside the mountain, Odin seduces Gunnlod, who guards the mead, and spends three nights with her. He persuades her to give him three drafts of the mead for each night he spends with her. This is all Odin needs to drain all three of the containers in which the mead is kept. Then he

transforms himself into an eagle and flies off toward Asgard. Suttung sees him escaping and follows, also in the shape of an eagle. Seeing Odin appear, the Aesir put out containers in Asgard's courtyard as instructed. Odin disgorges the mead, but Suttung is in close pursuit, and he inadvertently excretes some of the mead. This is not collected, but left for anyone who wants it.

The collected mead was given by Odin to the gods, and anyone who drank it became a skilled poet; but anyone who tasted the excreted mead produced only doggerel. As for Suttung, some versions of the tale say the sun's rays touched him just as he reached the walls of Asgard, robbing him of his eagle cloak, and he fell to the ground. In others, the gods built a fire, which singed his wings, again causing him to fall to his death.

Left **Pendant or amulet, ninth century A.D., Sweden.** The figure, possibly a priest of the cult of Odin, holds a sword and two spears and wears an adorned helmet. Odin is highly complex: god of battle, he is also god of wine and inspiration. Yet some see in his many sides a common thread: a loss of the self, be it through death or intoxication.

Above **Angel, on an altar of the Lombard King Rachis, eighth century** A.D. The Langobards (or Lombards) were originally from southern Sweden but settled in Italy, and gave their name to the region of Lombardia. Early tales explain how, when the numbers of the Winnili grew too big, they divided themselves into three and drew lots. The group led by Ibor and Aio lost, so they departed in search of a new homeland.

DESCENDED FROM THE GODS

Many of the Germanic tribes had myths linking their authority with the gods. Often this was Odin, the most powerful of the gods. One of the better known and oldest of the Germanic myths of origin comes from the Langobard historiographers of the sixth and seventh centuries A.D. They relate an old tradition that describes a battle between two Germanic tribes, the Wandali (Vandals) and the Winnili. The Wandali prayed to their chief god Godan (Wodan/Odin) for victory. The Winnili, however, were led by Gambara, the wise old mother of their leaders Ibor and Aio, who prayed to Godan's wife, Frea (Frigg).

Frea advised the Winnili warriors to position themselves in the east on the morning of the battle and for the women to stand with the men on the battle lines, arranging their long hair around their faces. Godan planned to give victory to the first army he saw in the morning. The next morning, on looking out his favorite window to the east, he spied the Winnili gathered, and called out, "Who are those Langobards (longbeards)?" Having named them, Frea said he had to grant them victory, and under that name they carved out their kingdom in what would later become known as Lombardia, in northern Italy.

In their description of this legend the authors reveal some influences from their understanding of the Classical couple that ruled the gods, Zeus and Hera, but the undoubtedly old story shows that even in the middle of the first millennium A.D., Wodan/Odin and his wife Frigg were already the powerful ancestral deities from whom Germanic royal families, as well as whole tribes, wished themselves to be descended.

Despite the fact that it was mainly Odin who featured as a divine ancestor in the genealogies of Germanic royal families, in Sweden at least it was the god Freyr who was widely celebrated, both as the ancestor and as the guardian and protector of the royal house of the Ynglings, the house from which even the Norwegian royal family later deduced their ancestry. Although Freyr was often seen as a god of fertility, mostly because Viking Age statues and pocket talismans show him with an erect phallus, he was really mainly perceived as the powerful and opulently rich epitome of Swedish kingship, as represented by the kings of Old Uppsala (a seat of power in Sweden in the sixth century and later, and still a religious and cultural center). His distinctive virility was surely part of this image of a young and powerful king, as was Freyr's attribute, the boar, which is another symbol of aggressively dangerous strength, and also of wealth. The soldiers of the Swedish royal guards of the seventh and eighth centuries, for example, wore helmets that were crowned with a metal boar. The connection with the house of the Ynglings was even reflected in a by-name given to Freyr when he was called Yngvi-Freyr, which may possibly be a very old name going back to the Germanic tribes mentioned by Tacitus who called themselves the Ingaevones.

Freyr and the Giantess Gerd

The story of Freyr, Gerd, and Skirnir is told in its fullest form in the Eddaic poem *Skirnismal*. Snorri Sturluson recounts a shorter more romanticized version of it in *Gylfaginning*. The story begins in Asgard. Freyr, god of wealth and fertility, sits in Hlidskialf, Odin's house, from where there is a view over all the other worlds in the universe. Looking down into the world of the giants he spots Gerd, a beautiful giantess, in the courtyard of her father's estate, and immediately falls in love with her. He languishes.

Freyr's servant Skirnir is sent to ask what is troubling him. Freyr explains, but feels his passion is doomed to remain unfulfilled. Skirnir offers to travel to Giantland and woo Gerd on his behalf. He borrows Freyr's magic sword and horse and, after negotiating mountains and a ring of fire around Giantland, arrives at Gerd's house but finds access to her prevented by savage guard dogs. Gerd, however, decides to receive him in her bower.

Skirnir communicates Freyr's love to her, offering as inducements golden apples and Draupnir, a magic self-reproducing gold ring, but Gerd has plenty of gold and spurns these gifts. Then Skirnir threatens her (and her giant father, Gymir, as well if he should he try to intervene) with death by Freyr's sword, but still Gerd resists. Skirnir describes in graphic detail the consequences of a curse that he will impose on her if she persists in rejecting Freyr's generous offer of love.

The curse will be carved in runes on a "taming wand." Under its terms, Gerd will be condemned to a veritable living death in Giant-land. Skirnir describes her life under the curse as a burlesque of the life she would enjoy with the gods were she to accept Freyr's hand. She will live on the edge of her world, like Heimdall does, the gods' watchman in Asgard; but whereas Heimdall is guarding his world against attack, Gerd will instead be a prisoner, staring outward and longing for the escape that only death can bring. Her only drink will be the urine of goats, a severe enough prescription, but made even more piquant by the reminder it will bring that the gods extract an excellent mead from the udders of the goat Heidrun, who grazes on the leaves of the world tree. Gerd will be regarded by others in this nightmare world as a freak and be stared at; and if she chooses to marry, the best she can hope for is a three-headed giant called Hrimgrimnir. Her days will drag horribly, as she is constantly persecuted by the trolls who constitute her only company. She will be assailed by tears, and desire will attack her with uncontrollable force.

Gerd caves in only when Skirnir begins to carve the runes that will turn this terrifying vision into her reality. She agrees to meet Freyr nine nights hence in Barri, a place described as a "calm grove." Skirnir returns to Freyr with this news, and the poem ends with the god complaining now about the delay Gerd has imposed on their union.

Different interpretations of this story are possible, but a symbolic reading of it as an agricultural fertility myth probably makes the best sense of it. Thus Freyr, established elsewhere in the mythology as a god of fecundity, represents the sun; Gerd is the unfertilized earth; and Skirnir, the go-between, whose name means "the shining one," represents the beams of the sun that bring about the germination of crops.

THOR AND HIS HAMMER

Thor was the god about whom the majority of myths from old Scandinavia were told, and who functioned as a cosmological protector of man and gods alike. As such, he was closely modeled in many of the stories on the Greek and Roman hero Heracles/Hercules, although in the Germanic translations of the Roman weekday names, he was even considered as equivalent to Zeus/Jupiter, the leader of the gods in classical mythology. Thor seems to have been very widely venerated as a god of thunder and lightning, as well as the weather generally. His popularity can be seen in the extremely frequent use of his name in the formation of many Scandinavian personal names, such as Thorleifr and Thorlakr. He has also survived in many of the Christianized folktales of St. Peter walking on earth. In southern Germanic areas he was known as Donar, the Anglo-Saxons called him Thunor, and in Viking Age Britain (in the eighth to eleventh centuries A.D.) he was usually called Thur or Thor, closely following the Scandinavian form of the name. In the tenth and eleventh centuries in Sweden, Thor and his hammer became pagan symbols that were used in opposition to Christ and the cross, and it can be seen that a number of grave stones from these late pagan times either show the hammer or invoke Thor to "hallow these runes."

THOR'S EXPEDITION TO UTGARD

This is the longest of the myths told by the Aesir to King Gylfi in Snorri Sturluson's *Gylfaginning,* and one of the most entertaining.

Thor and Loki are on an expedition in Thor's chariot, pulled by his two goats. They pass the night with a peasant family and repay their hospitality by slaughtering the goats and making a meal of them. Thor spreads out their skins on the floor and tells the peasant family to throw the bones onto the skins when they have eaten the meat off them but not to damage them. During the meal, Thialfi, the son of the family, splits the bones of one of the goats to get at the marrow. In the morning, Thor blesses the goatskins with his hammer and the goats stand up alive again, though one of them is lame in the hind leg. Thor is furious, but is mollified by the peasants' remorse, and he accepts the two children, Thialfi and Roskva, as his bondservants in compensation. Leaving his goats and chariot with the peasant couple, Thor, Loki, and the two children set off on foot toward Giantland in the east, with Thialfi, a fast runner, carrying Thor's knapsack. They cross the sea and then enter an extensive forest. They look for a place to spend the night, but can find only a large deserted building. In the middle of the night the travelers' sleep is disturbed by an alarming shaking of the earth.

Skrymir the Giant

They search the interior of the building for a place to defend themselves and find a side chamber halfway down one wall, which they occupy. A great rumbling and groaning is heard. At dawn, Thor goes outside to find a huge giant sleeping on the ground. His footsteps and snoring were what had woken them in the night. Thor prepares to kill the giant with his hammer, but before he can do so the giant awakes, rises to his feet, and introduces himself as Skrymir. He knows who Thor is, and jocularly accuses him of stealing

Right **Head of Loki, Denmark (A.D. 800–1050).** The thorn in the side of the gods at Asgard, Loki is mostly depicted as driven by jealousy of the gods, and of Thor in particular, but some of his escapades do end well for the gods. Thor's hammer is one such example, made by dwarfs in a bet with Loki.

Below **Dead giant, detail of a marble statue, 170 B.C., Pergamon.** In Norse myths, giants are the chief enemies of the gods, who they are destined to meet on the day of the Ragnarok. At the roots of Yggdrasill lies the "well of highest wisdom," guarded by the giant Mimir. In some stories, Odin, ever seeking knowledge, sacrifices an eye to have a drink from it.

his glove which, it now emerges, is the building the travelers had slept in. The side chamber in which they took refuge was the glove's thumb.

Skrymir obtains Thor's permission to travel with his party. The giant has with him a knapsack containing food and opens it to make his breakfast. He suggests that the whole party pool their food. Thor agrees to this, and all the food goes into Skrymir's knapsack. They resume their journey, Skrymir setting a cracking pace. In the evening they find a comfortable place to camp beneath a large oak tree.

Before he goes to sleep, Skrymir tells the rest of the party to help themselves to food from the knapsack, but so firmly has the knapsack been fastened that even Thor is unable to open it. He then becomes angry, takes his mighty hammer, and strikes at the head of the sleeping giant. His great blow has little apparent impact: Skrymir wakes up and asks if a leaf from the oak tree had fallen upon his head. Skrymir goes back to sleep and snores loudly. At midnight, Thor strikes again at the giant's head with his hammer and feels it go deep into the skull; but again Skrymir only wakes up and enquires if an acorn had fallen on him. He resumes his slumbers. Toward dawn, Thor aims a third blow at his head, this time at the temple. He feels the hammer sink in right to the handle, but Skrymir only wakes up and asks if a bird in the tree above has dropped some rubbish on his head.

Arrival at the Castle Utgard

Skrymir's journey takes him in a different direction, but before leaving Thor's party he indicates that a castle called Utgard is not far away to the east. He warns them that the castle's inhabitants are very large, and advises them to show humility in their presence if they pay them a visit. He suggests, however, that they might be better advised to go back to where they came from. With these words, he leaves them.

Later in the day, Thor and his party arrive at Utgard, a huge castle standing on open ground. The gates are shut and Thor is not strong enough to open them, so they are reduced to wriggling through the

gaps in the portcullis. We are now in a world where Thor and his companions are, in effect, miniature beings. They enter a large hall where many people, most of them immense, are sitting on benches. Their king, Utgarda-Loki, guesses Thor's identity, though he is surprised at how small he seems in view of all he has heard tell of his exploits. The king asks the visitors what feats they are capable of performing, explaining that every guest at Utgard castle must demonstrate some notable accomplishment. Loki steps forward, claiming the ability to eat faster than anyone else. The king chooses Logi, one of his men,

Above *The God Thor, on his Travels, is Teased by a Giant with Magical Illusions* from *Journal des Voyages* (1898). Unlike most adventures featuring Thor, those with the giant Skrymir leave him uncharacteristically abashed. His directness and ready strength are of no use to him in Giantland, also known as Jotunheim.

to compete with Loki. A large trencher is filled with food and set on the floor. Loki starts at one end, Logi at the other, both proceeding to eat furiously. By the time they meet in the middle, Loki has eaten all the meat off the bones; but Logi has eaten everything—meat, bones, and even the trencher itself. Loki is plainly the loser.

Utgarda-Loki then asks what Thialfi is good at. Thialfi, who has already demonstrated his ability as a runner, offers to race against anyone the king puts forward. Hugi, described as a small person by local standards, is chosen as his opponent, and everyone goes outside where there is a suitably level course for racing. Thialfi and Hugi run three races in a row and, although the king seems impressed by his speed, Thialfi still loses all three, performing ever less successfully as race follows race.

Utgarda-Loki finally turns to Thor and asks him to demonstrate just one among the many accomplishments for which he is famous. Thor decides to display his enormous capacity for consuming drink. A large horn is produced. Utgarda-Loki points out that some local drinkers are able to empty this horn in just a single pull, others take two, but no one needs more than three to drain it. Thor's first and second drafts produce very little change to the level of drink in the horn. With the third enormous gulp, under the provocation of some mild jeering from Utgarda-Loki, he manages to make quite a visible impression on the level, but the king declares himself very disappointed with Thor's overall performance.

Utgarda-Loki offers Thor a chance to prove himself in another kind of contest, though in view of Thor's evident weakness Utgarda-Loki can only suggest a game that the boys of the castle amuse themselves with: lifting his pet cat off the ground. A very large gray cat appears on the floor of the hall. Thor pushes its belly upward, but it arches its back so that he cannot reach high enough to exert much upward pressure. All Thor succeeds in doing is getting the cat to lift one of its feet off the ground.

Above *Thor Enthroned* by J. Rysbraeck (1693–1770). Thor's realm in Asgard is Thrudvangr, "plains of strength." In his hall, the tables are always groaning with food, for equal to his strength is his appetite.

By this time Thor, humiliated by his repeated failures, is in a fighting mood and offers to wrestle any local opponent. The king doubts if any of his people would not find it demeaning to take on such a weak opponent, but calls for an old woman called Elli, his former nurse. She wrestles with Thor and succeeds in forcing him down upon one knee, at which point Utgarda-Loki stops the fight.

Evening has come and the king makes his guests comfortable for the night. In the morning Thor and his party prepare to leave, but the king delays them with a generous breakfast to speed them on their journey. They set off, with the king, Utgarda-Loki, accompanying them for part of the way. He asks Thor if he has encountered anyone mightier than he during his expedition. Thor is frank about his sense of failure, but is most irritated by the damage to his reputation that has been done.

At this point, Utgarda-Loki comes clean about a whole series of deceptions that he has worked on Thor and his companions, and the whole story is transformed in retrospect. Thor, it now appears, was regarded as a serious threat to the giants. The giant Skrymir was none other than Utgarda-Loki himself

three races was Hugi, Thought, the speed of which no runner can hope to match. As for the horn from which Thor had drunk, its end was open and in the sea, so that Thor had no hope of draining it. His three drafts, however, had been prodigious enough to produce a new natural phenomenon: forever afterward the sea would be subject to the ebb and flow of tides. The giant cat that Thor had tried to lift was a transformation of his age-old enemy, the Midgard serpent, which lies wrapped around all the worlds of the universe. Thor did in fact manage to raise the middle part of its body to the sky, though the enchantment had concealed the magnitude of his achievement. Finally, Thor's seemingly feeble opponent at wrestling was Elli, Old Age, who brings everyone down in the end, though Thor had put up impressive resistance.

Utgarda-Loki then takes his leave of the party, warning them that any attempt to revisit Utgard will be resisted by similar tricks. Thor grabs his hammer for a last attempt to destroy the giant, but Utgarda-Loki has already disappeared, along with his castle. Thor and his party return home.

This myth was no doubt meant mostly as entertainment, though it is possible to see broader significance in some of the competitions. Perhaps the myth is meant to demonstrate human weakness in the face of natural forces and processes, for neither god nor man is able to defeat the natural power of fire (Logi), match the speed of thought (Hugi), or resist the slow onslaught of old age (Elli).

Left *Knight in Armor in Combat with Dragon* from *Historia de Gentibus Septentrionalibus* by Olaus Magnus (1490–1557). This masterpiece by Magnus was designed to bring the Scandinavian flora, fauna, history, and traditions to Renaissance Italy, which at that stage still thought of most northern folk as barbarians. This woodcut shows their pride in their fighting skills, against an ancient foe, though the warrior appears in armor more familiar to Italians.

in disguise. The provisions bag that Thor had failed to open was held by a magic wire that would defeat anyone who tried to loosen it. The three hammer blows struck by Thor at Skrymir as he lay under the oak would have killed the giant if they had in fact connected with his head; however, he placed a nearby mountain between himself and Thor's hammer in such a way that Thor failed to notice. The mountain is now dented with three square valleys where Thor's hammer fell. The defeats that were suffered by Thor and his companions in the games had all been engineered by Utgarda-Loki's magic.

Thus, in the eating competition Loki's opponent was Logi, a personification of Fire: Loki lost only because no one can consume anything as quickly as fire. Similarly, Thialfi's opponent in the

WARRIORS IN LIFE AND DEATH

The Germanic warriors emulated the fearlessness of their gods Odin and Thor, and were known to be fierce, brave, and proud fighters. Warriors followed their leaders out of choice rather than tribal obligations, according to Tacitus, and there was a strong code of honor and loyalty: "The chiefs fight for victory, the companions for their chief."

It was an honor to die in battle, giving a warrior almost godlike status: those who died of other causes went to the Underworld; while those who died in battle went to Odin's hall, Valhalla, to pass their days fighting and their nights feasting. Valkyries, fearsome and bloodthirsty female spirits, rode down through the sky on horses to bring the fallen to Valhalla, where they then served them food and mead. On the day of the Ragnarok, these warriors, called "Einheriar," would follow their leader Odin into the final battle.

Beserkers are said to be gifts from Odin, savage warriors that, in the frenzy of battle, become immune to pain, and may even turn into animals, or assume their qualities.

Left **Valhalla and Viking legends,** *bildstenar* (engraved stone), pre- A.D. 1000, Gotland, Sweden. Valhalla was the greatest of the twelve halls at Asgard. Some stories report that its roof was made of overlapping shields and that it had over 500 doors.

THOR'S FISHING

Of all the cosmological myths, none is better preserved than the episode of Thor trying to catch the Midgard serpent, known as Thor's Fishing. In the most detailed version, which is the version found in the prose *Edda,* Thor leaves Midgard in the disguise of a young man. When he reaches the abode of the giant Hymir, he spends the night there and next morning accompanies the reluctant giant on a fishing trip. When he is told to find his own bait, he pulls off the head of one of Hymir's bulls. Thor rows out further than the giant wants, then fastens the head of the ox to a sturdy fishing line, and the Midgard serpent bites at once. Thor pulls on the line with such might that his feet break through the planks of the boat and, standing on the bottom of the sea, he drags the monster up to the boat. The sight of the serpent fills the giant with terror and, as Thor tries to strike the serpent with his hammer weapon, Hymir cuts the fishing line and the monster sinks back into the sea. Thor throws his hammer after it, and, as the *Edda* says, "some people say that the hammer cut off its head at water level. I believe that the truth is that the Midgard serpent is still alive and out there in the seas which surround the world." Thor then hits the giant Hymir with such strength and anger that he falls overboard and must wade back to land.

I warn of his tree, while seeming slight, harmfully hurled ... will slay Odin's son

VÖLUSPÁ POEM c. A.D. 1100
(FROM THE POETIC EDDA)

This story was, however, known at least 400 years before it was retold in the poem called *Hymiskvitha* in the *Edda.* This was a common story recited by the Icelandic *skalds* (poets) working at Norwegian courts in the ninth and tenth centuries A.D. From around this time five separate allusions to this myth can be found, all brief, but clearly referring to a not very different version of the story. Even older still, from the eighth century, is a pictorial representation of the legend on one of the elaborate picture stones on Gotland (in Sweden), where two male figures in a boat seem to be baiting something with the head of an ox. Other, although later (but still pagan), pictures in stone in Scandinavia and Britain are partly more explicit in that they occasionally show Thor with his hammer raised and one of his feet breaking through the bottom of the boat.

Thus, the myth of Thor and the Midgard serpent was probably very widely known, not only across Scandinavia and Britain, but even throughout Germany in the fourteenth century, where the Midgard serpent (though without mentioning Thor) is referred to as being the source of earthquakes.

THE DEATH OF BALDR

One of the sadder stories from Snorri's *Gylfaginning* concerns Baldr, fairest of the gods, son of Odin and his wife Frigg. Baldr suffers from dreams foretelling his own death. The gods decide to protect him by extracting a promise from everything in the world not to harm him. Then, at assemblies, the gods amuse themselves by striking at him, or pelting him with missiles, in the knowledge that he cannot be hurt. Loki, envious of Baldr's immunity, visits Frigg in the guise of a woman. During their conversation, Frigg lets slip that the mistletoe has been excused from making the promise not to harm Baldr on account of its youth. Loki, resuming his natural shape, plucks some mistletoe and takes it to the assembly where Baldr is being pelted. Baldr's blind brother, Hod, is standing nearby. Loki encourages him to join in the fun, putting the mistletoe in his hand and pointing him in the direction of Baldr. Hod throws the mistletoe at his brother and it kills him. The gods are struck dumb with horror. Odin, Baldr's father, is especially grief stricken. Frigg asks who will go to Hel to offer a ransom for Baldr's release. Hermod, another of Baldr's brothers, offers to go. Odin lends him his horse, Sleipnir, and Hermod starts out.

An elaborate funeral for Baldr is prepared. His body is carried to the sea where his great ship, Hringhorni, is pulled up on the beach, but the ship cannot be moved. A giantess, Hyrrokkin, is summoned from Giantland. She arrives riding on a wolf, using vipers as reins. It takes four of Odin's warriors to restrain the wolf as she dismounts. Hyrrokkin launches the boat with a single touch, the rollers throw out sparks, and the ground shakes. Thor, ever ready to kill giants, becomes angry and threatens her with his hammer, but the other gods plead for her to be spared. Baldr's body is placed on the launched ship beside that of his wife Nanna, who has died of grief. The funeral pyre is lighted. Thor consecrates it with his hammer, Miollnir. A dwarf called Lit runs in front of his feet, and Thor angrily kicks him into the fire where he perishes. All the gods and goddesses, and many frost giants and mountain giants, attend the funeral. Odin places the gold ring called Draupnir on the pyre and Baldr's horse is also burnt, with all its trappings.

Opposite page *The Norse god Thor fishing for the Midgard serpent.* The Midgard serpent, Jorgamund, was a child of Loki. The serpent is usually shown circling Midgard, its tail in its mouth. On the day of reckoning, the serpent will emerge from the water for one final battle with Thor. The god will manage to kill the terrifying creature but its poison is too great: Thor will also die.

Above **Pendant, one of a pair, representing Baldr on his horse, Sweden.** Many interpretations for Loki's part in the death of Baldr have been proffered. Some have suggested that the gods, in seeking to free Baldr from death, are disrupting the natural order of things: everything must die. Loki's actions prove this.

Loki's Treachery

Below *Loki Punished* by
J. D. Penrose. For his
misdeeds, Loki is tied to
rocks below a serpent. His
wife is often shown with
him, catching the poison in
a bowl. When it fills, she
has to tip it out and the
poison falls on Loki.

Hermod, meanwhile, rides for nine nights through deep and dark valleys until he reaches a bridge over Gioll, the river of death. Modgud, a maiden who guards the bridge, comments that he does not look like one of the dead. She tells him that Baldr has recently crossed the bridge, and directs Hermod downward and northward to Hel. On reaching the gates of Hel, Hermod jumps over them easily on Sleipnir's back. He comes to a hall, dismounts and enters, and finds Baldr sitting in a place of honor. Hermod describes the gods' grief to the goddess Hel and pleads with her to allow Baldr to return to them. Hel agrees, on condition that everything in the world will weep for Baldr. Hermod immediately returns to Asgard, taking gifts from Baldr for his parents: the ring Draupnir for Odin, and a robe for Frigg.

The message goes out to the whole world to weep in order that Baldr can leave Hel. Everyone and everything begins to weep, with one exception. A giantess called Thanks, generally assumed to be the malicious Loki in disguise, refuses to weep. Baldr must remain in Hel. Loki is found hiding in a cave and is caught and chained, to remain that way until the Ragnarok.

This myth is another illustration of Loki's treachery; but it is more significant as a myth about a pagan Christ who dies but is not resurrected. The obvious inversion of the Christian myth is a clear sign of the author's exposure to the religion that eventually replaced paganism in Scandinavia.

CONTINUANCE AND CHANGE

Although much of the mythology of the various Germanic tribes was lost as they spread across Europe and intermingled with new peoples, some aspects of their culture and heritage were retained. Over time, new cultures arose and gradually developed into nations such as England, France, and Germany. Some of the early tales survived outside of the original homeland, or were developed to keep memories of the older culture alive.

One of the best-known stories of Germanic origin concerns the adventures of the mighty warrior Beowulf. However, this legend is not found in Norse mythology but in Old English. Beowulf's adventures were recorded by unknown scribes in a tenth-century A.D. manuscript, itself a copy of earlier manuscripts. There is only one manuscript in existence, and this epic poem is now regarded as the oldest known work of English literature. The story most likely comes from the seventh and eighth centuries and may have been created to keep alive the history and culture of the Anglo-Saxons, who

Below *Loki Punished* by J. D. Penrose. For his misdeeds, Loki is tied to rocks below a serpent. His wife is often shown with him, catching the poison in a bowl. When it fills, she has to tip it out and the poison falls on Loki.

THE RAGNAROK

When Heimdall, the god who guards the entrance to Asgard, blows his trumpet, it will sound the beginning of the Ragnarok. The fate of the gods was predestined: at a future time there would be a great battle, gods against monsters and giants, and humans against humans, in which most would be destroyed.

It is said that the great battle will begin thus: after a winter lasting three years, wolves will devour the sun and moon. Loki and his children, the goddess Hel and Fenrir the wolf, will be released by earthquakes. With the frost giants, they will sail to meet the gods in battle. The Midgard serpent, another of Loki's children, will swell the waves and the water will engulf the land. Warned by Heimdall's horn, the gods, with the fallen warriors gathered at Valhalla in Asgard, will advance with Odin at their head. Most will die in the battle and a great fire will sweep the earth. Only the sons of Odin and Thor, and the daughter of the sun, will survive. Baldr and his blind brother Hod will be freed from hell and the world will begin again.

Left **The god Heimdall blowing his horn before the Ragnarok.** Heimdall is the god of light and the watchman on the Bifrost Bridge, the only entrance to Asgard and also the connection with the underworld. At the Ragnarok, he and Loki will fight, and though the victor, he will die of his wounds.

had invaded England in the fifth century A.D. While Beowulf is a legendary hero, some of the tribal kings mentioned in the story are known to have existed, and Heorot, where part of the story takes place, is an ancient seat of Danish leadership.

The Story of Beowulf

The great mead hall of Hrothgar, King of the Danes, at Heorot is attacked by a troll-like monster called Grendel. No one is strong enough to kill him and he keeps returning. Beowulf, nephew of the King of the Geats, sails with his warriors from Sweden to help Hrothgar, and determines that he must fight the monster without his sword. When the monster returns to the hall, a mighty fight ensues. The hall is shaken to its foundations, but Beowulf, with his incredible grip, mortally wounds Grendel, tearing off his arm.

There is a brief time of great rejoicing, but when Grendel's mother learns of her son's death, she soon attacks the hall, killing King Hrothgar's most beloved companion. Beowulf must swim to her cavern at the bottom of a lake to kill her. When he confronts her, he finds that his sword is useless and he must fight her barehanded. The monster fights back savagely, wrestling Beowulf to the ground and sitting on him. When she attempts to stab him, only his coat of mail saves him. He breaks free, and, grasping a giant's sword that he sees on the wall of the cavern, kills her. He cuts off her head and takes it to Hrothgar as a prize, along with the hilt of the sword, the blade having been destroyed by the monster's blood. Beowulf is rewarded with much praise and treasure. He later becomes King of the Geats, and, in his last battle, dies killing a cursed dragon.

Left *Grendel and Victims,* by J.H.F. Bacon (1865–1914). The monster Grendel has abducted two youths from Heorot, the court of the Danish King Hrothgar. Some stories say that such monsters lived in shadowy, fearful places within the moors, exiled from the rest of mankind by the gods.

FINNISH MYTHOLOGY

Right *Cornelius Tacitus,*
engraved by Freeman
from an antique bust
(1830). The writings of
Tacitus offer a detailed
description of the ancient
Finns, however, they need
to be read with care as
they are influenced by his
prejudices as a Roman.

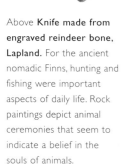

Above **Knife made from
engraved reindeer bone,
Lapland.** For the ancient
nomadic Finns, hunting and
fishing were important
aspects of daily life. Rock
paintings depict animal
ceremonies that seem to
indicate a belief in the
souls of animals.

Opposite page *Story of
Kullervo* by A. Gallen
Kallela (1865–1931). The
fable of Kullervo, as told
in the *Kalevala,* is an epic
of family feuding, revenge,
and regret. It has inspired
plays and musical com-
positions, including one
by Jean Sibelius, Finnish
composer (1865–1957).

The ancestors of today's Finns have inhabited the southern part of the country known today as Finland since as long ago as 5000 B.C. Some of the numerous tribes to which they belonged give their names to present-day Finnish provinces. The Estonians, from the southern side of the Gulf of Finland, and the Ugrians, from Hungary and western Siberia, are closely related to the Finns and share some of the same myths.

The earliest mention of a Finnish people is to be found in *Germania,* written by the Roman historian and politician Cornelius Publius Tacitus in A.D. 98. According to Tacitus, the Finns (Fenni) were "unimaginably barbarous and miserably poor." He reports that they had "no weapons, no horses, no houses, and nowt but wild plants for their food, skins for their clothing, and the ground for their beds." In spite of Tacitus's description it is likely, judging from their rock paintings, that the diet of the ancient Finns was not so simple, but also included elk and fish. During the Iron Age (*c.* 500 B.C. to A.D. 400), the distinctive features of their folk poetry were emerging, as well as a peasant way of life, which combined agriculture with hunting and fishing.

The early Finnish tribes spoke different languages that were dialects of the Uralic language, which spread to Finland in the period between 4000 B.C. and 2000 B.C. They did not live in towns but in family groups surrounded by neighboring races with whom they traded. Because the groups were relatively isolated from each other, a uniform set of

beliefs did not develop. As well, due to exposure to other cultures, their ancient tales exhibit a number of outside influences—particularly from Slavic, Norse, and Germanic mythologies.

THE SONG CATCHER

The majority of what is known today about Finnish mythology comes from the many songs and poems collected by Elias Lönnrot, which were originally published in 1835. Lönnrot conceived the idea of collecting the tales of ancient Finland in 1828. He traveled the length and breadth of Finland and Karelia for the next seven years, visiting even the smallest villages to record the songs and poems of the peasantry. He then compared and arranged these tales into the heroic epic that he called the *Kalevala.* This collection continued to grow until, by 1849, it contained nearly 23,000 verses.

The *Kalevala* is, in truth, part ancient mythology and part invention by Elias Lönnrot himself. In his eagerness to create an epic that would compare with Homer's *Iliad,* Lönnrot created entirely new poems from fragments of material he had gathered on his travels. The *Kalevala* describes a struggle between two peoples: the Kaleva from southern Finland, and the Pohjola from northern Finland or Lapland.

ELIAS LÖNNROT (1802–1884)

The man responsible for the *Kalevala,* Elias Lönnrot, was a true polymath: explorer, doctor, poet, and linguist. He was motivated to create the *Kalevala* by the idea, associated with the German scholar J.G. Herder (1744–1803), that a nation cannot exist without a distinctive cultural identity. The Grand Duchy of Finland had been annexed by Russia in 1809 and would not achieve independence until the Russian Revolution in 1917.

Together with the *Kalevala,* Lönnrot's dictionaries and periodicals earned him great fame during his lifetime. Today he is regarded as one of the fathers of written Finnish. His birthplace, the rustic Paikkari Cottage, is owned by the Finnish National Board of Antiquities and is operated as a museum. It can be found in the parish of Sammatti about 47 miles (75 km) west of Helsinki.

THE KALEVALA

The entire *Kalevala* is written in an unusual, archaic trochaic tetrameter, which means that each line has four pairs of syllables with a stress-unstress pattern in each pair. The opening lines describe how singers support each other during a recital that can last several hours.

> *Let us clasp our hands together,*
> *Let us interlock our fingers;*
> *Let us sing a cheerful measure,*
> *Let us use our best endeavours,*
> *While our dear ones hearken to us,*
> *And our loved ones are instructed,*
> *While the young ones are standing round us,*
> *Of the rising generation,*
> *Let them learn the words of magic,*
> *And recall our songs and legends,*
> *Of the belt of Väinämöinen,*
> *Of the forge of Ilmarinen,*
> *And of Kaukomieli's swordpoint,*
> *And of Joukahainen's crossbow:*
> *Of the utmost bounds of Pohja,*
> *And of Kalevala's wide heathlands.*

ENGLISH TRANSLATION BY W.F. KIRBY (1907)

Väinämöinen, the protagonist of the *Kalevala*, is a remarkable character, the greatest of sages and magicians. His mother was the divine mother Luonnotar, and the first part of the *Kalevala* describes how Väinämöinen carves the land of Kaleva from the primordial chaos. It is told that he spent 30 years in his mother's belly and, as a result, was wise from birth. As well, he was known as a warrior and an unrivaled musician and singer. When he played his kantele, a five-stringed harplike instrument that he made from the bones of an enormous pike, all the animals drew near to listen to his wondrous tunes.

IN SEARCH OF A WIFE

Despite his gifts, Väinämöinen was unlucky in love. The *Kalevala* tells how he and the black-smith Ilmarinen seek a wife—a search that takes them to the land of Pohjola, Kaleva's mysterious northern neighbor.

In return for her daughter's hand in marriage the Mistress of Pohjola requires a "many-colored" sampo (a talisman usually identified as a type of mill) that brings unlimited riches to its owner. Ilmarinen duly forges the sampo and marries the daughter in a wedding of great magnificence.

Above *Ilmarinen Ploughing the Field of Snakes* by Joseph Alanen (1885–1920). In Finnish mythology, Ilmarinen is the primeval smith: forger of the sky, sun, and moon. He taught mankind how to work with metals and brought them fire. He is also the patron of travelers.

Bad Blood

Soon after the wedding Lemminkainen, a petulant and proud young man also from Kaleva, takes time-out from his favorite pastime of seducing girls to make his own expedition north in search of a wife. His excursion is rather less successful and, after incurring the wrath of the people by killing one of their chiefs, he is chased out of Pohjola.

Largely as a result of Lemminkainen's efforts, relations between the people of Kaleva and Pohjola deteriorate into open conflict. When Väinämöinen discovers the prosperity that the sampo has brought to his northern neighbors he, together with his countrymen Ilmarinen and Lemminkainen, decides to retrieve it. Väinämöinen lulls his enemies to sleep with the aid of his kantele and they steal away with the sampo. As he sails home, the Mistress of Pohjola summons a terrible tempest; the sampo is smashed into many pieces and lost overboard. Väinämöinen is able to retrieve some of the fragments, and with these he brings fertility and prosperity to his people.

The Punishment of Pohjola

The Mistress of Pohjola does not take the loss of the sampo lightly. She brings a number of scourges down upon the people of Kaleva, culminating with her stealing the sun and moon and hiding them in a great mountain. Väinämöinen protects his people and retrieves the sun and moon by using his magic, skill in fighting and hunting, and great knowledge. With this achievement, however, Väinämöinen gets ready to depart. In the closing canto the aged, god-like Väinämöinen anoints his successor and sails away with his kantele for a well-earned rest.

Then the aged Väinämöinen
Went upon his journey singing,
Sailing in his boat of copper,
Sailed away to loftier regions,
To the land beneath the heavens,
There he rested with his vessel,
Rested weary with his vessel.

ENGLISH TRANSLATION BY W.F. KIRBY (1907)

ORIGIN MYTHS AND PRACTICAL ADVICE

In addition to recounting the many adventures of Väinämöinen, Ilmarinen, and Lemminkainen, the *Kalevala* describes in detail the origins of, among other things, iron and fire. These "origin myths" are in the form of incantations that confer mystical power upon the character that recites them.

The *Kalevala* also provides practical advice for readers and listeners. An entire section (Rune) of the *Kalevala* is devoted to advice for brides.

Hear, O maiden, what I tell thee,
What I say, and what I tell thee,
Do not go without thy clothing,
Nor without thy shift disport thee,
Move about without thy linen,
Or without thy shoes go shuffling,
Greatly shocked would be thy bridegroom,
And thy youthful husband grumble.

ENGLISH TRANSLATION BY W.F. KIRBY (1907)

ANCESTOR WORSHIP AND SHAMANISM

The ancient Finns believed in a tripartite world. Above were the heavens, where the gods lived, while the living inhabited an island surrounded by a great river. On the other side of the river was the kingdom of the dead, Tuonela.

The family unit was considered to include both its living members and those that had crossed over to the kingdom of the dead. Death did not relieve an individual of his or her familial duties; the deceased continued to take part in the lives of the offspring in a number of ways. In return, the living were required to observe faithfully the ancient rites and continue their ancestors' work. This practice lay at the heart of ancient Finnish understanding of family life.

If these rites of passage to Tuonela were not properly performed, the dead could become restless souls, known as *sijattomat sielut*, who haunted the house of future generations of their family, rather than become integrated into the larger family unit.

The Kingdom of the Dead

This land is not seen as a place of punishment in Finnish mythology. While it is darker than other lands, the sun does shine and plants grow. Its rulers are the king, Tuoni, and his wife, Tuonetar. Their two daughters are terrible to behold and cause all manner of disease and illness.

The ancient Finns believed that it is actually possible to travel to Tuonela although the attempt would be likely to end in a terrible death, if not in the thick dark forests on the way, then almost certainly at the hands of the inhabitants of Tuonela. Lemminkainen, as a young man, travels as far as the bank of the black river that surrounds the kingdom of the dead while pursuing a beautiful swan; he is tossed into the river and torn to pieces. It takes all his mother's skills as a magician to bring him back to life.

Väinämöinen alone is able to visit the kingdom of the dead and live to tell the tale. He travels to Tuonela in search of an incantation that will allow him to finish his magic copper ship. He is offered a horrible brew of frogs and worms by Tuonetar and told that he will never be allowed to leave. However, that night he changes into a type of snake and escapes.

Left **Eighteenth-century drum from Lapland.** The magic drums of ancient Finland, *quodbas*, were sacred objects, used by shamans to contact the spirits. To the Swedes, however, they were pagan objects that impeded their "civilizing" efforts.

Shamans

A family could communicate with their ancestors in the kingdom of the dead via a shaman who would contact the dead by beating his magic drum. A shaman might also eat certain types of mushroom to achieve the trancelike state required to communicate with the dead.

Successive neighbors and occupiers of Finland regarded the shamans with suspicion and fear. In the Middle Ages, the Norwegian kings prohibited their subjects from traveling to Finland to consult with the shamans. In the sixteenth and seventeenth centuries the Swedish authorities tried to render the shamans impotent by confiscating their drums (*quodbas*).

Left *Swan of Tuonela* by I.J. Belmont (1885–1964). This illustration, inspired by ancient Finnish tales and a musical composition of the same name by Jean Sibelius, evokes the eerie movements of the swan as it glides over the black waters of Tuonela.

ANIMISM

Care must be taken when using the *Kalevala* as a source for ascertaining the beliefs of the ancient Finns. While the songs are primitive in origin, they were collected in the nineteenth century and exhibit a number of external influences.

Analysis of the *Kalevala* has caused much discussion about the place of the Finnish gods in respect to their shamans. One commentator says: "The dead were the guardians of morals, the judges of customs, and they maintained the order of society. In this respect not even the god of the upper regions could compete with them." *The New Larousse Encyclopaedia of Mythology* (Hamlyn: London, 1968) observes that "shamanism … is scarcely compatible with the idea of gods who are essentially superior to humanity,

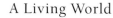

We are doomed to be eternal sentinels, our periods of rest have not been long.

ANON., FINNISH POET

because the shaman is capable of subduing everything with the magic of his spells."

It is now generally accepted that the gods of the *Kalevala* are too nebulous to have formed the basis of a "religion," and that it is probably more correct to suggest that the ancient Finns' beliefs resided somewhere between the worship of nature itself and the divinities that inhabited natural phenomena.

A Living World

The ancient Finns believed that every object had an "essence" or soul that was known as the *haltijat*. This essence is not like the Christian soul that lives on after the death of its host; the *haltijat* is inalienably linked to its physical form and dies along with the object that it inhabits.

The Finns understood even inanimate objects to have a type of life. There were spirits of the house and yard, the threshing shed, and of the cowshed. As long as these spirits were treated with adequate reverence and not "killed," they would watch over the activities of the people that lived and worked in these buildings. Hence, when Finns drew water from a well they would pour a little back in deference to the spirit of the well.

A Bond between Opponents

The souls of animals were believed to survive as long as the animal's bones existed. The *Kalevala* describes an intriguing "bear feast." After the bear had been killed and eaten, its bones were placed in a tomb with various objects. The dead bear was then treated like a friend and asked to tell other bears about the honors that humans had paid to it. As late as the seventeenth century a similar rite was described with some disdain by the Lutheran Bishop Isak Rothovius: "When they kill a bear they hold a feast, drink out of the bear's skull and imitate its growling in order to ensure plenty of game in the future."

FINNISH GODS

The creation myth in the *Kalevala* describes how Luonnotar, a virgin, grows tired of her lonely sterile life in the heavens and allows herself to fall from the celestial plane onto the surface of the void. She floats there for seven centuries until an eagle appears, builds a nest on her knee, and incubates its eggs. The eggs

Below *The Enormous Oak Tree is Cut Down* by Joseph Alanen (1885–1920). The *Kalevala* tells how the gnome of the plowland, Sampsa, is sent by Väinämöinen to find wood for his boat. He finds an oak tree with a "girth nine full fathoms," which he fells with his axe.

eventually drop from Luonnotar's knee—the yolk is transformed into the sun, the whites the moon, and fragments of the shell, the stars.

The heroes of the *Kalevala*, including Luonnotar's son, Väinämöinen, are left with the task of taming the wild lands that she creates.

Finnish mythology does not establish a detailed hierarchy of gods although some invocations name Ukko as the head of the pantheon. He is sometimes described as the "god of the sky and air" and other times, more narrowly, as the god of thunder. Indeed he gives his name to the Finnish word for thunder, *ukkonen*. In addition to thunder, he seems to be responsible for almost all natural phenomena that emanate from the sky: clouds, rain, snow, and hail. His wife was the divinity Rauni.

Other gods include Paiva (the sun), Kun (the moon), and Ilma (the divinity of the air whose daughter Luonnotar is named in the creation myth). Lesser divinities include Pellervoinen (the fields), Atho (water), Mannu (earth), and Metsola (forest).

There are numerous other Finnish deities. Even common activities such as dyeing and weaving are imbued with their own divinities (Sinettaret and Kankahattaret). As one commentator has observed: "Every deity, however petty he may be, rules in his own sphere as a substantial, independent power, or, to speak in the spirit of the *Kalevala*, as a self-ruling householder. The god of the Polar-star only governs an insignificant spot in the vault of the sky, but on this spot he knows no master."

HASTY ASSUMPTIONS

When Tacitus described the Finns as "unimaginably barbarous and miserably poor," he was unaware that their riches lay in their mythology. The *Kalevala*, with its poetic and vivid account of Väinämöinen's heroics, compares favorably with the best mythic tales of the Finns' neighbors.

The *Kalevala* was written to be recited rather than read in silence. Fortunately for lovers of the ancient Finnish tales, parts of the *Kalevala* are still performed by Finnish folk music ensembles today, although rarely, if ever, in English.

Above ***Witches Sell Winds*** from *Historia de Gentibus Septentrionalibus* by Olaus Magnus (1490–1557). The title of Magnus's work on the Nordic peoples means "History of the People below the Big Dipper, or the Plough." It consists of 22 books and describes how the harsh elements shaped both the people and their mythologies.

FROM FINNISH TO ELVISH

J.R.R. Tolkien (1892–1973) was Professor of Linguistics at Oxford University for 34 years. He had a genius for language, however, he is more famously known as being the author of *The Hobbit* and *Lord of the Rings*. Even as a child he was fascinated by words and was inventing languages. Later, his great "hobby" was to develop a complete language. Sound and the rhythm of the language was always very important to him; words should sound beautiful, as well as sound like the thing they describe. Tolkien was thrilled when he discovered Finnish which, for him, was filled with just such beautiful sounds. Elvish, or *Quenya*, one of the principal languages later used in the *Lord of the Rings*, was based on the sound of Finnish.

To develop a "real" language, not just one of invented words, Tolkien needed a mythology of the peoples who used it. Texts such as the *Kalevala* and the Icelandic *Edda* would have helped guide the way.

Also, just as the early Finns believed the forest was alive and venerated trees as well as animals such as the bear, the forests live in Tolkien's books. There is the wild man Beorn in *The Hobbit*, with his ability to turn into a bear. Tom Bombadil from *Lord of the Rings*, a character who sings constantly and has command over the trees, perhaps contains elements of Väinämöinen; and the Ents, the ancient forest beings Tolkien created in *Lord of the Rings*, could almost have walked out of ancient Finnish forests.

SLAVIC MYTHOLOGY

Right **Targitaj fighting a monster, bronze chariot ornament.** Slavic peoples cannot be considered a single group, though they share a common mythology. This piece was made by the Scythians, nomadic tribes who inhabited the Black Sea steppes from 500–300 B.C.

Below *Dragon of Krakow, Poland* from *Cosmographia Universalis* by Sebastian Munster (1489–1552). A long time ago, the town of Krakow was terrorized by a dragon. The wise Krakus smeared a sheep with sulfur, and gave it to the dragon to eat. The sulfur burnt the dragon, who drank water until it burst.

The Slavic peoples do not share a common ancestry, their bond is their culture, which has at its core a rustic mythology that has been passed between generations in folklore.

Probably originating in or near the Carpathian Mountains, and growing to incorporate tribes throughout eastern Europe, the Slavs were not recognized as a distinct people until the sixth century A.D. Today, the Slavs are arranged in three great blocs: south, west, and east, stretching from the Balkans to Russia. These blocs are divided into numerous ethnic enclaves including Russians, Poles, Czechs, Ukrainians, Belorussians, Serbians, Croatians, Macedonians, Slovenians, Bulgarians, Kashubians, and Slovakians. Although each of these groups has its own individual language, speakers of one Slavic language can generally understand much of what is said in another Slavic language.

OPPOSING FORCES

Slavic mythology does not provide a coherent system of gods, priests, and religious rites. It is best viewed as an attempt to make sense of the capricious forces of nature—storms, floods, and droughts—against which the ancients, gathered in small family groups, were largely defenceless. The myths are dominated by the opposing forces of chaos and malevolence on the one hand, and benevolence and order on the other.

Chernobog is the bringer of destruction. His name is a mix of the word *cherny* meaning "black," and *bog* meaning "god." He lives in shadows and the night. Conversely, Byelbog, from *byely* meaning "white," is the god of light and creative forces. He only reveals himself during daylight hours and is usually represented as a kindly old man with a white beard who protects those in peril from harm.

Dualism and Animism

The two forces of Byelbog and Chernobog were later
to be infused with the character of God and Satan
inherited from Christianity, but in their original form
they did not represent good and evil in the Christian
sense. On the contrary, Slavic mythology established
a kind of dualism that was opposed by Christianity,
so much so that most records of the ancient gods,
including writings and carvings, were destroyed after
the arrival of the Christian evangelists such as the
Saints Cyril and Methodius, as well as Orthodox
missionaries from the east. For example, a statue of
the god Dazhbog towered over Kiev until A.D. 988,
when Vladamir I converted to Christianity and
instructed that it be thrown into the Dneiper River,
together with statues of other pagan gods. Nevertheless, many of the ancient Slavic stories were
preserved in legends, tales, songs, and proverbs.

Slavic stories also describe a pantheon of animist
spirits—sometimes playful, occasionally cruel—that
inhabit the earth, sun, wind, and water. These spirits
are so rooted in the Slavic psyche that even today on
the eastern fringes of the Slavic world, there still
exists a mix of Christian and animist beliefs, which
is known as *dvoeverie* or "double-faith."

GODS OF THE ELEMENTS

The ancient Slavs believed that the unseen hands of
the gods guided all natural phenomena.

The Slavic sky god was Svarog. He had two sons,
Dazhbog, who was the personification of the sun,
and Svarogich, the god of fire. According to myth,
Svarog, after reigning over the world for countless
years, passed his power to his children, and
Dazhbog ultimately became the Slavs' supreme deity.

It is easy to understand how the gods of sun and
fire came to be at the head of the Slavic pantheon.
The Russians suffer some of the harshest winters of
any people in the world. Fire and sun, as providers
of warmth and light, were not just comforts but
lifesavers. It is largely for this reason that Dazhbog
also became synonymous with happiness and justice.

Dazhbog was said to live in a golden palace in the
east, in a land of plenty where summer never ended.
Every morning he would emerge from his palace on
a diamond chariot, drawn by fire-breathing white
horses, and traverse the sky. He was attended by two
beautiful virgins, the morning and evening stars, and
was counseled by seven judges (the planets). The
comets acted as his messengers.

In some myths Dazhbog is represented as being
born every morning, growing to become a handsome
young man at midday, and dying each evening.

THE CYRILLIC ALPHABET

The lack of any records written before the
ninth century by Slavic peoples led some
historians to suggest that the ancient Slavs
had no written language. It now seems
more likely that records of the early gods,
written in ancient Slavic runes, were
destroyed after the arrival of Christianity.
In the ninth century, the saints Cyril and
Methodius created the Cyrillic alphabet by
combining Slavic runes with the Greek
alphabet. With some modifications the
Cyrillic alphabet is still used by most Slavs
today although some, such as the Poles,
have adopted the Roman alphabet.

Below **Roman mosaic of the Saints
Cyril (A.D. 826–869) and Methodius
(A.D. 825–885).** These early evangelists of
the Byzantine Empire traveled to Greater
Moravia in A.D. 863 to spread Christianity.

The Quarrelsome Family

While the ancient myth relating to the sun god varies
only slightly between the different ethnic groups,
the god of the moon, known as Myesyats, is by turns
represented as either a balding old man who waits
patiently for Dazhbog to return from his daily adventure, or as a beautiful young woman who is married
to Dazhbog. The legends which represent Dazhbog
and Myesyats as husband and wife can be viewed as
a way of explaining a number of natural phenomena
through the vagaries of their rather tempestuous
relationship: for instance, tremors or earthquakes are
caused by their arguments and the barren winters by
their separations.

Above **Bronze votive figurine, from Strakonice, the Czech Republic, first century** B.C. Though Slavic mythology seems to suggest a world ruled by violent elemental forces, these forces could be appeased by giving due respect to the gods.

Opposite page *Baba Yaga, the Witch* by Dimitrii Mitrokhin (1883–1973), from Arthur Ransome's *Old Peter's Russian Tales.* Renowned children's author, Arthur Ransome (1884–1967) traveled to Russia to report on the Revolution of 1917. While there, he compiled a collection of 21 fairy tales.

Right **Anaitis, goddess of hunting, bronze statue, Romania, 700–600** B.C. This statue belongs to the Scythians, a hard-living group of fierce warriors. They believed that their wealth could be taken with them into the afterlife, and their burial sites have borne many treasures.

The Temperamental Winds

The ancient Slavs recognized at least three wind gods: north, west, and east. They were said to live on the island of Buyan and their tempers were reflected in the nature of the wind that they inhabited. For example, the west wind, Dogoda, was kind and gentle. *The New Larousse Encyclopaedia of Mythology* (Hamlyn: London, 1968) records the following spell, which would be uttered by a man experiencing difficulty wooing the woman of his affections: "On the sea, the ocean, on the isle of Buyan, live three brothers, the Winds: one is the North, the second is the East, the third is the West. Blow ye Winds, blow unbearable sadness to … [such and such a girl] so that she cannot live a single day, a single hour without thinking of me!"

Respect for the Earth

The Slavs also revered the earth beneath their feet, which was believed to be possessed by Mati Syra Zemlya or Moist Mother Earth, to whom great respect was given. Unlike other deities, Mati Syra Zemlya was always worshipped in her natural form, and was never represented as having human features.

In early spring the earth was considered to be pregnant and no one was allowed to strike Mati Syra Zemlya with a hoe or plow until the vernal equinox. If treated with adequate reverence she would reward the household with great bounty in spring, some of which she would expect to be returned to her by the pouring of wine into a hole or the burying of bread.

Sacred oaths were sworn while holding a piece of Moist Mother Earth, sometimes in the mouth. Wedding vows were taken with a small clump of earth placed on the head.

Mati Syra Zemlya was also considered to be a type of oracle. Peasants would dig a hole in the ground, speak into it, and listen for her reply. In fact, until the early years of the twentieth century, if no priest could be found, sins were told to Mati Syra Zemlya, and her forgiveness sought before death.

BABA YAGA AND THE CYCLES OF DEATH AND INITIATION

Baba Yaga, as she is called in Russia (from *baba* meaning "old woman," and *yaga* meaning "hag"), is a witch with the gifts of shape-changing and prophesy. She is known by other names outside Russia: Jezda in Poland and Jazi Baba in the Czech Republic.

Although most often depicted as a bony old crone with long sharp teeth, Baba Yaga is a highly complex character containing a number of facets. In addition to being the personification of death, Baba Yaga is also regarded as having an important role in relation to fertility and fate. Just as the ancient Slavs faced disease and death without warning or explanation, so Baba Yaga can fly into fits of rage on the smallest pretext, to the degree that she is wont to eat people that offend her or do not fulfil their duties.

Baba Yaga's house is one of the most evocative creations in the tales that involve her. It sits upon four chicken's legs—one in each corner—which allow it to turn and move about. Baba Yaga herself is often depicted inside at a spinning wheel (originally spinning thread from the innards of the dead). Some legends say that her teeth, nose, and breasts are made of iron and that her hair is a knot of writhing snakes.

Baba Yaga also has the gift of prophecy and can impart great wisdom. Those that wish to benefit from these gifts must undertake an arduous journey to Baba Yaga's house, which is in the most remote and inaccessible part of the forest. They must then survive Baba Yaga's demanding tasks and tests. The fence surrounding her house is made of the bones of those who failed to ask the right questions or satisfy her ruthless test of motives. Each picket is adorned with a skull.

Throughout eastern Europe, many tales involving Baba Yaga survived the advent of Christianity and continue to be the subject of great fascination. Despite years of analysis by academics, Baba Yaga continues to be an enigma. As one commentator has said, "Baba Yaga hails from the place where fear and wisdom meet, she straddles the gap between life and death and holds the secrets of both."

In the Christian era some myths that recorded Baba Yaga's unpleasant habits were altered to make them less gruesome. Some later legends even confuse her with Mary, Mother of Jesus—very strange to anyone who knows the original tales.

BABA YAGA AND VASILISA

Below *The Witch Baba Yaga* by Ivan Bilibin (1872–1942), from *Vasilisa the Beautiful.* Baba Yaga is found in stories and fairy tales throughout Russia and Eastern Europe. She is often shown flying in a mortar, steering with the pestle, and sweeping away her traces with a broom.

Vasilisa is a young girl when her mother becomes ill. Before she dies, her mother gives her a tiny doll. She tells her daughter that this doll will guide her; all she needs to do is ask, and the doll will answer.

Vasilisa is distraught when her mother dies. After a short time, her father remarries a woman with two daughters of her own. The stepmother and her children greatly resent Vasilisa. They torment and mistreat her when her father is away. Vasilisa says nothing of these abuses to her father, for she is too kind.

One day, when the father is away, the stepmother foolishly allows the fire to burn out. Without the fire there can be no food, no heat, and no light. Vasilisa's step-family entreat her to travel through the forest to the hut of Baba Yaga to fetch a flame with which to relight their fire. Although hesitant and fearful, the good Vasilisa agrees and sets off with her mother's doll in her pocket. The stepmother and her two daughters rejoice wickedly, since they believe that the fearsome Baba Yaga will devour the good Vasilisa, ridding them of the child that has become a constant reminder of their own shortcomings.

As she walks down the road through the darkness, Vasilisa consults the doll in her pocket. The doll gives her directions to Baba Yaga's hut by jumping up and down when Vasilisa guesses correctly. On her way three horsemen pass her, one dressed in white, one in red, and the last in black, rushing toward Baba's home.

When she arrives, Vasilisa sees that Baba Yaga's house is surrounded by a fence adorned with skulls that spew tongues of flame. Although terrified, she remembers her promise to complete the task, swallows her fear, and forges ahead. She is greeted by the repulsive hag, Baba Yaga, who flies down to confront the young girl.

Baba demands to know what the girl wants and Vasilisa replies that she has come for fire. Baba then asks the girl why she should grant her request. Vasilisa is speechless, and once again consults the doll. She replies as the doll suggests: "Because I ask it." Baba is surprised and tells the girl that this is the correct answer; she allows Vasilisa inside the hut. Baba Yaga says to the child that she must perform the tasks asked of her and that if she fails, she will be eaten.

Days go by, and the tasks become ever more difficult to perform until, finally, they seem impossible. Nevertheless, with the doll's help and reassurance, Vasilisa meets every challenge.

Baba Yaga is impressed, and one night at dinner allows the girl to ask some questions. Before the girl speaks, Baba warns her that too much knowledge makes a person old before their time. Vasilisa asks about the three horsemen, and is told that they are Day, the Rising Sun, and Night. They live within the hut, going forth each morning to bring day to the world. The child thinks to ask more questions but the doll stops her. When Baba Yaga inquires if she wants to know anything else, Vasilisa replies that too much knowledge will make her old. This answer pleases Baba Yaga, and she asks how the child came to be so wise at such a young age. Vasilisa touches the doll in her pocket, and replies cryptically: "By the blessing of my mother."

"No blessings in this house!" shouts Baba Yaga, and pushes the girl outside. Before Vasilisa leaves Baba Yaga hands her one of the posts topped by a flaming skull as payment for passing the trials. It is dark, and the skull casts an unearthly glow across the frightening forest as the child races homeward. She becomes frightened and thinks to toss the skull away but the skull speaks to her and assures her that everything will turn out fine.

Vasilisa returns to her home, to her shocked stepmother and sisters. They thought her dead because she had been gone for so many days. She enters the house feeling triumphant, for she had survived her dangerous journey and brought fire back to her house. The skull watches the stepmother and her daughters quite closely that day, noticing the terrible way they treat Vasilisa. That night the skull burns into the stepmother and her daughters, turning them to ash before morning's light.

CHRISTIAN INFLUENCE ON THE VASILISA TALE

The influence of Christianity upon the Baba Yaga legend can be seen in the fact that later versions of the Vasilisa tale emphasise the redemptive power of charitable works rather than the mystical power of a doll and skull. The version included in *Old Peter's Russian Tales* (Jonathan Cape Ltd: London, 1916) begins similarly but quickly diverges.

In this version, the stepmother wraps a little stale bread and some kitchen scraps in a handkerchief

for the girl's journey to the hut of Baba Yaga. When the girl arrives she notices a servant of Baba Yaga's is standing in the front yard, crying bitterly and wiping her eyes with her petticoat. The girl unties her handkerchief and shakes it clean. She puts the remaining morsels of food in her pockets and gives the cloth to Baba Yaga's servant, who wipes her eyes on it. Next to the hut is a wretched dog. Reaching into her pocket for her kitchen scraps, the girl offers them to the dog that eats them as if it had not eaten in a long time.

These creatures have never experienced such acts of kindness before and later they help the girl to escape. When the girl arrives home she tells her father that his new wife sent her to Baba Yaga's hut and he drives the stepmother out of the house.

Above *Three Women and Three Wolves* by Eugene Grasset (1814–1917). Fairy tales throughout Eastern Europe contain elements inspired by the Baba Yaga tale—the forest, and the creatures it held, had a particular potency to the ancient imagination.

Left *Firebird* by Dimitrii Mitrokhin (1883–1973), from Arthur Ransome's *Old Peter's Russian Tales.* There are various versions of this tale, one featuring a peasant girl Maryushka, who was turned into the firebird by a rejected suitor. In all versions, the feathers of the firebird are valued for their magic qualities.

SPIRITS OF THE HOUSE, YARD, FOREST, AND FIELD

There are no more curious spirits than those that inhabited the houses of the ancient Slavs.

One popular spirit is the Domovoi, from *dom* meaning "house." Members of the household often affectionately referred to him as "grandfather." He was a rather forlorn character whose stifled sobs could be heard in the creaking and groaning of the house at night. Legend has it that a number of Domovoi had revolted against Svarog soon after the beginning of time and had been banished from the heavens. They fell to earth, down the chimneys, and into the stoves of houses, where they now dwell.

The Domovoi was rarely seen. He was usually depicted as a small old man so entirely covered in hair (even on his palms and the soles of his feet) that his eyes were hidden. He may also have had horns and a tail. Some drawings depict him as resembling a bundle of hay. His wife, Domovikha, lived in the cellar.

The Domovoi and Domovikha were said to warn the inhabitants of a house about coming disaster. When someone in the household was about to die, the Domovoi could be heard crying at night. He was also said to pull a woman's hair to warn her that her husband was about to beat her. His wife, Domovikha, would tickle lazy children to wake them during the night. In contrast, the gentle furry touch of the Domovoi at night was a good omen.

Traditionally, peasants were highly respectful of the Domovoi and, for example, would not sleep in an area that would inhibit his noctural wanderings, such as near the stove. When changing house, peasants would acknowledge the Domovoi of the new house before they moved in.

The Slavs also recognized spirits of the yard (Dvorovoi), the bath (Bannik), and the barns (Ovinnik), which were generally less benevolent than the Domovoi and his wife. Dvorovoi was considered to be responsible for the death of animals in the yard, especially those with white fur for which he reserved particular dislike. After washing it was necessary to leave some water behind for Bannik to bathe. If this ritual was not observed, or a person entered the washhouse while the spirit himself was bathing, Bannik would take a terrible revenge. Interestingly, no Christian icons were placed in Slavic bathhouses, for fear of offending Bannik. Ovinnik, or barn spirit, was often depicted as a black cat sitting in the corner of a barn, and would set it alight if angered—sometimes with the owner in it.

Vodyanoi was a malevolent spirit who lived in an underwater crystal palace in lakes and rivers. From there, he would drown any careless maiden who trespassed on his territory. Once drowned, the maiden would become a water nymph known as Ruskala.

Leshy was the spirit of the forest. He amused himself by disorienting unfortunate travelers, making them stumble around in circles, sometimes for days, before finally releasing them. When forests were cleared, the resulting fields were inhabited by Polevik, who liked to punish drunkards and idlers.

VAMPIRES

The vampire may have lost much of his power to strike fear into us today but for the ancient Slavs, in whose mythology he originated, tales of his grizzly deeds must have been terrifying.

Bram Stoker based his famous 1897 novel *Dracula* upon the legend of a corpse, the *vampir,* which returns to life at night to suck the blood from the living. The victim then becomes a vampire himself. Stoker adopted a number of elements from the *vampir* legend, including the ability of Dracula to change into a bat or wolf.

The origin of the Serbian word *vampir* is uncertain. Some suggest it is related to the Turkisk word *ubir* meaning "undead," while other sources relate it to a fantastical creature from peasant Russian mythology, Upir, who himself was a type of vampire or werewolf.

Bram Stoker's book also drew upon elements of the story of the fifteenth-century prince, Vlad Tepes (1431–1477), known as Vlad the Impaler, a name bestowed on him by his subjects because of the fearful punishment he inflicted on his enemies. Living up to his title, he would bind his victim's hands and feet to four posts and rock them back and forth until they were gradually impaled on a sharpened stake. Ruling the area known as Walachia, south of Transylvania, Vlad's other name Dracula ("son of the devil") comes from his father, Vlad Dracul.

RISING FROM THE ASHES

The gods and spirits described here provide only a sample of the ancient mythology of the Slavic people. Recent studies have commented on the impact of Christianity on the culture, effectively suppressing the mythology before it had a chance to fully develop.

What remains gives us a tantalizing glimpse of what Slavic mythology once was, and what it might have become, if given the opportunity to mature. In the last decade there has been an upsurge of interest and research into Slavic history and mythology, deepening the knowledge and understanding of the myths, and restoring, if not their original power, then their significance in Slavic cultural history.

Above *Vlad the Impaler (Vlad VI of Walachia), German school, sixteenth century.* This portrait does not reflect the terror that Vlad Tepes, also known as Dracula, inspired among his subjects. One story tells of how he invited the needy to his castle, fed them, then locked them inside and set the castle on fire. He did this, he said, to solve the problem of beggars in the town.

Left *The End of a Vampire from Les Tribunaux Secrets by Paul Féval (1817–1887).* Vampires have fascinated people for centuries, and a detailed mythology has built up around them. Of the various ways to kill a vampire, driving a wooden stake through the heart is the most famous method, though in this picture a red-hot iron is used.

ROMANCE MYTHOLOGY

"Romance" is a many-layered word: it is a set of languages, a type of story, a form of courtship, and an outlook on life. All of these notions are related to each other, bound up in the narrative traditions of the Middle Ages (approximately A.D. 500–1500). The word originally referred to the Romance languages, those spoken languages that developed from Latin including French, Spanish, and Italian. The language of the Roman Empire, Latin, continued to be used in an official capacity throughout the medieval period for education, government, law, and religion. The languages of everyday life, however, were the vernaculars that had developed from it, and the two carried on, each in their own spheres, until modern times. "Romance" also came to be applied to the heroic tales, legends, and adventures that were recorded in these everyday languages, unofficial works meant for entertainment. Later, the title was applied to the courtly ideals and the knightly ethos recorded in them.

Romance mythology is not like ancient Greek or Roman mythology, where people speaking the same language shared tales about heroes and a pantheon of gods and goddesses. After the coming of Christianity, the nature of religion and religious narratives changed. The Bible was the ultimate reference for religious knowledge, and even though there were some disagreements about exactly which books formed the Bible or how best to translate them, a text-based religion meant that the basic religious narratives were codified and unchanging. Traditional tales about gods and heroes no longer formed the basis of religious beliefs as they had in pre-Christian times. Folk narratives continued to circulate, however, and continued to be important vehicles for expressing and shaping people's ideas of the world around them. Ancient stories, themes, tales of heroes, and even gods remained alive in oral tradition. Within Christianity, a new mythology arose to help the religion adapt to its new setting in post-Roman Europe, explaining inconsistencies and incorporating pre-Christian traditions.

Above **The Castle where a Dragon is Imprisoned, from Dioscorides Tractatus de Herbis.** This fifteenth-century French manuscript reveals how medieval tales incorporated a wide range of creatures—from human figures such as saints and pilgrims to mythical beings like dragons and unicorns.

Right **Lovers in a landscape by Marco dell'Avogardro.** This illustration, taken from the fifteenth-century illuminated *Borso d'Este Bible,* is said to be the most sumptuous work of its kind. While handwritten bibles replaced oral traditions in the medieval age, they, too, would soon be replaced, due to the invention of the printing press.

For the medieval period, the only records of that oral tradition are occasional references in historical documents and depictions in art and literature. The literature closest to oral tradition and most directly inspired by it, epic and chivalric literature, began to be written down in the High Middle Ages, from the twelfth century onward. Much of this material has also survived in the form of folklore in the modern Romance countries, and together they paint a clear portrait of medieval beliefs and legends.

EPIC NARRATIVES

As with Homer's earlier epic poems, the *Iliad* and *Odyssey,* the most important medieval narratives come down to us in the form of an epic, or cycle of epics (epic poems that form a complete history or story). New forms of old tales arose for the heroes of Classical tradition, but new heroes developed as well, often based on historical figures. Two of the

most enduring are the cycles surrounding the great Frankish king, Charlemagne (c. 742–814), and the Spanish hero warrior El Cíd (c. 1043–1099). These cycles are often expressed as conflicts between Islam and Christendom, probably under the influence of the persuasive language used during the time of the Crusades.

In France, these epics were written as *chansons de geste,* literally "songs about deeds." They are long poems recounting the adventures of a hero, most probably sung or chanted to an audience by a *jongleur* or wandering minstrel. The oldest and most famous is *The Song of Roland,* written around 1125–1150, but known to be much older. It chronicles the adventures and untimely death of the noble and brave Lord Roland, Charlemagne's nephew, at Roncevaux in the Pyrenees mountains in the year 778. The story pits Christians against Muslims, but the historical basis for the story was probably an attack on the Franks by the Basques, in whose territory the real events took place. Originally composed in Old French, the story spread across Europe and remains popular today.

The Song of Roland

The story opens with the revelation that Ganelon, Roland's stepfather and one of the twelve Peers of the

Realm, is jealous of Roland and is plotting his destruction. He gets his opportunity when Charlemagne's army is sent to fight Marsile, the Saracen King of Saragossa (northern Spain). Roland is captain of the rear guard, which Ganelon treacherously enables the Saracens to attack. Roland's friend and companion, Oliver, asks Roland to sound his elephant-tusk horn, Olifant, and call for help from the main army. Roland insists that it is better to die than suffer the shame of calling for assistance. They fight the Saracens bravely, but they are overcome. Only at the very end does Roland sound the horn, so that Charlemagne may find and avenge them. The effort of blowing the horn kills him. A thunderstorm and an eclipse of the sun signal Roland's death in France, suggesting that, like the heroes of Classical mythology, his death is significant on a cosmic level. Despite the tragic death of Roland, Charlemagne goes on to capture the city of Saragossa and conquer Spain. Ganelon's treachery is revealed, and he is punished by death.

Above *The Battle of Roncevaux,* fifteenth-century manuscript. While the real Roland has been largely forgotten by history, the noble Roland of legend became a figure so popular that it is said the song of his exploits was sung to the troops of William of Normandy in 1066 on the eve of battle.

Below *Death of Roland de Roncevaux,* from *Entre d'Espagne.* This epic has links to many cultures; the Danes sing *The Song of Ogier the Dane,* about a knight who died alongside Roland. In it, Morgan la Fée, better known from Arthurian myth, is featured.

Below **Alfonso VI, King of Castille and Léon.** In 1081, the King banished Rodrigo Díaz de Vivar, who then fought against Moors and Christians, often for financial reward. He seems more like an adventurer than a hero, using the spoils of war to buy back the king's favor.

El Cíd

In Spain itself, the most enduring medieval epic tale is that of El Cíd, based on the eleventh-century historical figure of Rodrigo Díaz de Vivar. The story of his deeds survives in just one manuscript from the fourteenth century, though again the story is older. The title "Cíd" comes from the Arabic word *Sayyidí*, meaning "lord, sir," and, in fact, the historical El Cíd served with the Moorish ruler of Saragossa for a time. However, the narrative is set in terms of the conflict between El Cíd's Christian overlord, King Alfonso VI of Castille and Léon, and the Moors of southern Spain. As with the story of Roland, the adventures of El Cíd center on the concept of honor. El Cíd is portrayed as the ideal vassal, doomed through lack of "a good overlord." Like Charlemagne, Alfonso makes poor decisions and therefore reveals himself to be a bad and weak king.

The story begins when Alfonso exiles El Cíd, on the unjust advice of his vassals. Undaunted, El Cíd tricks moneylenders into giving him 600 marks, which he uses to build his own army. He defeats the Moors in battle after battle, capturing Castejón, then Alcocer, all the while sending princely gifts back to Alfonso.

Won over by El Cíd's generosity and great military prowess, he forgives him and, to make up for his earlier mistake, arranges to marry El Cíd's two daughters to the two brothers Carrión. Like Roland's stepfather Ganelon, these young lords are cowardly and perfidious, qualities that contrast with El Cíd's bravery and heroism. When El Cíd's pet lion escapes, the two brothers run and hide. Later, in battle, El Cíd receives a good account of their bravery, but it turns out to be false—they had really hidden during the fighting. On their way home with the two daughters, the brothers Carrión stay with El Cíd's Moorish friend, Albengalbón. He

welcomes them hospitably and gives them horses and other fine gifts. More impressed by his wealth than anything else, they plot to kill him and steal his riches. Luckily, they are overheard by a Spanish-speaking servant, and Albengalbón sends them away in disgrace. El Cíd's daughters mock their husbands' base behavior, and in return are beaten within an inch of their lives and abandoned. The women are found by their cousin, and the brothers are brought to trial and killed. The daughters are then remarried to the Spanish princes of Navarre and Aragón.

MIXING MYTHOLOGIES

Romance mythology incorporated a number of mythical beings from the pre-Christian mythologies of Europe. Another epic centering on Charlemagne is the later medieval story of Renaud de Montalban and his three brothers, and includes characters from Celtic, Germanic, and Classical tradition. At one time, Renaud and his brothers were vassals of King Charlemagne, who gave them a magical flying horse, Bayard. Though it resembled

Right **Reliquary bust of Charlemagne, 1349, at Aachen, his capital and burial place.** Charlemagne was the consolidator and first ruler of the Western Christian empire and, thus, is central to many stories. Through him, the Romantic virtues of honor, courage, and loyalty are played out.

Left *Entry of Charlemagne into Spain in a Chariot*, thirteenth-century manuscript. Charlemagne led—mostly in person—over 50 campaigns. After one trip to Spain to fight the Moors, Charlemagne led his army back through the Pyrenees. There, the rear guard of his army was besieged by the Basques, who killed nearly every man. It was from this actual battle that the tale of Roland emerged.

a normal horse, it could also expand to hold all four of them, if necessary. Bay comes from the Celtic word for "yellow," and similar horses are found throughout Celtic folklore, the horse being revered by the Celts. Swayed by wicked councilors, Charlemagne acts unjustly toward the brothers, and as a result they wage guerrilla warfare on him. Their cousin, the sorcerer Maugis, uses his magic powers to procure the sword Flamberge for them. It was first forged by Wayland the Smith, a god from Germanic mythology. When the Devil kidnaps Bayard, Maugis pursues him via Mount Vulcan, widely believed to be the Mouth of Hell in the Middle Ages. It takes its name and imagery from the Roman god Vulcan, the god of fire and metalworking who dwelled under Mount Etna in Sicily. Eventually, the conflict moves to the Holy Land, where Renaud and Maugis fight the Sultan of Persia for control of Jerusalem. They are ultimately successful, but rather than assume the kingship they elect to return to Europe, where they become holy men. Renaud de Montalban is still recognized as a saint in Cologne and other parts of Germany and France, and many miracles have been attributed to him.

THE UNICORN

The medieval world of Europe was peppered with supernatural beings of all sorts. One of the most important of these was the unicorn, both for its practical uses and its religious symbolism. It was normally depicted as a white horse with a single spiral horn on its forehead. Drinking from a unicorn's horn would protect the drinker from poison and epilepsy, and because of this protection the unicorn was seen as an exceptionally pure beast. The tusk of the narwhal (a type of whale) was pressed into service as a unicorn horn. This fabulous beast, known from Classical sources, developed its own mythology during the Middle Ages.

Medieval tales of the unicorn describe it as a ferocious fighter that could only be captured if a chaste virgin were left alone in its territory. The beast would lay its head in her lap and fall asleep, at which point unicorn hunters would capture it.

Below *Unicorn,* from *Histoire des Juifs* by Flavius Josephus. The horn of the unicorn was considered a precious treasure, desired by medieval rulers.

Above *The Lover Standing before a Richly Dressed Lady* by Robinet Testard, from *Romance of the Rose.* Begun by Guillaume de Lorris, and continued by Jean de Meung, this poem (1487–1495) was highly influential to all who aspired to the ideals of courtly love. Ostensibly an allegorical romance, it also addressed all aspects of medieval life, from how a women should sit at table to the Church.

Right *The Nun's Priest* from the *Ellesmere Chaucer Facsimile* (1410). This hugely popular tale by Chaucer is itself based on another by Marie de France. The tale, told by "the nun's priest," concerns the rooster, Chaunticleer, which is carried off by a fox. Through his quick wits, Chaunticleer manages to free himself and escape.

COURTLY LOVE

Later in the Middle Ages, a new ideal arose featuring knights and warriors that centered not on their great prowess in the field of battle, but in the adventures they undertook for the sake of romantic love. Because marriages at the time were arranged and women were given over to men, often much older men, on the basis of their guardians' economic or political needs, neither young women nor young men of the ruling classes had much opportunity to choose a partner. These knights and ladies between them created and sponsored the notion of "courtly love," a love that transcended the bounds of marriage. The powerful stories told of the natural and super-natural obstacles men and women would have to overcome to be with each other.

One of the greatest storytellers of the tradition of courtly love was the poet Marie de France. Although she probably lived in England and claimed to be translating her material from Breton (the language spoken in Brittany, north-west France) tradition, she wrote in Old French and evidently came from Île-de-France, a small region that included Paris and was then considered to be the country of France. One of the greatest female writers of the pre-modern world, Marie's stories are simple and elegant, and contain an enticing blend of the supernatural with the prosaic. Although adultery is often celebrated in her stories, it can also be con-demned, as in the following tale. The overriding ethic is one of faithfulness and constancy to love, whether inside or outside of marriage.

Bisclavret the Werewolf

Marie's story of Bisclavret is known as a *lay,* as it was told in poem or song form. It is unexpected in that the hero is a werewolf, a young married knight in the service of the king. His wife, though she loves him, is concerned with his unexplained weekly absences. At last he admits to her that he is a werewolf, and that if his clothes were to be stolen, he would have to remain a wolf. His wife is repulsed, and takes a lover. Between them they plot to steal Bisclavret's clothes, which they do successfully, and with her husband's disappearance, the wife marries again. In time, the werewolf finds the king, who is so impressed by the beast's noble behavior that he adopts him as a sort of royal pet. The only time the wolf misbehaves is when he sees his former wife and angrily bites off her nose. The court nobles defend the beast's actions, and eventually the truth comes out. The werewolf is given clothes and a changing-room, and is restored to a human state, while the wife and her lover are exiled. Many of their female descendants are born without a nose, a condition well known in the Middle Ages as an effect of leprosy.

The tale expresses the medieval ethics of love, fidelity, and honor, with both positive and negative examples. It also showcases, however, the darker elements of medieval mythology, such as the belief that a disease like leprosy is a punishment for your own or your ancestors' sins.

PILGRIMS, SAINTS, AND WANDERERS

Travel was an often difficult and dangerous undertaking in the Middle Ages, but one of crucial importance. Pilgrimages, whether long or short, were conducted for a variety of reasons: to make amends for a sin, to atone for a crime, or to venerate a site or relic. Pilgrimage sites ranged from local holy wells dedicated to popular saints, to whole cities such as Rome or Jerusalem. Pilgrimages were often social journeys, as well; pilgrims banded together for safety and comfort, and as a consequence shared news and stories.

The fourteenth-century Italian literary work *The Decameron* by Giovanni Boccaccio (1313–1375) exemplifies both the stories travelers told and the circumstances under which they might be spread. Ten noblemen and women of Florence retire to the country to wait out an attack of the bubonic plague that was ravaging the city. With nothing to do, they spend the ten-day period telling each other stories, including a mix of material from legendary and folktale traditions. *The Decameron* was one of the inspirations for the *Canterbury Tales,* by Geoffrey Chaucer (*c.* 1340–1400), and contains a mixture of piety and humor, bawdiness and courtliness. The following tale is an example of a humorous piece.

Brother Onion

Frate Cipolla (or "Brother Onion") comes to the town of Certaldo, and offers to exhibit a relic from the Holy Land, a feather from the Archangel Gabriel. Two tricksters decide to steal this feather—really just a parrot's tail-feather—and see what happens when the friar is forced to explain its disappearance. They substitute coal for the feather in the casket in which it is stored and blend into the crowd. After much fanfare, the box is opened, but the quick-thinking friar is not in the least put out. He recites a long-winded speech about his travels "through the kingdom of Algebra and through Bordello, eventually reaching Bedlam," and lists the marvelous relics he saw, including "a phial of Saint Michael's sweat when he fought with the Devil" and "holes from the Holy Cross." He explains that he keeps his relics in small caskets, all alike, and that the coal he has by mistake is the coal from the fire over which Saint Lawrence was roasted. He then uses it to draw crosses on the foreheads of the faithful. The tricksters own up to their deed and return the feather, congratulating the fraudulent friar on his quick-thinking audacity.

Below *The Storytellers of the Decameron by Boccaccio (1313–1375),* painting by Francesco Podesti (1800–1895). A collection of 100 short stories, *The Decameron* is set against the threat of the Black Plague. Its stories range from simple moral fables to picaresque tales of illicit sexual adventures.

Above *Lucifer, Prince of Hell, with devils around him,* from *Livre de la Vigne nostre Seigneur,* France (c. 1450–1470). During the Middle Ages, the Devil was the subject of much attention. It was believed that the Devil and many other lesser devils were always abroad to create mischief, often appearing in the guise of an ordinary human being.

The previous tale of Brother Onion mocks the credulity of the people of a small town in northern Italy, but by doing so it also highlights the importance of saints. The Christian saints grew in fame as the Middle Ages progressed, and more and more saints were created, some simply from popular legend.

Saint Barbara

Barbara's father, a rich pagan man named Dioscorus, kept her locked away in a tower. Food and clothing were sent up to her in a basket on a rope. Unlike the folktale of Rapunzel, however, when handsome princes offered to marry Barbara, her father accepted but she herself refused. Later, when her father was away, Barbara came down from her tower and convinced some of her father's workmen to install a third window in a water cistern, as a symbol of the Holy Trinity: God the Father, God the Son, and God the Holy Spirit. Her father was very angry at this profession of Christianity, and tried to

punish her. She hid from him in a shepherd's hut, but the shepherd gave her away, and in revenge she changed his sheep into locusts and him into stone. Finally, her own father beheaded her. As the sword fell, he was stuck by lightning and also killed.

Like many medieval saints' legends, Barbara's tale had something for everyone. In addition to the drama, it highlighted the conflict between the young and their elders, and told of the power of faith.

DEVILS AND WITCHES

Strangers and outsiders were viewed with suspicion in the Middle Ages, in part because any human being was a potential danger, either as a brigand or as the devil in disguise. There are many narratives about identifying the Devil, who may inadvertently reveal his cloven hoof or his tail, and many more stories about ordinary people tricking the devil.

One Italian tale tells of a poor man who wanted to become rich. His neighbor, a rich man, said that he would give him all his wealth if he could only strike the devil in the back with three stones. On his way to see the Devil, the poor man is given a series of problems to solve: a fountain that gives only bad water, a gravely ill prince, and a garden whose trees no longer bear fruit. The man befriends the Devil's

Right *Dante Alighieri, 1265–1321, Italian writer, in Hell meeting the souls damned to be torn to pieces by wild beasts.* Dante's great work, the *Divine Comedy,* is intended as an allegory of human life, using the three stages of hell, purgatory, and heaven to gradually reveal God's presence to man.

wife, a hideous witch, and she agrees to find the answers for him. He throws his stones, and the Devil cries out. His wife pretends to have hit him because she is worried by three problems, and the Devil reveals the answers. To fix the fountain, it was necessary to resurrect the custom of the procession to the Madonna; to regain his health, the prince had to drink water containing the dandruff of a horse which had been run to a sweat and then dried; and for the trees, the wall the greedy king had built around them had to be removed, as it kept out the breeze and prevented pollination. Having tricked the devil, the poor man returns home and becomes rich.

Medieval Hell

The abode of the Devil, Hell, is also greatly elaborated on during the Middle Ages. The teachings of the church made it clear that the majority of people would die in a state of sin and, therefore, go to Hell. Medieval creativity was at its most gruesome when describing the tortures of the damned. *Inferno,* which comprises one third of the book the *Divine Comedy,* by Dante Alighieri (1265–1321), epitomizes the medieval idea of Hell. In the book, the hero is given a tour through the nine circles of Hell by the Classical poet Virgil. They spiral lower and lower, until they reach the bottom, which is covered in ice. There, a winged Lucifer is in the process of devouring the three greatest sinners: Judas, flanked by Brutus and Cassius. Religious literature of the time such as the Vision of Saint Paul also describes Hell in some detail.

The Devil's Servants

A more everyday supernatural danger for the medieval man or woman was the Devil's human servant, the witch. Witchcraft trials of both men and women became increasingly common in the fifteenth century, but isolated references to witches of either sex and witchcraft do occur throughout the period. The son of Chilperic, King of the Franks, died in the year 583 as a result of witchcraft, so the chronicles report; Jeanne of Navarre, Queen of France, was reportedly also killed by sorcery in the year 1305, by Guichard, the Bishop of Troyes. Two Germans, Heinrich Kramer and James Sprenger,

Where thou shalt hear despairing shrieks, and see spirits of old tormented

DANTE ALIGHIERI (1265–1321), INFERNO

ANTI-JEWISH MYTHOLOGY

Although medieval Christians knew very little about Jews, the Jews' existence held an important place in Christian mythology. Although Jews were important and productive members of European society, their existence as a minority in what was an overwhelmingly Christian and superstitious society made them prime candidates for scapegoats. The antiquity of their faith gave them a role as holders of wisdom and arcane knowledge, which made them both powerful and, to the Christian mind, potentially very dangerous.

Christians, encouraged by the Church, believed in the Blood Libel legend, which contended that the Jews engaged in ritualistic murder. Knowing little of their religion and practice, Christians suspected Jews used witchcraft and black magic, concluding that they conducted murder of Christians in order to drink their blood in a parody of the Christian mass, or for other magical purposes. The blood, or other substances, was sometimes believed to have been used to poison wells, and these poisoned wells were thought to have brought the Black Death. The rumors and legends of the Blood Libel resulted in the torture and expulsion or murder of Jews who were blamed for the deaths of Christians.

Above *Protestants and Jews Burned Alive, Accused of Heresy and Witchcraft,* German woodcut, 1493. Trials of witches existed as early as the 1300s and grew with the establishment of permanent judges.

co-wrote *Malleus Maleficarum,* "The Hammer of Witches," around 1486, and their work became a manual for witch hunters all over Europe. In order to identify witches and the practice of witchcraft, they collected the witchlore of Europe. For example, they describe how a witch will stick a knife into a wall and make milking motions, telling her familiar (a person or demon, sometimes taking the form of an animal such as a cat, who aids a witch) which cow she is milking. The milk pours into her bucket from the knife, and the farmer finds his cow dry. To steal butter, a male witch goes naked into a stream and sits with his back to the current, uttering certain words and moving his hands behind his back. He then returns with the butter.

ARTHURIAN MYTHOLOGY

Below *King Arthur, the Holy Grail, and the Knights of the Round Table.* As this fifteenth-century manuscript, *Le Roman de Tristan,* shows, Arthur and his Knights embodied all that was noble and good. On one level, the tales of their exploits are exciting stories of derring-do, but they also explore ideas of order and harmony in the world—between man, the land, and the spiritual.

Arthurian myth is a unique category of mythology. Myth is usually grouped by culture, such as the Sumerian or Aztec mythology, but the Arthurian mythos has developed over at least eight centuries from the repeated cross-pollination of a number of traditions. It combines Celtic, German, French, and other European pagan mythologies with esoteric Christian elements. We can even discern in the tales influences of medieval magic and the symbolism of alchemy. The result is a uniquely Western mythos, with distinct ideas about sovereignty and the almost mystical relationship of the ruler's wellbeing to that of his realm. Courtly and divine love both feature prominently. The myths explore how these loves can overlap, for example, when Perceval weds the Grail Maiden and becomes a king, or be at odds, when Lancelot and Guinevere's love destroys Camelot.

ORIGINS IN HISTORY

It is tempting to imagine that the mythological tales of Arthur are based on a real man, though it is hard to find conclusive evidence for this. If he did exist, the Arthur of history would have lived around the sixth century A.D. The Roman legions had just departed Britain after four centuries of occupation, leaving the native Britons undefended. Pagan Angles, Saxons, and Jutes invaded, and King Vortigern of the Britons requested help from other Saxons, paying them with land in Kent. Vortigern's "allies" shortly proceeded to attempt their own conquest of Britain, using the handy base that he had given them. Chaos reigned.

According to the tales, this was the power vacuum from which Arthur came. One of the earliest mentions of Arthur is in the eighth-century *Historia Brittonum,* attributed to a Celtic monk, Nennius. In it, Arthur is referred to as a "war leader" who fought with the British kings against the Saxons in a series of battles. Famously, in the Battle of Mount Badon around A.D. 516, he was said to have killed 960 men in a single day. Whoever the historical Arthur was, he was acclaimed as a hero or leader, and has subsequently been "claimed" by the Cornish, Scots, Welsh, French, and Irish as their own.

However, what we are most concerned with here is the body of myths and lore that grew up around him. Oral traditions would have come first. We know that

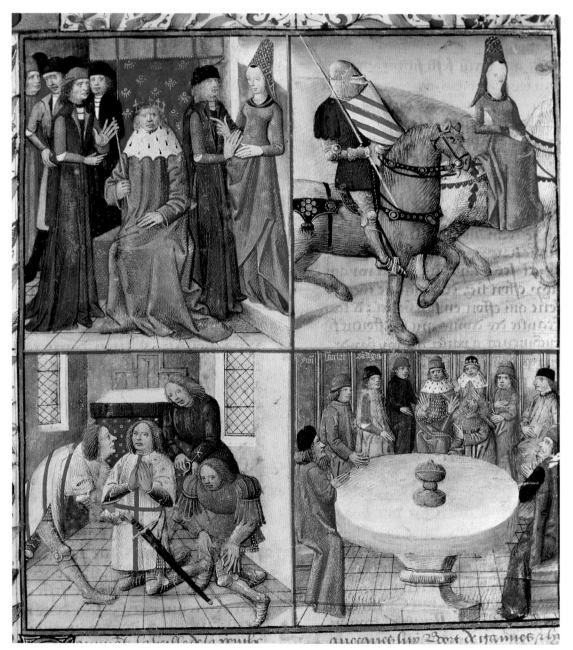

folk tradition associated Arthur variously with the "Wild Hunt," a nocturnal foray made up of supernatural beings accompanied by hounds, and also with cairns (piles of stones marking a spot, such as a grave) and cromlechs (prehistoric stone circles). He was said to sleep in "hollow hills" like Glastonbury Tor, or in various Welsh hills, and would return when Britain needed him. The Celtic bards, poets trained in myth as well as verse, no doubt also played a part in developing Arthur's heroic biography, and would have spread his stories on their travels.

THE CREATION OF A LEGEND

Geoffrey of Monmouth (*c.* 1100–1155) became Arthur's first fully fledged mythographer when he included him in his twelfth-century *Historia Regum Brittaniae.* Modeled on the great classical histories of Rome, and fleshed out with scraps of Welsh legend, it created a British king who ranked with the greatest known world leaders.

The Anglo-Norman poet, Robert Wace, born around 1100, wrote a French version of this history for Henry II and Eleanor of Aquitane, and French authors and audiences embraced and embellished the tale. In the retelling by Wace, we have the first mention of the Round Table. Chrétien de Troyes, working for Eleanor's daughter, produced the first written versions of Lancelot and Guinevere's love story, as well as the first mention of the Holy Grail. Both of these "new" elements, however, have earlier parallels in Celtic myth, so though it is known who first wrote them down, their origins are unclear.

The cross-pollination became still more complex after the Norman conquest of Britain in 1066, when the tales came back across the channel in their new forms and were further embellished by the bards—drawing again from native Celtic traditions.

The archetypal qualities shared by Arthur, Merlin, Morgan la Fée, and other figures in the myths, raise a question about their nature. There is some evidence that "Arthur" and "Merlin" may not be names as much as titles. Merlin's epithet "Ambrosius" or "immortal" and his association with many periods of history, may mean that there are actually several historical figures. These figures may have become "Ambrosius," an immortal deity, housed in a number of human oracles and mythologized over time as one

person. "Arthur" may come from the Latin *artos,* the "Bear," or the Welsh *arddu,* the "Lofty Dark One," an appropriate title for a war leader or war deity.

Upholder of Truth

In ancient Celtic culture, the divine king as warrior and ruler was the upholder of truth and cosmic order. The Old Irish word for king, *rí,* may come from a root meaning "to extend." Sovereignty was seen as a guiding force that extended over the kingdom. As king and upholder of the truth, Arthur enabled everyone else to maintain their true social and spiritual roles in relation to him. He created a stable base from which other adventurers, such as Perceval and Gawain, could proceed.

This makes the myths sometimes seem less about Arthur personally (except at the beginning, when he gains sovereignty, and at the end, when he loses it), and more about the sacred base he created and held at Camelot.

Above *King Arthur on his throne, surrounded by the Knights of the Round Table.* Chrétien de Troyes (died *c.* 1183) from France left an unfinished tale of Perceval, in which he first introduces the Grail. All of his Arthurian tales are full of chivalric detail, in particular, the codes and dress of battle.

Left *King Arthur, legendary British King,* from the *Chronicle of England* by Peter Langtoft (1325). The real Arthur was possibly a military genius or a tribal leader, but he came to be known as the "Once and Future King." Here, he is standing on a shield with the crowns and names of 30 kingdoms.

THE BIRTH OF ARTHUR

As with so much of Arthur's story even his very existence came out of the actions of the mysterious sorcerer Merlin.

Arthur's father, Uther Pendragon, King of the Britons, had fallen madly in love with Igrena the wife of his enemy Gorlois of Cornwall. This desire so possessed Uther that he persuaded Merlin to help him make it real. Accordingly, they went to Tintagel in Cornwall, Gorlois's castle, and waited for a time when Gorlois was away. Using his magical powers, Merlin transformed Uther into the likeness of his rival so that he could enter the castle and be with Igrena without her or anyone else suspecting his true identity. Their son Arthur was conceived from this magically assisted union.

After leaving the castle, having satisfied his lusts, Uther learned that Gorlois had been killed in battle just a few hours before. He lost no time in pressing his suit on Igrena and ultimately he married her. In this way, although Arthur had been conceived through a magical deception, he was legitimized as Uther's heir as he was born after the marriage of his mother to the man who was, in fact, his father. We do not know whether or not Igrena ever became aware of the truth of Arthur's conception, indeed she plays no further part in his story. Although Uther and Igrena had no other children, the marriage brought Arthur older half-sisters. The youngest, a girl called Morgan or Morgan la Fée, would grow up to be a powerful sorceress, and become in time a major force against Arthur and his kingdom.

Shortly after Arthur's birth Merlin came to Uther and, prophesying that the king did not have long to live, warned him of the grave dangers that surrounded his son from the nobles who would try to seize power after Uther's death. Uther was not a foolish man. He

THE LADY OF THE LAKE TELLETH ARTHVR OF THE SWORD EXCALIBVR

agreed readily with Merlin's plan to take the infant Arthur away and hide him with a foster family where he could come of age in safety. Not long after this meeting Uther died and, as Merlin had foreseen, the country returned to a state of violence, split into warring factions vying for rulership.

THE TRUE RULER OF ENGLAND

After fifteen long years of this conflict, a strange event took place. In a churchyard, there appeared a large stone with a heavy iron block, known as an anvil, on top of it. Thrust deep through both stone and anvil was a sword with the following words inscribed on its blade: "Whosoever pulls out this sword is rightful born King of Britain."

Seeing a chance to find peace with this wonder, the Archbishop, counseled by Merlin, announced a truce to be held over Christmas. During this time there would be a tournament in London followed by a test to see who among the assembled lords and gentlemen of arms could extract the sword.

Among those who made their way to London was the family of Sir Ector, including his son Kay who would take part in the tournament. The young Arthur, whom everyone thought was Sir Ector's younger son, was acting as Kay's squire. On the day

Right *Arthur Draws the Sword from the Stone* by Walter Crane in *King Arthur's Knights*. The sword, and weapons generally, had a symbolic role in medieval times. The sword in the stone and Excalibur represent Arthur's right to rule, and other weapons revealed the owner's fate or the bearer's worth.

of the tournament, Kay left his sword in their lodgings, so Arthur set off to retrieve it. Unfortunately, the hostel was locked as everyone had gone to the tournament. As he returned he passed the sword in the churchyard and, removing it easily from the stone and anvil, took it to give to Kay. Kay recognized the sword at once, and hurried to his father, claiming to have drawn it himself. Sir Ector knew this could not be so and revealed the truth about how Arthur had been brought to him by Merlin to be raised as his own. The following day, after many others had tried their hand, Arthur demonstrated that he and no other could draw the sword from the stone, and he was recognized by all who were gathered there as the legitimate ruler of the country.

Excalibur

Arthur set about establishing his court and trying to bring the rule of law back to his kingdom. This was not always possible without recourse to arms and in one early conflict the sword was broken. Merlin then came to him and took him to the Lady of the Lake, a powerful otherworld enchantress, who gave him the enchanted sword Excalibur, which made its wielder undefeatable, as its sheath gave its wearer protection from harm.

Thus armed, Arthur continued his campaign to rid the country of outlaws and conflict. During this time he and the knights that were accompanying him arrived one day at the besieged castle of King Leodegrance. Arthur and his men quickly drove off the attackers and rescued the castle's inhabitants.

MERLIN AS SHAMAN AND SAGE

We first hear of Merlin when King Vortigern sought a fatherless boy to sacrifice at the base of his fort. Merlin was such a boy—some tales say he was born of an incubus—but he revealed that the structure wouldn't stand because a red and a white dragon, symbolic of the Welsh and the Saxons, fought beneath it. He further prophesied that the red Welsh dragon would win. When King Vortigern asked his name, he responded that he was Merlin "Ambrosius"—Immortal. Like shamans the world over, Merlin sometimes wore a feathered cape and antlered headdress, showing he had the power of both natural and supernatural worlds. He was "taken out of himself" when he prophesied, "and like a spirit, knew the history of people long past and could foretell the future." From his birth to his magical "sleep," he fulfilled the shamanic role of bridging the human and divine realms.

Right *Tournament of the Knights of the Round Table,* from *Le Roman de Tristan,* a fifteenth-century manuscript. Knighthood was a semi-religious affair in the medieval age and knights were sworn to uphold the code: "to protect the weak, the defenceless, and helpless, and fight for the general welfare of all." Tournaments were a place to prove oneself and thus were serious events.

Below *Queen Guinevere* by William Morris (1834–1896). Guinevere's character is variously depicted as temptress or unwilling participant, both in terms of her affair with Lancelot and in Mordred's later attempts to marry her. In all stories, however, it is her role to be the ultimate cause of Arthur's downfall.

THE KNIGHTS OF THE ROUND TABLE

After the battle for the castle, among those who came to thank their rescuers was King Leodegrance's lovely daughter, Guinevere, who Arthur straightaway fell in love with. Merlin, acting as advisor to Arthur as he had to his father, agreed that she would indeed make a fitting queen, but warned that her very beauty might in time become a danger. Arthur was undeterred and in a short time the two were married. As part of her dowry, Guinevere's father gave Arthur a great round table that had originally been made for Uther Pendragon.

Arthur took the table to his court at Camelot and set it up in the great hall. He then made it known throughout the land that any knight of good standing who would swear an oath to uphold the good and protect the weak and innocent would be welcome to join his company of the Round Table, where no man sat higher than any other. Part of the power of the table was that, when a knight arrived at Camelot, if he was worthy, his name would magically appear on the seat. Many knights came to see if they would be judged worthy enough for their names to appear in gold across the back of a seat at the Round Table. Soon, only one seat remained without a name, which Merlin told Arthur was kept for the most perfect knight.

Arthur's marriage to Guinevere and the establishment of the Knights of the Round Table began the golden age of Arthur's court. Many quests and adventures would begin from that magical place.

THE ARTHURIAN WOMEN

There is much discussion over the various origins and meanings of the female characters in the Arthurian tales. Many aspects of the myths may hearken back to ancient Celtic deities, and this is certainly true of the female figures. The most prominent of these is Arthur's half-sister Morgan la Fée, (literally "Morgan the Fairy"), who may relate to the Irish goddess Morrigan or "Great Queen." Morrigan, like Morgan la Fée, is an ambivalent figure, who can both heal or destroy heroes. Some analysts of mythology have seen in Morgan's enmity toward Arthur the relics of a transition between goddess- to god-based religions.

The Lady of the Lake is supernatural as well, and as is the case with many figures of Celtic myth, lives in an otherworld beneath the waters. One form of her name, Vi-Vianna, suggests a connection with the Celtic water-goddess, Coventina. Even Guinevere's name can be translated as the "White Spirit." There are Welsh sources that call Guinevere the "Three Queens of Camelot," a possible reference to the Celtic "Triple Goddess"—maiden, mother, and crone—that is associated with the land. When the king married this goddess's representative, he symbolically married the land. Interestingly, however, early Welsh and Celtic stories also contain hints of the adulteress role Guinevere is to eventually play; Welsh triads name Gwenhwyfar as the worst offender of the "Three Faithless Wives."

THE PASSING OF MERLIN

Not long after the establishment of the Round Table Arthur was to lose the aid of his greatest helper. Merlin had warned Arthur that he would not be with him forever, and now the time for his departure came. A maiden, Vivien, who had been taught in the practice of magic by Morgan la Fée, came to Camelot to study with Merlin and so enraptured him with her beauty and wiles that he could refuse her nothing. Over time, she learnt all that he knew, until eventually her power rivaled his own. She then took him from Camelot to a wild place where she placed him in a deep sleep and sealed him within a cave.

This was not the only blow that Morgan la Fée was to strike against Arthur. While he was on a hunting trip she contrived through magic to capture him and pit him in combat to the death against one of his own companions. This battle went badly for Arthur as his half-sister had armed his opponent with Excalibur and its magic sheath. Though badly wounded, Arthur managed to prevail and regained his enchanted blade. While he lay recovering from his wounds, Morgan la Fée visited him. She attempted to steal Excalibur, but was unable to as he slept with the sword in his hand. She took the sheath, however, and threw it far into a lake, so depriving him of its protection.

Despite these setbacks, Arthur succeeded in bringing peace to his kingdom and establishing the rule of good, piety, and chivalry wherever his power extended. The fame of his court and that of the Knights of the Round Table spread far and wide, a shining beacon of noble virtues in an often-troubled world.

THE GREATEST OF KNIGHTS

There are many stories of the heroic deeds, the quests for justice, and the adventures in the name of Arthur's rule that the company of the Round Table embarked upon. It would take a large book to recount them all. They include Culwch and his wonder-filled wooing of Olwen; Tristan and his doomed love for Iseult; Bors the true; gentle Pellias; and many others that made up the court of Camelot.

However, despite the prowess of these knights, the greatest of the knights of the Round Table was Lancelot du Lac, the Knight of the Lake, so called as he was raised and trained by the Lady of the Lake following the death of his father. Lancelot's prowess was such that none could defeat him, and greater than his loyalty to Arthur was only his love of Guinevere: the flaw that would ultimately bring down Camelot and all that it had stood for. The introduction of Lancelot, more than any other character, into the Arthurian mythos highlights the shift over time from the values of the warrior king to those of romance and chivalry. Thus, Lancelot is a great warrior because he is pure.

> *but she wrought so there for him that he came never out for all the craft he could do*
>
> SIR THOMAS MALORY (1408–1471), *LE MORTE D'ARTHUR*

Below *Merlin and Vivien* by Eleanor F. Brickdale (1872–1945). Merlin's end varies but, in most cases, it is not peaceful. In some tales, the last we hear is of his imprisonment by Vivien and absence from Arthur's final battle. In others, he attends a later battle, but a vision sends him mad and he ends his days as a wild man living in the woods.

SIR GAWAIN AND THE GREEN KNIGHT

A typical Arthurian tale is that of Sir Gawain's encounter with the supernatural Green Knight.

On New's Year's Day, as there was great feasting in Camelot, a massive knight clad all in green rode into the castle hall, seated on an equally imposing and green horse. He challenged the knights: which one will take the

large axe he carries and strike him with it. Whoever does so will have to come, exactly one year to the day, and allow the Green Knight to return the blow.

Only the brave Sir Gawain offers to champion the honor of King Arthur. He strikes the Green Knight, cutting off his head. Unconcerned, the knight leaves the hall carrying the head, and reminding Gawain to meet him at the Green Chapel in a year's time.

Gawain later sets off on his faithful horse, Gryngolet, eventually arriving at a castle at Christmas. He is told the Green Chapel is nearby, and he stays as a guest at the castle.

The host strikes a bargain with Gawain: he will give him whatever he kills while hunting each day, if Gawain gives him whatever he receives during the day. The next morning, after the hunt has begun, the mistress of the castle comes to Gawain's room. She flirts with him and demands a kiss. Gawain does not want to offend the lady. Equally, he cannot dishonor his knightly vows, Camelot, or his host, but he offers a kiss. That night, the knight brings home a hart and Gawain passes on the kiss, without revealing its origin.

The next day the same thing happens and Gawain receives two kisses, which he duly passes on to the knight, who has killed a boar. On the third day, he accepts the lady's green belt, after she tells him it will protect the wearer from harm. That evening Gawain gives the knight three kisses but not the green belt.

On New Year's Day Gawain sets off for the Green Chapel, as agreed. The Green Knight is waiting for him and Gawain kneels to take the blows. The knight raises his axe twice without striking Gawain. The third time, he strikes Gawain on the neck, but cuts him only slightly. The Green Knight then admits that he is the knight from the castle, and that he had asked his wife to tempt Gawain as a test. If Gawain had given him the belt, he would not have cut him at all. He also says Morgan la Fée was behind the trick.

Gawain is mortified that he showed cowardice and disloyalty in accepting the green belt. He decides to wear it always to remind him of his failure and to keep him humble. After this, all the knights agree to wear green belts in his honor and to remember to keep their knightly vows.

THE SEARCH FOR THE GRAIL

Before the sad event of the demise of Camelot, there lay the greatest adventure yet to face the Knights of the Round Table: the search for the Holy Grail. The beginnings of this story were long before, in the early years of Arthur's reign. A rash and impetuous knight wounded the keeper of the Grail with a holy spear kept with the Grail. This wound would not heal, and because of it the lands around the Grail Castle were turned into a wasteland.

The only person capable of curing this evil wound was Galahad, the purest knight that ever lived. He

was conceived when the daughter of the wounded Grail King came to Lancelot disguised as Guinevere. Some years later the stage was set by two marvels: first, a stone floating in the river with a sword thrust into it bearing the words, "No man shall draw me save the best knight in the world." Then, Galahad's arrival at Camelot to claim the sword and take the final seat at the Round Table.

The story tells how, one evening not long after Galahad came to Camelot, while Arthur and his knights sat at the Round Table, a great light entered the hall. Floating over them was the Grail, draped in white cloth. It was there for a moment and then gone, leaving them full of wonder.

Sir Gawain was the first to swear that he would seek the meaning of this vision but the others were not long in following suit. The next day Arthur watched as the men who had made his dreams of chivalry a reality begin the quest for the Holy Grail.

THE GRAIL

The Grail is a complex object and its origins go far back. According to ancient tradition, the Dagda, Irish father god, possessed a cauldron of inexhaustible bounty accessible only to the brave. Several Irish stories feature goblet-bearing maidens, like the Grail Maiden, who dispense sovereignty to worthy candidates with a drink. In one Irish tale the sea god, Manannán, gives King Cormac a magical chalice that is shattered by falsehood and reunited by truth. The story's symbolism suggests that the chalice represents the vessel of self. The conception of the Grail as container of self is reinforced by the Welsh version of Perceval, "Peredur." In this version, Peredur sees the Grail not as a cup, but a human head. Some traditions speak of the ancient Celts using skulls as drinking vessels, and in later alchemical symbolism the *vas*, the crucible used by the alchemist, is sometimes identified as a skull. Thus, the Grail quest is, on one symbolic level, a transformative process carried out within the mind.

There is some evidence that the Grail is also connected with pagan fertility rites—the idea of a sickly land finding restoration only through the Grail, as well as the Celtic idea of a cauldron of plenty. Later, the Grail came to be associated with Christian ideas of the Holy Spirit: the Grail as a metaphor for the body containing the Holy Spirit.

Above *Temple of the Holy Grail* by **Wilhelm Hauschild (born 1827).** This painting is inspired by the opera *Lohengrin*, by Richard Wagner (1813–1883), in which the Grail has come to represent the Holy Spirit.

Above *Sir Bedevere Returns the Sword Excalibur to the Lake,* from a French manuscript (1300–1325). The image of an arm emerging from the lake to grasp Excalibur has captivated the popular imagination for centuries. Sir Bedevere was one of the first knights to join Arthur, and the only one to be left standing at the end of the fateful last battle, the Battle of Camlan.

Right *Sir Lancelot sneaking out of Queen Guinevere's room,* from *Le Roman du Roi Arthur* by Chrétien de Troyes (died c. 1183). The love of Lancelot and Guinevere was to prove the undoing of the Knights of the Round Table. Some sources say that Lancelot ended his days as a hermit, in penitence for his sins.

ENCOUNTERS WITH THE GRAIL

After many adventures Lancelot and Gawain came together to the Castle of the Grail. Gawain was allowed to enter the Grail chapel but Lancelot, a sinner through loving Guinevere, was denied entry. Gawain's actions removed the curse on the wasteland around the Grail Castle, which began to grow again.

After these two had left, Bors, Perceval, and Galahad arrived at the castle. All three were admitted to the Grail chapel, but only Galahad was given the Grail to drink from. Using the same spear that the young knight had used to wound the Grail King, Galahad cured the wound of his grandfather, and having fulfilled the divine role he had been born for, died. Perceval remained at the castle, married the Handmaiden of the Grail and became the new Grail King. Only Bors was left to return and tell Arthur of the success of the quest.

Perceval was the Grail King's nephew and he had been raised by his mother in the woods. He thought that knights were angels when he first saw them. When he discovered their true nature, he knew that he could not rest until he became as they were, and set off in a ragged outfit with just a small spear. Fortunately, his prowess matched his simplicity. In Camelot he became a great fighter and received a veneer of civilization. Unfortunately, his new manners worked against him in the Grail quest. On an earlier journey, he encounters the Grail at the

castle, in the Grail Procession, but remained politely silent, not uttering the question—what is the grail and whom does it serve—that would begin healing the wasteland. When he finally found his way back to the Grail, he was older and wiser. He was then able to take his destined place as the new Grail King.

Many knights never returned from the Grail quest, and times were changing. Arthur was getting older, his knights were elsewhere, and Camelot was no longer as happy a place. As well, certain knights were envious of Lancelot and determined to expose him and Guinevere as lovers. Chief among these plotters was Mordred, son of Morgan la Fée, and some say Arthur's bastard son born of incest.

The lovers were becoming careless and one night the conspirators caught Lancelot in the Queen's chamber. Seizing a sword, Lancelot fought his way free and escaped. Mordred demanded that Guinevere be burnt for her infidelity and, as sworn upholder of the law, Arthur had no choice. Sadly, he agreed.

On the day of the execution Lancelot and his followers appeared. Fighting their way to the stake, they released Guinevere and rode off with her. In the melee Lancelot unwittingly killed Agravain, Gareth, and Gaheris, brothers of Sir Gawain and Knights of the Round Table. They had been unarmed as a sign of grief at Guinevere's impending death.

THE LAST DAYS OF CAMELOT

Gawain, although always a friend of Lancelot and no supporter of Mordred, was incensed and swore to take revenge. Arthur's forces, led by Gawain, besieged Lancelot's castle. The castle could not be taken and Arthur was persuaded to take Guinevere back and allow Lancelot to go into exile.

For a while a troubled peace lasted, but the unity of the Round Table had been broken. Mordred and his followers continued to agitate against Lancelot, and Gawain brooded on the deaths of his brothers. Finally, arguing that Arthur must avenge his injured honor, Gawain persuaded the king to once again lead his forces against Lancelot, leaving Mordred behind at Camelot as regent.

The siege of Lancelot's castle went on for many months, Gawain all the time challenging Lancelot to single combat and taunting him as a coward. Unhappily, Lancelot finally accepted the challenge. He won but would not kill his former friend. As soon as he recovered, however, Gawain challenged Lancelot again, and again Lancelot defeated him. Then a message arrived from Guinevere asking for urgent assistance.

In Arthur's absence Mordred had set about consolidating his power. He spread the rumor that Arthur had been killed and, claiming the throne for himself, tried to force Guinevere to marry him. Arthur was furious and left for Britain with all his men, swearing vengeance. In the first battle Gawain's recent wounds re-opened; as he lay dying he wrote asking Lancelot to come to Arthur's aid. Sadly this message was too late. Arthur pursued Mordred until their two armies met. The slaughter was terrible. Surrounded by the dead knights of both sides, Arthur finally confronted Mordred face to face. They fought savagely and Arthur killed Mordred on his spear but not before he himself was fatally wounded.

In his dying moments, Arthur called his remaining knight, Bedevere, to him. Handing him the great sword Excalibur, Arthur ordered that it be cast into the nearby lake. Bedevere did as he was commanded, and as the sword flew out over the

water a hand broke the surface and caught its hilt. Flourishing the blade, the hand sank beneath the waves, returning Excalibur to the otherworld where it had been made. Bedevere returned to the dying king and helped him to the water's edge. There they waited as a black boat drifted toward them. On the boat were several women including the Lady of the Lake and Morgan la Fée.

Gently they picked up Arthur and placed him on board. Pushing off from the shore they took Arthur to the Isle of Avalon where he lies to this day, waiting to be roused from his slumber to once again assist Britain in its hour of need.

> *The sequel of today unsolders all the goodliest fellowship of famous knights*
> LORD TENNYSON (1809–1892),
> *MORTE D'ARTHUR*

Above *The Knights' March* by Dore Gustave (1823–1883). As important as any character in the tales is the land itself. While Arthur and the knights existed in peace, the land prospered. When this unity ended, so too did the fertility of the land. Today, much energy is spent trying to determine exactly where Camelot, Avalon, and Arthur's final burial place may be.

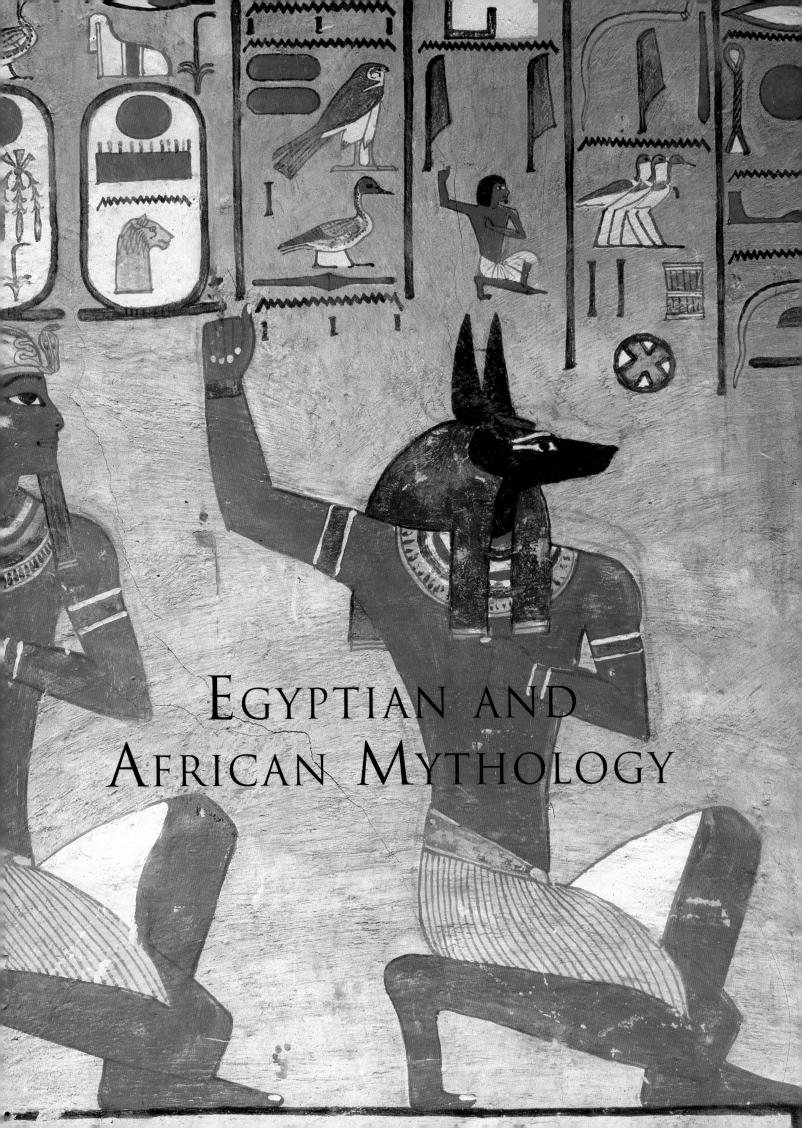

Egyptian and African Mythology

EGYPTIAN MYTHOLOGY

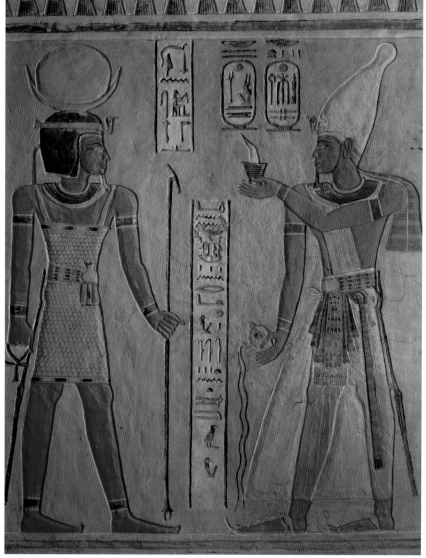

Below Ramesses III makes an offering to the god Re, tomb of Khaemweset (c. 1193–1162 B.C.). Ever since ancient Egypt was "discovered" by the ancient Greeks, it has fascinated. Its art, architecture, and the Nile itself, hint of treasures yet to be unearthed. Their religious beliefs, shrouded in ritual and mystery even then, retain much of that unique quality today, and perhaps always will.

The ancient Egyptian civilization was essentially conservative. Although it spanned more than 3,000 years, once a solution was found to a problem it seldom changed. As a result, most aspects such as art and technology can be studied as a unity. The only exception to this was their religious beliefs system. This developed slowly and changed, sometimes subtly, at other times radically. Consequently, it is one of the most complex areas of Egyptology, and the one that is most open to misinterpretation and debate by scholars and enthusiasts alike.

The reason for this misunderstanding is often a lack of objectivity in Egyptology itself. The scientific field of Egyptology is barely 200 years old; for the first century at least it was inspired by equal desires to prove the authenticity of the Bible and a lust for ancient Egyptian gold and precious treasures. The only sources early academics had were Classical—including Herodotus, Alexander the Great, Ptolemy, and the Bible—and they agreed that the Egyptians were simply "cruel taskmasters." This view has tended to color popular thinking to this day. However, modern scholarship has revealed a very different story.

Archaeology has shown that early settlers along the Nile valley came from a variety of places. We have very little evidence of a native indigenous stock; most immigrants arrived from Africa, the Hamitic region of North Africa, and the Semitic lands of the northeast. They formed isolated communities, developing their own languages, customs, and beliefs. These groups were unified into a single nation in a long series of conquests starting as early as 3400 B.C. and ending around 700 years later. Only around 2700 B.C. did a kingdom we can call Ancient Egypt finally emerge, with a single language under a single king. For the first 1,000 years afterward, their world was dominated by a king regarded as a demigod, feared by all. Myths were passed by word of mouth. Only with the demise of this form of monarchy, around 1780 B.C., was there seen a need to record the myths.

These myths created and supported the world the Egyptians occupied. Perhaps about 0.1 percent of the population could read and write; the others worked on the land and depended on storytellers for their entertainment. For those boys who attended school, writing down the traditional myths was a basic part of their education; and many myths thus survive to us only in schoolboy copies.

Earliest archaeological record shows that before and during the Unification, beliefs were dominated by a cattle cult. These cattle, huge and with great wide horns (similar to Ankole cattle today) were revered and the kings always remained identified with them. We can also see a firm belief in a life after death, as bodies, buried in a crouching position, lay with the head pointing south and facing west, in the direction of the setting sun, and accompanied by food, drink, and personal belongings.

Egyptian myths sought to explain to ordinary people how the world began and what may happen to them when they died. They were peopled with

a perfect replica of Egypt, without its problems. These two worlds were duplicates. It was absolutely vital to maintain these two worlds in balance, or Maat; if this balance were disturbed, even slightly, then primordial Chaos, or Isfet, was ready to return instantly. The king was the only bridge between the worlds. Daily, secretly, in the heart of the temple, he would reenact Creation. The Egyptians occupied a precarious world, trembling on the brink of disorder. The king's word had to be followed exactly to avoid chaos and devastation.

The myths, told popularly as folktales or as songs, undoubtedly gave comfort to ordinary people, assuring them that those who understood were in control and that their world was secure. They needed this comfort, for according to inscriptions, demons and evil spirits were waiting around every corner. Magic, in the form of amulets and special words of protection, was real to them and they used it to keep their fears of the darkness away.

long-dead heroes whose examples might both inspire them and terrify them. As one writer recently stated, national religion affected few outside the close royal circle; for most, religion was a mixture of magic and superstition. Tales explained to them how the world was created (the Creation myths); how man could overcome death (the murder and resurrection of Osiris); of the power and wisdom of women over villains (Isis); and of how right always triumphed over evil (the battles of Horus and Seth). There were also tales of sheer terror (the destruction of man).

BALANCE AND CHAOS

The Egyptians understood their cosmos as being two identical lands. This earth was created as a mound out of the waters of primordial Chaos. Beyond the western horizon lay the Other World, a parallel land occupied by spirits or the resurrected Dead. Every night, the sun left our world to shine in the Other World. As it sank, the newly dead would have to face the terrors of entry into that realm, and judgment beyond, before they could enter into a land that was

The Judgment of the Dead

According to Egyptian belief and law, no man could judge another in life or death. Under this unique system, they believed that after death the body, heart intact, was resurrected by the Opening of the Mouth ceremony, and thence passed westward into the hall of Osiris. The deceased there had to recite the deeds of his life. While his tongue may lie, his heart would know the truth. After he had finished speaking, he had to produce his heart for weighing (an amulet, a heart scarab, was placed in his tomb to enable him to do this). It was weighed against Maat, Cosmic Balance. If it was found heavy—full of guilt, because the tongue had lied—then the deceased suffered a second death by the Gobbler. The unfortunate individual then became a malevolent spirit, which could bring sickness and death to humans, and was driven away by physicians using words of power and amulets.

Above **Glazed terracotta amulet of dwarf god Bes** (c. 727–332 B.C.) Bes, an odd-looking dwarf god, is believed to have protected pregnant women and children. His gruesome expression and protruding tongue are intended to scare off evildoers.

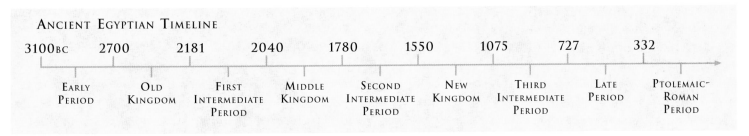

ANCIENT EGYPTIAN TIMELINE								
3100BC	2700	2181	2040	1780	1550	1075	727	332
EARLY PERIOD	OLD KINGDOM	FIRST INTERMEDIATE PERIOD	MIDDLE KINGDOM	SECOND INTERMEDIATE PERIOD	NEW KINGDOM	THIRD INTERMEDIATE PERIOD	LATE PERIOD	PTOLEMAIC-ROMAN PERIOD

Amulets

These talismans protected Egyptians in every aspect of their life and were believed to be very powerful. Images of the Wadjat Eye of Horus protected babies; images of Taweret, a pregnant hippo, helped women become pregnant; while a tiny frog assisted against miscarriage. The dwarf god Bes is linked with many kinds of misbehavior but he and his female counterpart, Beset, gave protection to the woman in labor and delivery. Flat or curved pieces of ivory, inscribed with words of magic and legendary figures of griffins and serpents, were laid over the belly of the woman in delivery to hasten the birth and drive away any evil spirits. After death, amulets were provided in great numbers to protect the dead. Kings and wealthy men had them included within their own bandages, from a tiny headrest to protect the neck, to a magical scarab placed directly over the heart, inscribed with words to enable the resurrected body to produce the heart for judgment. Lists were made prescribing the exact shape and type of material needed for the amulet to be effective.

the purchase, the buyer would kill and then mummify the animal so that its spirit would then be able to fly to the local god to ask questions and to demand assistance. Millions of these animals were killed and stored in catacombs, where they lie to this day.

Animal Cults

The Egyptians did not, as it is popularly believed, worship animals. In every town, they adopted an animal in predynastic times that represented aspects of local strengths. This might have been an animal such as a wild falcon, which was known for its predatory nature, swooping unexpectedly. Or it could have been a lion or crocodile, animals revered not only for their great strength but also for their tremendous power. In many cases, towns might adopt the natural enemy of their neighbour: if one town adopted a cobra, then the neighbouring town might adopt the ichneumon, Egyptian mongoose, that terrorized and killed snakes. In later times, the local god and the animal that represented it became inextricably linked together. Ordinary Egyptians could not enter the temple or participate in formal religion. However, each temple raised the local animals, which could then be exchanged for goods. After

THE CREATION MYTHS

Several versions exist explaining how the Egyptian world came into being, and these myths are popularly regarded today as having existed concurrently. This suggests that the ancient Egyptians either had a choice of what they might believe or that their beliefs varied across regions—a truly polytheistic basis for religion.

In fact, archaeology shows quite clearly that these myths did not exist side by side, but on the contrary developed one from another, each encompassing the previous myths and adding to them, to the advantage of the following god. This took the form of true "oneupmanship" where later gods literally added on sections to their own advantage. How did these myths come about? They centered, as did almost everything in Egypt, on the king himself. The king, once crowned, served his local temple of the town in which he was born. Here he made daily offerings to some ancient spirit, or *ka,* of a long-dead local hero. If he could persuade this *ka* to return to earth, even briefly, he could negotiate Maat. While a local chief might encourage this in his own temple with simple food and drink, a king could offer instead gold and gifts beyond their wildest dreams. These gifts were then handed over permanently to the temple staff to be stored in their treasuries or used to enhance the temple. So long as this family of kings remained in the ascendant, his temple would remain the richest in the empire. But when a new family took over the throne, then the riches of the previous temple would slowly be removed and a new temple and god would take its place. The cosmologies, or creation myths, exactly reflect the rise and fall of the ruling houses.

Temples and the Servants

The earliest layouts have been discovered as patterns in the ground at Nekhen (modern El Kab) and texts state that the layout of all subsequent temples faithfully copied this first one.

Essentially the temple was a large house, built of stone to last an eternity. Temples had an outer courtyard, accessed only by privileged staff; an inner hall of columns, open to the principal Servitor only; and an inner sanctuary, which held a shrine with the cult image of the god or goddess.

Temples were labor intensive, needing the sweat of thousands of men over many years. The majority of these worked in fields or workshops, though many were specialists, especially the scribes.

The principal temple staff were called Servants of the God, and only the foremost of these could enter the sanctuary. In theory, this would be the king, but others were appointed in his place, since he could not be everywhere. Around 1200 B.C., this post became hereditary in many places, and thus a few families eventually became political threats to the king.

Below **Bull God Apis, the incarnation of Osiris, with Isis and Hathor, bronze votive figurine, Ptolemaic era.** As the embodiment of power and strength, the Bull God Apis has long been worshipped in Egypt. In Memphis, Egypt, a tomb was found that had been carefully prepared for the burial of real bulls that had been specially reared as Apis-bulls. An avenue to the tomb was lined with stone lions, and recesses inside held the carefully entombed remains of the Apis-bulls.

Above **The pyramid of Cheops at Giza.** People have sought the scrolls of Thoth since the time of Cheops. From the Arabian tales of Scheherezade in the eleventh century to the European alchemists who tried to "rediscover" the lost wisdom through experiments, the legend of Thoth has tantalized with its potential for unlimited knowledge—and also the secret to making gold.

CREATION ACCORDING TO THOTH

Thoth was revered in Middle Egypt, in the location today known as Ashmunein. Archaeology may yet have to verify the true age of this site, it is so large and the remains are so deep, but it is agreed that the myths that originate from the city are much older than the unification of Egypt.

Although Creation was believed to take place within his city in a time too ancient to remember, Thoth played only a minor part in it himself. According to the myth, in the time before Existence, there was nothing but a deep, formless, and water-filled void. In this primeval "soup" there existed female and male demi-urges—primeval spirits that could combine together to create physical forms.

Atum, Lord of Completeness and supreme god outside time and space, summoned males and females together. There was Nun, and his counterpart Nunet, symbolizing Nothingness; Kek and Keket, Darkness;

Amun and Amunet, Secrecy; and Huh and Huhet, representing Silence. The males took the form of frogs, the females of reptiles; and from their reproduction, the seed of Creation was sown. Then Atum, in a supreme act of power, created a surface over the Deep and, within it, a mound of land. The centre of this mound was Egypt, and the Nile itself spouted directly from the primordial waters.

At the epicenter of this mound was Ashmunein, and here Thoth, created by his master Atum, set up effective administration, laid down all knowledge and science, and recorded it in 42 volumes of knowledge. These rolls were then hidden away in deepest secrecy until mankind was ready to discover them.

The interplay of the eight demi-urges brought forth Creation on the mound of Ashmunein. Plants, animals, and then mankind, came into existence. Much later, the Greeks identified Thoth with their god Hermes, the Greek messenger of the gods, and Thoth's city became known as Hermopolis. As for the texts themselves, do they exist? Who can say. They were recorded in legend as the Hermetic texts, and wise men and alchemists from the medieval periods to the present day, seeking "the wisdom of the universe," have longed to discover the originals.

Egyptian kings through the centuries longed more than anything else to acquire this original wisdom of Thoth. They looked back to his reign as a time of perfection, before mankind came along and ignored Thoth's rules—an age they called the First Occurrence. The Westcar Papyrus, in Berlin, Germany, tells how Cheops, a king from the Fourth Dynasty and builder of the Great Pyramid at Giza, is introduced by one of his sons to a great magician. The king asks him if he knows the whereabouts of the lost wisdom. The magician, Djedi, tells him that the rolls lie in a series of seven boxes, watched over by an immortal serpent curled around the outer box. This in turn lies in the deepest part of the river near Coptos. Cheops orders him to go and get it, but the magician has to refuse. Destiny, undeniable to all ancient Egyptians, had fated that it would not be found by him and his family but by the next family of kings, the Fifth Dynasty.

Did the kings of this fated dynasty find the lost texts? History does not record it, but at their center in Heliopolis, the seers became the inheritors of wisdom. They passed this knowledge from one generation of kings to the next, including the secrets of how to communicate with the land of the gods, and how to maintain Maat.

THE CREATION BY PTAH

The Unification saw the building of Egypt's capital city at Memphis (around 3000 B.C.), where the local god Ptah was identified with craftsmen. As the kings built and then served in the great temple there, the ancient story of the creation according to Thoth eventually succumbed to a new myth.

The Shabaka Stone, now in the British Museum, relates how the Libyan King Shabaka, about 850 B.C., found a "worm-eaten leather roll" in the library of the temple of Ptah and ordered it copied onto stone for posterity. The language in it is truly ancient, and could not have been written easily in the time of Shabaka— suggesting that the story was true.

The new tale maintains the previous Creation myth of the god Thoth almost completely, although the eight demi-urges were not part of the mythology any more. Instead, it tells how, on the mound of Atum, the god Ptah was brought into existence. His myth is interesting as he conceived ideas in his heart, considered them with his reason, and then spoke the words from his mouth. As the words dropped from his tongue, they turned into physical entities. This is the earliest account of Creation through logic, literally *logos*, the spoken word.

Later sources that have since been considered by many researchers to be far more orthodox and less pagan recorded this same tale with only very minor differences. "In the beginning was the Word; and the Word was with God; and the Word was God." Very few people today realize just how similar the opening sentence of the gospel of St. John is to the ancient Egyptian myth of Ptah.

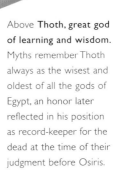

Above **Thoth, great god of learning and wisdom.** Myths remember Thoth always as the wisest and oldest of all the gods of Egypt, an honor later reflected in his position as record-keeper for the dead at the time of their judgment before Osiris.

Left *Ptah in his shrine,* from *Monumental History of Egypt* by W. Osburn (1854). The god Ptah is always shown in profile, wearing a tight-fitting skull-cap, false beard, and standing on a low plinth. He is a tall, slender figure wrapped as a mummy but holding a staff or scepter, which represents stability, life, and longevity. He is the creator god, builder of the boats to be used by the souls of the dead.

THE CREATION ACCORDING TO RE

Below **Mensuemsaf venerates the bennu bird, representing Re, papyrus (c. 1075–727 B.C.).** In this illustration, the god Re sits above the bennu bird. He is protected by a cobra in an upright position, the uraeus, symbol of Egyptian kingship and of the king's might. The bennu bird, an imaginary heron, was linked to the Nile and creation.

The cult of the sun as creator of life flowered at the end of the Fourth Dynasty (around 2600 B.C.) and lasted only briefly. It was centered on Heliopolis, under the Kings of the late Fourth and early Fifth Dynasty (c. 2350 B.C.), and was a turn toward solar worship for the first time.

At Heliopolis the religious celebrants were called the Seers. Their job was to interpret signs, to read dreams (included as the Wise Men and Magicians of Genesis), and also to instruct the crown prince in his future duties as king.

Re, or Ra, was the sun in all its varied aspects. We have no idea how the name was spoken—the nearest hint, from Egyptian Foreign Office archives of the later Eighteenth Dynasty, suggest it should have been "Ria." In Egypt, the sun has many faces, as it always had; the first faint light widening above the hazy eastern hills; then the tongues of light that bring day, but no heat; later comes the striking of power as mists dissipate and scorching power burns the earth; the kinder sun of mid-afternoon, when the intensity of the sun's rays starts to soften; and finally, the fabled scarlet sunset and the sun's disappearance into the Other World. In mythological terms, Re was brought up into the physical world by Khepri, a cosmic scarab beetle pushing the ball of the sun upward into the mortal realm. The first light was Re-Hor-em-akhet, or Harmachis as the Greeks called it, "Re who is Horus of the horizon," where Horus is depicted as a falcon, wings outstretched, its pinion feathers mirroring the rays of the sun. As the sun grows stronger, the god Re himself was believed to steer the sun's boat into the mid-heavens where, at its zenith, it became Aten. As it set toward the western horizon, he took the form of Re-Hor-akhetwy, or Horakhte, the "Falcon of the second horizon." As the sun set, Re entered into the night barque and sailed into the parallel world of the spirits of the dead, becoming one with Atum, great lord of Creation and Completeness.

On the first mound of existence, the myth recounts, there grew a lotus flower. As the bud opened into sweet heady fullness, Re, the sun, emerged from the heart of the flower, bringing first light into the world. The bennu bird then emerged, the legendary phoenix of later Greek legend. Created in the image of a heron, the bennu was the first life to appear on this original

mound of existence and its cries broke the first silence. Re, the sun and greatest god of them all, brought into existence first Shu, air, and then Tefnut, moisture, to be brother and sister. In time, they married and soon bore two children: a son, Geb, and a daughter, Nut. Geb and Nut grew to love one another and wished to marry, but Shu, their father, opposed the match. One day he found them in a passionate embrace; angry, he separated them, forcing Geb to remain lying down while he held up Nut away from the body of her beloved brother. Geb became the earth; while Nut, with only the tips of her feet and fingers allowed to touch Geb, became the arch of the heavens above, her dress sparkling with the stars. So there she has remained, forever driven apart from her brother-lover by the power of air, her father.

Finally, Re, sorrowing because he needed to be banished from the earth every night, commanded that Thoth be the moon, a colder light than his own but maintaining a little of the old myth of Thoth.

In time Nut would give birth to four children, Osiris, Isis, Seth, and Nephthys. Isis later gave birth to Horus. These became the Nine gods of Heliopolis, and were known as the Great Ennead: Shu, Tefnut, Geb, Nut, Osiris, Isis, Seth, Nephthys, and Horus.

Left Line fishing in the reeds, bas-relief, tomb of Kagemni, Sixth Dynasty. The Nile teemed with life, in and out of the water, but no more so than after the annual inundation. This bounty was considered to be a gift from Hapy, the God of Inundation. He is normally shown as a man with a round belly and a headdress of reeds and lotus blossoms.

THE REVENGE OF RE

A favorite recurring myth relates how Re created a partner for himself, Sekhmet. This word in ancient Egyptian means "power, might" and the word became reality in the form of a wild lioness.

Re became angered with mankind, believing that they plotted against him continually. He is persuaded by the Great Ennead to send his Eye, seat of his power, in the form of the lioness Sekhmet, down to earth. Sekhmet kills humans relentlessly until all the land is filled with their moans of terror. Re, now calmer and ashamed of his anger, summons Sekhmet back to him. But she is now filled with blood-lust and will not come to his call. Re therefore tricks her. He changes the river Nile into the color of blood, which attracts her, but turns the water into beer. The lioness drinks deeply until, sated, she falls into a drunken slumber. When she awakens, she forgets why she has been sent and returns quietly to Re.

This myth reflects many aspects of Egypt itself. Every year, the Nile did indeed run the color of blood, as the first water of the Inundation arrived colored with the rich red topsoil from the southern mountains of Ethiopia (a potent image that was to be repeated in the stories of the plagues in the time of Moses). Sekhmet is a metaphor for plague of some kind or another, which occurred regularly before the coming of the new waters, and would have terrified the Egyptians. In Egypt during the summer months the temperature often soars, and in the past the river at this time would have been little more than a bare trickle, fetid and infected. Food and water would have been running out, with disease and famine ravaging the land until the coming of the fresh water banished disease.

Despite its great status, the sun was never popular as a single focus for worship, probably because it was open to view; the secrecy associated with ceremonies in darkened rooms brought power to those inside and mystery to those outside. Instead, Re was syncretized with other gods: Sobek (local god of the village Kom Ombo and the lake Fayum), Amun ("the hidden"), and others.

Left Sandstone statue of Akhenaten, from Tell El Amarna. In the mid-Eighteenth Dynasty (c.1350 B.C.) the sun-cult reappeared in a new guise in Middle Egypt under a king born as Amenhotep but renamed later on as Akhenaten. The Aten was not the disk of the sun, as some say, but the power of the sun at its zenith at midday. It was believed that you could no more look upon the face of the god than look upon the sun at noon, and that the god gave life to the earth just as the sun's rays touched everything on earth. The cult aroused political antagonism and fierce opposition from the army, who, after the death of Akhenaten, tried to eradicate all traces of it.

Center *Hypostyle Hall at Karnak, from Panorama of Egypt and Nubia* by H. Horeau (1801–1872). Karnak was a magnificent complex, containing about five temples. The hypostyle hall—the roof no longer exists—was supported by massive columns, 134 in all, entirely covered with hieroglyphs. As a monument to a god, it ranks as one of ancient Egypt's greatest achievements.

THE STORY OF AMUN

Although Amun was once one of the eight demi-urges of Ashmunein, he seems to have been a local god also, in Tod, south of Luxor. The Kings of the Twelfth Dynasty (approximately 1780 B.C.) were born here, but took the city of Luxor, a wide and fertile area on both banks of the Nile, as their place of rule. Here they overlaid the attributes of their Amun over those of the local god. The local god had been represented by a goose; their Amun was represented by a curly-horned ram.

The foundations of the great temple complex of Amun, today called Karnak, most probably began before the Twelfth Dynasty; but it was only now that real greatness first came to Luxor.

Amun wholeheartedly adopted the earlier myths of Thoth, Ptah, and Re. He united with Re, to become the supreme god Amen-Re, uniting Creation and Wisdom into a single force for the first time. He appeared upon the mound formed by Atum and created mankind himself, either by spitting—the Egyptian word "to spit," *remetch,* was the same as the word for mankind—or, as is more frequently believed, by masturbation. His seed then formed the very essence of all Creation.

Within the temple of Karnak, the rite celebrated daily by the king had this act of Creation at its center. Images show Amen-Re with an engorged phallus, while a succession of kings kneels before it and venerates it. In this version of the story, however, Amen-Re becomes head of the Nine Gods, supplanting and removing Horus, son of Isis, from the story as told earlier in the myths of Heliopolis, the cult-center of Re. During the Eighteenth Dynasty (around 1550–1075 B.C.), the period of Egyptian imperial expansion, warrior kings came to Karnak to beg victory from the hands of Amen-Re. Later, in thanks for their success, they poured booty plundered from foreign lands into the coffers at the Karnak temple.

Successive kings added to the temple building complex for more than 500 years, until eventually Karnak became so rich that it challenged the wealth and therefore the very authority of the king himself. As a result, in the Late Period, kings living in the

Above **A young Ramesses II supports a staff that bears the ram's head of Amun, granite statue, Karnak.** It was believed that Amun could assume any form that he wished, including other gods. At the height of his powers, in the Eighteenth Dynasty, he did subsume many of the lesser gods. Apart from the ram, Amun is often represented as a bearded man wearing a cap from which two plumes emerge.

He created "five days that were not days, and five nights that were not nights."

PLUTARCH (C. A.D. 45–120), *DE ISIDE ET OSIRIDE*

north managed to dominate the temple and control its enormous wealth by "marrying" their daughters to Amen-Re. These god's wives lived as virgins and assisted the king or his appointed deputy in the temple in the daily enactment of the first act of Creation. They became known as the "God's hand." As wife of Amen-Re, they controlled the wealth of the home, as did every Egyptian woman. The wealth of Karnak became theirs, which they were then able to divert into the coffers of their fathers in the north.

THE OSIRIS LEGEND

Amen-Re, ruler of Egypt, grew old and weary. Thoth, oldest and wisest of the gods, attempted to persuade him to retire to his solar duties in the heavens, but Amen-Re adamantly refused.

Thoth challenged him, predicting that Nut, the sky, would give birth to four children, and that the first-born would rule Egypt in his place. Amen-Re remained stubborn and swore that Nut would never give birth, not in any day or night of the month.

Thoth's prediction seemed doomed. But he had a plan. Khons, son of Amun and his divine consort Mut, now occupied the Moon, where he resided alone, playing *senet,* a favorite and most ancient board game in Egypt that is almost identical to modern backgammon. Thoth challenged Khons to a game, but demanded a parcel of moonlight if he won. They played and, of course, Thoth won. With the moonlight, he created "five days that were not days, and five nights that were not nights." The five days and nights, not part of any month, were then added between the end of one year and before the next, bringing the days of the year from 360 to 365, righting the calendar. The moon, weakened by the loss of some of its moonlight, has waned a bit every month ever since.

Finally Thoth could fulfil his prophecy. On the first day, Nut bore Osiris; on the second, a daughter Isis; on the third, a son Seth; on the fourth, a daughter Nephthys; and on the fifth day, she rested to recover from the strange multiple births. It is said that when Osiris was born a voice cried out from the heavens proclaiming his birth.

A New Ruler

Osiris and Isis grew in beauty and wisdom. Isis, known as Great of Magic, was both beautiful and very strong, and was the loyal protector of her handsome and fit husband Osiris. For his part, Osiris brought agriculture and wealth to Egypt. But still Amen-Re refused to retire, despite the pleas of Thoth and Isis.

ISIS

Isis, sister-wife of Osiris, was revered as the perfect wife and mother. At the same time she was called Great of Magic for her part in the drama of her husband's life and death. In the Late Period (727 B.C. onward) her cult grew and temples to her were built all over Egypt. The Romans (30 B.C. onward) found her cult appealing, and Iseums (Isis temples) were built throughout the Roman Empire, as far as the northern reaches of Britain.

Above **The golden Isis, sarcophagus of Ramesses III (c. 1184–1153 B.C.).** Isis was, and still is, worshipped across Egypt. She is the protector of the dead, and her winged form often graces sarcophagi.

At last, Isis tricked him. In his old age, as Amen-Re walked, he drooled. Isis gathered his spittle, mixed it with dust and created a snake, which bit him on his heel. Amen-Re seemed in danger of dying. He called for help from Isis, Great of Magic. Isis, however, could only heal him if he told her his secret name.

According to Egyptian mythology, everyone has a secret name; if this is passed to anyone else, they can assume total control over you. Amen-Re knew this and therefore resisted. At length, weakened, he had no choice. He spoke the name; Isis pronounced it and was thus able to banish him to his barque to rule the heavens and guide the sun. She handed the throne to her husband Osiris.

The legend of Osiris is one of the most enduring of Egyptian myths; the classic good versus evil. Though murdered, Osiris would rise again. Anubis, as the patron of embalming, provided rare herbs and ointments for the preparation of the body. He also supplied linen, specially prepared so that it would never decay.

Right **Anubis as a jackal, terracotta pectoral pendant (*c.* 664–525 B.C.).** The cult of Anubis is very old and probably precedes that of Osiris. His role has always been connected with the dead, and in the Osiris legend it became more directly linked with guarding the dead in the Other World. Nephthys is always given as his mother, though the father varies—usually Seth or Re.

THE MURDER OF OSIRIS

Osiris, now King of Egypt, was beloved by all, while Isis, shining in gowns and crowns of brilliant gold, was always at his side, always the loyal and devoted sister-wife. She became the role-model for all women of Egypt. Seth, however, grew ugly, contorted with anger and jealousy at his successful brother Osiris and resentful that, as second son, he was entitled to nothing. His life filled with hate, which he focused on Osiris. He was united reluctantly with his sister Nephthys, although she, like most people, adored Osiris and Isis.

Osiris went away from Egypt into battle while Isis remained and ruled on his behalf, much to Seth's fury. As Osiris returned victorious, Seth with 72 loyal friends came to greet him and welcomed him to a grand banquet that they had organized in his honor. At the end of the banquet, doors opened and a coffin of solid gold was wheeled in. As everyone gasped in awe at its beauty and great weight, Seth called, "It shall belong to he who fits it best." The coffin had been made deliberately to fit the exact size of Osiris, bigger, broader, and stronger than all other men.

Each man tried, but none of them fitted it. At last it was Osiris's turn. As he stepped into it, Seth and his cronies slammed the lid shut, bolted it down, and fled with it to the Nile. They threw it in the river, so the coffin containing the body of the dead Osiris was swept north by the current and was lost.

Eventually, the coffin was washed by the currents of the river onto the shore of Byblos, where a great tree grew around it, enclosing it within the trunk.

The King of Byblos came and marveled at its great size and straightness and ordered it cut down to form a central column within his palace. The column-trunk emitted lights and sounds, and everyone who came near it was mysteriously healed.

In Egypt, Seth now ruled the land with terrible cruelty, while Isis, desolate, wept and mourned in a secret invisible island in the Nile delta called Chemmis. She heard of stories of the miracles of Byblos and knew at once what had happened. She sailed north at once, but on the way transformed herself by magic into an ugly old crone. When she arrived, she went straight to the palace and offered her services to the King and Queen as nursemaid to their son. They, impressed by her age and apparent wisdom, accepted happily. Isis stipulated one condition, however; they must give her full charge of the child and never question or observe what she did. The couple reluctantly agreed.

Every night, strange cries and lights came from the child's room. At last, unable to control herself a moment longer, the Queen made a tiny hole in the door to watch what was happening. As she watched, Isis spoke words of power, and was transformed from an ugly woman into her beautiful self, clad in gold clothes with a cloak of feathers that formed great wings like a bird. She then flew up like a kite over the child, swooping and crying. At last, she picked up the child gently in her wings and placed it straight on a brazier of burning coals.

The Queen, in terror, burst open the door and confronted Isis in her power. Isis, dismayed, rebuked the Queen, saying that she had been burning away the child's humanity, making him an immortal, but that the Queen's entrance had destroyed her work. The Queen, desolate, offered Isis anything in the palace as recompense. Immediately, Isis asked for the giant pillar in which her husband was encased.

Isis freed the coffin containing the body of her husband and took it back with her to Chemmis. That night, she transformed herself once again into the golden kite, but with her wings breathed life into the phallus of Osiris, and conceived a child of his spirit. Later, under the cover of darkness, Seth crept in, seized the body and tore it into 14 pieces, which he flung into the Nile.

From that day, Isis, pregnant and loyal to the last, sought out the torn pieces of her husband's body. At Philae, she found his head, at Abydos, she found his spine, and wherever she found a piece, a temple was erected. But the phallus was eaten by a fish, forever

OSIRIS AND ABYDOS

It was believed that the dead became *akh*, or transfigured spirits, and took the form of stars. According to inscriptions, in earliest times Osiris was associated with the constellation of Orion, seen by the Egyptians merely as the "belt" of the hunter we see today.

Long before Egypt was unified, the site of Abydos became holy to Osiris. The first Kings of Egypt, who originated further south in Nekhen and who also built Memphis, the capital in the north, chose to be buried here because of the sacredness of the site. At Abydos, probably at around the time of the building of the pyramids—the Old Kingdom (2700–2181 B.C.)—a shrine was built for Osiris. The site later fell into disuse.

Around 1500 years later, Seti I, the second King of the Nineteenth Dynasty, decided to renew it. Workmen uncovered the old shrine, now underground, and carved the ancient walls with his name. Every year, in a special secret series of rooms, the resurrection of Osiris was reenacted, giving hope to every Egyptian that they too would have life after death. Thus Abydos became the first true pilgrimage site.

lost. Isis now bandaged the pieces together, forming the first mummy, and placed it in a tomb at Abydos. She said words of magic over the body, the words of the Opening of the Mouth, thus freeing it as an *akh*, a resurrected body. Thus was the resurrected Osiris, the first to travel over the western horizon where he settled at the entrance to the land of the dead, giving the promise of an eternal life to all mortals afterward. The care lavished on the dead in ancient Egypt is the same care that was first bestowed on Osiris.

Nearby towns to Abydos yielded their own local gods, which became part of the legend. From Assiut, the local god Wepwawet, the Opener of the Ways, became Anubis, the guardian dog that crouched at the western horizon, ensuring that no living person could accidentally travel across to the land of the spirits. He had to inspect the body, check it was dead and was properly prepared for resurrection. Paintings show a priest wearing a mask of Anubis carrying out the inspection. Thoth of Ashmunein now became the Recorder of the Verdict.

Below *Anubis Weighs the Heart of the Deceased Hunefer* from *Book of the Dead*, known as *Papyrus of Hunefer* (1294–1279 B.C.). On the left, Horus guides the deceased to the Great Scales, which are weighing his heart against Maat, to determine if he has told the truth. On the right, Horus leads the deceased to his father Osiris, who sits in a shrine protected by Isis and Nephthys.

THE BATTLES OF HORUS AND SETH

Below **Personified Wadjat Eye of Horus holding the sacred flame, fresco, tomb of Pashed, Thebes, Ramesside period.** The Wadjat Eye, or healed eye, is shown here offering incense, as it emerges from the hills of the west bank of Luxor. As an amulet, the Wadjat Eye was usually placed over the embalming incision of a dead body, ensuring evil spirits could not enter it.

With Osiris removed into the land of the dead, Seth continued to rule Egypt, though this inheritance rightfully belonged to Horus, the son of Osiris. Isis had raised her son in secret on Chemmis, an island near Bhutto. As soon as her son became old enough, Isis, his mother and protector, made him swear he would avenge his father's murder.

Horus thus declared war on Seth. Bloody battles were fought, lasting many years. Every time, Horus triumphed and then demanded of the Great Ennead (of which he was not part, according to this myth) the return of his father's land and title. The Ennead always prevaricated.

Seth appeared in a variety of different guises—sometimes a pig, or a hippopotamus, sometimes a crocodile. Always Horus sought him out and killed him, but to no avail. On one occasion, Seth put out the left eye of Horus. His mother replaced it with the healed eye, or Wadjat Eye. This had power and magic of its own, and could be sent out against those who opposed him, always returning to its master. It was said that the eye Horus lost represented the moon, and that the time it took to heal equaled one full revolution of the moon.

The Creation of Hathor

Horus went to his mother and demanded that she represent him before the tribunal of the Ennead and help him win his inheritance. She once more wavered and urged him to yet more fights. Horus became enraged. Later that day, Isis fell asleep on the hills of the west bank of Luxor. Horus came to her, cut off her head and buried it in the sand. From one eye grew the white lotus, from the other, the blue lotus.

When she awoke, she sought her head, in vain, and, at last, in desperation, took the head of the only animal she could find, a cow that emerged from the hillside. Isis was thus transformed into Hathor and became the consort of Horus. As a result, Horus now took the title Kamutef, or "bull of his mother."

One explanation for this unusual story is that every member of the Ennead, except Horus, had a partner. To rectify this, Hathor was created, and was therefore a later addition to the myth-cycle.

The Victory of Horus

After 40 years of fighting, Horus was finally vindicated by the tribunal of the Ennead. Seth and all evil was banished and Horus was granted kingship over the entire land of Egypt, with Isis-Hathor at his side as Queen. From this time onward all kings were identified with Horus. The double crown, symbol of political unity in Egypt, even took the form of the Wadjat Eye. This became the basis of the evil eye of later legend.

Origins in History

The story of the battles between Horus and Seth is told on a later papyrus to that of the legend of Osiris and does not fit entirely with the older myth of Osiris and Isis. In the original story, Horus was the son of Isis, conceived with the spirit of her husband, thus making Seth his uncle. In the account of the Battles of Horus and Seth, the two are brothers, Horus fighting for his rightful place as Elder Brother. The Greeks sought to separate the two, calling Horus the Child, Hor-pa-khered or Harpocrates. In the story where he and Seth are brothers, he is called Horus the Elder, Hor-wer, or, in Greek, Haroeris.

The myth of the battles is a folk-memory of the war between two cities, Nekhen and Naqada, fought to unify the Nile valley in ancient times before the first unification. Horus was the local god of Nekhen, and Seth of Naqada. The military supremacy of Nekhen, whose leader became the first King of Egypt, over the defeated Naqada was thus remembered in this myth where Horus finally manages to vanquish the evil Seth.

In Edfu, home of Horus, every year festivals were held to celebrate the victory. Reliefs show an actor playing Horus who, publicly and no doubt to great acclaim, hunted down the creatures associated with Seth in the streets of the town. As well, images of kings show them as Horus, hunting Seth the evil one. In the Roman era, a statue now in the British Museum shows Horus dressed as a Roman Centurion, riding horseback and spearing Seth, the crocodile, beneath him. In time, this first became the story of St. Menas, and later St. George and the Dragon. The Egyptian name for Seth, *Sutekh*, may have evolved into the word Satan.

Horus, Fighter of all Evil

As a triumphant figure it is not surprising that the might of Horus was turned toward earthly illness. It was believed that nature destined everything to be perfect, according to the First Occasion, but demons existed that would bring illness and much chaos to humans and to the world. These had to be driven out. Papyri listed symptoms of the sick, a diagnosis, and a prognosis, this being either "something against which I can struggle" or "something against which I can do nothing." Lists then gave external or internal remedies, amulets, and words of power. Horus-cippus figures—small, rounded, upright stela carved with reliefs of Horus—were used in the treatment of illness. They show the child of Isis with a serpent in each hand, often standing upon two crocodiles, the whole covered with magical texts. Most of them were nonsense: the word "abracadabra" came from one of these. Water was poured over the cippus figure, absorbing the power of the words, and collected in a dish at the base. The water could then be used as a powerful remedy to drive out evil. Egyptians believed in the figures and would position them at the front of the house or in the garden as protection.

Left **The god Horus in the form of a falcon, wearing the double crown, temple of Horus, Edfu, Ptolemaic era.** Ancient Djeba, today's Edfu, was believed to be the location of the battle between Horus and Seth. The temple complex was begun around 237 B.C., and two huge granite statues of Horus as a falcon stand at its entrance. A number of Horus gods exist; the oldest was believed to be a creator god, represented by the falcon who flew at the beginning of time.

Below **Sarcophagus with eye of Horus, Anubis, and mourners, c.1450 B.C.** This sarcophagus of Lady Madja, Eighteenth Dynasty, is from the western necropolis of Gurnet Murrai, Egypt. The eye of Horus has, and still does have, great potency. Of the many Horus gods, subsumed into this one, all were connected with the sun. The Wadjat Eye has been linked by some with the "eye in the sky," seen at eclipses of the sun.

AFRICAN MYTHOLOGY

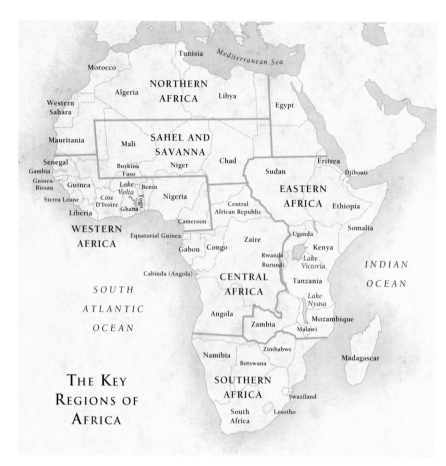

THE KEY
REGIONS OF
AFRICA

lines of humankind who may once have been more widely spread across the continent. Later migrations of Negroid people, taller in stature and more varied in physical type, moved south and east at different times in the last two millennia, taking up empty land and infringing on lands of the earlier inhabitants.

ORAL TRADITION

There was no written language in Africa until Islam spread westward across the Mediterranean plains in the eighth and ninth centuries A.D., and southward in the twelfth century across the Sahara Desert, into the interior of Western Africa, and through the Sahel. Europeans brought their own written scripts, along with the Christian missionaries, shipping agents, and trading companies in the fifteenth and sixteenth centuries, to the coasts of Western Africa, then around to the southern and eastern shores, and eventually into the interior. Writing impinged only slightly on the mass of the population, for whom an oral tradition had long existed. Written language and knowledgeof the Koran (Qu'ran) and the Bible had a social impact, associated as they were with external influences, power, and the rise of elite individuals or groups, but a resilient oral culture survived into the twentieth century, albeit with lessening prominence in a technologically-advanced world.

The stories that are examined here cover a range of African societies from north to south, and east to west, from coastal and island people to those of the interior, the vast savanna lands, forests, and mountains. They come from differing economies, many containing symbolic references to pastoralism, agriculture, fishing, metalworking, and other livelihoods. Some are sacred, and others secular. Invariably the stories have significance to the tellers and the listeners in terms of the history, or the origins of the people themselves, or their beliefs in the creation, or the origin of their worlds.

African creation stories have some similarities with understandings of creation in Western preliterate cultures. Knowledge of a supreme being is common to most African traditions. There is an array of lesser gods,

Africa is a vast continent comprising a diverse range of landscapes and economies, and a history of mankind traced, archaeologically, through more than a million years. There may be no connections between those distant days and the present, but there is certainty about the long histories of some of the people who currently inhabit the continent. While northern Africa, the Mediterranean, and the Red Sea shorelines were in trading contact with southern Europe and western Asia 4,000 years ago, the southern part of Africa was remote, and isolated from the Western world, until European exploration brought seafarers and traders to the country in the fifteenth century, and settlers thereafter.

The Khoi-San people of southern Africa and the Pygmy people of the great forests of central Africa represent ancient

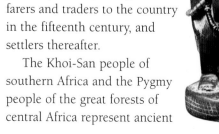

Right **Yoruba twins.**
In African mythology the theme of twins is common. The original placenta of Amma, the supreme being of the Dogon people, was a double one to attach the pair of twin Nommo, her offspring. This doubling up or twinning represents the formation of the earth and the sky, the creative act of Amma.

goddesses, and spirits that bridge the gap between the supreme being and men and women in their daily lives. Embedded in some of these stories is the history of specific ethnicities—ancestors form a central part of the mythology, forming a link between the present day and the origins of both the people and their world.

Christianity and Islam have been newcomers in the history of African religions, and although they have made quite a powerful impact on African people, there has been a very strong resilience toward these influences in some of the older traditions and mythologies.

THE IMPORTANCE OF MYTH

The stories included here are categorized under a series of headings, but these are artificial categories, and there is a crossover between types of stories. The mythology of the African peoples has evolved over very long periods of time, and has retained some consistency within the changing worlds. Creation myths and stories of the origin of a people tap into historic, even ancient understandings of where people came from, and how they perceived their world in earlier times. Myths that involve animals are often about people, their faults, weaknesses,

Left **Obas (kings) of Benin performing for the supreme god.** This war ritual was done to honor the god of creation. The acrobatic dance, Amufi, recalls a legendary war of the gods against the sky.

Below *North Africa and the Sahara* by Alberto Cantino (b.1502). This map shows the populations of the north of the African continent, and traces the movement of the cultures. Strong storytelling traditions were resistant to outside influences.

strengths and foibles. Heroic stories, likewise, tell of people who capture the imagination and provide an empowering model for ordinary mortals. Trickster myths can have close relevance for people in today's world of the misuse of power, and in their dealings with authority in various forms. Some myths are relevant to people of all times.

Today, as in earlier times, the mythology of the African peoples has significance in the socialization and education of children and young adults. In addition, it provides entertainment, a function that was of more importance in times when there was no mass media, but which continues to be significant, in some areas more than others. In parts of Africa the telling of creation myths and stories of origin is under pressure where schooling in Western methods puts emphasis on rational thought. The telling of stories in the homestead or village used to be performed by the elderly, which gave them important roles in educating the younger generation. In a changing world, this tradition is not always maintained.

Right God of the sun. There are a number of myths that credit a supreme being with the creation of night and day. According to some legends, it can be the messenger of the god, who misreads the god's instructions, that throws the sun's motion into chaos.

SIGNS, KNOWLEDGE, AND CREATION

The history of an extensive region of Western Africa is known through the oral traditions of the Bambara, Malinke, Diala, and Kassonke language groups and through the stories of populations that now inhabit the lands that lie between the Atlantic coast of Senegal and the deserts of northern Nigeria and the countries that border the Gulf of Guinea.

Providing a common thread, the mythology tells of an original homeland in the Mande, the upper reaches of the Niger River, and of 30 related families that dispersed from the Mande in the twelfth century to found the Mali Empire. Subsequently, they returned to their land of origin at intervals, recording their genealogies and performing certain rituals. The Dogon were, and are still, settled in the rugged mountains of Bandiagara, and maintain much of the traditional religion and mythology. Remote from the influences of modernity in their mountain homes, the Dogon practice a sign system of communication that links back to their earliest history, bringing together an understanding of creation, and with it, knowledge.

The Creation of Day and Night, The Bat Myth

There are many stories that tell of the creation of night. One, from the Kono people of Sierra Leone, relates how the creator provided light from the Sun by day, and twilight from the Moon, so that it was never dark, nor was it ever cold. The deity asked the Bat to take a basket of darkness to the Moon, but the Bat became tired, put down his load to rest, and to feed. Meanwhile, some animals discovered the basket, and opened it, causing the darkness to escape. Since that time, the Bat has slept through the day and woken at twilight to start his eternal journey in search of the darkness that had escaped, and to try to resume his futile attempt to put it back in the basket, and continue his errand to the Moon.

Among the Yoruba pantheon of gods, it is the supreme deity Olorun, creator of the universe, who is responsible for the creation of day and night. The supreme being also features in the separation of day from night among the Abaluyia people of Kenya, where Wele, the creator god, put the Sun and the Moon in the sky. But the Sun fought the Moon, and thrust him from his position, then the Moon knocked the Sun down. Finally, Wele decreed that the Sun

MARKING SIGNS

For the Dogon, signs are inscribed on rocks, on the ground, in caves, and on gourds. The first signs that were created were those of a placenta on which were marked signs denoting seeds and beings—two pairs of twins, the antecedents of man and woman. Inscriptions on the landscape are reminders of the power and meaning of features of the land to ancient people, and to the dependence of all people on the land.

A symbol of significance in Dogon understandings of creation is the placenta; they believe every human placenta to be a replica of the placenta of the womb of Amma, the supreme being, who conceived the universe.

According to various stories, the egg within which primordial events occurred was divided into a double placenta, each part of the placenta containing a pair of twin Nommo—the offspring of Amma. Each twin was made up of both male and female principles, with one principle more dominant than the other. The male Nommo, Ogo, forced his way out of the egg. He hurtled through space clutching a torn fragment of placenta that became the Earth with a predominantly male soul, creating an imbalance and an impurity. Ogo realized he couldn't rule without his twin, and tried to find her, but could not. According to legend, he still searches for her.

should be out in the day, and the Moon would shine at night. An ancient Twa story also gives responsibility to the supreme being, Khonvum, for the ordering of creation of the earth and the sky, the forests and the animals. At night, it is the task of Khonvum to ensure the regular renewal of the Sun in the morning. Twa storytellers say that he collects together broken fragments of the stars, and hurls them at the Sun to ensure that it will rise again.

In another range of stories, night and death come together. A Maasai myth tells of the ancestral figure

There is always something new out of Africa.
PLINY THE ELDER (A.D. 23–79)

Le-eyo, who was responsible for proclaiming on the death of a child that the child should go away, and then come back; and also had the job of telling the Moon that it should go, and stay away. Poor Le-eyo became extremely confused when his own child died. In his confusion, he incorrectly told the child to go away, and stay away, and told the Moon to go, and then return. Because of this error, say the Maasai, the moon has continued in its cycle of continually rising and setting, waxing and waning.

Above **Dogon cave paintings.** These early examples of rock inscriptions show the progression of creation myths through the ages, and illustrate Amma, the supreme being, giving birth to the universe.

Opposite page **Upright Nommo (an offspring of Amma).** A Nommo figure with raised arms symbolizes the close connection of the land, river, and sky. It also represents the male Nommo twin, Ogo, who falls from the heavens to earth.

Below **Mask of Gu.** Ogun, the god of war, is recognized by different culture groups, such as the Yoruba. He is the protective god of blacksmiths and hunters. "Gu" refers to the metal used for making tools or swords.

The Myth of the Sky God

Across the length and breadth of Africa, people of widely different origins and cultures have a mythology which gives the founding ancestors divine status. They are honored in terms of social relationships, and provide a harmony that holds societies together. The converging of social organization and mythology are well demonstrated by the pastoral Nilotic people inhabiting the floodplains of the upper Nile basin in Sudan, western Ethiopia, and northern Uganda, among whom are the Dinka, Shilluk, Nuer, and Anuak. Social organization is dependent on close-knit ties with land, river, and sky. The changing annual pattern of seasons, alternating between rain that floods the river and the drying out of the land, are essential to the survival of their cattle herds and themselves. As in all flat lands, the horizon is close, and the arch of the sky is more extensive than in landscapes of hills or mountains. A common thread of belief in a powerful sky god is found throughout these groups. Offerings and sacrifices are made in simple shrines throughout the land, which are situated on forked branches, small mud-constructed altars, rocks, man-made stools, and pots. A narrative mythology gives praise, through songs and poems, to the god-kings who are also the ancestors. Central to this is the organization of clans, and lines of descent that link the present-day people with their ancestors.

At the core of the mythology is the world of earth and sky, which were believed to have joined so that the first humans could move between earth and sky, and have access to the sky god. The sky and the earth were linked with a rope, just in reach of a man with outstretched arms. In one myth, the first humans, Garang and Abuk, had to be careful not to lift their hoes or pestles in case they touched the sky god. The founder of the Shilluk royal dynasty, Nyikang (or Nyikango), is, in one story, descended from a man who came from the sky.

Each new king is immortalized as Nyikango, and becomes both king and priest. In another telling, Nyikango was created as a cow, and married a female crocodile, or a womanlike crocodile.

THE STORY OF GU

The Fon stories of Mawu and Lisa vary. In one, the use of metal as a source for making tools is told. Mawu sent his "child" Lisa to the earth with a metal sword to show the people how to clear the forests, plow the cleared land, and cultivate crops. A metal sword is called "*gu*", a word that is associated also with the Yoruba god, Ogun. *Gu* is the name of the god of metal to this day among the Fon people. He protects warriors, blacksmiths, and hunters; today he is also the protector of trucks, bicycles, and cars.

vanquished foes, which may be a partial explanation for their composite pantheon of gods. In war, the gods of the vanquished had to be appeased, so they were assimilated into the Fon pantheon. Mawu-Lisa was from the Aja people in western Dahomey.

In another myth, Mawu and Lisa are said to have been born to a primordial mother, Nana Buluka, who was creator of the world. In this telling, the division of night and day is narrated, since Mawu lived in the west and was the Moon, and Lisa lived in the east and was the Sun. The division of male and female is also implied, for the female Moon came together with the male Sun in an eclipse. The Sun is fierce and fatherly; the Moon is gentle and motherly. The Fon associate eclipses with Mawu and Lisa coming together and making love, which in the past resulted in the birth of a hierarchy of gods, all of them twins.

Above **A Dogon cosmology stool.** The three parts of the stool reflect the concept of the cosmos. The seat (sky disc) is connected to the base (earth), by a central tree. The figures represent ancestral twins.

Left **The heavenly blacksmith.** This Dogon cultural hero, also known as the thief of fire, was the bringer of the art of metal work to the people.

Mawu-Lisa Myth

Among the Fon people who inhabit a region that used to be called Dahomey (now Benin), is a story of Mawu and Lisa, the Moon and her twin brother, the Sun. They combine to form the androgynous creator figure, Mawu-Lisa, who oversees a range of gods of the weather, the earth, metal, and the forests, and has a daughter called Gbadu. Mawu-Lisa created the world, and then delegated different duties to the other gods. This story of creation is like those in other traditions, invoking an evolving order of creation over a period of days leading to the creation of man on the final day.

The Fon are a warlike ethnic group with a complex history of fighting. Some scholars believe that the Fon may have appropriated the gods of their

Above **Benin butchers.** In the palace of the Benin Obas (kings), cows were the most prestigious of animal sacrifices. Special butchers were used to prepare the offerings.

Right **San rock paintings.** San cultures of Zimbabwe died out many centuries ago, but the stories of people's spirits going up to the sky, to become "star" ancestors, after their death are recorded in rock art.

THE KHOI-SAN PEOPLE

Like the Pygmies, the San, or Bushmen, are descended from an ancient line, and used to be spread more widely across southern, central, and eastern Africa. The San, like Pygmies, are small of stature, and come from a late Stone Age culture that are hunter-gatherers in their traditional lifestyle. Evidence of their former habitations is found not only in collections of stone tools distributed widely across the southern half of the continent, but also in rock paintings, which are also abundant. Later, southward migrations of Negroid people, with a different language and culture, established contact with these people. It was customary to believe that the new arrivals destroyed the existing communities. Recent research suggests that the San

established trading contact with the new arrivals, taking on new practices and a modified culture. Over time many of their communities merged.

One such modification was pastoralism. The Khoi people, with languages of a similar type to the San, became herders of cattle and sheep. Groups of the Khoi and San people were encountered behind the coastal lands of the Cape of Good Hope and in the high plateaus of the veldt when Dutch settlers arrived after A.D. 1650. Competition over land drove the San and the Khoi to the margins of good land, the San more able to survive in the dry semidesert of the Namib and the Kalahari. In these remote areas, their distinctive culture—including their mythologies—endured, though under pressure from external influences, at least into the twentieth century.

One story tells of a man or a woman's spirit, on death, going up to the sky and becoming a star. Stars are seen by some as the ancestors of the San. There is, however, as with the Pygmies, a wide range of stories about death, rather than a single myth. Death is also associated with water holes, and the belief that people's spirits go to a huge hole in the ground after death which they find by going along a "Bushman's path." In this version, it is the heart that goes to the sky. In the wide, open spaces of veldt and semidesert, the sky is expansive, and it is unsurprising that a cosmology of sun, moon, and stars is very prominent.

The supreme being, called Nladima by some San groups, is the creator. The word Nladima also means "sky." Nladima and his wife are believed to live in the sky, and humans and animals are their children. Another figure, with more evil characteristics, is Great G'mama, who shoots arrows of evil at humans.

MYTHS OF ORIGIN

The following myth is just one example of many myths that have a similar central figure, a crucial link between the sky god and ancestral origins. Variations on this myth would be dependent on the particular oral traditions and culture groups.

Efé, the First Man

Among the Pygmies, there is a story told of the first man, Efé. The story combines elements of a sky god with ancestors, and the forest environment in which the Pygmies live. The creator god placed Efé on the earth, but recalled him to heaven to hunt, drawing him out of the forest on a liane (vine) that festoons the tall trees of the forest. Efé went across the heavens until he found, and killed, an elephant whose tusks were the size of trees. Everyone was happy, especially the women, and they feasted to satisfaction. Efé was eventually sent back to his forest home where nobody recognized him, but there was some fear because of the spears he carried. After some time, Efé's brother recognized him, and asked him why he had been away so long. Efé told him of their father in heaven, and of the gifts, including spears, their father had sent. At this discovery, there was much joy and wild celebration. Pygmy myths are manifold, and vary across a large geographical area. Like the San and Khoi people, much of their mythology centers on the universe—

Above **Pygmy mask.** Although little is known about the Pygmies, they are believed to be an ancient race of African peoples. These hunter-gatherers probably used this mask as part of an initiation ceremony.

Left **Ceremonial cow head from Nigeria.** Cattle have great symbolic significance in many African cultures, and have a special place in the language of the Shilluk, Nuer, Dinka, and Auak people. In traditional African economy, cattle were the sole measure of wealth and status.

Above **The chameleon bringing death.** The chameleon is a wayward messenger of the supreme being. One legend sees the animal forgetting to deliver his message of immortality to human beings. Another sees him being tricked into handing over new skins, intended for humans, to a snake.

stars, the sun, and the moon over which the supreme being reigns, and from which man gains his spiritual essence. Spiritual fire is part of this, coming from the heavens at birth, and returning with death. Fire is sacred, and Pygmies maintain fire in fireboxes, and carry it with them on their journeys.

Pe, the Moon, is associated with fecundity, and feasts of the Moon are women's celebrations, while those of the Sun belong to men. Many myths incorporate the founding ancestral figure, Efé, and can be seemingly read with an historical meaning concerning the origins and movement of the people. Some tell of Efé crossing a vast stretch of water in a boat, others tell of frozen lands far away. Some have associations with the creation stories of Koranic (Qu'ranic) and Biblical origins, such as those telling of the coming of a great flood.

In one story, Efé escaped from the chaos of war by climbing into a tree through a hole in the trunk, staying there while the battles raged throughout the area. A chameleon man came along with his axe, and cut into the trunk of the tree. From this hole, water flowed, forming a river. Efé emerged completely dry from this watery hole.

MYTHS OF DEATH

Myths concerning death and the origin of death come in different forms. The eminent anthropologist J.G. Frazer, in a study of African myths, divided them into four types: those that described "the two messengers," those concerned with the waxing and waning of the moon, those about the serpent and the casting of its skin, and those about the banana plant. Over and above these are individual stories that are specific to a people or an area.

The story of the two messengers and the origin of death is widely told throughout Africa. The creator god sent the chameleon to earth to tell humans that they would live eternally, and he sent the lizard with a contrary message that humans would die. The chameleon dawdled on the way, but the lizard scurried to deliver its message, arriving before the chameleon. Thereafter, death became the destiny of all humans.

A variation of this myth is found in Liberia. The creator, Sno-Nyosa, sent four sons to visit the Earth. When he wanted them to return, they declined as they wanted to stay. The Earth also wanted them to stay. One by one they were recalled by Sno-Nyosa's magic power of death. It is said that before the creator quarreled with the Earth about the return of his sons, there was no death.

A different story of death comes from the Kabyles, a Berber people from Northern Africa. Here, in an ancient myth believed to predate Islamic influences introduced in the seventh and eighth centuries A.D., there is a woman described as the First Mother of the World. A woman known in many regions, she is responsible for bringing bad omens, misfortune, and ultimately death.

In an interesting analogy with Greek mythology, the Mende of Sierra Leone have an understanding that, after the rites of death have been performed, the soul crosses the water to reach the country of the departed. In this journey the soul is assisted by the ancestors who inhabit the territory in between, and by the burial goods that accompany the body in the grave. Among the Mende, as is found among the Baganda in Eastern Africa, the ancestors are part of the spirit world, mediating between the supreme being and humans, sometimes meeting with humans in their dreams, when the Baganda believe that the human soul leaves the body temporarily.

A PANTHEON OF GODS

In Western Africa around the Gulf of Guinea, an extensive mythology has evolved around a supreme being and a pantheon of minor deities. Among the Yoruba of southwestern Nigeria there are cults of minor deities, the Orisha, who stand as intermediaries between Olorun, the supreme deity, and human beings. Olorun is also "Lord of Heaven" and he is Olodumare, "Almighty." In the creation myth, the Yoruba describe Olorun inhabiting the sky while the earth was still too wet for human habitation. With Olorun in his heavenly realm were other minor divinities that sometimes descended to the Earth to play. Olorun decided to create dry land, and gave this task to Orisha Nla, the chief of the Orisha, who descended to the wet Earth with a snail shell that held some dry soil, a pigeon, and a hen. He emptied the soil on a flat, marshy area, and soon the hen and the pigeon scattered it around

Left **Celebrations of death.** Death rituals are seen by some African groups as an affirmation of life. Colorful funeral fabrics are often used to reflect the vibrant approach to death and mourning.

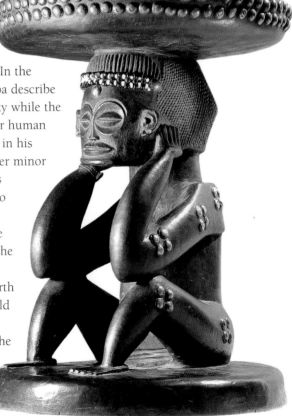

Below **A matriarchial ancestor, Chokwe people.** The seated posture of this figure, with its hands behind its ears, indicates the ritual of mourning. Carvings like these remind the living of the necessity of sacrifices to the dead, to appease the spirits.

307

Far right **Shango, god of thunder.** Olorun, supreme deity of the Yoruba people, sent Shango to Earth as a baby. When the people on Earth started to steal from each other, Olorun commanded that Shango create thunder to punish them.

Right **Eshu, the Yoruba messenger of the gods.** It is agile and quick-witted Eshu who delivers the sacrifices prescribed by Ifa, the divination god. Eshu's long hairstyle is a symbol of his close bond with Ifa.

earth were brought to life by Olorun. The first men and women were then sent to occupy the dry land, to till the soil, and produce crops.

The realm of Olorun is a remote place, beyond the human world, where he reigns supreme, and is too far away for mortals to access him, or present their supplications. But like the Orisha, Olorun is served by priests who enjoy high social status, and are consulted about the happenings of everyday life. The Orisha are the intermediary divinities, appealed to with offerings and sacrifices.

The creation stories link with those of the origins of mankind, the Orisha regarded as ancestral figures to the Yoruba, each with a special connection with natural forces, such as thunder, rain, and disease. This pantheon of gods is still central to the ceremonial and celebratory life of the Yoruba today.

Spear Master Myths

A myth from the Dinka people of southern Sudan includes a range of stories of the origins of a priestly lineage, stories that tell of relationships between religious or cosmological concepts, and the political histories of traditional people. The Dinka, like the Shilluk, live on the floodplains of the Upper Nile, an environment dependent on the annual flooding of the river and prone to extreme drought, which dries out of lands, including the grazing areas for the all-important cattle. The spear master myth has many variations. One tells of a woman, who, being without a child, caused her husband's lineage to have no line of succession. Bemoaning her barrenness by the river, the woman was told by the spirit of the river to go into the water, and to allow the water to ripple into her. The river deity gave her a spear, symbolic of giving birth to a boy. The woman became pregnant, and produced a son named Aiwel. Born with a full set of teeth, a sign of spiritual power, Aiwel performed feats, even as a baby.

One story tells of him rising from where he was lying on the floor, picking up a gourd of milk, and then drinking from it. Amazed at this achievement, his mother is sworn to secrecy on pain of death by Aiwel. But she cannot contain her secret, and dies. In this, the ability of the spear masters is preempted, for

Left **Yoruba Orisha.** Representations of these lesser gods are carried in rituals. It is believed that the deity will enter and live in the figure, bringing protection to the fortunate owner of the carving.

Below **Yoruba Orisha shrine.** Orisha, or minor deities, are seen as intermediate figures who mix with gods and mortals. This shrine figure displays the attributes of wealth (the horse), fertility (mother and child), and power expressed by the number of followers at the base of this statue.

to create a patch of dry land. A chameleon was then sent to test the dry land, and he returned to say that the land was not completely dry. After his second visit, the chameleon declared that the land was dry.

This creation, like that of other creation stories, was measured in days, and on the fifth day, Orisha Nla was worshipped, as has happened ever since in the Yoruba calendar. Then, Olorun sent Orisha Nla to create forests and land suitable to grow food while, in heaven, people molded from handfuls of they are known for their amazing powers to foretell the future of others in their early childhood.

Aiwel's powers stay with him as he grows. During a drought, Aiwel makes water pour from a stump of a tree. In another telling, he takes the cattle out to the dried-up pastures beyond the village, pulls up tufts of grass, and from beneath them the water gushes. After a severe drought, Aiwel offers to lead the people and their cattle to better pastures. The elders of the village do not want Aiwel to lead them, and they move off alone. As they cross a river a fence made of reeds—the sort used by the Dinka to trap fish—blocks their way. As they attempt to cross over it, Aiwel appears on the riverbank, spears each of them with his fish spear, and kills them all.

Spear master Aiwel was the founder of Dinka clan groups related through male lineage descent. These stories combine notions of the supernatural with the origins of the people.

ANCESTRAL ORIGINS, MOUNT KENYA

The people who live in the foothills around Mount Kenya all believe that they are descended from Gikuyu. Gikuyu was called to Mogai (the supreme being), and given a large stretch of land that included rivers and valleys, forests, and all the animals and plants that lived there. Mogai had also created the mountain, called Kere-Nyaga (Mount Kenya), which became the resting place for Mogai when he traveled around the world. Mogai took Gikuyu to the mountain top, and showed him all the land that had been given to him, and pointed to a place where wild figs were growing near the center of the country. it was here that Gikuyu created his home.

Every Gikuyu child knows this story of the origin of the Gikuyu people. They also know the next chapter, in which Mogai gave to Gikuyu and his wife, Mumbi, the promise that their sons and daughters would roam

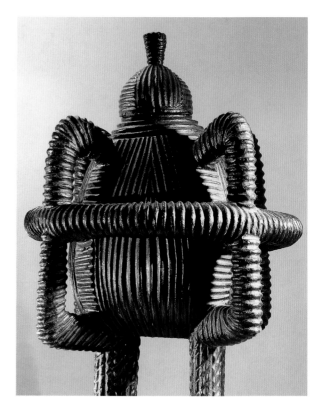

and multiply. Nine daughters were born to Gikuyu and Mumbi, but how were they to multiply in the absence of husbands?

Again Mogai brought deliverance, telling Gikuyu to sacrifice a fat ram, which would bring nine handsome young men into being. There was a great celebration when Gikuyu brought the young men home. The daughters accepted the men as husbands, on the one condition that they allow the women to be head of the household, and all live together in the same village. All Gikuyu, to this day, believe that they are descended from one of the nine clans named after Wacheera, Wanjiko, Wairimo, Wamboi, Wangari, Wanjiro, Wangoi, Waithera, and Warigia.

It is told by the Gikuyu, that for a number of generations all the women served as the rulers in their particular households. However, the men's telling of the story suggests that the women were harsh rulers, and eventually the original agreement was broken, the status quo was shifted, and the men were given the role as the head of their household.

THE KING AS GOD

The African king is the active representative of the supreme god, incorporating mystery and remoteness among his characteristics, and these are expressed within a context of rites, symbols, and a complex formula by which the royal person is identified with the nation. The king is the medium for supernatural elements that are a common feature of Bantu conceptualization. Whatever happens to the king affects the nation as a whole. If he is wounded, the entire country is affected. If he dies, everything comes to a standstill.

SACRED KINGSHIP

Stories of sky gods introduced the idea of divine kingship to many African cultures. Viewed through filters of rationality, kingship with divine attributes can give stability to social structures.

Kingship stories are widespread among the Bantu-speaking populations of central and southern Africa. Among the Zulus of South Africa, myths concerning the origins of the kings are also those of the origins of the people. One story tells of the son of a deity who was expelled from heaven for stealing his father's favorite white cow. He was lowered through a hole in the sky by an umbilical cord tied round him, and was later sent a wife from his father. These two became the founding couple of the Zulu people.

In the Great Lakes region of central-eastern Africa, several kingdoms, each with its own distinct language and culture, have their own myths concerning the foundation of their dynasties. In Ankole, a district of southwestern Uganda, an oral tradition traces the Bahinda dynasty of the Banyankole back through

We carry with us the wonders we seek without us: there is all Africa.

SIR THOMAS BROWNE (1605–1682)

several centuries. The founding myth describes the supreme being, Ruhanga, descending from heaven to rule the land. He bore three sons: Kakama, Kahima, and Kairu. To test them, Ruhanga gave them each a pot of milk to be left untouched through the night. Kakama spilt some of his, but the other brothers re-filled his pot from theirs. Kairu later fell asleep, and knocked his pot over, losing all his milk. In the morning, Ruhanga called the brothers together to determine the results of their testing. Ruhanga then decreed that Kairu should be the servant to his brothers, Kahima should be the herdsman of Kakama, and Kakama should be Ruhanga's heir. This was how the main divisions of the people of the Ankole region were created, the lineages of which were fixed when British explorers and colonial administrators came in contact with the Banyankole at the end of the nineteenth century, and continue to be relevant in the social structure.

Even today, the stories and rituals surrounding the milk pots and the protection of these sacred rituals are an important element of the Banyankole culture in this primarily pastoral society.

Above **Oba (Benin king), flanked by two attendants.** The Oba is considered to be the descendant of a god, and is therefore divine. He is said to have amazing mystical powers, and is an object of great reverence, awe, and fear.

311

STORIES OF THE RAINBOW

As in the mythologies of other parts of the world, the rainbow features widely in African myths. Associated with rain, the colorful rainbow sometimes has good meanings, though it can also be regarded as strange and ominous.

Among the Luba people of the Democratic Republic of the Congo, another society in which kingship is connected with divine origins, the founder of the kingdom was Kalala Ilunga. Kalala Ilunga was born in the court of the Rainbow King, Nkongolo. His mother was Nkongolo's sister, and Nkongolo brought up Kalala Ilunga as his own child, after sending the father away. Kalala Ilunga became a good runner and dancer, and was so popular that Nkongolo became jealous, and planned to kill him. Kalala Ilunga heard about this, escaped the kingdom by crossing the Lualaba River, and found his real father, who gave him an army to destroy Nkongolo. Nkongolo's spirit is the serpent, which is often intertwined with the rainbow.

This story has much that resonates with the significance of the mother's brother in the stories of many Bantu-speaking people.

Among the Fon people in Benin, the rainbow is again linked with the serpent, and may be seen as a portent of danger. In this legend, the serpent is intertwined with the rainbow, the red part being the male part of the serpent and the blue part, the female. Among the Pygmies there is also an association between serpent and rainbow. Khonvum, the supreme being, is, in some stories, cast as

Above **Kalala Ilunga, a legendary Luba hero.** Nkongolo, the Rainbow King, invited his nephew, Kalala, to perform a dance over a concealed pit full of upright spears. Kalala avoided being impaled by uncovering the pit with his own spear.

the great hunter carrying a bow made of two serpents, and this appears to those living on earth as a rainbow.

In Kenya, the Luyia have many stories about rain, and the control of rain by rainmakers. They believe that the rainbow is magical. The supreme being's creation of the rainbow is in two parts, a narrow male part, and a wider female one. If the male part occurs first, then the rain will stop.

The San people, found mainly in the dry lands of southern Africa, have a story that rain was once a beautiful woman who girdled her narrow waist with a brightly colored rainbow.

WATER SPIRITS, GODS, AND GODDESSES

Across Africa, people living close to major watercourses, lakes, and the sea believe them to be the dwelling place of water spirits. The Songhay, of the upper reaches of the Niger River, have many stories of water spirits known as Zin. One tells of a snake that inhabited a lake, and wanted to marry a woman. Her parents agreed, and for the bride-price payment, they asked for ownership of the lake. The snake agreed to this, and left the lake in the care of his wife's parents, returning from time to time to control the fish, the crocodiles, and the hippopotami. The guardianship of the creatures of the lake passed down from the snake to his son, and then on through the generations to this day.

The stories of the birth of Aiwel, founder and spear master of the Dinka, are associated with barrenness, and in this myth the river god plays a part in bringing fertility to Aiwel's mother. Among the Baganda people, the god Mukasa is associated with the waters around the shores of Lake Victoria,

and Mukasa is said to inhabit an island. The rivers, too, are believed to have sprung from spirits, or from humans. One river began when a young woman, after being deserted by her lover, gave birth to their child. On either side of the river, offerings are made by those wanting to cross the river safely.

Water spirits and gods or goddesses of water are often linked with birth, fertility, or infertility. In Nigeria, the Yoruba and the Ibo people have a tradition of water goddesses. In the Yoruba pantheon, the mother god, Yemaja, married her brother, Aganju, and gave birth to a son, Orungan, who later fell in love with his mother and, in the absence of his father, raped her. In a continuing struggle, Yemaja fell to the ground, swelled up, and poured two streams of water from her body to create a lagoon. From her abdomen, a number of minor deities emerged. The place where this happened has remained a sacred place for the Yoruba. The novels of the Ibo writer,

Flora Nwapa, describe the lives of Ibo women within traditional contexts. The cult that focuses on a river goddess, and the honor given to her chosen worshippers, is an aspect of Nwapa's novel, *Efuru*.

MYTHOLOGY OF MOTHERHOOD

The bearing and rearing of children, as in many other parts of the world, is celebrated in a wealth of stories told throughout Africa. Marriage and child-bearing are essential to the realization of identity for women in all regions. When a woman is childless in marriage, her condition of "barrenness" is a problem for her. Rituals and myths surround these stages and states throughout women's lives.

Traditionally, initiation rites at puberty had an educational purpose. Stories were used to convey the meanings of womanhood to young girls, or, in some cases, the meanings of manhood to young boys.

Above **Olokun, god of the sea.** Seashells and animals were often used as offerings and sacrifices to this god. He rules from the depths of the ocean, and has similarities to the Greek god, Poseidon.

Opposite page **Mythical python.** Snakes symbolize the power of Osun, the god of nature. The python is also a symbol of Olokun, the god of the sea. It is said that pythons are sent from Olokun to punish wrongdoing.

In Western Africa, there is a widespread tradition of life coming from water, and of women's fertility associated with water. In the oral traditions of the Ibo people of eastern Nigeria, the mythical figure of Ogbuide is a mother to all. As a goddess of lakes, Ogbuide is associated with women, who come to the river to collect drinking water, and to bathe. Ogbuide is known as a goddess of great beauty, and is believed to leave her watery home and wander through the marketplaces, mingling with women. She calls on women to serve her as priestesses, and through these special few, women bring their fertility problems to Ogbuide, and seek advice or consolation from the goddess. The divine women of African mythology, or goddesses of rivers, lakes, and the sea, are often beautiful women. They live beneath the water, and are very rarely seen.

The idea of water as a source of life is also a part of the belief system of the Oromo of Ethiopia. The

Below **Yoruba mother and child.** African mythology places importance on the stages of a woman's life cycle. Various fertility Orishas are given offerings to ensure that the lineage of a family continues.

dead are spoken of as having become dry, and a barren woman is also described as a dry woman. A barren woman will beseech the supreme being, Waqa, to make her womb wet so that she might sprout children. More important than Waqa to women is the goddess Maram, who is called on in all the rituals of childbirth, and is seen to look after women during their pregnancy and labor.

As mothers, women became involved in issues of heirship and inheritance. The mother of a king, or an elder, was often highly honored. In the history of the Bafokeng people of Lesotho, there is a story of a chief, Tshukudu, who, practicing polygamy, as was customary, would visit his three favorite wives and tell each of them that her son would be the chief after he died. Such an honor was thrilling to each of the women, but woeful after the old chief's death. The warring factions, named after the mothers of the three contenders, fought each other, leading to the splitting of the people into the three groups, who settled on different tracts of land. This story is also part of the mythology of the Sotho people.

HEROES AND MYTH

The stories that tell of heroes often merge myth with history. This is true of many heroic tales of southern African people, for whom the last 200 years has witnessed a turbulent struggle for land and resources, not only between various African people, but also between Africans and Europeans.

This is a complex and fascinating history, involving the movement of Bantu-speaking people into southeastern Africa, their dispersal into a range of scattered chiefdoms, then the merging of chiefdoms under the power of a paramount ruler.

From the late eighteenth to the second half of the nineteenth century, there were momentous happenings, battles, and epic migrations over extensive tracts of country, the essence of stories that have

Above **Battle of Isandhlwana, 1879.** The British invaded Zululand in 1879, which was at that time ruled by Cetewayo. The six companies of the 24th Regiment and a force of Natal volunteers were overwhelmed and massacred by the Zulus, who were inspired by the legend of the heroic figure, Shaka.

come down to the present day as part of the myth-ology. History has been interwoven with and reflects the traditional stories of the past.

Zwide, Soshangane, and Zwangendaba of the Ndwande people, and Dingiswayo of the Mthethwa people are heroic figures competing to extend their kingdoms in the area of what is now southern Mozambique. The Ndwande under Zwide were defeated by Shaka in the area close to what is today the heartland of the Zulu people. Their defeated force split into two groups, one under Soshangane that moved into and settled in what later became southern Mozam-bique. The other force led by Zwangendaba spread north and west, fighting local populations, suffering defeats and gaining victories, resting awhile, and marching on, eventually covering more than 1,000 miles. This group, in their original homeland described as Jere, became known as the Ngoni, and used the military skills they had

acquired in their fighting further south, and also developed political inclusion of the people they con-quered. Thus the Ngoni increased their power. They moved through the territory of the Shona in modern Zimbabwe, then crossed the Zambezi River, moving north toward Lake Nyasa. Where they might have gone after reaching the southern area of modern Tanzania is anyone's guess, but it is told that Zwangendaba was tired, ageing, and ill, and his people had become weary. Zwangen-daba died before any further moves could be accomplished by his people. This was only 20 years after the great migration had begun so far to the south, ending in the defeat, and dispersal of the Ndwande.

Stories of the heroic leader Zwangendaba have been told from the mid-nineteenth century to the present; he was a figure of history who became envel-oped by myth. But it is the hero, Shaka who has captured the imagination of, and is familiar to, many Western observers and history readers. Shaka was the younger son of

Left **Ashante fertility symbol.** Legend tells of a young woman, Akua, who was unable to become pregnant. On the advice of a wise man, she carried a wooden carving of a child around with her, and very soon she conceived.

Right **Ivory leopards.**
In Benin cosmology, the
leopard is a symbol of
royal power. At one time,
leopards were sacrificed
to ensure the well-being
of the kingdom.

Below **A leopard plaque.**
The Obas (kings) of Benin
surrounded themselves
with images and statues
of leopards. The power
and strength these animals
represented were quali-
ties passed onto the
Obas and their offspring.

the chief of the small kingdom of the Zulus. Shaka's
prowess as a military leader was widely known during the Zulu–British war of 1879, although he was
no longer alive. Shaka established an enlarged Zulu
kingdom by incorporating all the neighboring chiefdoms into Zululand, and eventually worked on over-
throwing the Ndwande chiefdom, to great success.

ANIMAL MYTHS

In African mythology the natural world is close to the
social. In the same way that the landscape, the sky,
the mountains, and the forests feature in stories, so
too do animals, birds, and reptiles. Some creatures
are more prominent than others. The chameleon and
the serpent have eminence over
wide areas of Africa. Others, such
as the leopard, the hare, the rabbit, and the tortoise, are featured
over more limited areas, perhaps
determined by the environment.
There are stories about hares
and tortoises that tell how their
cunning can, at times, be used
to get the better of larger, more
powerful animals. Often these
tales are actually about the
features of human beings, but
are often told to entertain and
serve as moral tales.

A small child asks his father
why a little snake comes to visit
him, the one that the child's
mother forbids the family to kill.
The father answers that the snake
is the guiding spirit of their race, and

explains how the snake came to make itself known to the family. First, the snake appeared in several of the father's dreams. Then, one night in a dream, the snake tells the father that he would appear in reality, giving the time and place for the meeting. However, the father sees the snake, and is filled with fear as the snake looks like any other snake. The father fights hard to stop himself from killing the snake. Seeing the father's reaction, the snake turned and disappeared the way he had come. The following night, the snake appeared again in the father's dreams, and asked why the father didn't receive him kindly, telling him that he, the snake, was the guiding spirit of the race, and if he was accepted, he would bring good fortune. The second time the father saw the snake, he received him without fear, and accepted him with kindness. From that day on, the kindly snake has brought the family nothing but good fortune.

Relations between human beings and animals may be expressed in other ways, such as in the stories from Malagasy (Madagascar). Certain clans in Malagasy call their menfolk "Sons of crocodiles," explained by a tale about a crocodile that lived in a river, whose wife was a human female. She became entangled in a fish trap, then was removed from the river and taken away by a man with whom she lived for a period of time. After bearing him two sons, she returned to the river.

A story about Gina tells how the crocodile came to have a humpy, ridged back. Gina, who was a man, was sleeping under a tree when a fire overtook him, and badly burned his back. Gina jumped into the river to put out the flames, and turned into a crocodile. This is a common story of animal origins that explains the characteristic features of a species. Another story tells of how the crocodile moved through the hills, and when as became tired, he turned himself into a rocky ridge to rest.

TRICKSTER MYTHS

There is a type of story found throughout the continent that is more secular than those with sacred connotations of creation and origins. Such stories contain circumstances in which the guileful, seemingly weak or innocent character is pitted against one with more power. In Western Africa, these stories reach a high level of importance, sometimes transferring from the traditional into a situation of modernity and current political significance. When ordinary men or women get the better of officialdom, there is entertainment, even though a more complex situation of deception or suffering may be involved.

A genre of tales about Ananse, the spider trickster, concerns the most popular characters in the mythology of the Akan and Ashante of Ghana, which are told more widely through Western Africa. One story tells of Ananse promising to cure the mother of Nyame, the supreme being, of her illness. She dies, and Nyame, holding Ananse to his vow that he would forfeit his own life in the event of failure, sentences him to death. Ananse performs his trickery, using his son, who burrows under the place where Ananse is held captive. The son cries out, as Ananse has instructed, that the Ashante will not survive if Ananse is killed, but will thrive if he is given a reprieve. Through these means, Ananse survives to perform further acts of a dubious nature. Many Ananse stories are coarse, even crude, with sexual misadventures, and they often demonstrate human foibles and weaknesses.

Another trickster, associated with the Fon people of Benin, is Legba, who is both a god and a mediator between the gods and humans, and between humans themselves. Legba, a linguist, knows the languages of all the gods in the pantheon, as well as the language of Mawu-Lisa, the supreme being of the Fon. As each god knows only his own language, as does Mawu-Lisa, this attribute enables Legba to move between the deities and, in effect, to manipulate situations to his own ends. Legba's nickname is Aflakete, which means "I have tricked you."

Left **The elephant as a wise chief.** Ashante legend says that this enormous animal can only be defeated with magic. The elephant is also believed to be a human chief from the past. When a dead elephant is found, it is given a proper burial.

WHAT IS A TRICKSTER?

The trickster is portrayed as a character that anyone can identify with: humorous, lawless, and something of a "jack-the-lad." Trickster figures appear in the myths and stories of many traditional societies in Africa. He sometimes appears as a god, sometimes as an animal. Trickster figures are well loved for their unconventional behavior.

Right **Trickster shrine figure.** While the trickster is playful, there is often a tragic side to some stories, with people being hurt. Tricksters appear in many forms, such as Ananse, the spider in Ghana; and Ajapa, the dog, of the Yoruba people.

317

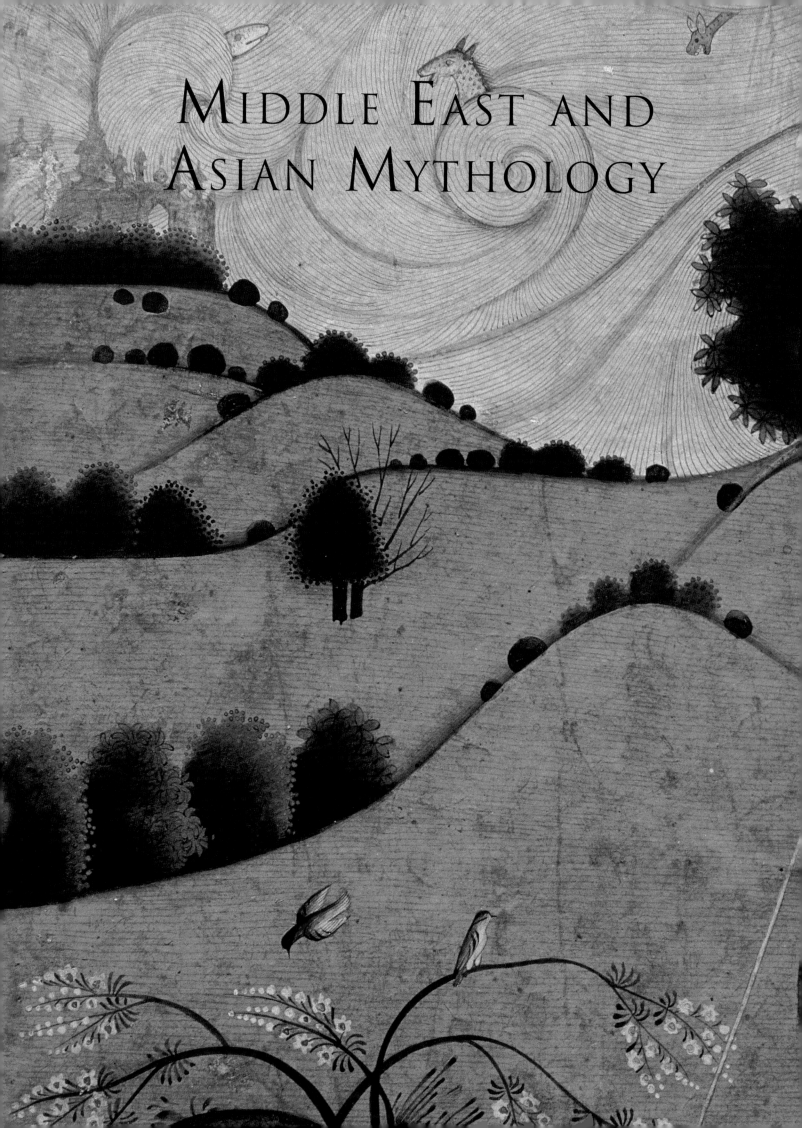

Middle East and
Asian Mythology

MESOPOTAMIAN MYTHOLOGY

Mesopotamia is Greek for "the land between the rivers," referring to the Bronze Age world of the ancient Middle East circa 3500 to 330 B.C. Mesopotamians lived in mud-brick houses behind protective city walls, and built palaces and temples of stone that towered into the sky. They were an industrious people in a difficult landscape, and they struggled together there to create magnificent empires and armies, noted for their opulence, gold, and monumental grandeur. Theirs was the era of epic heroes and fabulous beasts, of kings and divine powers.

The Mesopotamian region stretched from the Mediterranean Sea in the west to the Iranian plateau in the east, bordered on the north by the Caucasus mountain range, and on the south by the Arabian Desert and the Persian Gulf. Permanent cities had begun to appear as early as 3500 B.C. in the area referred to as the Fertile Crescent, known as "the land between the rivers," the Tigris and the Euphrates. These emerging cities expanded into powerful city-states, such as

Uruk, Ur, Eridu, Kish, Babylon, Lagash, Susa, Nimrud, Kadesh, Assur, and Nineveh. The Assyrians and the Mittanis were the principal northern tribes. The main southern tribes were the Sumerians and the Akkadians. Over the centuries, these city-states rose and fell—at times coexisting—and created the ruling nations of Sumeria, Akkadia, Amorite, Assyria, and, later, Babylonia. By the end of the third millennium B.C., for example, the Sumerian city of Ur (in the area of present-day Iraq) was politically dominant, and a great many of the recorded Sumerian texts date to that golden era. The Akkadians followed, under Sargon the Great (c. 2334–2279 B.C.). Various minor states followed, but by the eighteenth century B.C., the Semitic tribes of the Amorites and their related clans had swept through the region on the thunderous wheels of horse-drawn chariots. King Hammurabi made the city of Babylon their capital and their god Marduk king of the gods. The Sumerian language was exiled to temple texts and religious ceremonies, surviving there in written form for another 1,000 years.

CRAFTSMEN AND SCHOLARS

From the earliest times, the people of Mesopotamia have proved themselves to be superior metalworkers and tool-makers. They were responsible for major improvements in agricultural technology, inventing plows and hardware that made it possible for peasant-farmers to harvest enough for their own families, as well as support vast armies of soldiers and builders.

Mesopotamia is sometimes hailed as the birthplace of the written word and the cradle of Western civilization. Cuneiform script, which is the earliest known writing system, evolved here, and recorded, for more than 3,000 years, many of the details of life of the various Mesopotamian cultures. As a tool for organizing trade, business, and bureaucracy, the use of permanent standardized record-keeping reached its first zenith in the Mesopotamian empires. Weights, measures, and values made it possible to trade even in unstable regions, and meticulous inscriptions on clay tablets and stone walls controlled and maintained extensive temple complexes and populations of workers.

Around 1800 B.C., King Hammurabi of Babylon ordered that a list of laws, known as The Code of Hammurabi, be carved in stone in order to erect a

ANCIENT MESOPOTAMIA

permanent system that applied to all, from king to commoner. In this way, the Code established the enduring concept of written law as a formal guide for society, and is considered to be a prototype for the Ten Commandments.

This sense of permanency extends to their myths. Many Mesopotamian mythological themes can be seen in the later Homeric epics and in the stories of the Old Testament. The Tower of Babel, the slayer of Leviathan, the sieges of walled cities, tales of heroes that are part-god and part-man, quarrels among the gods, and a flood that cleansed the world at divine command can be found in their earliest forms in Mesopotamian myths and epic tales.

Above **Mesopotamia, the land between the rivers.** The Sumerian empire was centered in the city of Ur, and included Akkad and Elam. Under Ur-Nammu (ruled 2112–2095 B.C.), it saw the construction of the first ziggurats. After the fall of the Sumerians, the Amorites, Assyrians, and Babylonians rose to power. By 1757 B.C. all of Meso-potamia came under the rule of King Hammurabi, with Babylon its center.

THE ZIGGURAT, STAIRWAY TO HEAVEN

The great stepped stone terraces of the Mesopotamian temple, the "ziggurat," are as immediately connected with Mesopotamia as the Great Pyramids or the Sphinx are with ancient Egypt. These massive buildings dominated the view, rising tier upon tier over the city. The architectural form dates back to the earliest days of the city-states: whenever the walls of a temple collapsed because of age, earthquake, flood, or fire, the rubble was not cleared, but instead faced with stone, and used as the base for a new temple to sit on top. Thus, generation upon generation, the temples stood taller, lifting the priests and the aristocracy to ever more remote heights above the common people in their mud-brick houses below.

Ziggurats were covered in fine stone and magnificently painted and decorated inside, reflecting the wealth of the temples and royal courts. Wide staircases on the outside were platforms for seasonal processions and religious ceremonies. Divine beings stepped down from the sky to the tip of the ziggurat. The royal marriage bed of the king and his goddess was up there in a splendid temple room. Their nuptials linked earth to heaven and heaven to earth, and established the divine right of the king.

Left *The Ziggurat of Marduk, at Babylon,* from P. Spamer's *Illustrirte Weltgeschichte* (1880). This wondrous seven-staged tower probably inspired the biblical Tower of Babel.

Above **Babylonians bringing a humpbacked cow as tribute to Darius I, King of Persia, relief, fifth century B.C.** Just as the gods demanded propitiatory tributes so, too, did the human rulers. Darius I (550–486 B.C.), "King of Kings," founded the Achaemenid dynasty in Persia, which is present-day Iran.

APSU, THE WATERY ABYSS

Different city-states, empires, and language groups in Mesopotamia shared many of the same gods, though they used a bewildering variety of names for them. Indeed, the fundamental elements of religious belief were very consistent throughout the entire ancient Middle East. This created a continuity, a recognizable "Mesopotamian" culture that existed over three and a half millennia and across a vast territory, even in times of conflict. Marduk of Babylon replaced earlier gods, such as Assur in Assyria and Ninurta in Sumer, yet he fought the same battle, defeated the same cosmic enemies, and was responsible for the creation of the living universe of god and man.

The cosmos itself, Mesopotamians believed, floated upon Apsu, the watery abyss, which existed before creation. The divine power of gods and monsters was drawn forth from these primeval waters by magical recitations and heroic acts.

The Mesopotamians, particularly the early Sumerians, were among the earliest and best sailors. They had an intense relationship with the borders between land and water, and the stories of their gods are rich with the power and potential of water in a dry land. In the cycles of Gilgamesh, one of the most ancient and enduring of their stories, the hero

conquers the might of mountain, desert, dark forest, and wild beast, yet the magic of immortality in the waters of the world remains forever beyond his grasp.

Golden Gods and Human Clay

Mesopotamian origin myths show a belief in human servitude to divine powers. Even with the passage of time, this theme remained central to their myths. Humankind was created to be the slave of the gods, toiling in the fields and gardens of the gods, building their temples, and digging their irrigation ditches. In order to create these human servants, the gods had to kill one of their own and mix his divine blood with clay and ashes.

Mesopotamians envisioned reality as ascending hierarchies of order built out of chaos by the labors, loves, betrayals, and heroics of gods and humans. Generation was piled upon generation, struggling for the limited resources of a dramatic environment: a land of fertile soils and flooding rivers, searing deserts, muddy shores, and inhospitable mountain heights. They patterned their gods on the caprice and majesty of that environment. Their heroes, both human and divine, were inspired by the strength of the wild beasts around them: powerful bulls with massive horns, lions, eagles, serpents, and scorpions.

The primary gods and goddesses were the supreme deities of the spheres of heaven, air, earth, and water. There were more than 3,000 in all: a god for every aspect of human interaction with nature, with the gods, and with each other. Every kind of tool, product, or activity had a god, even if only a minor one. The gods watched carefully over everything their human servants did, ever ready to provide divine guidance or to deliver divine punishment. Statues of their gods had wide-open staring eyes to emphasize this supernatural surveillance.

As well as gods, demons and angels also influenced the human world. The supernatural forces of demonic chaos, seething in the underworld depths and in the watery abyss of Apsu, were balanced by the equally supernatural forces of divine light. The tales tell of the struggle of humans to keep their backs safe from the one and their faces turned to the other. Their safeguards: ritual, prayer, hard work, and sacrifice.

Right **Limestone statuette of a bearded god, third millennium B.C., Sumerian.** The staring eyes of this statue evoke the belief that the gods are all-seeing deities. It was believed that the statue of a god provided a direct physical link to the god's awareness.

CREATION STORIES

The Mesopotamian story of creation is best known today from several Babylonian editions of the *Enuma Elish*, the Poem of Creation, recorded in temple archives from the twelfth to the seventh centuries B.C. These versions are themselves based on translations, expansions, and adaptations of even older Sumerian, Akkadian, and Assyrian texts. The basic elements, no doubt, had been part of the cultural and oral tradition throughout the region long before they were written down. The imagery in the stories comes from the time when the first city-states of the Fertile Crescent were being established. The tales reflect the conflicts that grew with the rise in power of the towns and cities as they grappled for land and water, and the demand for the most vital resource of all: human laborers. In these early tales, the primordial world had a dark and savage nature to it. Generations of gods and demons were tossed together in a swirling darkness, living on each other's spilled blood and torn flesh, child gods devouring parent gods in order to acquire their divine powers.

The early myths provide various scenarios for the separation of earth, sky, and heaven, as well as for the creation of man. The supreme Sumerian deities were the heaven god, An, ruling the sky; Enlil, ruler of the air and earth; and the mother goddess Ninhursag. The fourth god Enki, ruler of the meeting-place between water and land, had different roles in different myths. The Babylonians altered their names but not their primary roles. An, for example, became Anu; Enlil became Ellil; and Enki became Ea.

In the *Enuma Elish*, the old gods fought a great war against the young gods. The demon goddess Tiamat, the female deity of chaos and consort of Apsu, rode at the head of their army. Champion for the young gods was Marduk, a divine warrior with four eyes, four ears, and fire in his breath. He rode a horned dragon, and used the winds and thunder as his weapons. In the terrible battle that ensued, Marduk trapped Tiamat in a net. Each time she screamed in rage, he forced one of the seven winds down her throat, until she was distended and helpless.

Marduk split Tiamat, and formed the sky, stars, and planets from her upper body, and the earth from her lower body. Her many breasts were piled up as the mountains. The Tigris and Euphrates Rivers flowed from her eyes. Marduk then organized the landscape revealed by this creation, and set the sun, Shamash, on its course. Marduk was made leader of the gods in return for these labors.

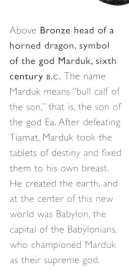

Above **Bronze head of a horned dragon, symbol of the god Marduk, sixth century B.C.** The name Marduk means "bull calf of the son," that is, the son of the god Ea. After defeating Tiamat, Marduk took the tablets of destiny and fixed them to his own breast. He created the earth, and at the center of this new world was Babylon, the capital of the Babylonians, who championed Marduk as their supreme god.

Left *The Hero Marduk Defeats Tiamat, the Fearful Goddess of the Deep,* from *Gilgamesh* by Zabelle Boyajian. Tiamat is an intriguing figure: though represented as a female dragon and the bringer of evil and chaos, she is also the source of all that exists in this world.

THE CREATION OF MAN

The younger gods celebrated the defeat of Tiamat and the design of heaven and earth. However, their elation faded once they discovered that their various duties involved hard work, and they did not like to work. Gods of earth and air bore the brunt of the work, digging riverbeds and irrigation ditches, planting, and harvesting crops to feed the gods. They complained bitterly about these burdens to the sky head god, Anu (An), and to the large pantheon of major gods. The hierarchy of divine workers needed a broader base.

Ea (Enki), god of magical spells, with the help of a mother-goddess, made little clay figures that would do the work for them. As punishment for his role in the great war between the gods, Tiamat's general, Kingu, had to be sacrificed to provide the vital force for the slave race that would serve the gods. So Marduk killed him and Kingu's blood was used to animate the clay figures.

The various versions of the creation of humankind reflected the demanding lifestyle imposed by the climate and landscape, and behavior in heaven to some extent reflected the social structure on earth. It was not enough that these human slaves must do the gods' work; they must also endure the gods' whims and caprices. In the oldest stories from Sumerian times, the gods played cruel and careless games with the clay figures, creating them just for the drunken entertainment of lazy overlords. Perhaps evident in these tales is an attempt by the ancient Mesopotamians to explain the difficult nature of their lives, to find some sort of rationalization for the unpredictable violence of the weather and the random violence of men. Some clay figures were deliberately deformed so that the gods could bet on the resulting creature's behavior in life. In another early story, a herder and a farmer were tricked into a ruthless competition so that the gods could bet on who was the more valuable to them.

As Mesopotamian civilization expanded and became more successful, the officials recording these stories modified them, putting greater emphasis on loyalty to the gods and on the ruthless power of their revenge if offended or betrayed by their mortal slaves, than on cruel games. Even so, humans remained the mortal playthings of the immortal gods, seemingly valuable only for the hard work they could do—tools to be discarded once they wore out.

ISHTAR AND THE SEVEN VEILS

Arabian women around the world today honor this ancient story in the "Dance of the Seven Veils," even though the cosmic power involved is no longer of religious significance.

In the oldest, Sumerian, versions of the myth, the goddess Inanna was tricked into the underworld by the gods. Her story was later transformed into a tale of divine romance: the tragedy of an immortal goddess in love with a mortal, Dumuzi. He is the supreme farmer, the superlative herder, fairest of all humans, and ruled by his complete devotion to his goddess wife. Yet other versions recount that Dumuzi was banished to the underworld by Inanna for some months of every year for his lack of feeling for her. During this time, the earth became barren, only returning to fertility when they were reunited.

In the later Akkadian version, these same roles were played by the goddess Ishtar and her beloved Tammuz. In this version of the tale, when Tammuz died, Ishtar followed his corpse into the underworld, the realm of her rival Ereshkigal, a gloomy place where the dead fed on dust, wore feathers, and stood about as servants in the hall.

Massive walls protected this multilayered underworld, one within the other, with locked gates and monstrous guards. Ishtar not only had to name each part of the gate and the staff who maintained it, she also had to pay to cross its dimensional threshold. One by one, she took off her jewels and garments as payment.

When Ishtar finally passed through the seven gates and reached the throne of Ereshkigal, she was naked and defenseless, and had only a glimpse of her beloved husband before she was slain. Her death left

The goddess—with her there is counsel. The fate of everything, she holds in her hand.

HYMN OF ISHTAR

the earth in turmoil: the soil would not yield, and no womb could conceive. Ishtar, however foolish in love, was no fool. She had left her faithful lieutenants prepared. A comely transvestite priest was trained and equipped, and sent as messenger of the gods to beg for Ishtar's corpse. Through flattery and eloquence, the priest reached Ereshkigal and won her heart. He carried in secret a vial of the water of life, provided by Ea (Enki), and with this he revived Ishtar.

In the complex bargain that was ultimately struck, Tammuz agreed to take Ishtar's place in the underworld for half of every year, during which time Ishtar's great grief brought on winter. Tammuz' sister took his place for the other half, and then Ishtar's happiness and sexual activity made the earth flourish.

At each gate on the return, Ishtar recovered another piece of her wardrobe. In the same way, the world of nature redressed itself as the seasons went through their cycles.

Above **Alabaster statuette of a lady, 2500–2400** B.C., **from the Temple of Ishtar, Syria.** The goddess Ishtar appears in many guises and across many cultures. In Syria, she is connected with their goddess Astarte, and in Egyptian mythology the goddess Isis and her beloved husband, the god Osiris, similarly represent the cycles of fertility.

Left **Soldiers, from the Stele of the Vultures, circa 2450** B.C., **Sumerian.** This famous stone relief is dedicated by Eannatum of Lagash, celebrating his victory over the city-state of Umma. These soldiers, so uniform in appearance, are similar to the little clay figures of men made for the gods' pleasure.

325

GILGAMESH, THE ORIGINAL SUPERHERO

Gilgamesh is thought to have been an early king of Uruk, and with mythical additions, he was a legend throughout Mesopotamia for millennia. The story of his exploits was told and retold in every household and inn, by those working in the ports and harbors of the Mediterranean, and by the herdsmen in the hard lands of the Caucasus Mountains. His adventures were parables of heroics and hubris, and many of the themes in the Homeric epics (c. 800 B.C.) and in the Old Testament are rooted in these tales. The standardized version of this oral epic was recorded in the Akkadian era, around the third millenium B.C.

The cornerstones of Mesopotamian faith are to be found at the heart of this story: the separation of human and divine; the absolute nature of human mortality and of human servitude to the gods; the assignment of roles to gods and to men for the maintenance of order against chaos; and the need to be obedient to one's divinely assigned role. Gilgamesh challenged these for the sake of human loyalty to the life of his beloved other self, the forest man, Enkidu.

Gilgamesh was unique because he was two parts god and one part man. The beauty of the sun god, Shamash, shone in his face, and the courage of the storm god, Adad, was in his blood. He was a man born of woman, yet endowed with divine attributes and supernatural powers; thus he represented a living link between gods and men.

In his youth, however, he abused these powers. He made stormy assaults on the lands and peoples around Uruk. There was a divine irony in his search for battle and adventure: he was created to be the greatest warrior of the world, yet that very fact denied him the fulfilment of that position because no one could stand up to him. There were no challenges worthy of his nature and, in frustration, Gilgamesh turned to excess and indulgence. He celebrated his victories with too much debauched partying, disturbing the folk in the city and the gods in the temples. He wasted food supplies with his revelry. He demanded the royal right to be first in every virgin's marriage bed, and he led men to their deaths in useless wars. The gods began to worry that someday Gilgamesh would ask for a greater part of his divine heritage. He could challenge the gods and rock the pillars of heaven if he wasn't controlled.

Enkidu, the Equal of Gilgamesh

The gods devised a plan. They believed that, if he was provided with an equal, Gilgamesh would divert his dangerous energies toward that rival and cease challenging heaven. The sky god, Anu (An), and the mother goddess, Ninlil (Ninhursag), created a mirror image of Gilgamesh from clay and gave it life. They sent a dream to Gilgamesh in which the stones of heaven fell at his feet, announcing the arrival of his new companion, Enkidu.

Dreams play a major role in the story. At crucial moments Gilgamesh performs elaborate rituals to evoke dreams to advise and guide him; indeed, he follows this internal guide over every other counsel. In a world dominated by the command of the gods, kings, and priests, this represented a dangerous course of individual willpower and self-determination.

The gods dropped Enkidu into the wilderness, where he lived and ate like an animal. He became beastmaster there at once, as dangerous in the sphere of nature as Gilgamesh was in the sphere of men. Herdsmen and farmers felt threatened by Enkidu's presence, and asked Gilgamesh for help.

Gilgamesh sent a wily temple courtesan to tame Enkidu, since the wild man retained his powers only so long as he remained innocent. Six days and seven nights passed with this educated lady, who changed Enkidu into a civilized man. She cleaned him up and brought him to Uruk, where the people were greatly excited by his likeness to Gilgamesh. They threw a great party for him, and Enkidu became boastful the more he drank. He announced himself as the man born in the hills, come to change the old order, and the people begged for his protection.

Enkidu intercepted Gilgamesh as the king set out to invade yet another bride's marriage bed. Enkidu issued his challenge to the king who was part god. Their fight is glorious, full of awe-inspiring deeds and destruction, but neither could prevail against the other. Finally, Gilgamesh succeeded in tossing his rival Enkidu to the ground.

The gods had not considered that, by creating Enkidu from a mirror image of Gilgamesh but without the divine portion, they had emphasized in him the humanity of Gilgamesh. That which inspired arrogance in Gilgamesh sparked humility in his alter ego. Enkidu did not become the rival, as the gods had planned him to be; instead he became Gilgamesh's trusted and loved companion.

An Inseparable Team

With Enkidu beside him, Gilgamesh prepared for his greatest adventure yet. He prayed and wept, begging Shamash, the sun god, for support. Shamash relented, and ordered that weapons be forged that had never been forged before. This part of the epic is told in loving detail, a warrior's adventure told by people who were proud of their skills and of their weapons. Together, Gilgamesh and Enkidu set off, entering new territory and accomplishing what no one else could.

Guided by powerful dreams about gods, falling mountains, and showers of glory, Gilgamesh and Enkidu set out for the divine mountain. This place was covered in a magnificent forest of cedar trees, and guarded by an ancient, primordial being, Humbaba, who radiated seven kinds of savage glory. Like Ishtar, Humbaba loses these one by one and, in an echo of the battle with Tiamat, Shamash sends the winds to immobilize Humbaba. Gilgamesh strips Humbaba of his magic weapons, and beheads him despite his pleas for mercy. Humbaba's wild radiance is absorbed by the lion, the hot dry lands, and by Erishkigal's dark and gloomy underworld.

The magnificence of Gilgamesh's victorious return inflamed Ishtar's passion, and she tries to seduce him. Gilgamesh scorns her, naming the many men she has ruined and the gods she has scorned in the past.

Ishtar is furious. Worse, she is humiliated and she demands revenge. The gods create the Bull of Heaven, but Gilgamesh and Enkidu were not to be defeated. They throw the bull's bloody thigh at Ishtar in her temple, and take its head home in triumph.

The rage in heaven could not be contained. Someone had to die. The great gods argued over which of the two should be punished, but they finally decided that Enkidu had to die for the sins of Gilgamesh.

Enkidu's dream of the underworld and the fate of the dead that reside there is one of the most moving passages of literature in the ancient world, and expresses the underlying angst that drove the entire culture. Cursed by the gods, Enkidu had to die, not as a warrior, but as he lay trembling and weak with fever. Disease in that era was powerful beyond the strength of even the greatest of warriors. Gilgamesh, overwhelmed by grief, sings a long beautiful lament for Enkidu, and gives him a hero's funeral. Gilgamesh has learned, at last, to fear death.

The Search for Immortality

The mightiest warrior in the world, who had challenged heaven and the gods with the might of his arm and the power of his will, could not bear sorrow. Gilgamesh set off alone on his final adventure. Like Ishtar, he could rule the world but not his heart, and was fated to travel through hell in the hope that he might revive his dead friend, his mortal half.

Grieving Gilgamesh wanders the world, seeking Utnapishtim, "The Faraway." Only this man and his wife, of all humanity, were graced by the gods with eternal life. Gilgamesh travels through the Mountain of the Rising Sun, somewhat like the Egyptian god Re's underworld journey, arriving at the garden of the gods. There he persuades Ursanabi, ferryman of the dead, to take him to Utnapishtim.

Gilgamesh begs to learn how to acquire immortal life. Utnapishtim answers first with a stark answer that nothing is permanent, that everything living must die. Gilgamesh rejects this, demanding to know how Utnapishtim had achieved immortality. The wise old man responds with the story of the great flood—startling in its similarity to the later biblical story of Noah and the flood, complete with ark.

The story goes thus: the constant noise of human multitudes annoyed the gods, and Enlil decided to flood the earth entirely and silence them. Ea (Enki), secretly warns one human, Utnapishtim, instructing him to build an ark, to fill it with livestock, goods, family, and craftsmen, then to seal it up and ride out the flood inside it. Six days and six nights of storm raged, but the seventh dawned clear. Utnapishtim then sent out a dove, but it found no land and so returned. At last a raven flew off without returning, and the people, plants, and animals in the ark went forth to rebuild. The gods were angry until the god Ea reminded them how much they needed their human slaves. Utnapishtim and his wife were made immortal, and allowed to dwell in the Garden of the Sun with the promise that the gods would never again attempt to destroy the human race.

Utnapishtim did not give Gilgamesh the secret of immortality, since that could only be given by the gods. Instead, he gave Gilgamesh a plant to revive Enkidu but, as Gilgamesh slept, a serpent stole it.

Gilgamesh had failed, and he spent his last days upon the walls of his city, brooding on the tragedy of life and death. After his death, he is mourned by all.

Scholars of Mesopotamia have often commented on the unusually pessimistic nature of the themes and conclusions found in the mythological and epic material, referring to Gilgamesh as "the first tragic hero." Some say that Egypt gave the world a vision of heaven and Mesopotamia gave the world a vision of hell. At the very least, the Mesopotamian view of the afterlife was starkly different from that of nearly all the other cultures of the time. Such a grim ending to a life of hard work—an eternity without light or hope—must have been a difficult future to anticipate.

Y

Right **Persian Empire,
600–500 B.C.** At its peak,
the expansive Persian
Empire stretched from
Egypt to Afghanistan and
central Asia. This diverse
range of cultures con-
tributed to a rich tradition
of storytelling, and fueled
ideas that still influence
the region today.

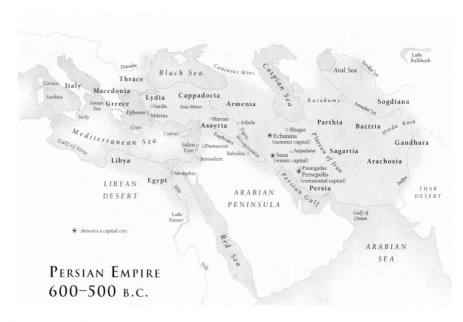

PERSIAN EMPIRE
600–500 B.C.

Most readers would
not be surprised
to find that the biblical
stories of Creation and
Eden are often considered
mythological. What would
surprise quite a number
of readers would be to
find a collection of biblical
stories of patriachs, kings,
and prophets included in a
section on Middle Eastern
mythology. These stories,
found in what Christians
call the Old Testament,
play a fundamental role in
the Jewish, Christian, and
Muslim religions. However, there is no archaeological
or historical evidence for most of the events and
characters found in these stories. Furthermore, we
still do not know when, where, or by whom these
stories were composed and collated to form the books
of the Bible. Most schol-
arly opinion would see
this process taking place
in the periods of the
ancient Persian or Hel-
lenistic Empires in the
Middle East, that pre-
ceded and succeeded
the era of Alexander the
Great (356–323 B.C.).

Seen from this per-
spective, the biblical
stories can be located as
part of major religious
movements that were
then occurring in the
ancient world. The
millennium preceding
the time of Christ was
marked by the rise and fall of empires and the resulting intermingling of cultures and religions. Questions
of universalism and diversity, the One and the Many,
arise, together with the questions of justice, good and
evil, suffering, and death. It is this dynamic inter
action of Babylonian, Palestinian, Assyrian, Egyptian,
Syrian, Persian, and Greek religious ideas that resulted
in the biblical narratives.

THE INFLUENCE OF
THE PERSIAN EMPIRE

The Persian Empire was the first to bring together,
under one rule, these diverse cultures. Established
under Cyrus the Great in 559 B.C., at its peak the
empire would stretch from Egypt and the Balkans
in the west to Afghanistan and to central Asia in the
east. The importance of Persia for the biblical writers
is attested not only by Cyrus being credited with the
release of the Judeans from Babylonian captivity and
authorizing the restoration of the Jerusalem Temple,
but also by his being declared, in Isaiah, as the divine shepherd and the Lord's anointed or the messiah.
What then were the religious beliefs of this messiah
and of his successors?

The evidence is unclear for Cyrus, but it seems
certain that his successors practiced a form of the
Zoroastrian faith, a religion which continues today
in small communities in Iran, among the Parsis of
India, and elsewhere. Zoroaster was the great Iranian prophet who probably lived around 1000 B.C.
He did not so much start a new religion as transform existing Iranian religion. Central to the Prophet

Left **Alexander the Great
and the Talking Tree.** An
illumination from *The Book
of Kings*, an epic poem by
Firdowsi (A.D. 941–1020).
According to legend,
Alexander came across
this tree as he searched
for the Fount of Life.

Middle Eastern rhyme, the *Shahname* (*The Book of Kings*), completed by the poet Firdowsi in A.D. 1010.

TELLING THE STORIES

The Islamic triumph shows how the biblical narratives, originally shaped by ancient religious processes, came to shape those same processes themselves. While the biblical texts were authoritative for ancient Judaism, there was not the rigid, literalist approach to reading sacred texts that is found in Christian and Islamic fundamentalist groups today. Ancient Judaism was diverse and complex, and had an active folkloric relationship with these stories. The biblical narratives are often full of gaps, and the Jewish tradition, from the very earliest times, has not been afraid to fill those gaps, and to expand and develop the biblical stories. By the practice of *midrash*, the Jewish people have retold and expanded on these stories and continue to do so. Consequently, these expansions have become part of authoritative scripture. The Sages say that everything one finds in scripture, and every interpretation, was originally revealed to Moses on Mount Sinai. The meanings of the scriptures are infinite—it is through reading, interpretation, and *midrash* that these meanings are uncovered.

By the time of the Prophet Mohammed, there was a rich Jewish story world derived from the biblical narratives. Much of this material was then incorporated into the Islamic scriptures, the Koran (also known as the Qur'an), which is itself a *midrash*, or retelling of the Jewish and Christian biblical narratives. This retelling process continues today within Islam. Despite the Islamic suppression of Zoroastrianism, the encounter of the two religions sparked a new creativity in the retelling of the biblical narratives, and in the weaving of new stories such as those found in the epic tale *One Thousand and One Nights*.

A sto[...] *Kings* tells of the great kin[...] Surrounded by his family and loyal subjects, with his last breath he asks them to follow him in death. They did, and were saved from the brutality of the invading Iranian army.

Below **Zoroaster dying in the flames of a temple fire.** Zoroaster was an Iranian prophet, whose teachings were recorded in the scriptures called the *Zend Avesta*. Zoroaster's death is often portrayed in a spectacular manner, surrounded by flames and worshippers. It is believed that he was murdered, at the age of 77.

Zoroaster's teaching was the struggle between good and evil, a struggle in which everyone had a part to play, and would ultimately see the triumph of good. The Zoroastrian religion was the main religion of Persia up to the Arab Islamic conquest of A.D. 642.

Following the conquest, Islamic supremacy led to the decline of Zoroastrianism, which was regarded as an infidel religion. It was only then that some of the ancient Zoroastrian traditions were compiled in the scriptures known as the *Zend Avesta*. Other traditions were translated from the ancient Avestan language and compiled in the Middle Persian texts, *Bundashihn* and *Denkard*. Many other mythical tales of kings and heroes were written down in the epic

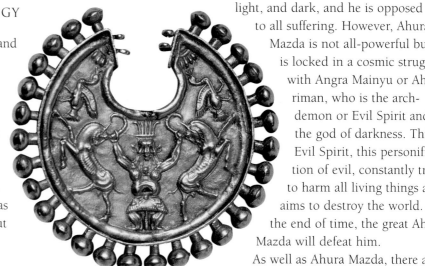

PERSIAN MYTHOLOGY

It was the Persian Empire and the bringing together of a diverse range of cultures that began a rich tradition and the development of mythological stories. Ideas of good versus evil, life versus death, and explanations of how the natural world was created remain as constant themes throughout these narratives.

The Divine and the Demonic

The Wise Lord, Ahura Mazda, is the god of gods, the supreme goodness, wisdom, and light. He is the Creator of all that is good: sun, stars, humans, animals, light, and dark, and he is opposed to all suffering. However, Ahura Mazda is not all-powerful but is locked in a cosmic struggle with Angra Mainyu or Ahriman, who is the arch-demon or Evil Spirit and the god of darkness. This Evil Spirit, this personification of evil, constantly tries to harm all living things and aims to destroy the world. At the end of time, the great Ahura Mazda will defeat him.

As well as Ahura Mazda, there are a number of divine figures that form his heavenly court. Most prominent are the Amshaspends, the Sons and Daughters of God, who are seven aspects of the divine, directly willed into being. These are Spenta Mainyu (Bounteous Spirit), Vohu Manah (Good Mind), Asha (Truth), Kshathra Vairya (Desired Kingdom), Armaiti (Devotion), Haurvatat (Integrity), and Ameretat (Immortality).

Below them are the Yazatas, the Worshipful Ones, who are the older gods and goddesses of the Iranians. Most important are Anahita, goddess of all the waters, and Mithra, the god responsible for controlling all of the cosmic order.

Similarly, the Evil Spirit is assisted by a variety of demonic beings whose diabolical nature consists of their devotion to trickery and falsehood. Their vocation is to "thwart" all efforts to achieve good. Demons or *div* included Aeshma, demon of fury, and the *Druj*, who were creatures of deceit, often female, always monstrous. The most vicious of these beings was Azhi Dahaka, who evolved into a serpent with three heads. Pairaka, a class of female evils, disguised their malevolence under beauty and charm and became most active in the darkness of night, seducing and harming men.

The Created World

At first creation was good. Ahura Mazda began with the sky, followed by the water and the earth. He created the Primal Tree without bark and thorn, the white ox, and then the archetypal human, Gayomart. However, the forces of evil attacked heaven and earth, devastating all that was created. Drawing from the victory of evil, the forces of life and of good used these lessons as a way of defeating the Evil Spirit. From the body of the ox came corn and medicinal plants, and from the purified seed of the ox came the different animal species. Gayomart was killed in the first battle between good and evil, but from his

SATAN

In the Hebrew Scriptures, Satan is not the name but the title of a functionary of the heavenly council, the Satan. This title may come from an ancient Semitic word meaning, "to obstruct." The main role of the Satan seems to be that of an accuser. Possibly due to Persian influence, by the time of Christ the Satan was transformed into an arch-demonic figure, also known as Beelze-bub. In Judaism, the chief demonic figure is known as Sammael, the angel of death, who led his angels in rebellion against the creation of humanity. A similar account is found in the Koran (Qur'an) where Satan, also known as Iblis and the mightiest of the angels, refused to prostrate himself before Adam, and was expelled from heaven. He was given the power to roam the earth to lead astray those who are not true servants of God.

preserved seed grew the first human couple, Mashye and Mashyane. Undeterred, Angra Mainyu infected their thoughts, forced them to cleave unto him, and tricked them into uttering the first lie—that the world was created by an evil being. This was the first human sin, and from that point on humans lost their orientation in life.

Humans were created as God's helpers in the struggle against evil. Humans and God need each other. The Prophet Zoroaster was crucial for bringing the Good Religion to humanity, restoring them to the path of their true purpose. Zoro-aster's divine conception and birth signaled the beginning of the era when evil would be defeated. His conception and birth were mira-culous works of the divine, and throughout his life the forces of evil struggled to thwart his acts of kind-ness. During his childhood, many demonic attempts were made to destroy him. According to the *Zend Avesta* (Zoroastrian scriptures), the final days before the defeat of evil will see the coming of three successive, savior figures or Saoshy-ants, each of whom are descended from the Prophet, whose seed has been preserved in a lake. The first two figures, Aushedar and Ashedar-mah, will bring

about the destruction of some of the evil in the world. With the third, Astva-terata, all disease, death, and suffering will be overcome, the dead will be raised, and the original Good Creation restored. The over-throw of evil will see the last judgment of humanity. The wicked will be consigned to hell, but not for eternity as this would contradict the divine goodness.

Above **Iblis (Satan).** Some myths say that Iblis was actually a Jinn (a nature spirit). After he was captured by angels, he became one of the mightiest of their kind.

JEWISH AND ISLAMIC MYTHOLOGY

Powerful religious influences filtered into the Arabian peninsula from Syria and Palestine, as well as from Christian Abyssinia (known as modern-day Ethiopia) just across the Red Sea. It is from these extensive sources that tales from the Jews and the Christians merged with ancient Islamic stories.

In the Beginning

The Hebrew Bible contains two creation stories in the opening chapters of Genesis. The first in chapter one is a beautiful, poetic account of creation out of a watery chaos over six days. These days are structured in matching pairs. The first day God creates light and separates the light from the darkness, to form day and night. On the fourth day, God creates the sun, moon, and stars, giving rulership of the day to the sun, and of the night to the moon. Similarly, on the second day, God creates the hard vault of the sky to separate the upper waters from those below, while on the fifth day God creates the creatures of the sea and the birds of the air. On the third day, God separates the dry land from the lower waters, and causes all manner of plants and trees to grow. This act is balanced, on the sixth day, by the creation of all the creatures that live on the land including, of course, humans who are created male and female in the likeness of God. Echoing Ahura Mazda in Persian mythology, God declared he brought humanity into being to be good and blessed it. On the seventh day, God decided to rest, instituting the tradition of Sabbath.

Sex and Death

The second account in Genesis is really about the origins of sex and death. It begins as a dry land creation with God creating a human being (in Hebrew *adamah* or groundling) from the ground. God plants a garden

Below *The Creation* by **Miguel Gonzales.** On the sixth day God surveys all he has created. He then rests on the seventh day. The animals are led to Adam so that he may name them, and choose from them a companion. None are suitable, so God creates woman from Adam's side.

LILITH

Lilith is a female winged night demon, who preys on men, endangers women in childbirth, and strangles children. She seems to be derived from ancient Babylonian demonology and a class of female evil spirits called *lilitu*. In Jewish tradition, it is said that when Adam and Eve separated, he fathered demons from the spirits that were attached to him. At this time, Lilith bore him many male and female demons. Most famous is the story that Lilith was Adam's first wife and created before Eve. Lilith refused to submit to him and, pronouncing the divine name, she flew away from him. Later she became the permanent partner of Sammael. Another story says that for a time she became a consort of God.

in Eden, places the male human being in the garden, and tells the human being that it may eat of any tree in the garden, except for the Tree of the Knowledge of Good and Evil. God warns that the fruit of this tree will bring death.

God creates all the animals from the ground as potential companions for the human being. Each of the animals is brought to the male human being to be named, but none of them are suitable companions. Finally, God puts the human to sleep, takes one of the human's sides to shape into a woman (the original Hebrew is better translated as side instead of rib). God brings this woman to the male human, who rejoices for he now has a true companion. He names the woman Eve, from the Hebrew word for being, for she is the mother of all the living. In Jewish tradition, Adam and Eve were originally two sides, or two faces, of the one being, which God finally separated to form woman and man.

The story goes on to describe how death entered the world. Firstly, the serpent tempts Eve to taste the fruit of the Tree of the Knowledge of Good and Evil.

She eats, and convinces Adam to follow her example. The fruit causes Adam and Eve to gain knowledge of good and evil. They become aware of their nakedness, and they hide from God, who realizes that they have eaten the forbidden fruit. God curses the serpent, and as punishment condemns Adam and Eve to a life of struggle and pain. They are expelled from Eden, and are then unable to eat from the Tree of Life which grows in the Garden of Eden. The fruit of this tree provides immortality to all that eat from it. From this point, death becomes a part of human life. Eden is placed under the watchful guard of the Cherubim. In Jewish tradition, Sammael took possession of the serpent, in order to deceive Eve and to gain supremacy over humanity. Sammael is said to have slept with Eve, and Cain was the child of this union. After the birth of Cain and Abel, Adam and Eve separated for 150 years before they came together to conceive Seth, who was born in his father's image, unlike his earlier brothers. In Arab tradition, Iblis tempted Eve. To gain access to Paradise he asked the peacock to smuggle him in but it refused. The peacock told the serpent of Iblis' promise to give the animal that helped him to get entry into the garden, the knowledge of the three sacred words for immortality. Hearing this, the serpent hid Iblis in his mouth and carried him into Paradise. From his hiding spot, Iblis spoke to Eve, who mistakenly believed it was the seemingly magical serpent speaking to her.

Left **Expulsion of Adam and Eve from Paradise.** This Turkish miniature illustrates the Arab tradition of this tale. In the background stands a peacock, whose haunting cry is said to be a warning or a bad omen. It was the peacock who refused to help Iblis, but inadvertently gave Satan an opportunity to find another creature to take him into Eden.

Below **Adam and Eve forbidden to eat from the Tree of Life.** This twelfth-century bronze portal shows the couple being escorted out of the garden by an angel. As a result of eating forbidden fruit, immortality is now lost to humanity.

Above **Scenes from the life of Abraham.** At the top of this illustration, Abraham proves his loyalty to God by preparing to sacrifice his son Isaac. Abraham is also pictured burning in the furnace—his punishment for refusing to recant his belief in God to King Nimrod.

CHERUBIM AND JINN

The biblical Cherubim are huge, supernatural, eagle-winged beings with lion-shaped bodies and humanlike faces. They guard the gates of Paradise, protect the Ark of the Covenant, and support the Divine throne with their wings. It is believed that they are the beings who enable the Divine throne to fly. God is also said to ride on a Cherub.

The Jinn are invisible nature spirits of Arabian tradition. Before Mohammed, they were revered almost as gods. While angels are made from light and humans from clay, the Koran (Qur'an) says that the Jinn are made from smokeless fire. Mohammed proclaimed a message that both humans and Jinn, can be either Muslim or non-Muslim.

Abraham, Primal Father of Arabs and Jews

Jewish and Islamic accounts agree that Abraham was a prophet of God who attained the highest degree of prophecy. He vigorously preached monotheism. When Abraham was born he was hidden in a cave because the king of the time, Nimrod, was warned that a child born in that year would dethrone him. Nimrod decreed the killing of all newborn male children. Abraham was nursed in the cave by the angel Gabriel. At the age of 13, he emerged from the cave committed to the worship of God. His constant struggle against idolatry brought him into conflict with his father and with the authorities, causing him to smash the idols of his father. In the Islamic account these are the idols of the city. Jewish and Islamic traditions agree that Nimrod eventually ordered the building of a great fiery furnace, threatening Abraham to recant or be cast into the fire. Abraham refused and was thrown into the furnace, but was saved by the intervention of God.

At God's command Abraham and his household move to the land of Canaan. Abraham finds he is without an heir because his wife, Sarah, is barren. To remedy this she sends him her handmaiden, Hagar, and from this union Ishmael, father of the Arab people, is born. God once again intervenes and Sarah miraculously conceives, giving birth to Isaac, father of the Hebrew people. However, Sarah becomes fearful of the enmity from Hagar and Ishmael toward her, so she asks Abraham to take them both into the wilderness. Almost dead from thirst, Hagar and Ishmael are saved by an angel who leads them to a well. According to Islamic tradition, this is the well of Zamzam found at Mecca.

As a test of faith, God demands that Abraham offer up Isaac in sacrifice. Abraham takes the boy to Mount Moriah, and just as he is about to kill him an angel saves Isaac and offers a ram in his place.

According to Jewish tradition, Sammael instigated this angelic intervention, accusing Abraham of selfish piety to God. It is God who decides to test Abraham by asking him to offer up his beloved son. Sammael persuades Abraham not to sacrifice Isaac, and to get Isaac to rebel against this trial. When he saw that Abraham would not disobey God, Sammael revenged himself by telling Sarah that Isaac had been brutally slain, causing her to die of grief and terror. After Sarah's death, Abraham marries Hagar.

Solomon and the Queen of Sheba

In both Jewish and Islamic traditions, Solomon is the great wise king and ruler of a mighty empire. He could speak all the languages, including those of the animals and birds, many of which submitted to his

judgment. He is believed to have built the first temple in Jerusalem with the help of angels and demons. In the Islamic tradition, Solomon ruled over all the Jinns, as well as humans, animals, and birds. It is the hoopoe bird that tells Solomon of a land to the south that does not know of him, and is ruled by the beautiful Queen of Sheba. Solomon asks the bird to deliver to the queen an invitation to come and honor him. Before her arrival, treasures and 6,000 beautiful boys and girls are sent ahead. After a journey that takes three years, the queen arrives in Jerusalem. On meeting Solomon she tests him with many riddles, all of which he answers and proves his wisdom. Solomon then tests the queen by receiving her in a hall with a floor made of crystal. Believing the hallway floor to be a waterway, she raises her skirts, exposing hairy legs and feet, proving to Solomon that she is not a demon. Islamic tradition says that Sheba was Queen of Yemen, where she is commonly known as Bilqis. It is also said that on her arrival at court, she found that a Jinn had set up her throne beside Solomon's. The Ethiopians claim she ruled their city of Axum, and her name was Makeda. After marrying Solomon, she gave birth to a son, Menelik, who became the founder of the Ethiopian royal lineage. Jewish tradition says that Nebuchadnezzar was descended from Solomon and Sheba.

Above **Detail from a nineteenth-century Ethiopian painting.** Solomon meets the elusive Queen of Sheba. According to Ethiopian legend, the son of this union was the founder of the Ethiopian royal family.

Left **Bilqis, the Queen of Sheba, showing her hairy legs to King Solomon.** The Queen of Sheba was tricked into revealing what her legs looked like. Hairy legs and feet were viewed as an aspect of womanly beauty and purity.

One Thousand and One Nights

Also known in English as the *Arabian Nights,* this epic brings together a wide variety of tales from Persian, Arabian, and other backgrounds that draw on biblical, Iranian, and other Middle Eastern mythological elements. The collection is framed in a story about a king, Shahriyar, who discovers that his wife is unfaithful to him and orders his grand-vizier to execute her. Fearing the repeat of infidelity and declaring that all women are as wicked as his first wife, he seeks his revenge by marrying young virgins, and then executing them the morning after the wedding night. Every day the grand-vizier is asked to find a new wife for the king, each day a girl is married, and a wife is dead. The city is filled with the pitiful cries and lamentations of the doomed young women and their grief-stricken families.

One day, Shahrazad, daughter of the grand-vizier, volunteers to marry the king in attempt to stop his barbarous practices and to change the fate of the young girls in the city. On her wedding night Shahrazad wins a promise from the king that he will not kill her until she has told him a story. She begins to tell a story that Shahriyar has never heard before, but the sun rises before Shahrazad can finish this spellbinding story. The king is captivated and halts the executioner's hand so that he might hear the rest of the story. This continues for a thousand and one nights and many different stories are told over this time. After the many nights of storytelling, the king asks Shahrazad what she would wish for and she asks that her life be spared for the sake of the three children she has borne him. He grants her this wish and they live happily ever after. The tales she tells are stories of magic, fantasy, love, and heroism, including the stories of Sinbad, Ali Baba and the Forty Thieves, and Aladdin.

The Fisherman, the Jinn, and the Enchanted Prince

One such tale is the Fisherman, the Jinn, and the Enchanted Prince. An old fisherman hauls in a bronze jar that bears the seal of King Solomon. The poverty-stricken fisherman decides to sell the jar at the bazaar to make a small amount of money to cover his lack of fish. On finding that the jar is quite heavy he breaks the seal and releases a Jinn who has been imprisoned for rebelling against Solomon. Once freed, the Jinn threatens to kill the fisherman, but the wily fisherman uses his wits and tricks it back into the jar, threatening to throw it back into the sea. Finally, the Jinn swears by the divine name not to

harm the fisherman if he frees him and promises to show him how to become a prosperous man. The Jinn leads the fisherman to a lake containing the most remarkable fish that have ever been seen—they are brightly colored red, white, blue, and yellow.

The Jinn tells the fisherman to sell his fish to the king of the land. As the king's maid cooks the fish, apparitions of a young woman and a slave appear and call out to the maid. Seeing these strange things happening, the curious king is determined to find out why these fish are enchanted.

He sets off for the lake and walks until he finds a palace whose only occupant is a melancholy prince whose lower body is made of stone. The prince tells how he found his wife to be unfaithful, and in a jealous rage he maimed her lover without his wife's knowledge. For three years she mourned, building a tomb where she hides her sick and mute lover.

Discovering that her husband, the prince, has injured her love she enchants the prince to become half stone, half man, as well as turning the city into a lake, and its people into fish. Every day she tortures the prince by whipping him brutally 100 times.

Outraged by the injustice, the king kills the sick lover, then tricks the wife into freeing the prince and the city from her spell. The king then kills the wife, and makes the prince his son and heir. The fisherman is rewarded handsomely, for being the first person to alert the king to the dreadful enchantment.

Vistas of fairy-land, where beauty reigns ... Of life in tents and palaces and fanes.

ISABEL BURTON (1831–1896)

Above **Mohammed and Fatima.** In this eighteenth-century Turkish painting, Mohammed is pledging his daughter Fatima to her cousin Ali. Mohammed and Fatima's faces are covered with divine light. Fatima is said to be one of the most important women in Islamic mythology.

Opposite page **Saif ul-Muluk, an Egyptian prince, and Badi'al-Jamal, a Jinn princess.** According to *One Thousand and One Nights,* the lovers are brought together by the Jinn, and carried off in a golden carriage.

THE FEMININE DIVINE

The Shekinah (from the Hebrew word for presence) is the female face of God in Judaism. The Shekinah is the presence of God in the world and is the glory of God that dwelt in the first temple in Jerusalem. She led the Israelites in the Exodus from Egypt, protected the infant Moses, and became his bride, appearing in the burning bush. God preserved Moses from the Angel of Death so the Shekinah took his soul with a kiss.

In Islam, there are two women who are very important. Mary, the virgin mother of Jesus, is a spiritual example for humanity. A whole chapter is devoted to her in the Koran (Qur'an). Of equal importance is Fatima, the youngest daughter of the Prophet Mohammed. She is the first believer to enter Paradise after the Resurrection. For Shi'ite Muslims, she is the wife of the true Imam, Ali, and foremother, through her two sons, of all the true Imams.

INDIAN MYTHOLOGY

Right **Writings from the**
Sri Bhagavata **(ancient**
text). A story from the
Bhagavata Puranas is written in Sanskrit on a roll
of silk paper. *Puranas* are
legendary texts and the
most extensive sources
of Hindu mythology.

Below **The wedding**
procession of Rama.
The epic Sanskrit poem
the *Ramayana* narrates
the adventures of Rama,
a mythical hero. In this
scene, the celebrations
for his wedding spill on
to the village street.

The Indian subcontinent is a vast, highly populated region with a rich and colorful mix of cultures. Many different ethnic groups exist side by side. Throughout India's long and tumultuous history, it has been invaded and colonized on numerous occasions, initially by the Aryans from the north, and later in the fourth century B.C. by Alexander the Great. Invasions by the Muslims followed, and later the Mongols from central Asia, and then colonization by the British also helped to shape the face of modern India. All these different influences have been incorporated into the fabric of Indian culture.

India's earliest religious scripture, the *Rg Veda,* appeared some time in the second millennium B.C. This consisted chiefly of hymns to a host of deities—the war god; the fire god; and animistic spirits of the sky, sun, and moon, of rivers and storms, of animals and trees. Some of the Vedic hymns, however, expressed a spirit of philosophical inquiry. After the composition of the *Rg Veda* came a significant portion of literature, a collection of philosophical speculations. This collection of writings, begun about 700 B.C. and called the *Upanishads,* contained many of the themes that inspired the originators of Jainism and Buddhism,

and provided the religious foundation for Hinduism.

Throughout the centuries, Hinduism, with its pantheon of gods and goddesses, has remained the most widespread of Indian religions, and its exciting mythical dramas seem like a mirror for the eventful history of this region. In practice, different gods and goddesses from this mythology have become the focus of the many different cults and traditions found within Hinduism.

The body of Hindu mythology is gigantic, and is found in numerous religious and literary texts from as far back as 1200 B.C. until the present day. Much of this mythology was told by the storytellers in villages and towns, and became very widely known by the majority of the Indian population.

In its variety lay Hinduism's strength. By accommodating all classes, all intellects, and all personalities, it became more than a religion; it established the framework for the uniquely Indian society, in which people of widely varying backgrounds, beliefs, social standing, and education go their own separate ways—together.

A full pantheon of gods can be identified in the earliest (Vedic) literature, and is added to via the great epics, the *Mahabharata* and the *Ramayana,* and the texts of legendary stories called the *Puranas.* Of the millions of deities in the pantheon, five stand out—Brahmã, Vishnu, Shiva, Ganesha, and Pārvāti, also known as Umā or the Mother Goddess. Myths associated with the Hindu gods are, at once, heroic tales and moral lessons. These gods are often just symbols of the interplay of larger themes—focused on the creation, preservation, and destruction of the world; tensions within families; and on the nature of the devotional relationship between god and devotee—explored in the narratives, in the same manner that problems in contemporary societies are often explored today across many soap operas.

Left **A mythological universe.** This diagram shows the great Mount Meru at the center of the universe. The writing outside of the circle tells of the importance and beauty of the mountain, which is also a meeting place for the gods.

India is the birthplace of several religious traditions. These new religions often adopted the creation myths from Hinduism, but sought social change through new religious expression, just as it happened with the development of Christianity. Buddhism has become a great world religion; Jainism has remained largely confined to India, probably because of its extreme asceticism; and Sikhism initially strove to overcome the conflict between Hinduism and Islam. All of these religions developed on Indian soil through the activity of spiritual teachers or gurus. Numerous myths are associated with these teachers; many are recorded in sacred texts, but many more myths are told within the practice of the various Indian religions.

Pilgrimage is an important part of the religious practice in India. Pilgrims enjoy hearing accounts of the trials and tribulations of their gods, sages, and gurus—events from the mythical or historical past that took place at the holy pilgrimage sites. There are many sacred sites throughout India that are shared by peoples of different faiths, and visited by pilgrims from different spiritual traditions. The last three myths included in this chapter are all associated with Rewalsar, in Himachal Pradesh, in the foothills of the Himalaya in northern India.

SOME OF THE HINDU PANTHEON

BRAHMĀ THE CREATOR was once thought to be the greatest of gods because he set the universe in motion. He has faded in importance with the rise of Shiva and Vishnu.

VISHNU THE PRESERVER is also known as the universal god. Whenever mankind needs help, this benevolent god appears on earth as an avatar or reincarnation. He is often represented by the color blue.

SHIVA THE DESTROYER is one of Hindu's two mightiest gods, and represents power, whatever his aspect.

GANESHA is the roly-poly elephant-headed son of Shiva, and is probably the most popular god in the pantheon.

PĀRVĀTI represents the unity of god and goddess. She is the daughter of the Himalaya Mountains, and sister of the River Ganges.

Above **The churning of the sea of milk.** Vishnu plans cosmic order by instructing demons and gods to wrap the cosmic serpent, Vasuki, around Mount Meru. They all pull together to churn the sea to create ambrosia, the source of immortality.

THE CHURNING OF THE OCEAN FOR IMMORTALITY

One creation myth is focused on defining the roles of the gods and demons, and distinguishes them on the basis of who possesses the gift of immortality, and who is stuck with mortal death.

In ancient times, the gods and the demons fought, and when the demons died they were revived with a magical potion provided by the god Shiva. The other gods sought advice from Brahmå. He said, "Make peace with the demons, and churn the ocean for the nectar of immortality, ask Vishnu to help. Use the Meru Mountain as the churning stick, and the serpent Vasuki as the string attached to the churning stick."

All the gods and demons went to the ocean, and different ones took hold of the mountain, and turned it around for 100 divine years. Animals and plants fell into the ocean, thickening up its waters, and wine was produced. The rubbing of trees on the mountain caused fire, which began driving out the rest of the animals. The ocean turned into milk, and clarified butter came out of it.

Various gods came out of the ocean holding many precious objects, then came fire and snakes. As the churning continued, the dreadful *Kālakuta* poison was created and enveloped the universe. This potent poison threatened to destroy all the gods and demons, so Shiva swallowed the poison, which turned his throat black.

Finally, Dhanvantari appeared with a pot of ambrosia, the nectar of immortality. Both gods and demons cried out "It's mine!" Vishnu assumed the form of a woman named Infatuation, who bewitched the demons so that they gave up the ambrosia to the gods, who then began to drink it. One demon, Råhu, took the form of a god and drank from the pot, but when it reached his throat Vishnu cut off the head of this demon with his discus. The demon's severed head rose into the sky, causing the eclipse of the sun and moon.

After the gods finished drinking the nectar, Vishnu assumed his normal form. A great battle erupted as he began savagely attacking the demons. Terrified, the demons fled and disappeared into the underworld and the ocean. The gods honored the mountain, put it in its proper place, and returned home like water-bearing clouds, making the heavens resound with their thunderous shouts. The precious nectar of immortality was given to Vishnu to guard and keep safe.

SHIVA'S DESTRUCTION OF DAKSA'S SACRIFICE

Shiva, often called Rudra in Hindu mythology, is associated with destruction, nonconformity, and ascetic practices, all of which are regarded as being, in some way, antagonistic toward the order that creation needs to survive, and it seems that these practices will always appear to be on the outskirts of the ordered world. In this myth, Shiva threatens Daksa's sacrifice. The sacrifice is always identified with the capacity to create, and also functions as a model of the ordered world.

Rudra was born as a result of Brahmå's anger at being unable to create. Brahmå then gave Gauri, as a wife, to Rudra, forbidding him to perform ascetic practices, instructing him to create the world instead. Rudra refused, and plunged into the water. Brahmå took Gauri back, and from his mind created seven sons, including Daksa, so that these offspring would, in turn, create. Brahmå offered Gauri to Daksa as a daughter, causing Daksa to rejoice, and he enthusiastically performed the supreme sacrifice to the pleasure of Brahmå.

After 10,000 years Rudra came out of the water, wishing to create the universe and the gods, but saw that the world had already been created, as a result of Daksa's sacrifice. Overcome by anger, Rudra violently destroyed Daksa's sacrifice. Eventually, he restored it at the request of the gods, and went with Gauri to his own dwelling place.

THE CREATION OF DEATH

In Hindu mythology, Death is always represented as a divine figure named Myrtu or Yama. He presides over one of the worlds of the dead, and supervises the enumeration of the good and bad deeds (karma) of all of the people who have died. The nature of these deeds directly affects where people are born in subsequent lives.

Sometimes Death disappears or takes a holiday, and the Earth becomes overcrowded and has to ask Brahmå to do something about the huge number of people on her surface. Brahmå's response is to either create Death, or to arrange Shiva to create Death, and place it among people as the origin of evil actions and the outcomes of these actions.

The gods in heaven also experience great fear when Death is absent because humans, characterized by their mortality, become immortal—thereby undermining the gods' own unique status.

Below **Vishnu the Preserver.** This god is also known as the solar god. The story of the "Three Steps" illustrates how Vishnu can clear the sky, the earth, and the lower world with three steps. He drives away the darkness as he travels.

343

Some of the most devotional stories of this mythology center on the pranks of Krishna as a child, and his capacity to disguise his true form as the most powerful god in the universe.

Balarāma and Krishna used to play in the village, crawling into the fields, and come back to their mothers covered in mud. But their mothers loved their sons, and would hug them and put them to their breasts. When they were boys they used to play tricks on the village animals, and when Krishna was a little older, he became the leader of a group of youths who used to get up to all sorts of pranks. The wives of the cowherds would tell Yashodha, Krishna's mother, that he had been untying calves, stealing curds and milk, and was being a general nuisance.

One day the other boys told Yashodha that Krishna had eaten dirt. He denied this, and told her to look in his mouth. When she looked into his gaping mouth she saw the whole eternal universe, including heaven, the regions of the sky, and the earth with its mountains, islands, and oceans. She saw the whole universe in all its infinite variety, with all the forms of life, and time, nature, action, hopes, her own village, and herself. Then she became afraid and confused, wondering, "Is this a dream or an illusion wrought by a god? Or is it a delusion of my own perception? Or is it some portent of the natural powers of this little boy, my son? I bow down to the feet of the god, whose nature cannot be imagined or grasped by mind, heart, acts, or speech; he in whom all of this universe is inherent, impossible to fathom. The god is my refuge."

When his mother came to understand the true essence, in this way, the Lord Krishna spread his magical illusion in the form of maternal affection. Instantly, his mother lost the memory of what she had just seen, and the fear and confusion she had experienced, and lovingly took her son on her lap.

Above **Krishna (right) and Balarāma in the forest.** In one story involving Krishna, to protect him from the murderous anger of his uncle, Krishna's parents exchange him for the daughter of a poor cowherd.

KRISHNA AND BALARĀMA

A later body of mythology, not found in the earliest literature, focuses on the important devotional god Krishna, one of the many forms of the god Vishnu. The Krishna myths combine a set of graphic word images containing strong theological and devotional messages for the devotees who read and hear them.

become a bull pulling a plough. Samudrå cursed the *brahmin* to become a donkey. She was cursed by the beggar to become an outcast woman. The curses became true, and Sulabha, Samudrå, and the poor *brahmin* beggar changed form.

Wandering in the city on the day of a festival of Ganesha, Samudrå saw a Ganesha temple. Suddenly, a violent storm started up, and the terrified Samudrå approached many houses in the city for shelter but was thrown out of every one she came to. Despairing, she made her weary way to the temple.

Samudrå started a fire with some *durva* grass so she could warm herself. Wind moved a blade of grass and, driven by fate, the grass fell on Ganesha's head. At the same time the cold, frightened donkey came into the temple, as did the bull freed from the plough. The animals ate the woman's grass, and then fought near the image of Ganesha. From their mouths two blades of *durva* grass fell onto Ganesha's trunk and foot, which pleased him. To stop this calamity, Samudrå struck the donkey and the bull with her staff, and then began worshipping Ganesha.

Watching the three of them, Ganesha considered that they had worshipped him well enough, and decided to send them to his own special heaven on a remark-

GANESHA AND SULABHA

Ganesha has been one of the most important Hindu gods for the last 1,000 years, largely because he is the god responsible for creating and removing obstacles. Many myths show devotees worshipping him for the removal of obstacles, whereas other myths show how the unwitting worship of him will also produce positive results.

In the city of Jamba there lived a warrior named Sulabha who constantly sang hymns of praise to the god Ganesha. Sulabha's wife, Samudrå, was virtuous and beautiful.

One day a very poor *brahmin* beggar named Madhusudana appeared. Sulabha bowed, but laughed at the *brahmin*, who then cursed him to

able flying vehicle. Worshippers at the temple saw this benevolence, and were astonished, believing this had come about because of good *karma*.

Some of the great *yogins* approached Ganesha's entourage, and asked why the result was such a happy one, despite the depravity and obvious bad *karma* of the three misfits. The *yogins* couldn't understand why their devotion to Ganesha hadn't rewarded them. Incensed, they declared that they would stop their own worship immediately so that they, too, could find out how to reach Ganesha's home.

Left **Pārvāti, Hindu goddess and wife of Shiva.** A feminine divinity who personifies the power of Shiva, this goddess is often portrayed with 10 arms brandishing various weapons, which signify the destructive side of her nature. In this image she gently nurses her baby son, Ganesha.

Below **Ganesha, son of Shiva and Pārvāti.** This elephant-shaped god is worshipped as the god of wisdom, good luck, and the remover of obstacles. He was born from the dew of Pārvāti's body, mingled with dust. Shiva, in anger, cut off Ganesha's human head. In remorse, Shiva replaced it with the head of the first animal he came across—an elephant.

Above **Detail of the Hindu trinity or Trimurti.** The absolute god manifests himself in three different aspects: Brahmå the Creator, Vishnu the Preserver, and Shiva the Destroyer. The sound of the mantra "om," comes from these gods' names.

HINDU: HOW MAHA-RISHI LOMAS REALIZED THE EXISTENCE OF GOD

We learn in the *Skanda Purana*, a very ancient text (the earliest known manuscript of the *Skanda Purana* dates from the eighth century A.D.), that the name of a particular mountain lake is Hridalayesh, meaning the "lake abode of the master," indicating its spiritual value. However, no one these days uses that name. This place is now called Rewalsar.

The oldest sage in the universe, great Rishi Lomas (also known as Maha-Rishi Lomas, as Maha means "great"), through the power of his meditation was rewarded with an exceptionally long life,

What is found in this epic may be elsewhere; What is not in this epic is nowhere else.

THE *MAHABHARATA*, THE BOOK OF THE BEGINNING

for only one hair on his body had decayed in each age (*Kalpa*). Rishi Lomas appears in the well-known Indian epic, the *Mahabharata*.

Rishi Lomas went to meditate on the Infinite, in the caves on the mountain Brahmå-Pārvāti, from where he saw this wondrous lake, with magnificent geese, ducks, and other water birds swimming and making beautiful sounds. Lovely young maidens were playfully splashing in the water. In the middle of the lake an exquisite blue lotus was blooming. The lake itself was surrounded by thick groves of trees, and Rishi Lomas recognized that the trees were actually forms of the gods, and the creepers entwined around them were the goddesses.

Rishi wandered down to the lake, and found a place conducive to meditation on the western bank. Controlling all his senses, Rishi dedicated his practice of penance to the Lord Shiva. Rishi Lomas received special teachings from Shiva, so that he really understood the existence of God. Sometimes he saw Lord Shiva and Pārvāti seated on a floating island in the middle of the lake, enjoying divine play. He also witnessed Lord Shiva sailing on the lake on a huge snake called Sheshnag. Lord Shiva gave this lake and seven others nearby to Rishi Lomas. The floating islands on the lake remind pilgrims of Rishi Lomas's realization of the existence of God, and flags are placed on the islands as offerings.

Rishi Lomas's meditation led him to experience the presence of all five gods: Vishnu, Brahmā, Ganesha, Shiva, and Pārvāti, who all reside together at this lake, having met there and enjoyed its great beauty, as told in the *Puranas*. There is a single image of these five gods together in the temple at the lake, as well as various representations of Brahmā-Pārvāti and Rishi Lomas. It is an extremely beneficial place for the pilgrim, particularly if they take a dip in the lake on special days associated with Shiva, as this purifies all sins.

BUDDHIST: HOW MANDARAVA, PRINCESS OF ZAHOR, MEETS HER VAJRA MASTER, PADMASAMBHAVA, AND THE ORIGINS OF THE SACRED LAKE TSO-PEMA

The city of Mandi was the capital of the ancient kingdom of Zahor. The King and Queen had a beautiful young daughter, Mandarava, who developed great faith in the teachings of the Buddha. She refused marriage to the princes of all the neighboring kingdoms, devoting her life to meditation, along with 500 other young women.

One night, Mandarava had a dream where she saw the Buddha, sitting on a lotus in rainbow light, who told her to come to a beautiful grassy hill nearby to receive teachings the next day. Mandarava, accompanied by the other female devotees, went, as instructed in the dream, to the hill that was covered in sweet-smelling flowers. Padmasambhava, whose name means "Lotus

Above **Padmasambhava.** An eighth-century mystic whose background has a princely origin, he is believed to be the son of the blind king, Indrabhuti. Padmasambhava imitates the Buddha in his desire to abandon the world.

Born," appeared before them in a rainbow light. All in his presence were filled with great devotion on seeing him, and hearing his sacred teachings of the secret-mantra *Vajrayana*. They invited the Master to come to their convent. Each day Padmasambhava instructed them in the esoteric teachings. Princess Mandarava, being a truly spiritual and blessed being, was the foremost disciple, quickly understanding the real meaning of her guru's chosen words.

Sometime later, a no-good, layabout cowherd came across the female devotees and their Master rejoicing in the teachings. He continued on into the city, spreading rumors about the Princess, saying she was keeping company with

Left **Buddha Sakyamuni.** The founding Buddha was born on the banks of the Ganges in 563 B.C. He was never portrayed in carvings or statues until A.D. 300, when the first sculptures of the Buddha were created.

some ordinary fellow instead of practicing meditation. The King heard these rumors and was infuriated, not believing that his daughter would behave in this way. However, the rumors persisted, and when the King investigated the situation, he did not believe his ministers who informed him that a great teacher was in his daughter's company. He thought that some ordinary man was courting his daughter, and was outraged because he had refused the advances of the neighboring princes so that his daughter could meditate.

The King ordered that the man be caught and burnt alive on a funeral pyre, and that Mandarava be imprisoned. Padmasambhava was very easily captured, taken to the grassy hill, and set alight on a pyre. The flames burnt high. Padmasambhava was

seen as an eight-year-old boy, sitting on a splendid lotus, surrounded by rainbows. The fire continued to burn for many days. A lake formed around the flames, and the lotus throne of Padmasambhava rose out of the lake.

That lake is Tso-Pema, the Lotus Lake, called Rewalsar by the Indians. The nine floating islands on the lake move contrary to the wind, and were formed from the ashes of the pyre that burnt so fiercely, yet did not harm Padmasambhava. These islands are covered with greenery, and the reeds offer protection to many beautiful birds.

The King's ministers heard about this extraordinary scene and came to investigate. They were totally convinced that this was a great Vajra Master, and reported this back to the King who also came to investigate. He realized he had made a grave error of judgment, and confessed to Padmasambhava, requesting him to take his place as King and spiritual teacher of Zahor. Padmasambhava consented, and wore the fine silk clothes and crown that the King supplied to him. Padmasambhava was, from then on, known as Guru Chimé Pema Jungné—the Immortal Lotus Born Teacher.

Mandarava was freed. She became one of Padmasambhava's closest disciples, and one of his two main consorts, later practicing with the Master at Maratika Cave in Nepal, where they both realized and came to understand the Long-Life Practice.

Now Tso-Pema is a great power-place of pilgrimage, where Buddhists from all over the world come to visit. There are several caves near the lake where *yogins* and *yoginis* meditate. Pilgrims also circle the lake many times, saying their mantras.

SIKH: THE NAMING OF THE REWALSAR, AND THE UNIFICATION OF THE HILL STATES

Rewal, the son of King Reva, ruled over the Kingdom of Mandi. He had a few enemies. The one that caused him the greatest fear was Yaksha, who lived in the dark forest, Naina Dhar. Yaksha caused many problems for Rewal, including engaging him in battles. Unfortunately, because of his fear, Rewal lost his kingdom to Yaksha. He then became a wandering beggar, and through his meditation lived for a very long time, moving from place to place.

Sikh Guru Gobind Singh (1675–1708), the tenth and last Sikh Guru, came to Mandi at the same time that Raja Ajmer Chand from the Kingdom of Bilaspur was being installed, sometime in the seventeenth century. On this occasion all the Rajas from the surrounding 22 Hill States from Garwhal to Chamba

JAINISM

The last of the prophets of the Jains was Mahavira (born 540 B.C.), a contemporary of Buddha Sakyamuni. It is likely that these two men were aware of each other's teachings, although no records of their meeting have been found. Mahavira was important in the development of the Jain community and philosophy, but he was not the founder of Jainism, as is sometimes claimed. The previous prophet, the twenty-third, was Parsva, who ruled in the thirteenth heaven in his previous incarnation as Indra. He was born

to King Avasena and Queen Vama, who saw a great serpent at her side one night during her pregnancy. Her child was called Parsva, meaning "flank." Parsva renounced the world, and through his asceticism overcame his *karma* and achieved omniscience.

Below **Jain wheel of life.** Devotees of Jainism believe that the soul is constantly being re-born on either a higher or lower plane. The circles represent these levels, and outline the worship of the relevant deities.

WHERE DID JESUS CHRIST DIE?

In Kashmir, in the Himalaya of northwest India, many stories are told about Jesus of Nazareth that say he did not die on the cross—that, although horribly wounded, he actually recovered. There is some historical evidence supporting this tradition. Jesus is said to have fled Palestine with his mother Mary, and traveled by foot through several countries in the East, preaching as he went. Mary died in Pakistan. The small village is now called Murree, where there is an ancient tomb locally known as "the resting place of Mother Mary." Jesus continued his journey to Kashmir. He continued preaching in parables, dying when he was 82. In Khaniyar, one of the oldest areas of Srinagar, the capital of Kashmir, there is a simple tomb, which local tradition believes houses the body of Jesus.

Left **Jesus Christ in India.** A miniature illustrates the legend of Jesus traveling through India. The robes and the small winged angel show the distinct characteristics of an ancient Indian influence.

hiding in the forest, for he could not attend the coronation since the loss of his kingdom. He saw the Guru, and prostrated at his feet, beseeching the Guru to help him. Although he had meditated for a long time he had not obtained any blessings. He knew this was because of his long-standing fear of Yaksha.

Guru Gobind Singh, being a true King, freed Rewal from his fear by killing Yaksha. He also instructed Rewal that if one meditated with a selfish motive, such as that of regaining one's kingdom, one never received blessings. Instead, one should always meditate on God-the-Timeless-Being, without any selfish motives. Only in this particular way can salvation be gained by a person. Subsequently, Rewal overcame all his worldly attachments and fear, and gained true understanding.

The beautiful lake, beyond the dark forest, is now called Rewalsar. This is a special place, and anyone coming here on pilgrimage will purify all sins. At times of great disturbance, when the whole land is flooded, this sacred place of Rewalsar is believed to be a haven for all Sikhs.

Below **Twenty-four** *Tirthankaras*. This sculpture represents saints who have reached perfection and absolute freedom. *Tirthankara* means "fordmakers," people who have managed to find their way across the swirling current of *samsara* (the eternal cycle of life and death).

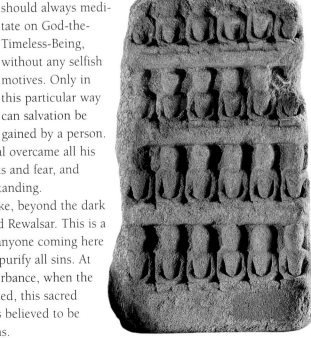

had gathered together. Fearing the tyranny of the Muslim Emperor, they decided to meet with Guru Gobind Singh. This great Guru formed the community of the Sikhs, the Khalsa, who were devout warriors prepared to unite together and fight for their Hindu religion against the Muslims. All the Rajas of the Hill States formed a united group, under the guidance of Guru Gobind Singh and the Sikh Khalsa.

While in the area, Guru Gobind Singh went hunting in the dark forest, Naina Dhar. Rewal had returned to the region near his kingdom, and was

Chinese Mythology

In most civilizations, the earliest traditions and often the earliest literature are mythological, and deal with ultimate origins, or the creation of the world, as well as tales of supernatural beings. China, at first sight, seems an exception. In the *Classics,* the most ancient Chinese books, and the textbooks of the Confucian school, we find stories of men, kings and nobles, soldiers, and peasants, but not gods.

The *Book of History,* although probably partly legendary, has no record of creation stories, and deals mainly with human activities. The famous *Book of Changes* is symbolic, but is not in story form, and was traditionally interpreted as relating to real events. *The Book of Songs* mostly consists of folksongs, but there are traces of mythology in the ritual hymns. The *Classics* are resolutely antimythological, reflecting the ideals of their Confucian editors.

The founders of the early dynasties are claimed to have had miraculous or divine origins, and these were alluded to in the *Classics.* For example, the first emperor of the royal lineage, that became the Shang Dynasty, was conceived when his mother swallowed an egg. Jiang Yuan, the mother of Hou Ji, ancestor of the Zhou rulers, became pregnant when she inadvertently stepped in a toe-print of God. Such stories probably reflect much earlier myths, which can only be glimpsed between the lines of the official literature that is available.

The myths collected from tribal peoples (the so-called national minorities) in modern China, probably represent the traditions of the various peoples out of which developed the Han, or core Chinese group in north China, and these are certainly full of creation stories and prominent heroic mythological figures.

Right **Mystical dragon.** The dragon was long regarded as a god in China. The Dragon Kings rule the seas, and are approached in times of drought and to avert flooding. The clouds around the dragon are symbols of eternal youth.

Right **Oracle bones.** Rulers of the Shang Dynasty (1766–1122 B.C.) would inscribe divinations on bones or tortoise shells, and ask the gods for solutions to rain, flood, and famine, or predictions on the outcomes of wars.

Mythical Figures

What is clear in the records is that the ancient Chinese seem to have historicized mythical figures. Unlike the ancient Greeks who, according to Euhemerus (*c.* 300 B.C.), turned men into gods, the ancient Chinese turned gods into men. The interest of the Confucian scholars, who were the keepers of the tradition, was in society, government, and morality; and history served these scholars better in these areas rather than the ideas of mythology.

The very earliest writings we have from ancient China are the short inscriptions on the oracle bones from the second millennium B.C., and they reveal a variety of spirit-beings to whom sacrifices were offered. Very little is known about any of them. They must have been regarded as powerful, and their names suggest they arose from nature myths, but their stories are lost forever. As Derk Bodde, an authority on Chinese myth and ritual, says, there were certainly myths in ancient China, but not a systematic mythology.

The earliest writings of the Daoist tradition, the *Daode Jing* and the *Zhuangzi,* contain references to mysterious figures that may come from traditional mythology. Their names suggest they are allegorical or symbolic figures. For example, in *Zhuangzi,* there is a story about Chaos, whose friends try to help him out by boring apertures into his body so that he is able to breathe, see, hear, and eat. He is literally bored to death by his friends. Such stories make their point well, but are really only conscious literary productions rather than the stuff of myths, which come from deeper sources in the unconscious and preliterate Chinese traditions.

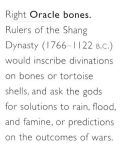

FOLK MYTHOLOGY

Among the popular local cults of female deities, one stands out, with variants along the Chinese coast, in Taiwan, and in Southeast Asia. She is known by various names, with Mazu and the Queen of Heaven (Tian Hou) being the most popular. The associated mythology varies widely, but the basic details are similar. A woman mysteriously appears to still a storm, and saves the lives of sailors; in one popular version, the sailors she saves are her brothers. Her festival on the twenty-third day of the third lunar month is the major festival of boat people throughout China. The name of Macao is derived from a famous old temple dedicated to her on the peninsula's harbor.

There is one popular god everyone will have seen in Chinese restaurants and businesses—Guan Di. He was an historical figure, Guan Yu, a general of the Three Kingdoms period (third century A.D.). Logically enough, he became God of War, but because he was so powerful he was worshipped by students wanting to pass examinations, and then worshipped by shopkeepers wanting to increase their profits. This is what Chinese mythology is about: a projection of human desires, especially for success, wealth, and children.

INFLUENCES ON CHINESE MYTHOLOGY

The arrival in China, in about the first century A.D., of the Indian religion, Buddhism, transformed Chinese mythology. The stories of the life and previous lives of the Buddha, of Indian gods, and miraculous events found in the Buddhist sutras were translated into Chinese, and became the stock in trade of the marketplace storytellers. They influenced popular literature, folk religious practices, and organized Daoist religion which systematized and developed old Chinese traditions. They also brought a new interest in ultimate origins, in cosmogony (where the world as we know it came from), and in cosmology (what the world is like).

In Chinese popular religion it is impossible to disentangle sources deriving from the great traditions of Confucianism, Daoism, and Buddhism from those that come from local and very ancient sources. Every village or area has its own God of the Place (Tudi Gong), and their shrines can be seen in streets and in temples throughout the Chinese diaspora, and now in the People's Republic. These all have their stories and their myths. But, once again, especially in the case of City Gods, they are often found to be deified humans, upright officials, generals, and heroes from the past. The Chinese gods even have birthdays, wives, and children, and a bureaucracy to serve them. As in all societies, Chinese myths are closely related to the involvement of rituals and festivals.

There are myths and practices associated with the New Year; the coming of spring (Qing Ming); harvest

time; the birthdays of the Jade Emperor (the Daoist high God), Confucius, Buddha, and Laozi; the lantern festival; the dragon boat festival; and the "Hungry Ghosts" festival.

CONFUCIAN MYTHOLOGY

In Song 245 of the classic *Book of Songs*, there is a hymn that probably accompanied a sacrificial ritual of the kings of the Zhou Dynasty (traditional date from 1122–221 B.C.). It celebrates the origins of the

Above **Laozi, Confucius, and baby Buddha.** Laozi wrote the text which forms the basis of Daoism. He is said to have been a contemporary of Confucius, the scholar and a teacher of Buddha. Daoism, Confucianism, and Buddhism all have contributed to Chinese mythology.

Opposite page **Emperor Ming Huang on his journey to Shu.** Legend has it that while on a journey to another province, Emperor Ming Huang (A.D. 713–756) dreamed that a small demon stole his belongings. A larger demon appeared, grabbed the smaller demon by the throat, and gouged out its eyes.

Right **Confucius, an influential scholar (551–479 B.C.).** Renowned as a philosopher and an advisor to the Zhou Dynasty, Confucius's teachings impacted on Chinese mythology by creating culture heroes, that is, men that were worshipped as gods.

Below **Emperor Xuanzong and his horses.** Legends of the various ruling dynasties are important as they reflect the divine selection. The tales also relay the idiosyncrasies of these godlike men. An indulgence of Xuanzong was a stable of 40,000 dancing horses.

Zhou royal house, and the founding of their first capital in Tai, long before they conquered all of north China. It is a classic hero myth in which the protagonist has mysterious, possibly divine origins, an extraordinary birth, is abandoned, rescued, develops precociously, and performs great deeds. His great achievement, though, is characteristically Chinese—he invents farming, and establishes the agricultural way of life. This hymn shows how the Hou Ji myth became the basis of an annual spring sacrifice to sanctify the coming agricultural year. Much more typical in the *Classics* are stories about the founding Sage Kings of China, discovered in the *Book of History*. In the beginning, some 5,000 years ago, there were the Three Sovereigns named Fu Xi, Shen Nong, and Huang Di (the Yellow Emperor).

They were the inventors of, respectively: writing, agriculture, and the calendar—all fundamental features of Chinese civilization. There is no historical evidence for the existence of such individuals, but some time around the third millennium B.C., perhaps even earlier, all three basic inventions undoubtedly occurred. They were probably gradual developments rather than inventions by individuals, but they marked the beginning of civilization in the strict sense in China. So these figures are "culture heroes" by whom the main features of Chinese civilization were fathered. (There are no "mothers" as in many other national mythologies.)

The Three Sovereigns were followed by the Five Emperors, the last two of which, Yao and Shun, were the first two of the Three Sage Kings who began the Chinese empire. Yao chose Shun as his successor when he heard how he managed to live peacefully with his dreadful family who, among other things, tried to kill him by dropping a rock on his head when he was down repairing a well. Yao tested Shun with various administrative tasks, and gave Shun his two daughters in marriage, to see whether he could keep both of them happy. Shun passed these difficult tests and was chosen as king, rather than Yao's useless eldest son. And so began the custom of choosing the most virtuous man to rule the empire. Shun's successor was Yu, the founder of the first dynasty, the Xia. Yu's great achievement, it is said, was to implement measures for flood control. "If it wasn't for Yu we would all have been fishes," states an old Chinese saying.

The *Book of History* goes on to tell how the Xia kings became degenerate, and were replaced by the virtuous Shang kings chosen by the High God. In turn, the Shang lost the Mandate of Heaven, and were replaced by the founders of the Zhou Dynasty, ruling when the *Classics* were written. If this is mythology, rather than legend (or the elaboration of the stories about actual people), it is political not religious mythology. Given its emphasis on legitimacy and divine sanction for ruling China, its purpose is clearly ideological. It would not fit the Chinese definition of "myth," which is *shenhua*, (talking about spirits). However, it is not history, and clearly falls within the boundaries of what the West calls "mythology." For example, the story of the last king of the first dynasty, the Xia, is obviously mythological, as Jie Gui is depicted as a monster of vice. He

was strong enough to twist iron bars into rope, and he made war on everybody, wearing out his subjects with his tirades. To buy him off, one of the great chiefs presented one of his daughters to him for marriage. Jie Gui was so infatuated with his new wife, that he made her a bed of ivory and gems, and created a garden in which they could enjoy themselves during the summer months. He built a pool and filled it with wine, he hung meat in all the trees, and surrounded himself with exotic foods. Jie Gui became so debauched that his subjects, the Shang, now became tired of his self-indulgent behavior, and realized they had no choice but to overthrow him.

HOU JI, FATHER OF THE PEOPLE

Once there was a woman called Jiang Yuan, who became the mother of the people. Childless, she conceived her son, Hou Ji, by stepping in the toe-print of God. She suffered no pain in giving birth, but her husband disowned the child who was abandoned in the lane outside the house. The farm animals came and kept him safe. He was then thrown out into the forest, but the woodsmen found him and saved him. He was left in the ice and snow to die, but birds came and warmed him with their wings. He grew strong and tall, and began to grow his own food. He taught the ancient people how to grow beans and rice, wheat and melons, all the crops that feed the people today. So every year at harvest time, in honor of Hou Ji, grain is harvested to make wine and cakes, then a ram is sacrificed and eaten. Hou Ji is seen as the founder of the dynasty that taught people how to live the Chinese way.

Above **Flying apsara, a mythological nymph.** These flying beings come from Hindu mythology, but were adopted by the Chinese. Tang Dynasty (A.D. 581–755) emperors used these carvings as curtain raisers, to re-create a Buddhist paradise within their lavish palaces.

Right **Mythological sea monsters.** *Classic of the Mountains and Seas* is an anthology of stories collected in the first century B.C. It lists fantastic creatures that combine the physical attributes of a number of animals, such as whale with elephant tusks, or crocodiles with tiger tails.

CREATION MYTHOLOGY

Chinese creation mythology is not found in the very earliest sources, but has to be reconstructed from later writings such as the *Classic of the Mountains and Seas*, where Chinese myths are already influenced by Buddhism and Confucian historicizing. However, they can be checked against surviving oral traditions of tribal peoples like the Miao.

Records of creators, as opposed to an impersonal process of creation, were first found in the third century A.D.—significantly after the introduction of Indian ideas—in the form of a male creator, Pan Gu, and a female, Nu Gua. Pan Gu is similar in many respects to Mesopotamian and Indian creator figures. In one account, he separates heaven and earth; and in another the world develops out of his body.

Pan Gu

Pan Gu, fearing that the earth and sky might merge together, stood between them, his head keeping the sky aloft, and his feet treading down the earth. For 18,000 years, the distance between heaven and earth increased at a rate of 10 ft (3 m) a day. Pan Gu grew at the same rate to continue to hold heaven and earth apart. Eventually Pan Gu considered there was no risk of the sky and earth joining, so he fell asleep and eventually died. From his corpse came all the world's elements. His breath became the wind and clouds, his voice became thunder, his left eye became the sun, and his right eye became the moon. His four limbs and his trunk were transformed into the cardinal directions and the mountains, his blood became the rivers, and his veins became roads. His flesh became trees and soil, the hairs on his head became the stars, and the hairs on his body were transformed into grass and flowers. Finally, the fleas on his body became the ancestors of the different races of human beings.

Nu Gua

In another myth, Nu Gua is responsible for the creation of human beings, and is known from much earlier (pre-Buddhist) references to her as one who changes shape and transforms things. She may be, as with female beings in other societies, the original Chinese creator. Nu Gua wandered through the

world longing for companionship. She sat down at the bank of a river, and began to model the river clay into a little figure. When Nu Gua stood the finished figure on the ground, it immediately came to life, dancing and laughing with happiness. Nu Gua was so happy she decided to fill the whole world with people, working until it grew dark. Nu Gua worked and worked, but realized that she could not possibly create enough people to populate the whole world. She called on her magic power, and taking a length of vine, she trailed it in the mud, and then whirled it about in the air. As soon as the drops of mud touched the ground, they were transformed into human beings.

In time, the Pan Gu and Nu Gua myths were combined, with the two represented as brother and sister. The problem of how to allow them to mate and produce human beings was solved by a special message from the Heavens authorizing this dramatic departure from propriety.

The mythic world of early China is best seen in a Han Dynasty work that purports to be a geography but is better described as a mythography. The *Classic of the Mountains and Seas,* in the manner of European travelers' tales, describes weird animals, monstrous human beings, gods and goddesses, and very strange far-off lands. The figures that are met in this tour of the world include a god of luck, a human figure covered in fur with a tiger's tail, the Ape God Howl, a snake god with nine human heads, and the nine-tailed fox. And the lands found included the land of the hairy folk, the land of the lop-eared people, and the land of the low people with fish tails for feet.

DAOIST MYTHOLOGY

The fourth century B.C. Daoist work attributed to Zhuang Zhou or Master Zhuang (Zhuangzi) opens with a myth of the world in constant transformation.

In the northern abyss there is a fish. Its name is Kun. It is gigantic, and no one knows how many thousands of *li* (a mythical measurement) it stretches. It is transformed and becomes a bird called Peng with a back so large that no one knows how many thousands of *li* it is wide. Peng springs into the air and flies, and its wings are like clouds floating in the sky. This bird floats above the waves toward the Pool of Heaven. This may be a product of Zhuang's extraordinary imagination, but it reads like a cosmological myth.

From the second century A.D. on, Daoism became an organized religion complete with priests, disciplinary and moral rules, rituals, and penitential practices. It quickly developed a pantheon of gods and goddesses. At the top was a trinity comprising the Celestial Venerable of the Original Beginning, the Jade Emperor, and Lord Lao up in Heaven, who was none other than Laozi, the alleged author of the *Book of the Way and its Virtue* deified. These figures, and a bewildering array of spirit beings, are described in a vast body of scriptures only explored in recent times.

One striking feature of the Daoist tradition is the emphasis on the female, something which goes back to Laozi who, in the *Book of the Way and its Virtue,* described the source of all as "the gateway of the mysterious female." This is reflected in the evolution of one cult with an extended mythology, that of the Queen Mother of the West, who lives on an enormously high mountain in the far West, and possesses the secret of immortality. The palace of the Queen Mother of the West has nine stories, and is believed to be built entirely of jade. Around the palace are magnificent gardens where the Peach Tree of Immortality is believed to grow. The Immortals are said to live here, in an endless series of amusements and banquets.

Daoism, too, developed the mythology and iconography of the Eight Immortals which have become an integral part of popular Chinese religion. Daoists believed that human beings can become Immortals (*xian*) through special practices, and many of these Immortals were revered. Finally, around the thirteenth century A.D., eight of these immortal humans were

Above **Wen Ch'ang, the god of literature.** This god was invoked for success in examinations. In a moment of despair, he threw himself into the sea, but a fish saved him. He is usually shown standing on a fish, with an inkwell and writing brush.

Left **A fantastic horned beast.** This animal plaque was inspired by an ancient geographical gazetteer that catalogued strange spirits and supernatural flora and fauna found in distant parts of the countryside.

THE CHINESE PANTHEON

The Chinese Pantheon is arranged in an imitation of earthly organization. It appears as a vast government administration complete with ministers and support staff. They keep registers, write reports for their superiors, and every year give an account of their administration to the sovereign god, the August Personage of Jade, Yu Ti. There is a definite hierarchy of rank and clearly delineated areas of power. The gods are promoted or lowered in rank, or even dismissed, depending on their performance. The gods are judged by the August Personage of Jade. This explains the large number of changing divinities which inhabit Chinese mythology. There are also many versions of the hierarchy, and differences over who is the High or Emperor God.

Opposite page **Guan Yin, Buddhist goddess of mercy and compassion.** This goddess is one of the best loved of all Chinese deities, particularly among women. She was sometimes portrayed as the Gentle Mother, carrying a child in her arms.

singled out, and their images and/or symbols are found in temples, while their stories are told and retold in print, in operas, and more recently in films. The Eight Immortals of Daoism are the following.

Lu Tongbin

This Immortal is portrayed as a scholar with a fly-whisk and a sword. Probably one of the most popular of the Immortals, Lu is the subject of a great number of myths, such as his killing of the Yellow Dragon; his conversion of the courtesan, White Peony; and the Yellow Millet Dream, a dream that foresees a successful career, that ends in his murder.

Zhong Liquan

The Immortal of longevity who is said, in ancient times, to have discovered the Elixir of Life, he always holds a fan to revive the dead, and sometimes carries a peach from the Tree of Immortality.

Cao Guojiu

This figure is always illustrated in court dress. He is said to have been the brother of an empress. As the patron of actors, he carries a pair of castanets. He has the reputation of being a bad-tempered murderer.

Into the grotto of the Spring of the Peachblossom invite the Immortal One.

CHINESE DIVINATION PRAYER

Li Tieguai

Li is always depicted as a beggar with a crutch and a begging bowl. He was the first Immortal rescued from his poverty by none other than the Queen Mother of the West. He is also known as "Iron Crutch."

Zhang Guolao

This Immortal is usually riding backward on a white mule, carrying a cylindrical musical instrument made of bamboo. He was born old, persecuted throughout his life by his family, and after many adventures, was rewarded with immortality by the Jade Emperor. He folds up his mule like paper and puts it in his pocket, taking it out when he needs to fly away to perform deeds of mercy.

Han Xianzi

This patron of musicians holds peach blossoms and a jade flute. He received the gift of immortality after falling from his favorite peach tree.

Lan Caihe

A beggar and a street singer of dubious gender, Lan holds a basket of flowers. The stories about this curious figure show him (or her) singing songs that attack the pleasures of life.

He Xiangu

A female Immortal, she is often pictured holding a lotus or a kitchen ladle. After many years, she was released from servitude in the kitchen of her wicked stepmother. She gained immortality by eating a peach from the ancient Tree of Immortality.

BUDDHIST MYTHOLOGY

Chinese Buddhism continued the process of mythologizing the historical Siddhartha into the mythical Buddha, that had begun in India. Ancient Chinese texts emphasized the miraculous events of his life in India, to a far-off China that did not know of Buddhism until five or six centuries later. For example, at the moment of his birth, Chinese rivers are said to have overflowed their banks, mountains collapsed, and meteors appeared. Wise men were consulted by the emperor of the time, and they told him of a great sage who had been born in the West. The Daoists had another version, that the Buddha was really Laozi, who disappeared, on the back of an ox, into the West after completing his work, *Book of the Way and its Virtue*. (The West to the ancient Chinese was India, not Europe.)

The most interesting of the Chinese Buddhist myths relates to Guan Yin, a popular female deity. Historians have traced the evolution of Guan Yin from the male Indian bodhisattva Avalokitesvara, via the influence of Chinese fertility figures. Serious-minded Buddhists saved her Buddhist credentials by arguing that a bodhisattva can change shape or sex at will. One story says that if she finds she is not taken seriously by the men she appears to, because of her femininity, she changes into a male, and back again to show that sex differences are irrelevant to spiritual power. Chinese women, however, find her femininity sympathetic when seeking good marriages or male children.

Above **Buddha Sakyamuni.** This Buddha is often pictured accompanied by the bodhisattvas, Mahakasyapa and Ananda.

Below **Guan Yin on a lotus flower.** A popular goddess, she is credited with the ability to release prisoners and remove poison from snakes.

JAPANESE MYTHOLOGY

Right Shinto goddess Nakatsu-Hime-Zo. Originally a consort to Emperor Ojin, a deified form of the war god, Hachiman, this goddess became an incarnation of the compassionate bodhisattva (enlightened being), Kannon.

Ancient Japanese mythology is primarily enshrined in two great collections from the early eighth century A.D., the *Kojiki* (Record of Ancient Matters), and the *Nihongi* (Written Chronicles of Japan). This makes reconstruction of earlier mythology very difficult because these works have a very special status not only in Shinto religion, but also in state ideology. They are devoted to establishing the divine origin of the Japanese emperors, and the uniqueness of the Japanese islands and people.

However, we can read between the lines to find their origins. Modern ethnology has established the mixed (Polynesian and mainland east Asian) origin of the Japanese people which suggests a variety of influences on Japanese mythology. The beginning of the Japanese creation story has remarkable similarities to Polynesian creation myths, while the emphasis on the divine origins of the imperial line is closer to Chinese and Korean origin stories.

THE NOTION OF KAMI

As organized in these very earliest of Japanese writings and in "the way of the Kami" (Kami-no-michi, or Shinto), the focus is on the kami, or spirits. This term has a far wider meaning than "gods," but the concept of kami is very elusive. Motoori Nori-naga (1730–1801), an important figure in the modern revival of Shinto, wrote that kami embraced not only gods, but human beings (especially emperors), natural objects, and "anything whatsoever which was outside the ordinary, which possessed superior power, or which was awe-inspiring." And he went on to say that powerful evil as well as exceptional good marked

Below Bodhisattva, from the Descent of the 25 Blessed. These beings accompany Amida, a great Buddha of wisdom, when he descends from paradise to lead his followers back to "the Lotus Land of Bliss."

a kami. The number of kami is indefinite, and the stories about them, the myths, are not necessarily religious, in our sense.

The Japanese deified the forces of nature because they felt these forces were more powerful than humans were, and venerated them under the name kami. Anything considered outside the ordinary, or a being that seemingly possessed superior power came under the name kami, including human beings, high mountains, tall trees, birds, beasts, plants, seas, and so on. The kami have bodies like those of human beings, and are endowed with all the human qualities and defects. When the kami die, their spirit lives on. At times, their souls can leave the body and manifest as an object. The kami can also do both good and evil. The successive generations of sacred emperors were also called kami.

SHINTO MYTHOLOGY

It might be questioned whether the ancient Japanese really believed that all men of the world were descended from the kami, or that this only applied to the Japanese people and the Japanese islands. In practice, of course, at the time that Shinto originated, there was probably no thought that any other land or any other people existed. In later times, during the national revival of the eighteenth and nineteenth centuries, the notion of the special and unique status of Japan was drawn from these myths by proponents of the *Kokugaku* (national revival).

The religion of the ordinary people, however, at the beginning of the Empire was a kind of shamanism, like that of most of northern Asia, and based on spirit mediums who contacted the spirits and were taken over by them to communicate messages from the spirit world to the physical world. Japanese mythology often refers to communications with spirits in dreams and ecstatic trances.

THE INTRODUCTION OF BUDDHISM

Shortly before kami mythology was organized and written down, Buddhism was introduced to Japan from China. Just as the original Indian Buddhism had been altered in China, in Japan Buddhism

underwent a further transformation into Japanese forms, which generated a new Buddhist mythology. This partially involved an identification of preexisting kami with buddhas and bodhisattvas, as well as the mythicizing of founders of Japanese Buddhist sects.

In the early literature, especially works such as the anthology of poetry, the *Manyoshu,* oral traditions of a mythological nature may be discovered which match more recently collected folk traditions, and probably precede both imperial ideology and attempts to match Buddhist stories. Rituals, festivals, folk customs, proverbs, and popular sayings also give clues to the myths now lost by the theologians of Shinto and Buddhism.

The invention of myths, however, still continues to the present day. The proliferation over the last century of what the Japanese call "New Religions," is often accompanied by new myths about their origins, founders, and special powers. The Japanese people frequently adapt, in their eclectic fashion and for their own purposes, the religious mythology of other traditions.

> *Make the offering to*
> *Buddha of cherry blossoms.*
>
> SAIGYO, TRAVELER-POET AND
> BUDDHIST MONK (A.D. 1118–1190)

A CREATION STORY

The kami, according to the Japanese, were responsible for the creation of the world as we know it. In the *Kojiki,* we are told that in the beginning there were the kami of the center of heaven, and then the kami of birth and growth appeared. The brother and sister kami, Izanagi, "the male who invites," and Izanami, "the female who invites," were the eighth pair of deities to appear after heaven and earth had been created out of chaos. Izanagi and Izanami were

Above **View of a Japanese landscape.** Ritual landscapes represent the harmony between people and the natural universe. Kami, or deities, are said to live in certain areas of the landscape.

Above **Amaterasu, the sun goddess.** Susano-o, the storm god, became so destructive that the sun goddess hid in a cave. The evil gods were delighted, because the world was thrown into darkness, which hid their wicked deeds. The good deities eventually persuaded Amaterasu to come out of hiding.

ordered to create the islands of Japan. They stood side by side on the "Floating Bridge of Heaven," lowered a heavenly jeweled spear into the ocean, and began to stir. When the water began to coagulate they lifted the spear out of the water, and the droplets fell from its tip and became an island, the first solid land. The two gods then descended onto this island, and built a heavenly pillar and a splendid palace. Izanagi and Izanami circled the pillar until they met. They examined each other's bodies, and realized that they fitted together. The first result of this union was a deformed creature called "Leech Child," who the couple abandoned at sea on a camphorwood boat. Izanagi and Izanami were told by the gods that the reason for this unfortunate birth was the result of Izanami speaking first during their courting ritual. Once again, the couple circled the pillar, and gave

birth to the Eight Great Islands of Japan, as well as the other great kami. Amaterasu, the sun goddess, was their favorite child, and was sent up on a ladder to her place in the heavens. The moon god Tsuki-yomi came next and was sent to heaven to complement and as a consort of the sun. Then came Susano-o, a cruel and badly behaved god given to destruction and to making loud noises, so he was expelled to become the storm god.

Death of Izanami and Izanagi's Descent into Hell

While giving birth to the god of fire, Izanami was so badly burnt that she died. Before her death, she managed to give birth to the water goddess, the earth goddess, and the gourd of heaven, who together could control the god of fire, and prevent the world

RUSTIC GODS

All aspects and phenomena of nature are considered manifestations of different divinities. In addition to generalized divinities, each species of tree has a special god. Large and beautiful trees are worshipped, and are often decorated with a rope of plaited straw, from which hang little pieces of paper letting people who pass by know of the divine quality of the tree. Offerings are also placed in front of the tree for those faithfully devoted to specific rustic gods.

from being destroyed. A desperately unhappy Izanagi came to the land of Yomi (the land of the dead) to see if he could reclaim Izanami, but he was refused. Izanami told Izanagi not to look at her, but against her wishes, he broke off a tooth of his wooden comb, lit it, and used it as a torch to see her. He was shocked at her horribly transformed appearance. In revenge, Izanami created eight female spirits, who pursued Izanagi to the end of the world. He bathed and purified himself from the contamination of his contact with death, and from his bathwater a number of other kami were produced.

Amaterasu and Susano-o

Amaterasu and Susano-o had a stormy relationship. Susano-o delighted in destroying his sister's creations. He broke down the earth walls of her rice fields in spring, and at harvest time made "the heavenly piebald colts" lie down in the fields. He filled irrigation ditches, and deposited excrement in the temples built for the Festival of the First Fruits. The storm god also destroyed all the crops. Despairing, Amaterasu hid in the rocky cave of heaven, blocking the entrance with a boulder, and as a result the world was plunged into darkness. This conflict of the siblings gives an explanation for the change of the seasons, from spring, to autumn, to winter.

Amaterasu was enticed out of hiding by a display of hanging jewels and a mirror in the tree outside her cave; a wild and obscene dance by the other kami also attracted her curiosity. She was persuaded to come out of the cave, and once more the world was lit up by the rays of the sun.

The last, but certainly not least, of the creations of the kami is the Japanese imperial line. Amaterasu sent her grandson, Ninigi, down from heaven to rule Japan. Ninigi's great-grandson, Jimmu, eventually became the first emperor of Japan, and all Japanese emperors since this time have been considered divine. Amaterasu's image and her emblems, now the insignia of the emperor, are enshrined in the great imperial shrine of Isé, which became the center of her cult and is considered the most sacred place in Japan.

BUDDHIST MYTHOLOGY

When Buddhism came to Japan, on the whole it did not oppose the kami, but sought to assimilate them into the beliefs of Buddhism. For example, a story arose that the Emperor Shomu had a dream, in 742 B.C., in which Amaterasu herself said: "This land is the country of the kami. The people should worship them, but the wheel of the sun is Dainichi Nyorai. The true nature is Vairocana (Illumination). If sentient beings understand this logic, they should convert to Buddhism." This passage introduces a distinctively Japanese Buddha, Dainichi (the Indian Vairocana), and identifies him with the sun, subsuming and subordinating Shinto to Buddhism. However, it does not seek to completely eliminate the kami.

Temmu, the emperor who first promoted Buddhism in Japan, was influenced by a Buddhist sutra (The Sutra of the Golden Light), which depicts the Buddha appointing four God Kings to protect any king or kingdom that accepts his teaching. These God Kings are also known as the Four Heavenly Kings, Guardians of the Four Directions, Protectors of Buddhist Law. They

Above *Izanami and Izanagi Creating the Japanese Islands* by Kobayashi Eitaku (1843–1890). These divinities also produced the major deities. The death of Izanami marked the in-trusion of death into the world. The grief felt by Izanagi introduced the notion of mourning.

Left *A Snowstorm at Kinroyzan Temple* by Kuniyoshi Utagawa (1796–1861). The conflict between Amaterasu and Susano-o set in motion the change of seasons. When the storm god became too boisterous, the sun goddess would hide her rays, and winter would begin.

Opposite page **One of the four God Kings of Buddhism.** These characters were the protectors of Buddhist law. Images of them are found within temples. Traditionally, these guardians hold a sword to conquer greed, anger, and ignorance. The other hand holds a rope to catch those who oppose Buddha.

Right **Amida seated on a lotus flower.** Amida, which means Infinite Life, is one of the great savior figures in Japanese Buddhism. Followers believe that, at the hour of death, Amida will take them to an idyllic place called the Pure Land.

Below *Calligraphy* by Matsuo Basho (1643–1694). The development of Zen Buddhism influenced many aspects of art and life. The Sixth Patriarch, Huineng, wrote two poems on a monastery wall. This form of poetry is now known as Haiku, and expresses the essence of nature.

are often realized standing at the corners of altars. Ferocious looking, sometimes portrayed with fiery halos, and often stepping on *tentoki* (tiny creatures), they are depicted as warriors protecting the Buddhist realm.

The most influential text in Japanese Buddhism is undoubtedly the Lotus Sutra, which is a powerful story of miraculous events and a vision of Buddha-worlds, revealed by the Sakyamuni on Vulture Peak before he enters Nirvana. It has something for everyone from sophisticated metaphysical notions to simple faith-based practices which will enable anyone to achieve enlightenment. However, it is the mythological elements, the stories within it that have left the greatest impression on the Japanese. It has been called the "gospel" of Japanese Buddhism. For example, devotees are introduced to an extraordinary vision of a giant stupa (a Buddhist tower-temple), made of the seven kinds of precious stones, soaring into the sky, but floating in the air, unsupported. It is filled with millions of grotto-rooms and is decorated with ten billion jeweled balls. Gentle music echoes within it, and from this vision comes a voice that proclaims the glory of the Buddha.

Amida

The mythology of Amida, the savior Buddha, is another major element in Japanese Buddhism. It presents the Pure Land, "the Lotus Land of Bliss," a kind of heaven providing fulfillment, and filled with delights ranging from beholding the Buddha, to the satisfaction of all the senses. This land is presided over by Amida who, along with Kannon (the Japanese version of the Chinese bodhisattva, Guan Yin), is found represented in temples throughout Japan. Pure Land Buddhism also taught devotees about a graphically depicted hell especially reserved for murderers, butchers, and meat-eaters.

This idea was further developed in the Pure Land Sutra. Those who reach Amida's Pure Land have escaped, not only Hell but all suffering and rebirth. The Pure Land is full of fragrances, flowers and fruit, trees decked with jewels, and huge jeweled lotus flowers. This garden has no rocks or hills, but is crisscrossed with calm streams that have sweet-smelling water and floating flowers. The water feels hot or cold according to one's specific wishes, and once again, peaceful music is played throughout this glorious place.

Zen Buddhist Mythology

Zen Buddhism developed a considerable mythology and iconography around the figure of Daruma (Bodhidharma), the alleged founder of the Chinese Chan School of Buddhism, from which came Zen. Further back lay the founding story of Zen, how Mahakasyapa was the only disciple of the Buddha who smiled to show he understood when the Buddha held up a flower. Then came stories about the succession of Indian and Chinese Zen Patriarchs, and, finally, the Japanese teachers. Perhaps the most famous one of all is the story of the Sixth Patriarch, the Chinese monk Huineng, and the real founder of Zen. He was a poor man from South China who went north to find enlightenment from the famous teacher, the Fifth Patriarch, Hongren. He was set to work in the kitchen, but only Hongren recognized his qualities. The master, who was dying, announced that the monk who wrote the poem best expressing what Buddhism was about would be his successor. The favorite of the monks wrote a poem about polishing the mirror of the mind to reflect reality. In the middle of the night, Huineng awoke, and wrote two poems on the wall of the monastery. They argued that there was no mirror, that the Buddha-nature was in everybody, just waiting to be discovered, so no polishing was needed. This is the essence of Zen told in story form.

Another famous story is told of how the child monk, Toyo, solved the problem set by his Master

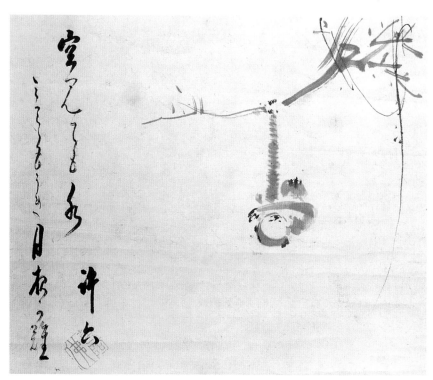

Mokurai, who asked, "What is the sound of one hand clapping?" First, he suggested it was the music floating up from the geisha quarters; then the sound of water dripping; then the whisper of the wind; then the hoot of the owl; and finally the chirping of the cicadas. The Master rejected them all. Finally, he achieved *satori* (enlightenment) when he realized that it was a "soundless sound," that all sound is illusory.

Dogen, founder of the Soto school of Zen, translated and commented on Chinese collections of sayings and stories of the Zen masters. Whether one calls such stories myths is a matter of definition. Some incidents may actually have occurred. They teach a lesson through the words and actions of a great and illustrious Master.

One favorite is the story of Nanquan killing the cat. One day the monks in Nanquan's monastery got into an argument about a cat. Nanquan called for the cat to be brought, and he held it up. "Can anyone tell me," he said, "why I should not kill it?" No one spoke up, so he cut the cat in two.

The point of such stories lay in the commentaries. Some say Nanquan didn't actually kill the cat, as the action of killing is shocking to Buddhists. Some say he did it to teach a lesson, but commentators differ greatly on what the lesson is: Don't argue? Life and death are relative? Worry about the things that

matter? Others still point to the action, a sudden violent act to induce enlightenment, which is akin to the Zen practice of the Prior striking meditating monks, sharply, with a stick.

FOLK MYTHOLOGY

There are many local cults in Japan which are not part of State Shinto, and which are not based on the ancient writings. Jean Herbert, an academic, has described the process of "kamification" by which people, who in life were thought to have displayed special powers, came to be worshipped in death. While many of these figures are clearly historical, others appear to be the product of myths. The stories about the Uji-gami, or ancestral kami of clans or families, and the particular patron kami of various professions often appear to have been borrowed from myths. For example, Nomi-no-sukune, the patron of Sumo wrestlers, is said to have been famous in his home village for his prodigious strength. He was brought to court where he was tested against the Grand Champion and killed him with one blow. He became a high official and was responsible for abolishing human sacrifice.

Rain Gods
Rain also had its special gods, such as the god Taka-Okami, who lives on mountains, and Kura-Okami, who dwells in valleys, and can cause snow as well as rain. In the description of Izumo province, it is stated that, to the west of Mount Kaminabi, the wife of the god Aji-Suki-Taka-Hikone gave birth to the god Tak-Tsu-Hiko, and advised him to build a temple, as a mark of respect to the rain gods.

Mountain Gods
The sacred Mount Fuji is worshipped as a kami by many Japanese sects, and has an enormous and complex mythology. It is said to be the axis of the world, and the source of heaven and earth. It is claimed to have arisen miraculously out of the earth in the third century B.C. A story tells of how an emperor was once enticed into the crater by the goddess of Fuji, and he was never seen again.

Sea and River Gods
Most Japanese rivers have their kami respected and feared because of their creation of floods. A fearsome dwarf god, Kappa, is blamed for drownings, but

Right **Mount Fuji, home of the mountain gods.** The extinct volcano is the sanctuary for mountain gods and goddesses. Chief god and lord of the mountains, O-Yama-Tsu-Mi was born from the dismembered parts of the fire god's body.

Below **The Feast of Inari.** The god of rice is called Inari. He is closely related to the food goddess, Uke-mochi. Inari is a symbol of prosperity, and many festivals are held to celebrate and encourage his benevolence.

called Namazu, which lay bound underground with wisteria vines under a stone until he escaped. His movements were said to have caused the all-to-frequent earthquakes.

Left *The Waterfall* by Kasushika Hokusai (1760–1849). Kappa, a river god, is responsible for waterfalls. The symbol of water also represents purification, which came into existence when Izanagi washed himself after being contaminated by death.

Wind Gods

From the breath of Izanagi came the wind god, Shina-Tsu-Hiko, who blew away the mist which covered the land. There are actually many wind gods. Some are responsible for gentle breezes. Fishermen believed in Haya-ji, the typhoon god, who carried wind in a bag on his back.

Thunder Gods

There is a curious mythology relating to "thunder-trees," which are protected against lightning by Kami-nari, the thunder god. One story in the *Nihongi* is about the felling of a forest to build an imperial fleet. The official in charge, Kahabe-no-omi, refused to stop operations when told by the thunder god that they were attacking thunder-trees. He persisted, despite torrential rain, thunder, and lightning, and the official eventually burnt the thunder god, who had taken the form of a fish. There is another story that relates the punishment of the Empress Saimei for daring to cut some sacred trees to build her Palace of Logs.

In many places rocks are worshipped as kami because of their striking shapes. One is especially venerated as the stone which Empress Jingo (A.D. 170–269)

people can escape his wrath by bowing to him, which forces him to bow in return, causing the flood water to pour out of his skull. Many waterfalls have water goddesses, complete with stories and shrines. There are several sea gods who were created when Izanagi washed off the impurities of death, such as the god of the bottom of the sea, the god of the middle waters, and the god of the surface.

Earthquake Gods

Earthquakes are sometimes attributed to Nai-no-kami, the earthquake god, and sometimes to a giant fish,

Below **Snakes and serpents.** One legend tells of an eight-headed snake who visited the province of Izumo once a year to devour a daughter from each family. The storm god eventually defeated this terrifying creature, by putting out eight cups of wine for each of its heads.

Below **The accomplished and lucky tea kettle.** An abbot bought a tea kettle. When water was boiled in this kettle, it turned into a raccoon, and ran about the room. The savvy abbot decided to take it around the countryside as a performing show.

carried on her belly to delay the birth of her child until she had completed a military expedition against her foes, the Koreans.

Goddess of Food

There are several food gods—of rice, of fish, of vegetables—each with their accompanying stories. Uke-mochi is the general goddess of food. Amaterasu is said to have sent her brother/consort, Tsuki-yomi, to seek her secrets. Uke-mochi produced a meal from her mouth, which so disgusted him that he killed her and threatened to stop the the food supply. Amaterasu intervened, and ordered that a shrine be set up next to her own great shrine of Isé. From the corpse of Uke-mochi, seeds and crops, farm animals, and silkworms were produced.

DRAGONS AND SNAKES

In ancient Japan, the people believed in a snake god, Orochi, who lived on the very top of mountains. The Buddhist religion told of the dragon god, Ryujin, who ruled the clouds, the rain, and the water. There was the dragon, Yasha, one of the demon-gods who protected Buddhism. All of these deities have wide mouths, sharp fangs, pointed horns, and all-seeing eyes.

In Japanese folklore there are tales told of people who turned into snakes after death because of their evil ways and miserly habits. A male becomes a serpent because his desires are not satisfied. Women are often associated with snakes because of the tales told

ANIMAL MYTHS

The Japanese raccoon (*tanuki*) and the fox (*kitsune*) are the most popular animals in Japanese mythology. One story tells of an abbot of the Morinji Temple. He instructs one of his monks to clean a tea kettle he has bought. Suddenly a voice from the kettle says, "Ow, that hurts, please be more gentle." When the abbot boils water in the kettle, out pops the tail and legs of a *tanuki*, and the kettle runs about the room, while the abbot vainly tries to catch it.

The *kitsune* also have the ability to change shape, but their faces always remain foxlike. In folklore, foxes pretend to be humans so that they can lead men astray, by either hypnotizing people and leading them into perilous situations, or seducing men by pretending to be beautiful women.

of them being fierce and possessive toward their lovers. Snakes are not always thought of as symbols of evil, but also of love with no bounds. Long ago in the Keicho era, there lived a beautiful girl in Senju, in the province of Musashi. A bachelor called Yaichiro fell in love with her, and sent her many letters of love, but she did not respond. Yaichiro died of sorrow, and the girl married someone else. On the morning after the wedding, the couple didn't emerge from their room. When the bride's mother entered, she found the bridegroom dead, and a snake crawling out of the bride's eyes. The villagers believed that the snake was the heartbroken Yaichiro.

Serpents and dragons are also associated with nature. Natural disasters, especially devastating floods, are linked to them. It is believed that after storms they are washed out of their dens and come into the open. There are four types of dragons in Japanese mythology: the heavenly dragons who guard the palace of the gods, the spiritual dragons who bring the blessed rain, the earth dragons who determine the course of rivers, and the dragons who are the guardians of all the earthly treasures.

HELL AND DEMONS

Hell, or Jigoku, is underground, and is divided into eight regions of fire and eight regions of ice. Emma-o is the ruler of Jigoku, and the judge of the dead. He is identified with the Chinese deity, Yanluo Wang, and his origins are from the Hindu god of death, Yama.

In Jigoku, Emma-o is surrounded by 18 generals and thousands of soldiers, as well as nasty demons and guards with horses' heads. According to one tradition, death begins as a journey across a vast, empty

Opposite page **Oni (demon) skewering the damned.** These demons work alongside Emma-o, the ruler of Jigoku. They are responsible for keeping the tortured souls of the underworld under tight control.

plain. In other versions of the tale, infernal beings guard the dead during their journey. At the entrance to Jigoku lies a steep mountain, which the deceased have to climb, and on the other side of the mountain is a river with three crossings. One of the crossings is a shallow ford, which those who have committed only minor sins may cross. Another is a bridge over which good people may pass. The third is a horrific torrent filled with monsters, through which evil sinners must struggle. On the other side of this third crossing waits a horrible old woman who strips her victims naked. They are then taken by the Jigoku guards to Emma-o, who judges only men; his sister decides the fate of women. The god sits between two severed heads, and a magic mirror reflects the sinner's past wrongdoings. Emma-o then judges the individual's sins, and allocates them to the appropriate part of Jigoku. The souls of the dead can, however, be saved with the help of a bosatsu, the Japanese form of the bodhisattva.

The Oni

The Oni are giant, horned demons. They are said to have come to Japan from China with the arrival of Buddhism, and Buddhist priests perform annual rites to expel them. The Oni can be a variety of colors, and they have three fingers, three toes, and sometimes

three eyes. They are usually cruel and lecherous, and they are said to sweep down from the sky in chariots, to steal the souls of people who are about to die. One story tells of how the diminutive hero Momotaro freed young girls whom the Oni had captured.

The Oni of Jigoku take sinners to Emma-o, and are said to be responsible for creating illness and disease.

Above **Woman reading a love letter in front of her servants, Edo period (1614–1868).** In one Japanese myth, a beautiful girl rejects the advances of a lovelorn boy, with fatal consequences.

367

TIBETAN MYTHOLOGY

Right **Padmasambhava and his wives.** Padmasambhava was called to Tibet by the Dharmaja (King of Law) in the eighth century. This Indian monk introduced Tantric Buddhism to Tibet, and is often represented seated on a lotus, holding a thunderbolt *(vajra)*, a skull, and a trident.

Folk history, with its broad range of exciting and instructive myths, is an important part of Tibetan culture. These traditional accounts explain the stuff of existence— the origins of the world and of their people, the development of agriculture and technology, the might and splendor of their kings and their realm, and their conversion to Buddhism. These stories are not fixed, but part of a living, evolving, oral culture, open to embellishment and elaboration. Traveling bards spread the stories far and wide, although different regions in the vast Tibetan cultural arena have their own particular traditions. Some of these myths have been written down, and are often further embroidered through episodes rediscovered in the various visions of the historiographers.

The gradual taming of the environment and its forces is an important theme in the mythological history of Tibet. Padmasambhava, or Guru Rinpoche, the eighth-century tantric master revered for bringing Buddhism from India to Tibet, epitomizes this process. Similarly, the exploits of the warrior hero of Tibet, King Gesar of Ling, are far too numerous and extensive to be included here.

The core of the epic of Ling, which might well be compared to the *Iliad* and the *Odyssey,* or the Hindu tale, the *Mahabharata,* tells of the stories of Gesar's birth, childhood, and marriage; how he became ruler; and his wars against the demon king of the

north and the Turkic peoples. Typically, King Gesar and his army defeat the foe, often through trickery and cunning, as much as might, returning home with a booty of medicinal herbs, cattle, magic jewels, and other treasures. Gesar allows the defeated tribes to maintain their autonomy, causing them to become allies. This process can be seen to mirror the political process of "Tibetanization" through adopting Tibetan Buddhism. There may be kernels of factual history embedded in these myths, however, the Tibetan idea of historiography is more about instilling desirable values, glorifying the people and their complex society through the triumph of good over evil, and bringing the past to life. For the Tibetan people, this folk history is real, no matter if there are variations on names, places, and motives in different sources. This extensive genre consists of a rich tapestry of verse and prose that are performed in dramatic dances, in

THE MONKEY DESCENDANTS AND EVOLUTION

We can speculate about this myth of the origin of Tibetan people, and look at what we understand from scientific evidence about the processes of physical and cultural evolution. Does this origin story contain some kernel of prehistoric truth?

Old and Middle Stone Age tools and the evidence of habitation have been discovered at archaeological sites on the Tibetan plateau. Genetic mapping suggests that modern humans may have originated about 40,000 years ago, west of Tibet and north of India. Clear evidence for early modern human inhabitation on the northern edge of the Tibetan plateau in the Tsaidam Basin dates from 33,000 years ago.

Right **Map of the world, according to Tibetan cosmology.** Mount Sumeru, the axis of the universe, is in the inner circle. It is surrounded by four continents with their four islands within the cosmic ocean. The guardian of the north sits on a white lion on Mount Sumeru.

song, and also in simple story-telling. The following origin myths are well known throughout Tibet, and were recorded by Tibetan historiographers in the first section of the *Mani Kabum,* a twelfth-century ancient text that has been "rediscovered" and is currently being studied.

THE ORIGINS OF THE TIBETAN PEOPLE

There was once a magical monkey, living very high up in a very fine cave on Mount Kongpori, a sacred peak in the Yarlung Valley in central Tibet. Because this monkey had visited the high realm of the Buddhas and made contact with Chenrezig, a great compassionate Buddha-to-be, he spent all of his time in meditation, patiently developing his skills in compassion, peace, and loving-kindness.

One day his sublime practice was interrupted by a passionate rock srinmo-demoness, who was overcome with lust when she saw the radiant monkey. The monkey, however, had vowed to meditate until he reached enlightenment, and was not attracted to this rock srinmo-demoness. She threatened that she would marry a violent rock demon, and produce many destructive offspring who would destroy many living beings, if the monkey did not succumb to her wishes, and take her as his wife.

The monkey was stuck. He knew he could prevent this great destruction, though it would cost him his vow. Because of his com-passion he united with the rock srinmo-demoness, and she bore him six wild red-faced monkey-children. Their father took them to a bountiful forest full of many fruit-bearing trees so they could eat well, and grow up happily. But before long there was no more food left to eat, and the youngsters became hungry.

Filled with great compassion for their plight, the monkey sought assistance from Chenrezig, who intervened by producing grains including barley, rice,

and buckwheat. As the monkey-children satiated their hunger, their hair and tails grew shorter, they learned to speak, and became human. The six original tribes of the Tibetan people are descended from these children. This is why Tibetans are both spiritual and compassionate, traits inherited from their monkey ancestor, an emanation of Chenrezig; and strong and courageous like the srinmo-demoness, an emanation of Tara, the Buddhist protectress of Tibet.

Above **Green Tara.** This goddess symbolizes com-passion, and is the Buddhist protectress of Tibet. Ancient legend has it that Green Tara was a Nepalese princess, reincarnated because of her study of and devotion to Buddhism.

CONVERSION OF TIBET TO BUDDHISM THROUGH PINNING THE DEMONESS

Right Skull decoration from Jokhang Monastery. King Song-tsen Gampo built the Jokhang Monastery. The symbol of the skull serves as a reminder of life's impermanence, and the use of skulls as cups played an important part in Tibetan rituals.

Below Buddha's first sermon. This seventeenth-century fresco shows five high-caste followers gathering around Buddha in a deer park. This represents the beginning of his public life. Buddha is seated on a lotus flower, and the scene below him illustrates the ever-widening circle of Buddhist devotees.

The Tibetan Empire had become great, and the ruler King Song-tsen Gampo, who reigned between A.D. 627–649, commanded respect from all the neighboring countries. Despite his already happy marriage with the Nepalese Princess Khri-tsun, he desired a second refined and beautiful younger wife. So, a marriage was arranged with Princess Kong-jo from the nearby country of China.

With negotiations finalized, and wedding plans in place, the young princess and her entourage embarked on the long journey to Lhasa in central Tibet, protected by two strong Tibetan bodyguards, Laga and Luga. The princess carried a beautiful statue of the Buddha Sakyamuni, her most precious offering to the Tibetan court. She encountered many difficulties on this journey, and the special chariot that carried this statue seemed to be particularly prone to mishap. On reaching the plains of Lhasa, the chariot became completely bogged, and nothing Laga and Luga did could free it. Despairing, Princess Kong-jo consulted her feng shui charts to determine the cause of the problem. To her dismay she discovered that the very energy of the earth of Tibet was trying to repel this statue of the Buddha Sakyamuni and, with it, all the teachings of Buddhism.

Reflecting very deeply, Kong-jo realized that the very earth of Tibet, Land of Snows, was actually a huge and powerful reclining srinmo-demoness. To add to the Princess's troubles, there were also treacherous otherworldly beings inhabiting the land and supporting this demoness. Despite these considerable obstacles, other aspects of the landscape were proven to be quite favorable. Kong-jo's feng shui calculations determined that a series of Buddhist temples and stupa-reliquaries could pin down the negative earth forces and otherworldly beings, and curtail their destructive activity. She could then get started on building the temple to house the precious Buddha Sakyamuni statue.

Princess Kong-jo was received with much celebration by the Tibetan court. It was only Queen Khri-tsun who was not so pleased with the arrival of this second wife. On hearing of Kong-jo's plans to build a temple in Lhasa for the precious Buddha-statue, Khri-tsun claimed the right, as senior consort, to build her temples first. Kong-jo suggested that Khri-tsun build a great temple in the middle of the lake near Lhasa, which, along with other protective measures, should, firstly, be filled with earth. This angered the jealous Queen Khri-tsun, who then asked the King for permission to build 108 Buddhist temples wherever she wanted.

Foundations were dug, and stones were laid, but no matter how much was built by day, the malignant beings in the earth destroyed the work by night. In desperation, Khri-tsun consulted Kong-jo, knowing that her feng shui skills would resolve the impasse. Kong-jo again explained the remedies, including the filling of the lake with earth, which would enable the great temple of Lhasa to be built. Khri-tsun didn't fully understand the instructions, and when she tried to fill in the lake it became a muddy mess. This confirmed the Queen's sneaking suspicions that Kong-jo was deceiving her out of spite.

Queen Khri-tsun explained her difficulties to the King, who comforted her. Through his own divination he realized that a temple should, indeed, be built near the lake. So, the King and Queen rode to the lake, and taking a ring from his finger, the King told Khri-tsun to build a temple wherever his ring fell. The ring flew high into the air, bounced from

the Queen's saddle, and fell into the lake. Khri-tsun was dismayed, but the King promised to help her. Together they did their best, but whatever was built by day, was again, crumbled by night.

With all building attempts thwarted, the frustrated King reconsidered Kong-jo's scheme. With reflection he gained a full understanding of the supine srinmo-demoness. As the demoness flailed her limbs about, the newly built temples were destroyed. The King decided to build 12 Buddhist temples, successfully pinning the srinmo-demoness by the hands, feet, knees, elbows, shoulders, and hips. These Buddhist temples were built throughout the entire Tibetan domain and finally, both queens were able to build their temples. The precious statue of the Buddha Sakyamuni, also known as Jowo

KING GESAR OF LING

King Gesar is also known as Gesar of Khrom. Some historians suggest that this name was adapted from Caesar of Rome, speculating that the tales of the King of Ling were overlaid with exploits told by Arabs in west central Asia, during the time of the great Tibetan Empire (seventh to ninth centuries A.D.). The might of Tibetan military power spread to Mongolia, through Turkestan, and even further west to the Arab conquerors of the old Persian dominions; south through the whole Himalayan region into Nepal and the plains of India; and in the east into Gansu, Qinghai, Sichuan, and Yunnan Provinces in China.

Rinpoche, found its final place in the great temple of Lhasa, called the Jokhang Monastery. Finally, the compassion of the Buddha's teachings radiated through the Land of Snows.

Above **Life of Buddha Sakyamuni.** After his birth from his mother's right side, the Buddha takes seven steps on seven lotus flowers. Two god figures receive him with a sacred cloth. When the Buddha Sakyamuni statue was enshrined, compassion filled the country of Tibet.

MYTHOLOGY
OF OCEANIA

OCEANIC MYTHOLOGY

Right **Tortoise shell spirit carving.** The sea spirit or *adaro* appears in many Polynesian and Melanesian myths and legends. Sharks, fish, and turtles merge in a sea spirit, which appears as a humanlike figure.

Oceania, according to the well-known Tongan anthropologist Epeli Hau'ofa, can be considered a sea of islands. The peoples and the cultures of Oceania have been conveniently divided into three main culture areas: Melanesia, Micronesia, and Polynesia. This classification, while problematic in many ways, is made mainly on the basis of a number of things, such as geography, race, art, mythology, religion, and language. Oceania, contrary to stereotypical portrayal, is far from static and uniform—it is quite complex and made up of different elements. While there are cultural and historical variations within and across Oceanic societies, these cultures share a lot in common, respectively exhibiting both differ-ences and similarities. The same applies to particular mythologies found in Oceania.

Numerous differences are mingled with similarities of the gods and within storylines. Sometimes, in the different islands of an archipelago, in the different districts of an island, or even in a single tribe, and according to different individuals, the same god is endowed with different attributes, or unites in himself, or herself, the attributes which belong to different gods in other places within Oceania. This can also work the other way around, where different gods in different populations have the same, or at least very similar attributes.

Below right **Symbols of fishing and the sea.** The sea is an important element throughout Oceanic mythology. Some existence myths attempt to explain the beginnings of the sea as coming from the sweat of the god of the oceans, Tangaroa, as he works at creation.

Below **Marakihau, a sea monster.** Marakihau are female sea monsters, and often turn into human women to marry men. When their husbands discover their true nature, the Marakihau are forced to return to the sea.

As in all cultures, mythology in Oceania is seen as a system of knowledge where people organize themselves in relation to nature and the environment. Obviously, as in the case of Oceania, mythology functions as an instrument of both investigation and explanation, as it symbolically explains how things work in reality, but mythology also works as an excellent means of communication, or oral tradition. This brings nature, mind, and society, as is evident in the retelling of a number of Oceanic myths, into conflict as different themes are stronger than others within mythological stories. The form and content of these many Oceanic mythologies vary from one place to another, and all have common narrative threads running through the stories and linking all cultures.

In Oceania, myths differ in both structure and subject matter, and from one locale to another. Generally, myths reflect the individual and society, as well as major events taking place in nature, and feature volcanic eruptions, landmarks, exploits of great ingenuity, war and peace among the gods, and romance between famous lovers. There are also variations between the local and the regional, where local versions happen to express themes relevant to the specific region. For example, some regional myths—such as the Maui, Tawhaki, and Tangaloa hero cycles—occur in Polynesia, but there are different versions of the stories throughout the whole Oceanic region. New myths, such as the Origin of Kava, Tonga's Lament for his Daughter, and the Fight with Oroi, are seen as being specific to Tonga, Mangareva, and Rapanui. These myths may

dreams, both as worlds without logical consequence, and where anything, and almost everything is possible.

These myths can be viewed as a work of art, especially the way in which their form and content are specifically organized. As seen in most highly developed myths, the elements of the myths are formally organized in sequences, and are made up of closely related episodes, which then combine to create the central plots and themes of the myths.

All myths tend to have investigative approaches, or they aim to change the way people look at a story or at history and its meaning. These myths provide an important source of knowledge for future generations.

represent an older social order, which diversified as people moved to new islands and adjusted to a new life. This shift is reflected in the substantial change in the form and content of new myths.

MYTHS AND HISTORY

Myths are a social institution, and they exist within and across all human cultures. The following general descriptions are specifically true of all Oceania. Being a hallmark of mainly verbal cultures, myths are transmitted through generations by word of mouth. Generally, myths can be considered as an aid to human memory in recording major historical events of extreme natural, mental, and social significance. Specifically, however, myths record in magical ways the major historical occurrences that concern, and influence, types of social activity, and characterize the relationships between people and their environment. In this respect, myths can be said to be storage boxes of human knowledge about nature, mind, and society. Similarly, material artifacts and languages can be effective sources of history, capable of holding vital information about the past of a group of people.

Oceanic myths are symbolic accounts of actual historical events. Conversely, actual events taking place in time and space are retold using symbols to represent ideas, the meanings of which are widely shared by members of a particular culture.

This is clear in the Oceanic myths retold here, where a number of symbols are used as pointers, or markers, to real occurrences taking place. This leads to myths having no connection to cause and effect, and creates a world of pure possibilities. Some Oceanic examples include Tanematua's pushing of the sky upward, the mortal woman Fataimoeloa being impregnated by the Sun, and Maui's fishing-up of lands, among many others. In this respect, myth tends to share a lot in common with

Below **Protective figure from the prow of a war canoe, Solomon Islands.** It was believed that the figure represented an ancestor that watched over the warriors while they were at sea, and the bird kept the boat on the right course.

Right *The Birth of Maui*
by **Wilhelm Dittmer**
(1866–1909). This hero
represents the power of an
individual to fight against
oppression and defeat the
enemy. Maui and his adventures reflect historical and
geographical changes in the
landscape, and their effects
on the people of Oceania.

MAUI AND TAWHAKI HERO CYCLES

In Oceania, the Maui and Tawhaki hero cycles exist
on both the regional and local levels. Maui and Tawhaki represent actual powerful individuals or dominant ideologies. As individual protagonists, who are
featured either as gods or demigods in many myths
throughout the region, they have been described as
nonconformist and aristocratic culture heroes. In
terms of ideologies, Maui and Tawhaki represent the

liberal and conservative tendencies as permanent
aspects of the human context. As is always the case,
these opposing points of view exist in the form of a
constant struggle between social groups over the
control of both human and material resources.

These competing ideologies generally reflect the
two main social divisions in Polynesia, made up of
commoner and "chiefly," or higher social classes.
There were also "in-between" professional classes
that actively engaged in different forms of social

activity such as art, cultivation, navigation, religion, and housebuilding, among other things. These were very highly organized professions that were handed down from father to son. The conflicting relationships between these social relations of domination and oppression, and manifested in the Maui and Tawhaki cycles, highlight the resistance against social norms, and were the main driving force behind the expansive movement of Oceanic peoples.

Ranginui and Papatuanuku

This conflict of social class is evident in the Maori myth of Ranginui and Papatuanuku, gods of the sky and earth, symbolic of the combination of the priestly class and the landed aristocracy, highlighting this relationship as exploitation and oppression. In this myth, there exists an intermingling of the competing Maui and Tawhaki tendencies. Ranginui (Rangi), the Sky Father, and Papatuanuku (Papa), the Earth Mother, were inseparably embraced, with their children living between them in the dark. The children of the gods, Tanemahuta (Tane), Tawhirimatea, Rongomatane (Rongo), Haumiatiketike (Haumia), and Tangaroa—the gods of the forests, winds, kumara, plants, and oceans—had enough of living in darkness, and were eager to see the light of day.

One day, they had a meeting where they decided that the only way for them to realize their long-standing wish was to separate their parents by force. None of the children were eager to follow through with this plan. Some of the gods' children simply feared the consequences of their actions, while others were being respectful of their parents. However, Tanemahuta took on the challenge of separating the parents. He did this by kicking Ranginui skyward and placing Papatuanuku on earth permanently. The children of the gods saw light for the first time. Enraged by Tanemahuta's action against their parents, Tawhirimatea chose to be with Ranginui, his father. To punish his brothers, Tawhirimatea angrily sent his children, who were hurricanes and tornadoes, to ravage the forests, kumara, plants, and the oceans. Fearing the terrifying wrath of Tawhirimatea and his tempestuous children, the brothers all hid, clinging to the breast of their mother, Papatuanuku, for protection.

Like Maui, you are a deceiver.
MAORI PROVERB

Munimatamahae and Sisimataela'a

Like many of the Oceanic islands, the Maui and Tawhaki hero cycles, as opposed heroic entities, are more clearly found in Tonga. As local variants, they are expressed in the myths of Munimatamahae and Sisimataela'a, who were nonconformist and aristocratic heroes. Munimatamahae, literally "Muni-the-shredded-eye," was born to commoner parents, who deserted him at birth, after throwing him into the sea. He was eventually washed ashore on one of the islands, and as he lay abandoned, a seabird viciously pecked out one of his eyes.

A commoner couple found and adopted him. Munimatamahae grew up to be a solidly built, handsome young man of extreme power and exceptional athleticism, and became greatly feared, even by his adoptive parents. If the chiefs on this island assigned a task, the people had to attend to it immediately, with all their might, as failing to do so meant severe punishment. Whenever a task was set, no matter how big or how hard, Munimatamahae would single-handedly and secretively complete any task in less than no time.

Sisimataela'a, literally "Sisi-the-eye-of-the sun," was born as a result of the union between a beautiful woman of noble birth, Fataimoeloa, and her aristocratic husband, the Sun. Fataimoeloa always bathed in a pool near the beach. She would then dry herself, bending forward, and exposing her buttocks to the burning Sun. Over time, she fell pregnant to the Sun, and gave birth to Sisimataela'a. Sisimataela'a was considered to be extremely handsome, and had all the physical attributes of being a chief of high standing. He was also equipped with all the necessary social knowledge of etiquette and protocol.

It happened that one day, the Tu'i Tonga (the King of Tonga) sent a party of high-status people on a voyage to the outlying islands, in search of an appropriate husband for his daughter. They came across the islet of Felemea in the Ha'apai group, where they found Sisimataela'a. All of them were struck by his physical attractiveness and aristocratic manners. He was ordered to come to

Above **Ivory Tiki figure.** In some regions of Oceania, Tiki is believed to be a creator, while other regions use the symbol of Tiki to represent their ancestors. Tiki pendants were carved with care and presented to others as a gift of respect and acknowledgment.

Left **Ranginui and Papatuanuku.** The myth of the Sky Father and the Earth Mother describes how their tight, loving embrace kept light away from their children. Yearning for a break from the darkness, the children separated the couple and brought light into the world.

377

The First Tu'i Tonga

The myth of the origin of the first Tu'i Tonga, 'Aho'eitu, is another variant of the Tawhaki hero cycle. It symbolically records the historical rise of the most ancient Tongan dynasty around the tenth century A.D. In historical terms, the myth is a metaphorical account of the dynastic connection between the Samoan and Tongan elite families, and is generally symbolized by the casuarina tree.

The myth relates how 'Eitumatupu'a, one of the Tangaloa sky gods, regularly descended to earth by climbing down a casuarina tree. On one of his earth visits, 'Eitumatupu'a impregnated 'Ilaheva, an earthly woman of noble birth. Her name was later changed to Va'epopua, after knowing 'Eitumatupu'a. She was the daughter of Seketo'a, an aristocrat of high status from one of the northernmost Tongan islands of Niuatoputapu. The physical union between the heavenly 'Eitumatupu'a and earthly Va'epopua (which signifies the historical links between Samoa and Tonga) resulted in the birth of 'Aho'eitu, who inherited the sky and earth, and both divine (spiritual) and secular (material) position on earth.

MAUI THE FREEDOM-FIGHTER

As a nonconformist culture hero, Maui is renowned for his many heroic exploits. He has been described as a trickster, commonly as "Maui-of-a-thousand-tricks," a characterization of the ingenuity in the conduct of his great deeds. His multiple heroic exploits are allegorical references to his permanent struggle against, and constant opposition to, actual forms of political oppression in the particular society of his time. The Maui gods, or demigods, existed as one of the competing ideologies,

Tonga-tapu to marry the king's daughter, so his father, the burning Sun, and his mother gave him two magical packages, one of fortune and the other of misfortune, instructing him carefully on how to always use them to his advantage or disadvantage.

Right **A bonito fish carving from the Solomon Islands.** When turned upside down, this bonito fish becomes a shark. Annual fishing expeditions were a major ritual event in Oceania. Carrying this type of carving in a canoe served to lure the bonito, while repelling the predatory sharks.

several centuries before the rise of the first Tu'i Tonga, 'Aho'eitu. This was witnessed in the manner of Maui's life and, indeed, in the manner of his death. Maui's exploits were always done for, and in the name of, freedom for the people of the earth. Maui's heroic deeds, among many others, see him as a fire-bearer, a sky-raiser, a sun-snarer, and a land-fisher, all of which are symbolic of a real life of protest against tyranny, in place of autonomy. This becomes more obvious in Maui also being a god of the underworld, which is a symbol for people who are downtrodden.

In Oceania, fire is symbolic of freedom, the driving force behind all forms of creative and innovative works of intellectual, artistic, and technological significance. The concept that freedom is not something given, but rather a form of constant struggle, is the prevailing theme in the story of Maui. He was opposed to the oppression brought about by the sky and earth separating, which was symbolic of the aristocratic classes, as well as people bending their backs under the burden of their social obligations. Similarly, the sun is a symbol of power manifested in the person of either a monarch or an aristocrat. Maui's snaring of the sun, which allowed more time for working people, symbolizes the act of asserting one's self against the powerful, and agitating for more personal power for the underclass. As a land-fisher, Maui symbolizes the liberation of the people, metaphorically represented by the land; these stories also illustrate social transformation, and the changes in the way of life for people from working and fishing the sea for a living, to eventually farming the land. These stories can vary from place to place, but Maui's basic purpose always remains the same.

THE KAVA MYTH

One day the tenth Tu'i Tonga, Momo, King of Tonga, who lived on the easternmost part of the main island of Tongatapu, was game fishing. On this particular fishing trip, he and his royal party couldn't catch any fish. Exhausted and hungry, they landed on the islet of 'Eueki. Living on the island was a man of common status named Fevanga and his wife, Fefafa, and their only daughter, Kava'onau.

Having heard of the arrival of royalty, the couple had to make an offering. They decided to harvest their giant taro plant, but found the king leaning against it. This meant that the taro plant could not be used as it had become taboo, because the king had touched it. Instead, they killed their daughter and baked her in an 'umu (earth oven).

The king told them not to uncover the 'umu, but make it their daughter's grave. From this grave grew kava and sugarcane, which the couple harvested, and then used for a formal kava ceremony. Today this ceremony is performed as a dance.

Below *The Kava Ceremony* by Louis Auguste de Sainson (1801–1887). This ceremony is performed as a traditional sign of welcome for visitors and dignitaries.

MAUI THE FIRE-BEARER

Maui's grandfather, the old Maui, lived in the underworld, where he guarded the only source of fire—a huge log of burning wood. One day, Maui left earth to visit the old man, entering through the secret gate to the underworld. Maui found his grandfather jealously guarding the single fire source. He told the old man that he wanted to take some fire back with him to earth, so that people could use it for cooking, as a change from eating their food raw. The old Maui refused his grandson's request, prompting Maui to work out a plot to smuggle the fire away so he could take it back to earth.

Maui took a piece of burning charcoal, and carefully wrapped it up in a leaf. As he was leaving, his grandfather could smell the fire on him, and challenged the young man to a wrestling match.

Depending on who won, the fire would either stay in the underworld, or be taken to earth. The old Maui grabbed his grandson, and tried to throw him into the sky. Maui was flung upward, and reached the top of the trees. He then fell back down, landing safely on the ground. When it came to Maui's turn,

Left **Kings and dynasties.** A Polynesian statue of a kingly figure has an almost godlike appearance, complete with powerful arms and legs. This figure looks reverently toward the sky as a mark of respect for the ancestors.

went about their daily routine—men, women, and children were busy with their various day-to-day activities, such as fetching water and firewood, and getting food to cook. On his return to earth, Maui discovered a strange thing happening. He noticed that the sky and the earth had moved closer together. To his great dismay, Maui also saw that his fellow earth dwellers were walking around with their backs bent forward, unable to walk upright, and their movements were cramped and restricted.

Immediately, Maui began working out ways to deal with this troubling problem. He decided the best solution was to raise the sky by pushing it upward with all his might away from the earth, and put them into their proper positions. As a consequence of his wilful action, it was said that the people of the earth immediately regained their normal posture, and began walking about, and doing their work with greater ease.

MAUI THE SUN-SNARER

The earth inhabitants were used to a normal day, with the usual division of night and day, and their activities were based around this daily division. However, people could see that the days were strangely getting shorter and shorter. During the day, the sun would rise and set very quickly across the sky, giving people less time and space to carry out their normal tasks such as fishing and the tilling of the land. This meant that they were never able to finish their work. People became alarmed, and then started to complain loudly to the gods.

The people's concerns soon reached Maui and his brothers, Maui 'Atalanga, Maui Loa, and Maui Puku, who then held a meeting to discuss the matter, as it seriously affected life on earth. They decided that one way of alleviating this problem was to slow down the sun, giving the people enough time to do their work. Maui suggested that they make a huge net, which could be used to snare the sun, and anchor it firmly to earth. His brothers were fiercely opposed to the idea, as they feared both the enormity of the task and the fierce intensity of the sun's heat. Maui was unmoved by their concerns, and eventually won over the complete support of his brothers. They successfully managed to capture the sun. This limited the sun's rate of motion, and restored the pattern of normal daily life back to the people.

Above *Maui Snaring the Sun* by Wilhelm Dittmer (1866–1909). Maui conceived a plan to capture the sun, when the days on earth became shorter and the nights became longer. The sun was captured with a net, which then slowed its progress through the sky. As a result, the daylight hours were extended.

Right Jade *hei matau* or fishhook. The islands of Oceania were said to have been fished up by the hero, Maui. With deceit and trickery, he managed to find a magical fishhook, learn its secrets, and pull up land from the depths of the ocean.

he took hold of his grandfather with one hand, sent him up beyond the clouds, and watched him disappear into the heavens.

The young Maui took off with his hidden treasure, with his grandfather, who had landed, in pursuit. Just as Maui was about to enter the secret gate, the old Maui caught him. As the gate opened, young Maui threw the wrapped-up fire out to earth, instructing it to enter every tree. Old Maui was completely powerless to stop the fire from spreading. This was the origin of how fire appeared on earth, and how it is now used for cooking by its people.

MAUI THE SKY-RAISER

At one time, Maui descended from the earth above to the underworld below. As usual, people on earth

MAUI THE LAND-FISHER

The god of the sky, the old Tangaloa, and his children lived in the heavens above earth. One of his children, young Tangaloa, the artisan and god of the material arts, was responsible for the creation of many of the Oceanic islands. He would tip the wood chips from his workshop in the sky, down onto the earth, and these chips formed many of the islands. This is how Tangaloa the artisan became Tangaloa, the creator of lands. The word sky, *langi* or *rangi,* is, in Oceania, a symbolic name for Samoa. The creation of land is probably a metaphor for the secret knowledge involving the organization of people of this time. It may mean that Tangaloa was either an

SYMBOLS

Some common examples of symbols as actual markers to history in Oceanic mythology include the bending forward of backs for oppression; sun for power, monarchy, or aristocracy; sky for the priestly class; underworld for the down-trodden; fire-bearing for innovation; sky-raising for opposition; sun-snaring for contestation; and land-fishing for liberation.

influential person or a kind of social norm held up as an example to others in society.

The rest of the islands in Oceania were said to have been fished up by Maui from the depths of the ocean. The fishhook that Maui used for fishing up lands, including many of the Tongan, Fijian, and Samoan archipelagos, is said to have come from Manu'a, the easternmost group of islands in Samoa.

Maui desperately wanted the old, rusty, worn-looking fishhook for its magical qualities, specifically for fishing up lands. Tongafusifonua (literally "Tonga, the Fisher of the Lands") was the owner of the fishhook, and extremely protective of it. Maui set about working out a way to deceive Tongafusifonua so that he could steal the fishhook away. He decided to seduce Tongafusi-fonua's wife, Tonga.

While they were making love, Tonga was said to have romantically whispered the mysterious secrets of the fishhook to Maui, giving him all the information he needed to find it, as well as the details on how to use it.

This story cleverly illustrates that sex is not only a union of physical and social benefit, but it can also be used as an instrument of political manipulation.

Above *Pirogue, Vitu Islands* from *Voyage de la Corvette* by J.S.C. Dumont d'Urville (1790–1842). Canoes are important symbols within the myths of the islands of Oceania, signifying movement and survival. On many of the islands throughout Polynesia, Micronesia, and Melanesia, ancient canoes have been found beside rock paintings, and represent the travel and migration of ancestors.

AUSTRALIAN ABORIGINAL MYTHOLOGY

Right **Map of Australia's mainland.** Australian Aboriginal mythology is extensive and wide ranging. All the myths retold here relate to specific places and landscapes that are found on the Australian mainland.

Below **Clan ancestral mythology, Arnhem Land.** This bark painting represents an episode in an ancestral story. Aboriginal myth is considered as "living." Events relate to ancestral stories, and explain natural and social events. The stories are often recorded in artwork distinctive to each indigenous region.

Australian Aboriginal people see the social and physical aspects of their world as very closely interwoven. They believe that during a creation period, known in English as the "Dreaming," their spiritual Ancestors performed heroic deeds, and in doing so molded a relatively featureless landscape into the present form. These ancestral beings had human traits such as virtues, pleasures, and vices, and were also capable of dying and being transformed. The Ancestors often took the form of particular animals and birds, but were also diseases, plants, and atmospheric and cosmological phenomena. The Ancestors created the world as Aboriginal people experienced it, and laid down the rules and cultural practices that their descendants continued to follow. Although they were active in the past, the Ancestors are still considered to influence Aboriginal Australia today.

The Dreaming mythology comprises an Aboriginal system of beliefs that provides answers to the great universal religious questions of humankind, concerning the origin, meaning, purpose, and destiny of life. Aboriginal people can, through their participation in ceremonies and rituals, connect directly with the Dreaming. The Ancestors are generally seen as the totems for their clans, thereby providing a link to present-day people. Aboriginal people acknowledge the Ancestors' role in creating landscape features such as wetlands, hills, forests, and water holes. Some Aboriginal people have, through actual dreams, gained deeper insights into their past, and have had revealed to them the significance of particular places in their landscape. Nevertheless, the Dreaming and Dreaming Ancestors are not the direct products of dreams. To Aboriginal people, the power of the Dreaming is present everywhere, just waiting to be discovered. The "Dreaming" can loosely be described as the entire body of mythology that provides Aboriginal people with insight into their religious traditions. It therefore relates to the Ancestors, the customs, and sacred objects they introduced, and the

sacred places that they left in the landscape. Although chiefly concerned with past events, the Dreaming is still of primary importance to many Aboriginal people for making sense of their modern world.

THE DREAMING AS HISTORY

Across Australia the "Dreaming" was known by a number of language terms: for example, Ngarranggarni (Gooniyandi people, southeastern Kimberley), Djang (Kunwinjku people, western Arnhem Land), Wongar (Yolngu people, northeastern Arnhem Land), Tjukurpa (Western Desert region), Altyjerre (Arrernte people, MacDonnell Ranges, Central Australia), Muramura (desert groups, east of Lake Eyre, Central Australia), Bulurru (Djabugay people, northeastern Queensland), and Yemurraki (Wemba Wemba people, northwestern Victoria). A related word in Aboriginal English is "Law," which refers to the body of religious and cultural knowledge that is used to inform and direct Aboriginal society. A "law man" or "law woman" is a person who has been through the relevant initiation ceremonies where they have received important religious knowledge. In some northern areas, Aboriginal people refer to the Dreaming knowledge that they possess as their "history."

Dreaming Ancestors are central to Aboriginal religion and the sharing of beliefs and customs, helping to bind together Aboriginal people from a wide-ranging area. For example, in northeastern Arnhem Land, Yolngu people celebrate, in ceremony, the arrival of two sisters and a brother, collectively known as the Djanggau, during the Dreaming creation period. They came to the region by paddling a bark canoe from the Land of the Dead in the east. They traveled across Yolngu country, transforming the landscape, and after many deeds departed to the west where the sun goes. The first people were the children of the two sisters, who gave them territorial boundaries. Another sister pair in Yolngu mythology was the Wawalag sisters, who traveled north across Arnhem Land to Roper River. They arrived at a water hole, which was the home of Yulunggul, the Ancestral Python. After giving birth to children, they were all swallowed by Yulunggul, but later regurgitated. The Djungguwan ritual celebrates the Wawalag Dreaming, with young initiates being symbolically regurgitated. Both the Djanggau and Wawalag myths are ritually important,

and form the basis of the Yolngu religious system. It is impossible to speak of Yolngu culture without making reference to these particular mythologies.

Before the arrival of Europeans in Australia, all the different Aboriginal groups possessed religious beliefs that explained how people, the land, plants and animals, and their customs came into being. In south-eastern Australia, many of the main creation Ancestors were male figures, whereas elsewhere there was, typically, a much greater range of Dreaming identities. It is thought that this may have been a post-European development. These "high gods" had names such as Korna, Kulda, Ngurunderi, Nureli, Bunjil, Baiame, and Daramulun. Whether such male Ancestors were so dominant in southeastern Australian cultures before Aboriginal experience with non-Aboriginal people will never be known for certain. Nevertheless, there is a possibility that the rapid demise of the Aboriginal population on the frontier significantly enhanced the importance of their beliefs, in particular, Ancestors, especially those associated with death and living in the Skyworld.

Above **Three-masted European ship with trailing anchor.** After the arrival of non-Aboriginal people, the importance and strength of Aboriginal beliefs grew as the indigenous population started to diminish. Although based on the past, these beliefs are still very important today.

Left **Carved stone disk.** In some Aboriginal cultures it is believed that the Ancestors of the Dreaming and their weapons became disks. They represent each Ancestor's immortal spirit, and show the specific area that they came from.

Right **A hunter with two kangaroos.** In the Ngarrindjeri Dreaming, kangaroos were much bigger than they are now. The skins of these animals were used to form parts of the landscape. Kangaroos are also found in the Aboriginal Skyworld.

NGURUNDERI, A LOWER MURRAY DREAMING

In the Ngarrindjeri Dreaming, known as the Kulhal, Ngurunderi was the first Ancestor to wake. Three or four other Ancestors woke later, some complaining that they were cold and hungry. Ngurunderi told one Ancestor to make a fish, and then he taught the other Ancestors how to cook it. He then ordered the Ancestors to collect firewood and water. These Ancestors lived somewhere in the inland region of southeastern Australia, so Ngurunderi sent other Ancestors away to lands he was creating, while he and his sons drove an enormous Murray cod, Pondi, down the Darling and Murray Rivers. These rivers were just small streams, but as the giant fish pushed its way through the mud, it created the deep channels of the rivers, and with a flip of its tail it made lagoons. Ngurunderi was losing Pondi, so with smoke signals he managed to get the help of his brother-in-law, Nepeli, who was camped

downstream on the southern shore of Lake Alexandrina. They finally caught Pondi near Raukkan. Ngurunderi tore the large fish into small pieces, throwing each of the fragments back into the water, creating the different species of fish that live in the waters today.

Ngurunderi stayed in the Lower Murray region for a while. He was a large and very powerful man with two wives, who were sisters, and four children. Ngurunderi was a renowned hunter, along with Nepeli, and Nepeli's brother-in-law, Waiyungari. As evidence of their hunting prowess, Nepeli and Waiyungari were credited with having created numerous salt lagoons by pegging out fresh kangaroo skins, and denuding these places of grass. (The kangaroos back then were much larger than today.) One day, two of Ngurunderi's children strayed into the bush, and were lost. To escape the wrath of their husband, the wives ran away. The two sisters had also broken a food taboo by eating bony bream, which was forbidden to young women. Ngurunderi chased them

Right *The Murray, 1836* **by Thomas Mitchell (1792–1855).** After Europeans moved through the Australian landscape, different representations of the scenery appeared. According to the Lower Murray Dreaming, an Ancestor created these lands when he followed a huge Murray cod.

across the land, and, in doing so, created many geographic features. He made fresh water soaks by digging between sand dunes, and his brush shelters became hills. While he was desperately searching for his children, Ngurunderi quarreled with Parampari, a sorcerer at Salt Creek. Ngurunderi killed him and then burnt his body, the remains of which formed a large granite outcrop on the ocean beach near Kingston. After finding his children, Ngurunderi finally caught his wives and beat them, but they escaped again. He was tired of chasing the women, so he commanded the sea to flow and drown them. The bodies of the wives became The Pages islands, which can be seen in the Backstairs Passage near Kangaroo Island.

Ngurunderi had family connections to other Ancestral creators. The Barkindji people who lived along the Darling River knew that Ngurunderi's two wives had earlier been in their country, when married to Tulu, the Kingfisher Ancestor. Here, it was believed that Waku, the Crow Ancestor, had chased the women. Two warriors from Ngurunderi's group returned to the Upper Murray-Darling area, where their Dreaming adventures had begun, but were never heard of again by the Ngarrindjeri.

One of Ngurunderi's sons traveled further south, and was attacked and chased by a "big devil" named Mirka, who emerged from the Blue Lake at Mount Gambier. The son fled north, crossing the Mount Lofty Ranges to arrive at Willunga, near the present city of Adelaide. Here, Ngurunderi joined the fight and wounded Mirka. The congealing blood of the "big devil" formed a rich red ochre deposit at this place, which is now known as Red Ochre Cove.

After leaving Ngarrindjeri territory, Ngurunderi went on to create other lands to the west. Before leaving, he foretold the coming of Europeans and their destruction of the environment, saying "Beware of *puruki* (ants)." Leaving the Lower Murray, Ngurunderi swam to Kangaroo Island. One of his sons was accidentally left behind, but found his way by grabbing at the cord thrown toward him, the end of which was attached to Ngurunderi's testicles.

Ngurunderi and his family went to the western end of the island. From this point of land, he threw his spears out into the water, and they became rocky islets. The creation of new rivers, hills, and other features in the Lower Murray ceased after Ngurunderi left, and he went to live in the Skyworld, Waieruwar, which was a place where life was extremely comfortable, and there were many kangaroos and emus for him to hunt.

The legacy of Ngurunderi was tangible to Ngarrindjeri people. The present major landforms were shaped by his powerful actions. Another illustration

of Ngurunderi's creative power was to give numerous fine bones to the bony bream fish. Thunder was regarded as his voice, while rainbows showed him urinating. Customs attributed to Ngurunderi's law include the prohibition of young male initiates eating certain types of fish. He and his son, Matamai, are also credited with introducing mortuary rites, which involve smoking the dead, to Ngarrindjeri people.

Above **Aboriginal bark painting of two fish.** A number of Aboriginal Dreamings tell how enormous fish moved through small, muddy streams, creating rivers and lagoons with their gigantic fins and tails.

THE DREAMING LANDSCAPE

The landscape was an artifact that Dreaming Ancestors left behind for Aboriginal people. Through their actions Ancestors created the landscape, forming hills by killing a large kangaroo, making a quartzite rock formation with the fat of a cooked snake, or forming a water hole with their tears. After the main creation period was over, these places were thought to retain some of their Dreaming character, as well as part of the essence of the particular creator Ancestor. These sacred memorials, or "sacred sites," may be such things as a mountain, water body, plant formation, rock outcrop, or another environmental or geographical feature. They form part of the trails that knowledgeable Aboriginal people recognize, and are seen as evidence that the Dreaming actually happened. The sacred memorials are central places that provide connections that link present-day Aboriginal people with the Dreaming. The number of sacred places linked together through the webs of Dreaming traditions is enormous.

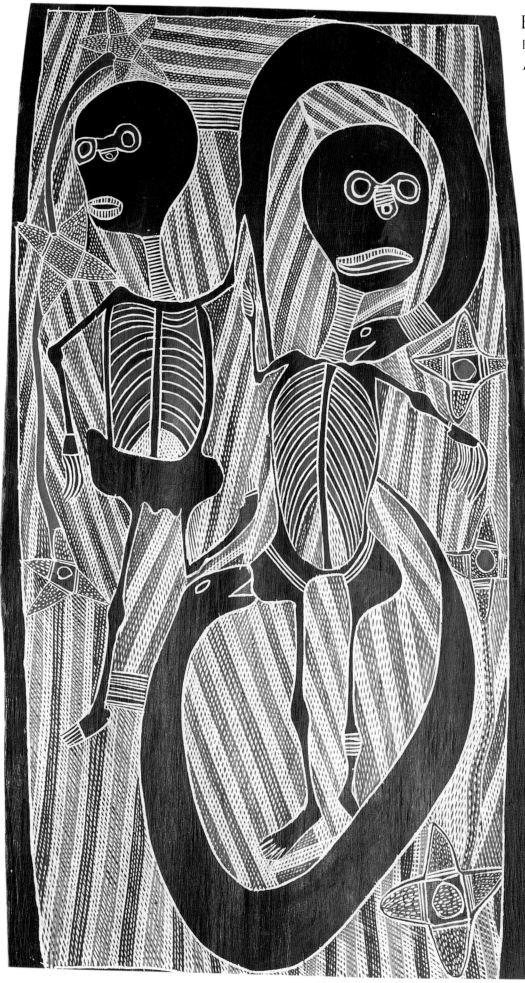

BUNYIPS, WATER SPIRITS FROM SOUTHEASTERN AUSTRALIA

Throughout southeastern Australia there are recorded accounts from Aboriginal people of water spirits, now commonly known as "bunyips." The early European settlers were convinced that bunyips existed. Although Europeans generally referred to them as "bunyips," there was much variation in how they were described; some looked like large and ferocious emus, seals, crocodiles, and serpents, while others were more like hairy humans. In the case of the latter, they appear to be related to the "yowie" spirits—apelike monsters from southeastern Australia. The term "bunyip" is from the Wergaia language in northwestern Victoria, where it was originally recorded as *banib*. The word "yowie" was derived from *yuwi*, from the Yuwaalaraay language of northeastern New South Wales. The European colonists recorded from Aboriginal groups in the Hunter River region of eastern New South Wales, the term "wowee" used for bunyips.

The variable descriptions of bunyips are not solely accounted for by the cultural differences between Aboriginal groups, as variation occurred even within the same region. For example, in the 1840s along the Murray River in South Australia, it was noted that local Aboriginal people had difficulty in describing the water spirit being, some thinking that it was like an enormous starfish, whereas others described a spirit with more humanlike features. Given that many Aboriginal

Left **Mythical figures surrounded by a sacred python.** Among the thousands of mythic paths that crisscross the Australian mainland are tracks commemorating the journeys of giant snakes.

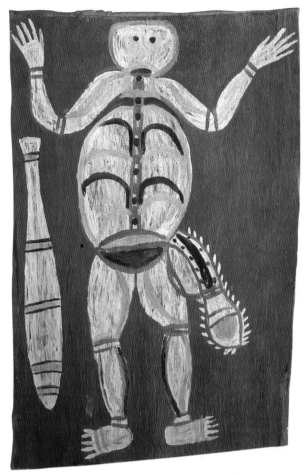

SKYWORLD

The belief in the existence of the Heavens or Skyworld as a region much like the world we live in was widespread across Aboriginal Australia. Various star constellations and planets were considered to be Dreaming Ancestors, while large features, for example, the Milky Way, were seen as celestial rivers or large canoes.

The association between the human spirit and the Skyworld is broad, involving both ends of a person's life. In many Aboriginal cultures it was believed that the spirits of babies fell down from the sky and that secret knowledge could be gained through visits to the Skyworld, usually using special ropes. Aboriginal people considered that the spirits of their dead followed the Ancestor's path into the Heavens. The Skyworld was considered to begin at the height of a large tree or small hill, and was therefore part of the landscape, which meant that it was not beyond the physical reach of Aboriginal people.

rheumatism. The booming noises were also linked to the broken up gum trees that often floated down the Murray River into the lakes, particularly during the heavy seasonal floods.

In the Lower Murray, bunyips would lie submerged in the shallow waters near the edge of the lakes waiting for human victims. When children washed their hands in lake water after eating, the smell of grease from fish and duck meat was said to attract the bunyip. Ngarrindjeri people claimed that a man was able to rescue a child abducted by the bunyip, by rubbing a magical substance over his body and descending, by a rope, to the bottom of the lake. He could then drag the child out from among the sleeping bunyips, and get back safely. If he was unsuccessful, it was thought that the child would eventually be transformed into a bunyip. Ngurunderi, the main Dreaming creator of the Lower Murray region, also suffered from the actions of these water spirits. A bunyip tore holes in his nets, which prevented him from fishing for his family.

Certain spots along the Murray River, often at the base of cliffs, were considered to be the main refuges for bunyips. Understandably, Aboriginal people did not swim at these places, and avoided passing by on reed rafts and in bark canoes at night. Bunyips were said to produce the bubbles that were sometimes seen in the lake water, and when they were swimming they made the unexplained ripples often seen in the river. Ngarrindjeri people claimed that whirlpools were bunyips cleaning out their homes.

One Ngarrindjeri man believed that a particular hole he found along the edge of a lake was another bunyip lair. This water hole had a foul stench, along with a strange whooshing noise.

Left **Warrior spirit from Croker Island.** These spirits in the landscape are sometimes threatening. This makes certain areas, such as deep water holes, very dangerous to venture near at particular times.

Below **Horned spirit figures.** Depending on the place of Dreaming, spirits can either live within part of the landscape, such as in rocks or caves, or their bodies might create significant landforms, such as mountain ranges.

spirits had the ability to change shape and use sorcery, it is not surprising that the bunyip beliefs have a myth-like quality. Due to the wide-ranging descriptions, it is best not to treat the bunyip as a single entity, but as a class of spirit beings based around permanent inland water bodies.

Aboriginal people living in the extreme south of Victoria, near where the city of Melbourne now stands, believed that an amphibious "bunyip" spirit was the size of a full-grown calf, and had dusky gray feathers. The bunyip here was considered to have a magical power over humans, causing them considerable misfortune. Places where there were many eels tended to be where bunyips lived, as this was their food. On one occasion, Aboriginal people claimed that a bunyip lured a woman to her death by distracting her with a large catch of eels. It was considered extremely bad luck to kill or injure a bunyip.

The best-recorded traditions concerning the bunyip are from the Lower Murray region of South Australia. Here, the bunyip, known by Ngarrindjeri people as the *mulgyewonk,* had some humanlike features. It was said to have a body resembling a seal, a bearded face like a man, and very long, trailing hair that looked like waterweed. This water spirit was generally thought to be a threat to people. The bunyip could hurt people with sorcery, and the booming noises it made were thought to cause

Above **An incised hair ornament.** As part of various rituals and ceremonies, certain body decorations and headgear are worn.

PURRUKUPARLI, WHO BROUGHT DEATH TO THE TIWI

The Tiwi people live on Melville and Bathurst Islands, north of Darwin in the Northern Territory. Before European settlement, they were largely isolated from the Aboriginal cultures on the Australian mainland, due to the large breadth of Clarence Strait, and to the roughness of the seas for canoe travel. The Tiwi believe that during the Parlinari creation period, an elderly blind woman named Mudunungkarla rose out of the ground at Murupianga, in the southeast of Melville Island. She had three infants—two girls, Wuriupranala and Murupiangkarla, and a boy, Purrukuparli. Mudunungkarla crawled northward, carrying her children from her breasts, and while doing this she created many of the major landforms, and finally separated the islands from the mainland. Before leaving the islands, she also made the numerous freshwater wells, and left behind plants and animals for her children to survive on.

In order to start creating families, Purrukuparli visited the homes of the various spirit children, to bring some of them back to become people. He lived at a place called Impanari on Melville Island with his family—a wife, Pima; his much-loved baby son, Tjinini; and his unmarried "brother," Thaparra. Purrukuparli, like his mother, was a major creation Ancestor. On one occasion, Jurumu, the Wedge-tail Eagle, and Mudati, the Fork-tailed Kite, accidentally made fire when they rubbed two sticks together. They decided to approach Purrukuparli, and wanted him to put it out. However, he recognized the value of the fire in keeping them warm and for cooking

We are all visitors to this time, this place...Our purpose here is to observe, to learn, to grow, to love...and then we return home.

AUSTRALIAN ABORIGINAL PROVERB

their food. Purrukuparli lit a large bark torch and gave it to his sister, Wuriupranala, the Sun Woman. He gave a smaller torch to his "brother," Thaparra, the Moon Man. Today, because of the differences in torch size, the light from the sun is stronger than the light from the moon. Purrukuparli made the first large painted poles for the Tiwi people, and created songs and dances, and established the Kurlama initiation ceremonies.

As was typical of most Aboriginal families, Purrukuparli and Pima were apart during the day. Pima would go into the bush each morning to gather food, carrying the infant Tjinini, while Purrukuparli went away hunting. She would return to camp with Tjinini and the food in the late afternoon. It became an illicit practice of Thaparra's to meet up with Pima

PERFORMANCE

Aboriginal people hold ceremonies that may be both sacred and heavily ritualized, or on other occasions, secular and less formal events. They often involve widely dispersed groups coming together at a single place, which may be an area of sacred Dreaming significance. In sacred ceremonies, the dancers will act out events associated with particular Dreaming Ancestors, while secular ceremonies usually relate to everyday incidents or historic events. Aboriginal people hold ceremonies associated with births, initiations, and mourning, which might last many days. They may involve singing, playing musical instruments, and performance. The participants typically wear special decorations, headgear, and feathers, and have totemic designs painted with ochre on their bodies. At larger events, occurring over several days, there are opportunities for people to arrange marriages, settle disputes, and to trade. Some ceremonies are formally passed on to neighboring groups, establishing good relations between potential enemies.

Above **Ritual dance ceremony.** Ceremonies and performances serve as living records of the past, as well as being vital in ensuring that the stories of the Dreaming are passed down to younger generations.

during the day. They would leave Tjinini in the shade, while they went off together to be lovers. This had been going on for some time when, on one particularly hot day, Pima was late getting back. As the sun shifted, Tjinini was exposed to the sun and died.

Purrukuparli was enraged and stricken with grief when he returned to find his son dead, and his wife was nowhere to be seen. When he found Pima, and discovered what had happened, she was severely beaten with a club. Pima was remorseful, chanting a song that means, "Evil woman am I to have caused the death of my son." Purrukuparli refused to allow Thaparra the three days it would take to bring Tjinini back to life. The two male Ancestors then fought with forked clubs, from one end of Melville Island to the other. Both were injured about the face and body. When the fight was over, Purrukuparli picked up his son's body, which was wrapped in paperbark, and walked backward into the sea. As he did this he uttered, "As my son has died, and will never return, so shall all men." The creation period was coming to a close. At the place where Purrukuparli drowned a whirlpool appeared, and his footprints

remained visible on the ground nearby. Before Purrukuparli died, he stabbed Thaparra in the eye and killed him. Thaparra became the moon, and although he died, he is able to come back to life, as the new moon, after three days of darkness. The dark spots on the moon's surface are the wounds he received from fighting with his angry "brother," Purrukuparli.

Pima was left alone in the bush, and became a stone curlew. This bird has a wailing call, which, when heard by the Tiwi people at night, is said to be Pima calling out for her dead son. The curlew

as a dark mark on its head where Purrukuparli's club had violently struck Pima.

The Tiwi people also have a song that they say was sung by Pima in mourning, after Purrukuparli had killed her lover, Thaparra. In more recent times, a woman would sing this when goading her husband to take action, in response to her illicit affairs becoming more widely known within the community. Tokampini, the Honeyeater Bird Man, established the first Pukumani mourning ceremony, as a mark of respect after the death of Purrukuparli.

Above **A distorted female figure.** Images like this were thought to be used in magical processes to inflict harm, or gain revenge. Some Dreaming stories tell of dangerous women feared by men because they are drawn to them, similar to the Sirens of Greek and Roman mythology.

Right **A rock painting of mimih spirits.** Mimih and men come together in many Aboriginal stories from Arnhem Land. Although sometimes shy, the mimih spirits did make themselves known to Aboriginal people, teaching humans the arts of painting, water divining, and cooking.

MIMIH SPIRITS OF THE ARNHEM LAND ESCARPMENT

The mimih spirits are important to the Kunwinjku people of western Arnhem Land, although they are not Dreaming Ancestors. They are similar to humans in form, but very long and thin, and so delicate that out in the open, a slight breeze causes them to face into it and brace themselves, and a very strong wind would break their slender necks. The mimih spirits have excellent vision and hearing, and are able to avoid contact with people they detect coming their way by disappearing into rock faces, which they open like a door by speaking to the rocks or by blowing onto them. They have pets, which may be possums, rock wallabies, geckos, rock pythons, or echidnas. If these are killed, the mimih spirits are believed to feel grief, and to want retribution. The mimih are considered to lead separate lives to humans, with a culture of their own. They live inside a landscape embedded in escarpment rocks, and this landscape has its own plants and a sun.

Unlike many other spirit beings, Aboriginal people generally regarded the mimih as harmless to people. Some Kunwinjku hunters have claimed to have met mimih, and also talked to them. The mimih are believed to have painted their images in the rock art galleries of the escarpment. The Kunwinjku also believe that their Ancestors were taught how to paint by the mimih spirits, who showed them by painting on rock. The mimih also instructed them on how to find water when it was dry, as well as how to cut up animals and cook them for food.

Mimih spirits and people both fear Namarrgon, the Lightning Man, who is shown in paintings as having stone axes,

Below **A male spirit painting.** Mimih spirits are often painted on bark. These spirits generally do things that humans do, but they live in a special landscape behind rocks. Mimih spirits are usually portrayed as very fragile and delicate.

which make lightning, that stick out from his head, elbows, and knees. The mimih spirits bury their own axes when he is about, so as to avoid his anger. When visiting the "stone country" (western Arnhem Land escarpment), Aboriginal people typically call out to the mimih spirits, announcing who they are and why they are there. Aboriginal people were warned not to follow the mimih to their homes in the rocks, as they might never return. In one myth, a young man followed a mimih spirit into his cave so he could sleep with the mimih's sisters. The young man was trapped there until his father, who had special powers, was able to break into the cave to kill the mimih.

Left **The kangaroo and dog.** These animals are enemies because the kangaroo promised to paint the dog to make it look beautiful. The kangaroo made the dog look ugly, so, for revenge, the dog will always chase the kangaroo.

The red paintings commonly found in the rock art caves on the western edge of the escarpment, which archaeologists refer to as the "dynamic figure style," are considered by the Kunwinjku to be mimih spirits. They believe that some of them are painted in blood. The mimih spirits are often painted on bark, where they are seen hunting, giving birth, and participating in ceremonies that regenerate kangaroos and people. Aboriginal people believe that these spirits were able to magically bring down a vertical rock wall to a horizontal level, paint on it, and return it to its original position. Strange things that present-day Aboriginal people see in the rock art are said to have been painted by the mimih. Today the bark paintings of the spirits are important for teaching younger generations about the Dreaming, especially those who no longer have the opportunities to visit rock galleries.

The Kunwinjku have a myth about two mimih spirits, Ngurdyawok and Nawalabik. The following account shows that their lives were parallel with humans, having all the pleasures and vices normally associated with people. Ngurdyawok was attracted to Nawalabik's two wives, despite them being his sisters. One day, when Ngurdyawok and Nawalabik were out collecting sugarbag (native bee nests), Nawalabik cut off Ngurdyawok's head with a stone ax. Back at camp, Nawalabik told his wives that Ngurdyawok had gone hunting. Then, Nawalabik went away with his dog to hunt echidna.

The birds eventually told the women what had happened, and they got their father's relatives together to punish their husband. Nawalabik was confronted, and for three days managed to dodge spears that were thrown at him by the relatives of his wives to resolve the dispute. When it was over, he slept at his wives' camp, but his father-in-law killed him with a club.

Nawalabik's dog saw all this happening, and after snapping the rope that had him tied to a tree, he covered himself with his owner's blood and fled to the camp of Nawalabik's brother. A large number of warriors, Nawalabik's relatives, gathered and followed the dog back to the body of Nawalabik, and respectfully buried him. They then went to the camp of Ngurdyawok's people, who were holding a ceremonial dance. They hid in the shadows, and as soon as they got their chance, the relatives of Nawalabik revenged his death by rushing the people of the camp and killing them all.

PUKUMANI MOURNING CEREMONY

The Tiwi people of Melville and Bathurst Islands in northern Australia hold Pukumani ceremonies in honor of the deceased, and in celebration of their Dreaming Ancestors. These ceremonies are held as a series of mortuary rituals that release the spirit of a recently deceased person. To those outside their culture, the distinctively carved burial poles, which are erected vertically near the grave, have become widely recognized symbols of Tiwi culture, and are often made today for sale to art galleries and museums. The poles are cut from the trunks of ironwood trees, and may be up to 10 ft (3 m) in length. They are decorated with designs that relate to the mythology and the land. Heavily decorated spears and bark containers are also made for ceremonies. The mythology behind the Pukumani ceremony is based on the Purrukuparli Ancestor who, in Tiwi Dreaming, first brought them death.

Right **Aboriginal bark painting of a funeral ceremony.** Funeral rituals vary. Some rites involve smoking, which clears away unwanted spirits.

WANDJINA, SPIRITS FROM THE KIMBERLEY

The wandjina spirits are important, as they control the monsoon clouds that bear rain. Aboriginal people consider them to have both humanlike and cloudlike forms. In one sense, the wandjina represent the monsoon clouds. In the Kimberley, Aboriginal people sing to these spirits to keep them calm during the monsoon. In some areas, the wandjina are also considered to be major creators of the child spirits that enter the bodies of women to become babies. Similarly, the wandjina control the child spirits of animals, such as kangaroos and emus. Like people, they have been involved in many adventures, which are illustrated in Kimberley rock art. The wandjina have, at various times, fought with people. They have also had fights among themselves, over such things as the stealing of wives. Each wandjina spirit had at least one personal

name. The mythology behind them is extensive, with their intersecting paths spread throughout much of the Kimberley region.

The wandjina spirits are featured in some of the most spectacular examples of rock art surviving in the world today. The wandjina figures are often very large, some measuring over 20 ft (6 m) in height, and typically painted in black, red, or yellow lines over a white background. Their figures may be represented in full, with arms or legs, or as just the head and halo, or reduced to the extreme as eyes peering through the halo. Their headdress can be described as their hair, but can also be seen as cloud. The strands of material coming from the hair may be feather decoration, or the lightning under the control of the wandjina.

Protocol demands that caves of wandjina paintings be approached properly, with the names of visitors announced, and by telling the spirits that they have upheld their religious obligations since the last

ROCK ART

Rock art sites occur widely, but unevenly, across Australia, and are part of traditions that stretch back over 40,000 years. The techniques are rock painting, stenciling, and engraving. It is estimated that there are presently over 100,000 examples of surviving rock art in Australia, representing a small part of all the rock art ever produced here. The use of "rock art" to describe these traditions presents a problem, as it is generally not known why individual pieces were produced. In general, from the few accounts received directly from Aboriginal artists, it is known that rock art sites collectively contain images of people, Dreaming Ancestors, spirit beings, animals, plants, artifacts, and cosmic phenomena, and are often linked to particular cultural sites. Some rock art contains images of extinct animals, such as Thylacines. Aboriginal rock art painting traditions continue today, particularly in central and northern Australia, where they are strongly connected to Aboriginal ceremonial life.

Left **Aboriginal rock paintings near Alice Springs, Northern Territory.** These particular paintings mark the place where women of the Dreaming watched the performance of a sacred ceremony by men of the tribe. In the Dreaming women shared the knowledge of important tribal rites.

visit. At some sites, visitors burn tobacco for the spirits. As with many important painting sites across Australia that have mythological significance, there must be no unruly behavior or any physical damage done to the paintings. Tradition demands that the wandjina paintings are regularly repainted to conserve them, which apart from maintaining their galleries, helps to maintain the fertility of the region. Nevertheless, most Aboriginal people believe that people did not do the original wandjina rock paintings, but that they represent the image of each spirit as they died. If the above practices are not kept, and the wandjina become angry, it is believed that they will strike down people with lightning, cause a flood, or bring on a cyclone. The wandjina art has also appeared on carved boab nuts, and on artifacts such as bark containers.

The following account of a wandjina named Wodjin is from the Ngarinyin, Worora, and Wunambul people, but is also widely known across the Kimberley region, with many variations.

Two boys were playing with a bird named Tumbi, which they thought was a honeyeater, but it was actually an owl, and the son of a wandjina. They mistreated Tumbi very badly, plucking his feathers, flicking him with speargrass, and throwing him naked through the air. When the bird spirit eventually escaped, he flew into the sky to complain to the wandjina spirits. In revenge, a wandjina known as Wodjin brought together his fellow spirits. Although he sent out animals to find out where the people of the boys were, they were not initially found, as the animals did not want to reveal them. Eventually, Wodjin created a bicycle lizard from his penis, and the people were finally located at a spring near Tunbai. The wandjina spirits came together on top of a nearby hill, and held ceremonies in secret. Although

Wodjin had become too ill to fight, the other spirits formed themselves into two groups and attacked the people. Afterward, the tracks of the wandjina remained as two scars running down the hill. A great flood was called, and most of the remaining people were drowned.

The two boys who had caused the conflict through their mistreatment of Tumbi managed to escape. Some people say that they hid from the wandjina spirits in the pouch of a kangaroo, and were later able to start their whole tribe again. Others assert that they eventually crawled inside a split boab tree to hide from the rain and lightning. Unfortunately for them, the tree was a wandjina, and once they were inside they were crushed to death. After the massacre, the wandjina spirits split up and went their separate ways.

Most traveled westwards, some to as far north as Kalumburu, others south to Fitzroy River. Wodjin hurt his foot in a cave known as Wanalirri, and decided to stay there.

Today, this site is a major rock art gallery containing powerful images, among which local Aboriginal people identify Tumbi the owl and the bicycle lizard. It is at this site that the image of the powerful Wodjin is particularly large and imposing.

Left **Spirits on a hill.** This abstract bark painting is said to represent the gathering of Wandjina spirits before they decide to fight with the people who have offended them. Wandjinas call on the help of animal spirits when they are trying to find people.

Opposite page **The "Lightning Man" of northern Australia.** This bark painting depicts the legendary Wala-Undayna spirit with axes growing out of his knees. He moves across the land terrifying humans and other spirits.

BARK PAINTINGS

The bark painting art styles of Arnhem Land are directly related to the extensive rock art galleries found elsewhere in the region. Many of the early bark paintings collected from this region were on bark slabs that had been used in making the roof of wet-season shelters. Bark paintings convey information about the landscape, and are often based on local myths, containing images of major Dreaming Ancestors such as the Djanggau and the Wawalag Sisters, or of spirit beings such as the mimih. Food animals, such as kangaroos, turtles, and barramundi fish also appear in bark paintings, as do images of past contact with strangers, like the Macassans and European buffalo hunters. From the early twentieth century, European interest in bark paintings has placed them in the international indigenous art market. Since then, this art style has spread to many Aboriginal groups that formerly did not produce bark paintings.

Right **Bark painting in an x-ray style.** The cross-hatching relates to a specific tribe.

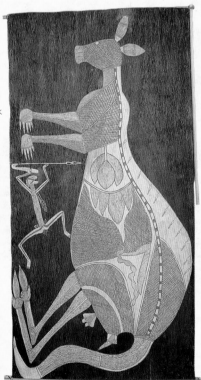

Right **Hunting kangaroos.**
Legends tell of "taboo"
areas that are found on
the land. One story re-
lates how a man hunted
a kangaroo. When the
man was swimming, the
kangaroo came back to
drown him. This unusual
and immoral behavior
made the area where this
happened "taboo."

FIRE DREAMINGS

Fire is important to Aboriginal people as it provides warmth, protection against darkness and spirits, and is a means to cook food and make artifacts. Aboriginal people practiced "fire-stick farming"—burning bush to help with hunting, to make traveling easier, and to produce food plants for the animals they hunted. Fire Dreamings are widespread throughout Australia, and typically have one Ancestor who knows how to make fire, but who selfishly keeps it secret from other Ancestors. Eventually, this knowledge of fire is discovered and stolen, and becomes widely known to people. As a result of this, fire escapes and is now present as bushfires.

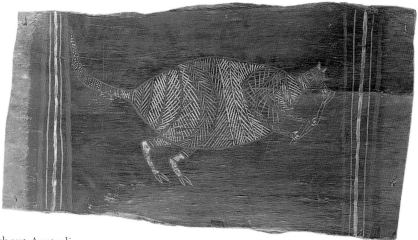

Aboriginal people living near Katherine, in the Northern Territory, have a myth where only the Crocodile Ancestor possessed fire. The Rainbow Bird kept asking him to share it, but he was repeatedly denied. The Rainbow Bird had to camp without fire to cook his meals. This made him angry, so one day he swooped down from a tree to try to snatch the fire-sticks. He missed the first time, but he later managed to steal the fire-sticks when the Crocodile Ancestor had turned the other way. The Rainbow Bird Ancestor flew into the trees, telling the Crocodile that he would give fire to all men. The Rainbow Bird placed the fire-sticks in his rump. From that time onward, rainbow birds live in dry country, and crocodiles are restricted to living in water.

The Western Desert people of central Western Australia have a Dreaming myth where Tjilpi, meaning "old man," remained in camp while his son, Yilgadidi, went hunting with other young men. The hunters returned with kangaroo and possum meat, which was cooked and eaten, but none was given to Tjilpi. The old man was both hungry and angry, so when the young men left again to hunt, he put out all the fires by covering them with sand. He then took the fire-stick with him on a long trip east, camping first at Walangara. On returning to the campsite, the young men were unable to start their fires, and they became very cold during the night. Alone, Yilgadidi tracked his father to Walangara, but discovered that his father had already left, and his campfire was cold.

Tjilpi continued on his journey, finally heading south toward the Southern Ocean. He entered the sea near Eucla. Yilgadidi caught up with Tjilpi when the water was up to his neck, with the fire-stick held above his head. Tjilpi was dragged from behind, back to land. Yilgadidi saved the fire-stick, and then camped with his father nearby, where they eventually turned into rocks. In a related account, it was the Turkey Bustard Ancestor who had fire and fled to the coast near Eucla. Here, he intended to hide the fire

Right **The origins of the
whale.** The creation of
animals comes from con-
flicts between, and the
changes in form of, the
Ancestors. One Ancestor
of the Booandik people,
Kounterbull, became a
whale after he was
speared in the neck
during the battle over fire.
The wound became the
blowhole of the whale.

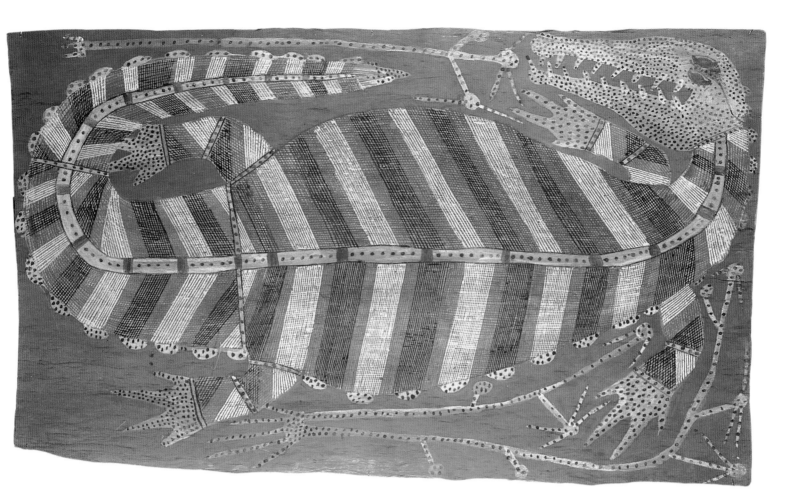

in the flint nodules under the sea. In this account, it was the Hawk Ancestors who rescued the flints, which are still accessible today, but only at low tide on extremely calm, windless days.

The Booandik people in the southeast region of South Australia believed that the Ancestor Mar was the one who solely owned fire in the Dreaming period, and that this was hidden inside an ornament on his head. Other Ancestors met to discuss how they could discover the secret of fire. Several of them tried to spy on Mar, and the Ancestor Tatkanna had his chest singed red from the heat of Mar's fire. When fire was at last caught in a dead grasstree flower spike, it accidentally spread to dry grass and shrubs, where it quickly grew into a bushfire.

When he realized that the fire was stolen, Mar rushed to where the other Ancestors were camped, and started a fight. One of the Ancestors, a large man named Kounterbull, received a deep spear wound in the back of his neck. He rushed into the sea where he became a whale and was later seen spouting "steam" from his wound. Mar flew up into a tree and became the sulfur-crested cockatoo, which has yellow feathers ("fire") on the top of its head that are only visible when the crest is extended. Tatkanna turned into the scarlet robin, which has a red breast.

Ever since this happened, Aboriginal people have been able to continue to make fire, using the fire-sticks made from dried grasstree flower spikes and dry shrubs that dot the landscape.

In western Victoria, Aboriginal people believed that during their Dreaming period, fire had been the property of the Waa, Raven Ancestors, living in the Grampian Mountains. The Ravens enjoyed the ability to make fire, and would not let any of the other Ancestors get a light. An Ancestor named Yuuloin Keear, described as a Fire-tail Wren Ancestor (probably the Beautiful Fire-tail), saw a group of Ravens throwing fire-sticks about as they played. He picked one up and flew away. Tarrakukk, the Hawk, robbed Yuuloin Keear of his fire-stick, but in the process he started wildfires that raged across the country. Since that time, Aboriginal people have been able to start fires.

Above **Ancient crocodile.** Stories from Aboriginal people living near Katherine, in the Northern Territory, tell of the great Crocodile Ancestor who possessed fire, but did not want to share it with anyone else. The wily Rainbow Bird tricked the crocodile into sending out the fire to all men.

WESTERN DESERT ART

The Western Desert is a large region where Aboriginal people speak one of dozens of related dialects, and share many of the same Dreaming traditions and cultural practices. Here, Aboriginal art appears on artifacts, rock paintings, on bodies, and directly on the ground. In the case of ground paintings, these were often associated with ceremonial activities, such as dancing. Western Desert art is distinctive in its predominant use of dots and concentric circles.

On less formal occasions, people draw in the sand when telling stories. Here, the sand acts as a slate on which pictures related to the myth or event are illustrated, and then erased. All these art forms are still widely practiced today, with canvas and acrylic paints being the preferred media to produce art for sale. Several painters may collaborate to produce an individual piece, particularly if it is large and is associated with a special ceremony.

Right **Rainbow Serpent with a lizard.** Rainbow Serpents are powerful Ancestors. A young man was once forced to ride on the back of one, holding onto the stingray nails behind its head. When he was returned to his family, the Serpent forbade him to wash. The man ignored this advice, and died.

WATER SERPENTS

Across Australia Aboriginal people associated large snakes with water and rain. Often called Rainbow Serpents, these Ancestors are generally thought to live in bodies of fresh water. They are associated with rainmaking, and are considered very dangerous to people. In Arnhem Land, rock art featuring serpents has been dated at more 8,000 years old. The Dreaming Tracks of the Water Snake Ancestors crisscross the whole of the Western Desert, and are generally associated with water holes. Aboriginal people believed that certain men were rainmakers, having the ability to bring on a change of weather. In some regions, rainmakers wear shell ornaments that are symbolically linked to the Rainbow Serpent.

Although the mythology connecting snakes with water is large and varied, the common themes are control of water and danger to people.

In western Arnhem Land, the main Rainbow Serpents are Yingarna and her son Ngalyod, who are believed to live in the deep water holes. These Serpents represent the monsoon weather, which fills the inland waterways when the heavy rain comes. In particular, the rainbow that appears after the rain is identified as Ngalyod. This Rainbow Serpent is still, in a sense, a creator, as he increases plants and animals with the change of the season. The Rainbow Serpent is also believed to possess the power to send spirit children to water holes, to wait before becoming human. Ngalyod is like a Supreme Being to all Ancestors, and because of this is connected to most mythological sites in the western Arnhem Land region. In myth, Ngalyod swallows people for their failure to observe the sacred Law. The Rainbow Serpent can also cause floods, storms, and even drought. The Rainbow Serpent is part of the major rituals of western Arnhem Land, including the Wubarr, Marrayin, and Kunapipi.

The Western Desert people living on the northern edge of the Great Victoria Desert have a Dreaming account involving a large number of Geniga, Spotted Native Cat Ancestors, camped at Beril-beril water hole near a lake where two Wanampi, Snake Ancestors, lived. Minma Murulu, Marsupial Rat Woman, came down from the north looking for water. She found that the Geniga Ancestors were away hunting and gathering, apart from an old Geniga woman still in camp. Minma Murulu offered to delouse the elderly woman, who accepted and then fell asleep. Going to the lake, Minma Murulu dipped her wooden container, which was extremely large, into the water. By filling her container, she completely drained the lake and everything that lived in it.

Minma Murulu then headed back north toward the Kimberley, managing to escape the Geniga men who were tracking her. Once she got back home, she went hunting, and carelessly put her wooden container with the water still in it on top of a spinifex grass tussock. The dish tipped over, and all the water poured out and formed the Fitzroy River in the southern Kimberley. The Wanampi came out of the wooden container, and one of them swallowed Minma Murulu. The large serpents then traveled toward the sea, making the rivers and the streams, with their meandering courses.

The Kaurna people of the Adelaide Plains believed that the dark spots seen in the Milky Way were water lagoons, where a large serpent named Yura lived. These dark areas in the sky were known as Yurakauwe, which translates as "monster-water." The Milky Way was considered to be a large river with reeds growing along the banks. Aboriginal people feared Yura would swallow them if they did not hide. When he appeared on earth, an abundance of water was created. Yura gave the Kaurna people some of their initiation rituals, and would severely punish those who neglected these practices.

The Akurra spirits of the Adnyamathanha people of the Flinders Ranges are considered to be very large, with scales, beards and manes, and fangs. On the back of the Akurra's neck are ticks that cannot be removed by the spirit. In some accounts there are two Akurra spirits—a smaller male and a large female. The eggs, feces, and vomit of the Akurra became landforms in the Flinders Ranges. A large ring of mountains, known as Wilpena Pound, represents the bodies of a pair of Akurra. The male forms the northeastern wall of the Pound, while the body of the female makes up the southwestern side.

Adnyamathanha people believed that the Akurra moving underground caused earthquakes and rock falls. They are creators and guardians of the large permanent water holes in the region. When camping near these water holes, people must always remember not to cook meat near the water, as this could bring the local Akurra spirit out, and encourage it to attack them. Swimming at such places is also very dangerous. It is also believed that at the water holes that have dried up, the Akurra spirits are considered to be dead.

Above **Pearl shell ornament.** In some regions, these ornaments are linked to the Rainbow Serpent and are used by rainmakers. A story of a man who came from the clouds relates how he used the lightning that he carried to create rain. Areas where he rested are called "soaks."

Left **Totemic stone.** Totemic patterns carved on stone relate stories of the Dreaming Ancestors. Sometimes these stories are told through aerial drawings of the mythical landscape. These carvings are used in ceremonies and rituals.

SKYWORLD OMENS

Aboriginal people were keen observers of the movements of celestial bodies in the night sky. Changes in the Skyworld signaled the timing of events on earth. For example, the halo of the moon was considered by some Kimberley groups to signify the time for the initiation of boys. In the MacDonnell Ranges of Central Australia, the lunar halo was believed to be string being made by the Moon Ancestor from possum fur, which is spun by running a flat hand along the upper leg. Such string is used in the making of ceremonial ornaments. Across many regions in Australia, the arrival in the Skyworld of the Pleiades constellation, which was often seen as a group of sisters, and perhaps one younger brother, was taken as a cue for commencing major ceremonial activities such as initiations.

Many of the planets and constellations were considered by Aboriginal people to be their Ancestors, linked together through kinship and Dreaming events. For instance, the Kaurna people who lived on the Adelaide Plains of South Australia believed that Tindo Yerle, or Sun Father, had a pair of sisters who were "long," and probably comets. Aboriginal people here considered most of the strange events they saw in the sky to be bad omens. In March 1843, a comet seen by Aboriginal groups along the Murray River in South Australia was believed to have been created by powerful sorcerers in the north. Aboriginal people considered it had arrived to punish Europeans who had taken away land from Aboriginal people. The same comet seen in the Port Lincoln area of the Eyre Peninsula in

Above **Female ancestral figure.** These painted figures are said to represent sacred beings described in tribal mythology. The designs depict seasonal changes.

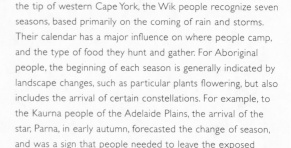

SEASONS

Australian Aboriginal people generally recognized the existence of more seasons than Europeans. For example, at the tip of western Cape York, the Wik people recognize seven seasons, based primarily on the coming of rain and storms. Their calendar has a major influence on where people camp, and the type of food they hunt and gather. For Aboriginal people, the beginning of each season is generally indicated by landscape changes, such as particular plants flowering, but also includes the arrival of certain constellations. For example, to the Kaurna people of the Adelaide Plains, the arrival of the star, Parna, in early autumn, forecasted the change of season, and was a sign that people needed to leave the exposed coast to build large and waterproof huts in the Adelaide foothills. Aboriginal movements across the landscape were not random, but followed a pattern where they could maximize seasonal food sources.

South Australia caused Aboriginal people to hide in caves. In Central Australia, comets were sometimes believed by desert Aboriginal people to be spears thrown by particular male Ancestors.

In the Adelaide region of South Australia, the exceptions were meteoric lights (a "shooting star" or "falling star"), which the Kaurna people described as "orphans." The rarity of their appearance, and their random pathways across the Skyworld, would have contributed to their status as outsiders. Across Australia, meteors were generally treated as bad omens. In the Lower Murray region of South Australia, an Ancestor named Kulda was believed to be a meteor, who had came out of the Southern Cross. Kulda foretold the coming of a disease epidemic. Whenever a falling star was seen, the Lower Murray people reportedly said *Peika baki*, meaning "Death is coming." Similarly, to the Gundidjmara people of southwestern Victoria, a meteor represented "deformity." The Southern Lights (Aurora Australis) and the eclipse of the moon were also widely treated as bad omens across Aboriginal Australia.

Left *Fishing by Torchlight* by Joseph Lycett (1775–1828). Aboriginal people looked to the sky and stars for signs of change in the Skyworld. These changes indicated the time for special ceremonies, events, or movements of the tribe.

Opposite page **Hunter with spear surrounded by spirits.** Hunting was dictated by the seasons. Aboriginal people used the constellations to predict the change of seasons, as each season influenced the types of animals they could hunt.

MAORI MYTHOLOGY

The main body of Maori mythology contains three great complexes. The first is the traditions of creation, concerning the genesis of the universe, the heavens and earth, gods, humans, and all animate and inanimate forms. Many of these myths derive from the Polynesian pantheons of creation, and were adapted and localized in Aotearoa-New Zealand. The Maori mythologies of creation are a blend of allegorical explanations, moral codes and prescriptions for behavior, precedents for the existence of social institutions, deep-seated beliefs about the nature of being and non-being, the relationship between the known and the unknown, and the origins of all things seen and unseen. They are a template of deep philosophies and important religious, cultural, and social beliefs.

The second complex involves the demigod cycles, headed by Maui and Tawhaki, and follow on from the creation cycle. Many of the figures in these myths also come from the wider Polynesian body of oral lore. They make an important connection between the gods of creation and humans in the terrestrial world. Gods are the source of all things. Demigods, such as Maui and Tawhaki, therefore act as intermediaries between the gods and humans, fetching knowledge from the deities and transmitting it to humans. This adds order and sense to the world. Demigods also test the parameters of creation by revisiting the threshold laid down in the genesis traditions. Typically one demigod will test the darkness of creation and death by attempting to gain immortality. In the Polynesian pantheons this figure is Maui. Another demigod will characteristically revisit the origins of creation by attempting to ascend into the heavens. In the structure of the numerous Polynesian pantheons, this

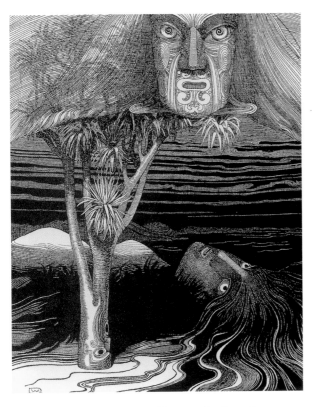

Left *The Birth of Tawhaki* **by Wilhelm Dittmer (1866–1909).** The Maui and Tawhaki cycles illustrate the lives of these demigods, who were able to travel between the world of the gods and the world of the humans. Their adventures also serve as moral instruction.

figure is Tawhaki. A second layer of culture hero myths underpins the Maui and Tawhaki cycles. These lay down particular rules, and include the traditions relating to Tinirau, Rata, and Whaka-taupotiki, among many others.

A third body of myths relates to the natural world and includes tales involving Maori astronomy. These traditions reflect a deep-seated intimacy and under-standing of the natural world, presenting sophisti-cated knowledge in poetic form.

CREATION TRADITIONS, DARKNESS AND LIGHT

Maori beliefs about the evolution of the universe are embodied in genealogical form. There are many types of these genealogies, with quite a number of recurring themes. Creation was likened to a series of periods of unknown darkness, light, and primal source or pri-meval potentiality, each qualified by some descriptive term and/or quantitative sequence. These distinctive periods of time corresponded to eons of cosmologi-cal time, when the seeds of the universe scattered throughout the vast emptiness of space came together to form the Sky Father and Earth Mother.

Many creation narratives began with Te Po (Un-known Darkness) which likens creation to the dark-ness of the womb, an absence of knowledge, and the unknowable nature of ultimate origin. Te Po was timeless with internal divisions: Te Po-nui was the great unknown darkness; Te Po-roa was the extensive darkness; Te Po-kerekere, Te Po-tangotango, and

Te Po-uriuri, represented different shades and depths of the darkness; and Te Po-te-kitea was the dark-ness within which nothing was known or seen. The descriptions of Te Po sometimes culminated in a numerical sequence of darkness, from Te Po-tuatahi (the First Darkness) to Te Po-tuangahuru (the Tenth Darkness), and on to the hundredth and thousandth darkness, which implied a progression rather than a static state. This great period of darkness is also a metaphor for the mind. Without light there was no knowledge. The abyss of darkness prevailed.

Te Ao (Light) followed and represented the birth of the world and life, the emerging understanding of increasing knowledge, and awareness. Te Kore (Primal Potential, Primeval Source) represented a state of un-formed phenomenology or chaos within which lay the latent potential for all things to exist. Te Kore was the source from which all animate and inanimate things took their substance and form. Like Te Po, Te Kore was also characterized by divisions, each with its own descriptive terminology. Te Kore-te-whiwhia (the Source of all Things), Te Kore-te-rawea (the Source of all Forms), and Te Kore-te-matua (the Parental Source) were typical characterizations.

Other versions likened the evolution of the uni-verse to a tree, with its base, tap roots, rootlets, and branching roots reaching out to form a forest. Another theme characterizing evolution was one that connected the emergence of thought to conscious-ness. Some, or all, of these concepts appear in the same genealogy.

MAORI GENESIS TABLE

CREATION AS THE GENESIS OF A GREAT FOREST

TE PU	THE ROOT CAUSE
TE WEU	THE EMERGING ROOTLETS
TE MORE	THE FIRM TAPROOT
TE AKA	THE SPREADING VINE
TE TIPURANGA	THE MATURING GROWTH
TE WAONUI-A-TANE	THE GREAT FOREST OF TANE
RANGINUI = PAPATUANUKU	SKY FATHER AND EARTH MOTHER

CREATION AS THE GENESIS OF KNOWLEDGE

TE RAPUNGA	THE SEEKING
TE KUKUNE	THE INCEPTION
TE PUPUKE	THE SWELLING
TE HIHIRI	THE PSYCHIC ENERGY AND DESIRE
TE MAHARA	THE THOUGHT AND REMEMBRANCE
TE HINENGARO	THE CONSCIOUSNESS
TE MANAKO	THE LONGING
KA HUA TE WANANGA	THE FRUITFULNESS OF KNOWLEDGE
RANGINUI = PAPATUANUKU	SKY FATHER AND EARTH MOTHER

The Gods

After the darkness the creation of the gods began, along with a complex tradition of oral history that provides the background for Maori beliefs.

Sky Father and Earth Mother

Most versions of the cosmogonic genealogy culminated in the two names Rangi (Sky Father), and Papa (Earth Mother). Their marriage produced the gods and, ultimately, all life on earth.

One traditional chant refers to Rangi as the Great Sky Father (Ranginui), the Encompassing Sky Father (Rangiroa), the Heavenly Winds (Tawhirirangi), the Life-Giving Winds (Te Hauwhakaora), and finally the Winds that Caress the Skin of all People (Te Hau-e-pangia-te-kiri-o-te-tangata). Papa is referred to as the Earth Mother Trampled by the Ancestors (Te Papa-i-taka-takahia-e-nga-matua-tupuna), the Earth Mother Left in Remembrance by the Ancestors (Te Papa-i-wai-hotia-e-ratou-ma), the Earth Mother Stretching unto the Sunrise (Te-Papa-e-maroro-ki-te-itinga), the Earth Mother Stretching unto the

Below **Maori gods, Rangi and Papa.** This heavenly couple were separated by their children, so that the world could have light. Tane (God of the Forests) forced them apart, and soon Rangi became the sky and Papa became the earth.

Sunset (Te Papa-e-maroro-ki-te-opunga), the Embracing Earth Mother that Comforts all People (Te Papa-awhiawhi-e-awhi-ana-i-a-tatou), the Earth Mother Over Land (Papa-tuanuku), and finally, the Earth Mother Under the Heavens (Papa-tuarangi).

The concept of the Sky Father and Earth Mother is found deep within Polynesian philosophical thought and religion. In Samoa, Tangaloa-lagi was the God of the Heavens, Papatu was the Mountain Father, and Papa'ele was the Earth Mother. In Hawai'i, Rarotonga, and Tahiti, Atea (Wakea in Hawai'i) represented the Sky Father. In Hawai'i Papa was the Earth Mother; in Tahiti she was Papa-tu'oi and Papa-raharaha, the Life-Giving Earth; in Rarotonga she was Papa-i-te-itinga and Papa-i-te-opunga, the Earth Mother at the Sunrise and the Sunset.

The Separation

The most comprehensive account of the Sky Father and Earth Mother comes from the Te Arawa tribes of the central North Island of Aotearoa-New Zealand. This tradition says that the primeval Sky Father and Earth Mother caused darkness because of the close coupling of their bodies in the act of procreation. Their children longed for light to enter the world so that they and all of their descendants could flourish. Some of the children plotted to kill their parents, but one of the sons, Tawhirimatea (God of Wind and Storm), felt pity for his parents and argued that they should not be killed, only separated. One by one, Rongo (God of Cultivated Foods), Haumia (God of Uncultivated Foods), Tangaroa (God of the Oceans), and Tu (God of Human Martial Consciousness) tried to separate their parents. They all failed. Then, Tane (God of the Forests) lay on his back, pressed up-ward with his feet, with all his might, and gradually forced them apart, until one was far above and the other was far below. Tane's separation of the Earth Mother and Sky Father ushered in Te Ao-marama (the World of Light).

The Wars of the Gods

Tawhirimatea was angered by his brothers' treatment of their mother and father, and flew off to join the Sky Father. He carefully gathered together his many offspring, who included the hurricane, storm clouds, hail, rain, and sleet, and sent them to all corners of the heavens. Once they were in place, Tawhirimatea attacked his brothers. The great forest trees of Tane broke under the attack and fell to the ground, be-coming food for decay. Having defeated Tane, Taw-hirimatea then turned his wrath on the oceanic domain of Tangaroa. Tangaroa fled into the waters of the earth where he became the progenitor of all fish species, reptiles, and sea birds. Next, Tawhiri-matea attacked Rongo and Haumia, who were in great fear. However, as they were being attacked the Earth Mother reached out and drew them to the safety of her breast, leaving only their hair above ground. The storms raised by Tawhirimatea passed harmlessly overhead. As a consequence, Rongo and Haumia remained condemned to a lower estate. Rongo became the god of the kumara (the Maori word for sweet potato), agriculture, and peaceful arts. Haumia became the god of the fernroot and wild plants. Tawhirimatea finally turned his rage against Tu, and violently attacked with all his force, but Tu was able to stand against Tawhirimatea when all others failed. When Tawhiri-matea's anger finally abated, it

was then Tu's turn to become angry, and he attacked his brothers for failing to support him. He attacked Tane of the forests, felling the rest of his trees and trapping, spearing, and eating his birds; then he wove nets from forest plants, and cast them right out into the sea, so that the children of Tangaroa soon lay in stranded heaps upon the shore; he found Rongo and Haumia's hiding place, and dragged them by their long hair, that was exposed, from the earth, and then ate them.

The war of Tawhirimatea highlights the notion that all life is subject to the tempests of storms, winds, and rain. Tu's assertion of dominance over the natu-ral domains of his brothers reflects the natural order. It also introduced the fundamental dichotomy be-tween *tapu* (sacred) and *noa* (human use).

The world's resources emanated from the realm of gods. This made them sacred. Tu's subordination of the descendants of Tane, Tangaroa, Rongo, and Hau-mia resulted in their transformation from the sacred estate of gods to the profane level of human use as artifacts and food. Tu made these gods available for human use in the world of light, a task that could be repeated through use of the appropriate incantations and the act of mediating between the gods and their human progeny. Tu represents human consciousness, and the ability to com-mand the resources of nature.

Below **Carving of Rangi and Papa on a war canoe prow.** The carved spirals represent the light and the knowledge that entered the world when Rangi and Papa were separated. The figure also serves as a re-minder of the anger of the God of Wind and Storms, Tawhirimatea. The prow is a protective measure against turbulent seas.

Tangaroa, the Father of the Seas

Tangaroa (God of the Oceans)—known as Tagaloa-lagi in Samoa, Takaroa in Hawai'i, Tanaoa in the Marquesas, Ta'aroa in Tahiti, and Tangaroa in Raro-tonga—is the oldest of the Polynesian first order anthropomorphic gods. One of the better known West Polynesian accounts is that Tagaloa-lagi dwelt in the heavens from where he sent a bird named Tuli to soar across the seas. Tuli returned, and reported that there was only water, and no land. So Tagaloa-lagi decided to throw down stones, which became the islands of Manono, 'Upolu, Savai'I, Manu'a, and 'Olosega, creating the Samoan archipelago.

In East Polynesia, the god Tangaroa is usually associated with the oceans. To the Maori, Tangaroa was the progenitor of all life associated with the sea, and was also considered the great guardian of canoes. Whenever the people in canoes ventured out on the ocean to make long journeys, or to catch Tanga-roa's children, they were careful to perform the appropriate rituals and make offerings to Tangaroa, both on departure and arrival.

His numerous offspring included Hine-moana (the Ocean Maid), Hine-wai (the Water Maiden), and Hine-awaawa (the Maiden of the Rivers) who was responsible for the many tidal streams, inland lakes, and rivers of the region. Tangaroa-whai-ariki (Tangaroa the Lordly Chief) is one of Tangaroa's many expansive titles. He was also known as Tangaroa-whakamau-tai (Tangaroa, the Controller of Tides), whose breathing was said to control the ebb and flow of tides.

Tane, God of the Forests

The god Tane originated in East Polynesia, where he was a deity of creation, light, and life. He was known in Rarotonga, Tahiti, Tuamotu, and Hawai'i as Kane, and is identified as a son of Atea, Watea, or Wakea (the Space of Heavens). These names are remembered in one of the Maori titles for Tane's father Rangi-atea, meaning the Great Expanse of the Heavens.

In Maori tradition, it was Tane who separated the Sky Father and Earth Mother. When Tane separated the two, he placed props between them to hold them apart. The event is marked by the name Tane-te-toko-o-te-rangi (Tane with the Posts Upholding all the Heavens). Tane has other extended names that recall how he slowly stretched out his legs while raising his father; these include Tane-tuturi (Tane with Bent up Knees), and Tane-uatika (Tane with a Straight Backbone). It is said that these props can still be seen as the mighty kauri, rimu, kahikatea, and totara trees

TANGAROA AND THE ORIGIN OF MAORI CARVING

In some traditions, as well as being the father of all life in the oceans, Tangaroa also had human offspring. In one East Coast tradition, one of these human children, Rua-te-pupuke, is said to have discovered the art of carving. Tangaroa kidnapped Rua-te-pupuke's son, Te Manu, took him to his home in the sea, and placed him on top of his carved house as a *tekoteko* (gable figure). Rua-te-pupuke found the house and burnt it down after retrieving the carved posts from the porch. These posts became the models for carvers. In a more general way Rua-te-pupuke represents forms of knowledge, the desire for knowledge, and its acquisition. Rua-te-pupuke conveys the idea of the welling up of knowledge. Sometimes the personifications of Rua-te-pupuke are male, and sometimes female.

of Te Waonui-a-Tane (the Great Forests of Tane), or Tanemahuta (God of the Forests).

Tane is credited with giving form, and creating much life after the separation of the Sky Father and Earth Mother, through marriages to feminine aspects of creation. Tane married Hine-tumaunga (Mountain Woman). From this union came all mountains, hills, rocks, pebbles, and sand. He married Hine-parauri (Woman of Autumn Browness), whose children included all the great trees. From his marriage to Hine-waoriki (Woman of Small Foliage) came the small trees, shrubs, vines, and other plants. Tane also married Punga and their children were the reptiles and insects. His marriage to Kahu-parauri (Brown Cloak of Autumn) gave rise to the birds of the forests. The bird song of the *tui* (parsons bird), and *kokako* (bellbird) at the dawn of each day was called Te Putangitangi-a-Tane (The Songs of Tane).

The title Tanenui-a-Rangi (Great Tane of the Heavens) celebrates two mythological events. The Ngati Awa tribe of the Bay of Plenty say that he obtained the stars, the moon, and the sun from Tangotango (Blackness of Heavens), while the Ngati Kahungunu of the East Coast say the stars came from a cloak named Wehinui-a-mamao, with which he adorned the Sky Father. In other traditions, Tane is believed to have retrieved three *kete* (baskets) from the heavens that contained knowledge for humankind. One basket, Te Kete-tuauri (Darkness) contained the unknown; the next, Te Kete-tuatea (Light) contained the things we know, and Te Kete-aronui (Pursuit) contained the knowledge humans currently pursue through study.

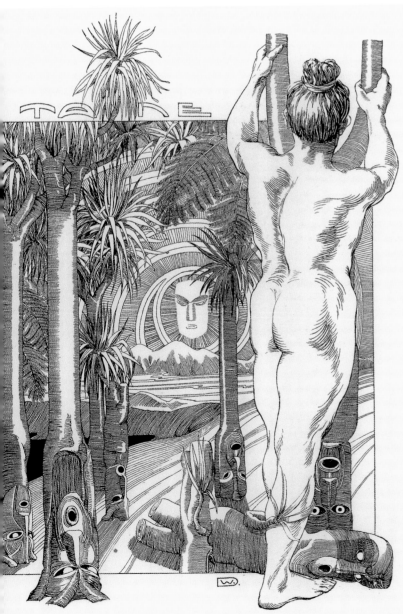

Below A *tekoteko* or gable figure. According to Maori legends, Tangaroa (God of the Oceans) accidentally revealed the secrets of carving to Rua-te-pupuke when he rescued his son from the top of the god's carved house. From that day, carving became central to Maori culture.

Rongo, the Origin of the Kumara

Rongo is another well-known East Poly-nesian deity. In Rarotonga, Rongo was one of the five sons of Atea and Paparoa. In Maori tradi-tions Rongo was the deity of all cultivated plants. Rongo became the progenitor of the ku-mara at the separation of the heavens and the earth. In the East Coast Ngati Porou traditions, Rongo-maraeroa (Rongo of the Long Marae) is the father of the kumara, while a secondary figure, Rongo-i-amo (Rongo of the Cere-monies), actually conveyed the kumara to human beings in Aotearoa-New Zealand. The Ngati Awa tribe say that Rongo is a son of Tane, and father of the kumara. Rongo's association with cultivation meant that he also represented peace.

Kumara, the main source of carbohydrate, was the most vital crop in Maori society. It was the equivalent of the potato to the Irish, the taro to the Polynesians, and rice in Asia. Kumara was also difficult to grow, as it needed to be specially propagated and prepared for cropping to be successful.

Precise planning was required to ensure success, therefore the association between the kumara and the stars was very strong. The mid-June rising of Matariki (the Pleiades) signaled the time when the earth was turned in preparation for plant-ing. The rising of Poutu-te-rangi (Altair) and Wha-nui (Vega) in late summer signaled the optimum time for harvesting and storing the kumara. Each tribe had their own account of the first human ancestors to bring the kumara to Aotearoa-New Zealand. Taranaki tribes say it was Turi and his wife, Rongorongo. Bay of Plenty tribes say the canoe Te Aratawhao fetched the kumara from Hawaiki. The Ngati Awa tribe say that Rongo-maui acquired the ku-mara from the star Whanui (Vega). East Coast tribes say Kahukura went to get the kumara on the canoe, Horouta. South Island traditions say Rongo-i-tua brought the kumara from Hawaiki.

Above *Taumata atua, the resting place of Rongo, the God of Cultivated Foods.* These stones were placed beside sweet potato crops. Using the correct rituals, Rongo is asked to enter the stone to watch over these crops.

Right **Tu, the God of Warfare.** This carving is believed to be a place where the spirit of the god lives. The *haka* (a dance) used to be per-formed in honor of Tu, before the warriors headed off for battle.

Tu, the Origin of Human Martial Consciousness

Tu is known in Tahiti, Tuamotu, and Rarotonga, and is known as Ku in Hawai'i. In Maoridom he is best known for the tradition of turning on his brothers—the terrestrial gods Tane, Tangaroa, Haumia, and Rongo—consuming them and their offspring. In this way, Tu set the pattern for the future, as he repre-sents human beings, and the brothers he killed and ate are the creatures and plants upon which humans depend for their survival. The martial nature of Tu also means that he is the god of warfare. Humans make war now because Tu did so in the beginning. Warriors were dedicated to Tu as were the chants or *haka* (war dance) they performed when warriors girded themselves for battle. The body of the first enemy warrior killed was often offered to Tu. Even though Tu was primarily the originator of warfare, every tribe also possessed other powerful gods such as Kahukura, Uenuku, or Maru, whom they sought assistance from in times of war. The name Tu is a personification associated with assertive, aggres-sive action, since the word "tu" literally means to "stand upright." He was honored with many titles, among them Tu-mata-uenga (Tu of the Fierce Countenance), Tu-ka-riri (Tu who Fights), Tu-kai-taua (Tu the Consumer of War Parties), and Tu-mata-kura (Tu with a Flushed Face).

THE FIRST HUMANS

According to various traditions, the gods are responsible for creating hu-mans that combine a human principle with the elements of the divine.

Hine-ahu-one and Hine-titama, The Woman Shaped from Sand

Tane and his brothers embodied *ira atua* (the divine principle). In the most well-known traditions Tane searched for the female element in nature to create *ira tangata* (the human principle). Many tra-ditions say that when Tane was unable to find a suitable female to bear human children, he decided he would create a female for himself.

He went to a beach, Te Oneone-o-Kura-waka (the Sands upon the Vulva) which was on the *mons veneris* of his mother, Papa. Here he modeled from the earth a woman that suited him. This woman was the first human, and was named

Hine-ahu-one (Earth-Formed Maid) or Hine-mata-one (Maid with Earth-Formed Face). Finally, Tane breathed his *mauri*, and now there is a duality of *ira atua* and *ira tangata* in human beings. But humans, unlike gods, are not immortal. When the *mauri* leaves the body death occurs. Only *the wairua*, the spiritual remnant, and *ira atua,* survive death to return to Te Po, back to the beginning from where all things came.

Tane cohabited with Hine-ahu-one, and from his merging with different parts of her body he created human sweat from her head, human pupils from her eyeballs, and mucus and saliva from her nose. In the final act, Tane produced a daughter named Hine-titama (Dawn Maid), also known as Hine-i-tauira (Patterned Maid) and Hine-manuhiri (Newly Arrived Maid). Tane then slept with his daughter to beget more children. On finding out that Tane was her father, Hine-titama fled to the portal of the underworld, Raro-henga. Tane pursued Hine-titama, but she commanded him not to follow as he was to remain on earth to care for their children in the world of light. Hine-titama promised to wait, and receive them into the world of night in the form of Hine-nui-te-po (Goddess Guardian of Death). Hine-titama's flight from Tane encapsulates the belief that humans came from an original incestuous relationship, as well as dramatizing the serious nature of incest, and sets a social prohibition against its continuation.

This myth also adds further continuity to creation. Creation began from Te Po, and culminated in the formation of the Sky Father and the Earth Mother. The food that springs from the bosom of Papa sustains life in this world. It is for this reason that the earth is loved and cherished as a mother. Tane then created humans out of the earth. The creation of human life also predetermined that death would eventually come into the world. Physical death and decay is therefore conceptualized as a return beneath Papa, the portal of Rarohenga, where Hine-nui-te-po awaits as a benevolent mother figure to receive the dead, before freeing their *wairua* (spirits) to return through the heavens of the Sky Father, back to Te Po, the origin of all existence. Rarohenga was not to be feared, as it was thought of as a pathway through which the dead would be reunited with their ancestors.

Tiki, the Origin of Sexuality

In other traditions, particularly on the West Coast and in the South Island, the first human made by Tane was a man named Tiki. In some traditions Tane

Right ***Kuwaha pataka.*** This is a symbol of the gateway to the underworld, or Rarohenga. The figure represents Papa, the Earth Mother, awaiting the arrival of the dead.

makes a wife for Tiki. In other accounts, it is Tiki himself who creates the first person. And some traditional accounts bring these ideas together by saying that Tiki is Tane's penis. When Tiki makes the first human he is sometimes regarded as a son of Rangi and Papa. In one account, Tiki's wife was formed from earth by the echo and the quivering heat of the sun.

Another story is that Tiki took red clay and kneaded it with his own blood, forming eyes and limbs, and gave the image breath. Tiki's main symbolism seems to be as the initiator of sexuality and human reproduction. Even when Tane was believed to have made the first woman, or slept with her, lovemaking was Tiki's specialty. In songs, Te Mahi-a-Tiki (Tiki's Work)

Right *Maui Fishing up the Land* by **Wilhelm Dittmer (1866–1909).** Using a magical fishhook, and some of his blood and hair as bait, Maui casts out to sea. With his mighty strength, he hauled up all of the islands of Aotearoa-New Zealand. Maui is a popular demigod of Maori mythology.

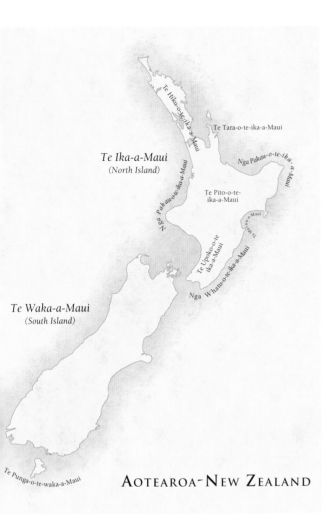

AOTEAROA-NEW ZEALAND

are caused by the cycles of the sun. Another of the main themes encapsulated in the Maui myth cycles is that he is a precocious youngster, an archetypal culture hero who overcomes the disadvantage of being the last born to gain fame and adulation as a benefactor of humankind. He also stands as a model to all *teina* (juniors) that they can succeed, provided they have the required personal qualities and traits exemplified by Maui—such as intelligence, cunning, initiative, boldness, and determination.

Maui and his Family

Maori oral traditions say that the human offspring of the gods increased and multiplied, and did not know of death, until the generation of Maui. They also say that Maui was abandoned at birth. The most well-known tradition from Te Arawa in the central North Island is that he was aborted by his mother, and cast into the sea, wrapped in her loin cloth, or in a basket made from her hair. Washed ashore, entangled in sea-weed and swarmed over by gulls and flies, Rangi is said to have rescued him and nursed him back to life.

On reaching adulthood, Maui's first exploit was to find his family. This dramatized the pivotal nature of identity because, in the Maori world, talent without identity is insufficient to succeed. On finding his kin, Maui legitimized his ancestral credentials. With his place in the world secured, Maui set about acquiring knowledge from his ancestors, because talent and identity are most effective when they are balanced with knowledge.

Maui and Knowledge

From his grandparent, Muri-rangawhenua, Maui acquired a jawbone symbolizing knowl-edge. From this, he was immedi-ately able to manufacture hooks and weapons, and began his journey as a benefactor for humankind. Maui also used a hook, fashioned from the jawbone, to fish up the North Island of Aotearoa-New Zealand.

Maui's fishing up of the North Island of Aotearoa-New Zealand is celebrated in the name Te Ika-a-Maui (the Fish of Maui—the North Island), and the South Island is called Te Waka-a-Maui (the Canoe

Left **Aotearoa-New Zealand as created by Maui.** This map shows the islands that Maui fished up. These ancient Maori names for the various parts of the country are still used today.

Below **Ancestor figure.** Having been abandoned at birth, Maui searched for his parents and ancestors. From these traditions, the importance of ancestry and knowledge is empha-sized in Maori culture.

was the act of coitus rather than procreation. The stories of Tiki and Hine-mata-one come from an cient accounts in the Marquesas, and Tuamotu and Tahiti archipelagoes.

THE MAUI CYCLE

This is one of the key demigod cycles that follow on from the creation cycle.

Maui in the Pacific

Maui is the most ancient figure in the pantheons of mythology carried by the ancestors of the Maori to Aotearoa-New Zealand. Maui is also widely known throughout the islands of Polynesia, Melanesia, and Micronesia. The full geographic extent of these tra-ditions range from the island of Yap in Micronesia to the west, to Mangareva in the east, and north from Hawai'i to Aotearoa-New Zealand in the south. The distribution of these traditions suggests a pre-Polynesian origin, meaning that they have been told for 3,500 years or more.

Across the Pacific, the Maui cycles explain how the things necessary to sustain life were obtained, in-cluding the acquisition of knowledge, the finding of land, the origin of fire, and the seasonal cycles that of Maui—from which he fished up the North Island). Stewart Island is called Te Punga-o-te-waka-a-Maui (the Anchor Stone of the Canoe of Maui). Te Hiku-o-te-ika-a-Maui (the Tail of the Fish of Maui) refers to the narrow stretch of land in the far north of the North Island. The thin stretch of the Coromandel Peninsula is Te Tara-o-te-ika-a-Maui (the Barb of the Fish of Maui), with the barb coming from the belief that the fish of Maui was a stingray. The coastal abutments north of Gisborne on the East Coast of the North Island and around New Plymouth and Mount Taranaki on the West Coast form Nga Pakau-o-te-ika-a-Maui (the Wings of the Stingray of Maui). Te Pito-o-te-ika-a-Maui (the Navel of the Fish of Maui) is Lake Taupo in the middle of the North Island. Te Matau-a-Maui (the Hook of Maui) is the curve of Hawke Bay. Te Upoko-o-te-ika-a-Maui (the Head of the Fish of Maui) is the Wellington area. The waters of Wellington Harbour and Lake Wairarapa form Nga Karu-o-te-ika-a-Maui, or Nga Whatu-o-te-ika-a-Maui (the Eyes of the Fish of Maui).

Maui also slowed the sun's passage across the sky, putting in place the customs for the working day, according to seasonal agricultural cycles. He also provided human beings with a valuable companion,

when he turned his brother-in-law Irawaru into a dog for beating him at fishing. The kuri (Polynesian dog) served as a valuable resource. Its flesh was eaten, the skin used to make cloaks, and its delicate bones crafted into ornaments and small tools. The event dramatized the uneasy nature of the relationship between the brothers-in-law.

Maui wrested the secret of fire from the fingers of another grandparent, Mahuika. He did this by extinguishing all the fires in the village, and asked for the fingers of his grandparent one at a time, until only one was left. Mahuika, realizing that Maui was tricking them, hurled the last finger at him, causing the world to catch on fire. Maui escaped by taking the form of a pigeon, and calling on Tawhirimatea to extinguish the fires with rain.

The fire then became embedded in the trees of the forest, and it was from these trees that the ancestors of the Maori were able to make fire to keep warm, and cook food.

Maui's adventures brought him closer and closer to the parameters of primeval forces. This adventure nearly caused his death, and is a lesson that the fullest extent of human ability cannot overcome the primeval forces of nature.

Below **Jade pendants.**
These pendants are a symbolic reminder of the fishhook that Maui fashioned out of a jawbone to create the islands of Aotearoa-New Zealand. Fishhook replicas were worn by chiefs and priests, and were seen as a mark of great knowledge.

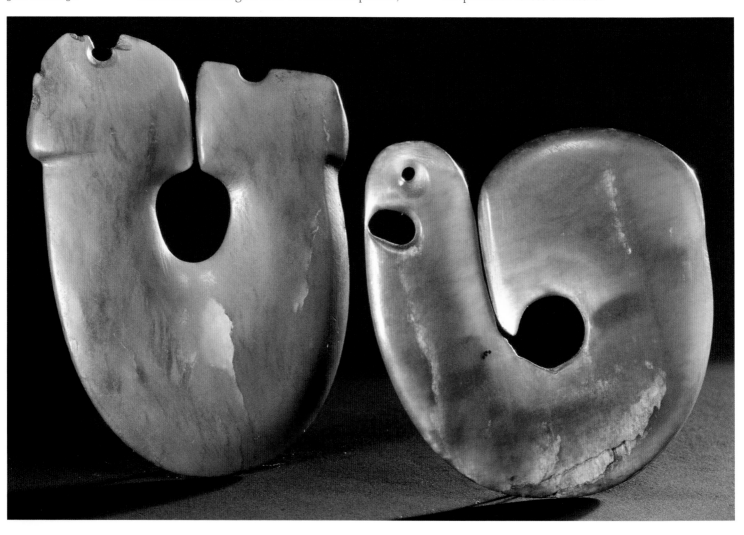

HINE-NUI-TE-PO

Maui and Death

Maui prepared himself for one last adventure. His parents told him that Hine-nui-te-po (the Goddess Guardian of Death) lay on the horizon. Her body was like that of a human being, but her eyes were greenstone, her hair sea-kelp, her mouth was like that of a barracuda, and sharp flints of obsidian and greenstone were set between her thighs. Maui took with him the smallest birds of the forest—the tomtit, the robin, the gray warbler, and the fantail—and set off toward the horizon. There he found Hine-nui-te-po

asleep with her legs apart. Maui was determined to enter Hine-nui-te-po's body, consume her heart, and then aimed to reappear from her mouth, reversing birth, so that people would be able to live forever.

As Maui started on his task, the feathered cheeks of the watching birds puckered with suppressed laughter. When his head and arms disappeared, the fantail burst out laughing. Hine-nui-te-po awoke, clapped her legs together, and cut Maui in two. Maui was the first being to die, and because he failed in his self-appointed task, all humans are born mortal.

The adventures of Maui reflect the human reality that great things can be accomplished through a combination of talent, secure identity, and the acquisition of knowledge, but only within the boundaries of life and death as laid down in creation.

THE TAWHAKI CYCLE

The Whaitiri-Kai-tangata, Hema, and Tawhaki cycle is the most enduring genealogical sequence in the East Polynesian pantheon of demigod traditions. This bespeaks the power of Whaitiri, and the regard in which she was held. Whaitiri was called Hina-hana-ia-ka-malama in Hawai'i and 'Ina-ma-nguru-nugru in Rarotonga. Hema was also known in Hawai'i, Tahiti, and the Tuamotu archipelago, and as

Left *Hine-nui-te-po, the Goddess Guardian of Death* by Wilhelm Dittmer (1866–1909). Maui bravely braced himself to face this terrifying goddess, but he was fatally defeated by her. As a result, death became part of the life cycle of humankind.

HEITIKI

Heitiki are traditional ornaments made out of *pounamu* (greenstone), or whalebone, and worn around the neck as items of adornment. In traditional Maori society Heitiki represented fertility, birth, and life. They were often associated with formal betrothals, marriage celebrations, and important births. The first Heitiki was said to have been worn by Hine-te-iwaiwa (Woman of Subtle Light). Hine-te-iwaiwa appears in many myths. She is often associated with the origins of female action songs, and is one of several female personifications of moonlight, linking the cycle of the waxing and waning moon with that of female menstruation. Heitiki also represented ancient genealogies, and were therefore highly prized as gifts of honor and

respect. In modern times, Heitiki continue to be presented as gifts to respected elders, visitors, or dignitaries. Older, and much more valuable, Heitiki presentations from Maori people never become absolute personal property as it is expected that the Heitiki will be eventually returned to the presenter's tribe.

Right **Heitiki pendant.** Prized as personal ornaments, some heitiki became clan heirlooms passed down for many generations. They are believed to embody *mana*, or the spirit of the tribe.

413

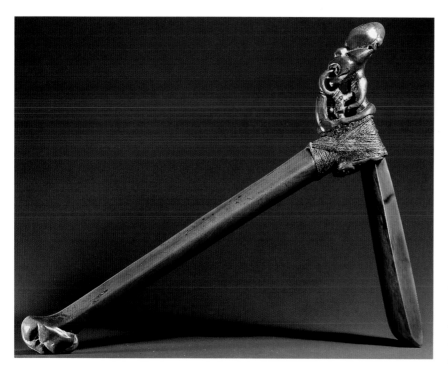

Above **Tokipoutangata, ceremonial adze.** This is a ritual tool used to invoke the gods when the first chips of a canoe are carved.

actions made certain that her grandson, Tawhaki, would become a great leader. After his birth, Whaitiri set in place a sequence of events leading Tawhaki on a series of adventures that culminated in his ascent into the heavens where he was finally reunited with her at the point of creation.

Tawhaki

Hema had two sons, Tawhaki and Karihi. As guided and predicted by Whaitiri, Tawhaki became a great leader. Where Maui tested the parameters of life and death by exploring the pathway to Te Po guarded by Hine-nui-te-po, Tawhaki retested the parameters of creation by ascending to the heavens. Each significant event in Tawhaki's life represents a step toward this goal and reunification with Whaitiri. Tawhaki overcame the many challenges that faced him through the assistance of a number of benevolent female figures, such as a sister, mother, or aunt who, as representations of Whaitiri, his grandmother, increased in potency from one adventure to the next, only revealing their true identity when Tawhaki was considered ready to know.

'Ema in Rarotonga. Tawhaki was known as Kaha'i in Hawai'i, Tafa'i in Tahiti, Tahaki in Tuamotu, and as Ta'aki in Rarotonga.

Whaitiri, Kaitangata, and Hema

Whaitiri or Whatatiri (Thunder), a cannibal, is the most potent female demigod figure in Maori oral traditions. Some Maori accounts hold that it was she who performed the *karakia* (ritual chants) that allowed Tane to separate the Sky Father and the Earth Mother. Other myths say that she came down from the sky, and married the man Kai-tangata (Man-eater), thinking that he shared her taste for human flesh because of his name. Disappointed at finding that this was not so, she left him to look after their son, Hema. Whaitiri guided Hema toward marrying a woman of high status so that the genealogical lines of her descendants would increase. Her

> *Many stars cannot be concealed by a small cloud.*
> MAORI PROVERB

Maori myths say the first significant event occurred when Tawhaki was attacked, injured, and, in some of these myths, killed by his relations who were jealous of his high status. In some accounts Tawhaki was revived by his wife Hine-piri-piri, in others it was his mother, sister, aunts, or other women who rescued him. In another adventure Tawhaki is said to have married Tangotango, the Blackness of the Heavens found in the very boundaries of Te Po. On returning to the heavens she indicated that Tawhaki should follow. Eventually, Tawhaki and his younger brother, Karihi, started to climb into the heavens. Traditions say that at the beginning of their journey they found an old blind

woman named Matuku-mata-kamo-kamo. She sat counting sweet potatoes, her only food. The brothers tormented her by snatching the food away, upsetting her tally. Eventually, they made themselves known to her, and Tawhaki restored her sight. In return, the old woman gave them advice about the ascent to the sky. Karihi tried first, but made the mistake of climbing up the *aka taepa* (hanging vine). He was blown about by the winds of heaven, and was killed. Tawhaki climbed up the *aka matua* (parent vine), reciting the appropriate chants, and entered the heavens. Here, he was reunited with Whaitiri, who rewarded him with chants from Tama-i-waho, and with remarriage to Tangotango. Some traditional accounts say he was imbued with supernatural powers in warfare, and that lightning emanated from his armpits. The tenet of the Tawhaki cycle is one where humans cannot defeat death, but they are able to, and can, attain extraordinary heights in life through their respect for its gifts, which ultimately came from the heavens through the Sky Father.

OTHER CULTURE HEROES

There are a number of demigods that play a role in Maori traditions. Here are some key heroes, and their influence on the importance of rituals for humans when negotiating with the gods.

Rata

After Maui, Rata is the mostly widely known demigod in the Pacific. The Tongans speak of him as Lasa, the Samoans as Lata, the Hawai'ians as Laka, and the Rarotongans as Raka. Rata's most famous adventure is the construction of a canoe to be used to avenge his father's death, which happened at the hands of ancestral enemies. By forgetting to follow the appropriate rituals, his first attempt to fell a tree for the hull of the canoe failed. When this omission was fixed, the guardians of the forest stopped obstructing the work, and helped Rata complete his canoe. Rata sailed off and defeated his enemies. Rata reinforced the sanctity of nature, and reminded the Maori that the resources of nature came from the gods, and permission of the gods must be sought before they could be used. This also clarified the idea of *mana* (mandated spiritual power) and *tapu* (sacredness of creation). Rata was highborn, and had a just cause to build the canoe; this gave him *mana*. However, *mana* could not be exercised without negotiating the *tapu*, the power of creation through mediating rituals.

Tinirau

Tinirau is another important Polynesian culture hero known in Rarotonga and Tahiti; he is also known in

Above *Ta Moko,* or Maori tattoo. The distinctive patterns of these facial tattoos represent specific ancestors. They are also a sign of great courage, and are regarded as the key to revealing a person's true spiritual identity.

performed amorous dances to make Kae laugh, they put him into a trance, and then carried him off to be killed by Tinirau. Kae's teeth are remembered in the carving pattern Te Kata-a-Kae (the Laughter of Kae) where the edges of the traditional spiral patterns are indented to represent his crooked teeth. This pattern also represents the wealth of the whale, which was an important commodity in pre-European Maori society, as it was a source of bone for tools and weapons, and provided meat for food.

Whakataupotiki

Whakataupotiki is another important figure whose adventures laid down the dictates of warfare. In one of his main adventures Whakataupotiki adopted a disguise to enter the camp of his enemies. There, he kidnapped one of them for interrogation to gain intelligence about his enemies. Having done that, he organized his men into attacking columns and ambushed his foes while they slept at dawn. In another campaign, Whakataupotiki defeated 10 men in successive single-handed combat.

For the commander of warriors, the dictates of Whakataupotiki included careful selection of personnel; military drills, practicing orders of battle; the disposition of warriors into assault, supporting, and reserve columns; disguise; spying and reconnaissance to gain intelligence on the enemy; interrogation of prisoners; denial of intelligence to the enemy; and other exploits. Maori war parties were called Te Hokowhitu-a-Tu (the 140 of Tu—the God of War), after the tenets of Whakataupotiki. These tenets of war were followed, and explain the successes of Maori leaders in the colonial period against the British army that outnumbered and outgunned them. Maori war strategies were subtler than the European traditions of bombardment and the wasteful expenditure of human life by frontal assault.

ASTRONOMICAL KNOWLEDGE

This is an essential knowledge that explains and gives expression to the change of season, traditional farming practices, and respect for natural cycles.

Tamanui-te-Ra, the Sun

Traditions say that the sun (Tamanui-te-Ra) was placed in the sky by Tane after he had separated the heavens and earth. Some traditions claim there is a bird in the sun, but others say that Te Manu-i-te-Ra (The Bird in the Sun) is the sun itself. Sunrise was associated with life and well-being, and the sunset with waning health and death. The east was a propitious direction. At divination ceremonies, it was a

Bellona (a remote Polynesian region) as Tinipau, in Samoa as Tigilau, in Tonga as Sinilau, and as Kinilau in Hawai'i. He is associated with traditions about the origin of performing arts.

Maori traditions say that Tinirau married Hinauri, a sister of Maui. When her child was born, a priest named Kae performed the ritual birth ceremony. After this was done, Tinirau lent Kae his pet whale, Tutunui, to take him home. In spite of strict instructions to the contrary, Kae foundered the whale in shallow water, where it died, and was eaten by Kae and his people. Tinirau sent his sisters to capture Kae, telling them that they could find him by getting him to reveal his overlapping front teeth. To make sure they had found the right man, the sisters

THE ORIGIN OF *TA MOKO* (MAORI TATTOO)

One day, the chief Mataora (Face of the Living) was visited by young people from Rarohenga (the underworld). With them was the daughter of Hine-nui-te-po (Goddes Guardian of Death) and her husband, Uetonga. Her name was Niwareka, and Mataora fell in love with her. They married, and were happy together until one day Mataora became jealous of Niwareka, and hit her. She returned home to Rarohenga. Grieving, Mataora followed her to Uetonga's house. Uetonga agreed to tattoo Mataora, using the technique of deep puncturing. During the tattooing, Mataora sang of his sorrow and his search for Niwareka. Niwareka heard him, and returned.

Permission was granted for Mataora's return to his world. However, he forgot to leave an appropriate offering for Kuwatawata, the guardian of the portal between Rarohenga and the human world, so a decree was set that living humans should no longer enter the underworld. *Ta Moko* reminds Maori people of the boundaries between life and death, the ancestors who have already departed, and the guardians that await them. The honor of being tattooed requires wearers to treat others with respect.

Left *Ta Moko* funnel. A feeding funnel was used to prevent food from touching the tattooed person's lips. Any contact with food before the tattoo work had healed would remove spiritual power.

good omen if the ceremonial rods fell toward the east, a bad one if they fell toward the west. One tradition from the Ngati Awa tribe of the Bay of Plenty demonstrates the awareness the Maori had about the movement of heavenly bodies. Te Manu-i-te-Ra was married to two sisters, Hine-takurua (Winterwoman) and Hine-raumati (Summerwoman). During summer he lived with Hine-raumati, whose house was on land in the south. During autumn he would venture northward, having affairs with several female stars, before living with Hine-takurua, whose house lay in the sea to the north. This tradition is a clear allegorical depiction of the summer and winter solstice.

From the Bay of Plenty, where this tradition is told, the sun rises over the hills from the land during summer, and from the ocean to the north during winter.

Hine-raumati bore Te Manu-i-te-Ra a son named Tane-rore (Shimmering Tane), who composed the first *haka* (action dance) celebrating the fine weather and the bounty of summer. The quivering movements of his dance are still seen in the shimmering heat of summer days.

Te Manu-i-te-Ra sent Auahi-tu-roa (Long Current of Smoke) to earth as a comet, where he married a beautiful woman named Mahuika, and gave her the gift of fire. Mahuika held the gift from her husband in her fingers, before implanting the fire in a number of softwood and hardwood trees. The rubbing of a hardwood stick against a flat piece of softwood was used to make fire. This myth explained the origins of a form of dance, the heat of summer, the existence of comets, and the gift of fire.

Left *Battle of Gate Pah* by Orlando Norie (1832–1901). Whakataupotiki is a Maori hero who developed specific approaches and strategies toward war. These principles saw the success of Maori leaders in battles against the Europeans.

417

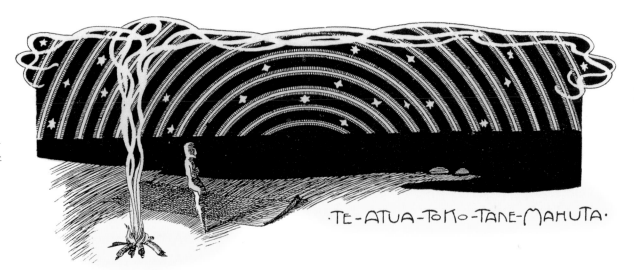

·TE-ATUA-TOKO-TANE-MAHUTA·

Te Marama, the Moon

All living beings beneath the moon will die, while those above it will live forever. The fate of Te Marama (the Moon) is different, because every month the moon dies, then lives again. The moon was also associated with the menstrual cycle of women, and often referred to as Hina (Maiden), hence the saying, "Na Hina te po, na Hina te ao" (By Hina is the day and the night).

Traditions from the far north of the North Island say that Rona, a woman, set out one night carrying her gourd to go and draw water. When the Moon passed behind a cloud, she stumbled among the bushes and cursed the Moon for not giving light. This enraged the Moon, who came down and seized her. Rona clung to a nearby tree, but this tree was suddenly pulled from the ground, roots and all. When the Moon is full, Rona can be seen with her tree and her gourd. The insults she shouted at the Moon were sometimes regarded as the origin of curses and vilification in this world, and a saying warned "Ka mahara ki te he o Rona" (Remember Rona's mistake). Rona was thought to regulate the tides, so another of her names was Rona-whakamau-tai (Rona, the Controller of the Tides). The tribes along the West Coast of the North Island tell a similar story, except that Rona is a man, a *rangatira* (high chief) who is annoyed that he has to draw water in his wife's absence. In the southern Bay of Plenty and the Urewera region, Rona went searching for water with her sister

Tangaroa-a-roto, and when Rona cursed, both women were carried up to become the Moon's wives. In the Hawke Bay region, and some parts of the South Island, the phases of the Moon, along with eclipses, were thought to be due to the constant struggles between the Moon and Rona.

Kopu (Venus) and Pare-a-rau (Jupiter)

Kopu (Venus—the Bowl) and Pare-a-rau (Jupiter—the Headband of a Hundred Lovers) are the two brightest bodies in the heavens after the sun and the moon. Kopu and Pare-a-rau were said to be husband and wife. Their house was on the horizon. Traditions say that Pare-a-rau would sometimes leave her husband, and embark on numerous affairs with other stars. Maori beliefs about these stars reflect an appreciation of planetary motion. The path of Venus is closer to the sun than that of the Earth, therefore it is only seen on the eastern horizon before dawn, and on the western horizon after sunset when the sun is absent from the sky. Jupiter, whose path around the sun is wider than that of Venus and the Earth, is seen tracking across the sky for much of the year. When Pare-a-rau is on the horizon with Venus she is at home with her husband, but when tracking through the heavens alone she is thought to be embarking on her amorous affairs. Venus was also called Tawera (Burnt Up) when seen on the eastern horizon, because the rising sun soon obliterated its appearance. Venus was called Meremere-tu-ahiahi (the

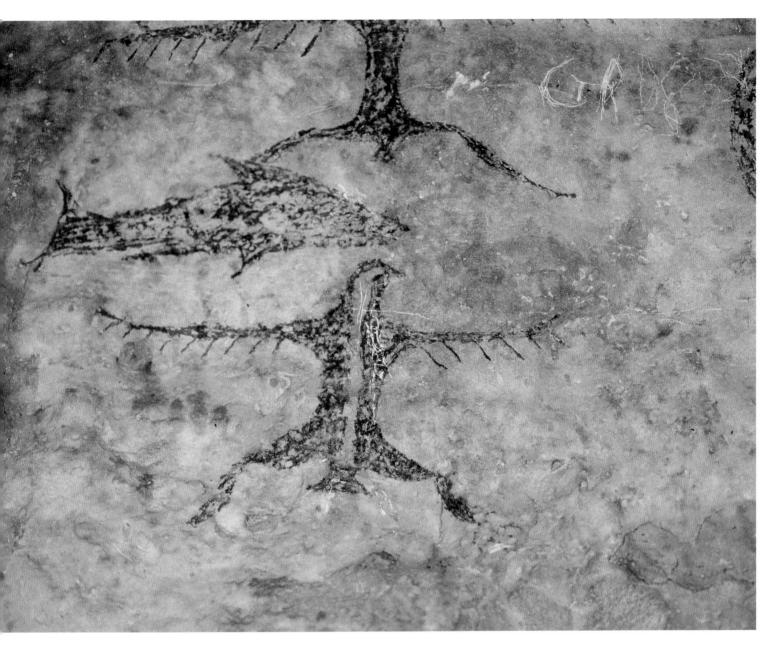

Above **Maori rock drawing.** Early records of these paintings show the hunting and gathering during the seasons. The birdlike ancestor figures are pictured with their arms outstretched as they try to trap a shark.

Evening Display) when on the western horizon, because he was able to show his entire luster once the sun had set.

THE NEW YEAR STARS

The Maori New Year is in the middle of June, when a line of stars including Atutahi or Atuatahi (Canopus), Takurua (Sirius), Puanga (Rigel), Tautoru (Orion), and Matariki (the Pleiades) rise in the morning on the eastern horizon.

Atutahi or Atuatahi is one of the brightest stars in the southern sky and stands out, so its name means to "stand alone." This was often the main New Year star for tribes in the South Island. Takurua is the brightest body seen in the heavens after the sun, the moon, Venus, and Jupiter, and its appearance signals the coming of winter. Puanga was said to be a daughter of Rehua (Antares), the chief of all stars. This star

was held to be of particular significance by northern tribes and was their marker of the New Year. Tautoru, meaning Three Abreast, referred to the belt of Orion.

The small cluster of seven stars known as the Pleiades has the Maori name, Matariki, which means Little Eyes. Matariki is often thought to be a woman, with her six daughters making up the seven star configuration. For many tribes, the appearance of Matariki at dawn (or sometimes the first new moon after their appearance) marks the end of the old year and the beginning of the new. When Matariki first reappeared, she and her daughters were greeted with laments remembering the loss of those who had died in the previous year.

Matariki also brought food supplies to human beings, marking the times to till the earth and signaling when the birds and other game, grown fat on berries and other foods in season, were able to be caught, collected, and preserved.

MYTHOLOGY OF
THE AMERICAS

NORTH AMERICAN MYTHOLOGY

Before European ships reached the shores of North America, life among the tribal communities was never marked by a fragmented existence. Tribal communities embraced a worldview in which all aspects of life were connected (language, teachings, ceremonies, food gathering). This, of course, is not to suggest that indigenous peoples lived in paradise. The ways of harmony included acceptance of social disruption, even unforeseen tragedy. And myth played a vital role in explaining the ways of the world, and the individual's place in it. In our modern world we note a conspicuous reality of detachment from the natural and spiritual world around us, and it is with this contextual understanding of historical tribal communities that we approach the role of myth among native North Americans—both yesterday and today.

Myth was once at the core of maintaining this harmonious balance in tribal life. Stories offered indigenous peoples an understanding of many different things: their origins; their relationship to land, water, and animals; and their connection to the spirit world. Myths also provided guidance for finding an individual's place within the village community. All of the above served to shape an expansive tribal worldview that informed tribal communities of collective values, and of a complex body of knowledge that served to direct tribes for a number of generations.

Storytellers (often elders) held a special place within the community, for they were the teachers, the bearers of these ancient stories. It was their duty to impart this knowledge to the villagers, especially the young ones—"indoctrinating" them into the fold with the

Right **Shield, Plains culture.** Important symbols were often painted on shields to enlist the help of spirits in protecting the shield's owner. In this case a bear is bravely coming out of its hole to face a barrage of bullets—giving the owner the strength of the bear spirit to face his enemies.

Left **Alaskan Eskimo mask.** Native North Americans celebrate their connection to the spiritual world. This Eskimoan mask represents the flight of a shaman's spirit, with the face in the center of the mask symbolizing the shaman's soul.

ultimate goal of perpetuating the tribal way of life. Often infused with sacred ceremonies or celebrations, tribal myths were the foundation of tribal existence, purpose, and identity.

The season of storytelling in tribal communities was held in high regard among tribal members. In these tribal worlds, context was critical to storytelling. How these tribal myths were presented was just as important as the message. In fact, one can observe that the true power of tribal myths rested on proper setting. Myth was delivered orally to tribal members. Parents and children reverently listened as their storyteller told great tales of how the Creator formed the world, or how evil was overcome with the help of kind spirits. From this intimate setting villagers would depart, deeply impressed.

THE INFLUENCE OF EUROPEANS

One of the most severe disruptions forced upon tribal communities by the presence of Europeans was the end of traditional tribal life as it was known. The dismantling of tribal village systems resulted in a massive rupture of social order. Traditions were lost at a rapid pace as the colonization spread. As Native Americans were displaced or dispersed (a number of tribes were wiped out entirely), so too were their ancient ways. The end of traditional tribal community life was evidenced not only by the loss of land, but also by the demise of culture, language, traditional knowledge, and vital ceremonies. Nearly every tribe on the continent faced a harsh measure of loss.

For those tribes that have survived it has been and will continue to be a different world. Though there are native communities living on partitioned land, the infiltration of European life (the institution of a nuclear family; modern technology; as well as political, social, and religious worldviews) have prevented nearly all native communities from returning in entirety to the tribal-centered world of the past. Today's tribal forms of government no longer function like ancient tribal governments. As "wards of the state," native communities have been forced to accept from the Federal Government systems of governance that are in direct contradiction to traditional tribal systems. And many would argue that these forced-upon forms of government have been, and are still today, aimed at

subverting or perhaps blocking any attempts by tribal people to rule over themselves in the original ways their ancestors once ruled.

But in this postcolonial world tribes are seeking to reclaim those old ways as much as possible, despite the change in landscape. Tribes are trying to recover that which was taken from them. And while many myths were scattered, or have been lost through the years, many stories remain alive—saved by memory and recorded in oral libraries hidden deep within the hearts, minds, and souls of tribal elders. These are the amazing stories that continue to be passed down from generation to generation.

THE IMPORTANCE OF CONTEXT

While native people across North America have held on to many of their greatest and most powerful myths, it is evident that the destruction of the traditional way of life has robbed these tribal myths of their full authority over the descendants of those who were first affected by European colonization. For if we recognize that the power of tribal myths is contingent upon a proper setting for storytelling, then we must wonder what role tribal myths play in these modern times for native North Americans, given this loss of traditional tribal communities?

This important issue of contextual loss begs the question: have tribal myths forever lost their highest influence, that of informing one's purpose, place, and direction in the world because there no longer remains traditional tribal villages? If the answer is yes, then is the retelling of tribal myths, at best, a glimpse into how indigenous North Americans once lived a life of balance with their world? Or, at worst, is the retelling of tribal myths merely an entertaining act of theater intended to humor the audience, to tickle the imaginations of children and adults alike?

And perhaps an equally important question to address is this: what role do indigenous North American myths play in the lives and belief systems of the rest of the world's populations? Of course, this and all such questions about traditional tribal knowledge are best left to those who study history, race, anthropology, and other related disciplines, but one must certainly wonder how it would be a different world if it were informed with a base of indigenous North American knowledge.

Above **Bentwood serving dish, Yup'ik culture, southwestern Alaska.** A male caribou is linked to his spiritual counterpart, which is shown with three strange legs. Native North Americans believe that all animals have a soul, and that hunters need to treat their prey with respect if they are to ensure continued success with their hunting.

Right **Sinister spirit figure, Eskimo culture, Alaska.** Many spirits—both benevolent and malevolent—inhabit the Eskimo world. Evil spirits of the sky would create devastating storms, while diabolical earth spirits could make unwary travelers disappear into thin air.

But for the purposes of this chapter we should consider what is to be gained in learning some of the many rich tribal myths of the native North Americans. Tribal myths are finding a place in the popular culture of modern North America. Not too many years ago a Native American playwright was commissioned by a theater company to write a special play for children based on a tribal myth of her choosing. Once the play had been written she stopped in to see how the rehearsals were going. She burst into tears when she realized just how the theater company had coopted her script, how they turned that myth into nothing more than a fairy tale aimed at amusing children. This tribal myth that was once greatly revered as vital knowledge was now, in fact, nothing more than shallow entertainment for the audience.

An editor and/or writer should have a sense of trepidation if committed to retelling indigenous North American myths in published form. Certainly publishers should be fully

aware of the fact that these stories lose so much of their power when removed from their original, traditional setting. Despite these concerns, it is apparent that if the reader pays close attention to these tribal myths, they will make a wonderful discovery. The reader will find that tribal myths still feature a wealth of ancient knowledge and wisdom—that not even the printed page could rob them of their secrets. If read carefully and thoughtfully, tribal myths still reveal age-old truths, no matter how removed they are from proper context.

A DIVERSE ARRAY OF MYTHS

The fascinating myths included in this chapter represent the tribal diversity of North American indigenous communities. There are well over 500 Native American tribes within the borders of the contiguous U.S.A., and more than 250 Inuit tribes in the North American Arctic, which includes Alaska, Canada, and Greenland. (Note that the definition of "tribe" is different in Native American and Inuit cultures—Native American tribes can be an amalgamation of several groups or "bands," while Inuit tribes usually only encompass a single village.)

Included in this anthology are myths from nearly every region of North America. From Greenland, Canada, and Alaska, to the northwest, down the Pacific Coast and to the southwest, through the mountains, across the Great Plains, around the Great Lakes, trailing the northeast and eastern region, then throughout the south the reader will find myths that are as similar as they are different. What these tribes share is a worldview that is based on their relationship to land. The stories of land-based "religions" instruct us on how to live in balance with our world. Tribal myths emerge from our knowledge of the land.

Many of the major themes found in native North American myths are covered in this chapter—there are stories about creation, hero journeys, tricksters, spirits, animals, love, humans, Mother Earth, the sky, and life's passages. Myths from various tribal regions are presented, and the panoramic retelling of the myths should give the reader a taste of the diversity and commonalities among tribal nations. Given that myth is a spiritual language, if it is accurately decoded

Below **Shell gorget (throat pendant), Mississippian Southern Cult.** Flourishing between A.D. 1000 and 1500 in the southeastern woodlands of the U.S.A., the people of this culture decorated much of their art with woodpeckers, their symbol for war.

it can open up the universe to any and all with an ear to hear. One might be surprised to learn that North American tribal myths trace themes similar to those of other ancient myth-making cultures, such as the good and evil of the spirit world, and how the earth was formed. As an example, there are many tribal creation stories that tell of a great flood that covered the earth, similar to the flood in the biblical story of Noah. One can also find an indigenous version of some of the myths told by the Greeks, such as the story of Pandora's box. The universality of these myths is fascinating, but upon closer reading of the stories one will find an entirely different world and worldview that is clearly from a tribal perspective.

These myths come from a wide range of sources, and are retold with noticeable differences to the stories that readers may have heard or read before. This is due to the fluid nature of the myths, which allows the storyteller to alter the stories based on his or her own knowledge and experience. It should be pointed out that even before the arrival of the Europeans, tribal myths were quite fluid. Stories evolved almost with each retelling, and storytellers often introduced new characters and plot lines, changing the myths over a period of years. And throughout native North American communities today, these myths continue to evolve. But their central truths remain and the ancient knowledge has stayed intact, despite the many changes during retellings.

Finally, it should be understood that traditional storytellers never told their myths in the manner in which modern Western readers are accustomed. Western structures of plot development—introducing conflict and gaining resolution—were not the indigenous ways of conveying knowledge. It was more common for a tribal storyteller to embrace a circular style of telling, which kept the myths fresh. This style allowed the storyteller to reveal knowledge when they felt it was

most important, or would have the most impact. However, the myths in this chapter are presented in a mostly conventional, Western form of storytelling. Though they have been reshaped, it is believed that the ancient knowledge still lingers within these pages.

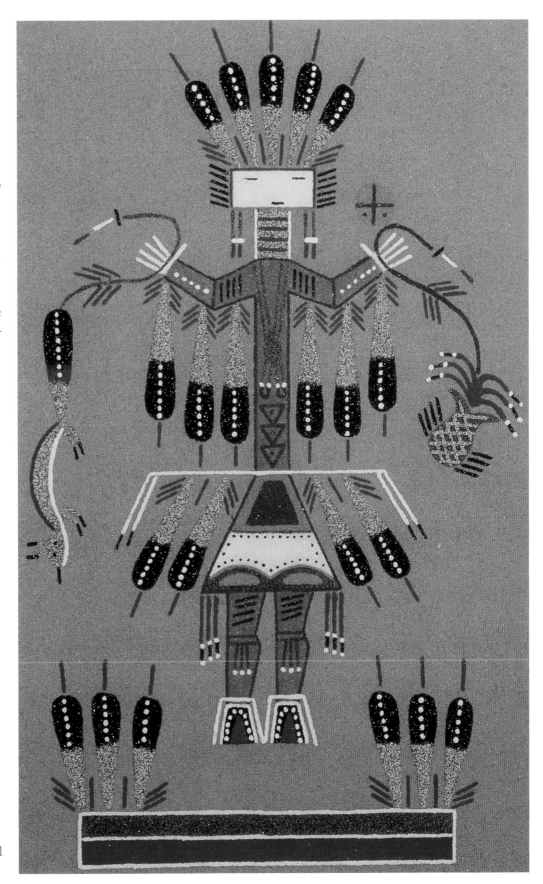

Below **Sand drawing, Pueblo culture.** Sand drawings were created by many different southwestern U.S. cultures as part of a shaman's healing ritual.

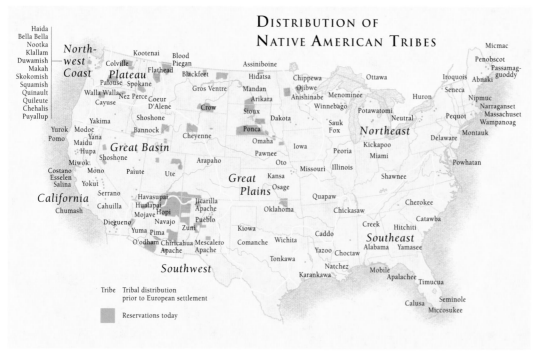

DISTRIBUTION OF NATIVE AMERICAN TRIBES

Haida
Bella Bella
Nootka
Klallam
Duwamish
Makah
Skokomish
Squamish
Quinault
Quileute
Chehalis
Puyallup

North-west Coast

Kootenai
Colville
Palouse Spokane
Flathead
Blood
Piegan
Blackfeet

Plateau

Walla Walla
Nez Perce
Cayuse
Coeur D'Alene
Yakima
Shoshone

Assiniboine
Hidatsa
Gros Ventre
Mandan
Arikara
Crow
Sioux
Dakota

Chippewa
Ojibwe
Anishinabe Menominee
Winnebago

Ottawa

Micmac

Penobscot
Passamag-
guoddy

Iroquois
Seneca
Abnaki
Huron
Nipmuc
Narraganset
Massachuset
Wampanoag

Northeast

Potawatomi
Neutral
Pequot
Montauk

Yurok Modoc
Pomo Yana
Maidu
Hupa
Miwok
Shoshone

Great Basin

Bannock
Cheyenne
Omaha
Pawnee
Oto

Sauk
Fox
Kickapoo
Iowa
Peoria
Miami

Delaware

Powhatan

Costano Mono
Esselen
Salina Yokut
Serrano

Paiute
Ute

Missouri
Illinois

Great Plains

Kansa
Osage
Quapaw

Shawnee

California
Chumash

Cahuilla
Diegueno

Havasupai
Hualapai
Mojave Hopi
Navajo
Yuma Zuni
Pima
Jicarilla
Apache
Pueblo

Kiowa
Comanche
Wichita

Caddo

Creek Hitchiti
Alabama Yamasee

Cherokee

Catawba

Chickasaw

Southeast

O'odham Chiricahua Mescalero
Apache Apache

Tonkawa

Yazoo Choctaw

Southwest

Natchez
Karankawa

Mobile
Apalachee
Timucua

Calusa
Seminole
Miccosukee

Tribe   Tribal distribution prior to European settlement

Reservations today

NATIVE AMERICAN MYTHOLOGY

Originating as oral stories, the engaging myths of the Native American peoples were first written down in the nineteenth century. And although taken out of their tribal context, these fascinating stories continue to be powerful legacies of a proud cultural heritage, with themes and lessons that are as valid today as they were centuries ago.

CREATION DREAMS: THE BIRTH OF PEOPLES AND THE EARTH

Tribal myths that reveal how the natural world came into existence can be found within every Native American community in the U.S.A. They are some of the most ancient of all stories, and explain the origins of the sun, stars, and moon, as well as the land, water, and the indigenous peoples. These rich stories are the very foundation of all other tribal myths, for they speak directly to a unique sense of place and identity. Though these tales vary greatly in structure and the use of imagery from tribe to tribe, they share the common theme of teaching tribespeople the importance of living in balance and harmony with their world.

Right **Mask, Bella Coola people.** Featuring a human-like face with an eagle's beak for a nose, this mask represents a revered ancestor. In Bella Coola mythology, the Creator sent four carpenters to earth from the sky to form the first human beings.

Father Sun, Mother Moon
OSAGE PEOPLE

Long ago in the land where the sky and earth met, in a time when the ancient peoples used to live in both worlds, there was a pair of brothers who grew up never knowing their father. Their mother often told them he died in a great battle while she was pregnant. But as the brothers grew older they heard rumors from among the other ancient peoples—rumors that their father had not died in battle. In fact, the ancient ones said their father was not even a warrior—that he was a stranger who wandered into their world one evening. But even more astonishing was one rumor that implied the sun, who sees all, was the only one who could tell the brothers the truth. And the boys were determined to find out that truth.

The day the brothers planned to embark on their great journey to meet the sun, some of the ancient ones warned them that it was too dangerous. They knew that no other ancient one had ever journeyed to see the sun. However, the warnings did not even make the brothers think twice. They started out on the long journey across the sky.

It was a long journey indeed. The brothers grew low on food. And as they considered that they had at least another week of travel, the younger brother wondered if they should turn back. The older brother, worried that the ancient ones would mock them on their early return from their quest, and gossip even more about their father, convinced the younger that they should continue toward the sun.

The brothers were nearly starving by the time they reached the sun. The sun got right to the point. He told them that he was their father. But that was not all he revealed.

"The woman who raised you both as her own children is not your real mother," he said. "The moon is your real mother. If you don't believe me then ask her yourself. She will be passing by tonight."

And so the two brothers approached the moon as night fell. Sure enough, the moon confirmed to them that she and the sun were their parents. The younger brother was very upset—he knew that the brothers could not return to the ancient ones, as they were not the brothers' people.

The moon lowered her eyes in silence. Then she pointed to the earth and told the brothers to live among the animals.

The brothers nodded and began the new journey to the earth. But as they neared the surface they realized that the earth was covered with water. The water lapped up against their feet, pulling them down. Suddenly they were surrounded by a herd of elk. The brothers begged the elk for help as they splashed in the water.

The leader of the herd turned to the brothers. In an instant the entire herd reached down and began to drink the water. It was not long before the waters were nearly consumed by the herd. The brothers soon found themselves standing on solid ground.

The brothers heartily thanked the elk leader for the animals' help, and invited the herd to live with them on earth. The elk agreed. In time the brothers would learn to grow corn and beans that they would share with the elk. But of course, the brothers politely turned down the herd's offer to share the grass.

Left **Shield, Cree people.** The central figures of this warrior's shield are Pisim the sun and Tipiskawipisim the moon, which are a brother and sister in Cree mythology. The design idea was probably received in a dream or trance.

Below **Nineteenth-century blanket, Navajo people.** One of the Navajo creation myths tells of the "Holy People," gods who were responsible for creating the four original Navajo clans. The first clan, Kiiyaa aanii ("Tall House People"), was produced from maize.

Above **Woven basket, Modoc people.** The Modoc culture is known for its baskets featuring simple geometric designs. The baskets were used to carry and store food and other items, and were traditionally woven by women from tule reeds and porcupine quills.

Basket of Bones
MODOC PEOPLE

There was a time when only an old man and his daughter roamed the hills and valleys of the west. One day the old man decided there needed to be more peoples living in the upper world, and told his daughter that they should go down to the spirit world and see if they could find a way to bring some of them back into their world.

The old man led his daughter down a dangerously steep hill into the lower world. The daughter was amazed at how many spirits lived below. "It's like looking at the stars," she said.

Indeed, at night, the spirits danced and sang— glittering like the stars in the sky. During the day they returned to their homes within the rocks. The old man and daughter noticed that the spirits turned to bones once they entered the rocks, and decided to gather some of the bones in a basket.

When the basket was full they began to climb up the steep hill. But the old man slipped and he lost his basket. The basket tumbled against the rocks, spilling the bones. Immediately the bones turned back into spirits. The spirits quickly raced back into the rocks, before turning back into bones.

Once again the old man and his daughter gathered up some of the bones into their basket. This time though the daughter carried the basket, but she too slipped and lost the bones. Again the bones turned back into spirits, fleeing to the safety of the rocks.

The old man decided they would try one more time to bring the bones to the surface. As they picked up the bones, the old man scolded the spirits. "You don't know how wonderful my world is for you. When you see the land, the sun, and the sky you will never want to return to this dreary spirit world again."

Right **Warrior's cloak, Apache people.** Painted with representations of Apache gods or spirits, who lived in a world where death and disease were unknown, this cloak served to invoke the power of the otherworld to protect the wearer from harm during battle.

The old man told his daughter that they should carry the basket between them up the slippery slope. Finally they reached the upper world. The old man scattered the bones on the ground. With great care he picked out certain bones, and threw them in each direction of his world to create more peoples.

And so it was that the world became filled with other peoples—in the mountains, the valleys, and along the water's shores. In order to help the peoples survive, the old man spoke the names of fish, animals, and plants. As he mentioned each name they appeared as if by magic. Then the old man instructed all the peoples to hunt and gather food to sustain them. The daughter marveled at how all the peoples heeded the old man's words.

The old man looked over his peoples and saw that his work was done. So he and his daughter traveled to the eastern sky to a place near the sun where they could see over the entire land below. Even today the old man and his daughter still watch over the peoples from the sky above.

The Great Chief
YAKIMA PEOPLE

One day the Great Chief decided he was tired of living in the sky, all alone. Even the world below held no life, as it was covered with water.

So the Great Chief came to the water below and began to make big fists of mud. He threw the mud across the waters, creating huge piles of land. Some of the piles grew so high that the tops became frozen

with ice. In only a short amount of time trees and grass began to grow on the large piles of land.

Then the Great Chief rolled a smaller ball of mud, shaping it into human form. Like the trees and grass, the human form came to life. The Great Chief told the man to fish and to gather food from the forest.

But before long, the man told the Great Chief that he was lonely. Taking pity on the man, the Great Chief created a woman for him. While the man hunted, the Great Chief showed the woman how to gather berries, how to sew, and how to cook fish.

One evening the woman had a dream that left her with the burning desire to please her husband even more. She prayed to the Great Chief. The Great Chief answered her prayer by blowing his special breath on her, giving her an invisible gift—the ability to have children. In the years to come, the woman found she could show her daughters and granddaughters all the wonderful home-making skills the Great Chief had taught her.

But as the people grew in number they began to quarrel among themselves. Jealousy and greed overcame many. Harmony among the people was entirely lost. Mother Earth became so tired and angry at all the constant fighting she savagely shook the mountains. Large rocks rolled down the mountains, crushing many of the people and burying them.

The remaining people knew that they had brought on the wrath of Mother Earth because of their fighting. Many raced to the bottom of the mountain hoping to find their loved ones alive. But alas, none of them had survived. Great mourning came over the people.

The people mourned for many days. When the season of grief had passed they returned to their lives—hunting, gathering, and preparing food. Some of the people would return to the mountain graves and they would report hearing the lost spirits of those buried call out sadly.

Many sought the Great Chief, looking to see if he would remove the rocks and allow the spirits to return to their remains. But he would not give them an answer. Instead, the people were instructed to keep the ways that they learned from their grandparents and to pass them on to their own children. It is only by keeping the old ways alive that the Great Chief will one day open up the graves and allow the spirits of the dead to return.

GODS OF THE NATIVE AMERICANS

Although they often have different names from tribe to tribe, certain gods and goddesses of the Native Americans are similar in function. The Great Spirit, Creator, or Master Spirit—known by a variety of names such as Awonawilona (Pueblo people), Isakakate (Crow people), and Tirawa-atius (Pawnee people)—is the omnipotent and omniscient deity responsible for the creation of the universe, and is sometimes represented by the sun. Mother Earth—known as Atira by the Pawnee people, Eithinoha by the Iroquois people, and Isanaklesh by the Mescalero Apache people, just three of her names—is associated with agriculture and fertility, and thanks are offered to her in times of bounty.

Other gods represent the elements, or facets of human life, and can be prayed to for help in times of great need or for relief in times of hardship.

Thunder—Heng (Huron), Hino (Iroquois)
Rain—Sio Humis (Hopi), To'nenile (Navajo)
Wind—Gaoh (Iroquois), Hotoru (Pawnee), Master of Winds (Iroquois)
Love—Ca-the-ña (Mojave)
Sex—Tunkan Ingan (Dakota)
Childbirth—Chakwaina Okya (Zuni)

Below *Sioux Myth of Ictinike* by James Jack. Son of the sun god, Ictinike was infamous for his lying, trickery, and love of war. In one particular myth, Rabbit has his revenge on the deceitful Ictinike by magically compelling him to leap higher and higher into the air with every drum beat—eventually breaking every bone in Ictinike's body.

HONORING WARRIORS: THE POWER OF BRAVERY AND SKILL

The journey of the Native American hero is, for the most part, not unlike that of hero journeys found in other mythologies. Along his quest, a young man must acquire the wisdom and skills he will need when he faces his most challenging test—usually slaying a formidable foe or waging a victorious battle. In many cultural myths the hero's journey is that of overcoming some inner, personal demons that are manifested in outer forms and threaten harm. But in almost every tribal myth the hero's journey is not merely a search for self-improvement. It is a journey on behalf of the community— one that seeks to improve the welfare of the tribal whole.

Bear and Boy
PAWNEE PEOPLE

There once was a boy who never knew just how poor he was until he visited the home of the village chief. The boy was invited to the home by his best friend, the chief's son. From that day forward the boy grew increasingly sad because of his family's poverty. Overcome with this deep sadness, the boy decided to

Right **Rock art, Plains culture.** Depicting an important warrior with a feathered headdress, this ancient rock engraving reveals the value placed on the warrior and his skills. Storytellers would often regale the tribe with tales of heroic deeds and great battles.

430

leave the village and journey into the woods, hoping to be killed by a pack of ferocious animals.

On the second day of his journey he came upon a cave. Thinking he was alone, the boy curled up on the cold ground to sleep.

"Who are you?" a voice said in the darkness.

The boy jumped up to flee but he was grabbed by a large furry paw. Immediately the boy realized he had entered a bear's cave. The boy begged not to be eaten, and the bear told him to keep his voice down, or he would wake the bear's cub.

Suddenly the boy realized that the mother bear had no interest in eating him. In fact, the bear offered to let him spend the night. But she warned him that her husband would eat him when he returned, unless the boy wrapped his arms around the cub.

And so it happened that the father bear returned. When he saw the boy he flashed his great teeth at the sight. But the boy did as the mother bear instructed. He grabbed the cub and stared straight at the father bear who quickly calmed down.

"I will now call you my son," the bear said. He told the boy that he would give him special powers that would make him a great warrior, and that he would take his cub's life and give the boy the cub's skin to protect him in battle.

In the months that followed this meeting the boy returned to the village and joined the war party. He performed many great feats in battle and was praised by the tribe's chief.

Over time the boy's affection for the chief's daughter grew, and he longed to make her his wife. But during the night the bear came to him in a dream and told him he could not marry her until he performed one more grand deed in battle. The boy heeded the bear's words. He led his war party into one final great battle and was successful.

But when he returned from war he found that the chief's son—his best friend—was deathly ill. The boy carried the chief's son to the edge of a cliff and left him alone to feed the birds with buffalo meat. After a few days the boy returned to find that the chief's son was well and that he had acquired particular powers from each of the birds.

The chief was so grateful to the boy for helping his son recover from sickness, he offered his daughter's hand in marriage to the boy.

For many years the boy, now a man, ruled over the village alongside the chief's son. When the time came for him to pass on to the next world, he held his young child in his arms and gave him a special gift—his remarkable bear powers.

Return of the Horses

BLACKFEET PEOPLE

One day an old chief watched as a young orphaned boy was being cruelly teased by a group of others his age. The old man had heard that the boy was deaf, and he knew that the tribespeople all perceived the boy to be stupid as well.

The old chief waited until the children grew bored with teasing the boy and went away. Once the boy was alone the chief approached the boy and offered him some dried meat. The boy knew by the gentle look in the old chief's eyes that he was welcome to live with him.

One day while the old chief and the young boy were walking along the shoreline of a nearby pond, the boy pointed to a herd of horses grazing in the distance. Knowing the boy could not hear his words, the old chief took a stick and drew pictures in the sand. He drew pictures of the tribesmen riding the horses, and then he drew a picture of the horses roaming the plains without the men.

Left **Bear claw necklace, Sac and Fox people.** Necklaces such as this could only be worn by men who had shown their bravery by making contact with the Bear Spirit. This is a deeply religious culture, with the belief that each person and animal in the world has its own guardian spirit.

Below **Horse effigy, Blackfeet people.** Effigies such as this were strapped to the back of Blackfeet warriors who sought visions of power, protection, and success during horse-raiding expeditions. Horses were seen as symbols of great honor and respect by the Blackfeet people, and were either stolen from their neighbors or obtained through trade.

Above *Grandson of Buffalo Bull's Back Fat* by George Catlin (1796–1872). Tcha-aés-ka-ding, the grandson and heir of the Blackfeet chief Buffalo Bull's Back Fat, is shown by Catlin in a robe of raccoon skin and grasping his bow and arrows. In Catlin's words he "stood forth like a tried warrior." Native American boys were encouraged from an early age to emulate the strength, bravery, and skill of the warriors.

the young man to the bottom of the pond where he was introduced to the man's grandfather.

The grandfather sat the boy down and told him he would help the boy bring the horses back to his people. He took off his belt and his robe and gave them to the boy, telling him that the belt and robe held magical powers that would allow the boy to charm the horses.

As the boy was putting on the robe and belt, he saw that the grandfather's feet were actually horse's hooves. Suddenly the young man put his hand on the boy's shoulder, telling him that he needed to return to the surface of the pond.

When he returned the old chief was gone and the boy knew that he needed to set out on his journey to capture the horses. When the horses saw the boy they were stunned and awed at the beauty of his robe and belt. The boy easily befriended the horses, who told the boy that they would only return to the tribe if he learned how to ride properly.

For many days the boy rode the horses across the prairies, gaining their trust and confidence. Finally the horses agreed that it was time to go back to the tribe.

When they returned the boy discovered the sad news that the old chief had died. But the tribe was so grateful to the boy they threw a large celebration to honor his great feat.

The Strong Infant

SENECA PEOPLE

The little boy watched his father grieve at the side of his dead mother. She had passed on while giving birth

The boy realized that the old chief was explaining how the horses decided to leave the tribe. Then the boy took the old man's stick and he drew in the sand a picture of a little boy riding a horse. The old chief knew that the boy wanted to do something great for the tribe. He knew the boy wanted to bring the horses back, something that no warrior had been able to accomplish.

The old chief led the boy a few feet into the pond. The boy lowered his head and stared into the waters. Beneath the surface he could see a young man bidding him to come into the waters. The boy looked at the old chief and then he plunged into the pond.

To his great surprise the boy found that he could breathe under water, and he found that he could hear all the sounds of life beneath the surface. He followed

Above **Pipe in the form of a frog or toad, Hopewell people.** In Native American mythology frogs were sometimes the demonic guardians of fresh water, or they could represent more positive things such as cleansing, regeneration, and fertility.

to her second child. And though the child lived, the father was distraught at the very sight of him. The child was such a painful reminder of the loss of his wife he decided he would take it to the woods and leave it to die.

The boy secretly followed his father as he carried his younger brother deep into the woods. He watched as his father placed the infant on a tree stump and then turned his back on the child and left. Quickly the boy ran for the child and took him in his arms.

The boy had not even thought of how he was going to keep the child's continued existence from his father. He only hoped his father's grief would fade and that one day he would welcome his child back. But as the boy sat in the woods holding the infant, it jumped from his arms. Before the boy knew it, the infant was walking, even running among the trees.

The boy realized that this was a very special infant with great powers. Suddenly the infant reached for a large branch and began felling trees with powerful swings.

The boy decided to keep the infant hidden in the woods, away from his father, but it was an impossible task. Upon hearing the loud crashes, the father raced to the woods to see what was happening. He saw his young boy and the strong infant standing among the downed trees.

Fearing that the villagers would not accept the unusual infant, the father instructed his son to take the child far away from the village, and to raise him alone. But he warned his son not to go north, as it was too dangerous due to the devilish frogs waiting there to eat unsuspecting travelers.

Right **Cradleboard, Pawnee people.** Featuring the symbol for the deity Morningstar—protector of the people's well-being—this cradleboard was used as a supportive base for a soft, skin baby-carrier. Cradleboards were traditionally cut from the center of a living tree to preserve the "heart of life."

But confident that the infant could overcome the frogs, the boy led the child into the north. And sure enough, the infant engaged the evil frogs in a fierce battle—killing all of them quite easily.

The boy believed that the infant could survive on his own, and decided to leave the infant to journey on alone. And indeed, the infant conquered a vast number of enemies who sought to destroy him. The infant defeated enemies in every direction he went. Whether it was east, west, south, or north there was no enemy that could match his powerful strength. Soon word grew throughout the land about the infant's remarkable strength.

When word of the infant reached a peculiar giant who lived farther north, he decided it would best to trick the child rather than fight him. When the infant entered the giant's territory, he agreed to an eating contest. The giant thought he would lure the infant into a deep sleep after feasting on the big meal. But as soon as the giant could eat no more, as soon as he

declared the infant to be the winner, the child ripped the giant into pieces.

It was not long after all of his journeys that the infant grew tired of waging wars with his enemies. One day he came upon some villagers playing ball. Curious at the sight of the infant, the villagers challenged the infant to a game. If the child should win they would give up their land. And, in fact, the child did defeat the villagers. The infant called for his father to come to the village and rule as chief. His father came and ruled for many years.

TRICKSTER TALES: COYOTE AND OTHER TEASING SPIRITS

The impulse for trickery or teasing is very strong within Native Americans. One of the most familiar characters and motifs in tribal myths is that of the trickster. Often showing up in different shapes such as coyote, spider, or beaver, the trickster is always creating havoc, even if his intentions may be good. Depending on his form, the trickster often seeks to deceive the other animals, people, and elements of the sky in order to satisfy his greed. His ever-constant presence in tribal mythology serves to always remind people that there should be a little coyote, spider, or beaver in everyone.

Coyote and the Boxes
HOPI PEOPLE

It had been another long day for Coyote. He had traveled for many miles in his search for food. As his stomach growled in hunger, he felt his luck had run out. He decided he needed to enlist the help of Eagle if he were to survive.

He told Eagle that he had a plan for them to work together in a hunt. With Eagle's eyes in the sky and coyote's nose on the ground he figured that they could catch enough prey to fill both their stomachs. Although Eagle was skeptical, he agreed because he was not having much hunting fortune on his own.

But the hunt did not go well. Coyote complained that Eagle's eyes must be growing old and weak. Eagle answered that he could see perfectly well under ordinary conditions, but there was a lack of good light—there was only so much that he could see in these very trying conditions.

Eagle was preparing to tell Coyote that his nose was failing him when they came upon a village of spirits. The two hunting partners were standing on a hill looking down at the village when Eagle saw that the spirits were gathering around two boxes. Eagle watched as they opened each box; one for more light and the other for less.

KACHINAS

Legend has it that long ago deities known as Kachinas came to earth to live among the tribes of southwestern U.S.A. At first they were honored as both educators and guardians of the people, but as time passed the Kachinas saw that they were being taken for granted and decided to return to their home in the sky. Before they left, however, they taught the tribesmen how to fashion clothing and masks in their images, so that when ceremonies and dances were performed in these costumes the tribesmen would take on the powers of the Kachinas—including the capacity to bring rain for the crops and health to the people.

Kachina dolls, also known as *tithu*, are created by the Hopi people to teach their children about the Kachinas, and are believed to contain some of the power of the particular Kachina they represent. They are carved from cottonwood roots, then brightly painted and decorated with colorful feathers and special religious symbols.

Below **Kachina dolls, Hopi people.** There are hundreds of different Kachinas, from those that represent the sun and clouds to special animal and bird spirits, and no two handmade Kachina dolls are alike. The most prized dolls are carved from a single piece of wood.

Coyote wanted to steal the boxes and keep them, but Eagle only wanted to borrow them for a short time. Coyote consented and it was agreed that Eagle would fly over the village of spirits to get a better look. When Eagle returned he told Coyote that the spirits were careful to not completely open the boxes, fearing that the contents would escape.

Suddenly Coyote's hunger gave way to curiosity. He desperately wanted to know what was in those boxes. It was decided that Eagle was the most qualified to seize the boxes. But they would have to wait until nightfall.

While Eagle went after the boxes, Coyote could think of nothing except the contents of the containers. Eagle returned, carrying a box in each of his two claws. Coyote offered to carry the boxes on the journey back home, saying that Eagle looked tired.

Eagle admitted that he was tired, but he was suspicious of Coyote. He decided to let Coyote carry the boxes only if he promised not to open them. Coyote faithfully promised he would not open the boxes until they returned home.

But as soon as Coyote had the boxes in his grasp he opened them up. In a flash the sun and the moon escaped from the boxes and they fled to the highest parts of the sky, out of reach.

"You fool!" Eagle cried. "Now we shall be at the mercy of the sun and moon. We will only be able to hunt whenever they decide to give us sufficient light!"

But that was not all the trouble that Eagle and Coyote caused. For now that the sun and moon were free to give the world light and darkness whenever they wanted, they also decided to create the cold winter.

Above **Wicker plaque with eagle design, Hopi people.** There are many Hopi myths featuring the eagle, including one where the eagle tricks the coyote into cutting off his own leg, and another where the eagle makes his nocturnal friend the owl hunt during the day, only to see the owl fall asleep and be shot by a human's arrow.

Left **Red argillite pendant in the form of an eagle, Sinagua people.** Living in what is now Arizona between A.D. 500 and 1300, the Sinagua people were influenced in both their artwork and mythology by the bald and golden eagles that soared overhead.

Right **Green quartzite effigy of a buffalo, Plains culture.** Figurines like this would have been used in rituals to honor the buffalo's spirit, ensuring that hunters were not trampled by these mighty beasts and that they came back to the tribe with a bounty of buffalo meat.

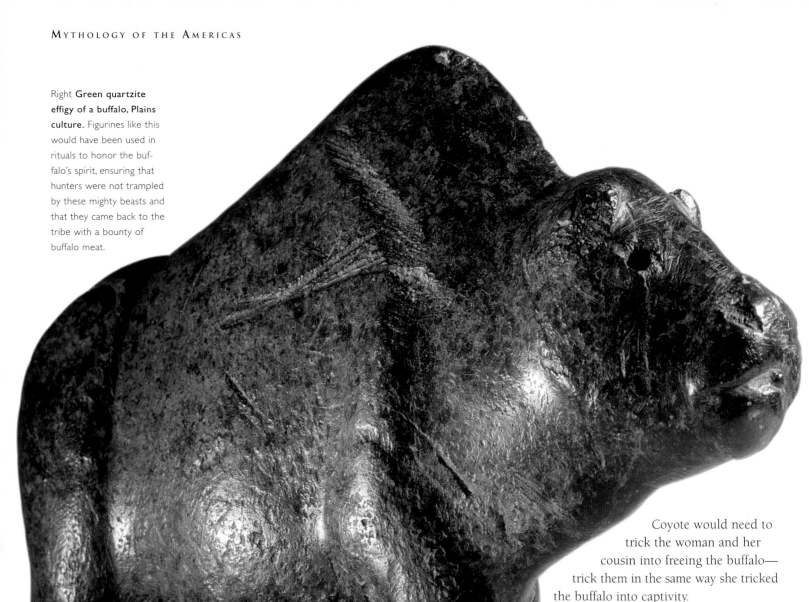

Freeing the Buffalo

COMANCHE PEOPLE

There was a time when the buffalo did not always freely roam throughout the land. Long ago an old woman and her young cousin found all the buffalo grazing on a hill. While the buffalo fed they built a large pen, fencing in the animals.

One day Coyote decided he needed to approach the people to complain about the woman and her younger cousin. He convened a council meeting and announced that as long as the buffalo were fenced in, he would starve. But while the council members were sympathetic to Coyote's concerns, they said the buffalo did not want to be freed for they were charmed by their captors.

From Wakan-Tanka, the Great Mystery, comes all power. ... Man knows that all healing plants are given by Wakan-Tanka; therefore they are holy. So too is the buffalo holy, because it is the gift of Wakan-Tanka.

CHIEF FLAT IRON (MAZA BLASKA), OGLALA SIOUX CHIEF (LATE NINETEENTH CENTURY)

Coyote would need to trick the woman and her cousin into freeing the buffalo—trick them in the same way she tricked the buffalo into captivity.

Coyote agreed and offered a clever plan to free the buffalo. The people would send a small animal to the watering hole where the young cousin went each morning. He would be so taken with wanting a pet of his very own that he would bring it home and convince the old woman that he should keep it. The buffalo would soon become jealous of the new pet and storm the gate, breaking it down. They would race down the hill, free from the old woman and her cousin.

Coyote convinced a small bird to go along with the plan. So one morning the little bird appeared at the watering hole. As Coyote guessed, the young cousin was completely taken with the bird and he brought it home.

"Take this bird back!" the old woman screamed at him.

"Can't you see that Coyote is trying to make our buffalo jealous!"

The young cousin, with much regret, returned the bird. Coyote was furious but not defeated. The next day he convinced a squirrel to try to win the heart of the young cousin. And the squirrel did.

Again the old woman called her cousin foolish, and told him to return the animal to the watering hole or risk losing their buffalo.

And, just like the bird, the squirrel reported to Coyote that he had failed to outsmart the old woman. Upon hearing of the failure of this second attempt, Coyote decided he would send just one more animal—knowing that if this last trick failed then he was unable to beat the old woman and retrieve the herd of buffalo.

For the third attempt Coyote sent a small rodent. The young cousin was so excited at meeting the rodent that he decided that no matter what the old woman said he was going to keep the little rodent as his precious personal pet.

The old woman was so angry she wasted no time yelling at her young cousin. Instead she reached for a large stick and charged at the rodent, trying to kill it. The young cousin screamed as the rodent ran out the door. Desperate to flee from the old woman's wild rage, the small rodent crawled under the fence to hide among the buffalo.

But as soon as the buffalo saw the rodent they were frightened. Chaos broke out among the herd of buffalo, and they charged the front gate, breaking it down easily. The herd roared down the hill, scattering throughout the land. Coyote was pleased with himself.

Fire Thief
NEZ PERCE PEOPLE

It was known for a long time that the pine trees were the only ones who had the secret of fire. And the last thing they ever wanted to do was let any of the animals in on their secret of how to create these great orange flames.

Each winter the animals would growl in anger at the pine trees as they struggled to keep warm. The cold could become so severe that not even the animal with the thickest coat of fur could stay warm.

Attempts to reason with the pine trees over the years were always to no avail. The pine trees were just simply selfish, not at all open to sharing with anyone except their own kind.

During a time of terrible cold air that came upon the land, the animals called a secret meeting to consider ways in which they could get the pine trees to give up their fire secret.

Beaver decided to sneak around on the outskirts of the pine trees the next time they held their council meeting. He knew that the pine trees always prepared a huge fire for their council meetings, and was sure he could snatch a stray coal or two. For once the animals were hopeful that they would learn the secret of fire.

Beaver was extremely patient and careful as he silently made his way around the outskirts of the council gathering. Before the meeting started he watched as the pine trees bathed in the cold waters by the river. He also watched as they dried themselves before one of the largest fires Beaver had ever seen in his life. But Beaver was smart, for he knew that the ancient pine trees were no fools. They had a number of guards posted around the area.

Left **Shell gorget (throat pendant), Mississippian Southern Cult.** The Mississippians worshipped a fire or sun deity, which was represented in their art by a cross. The spider is symbolic of weaving and balance, and was thought to have given the gift of fire to the people.

Below *The Beaver* by **Josiah Wood Whymper (1813–1903).** In Native American mythology, the beaver could be a trickster or a hard-working animal. There are also legends from northeastern tribes that tell of a giant beaver—fossil evidence has shown that a beaver as big as a black bear did once exist in the region.

Above *American Indian Sweat Lodge* by H.E. Sylvester. The sweat lodge ceremony is called *oenikika,* which means "breath of life." In order to reach a higher state of consciousness—and a closer relationship with the spirits—the participants must purify their body by fasting before the ritual, then use the ceremony to dispel negative feelings such as jealousy and hate.

SWEAT LODGES

Sweat lodges are found in most tribal cultures across the U.S.A. Skins or other materials are stretched across a simple wooden frame, and the air inside is heated by burning logs or hot rocks sprayed with water. The sweat lodge combines the four elements of the universe—earth, water, air, and fire—in a sacred structure that is as important to Native American culture today as it was centuries ago.

There are three main purposes for taking part in a sweat lodge ceremony: cleansing the body, purifying the mind, and connecting with the gods. Sweating removes toxins from the body through the pores of the skin, and the beating of drums or chanting during the ceremony focuses the mind. Once the participant has a clean body and mind, they are able to make contact with the spirits.

In the past, shamans (or medicine men) used sweat lodge ceremonies to call upon the most powerful spirits of the universe, and ask for their help in times of adversity.

Below *Blackfeet Shaman* by George Catlin (1796–1872). Many Blackfeet ceremonies—such as the sacred Sun Dance—were preceded by ancient sweat lodge rituals that were performed by the shaman of the tribe.

Beaver sat quietly as the council got under way. And as the fire blazed, a number of small embers burst from the flames and rolled down the bank of the river. Beaver cautiously crawled along the ground and down the bank. While one of the guards was not looking he snatched a handful of hot coals and placed them in a pouch. Beaver dashed toward the dark woods. But as he was fleeing the guards heard his heavy paws crunching the dead leaves beneath him. The council ordered an immediate pursuit.

Beaver tore through the thick woods, leaping over fallen branches and tearing through bushes. But even though he raced as fast as he could, the guards were gaining on him. Beaver decided to risk running along the rugged shores of the river in order to keep ahead. It was a good move. Soon some of the tree guards grew tired of chasing Beaver or fell along the banks, where they remain today.

But just as Beaver breathed a sigh of relief and thought he might be in the clear, a band of guards approached him from the front. Beaver started up the bank only to find another band of guards closing on him. Surrounded, Beaver had no choice but to venture across the river. He held the pouch of coals above his head as he swam across.

When he neared the other side of the river his eyes made out another band of guards waiting for him to arrive on shore. Beaver, though one of the best swimmers among the animals, was growing very tired from running and swimming.

He had only one choice to save the fire. Beaver let the river's current take him downstream. He opened the pouch and, as he floated along, he cast the coals ashore on either side of the river into patches of cedar and birch trees. It was a good move because these trees proved to not be as greedy as the pines. Today you can create fire very easily by rubbing together small sticks of cedar or birch.

SPIRIT WORLD: JOURNEYS TO THE OTHER SIDE

One of the most effective ways to maintain order among tribal villagers was to tell tales of good and evil spirits. Stories told about man-eating spirits that roamed the forest, or about an angry sun that sends a deadly fever to the peoples, proved successful in keeping villagers in line. There was a great belief in and respect for the spirits. Keeping on their good side could also mean help from the spirits as well. Myths about the spirit world were not simple fairy tales for the peoples. They were stories that gave tribal villagers guidance on how to properly conduct themselves while in the community.

Battling Sky Spirits
ANISHINABE PEOPLE

In the days when the land knew only freezing winter, Badger and his friends decided that they were tired of the cold, and they would work together to see if they could change the harsh season to something warmer.

Badger was the first to address the determined group, and told them he had been watching the high place called Skyland for quite some time. He proposed that they make their way up the mountains to Skyland—where it was warm—and bring some of that warmth to earth.

Well, of course, it sounded like a good plan except the other animals were not quite sure of how they were going to bring the warmth back to earth. Otter in particular was certainly not interested in staying in Skyland just to be warm.

Badger told Otter that the journey to Skyland was long, and that they would have plenty of time as they made their way up the mountain to think of a plan to capture some of the warmth and bring it home.

And that appeared to be a good plan for the animals. At once they started up the mountain on their way toward Skyland.

But try as they may, no one could come up with a plan for bringing the warmth back. And yet they had traveled so far that at the very least they were comforted by the fact that they would feel Skyland's warmth, if only for a few days.

Once they reached the place where Skyland met the mountaintop, they were discouraged to learn that they

could not break their way inside. Determined to get into Skyland, the animals took turns banging against the invisible wall. Finally—with one last, mighty effort—they broke through.

Skyland was a warm and beautiful place full of flowers and birds, just as they had expected. And to their joyous wonder they found the warm air of Skyland pouring down to the world below through the hole they had created. The warm air melted the ice and snow from the mountain.

Below *Sacred Otter* by James Jack. In a Blackfeet legend, Sacred Otter dreams of visiting the tipi of Es-tonea-pesta, Lord of the Cold Weather, who gives him special "medicines." Later, he is able to use those "medicines" to ask the Lord to save his people from a blizzard.

Above *Sioux Hare Myth* by James Jack. In this legend, Hare enters the cave of Pahe-Wathahuni and is swallowed by the monster. Hare cuts open the monster's stomach to escape.

But as the animals basked in the warm world of Skyland, a large number of Sky Spirits came upon them. The animals were surrounded by a flurry of arrows. Fearing for their lives, they raced to the hole. But when they reached the hole Badger stopped. He realized that they would have to make the hole bigger or else the Sky Spirits would seal it up again and never let the warmth come to earth.

As the animals hurried to enlarge the hole, one of the Sky Spirits' arrows hit Badger in the side. Badger fell, and as he neared death he told the other animals to go on without him as the hole was big enough.

The animals refused to leave without Badger but they knew they were no match for the Sky Spirits. Badger smiled as he watched the earth below melt away into summer. And then he closed his eyes for the last time. Saddened by his death, the other animals knew they had to flee down the mountainside.

Suddenly the Great Spirit Manitou appeared and took pity on Badger. He waved off the Sky Spirits and knelt at Badger's side. He placed healing medicine on his wound and brought Badger back to life—a different life, in which Badger ascended into the heavens above Skyland.

The inspiring story of Badger's courage is often told when he is spotted in the night sky—some know of Badger as the Big Dipper.

Cave Prophecies
SIOUX PEOPLE

It had been a long day of hunting for the young warrior—a day that yielded no kill. Deciding that he would try again the next day, the warrior started for home. Since it was growing dark he thought he would take a short cut through some hills. And that's when he came across a strange cave that he had never seen before.

Curious, he entered the cave where he found paintings of animals on the walls. And he found many necklaces and bracelets on the ground. He realized that they must have been offerings. Though it was getting darker the warrior wanted to explore the cave in detail. He found many chambers and wall paintings.

Suddenly, the air went black. The man could not even see a glimmer of light in the cave. Chills ran up his arms and he raced to find the cave's entrance.

When he returned to the village he reported what he had seen to the chief. The very next day the chief ordered five of his best warriors to venture to the cave and make their own report about it. Led by the young warrior, the men made their way to the cave.

But once they entered the cave the young warrior noticed that the paintings had changed. The animals were completely different. The young warrior showed the men many of the chambers he had found. Suddenly a sweet odor filled the room they were in. The men traced the delicious smell to a small opening leading to another chamber.

ANCIENT PETROGLYPHS

Native American petroglyphs are ancient forms of rock art found mainly in the present-day southwestern U.S. states of Utah, Arizona, Colorado, New Mexico, and Texas. Symbols and images were either scratched, carved, or pecked into the darkened surfaces of basalt and sandstone canyons, caves, and boulders up to 12,000 years ago, revealing the lighter colored stone underneath.

The specific meanings of many of these images have been lost in time, but it is generally thought that they represent historical events such as the arrival of the Spanish; day-to-day proceedings like hunting and fishing; the relationship between Native American peoples and nature; religious ceremonies, beliefs, or prayers; elements of warfare; or mythological characters and stories. For Native American tribes of the southwest, petroglyphs have been a vital part of their environment since the time of creation, and are still considered significant symbols revealing their ancient histories, intricate societies, and strong beliefs.

Below **Newspaper Rock petroglyphs, Canyonlands National Park, Utah.** Created by many different peoples—including Navajo, Fremont, Ute, and Anasazi—these symbols are said to record important rituals or events.

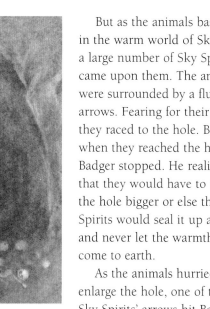

The group's leader decided that instead of exploring this chamber they would return to the camp and report what they had found to the chief. On their way out one of the other warriors decided to take one of the bracelets.

The leader told him to leave the bracelet, as the cave was clearly the home of some great spirit. However, the warrior argued that he wanted to prove to the chief that they spoke the truth about the cave and its many wonders. The leader insisted that terrible trouble would follow the warrior and the rest of the group should the bracelet be taken. But the warrior scoffed at his leader. He placed the bracelet on his wrist and stepped out of the cave. When they arrived home the warrior flashed the bracelet before everyone as proof of what they had discovered.

The next day these same men were setting a trap to catch some wolves. They raised several heavy poles above a piece of meat that rested on a patch of leaves that covered a hole. When the wolf reached for the meat, he would fall in the hole. The men would pull strings, releasing the poles to trap the wolf. But as they prepared the trap, the warrior who had taken the bracelet accidentally slipped. He fell against the poles, which tumbled on top of him. When the others removed the poles they saw that the warrior was alive, but that his wrist was broken.

Frightened about further angering the cave's spirit, the warrior immediately took the bracelet back to the cave. When he entered he saw new paintings on the walls—paintings of a wolf trapped beneath a pile of poles. He also saw paintings of women cutting up buffalo meat and hanging it out to dry.

Since that day the villagers would often come to the cave to see the paintings, to seek direction about how they should live their lives.

Above **Pictographs, Seminole Canyon State Park, Texas.** Produced between 2,000 and 8,000 years ago, these paintings on the wall of a rock shelter may have originally had a specific religious purpose. There are pictorial symbols of humans, animals, warfare, dancing, and other rituals.

Above **Navajo rug.** This early twentieth-century rug features the swastika, an ancient symbol found in the art of many cultures from around the world. In Navajo mythology it represents abundance, happiness, and well-being.

Twins of the Goddess

NAVAJO PEOPLE

When the First Goddess was fully grown she drew the affections of the Sun God. He came up behind her and nuzzled her neck. The warmth of his breath was very pleasing to her, and they were immediately joined in union at that moment. Soon she bore him a beautiful son and they seemed to be forever happy.

But one day while she was resting below a cliff, a drop of dew fell upon her head. It was not long before she realized that she was with child. When the child was born she knew that the Water God was the father. Despite this she raised both boys as if they were twins. They were known as the Twins of the Goddess.

As time passed word spread that there was an evil giant roaming the land, devouring every human he could find. One day he came upon the First Goddess. He was so taken with her beauty he did not want to

In the beginning of all things, wisdom and knowledge were with the animals, for Tirawa, the One Above, did not speak directly to man.

CHIEF EAGLE (LETAKOTS-LESA), PAWNEE
(LATE NINETEENTH CENTURY)

kill her. But when he saw the footprints of her twin boys on the ground he became very jealous and was intent on eating them.

She quickly ran into her home and hid the boys in a hole that was dug in the ground. The giant stormed into the house and demanded to know where the twins were. The First Goddess told him she had no children. The evil giant accused her of lying, as he had seen their footprints. In a sad voice the First Goddess replied that the footprints had been made by her own hands to comfort her as she was so lonely and wanted children of her own.

This seemed to satisfy the giant until the day he saw the boys. But the twins escaped and hid in the hills. Later, their mother came to them while the giant slept. She told them to travel to the west and find their fathers.

The twins did as she told them, but soon realized that their fathers were not in the west. They secretly returned home, and accused their mother of lying to them about where their fathers were. At that, the mother told the boys to go east and then south. And so they did, but they did not find their fathers. They returned only to hear that they must travel to the north to find their fathers. This they did as well but again, they could not find either of their fathers.

Finally the mother relented. She told her sons that in order to reach the place where their fathers were they would need to travel over a great canyon, an awesome place that they would never survive crossing. But the boys were determined to find their fathers, and so they journeyed toward the canyon.

Along the way they met Spider Woman who took pity on them. She gave them each a magic feather to hold up in the direction they wished to travel, and the wind would carry them across the canyon.

When the boys reached the canyon they held their feathers up. The wind carried them safely across the canyon to the Great Water. At the shores of the water a rainbow bridge appeared. The twins crossed the rainbow bridge and when they reached the other side they found their fathers, Sun God and Water God. They were warmly greeted and they stayed there, never returning to their mother.

ANIMAL RELATIVES: SOME OF OUR CLOSEST FRIENDS

There are numerous tribal myths that begin with a sentence like "Back in the days when animals used to speak." The ancestors truly believed there was a time when animals governed the world before the peoples arrived. In fact, many ancient ones would say that the peoples learned to create community among themselves because the animals taught them. These days the animals speak only to one another. But animal myths are still full of wisdom from Brother Wolf and other intelligent animals like him. Native Americans believe that some animals are wiser than even the smartest human in the land.

Day and Darkness
IROQUOIS PEOPLE
Porcupine seemed to be the best choice for leader over the other animals, given the constant division and arguments that always arose over particular concerns. Porcupine was greatly respected for his even temper, and was never one to be easily persuaded.

The first concern that was raised after Porcupine took up his post was a question about day and night. Many of the animals decided that daylight should be constant, while others insisted that darkness should rule the land. As expected, a huge debate erupted between the two sides during the special meeting porcupine had convened. Chipmunk was the most vocal proponent for daylight. He intensely argued that the light of day afforded more time to gather food, as well as for play and relaxation. He believed that there was no productivity at all when night fell, and that the animals wasted a lot of time when it was dark.

Bear matched Chipmunk's argument with his own appeal. He said that fish were easier to catch during the darkness, and that the animals spent far too much time trying to snare the fish that dwell deep in the waters to escape the light.

Left **Elliptical gorget (throat pendant), Glacial Kame people.** Dating from the Archaic Period (over 3,000 years ago), slate gorgets were placed in Glacial Kame burial complexes as offerings. Gorgets are ordinarily plain, but this one has been engraved with the likeness of an animal still bearing its umbilical cord.

Left **False Face Society mask, Iroquois people.** Carved from the wood of a living tree, the False Face mask depicts a mythical being with the power to cure ills. When the owner "feeds" the mask tobacco and sings the sacred song, he becomes imbued with the ability to heal.

443

But no matter how hard Porcupine tried to maintain order it was no use. The animals were so fiercely divided they spent the rest of the meeting time yelling at each other. Nothing was resolved.

The next day Porcupine decided the best way to find a solution would be to speak privately with Chipmunk and Bear. Fearing the debate would result in warring divisions, Porcupine was bent on finding common ground with his fellow animals.

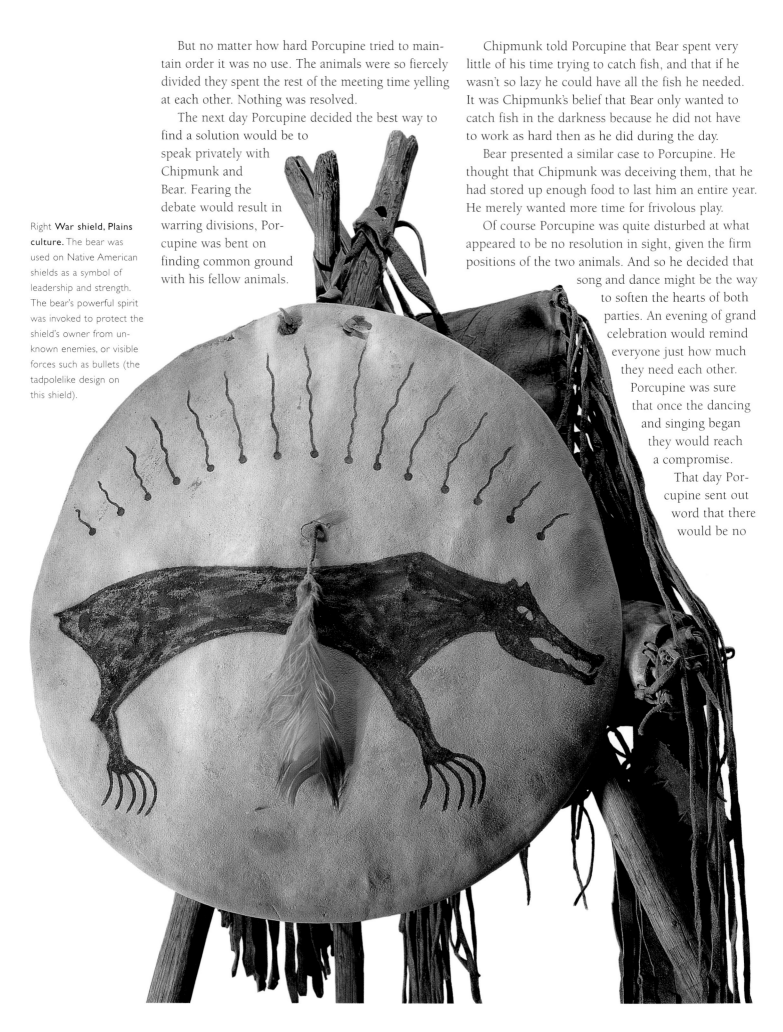

Right **War shield, Plains culture.** The bear was used on Native American shields as a symbol of leadership and strength. The bear's powerful spirit was invoked to protect the shield's owner from unknown enemies, or visible forces such as bullets (the tadpolelike design on this shield).

Chipmunk told Porcupine that Bear spent very little of his time trying to catch fish, and that if he wasn't so lazy he could have all the fish he needed. It was Chipmunk's belief that Bear only wanted to catch fish in the darkness because he did not have to work as hard then as he did during the day.

Bear presented a similar case to Porcupine. He thought that Chipmunk was deceiving them, that he had stored up enough food to last him an entire year. He merely wanted more time for frivolous play.

Of course Porcupine was quite disturbed at what appeared to be no resolution in sight, given the firm positions of the two animals. And so he decided that song and dance might be the way to soften the hearts of both parties. An evening of grand celebration would remind everyone just how much they need each other. Porcupine was sure that once the dancing and singing began they would reach a compromise.

That day Porcupine sent out word that there would be no

evening meeting—it would be an evening of song and dance. And as the evening progressed it seemed that Porcupine's plan was working, for Bear danced right alongside Chipmunk. You might never guess such friends could be so opposed to each other if you were there that night.

But the one thing Porcupine had forgotten about Chipmunk was how arrogant the animal could be. Out of nowhere Chipmunk broke into song, singing "We must have light, we must have light all day!"

Well, naturally, everyone was stunned. Furious, Bear broke into his own song, singing "We must have night, we must have night all day!"

In a matter of moments the singing gave way to yelling—each faction demanding Porcupine rule in their favor. In fact, things were so out of control that Bear lunged at Chipmunk. Chipmunk fled and Bear pursued. Just as Chipmunk was scaling a tree, Bear swiped at him with his paw—leaving a dark mark on his back that has stayed on the chipmunk to this day.

The only way Porcupine could settle the debate was to order that day and night would alternate. And that too remains to this day.

Alligator Wisdom
CHOCTAW PEOPLE

Among the people there was a hunter who was more skilled at the bow than anyone else. But despite this great skill he was terribly unfortunate during the hunt. He concluded that he must be cursed with bad luck.

Though he knew the forest well, and knew where to find huge herds of the most prized deer, something always happened, something that kept him from making the kill. For instance, one day the hunter spotted a large buck. Just as he aimed his arrow a flock of birds swept over the deer, frightening it away. The hunter could only grimace as he watched the animal fleeing deep into the woods.

The hunter's frustration was so great that he decided he would venture into the swamps and remain there until he succeeded. He decided he would not return to the village even if it meant facing his own death during the hunt.

He made his way through the swamps for a few days and finally came upon a very shallow pool. The hunter knew the long hot summer had reduced the ordinarily large pool to nothing more than a puddle. There, on the sand, was an alligator. The hunter was afraid of the beast, and he made sure he kept his distance.

The alligator told him not to be afraid, as he was too weak to harm the hunter. "My luck is worse than yours, friend," the alligator said.

The hunter replied by telling the alligator that there was a much deeper pool just to the east. But even the hunter knew that the alligator was too weak to travel that far east on his own. The alligator then proposed that if the hunter helped him get to the bigger pool, he would help the hunter make a great killing, thus reversing his hunting fortunes.

The hunter was suspicious about the alligator's motives, but the alligator convinced him that he would give him his word. And, to be sure, the alligator let the hunter bind his legs and jaws. Though the alligator was almost too heavy to carry, the hunter was desperate to put an end to his string of bad luck. He carried the beast to the large pool in the east, untied him, and watched him dive into the cool waters.

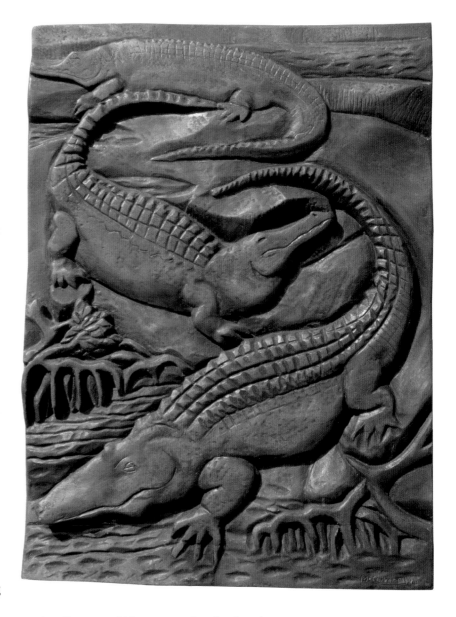

Above **Bronze plaque depicting American alligators.** These creatures are found in the southeastern states of the U.S.A., and influenced the mythology of many Native American cultures in the region. The Choctaw called them *chinchuba* and respected their wisdom and survival skills.

Left **Wooden deer head effigy, Calusa people.** The Calusa inhabited Key Marco in Florida between A.D. 800 and 1400. Discovered by Frank Cushing in the 1890s, this effigy was described by him as having been produced by someone who "loved, with both ardor and reverence, the animal he was portraying ..."

Above **Deer pendant, Sinagua people.** Made from abalone shell (obtained through trade) and turquoise beads, this pretty pendant may have been interred with the dead during burial as a symbol of the game that was hunted during life. The face of the deceased was stained or painted blue and green, and the body was clothed in cotton robes.

Right **Wooden mask with deer antlers, Mississippian Southern Cult.** Produced around A.D. 1200, this mask is made from cedar and inlaid shell. It was probably worn by a shaman during a special ceremony to promote good hunting. Deer meat was an important part of the Mississippians' diet, and a successful hunt was essential for the group.

After some time had passed, the alligator surfaced and swam to the shore. Making sure to keep his distance, the hunter waited for the alligator to speak.

Presently the alligator offered his reward for the help he received from the hunter. He told the hunter to go off into the woods, where he would see a small doe—but he should not kill it. Next he would find a young buck, but he must not kill that one either for the buck shall mate with the doe and she shall give birth to a fawn. If the hunter restrained from killing either animal, he would come upon an older buck, one that was ready to give itself to the hunter. That one the hunter may kill.

The hunter thanked the alligator and eagerly set out on his hunt. As the beast had told him he did indeed come upon the doe and young buck. And he did not shoot either of them. Finally he spotted the older buck and he raised his bow. His aim was perfect. The buck dropped to the ground as soon as the arrow plunged into his side.

Each time the man went out on a hunt he thought about the wise words of the alligator, which taught him about being patient. He never came back from hunting without a kill ever again.

Turned To Stone

NEZ PERCE PEOPLE

Long before the peoples arrived, the ants and bees used to live peacefully on a hillside. That peace was severely disrupted when the chief of the ants insisted on feasting on the chief of the bees' prized salmon.

Though he had plenty of food of his own, the chief ant was taken with jealous greed.

The chief bee liked to dry his salmon on a large rock on the hill. It was here that he returned to eat the fish. One day the chief ant called out as the bee was preparing to eat. He wanted to know what the chief bee was doing on that rock, as that spot was not his. The chief ant believed the chief bee had no right to it, and demanded that he leave at once. The chief bee replied that he ate at this rock all the time.

But the ant insisted the bee had no right to the rock. After a long exchange the chief bee realized the ant really only wanted his salmon. He knew that if he were to leave the rock he would have to leave some of his food as well for he could not carry it all.

Though the bee tried to ignore the ant it became impossible. The ant approached the bee and gave him one last warning to leave. When the bee refused, the ant engaged him in a fierce battle.

While the two were fighting, the coyote came along. He wanted to know why the ant and bee were fighting. But the bee and ant were too busy kicking and biting each other to respond to the coyote. It was only after the coyote roared his loudest that the two stopped long enough to hear the coyote out.

The bee told the coyote that he had always eaten his food on this particular rock, and that the ant knew it. He believed that the ant just wanted to steal his food. The coyote turned to the ant and said that there was plenty of food for all of them in this land.

But the ant was not interested in the coyote's words. He lunged at the bee, catching him off guard. The

bee then responded by biting the ant hard on his back leg. The coyote attempted to get the bee and ant to stop fighting. He warned them that if they did not stop they would cause great division between all ants and bees. If they became divided they would no longer be great throughout this land. But they refused to listen.

Fearing he had no choice, the coyote warned them that if they did not end their war he would be forced to turn them into stone. But the bee and ant were so caught up in their fighting they ignored the coyote's threat. The coyote warned them one last time to either stop fighting or be turned into stone. He knew that if that happened there would be great division between all bees and ants.

Every part of the earth is sacred to my people. Every shining pine needle, every sandy shore, every mist in the dark woods, every meadow, every humming insect. All are holy in the memory and experience of my people.

CHIEF SEATTLE (SEATHL),
DUWAMISH (1786–1866)

But his repeated threats were to no avail. The bee and ant continued to battle with each other. The coyote raised his paw and moved it in the air, calling upon some ancient magic. While the bee and ant continued to fight, the coyote pointed his paw toward them. The bee and ant turned to stone, just as the coyote had threatened.

And the fear of a great division growing between the bees and ants came true. By the time the humans came, the bees and ants were both reduced in power and greatness because of this division. Today, if you look carefully, you can still see the bee and ant locked in each other's arms on that rock.

Left **Pottery bowl painted with insects, Mogollon people.** Painted in the Mimbres style, this bowl dates back to A.D. 950. The Mogollon people of southwestern U.S.A. buried their dead beneath the floor of their home, and placed a decorated bowl over or near the head. The bowl was ritually "killed" at the time of burial by having its base punctured.

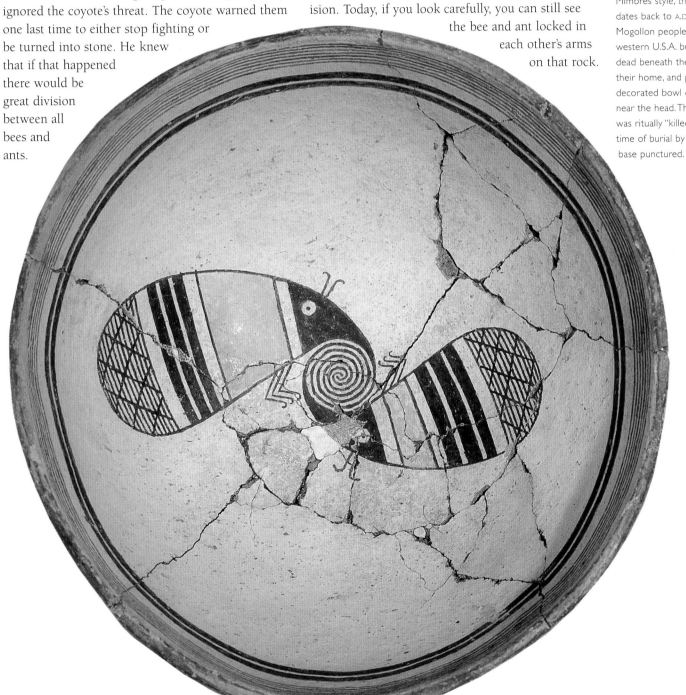

Love Visions: Deep Desire Within Their Hearts

Not many people know that some of the most appealing tribal myths are, in fact, engaging stories about true love. Myths reveal that tribes have always honored rituals of courtship and marriage. But many tribes had no spoken rules for runaway love or unharnessed lust. Rarely, if at all, can one find tribal myths that punished someone who fell in love with a person other than the one he or she was supposed to be with. Like Native

Certain things catch your eye, but pursue only those that capture your heart.

NATIVE AMERICAN PROVERB

American hero tales, many myths that seem to be about wild love are often really about preserving the tribal village's health and wealth.

The Star Lovers
OJIBWE PEOPLE

There once were two young women who longed to make love to the stars, as they thought that stars made the best lovers and they were eager for the experience.

They decided to dream about the stars in their sleep, and let their dreams carry them to the stars during the night. And so the young women put on their very best outfits and washed their hair in order to look their best for the stars. They covered themselves in heavy blankets of fur and drifted off into the dreamworld.

Suddenly they opened their eyes and found that they were among the stars. They were surprised to learn that they each had a new star husband. Excited by this, the young women wasted no time with small talk. They insisted on making love to their husbands immediately.

After many long hours of very intense lovemaking the men decided they had to escape from the voracious women, for they feared making love constantly for the rest of their lives. The star husbands found an opening in the sky leading to the earth below. In order to reach the world below, they lowered a long rope and began to climb down. But on the way down they got stuck in an eagle's nest.

Unable to free themselves from the prickly walls of the eagle's nest, the star husbands cried out for help to the animals that passed by beneath them. When no one was interested in helping them, the husbands tried to tempt the animals with promises of wild lovemaking sessions. However, the only one interested in their offer was the wolverine.

Thinking they would trade one night of passion with the wolverine for their freedom, the star husbands gave themselves to the animal. But when the wolverine was finished he refused to let them go. Instead, the wolverine stuck them back into the thick and prickly nest walls. "Now I shall make love to you whenever I like," he said with a devious grin.

Below *Algon Captures a Star-maiden* by James Jack. According to Shawnee legend, the constellation Corona Borealis is made up of 12 Star-maidens. The hunter Algon fell in love with the youngest Star-maiden and carried her off to his home. She fell in love with Algon but was homesick, and eventually returned to the sky. Algon followed her and became the star Arcturus.

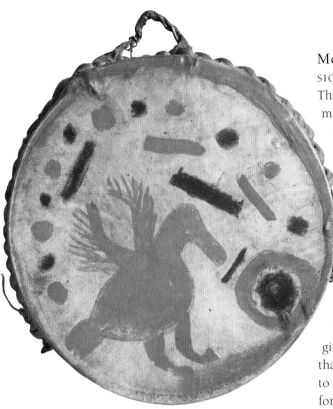

Moccasins of Love

SIOUX PEOPLE

The young hunter had never given much thought to marriage until he spotted the most beautiful girl he had ever seen. Just as he was returning from a hunt he saw her fetching water from the local stream. But even though he was a bold hunter he was very shy with women.

Unable to resist staring at her, the hunter hid in the bushes and watched the girl fill her bucket. After she was done she dried her feet in the warm grass. Then she put on her moccasins. The hunter was amazed at how superb the girl's shoes were.

The hunter lived with his grandmother, and when he returned he wanted to tell her about the girl at the river. He wished to tell his grandmother that he wanted to marry her. But he was even too shy to speak of his feelings to the woman who had cared for him his entire life.

Left **Hand drum with bird design, Ojibwe people.** As with other Native American cultures, the Ojibwe see the drum as the beating heart of the people. It plays a prominent part in social gatherings and religious ceremonies such as the Drum Dance, which is said to bring peace to the Ojibwe people.

The star husbands were furious with the wolverine and his trickery. After the wolverine left they once again called out to the other animals, pleading for their help. But they knew it was no use. They should have stayed with their wives—at least they would be free from the eagle's nest.

Not long after that a female wolverine came by and listened to the pleas of the star husbands. She promised to set the husbands free from the nest on one condition— that they help her in her quest to make passionate love to the male wolverine.

That night the male wolverine returned to the nest. The night was darker than most, and the wolverine had trouble seeing. But he concluded that he did not need his eyes to make love to the star husbands. After a long night of lovemaking, the wolverine woke up to the morning sun thinking that he had just had the best lovemaking he had ever experienced. But he also found that his lover was the female wolverine. Both wolverines were repulsed for they found each other to be terribly ugly.

But the wolverines were also practical animals. "Who else would have us," the female wolverine said. "Besides, I can't imagine either of us finding anyone who can make love as well as we can."

Above **Quilted moccasins, Sioux people.** Intricately decorated with colorful beads and porcupine quills, these leather moccasins feature a design of bear claws and buffalo heads. They may have been made for a Sioux hunter by his loving wife or proud grandmother.

THE SACRED PIPE

Often called "peace pipes" or "calumets," sacred pipes hold both religious and political significance for Native Americans. Tobacco symbolizes the wonder of creation, and in smoking it indigenous people show their respect for the Great Spirit who created all. As the smoke from the pipe rises, the thoughts, feelings, and prayers of the person holding the pipe travel upward to the Great Spirit. If the "keeper" of the pipe lives a good and righteous life, the pipe will reward him with honor and power.

Politically, the sacred pipe has played an important role in treaties between European settlers and Native American tribes. Smoking the sacred pipe signaled an agreement to seek out friendship and harmony between the cultures. To refuse to take part in the pipe-smoking ceremony was regarded by native people as a supreme insult.

Below **Pipe, Crow people.** The leader of a Crow war party would often sit apart from the other warriors to seek advice from the spirits by smoking his pipe. To this day the flag of the Crow nation features a pipe.

Below **Slate pipe, Santee people.** Many traditional Native American pipes were carved with figures of animals or people, who acted as spirit messengers between the earthly realm and the spiritual world. They carried the thoughts and prayers of the person upward in the smoke emanating from the pipe.

After supper the hunter's grandmother sat by the fire and started to sew up some holes in an old pair of moccasins. The hunter sat next to his grandmother, trying to work up the courage to tell her about the girl.

The grandmother knew something was on her grandson's mind, and asked him to tell her what it was. But he couldn't bring himself to confide in her. Instead he turned his attention to the moccasins. "Do women who make fine moccasins make good wives?" he asked. The old woman smiled, knowing exactly what was on her grandson's mind.

The next morning the young man again noticed the girl making her way down to the stream to fetch the day's water for her family. He looked at the pair of his grandmother's old moccasins. When she was not looking he grabbed the shoes, hid them in his shirt, and raced out the door.

Determined to meet the girl, he quickly put on the shoes and ran the entire way to the stream. Just as the girl had finished taking off her moccasins he slowed his pace and walked up to her, offering to fill the bucket for her.

Then he reached down and picked up her shoes, so he could give them back to the girl to put on again. But as he held her moccasins he could not help but admire how beautiful they were.

The girl looked at the hunter's old moccasins and noticed how worn they were. "You should have your grandmother make you a new pair," she said. But the hunter told her that his grandmother was nearly blind and could no longer sew.

Knowing the hunter was vying for her affection, the girl teased him by saying he should find a wife who could make him beautiful new moccasins.

Later the mother of the girl realized that her daughter had not returned from the stream. She set out to find her. When she arrived at the stream she saw the empty bucket. The mother was quite puzzled until she saw something in the sand that made her laugh. She saw two pairs of moccasin tracks leading toward the bushes.

Wolf Woman
DAKOTA PEOPLE

In the days and years that followed this story, the peoples remembered to replant the corn and to smoke the sacred tobacco. They did this to remember their First Mother and thank her for her sacrifice.

There once was a beautiful young woman who was not particularly interested in marriage. All the young men of the village attempted to court her, but none could win her heart. Finally she met a wonderful man to whom she found she could give herself in marriage. She had only one condition in accepting his proposal—he must always treat her kindly.

But not long after their marriage the man broke his promise. He often criticized her and he would beat her. Fearful for her life, the young woman ran away. The men of the village formed many search parties, but the woman was not found.

One day the woman came upon a strange man. Little did she know that he was not, in fact, a man at all.

450

He was the chief of the wolves. Feeling sure that he would not give her up to her cruel husband, she asked the wolf chief if he had any food as she was hungry. The wolf chief held out his hand and offered to take the woman to his village.

When they arrived at his village she found a pack of wolves gathered around a fire. It was then that she realized he was not a man after all. The wolf led her into a tipi and asked her what her pleasure for food was. The woman wanted buffalo meat.

The chief wolf ordered two in the village to go out and bring back some buffalo. When they returned the wolf asked her how they should prepare the meat, and the woman said the meat must be boiled. Then the wolf chief instructed that a large bundle should be opened up. The woman guessed that the contents of the bundle had been stolen from humans.

An iron pot and sharp knives were found inside the bundle. The wolf asked the woman what to do next. She replied that she sliced the meat.

And so she was given a knife and she began to slice away meat from the animal. She dropped the meat in the pot of boiling water. When the meat was ready, she prepared the meal for the entire pack of wolves. The woman stayed with the wild wolves for many months, always in charge of preparing each meal for them.

One night the chief wolf told the woman that her people were on a buffalo hunt, and if they continued in the direction they were heading, they would reach the wolves' camp by morning. The woman had to go to them and ward them off, as they would kill the wolves if they reached the camp.

Left **Wolf head effigy, Calusa people.** The Calusa were a highly religious people and believed in an afterlife. They used local shells and hardwood from nearby forests to create offerings to their ancestors in the form of statues and effigies of animals and birds.

Below *Mexican Coyote 1845* by Col. H. Smith, from Sir William Jardine's *The Naturalist's Library.* The coyote is related to the wolf, and is found from Alaska to Panama. Its wide distribution means that it has found a place in the mythology of many Native American peoples—mainly as a trickster.

Right **Wooden headdress, Nootka people.** Carved in the shape of a wolf and vividly painted, headdresses such as this were worn during the Wolf Society Ceremony (Tluukaana). As part of the ceremony, the elders would take the young men of the tribe away to teach them the heritage and rituals of the Nootka people. Legend has it that these rituals were given to the ancestor of the Nootka people by the all-knowing wolves.

The next day the woman went out to meet the hunting party. But when she neared the men she began to feel faint at the smell of the humans. One of the men recognized her. But the woman told them she had been living among the wolves and was not interested in returning to her people.

The men begged her to come back to the village. The woman was silent. Finally she told them to continue with their buffalo hunt. When they came back this way they had to give her the tongues and some of the best meat. The men agreed.

When they returned they brought her all the requested meat. The woman took the meat and spread it between two hills. Suddenly the hillsides were swarming with wolves who raced to the meat.

The woman returned to the village and eventually made up with her husband. She knew he would now treat her well for she had lived among the wild wolves.

HUMAN JOURNEY: STORIES OF DISCOVERY AND VICTORY

Two of the greatest gifts the Creator gave the peoples were the gifts of observation and humility. Native Americans have always paid close attention to the ways of the animals and plants. Many peoples found their way through famines and long, cold winters by watching how their relatives, the animals, managed.

But once in a while a human will be bestowed with special powers that can either be used for good or evil. Sadly, such humans can allow their pride to rise unchecked, causing great harm both to themselves and to others. But sometimes the gifted human does not allow their special powers to eclipse the simple gifts of observation and humility.

Buffalo Man
UTE PEOPLE

There once lived an old man and his wife. They were very frail and struggled to find food. They had no children to aid them with hunting and other food gathering activities because the woman was barren.

Facing starvation, the old man went out one last time to find some small game. Along the way he came upon some buffalo tracks. But he also noticed a small clot of blood that he guessed was something the buffalo had dropped. He wrapped it in a cloth and brought it home.

That night the old woman boiled some water and placed the blood clot in the pot. When she went to stir the pot she was shocked to see that a baby boy was inside. She lifted the boy from the pot and dried him in her arms.

THE IMPORTANCE OF THE BUFFALO

The buffalo, also know as the American bison, formed an essential part of the economy and culture of the Native Americans—particularly the tribes of the Plains—before the arrival of Europeans. They made use of virtually every part of the buffalo—from the hide and hooves to the bones and organs—and this bounty was believed to be a wonderful blessing from the Great Spirit above.

As well as being seen as a direct link to the Great Spirit, the buffalo was revered for its unique strength and power. Native Americans believed that incorporating "buffalo" as part of a child's name ensured that the child would grow up to be strong, while hunters who dreamed of buffalo regarded the beasts as their spiritual guides to successful hunting.

As befitting these important animals, there are many myths associated with the buffalo, such as "White Buffalo Woman" from the Sioux and Lakota tribes, and "Legend of the Buffalo Dance" from the Blackfeet people.

Left *Buffalo Hunt Under White Wolf Skin* by George Catlin (1796–1872). Men of the Great Plains tribes would hunt buffalo by either stalking them under wolf skins and using their bows and arrows, or by driving the herd over a cliff edge.

In only a few days the old couple noticed that the boy was growing very quickly. It wasn't long before the old man found the boy outside with his bow and arrow. The old man told his wife that the boy was an expert shooter, and he planned to send the boy out to hunt for their food.

The next day the old man instructed the boy to go on a hunt. The boy eagerly took the bow and left. Later that day he returned with nearly every kind of animal that lived in the land—from rabbits and deer to squirrels and birds. The old couple now had enough food to last them for many months.

Years later the boy had grown into a man. The old man soon realized that his adopted son needed to find his own tribe and live among his people. The young man agreed but before he left he wanted to make sure the couple had enough food to last them for their remaining days.

Not many days into his travels the man came upon a village, where he was greeted by the chief. The man told the chief he was looking for his tribe, for he didn't know where he came from. Feeling sorry for the man, the chief offered to let him live among his people.

It was not long before the young man fell in love with the chief's beautiful daughter. The chief allowed him to marry his daughter because he was such a great hunter.

One night the young man told the villagers that a great storm was approaching. He told everyone to fasten down their tipis. The next morning there was a dead buffalo in front of every tipi. It was then the young man realized that he was of the buffalo tribe. But he loved his wife deeply and he told her that in order for him to stay with her people she must not say the words "buffalo calf."

Many weeks later when the men were preparing for a buffalo hunt, the young man's wife forgot about her husband's words of warning in her excitement about the hunt. She cried out to the men, "Kill the buffalo calf!" At once the young man started to flee the village, turning into a buffalo as he ran. His wife called out to him to return, but he did not. He lived the rest of days among his own—the buffalo.

Above **Rattle with buffalo design, Plains culture.** Many ceremonial songs of the Plains region were accompanied by rattles that represented the sound of particular animals, such as the buffalo. In one ritual the Cheyenne utilized a rattle that sounded like the hoof beats of a herd of buffalo, while the Mandan people used a buffalo-calling rattle to bring the herds to them.

Raven Feast
APACHE PEOPLE

Long ago the peoples only had two kinds of seeds for food. They would grind the seeds in preparation for their meals. One day a raven noticed a woman and a man leaving their tipi. Not realizing that there were children inside the tipi, the raven hung his quiver on one of the poles.

Later, when the children came out to play they found the quiver hanging on the pole. They lifted it down and looked inside, seeing some meat. They eagerly ate the food and instantly became fat.

When their parents returned they were in awe at the strange sight of their fat children. While they were inside the tipi, the raven returned to fetch his quiver. The parents watched as the raven flapped his wings and flew away with his empty quiver.

When the rest of village heard the story of the raven's food, it was decided that a group of scouts should seek out the home of the ravens and discover where the birds got their special meat.

For four days the group traveled, and it was a distance that no one had ever traveled before. Finally they found the ravens' camp. They waited until the ravens left the camp, then discovered a bed of ashes where the birds prepared their meat. In order to get close enough to the ravens, a boy was changed into a puppy. They placed the puppy near the ashes, hoping the ravens would befriend him.

Indeed, when the ravens returned they felt great affection for the puppy and they wrapped him in a blanket. As night approached, the puppy watched as the ravens removed a large stone from the ashes, revealing a deep hole in the ground. The ravens descended into the hole and were away for a long time. When they returned they brought back a buffalo with them that was killed for supper.

The next day when the ravens departed, the boy turned himself back into his normal human shape. He found a black feather and a white feather near the ravens' camp. He removed the stone and climbed down the hole with the two feathers. Below he found four buffalo. He placed the white feather on the mouth of one of the buffalo, and commanded the animal to follow him to the world above.

But the buffalo told him he must go to the last buffalo among them. And so the boy went to the fourth buffalo, placed the feather on his mouth, and commanded it to follow him to the world above.

But the buffalo told the boy that he needed to stuff the feather in the first buffalo's mouth. And so the boy did, declaring to the first buffalo that it would be king of all the animals if it followed him to the world above.

Meanwhile the ravens had returned to find their puppy gone. Suddenly the stone in the middle of the ashes was overturned. The boy and a herd of buffalo

put it back in place at will. He could also turn himself into a pile of bones if he wanted.

Word spread throughout the village about the boy with the amazing special powers. Feeling threatened by his growing popularity, the chief attempted to belittle the boy and his powers. The boy refused to be treated in such a way, and soon a fight broke out between the two. The chief was no match for the boy, who was very strong. With a swift jab the boy managed to knock the chief down to his death.

The warriors were enraged and they raced to the boy. But the boy kicked a kettle of boiling water into the fire, causing a large cloud of steam to rise. The warriors were lost in the steamy cloud and the boy escaped from them. For days the warriors tracked the boy but they never got close enough to capture him. The clever boy managed to elude the men at every turn. It seemed to the warriors that the boy could disappear into the rocks of the mountainside.

One day, after the boy eluded the party of angry warriors by slipping magically into the mountainside, he realized that he was not alone. He turned to see a council of old men. One of the old men told the boy not to be frightened, as they were not there to capture or harm him. They were there to help him and his people.

Trusting the wise men, the boy—who was tired of constantly being pursued—asked if he could stay among them. For four years the men taught the boy many mysteries and secrets about the universe. When they felt his training was complete they gave him a bundle of arrows with special powers.

As the boy, who was now a man, neared his home, he shot and killed a buffalo. He thought that this act of goodness might help the village forgive him for killing the chief. Little did he know that a great famine had come over his people while he had been away. They not only welcomed him home, but they made him their chief as well.

came rising from the world below. The ravens scrambled to close the lid but it was too late. The boy and buffalo escaped.

As the ravens watched the boy leading the buffalo to his people's camp, they cried out for the boy to save the eyes for the ravens when the beasts were killed.

When the boy returned home with the buffalo, the chief slit the throat of the first buffalo and a feast was prepared. And the boy saved the animal's eyes just for the ravens.

Boy in the Mountain
CHEYENNE PEOPLE

It was the longest pregnancy that anyone in the village had ever seen. The woman was with child for four years. The elders in the village talked among themselves, musing that when it arrived the child was sure to have special powers.

Indeed, when the woman finally gave birth to the baby, she found the boy to have supernatural skills. Amazingly, the boy could remove his own head and

Below **Detail of a hide warrior's cloak, Apache people.** This cloak features an image of a Gan, one of the mountain spirits who were responsible for teaching the first Apaches how to govern themselves, hunt for food, and heal the sick. The Gans eventually returned to the mountains, but they can still be prayed to in times of need.

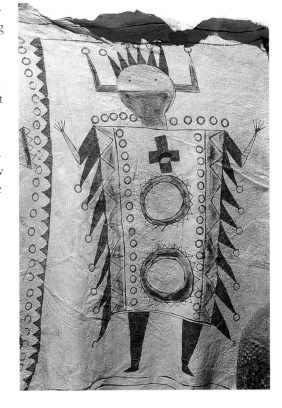

MOTHER EARTH: MYTHS OF LAND AND WATER

For many generations Native Americans have recognized that to truly live in balance with the world they needed to respect both the land and the water. For it is only in respecting and honoring Mother Earth that the peoples can be prosperous. Caring for the land and water has given tribes plentiful food and game. The stories and ceremonies of the peoples come from the land. Without a good relationship with the land and water, Native Americans believe there will be no world for their future generations.

Treat the earth well: it was not given to you by your parents, it was loaned to you by your children. We do not inherit the earth from our ancestors, we borrow it from our children.

NATIVE AMERICAN PROVERB

Monsters and Floods
CADDO PEOPLE

It was not uncommon for monsters to be born among the peoples. Usually they were killed immediately for fear of what they would do to the villagers. But on one occasion a chief's wife convinced her husband that the four monsters she bore him would make productive members of the tribe.

The chief, of course, was entirely opposed to his wife's desires. However, he relented after it was learned that she would not be able to have any more children. Convinced that she could raise the monsters to be good members of the tribe, she fed and nurtured them as any devoted mother would do.

Right *Nekumonta Collapses in the Snow* by James Jack. In this Iroquois myth, the warrior Nekumonta falls to the ground exhausted after searching for special herbs that will save his sick wife. As Nekumonta is a good person who respects the earth, the great spirit Manitou sends him a message in a dream, telling him of the healing waters that will cure his wife.

But it soon became apparent to everyone—as the monsters grew much larger than the rest of the villagers—that something had to be done to ensure the tribe's safety. It was decided that they would be banned from the village. But before they could be banished the monsters went on a rampage, devouring the villagers at will.

In just a few days the monsters killed nearly everyone in the village. Finally an old man in the village, who had been left alone by the monsters because of his skinny frame, heard a voice telling him that the monsters' parents needed to hide in a hollow tree trunk. A great flood was coming and the entire land would be covered with water, the old man told the monsters' parents. The mother wanted to know when this would happen.

"There will be a sign, a cloud of birds will form in the sky," the old man replied. "It will rain until the whole earth is flooded."

The old man was right. Just as the parents entered a hollow tree trunk near the village they saw a cloud of birds overhead. Suddenly the skies opened up with heavy rains that lasted for many days. The parents clung to each other in the floating trunk until the skies cleared.

Meanwhile a turtle was resting at the bottom of the flooded land when he heard a voice telling him to attack the monsters. The turtle thought he was no match for the monsters' great strength, but the voice assured him that the monsters were at a disadvantage in the deep, swirling waters.

The turtle took comfort in that, and he set out to ambush the monsters. He decided he would come right up under the monsters, who were staying afloat at the surface. The little turtle rammed the monsters and then with his sharp teeth he easily ripped them to pieces.

As the days continued the hot sun began to dry the land. Soon the parents were able to walk around again. It took some time but eventually the land was repopulated with a wealth of animals and plants. And

much to the joyous surprise of the woman she was able to have more children. So in time they repopulated the land with humans.

First Mother

PENOBSCOT PEOPLE

Before the time of the world's peoples there was only the All Maker. One day while standing on the shores of the great waters, the All Maker saw the unique shape of a young man emerging in the crashing waves.

He watched as the waves rolled up on the shore, tossing and turning the shape of the youth in the foam and sand. Finally the water yielded the young man. The sun dried his frame and the moist wind gave him breath. The All Maker decided to appoint the young man as his chief helper.

Above **Pottery bowl with hermaphroditic monster, Anasazi people.** Produced by women, the pottery of the Anasazi was made from smoothed coils of clay—which contained the spirit of Mother Earth—and was decorated with geometric designs, symbols of the artist's clan, or images of mythological creatures.

Left **Beaded buckskin pouch in the form of a turtle, Plains culture.** Associated with both fertility and long life, the turtle is a potent Native American symbol for women. This pouch held a female baby's umbilical cord, and was carried later in life to protect the woman from ill health.

Not many days later a young girl appeared to the All Maker and his chief helper. She said she was born from the earth, nourished by the plants, and given blood from the morning dew. She announced that she was the giver of life to all men and animals.

The All Maker thanked the Great Mystery for sending him the young girl. In time the young girl and young man were married. She conceived and gave birth to the peoples. She became the First Mother. The All Maker taught the peoples to live, and then he went north to live for the rest of his years. He returned only when called upon by the peoples for his help and guidance.

As the population grew in size, the hunger of the peoples also grew. There were not enough sources of food to feed all the world's peoples. The First Mother was saddened at the starvation facing her children, and promised to find food for all her young ones.

First Mother spent the evening alone, apart from the peoples, hoping that she could find a way to feed her children. As the evening wore on, her husband came to her, feeling her sadness and frustration. He asked her what he could do to help.

The First Mother knew that the only thing left to do was to have her husband kill her. But her husband refused. She looked her husband long in the eyes and he felt her sadness in a new way.

The next morning the husband traveled north to see the All Maker. The All Maker revealed to the husband that the First Mother would go on with her sadness forever unless he killed her—that the husband had no choice.

The First Mother was very specific about what her husband had to do after he killed her. He had to have his two older sons drag her body across a patch of land by her hair, until only her

bones remained. They must then gather her bones and bury them in a small clearing nearby. They were to wait seven moons before returning to the spot, and when they returned they would find her flesh nourishing the land.

And so, with great sadness, the husband took his wife's life. The sons dragged her body across the land until her flesh covered every part of the ground. Her bones were buried and many tears were shed by the

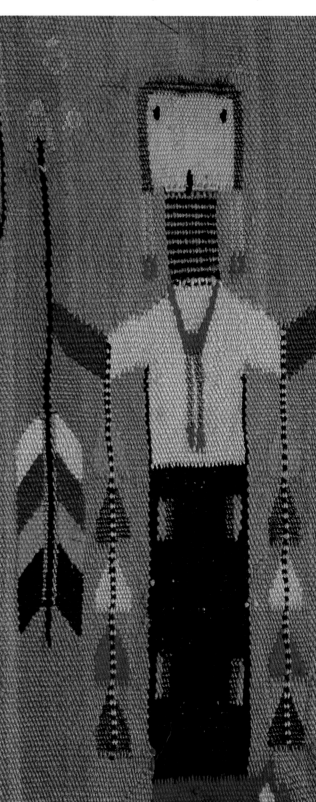

Above **Stone sculpture of a nursing mother, Coast Salish people.** Found along the Pacific Northwest coast of the U.S.A. and into Canada, the Coast Salish people created bowls and tools from local stone, as well as sculptures that were used in shamanistic rituals.

Right **Mother and child sculpture, Nootka people.** Nootka mythology is rich in stories involving mothers. In one, Tihtipihin and Kwat-yat are two brothers who rescue their mother from the stomach of a monster. A second tale tells of a woman whose children have been kidnapped by a malevolent forest deity named Malahas. As she cries, the woman's tears become a fully grown man, Andaokut, who saves the children by killing Malahas.

family. Seven months later they returned and found the land covered with tall green stalks bearing fresh corn. When they tasted it, they found that the corn was sweet. The husband instructed the sons to gather all the corn but to save some of the kernels so they could return them to the earth. He also found a new plant, called tobacco. Before they left they breathed in the sacred smoke of the tobacco plant and offered a prayer on behalf of the First Mother.

Traveling Tribes
CHOCTAW PEOPLE

There came a day when the people who dwelt in the west found their numbers had grown too big for the land. The land offered not enough food to support the tribe. Rather than face years of famine and death, the tribe sought the wisdom of their elders. The elders decided that the tribe needed to move from this land in search of a wealthier region to support them. And so two brothers were called upon to lead the tribe eastward in search of those more prosperous lands.

As the tribe prepared for the long journey, packing up their belongings, the elders called the brothers to a special council meeting. One of the elders presented the brothers with a magical rod that had been with the tribe as long as they could remember.

The elder told the brothers that the rod would guide them and the people to the right place. He warned the brothers not to rely on their hearts and minds, only to trust the rod. For if they did, they would find pleasant lands for the people, lands that would feed them for generations.

The brothers took great care of the magical rod as they led the tribe across the land. Like the elders had said, the rod guided the people on their journey. Each night during their long travels, the brothers would place the rod in the ground. Whichever direction it faced in the morning was the way the brothers would lead the people.

There were many tests along the way. Often many in the tribe liked certain places that they passed, and desired to settle there because there was a river and plenty of woods and animals.

But the brothers always reminded the people that they were not to settle on any lands unless the magical rod stood straight up. Though the people grew tired of the long journey and longed to end their traveling, they had faith in the brothers and in the wisdom of their elders.

Finally, after many weeks of traveling, they found a place that they hoped would be their new home. The land was rich with all the things they once knew in their old world. That night the brothers could only hope the magical rod would agree.

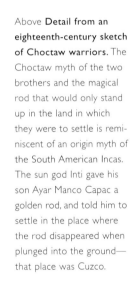

Above **Detail from an eighteenth-century sketch of Choctaw warriors.** The Choctaw myth of the two brothers and the magical rod that would only stand up in the land in which they were to settle is reminiscent of an origin myth of the South American Incas. The sun god Inti gave his son Ayar Manco Capac a golden rod, and told him to settle in the place where the rod disappeared when plunged into the ground—that place was Cuzco.

Left **Nineteenth-century blanket, Navajo people.** As a staple part of their diet, the maize plant featured prominently in the mythology of the Navajo. A deity called Estanatlehi (Changing Woman) created maize, which became the symbolic plant of the north. Later, the "Holy People" produced the first humans from the sacred maize.

THE THUNDERBIRD

One of the most well-known characters in Native American mythology, the Thunderbird is found in the stories of cultures right across present-day U.S.A., from the northwest coast through the Great Plains to the northeast. It is said to cause thunderclaps and windstorms by flapping its wings, while dazzling bolts of lightning are cast down from its eyes.

The Thunderbird is a creature of remarkable contrasts. It is sometimes viewed as a physical entity, with a number of researchers even believing that the myth is based on the existence long ago of enormous birds of prey, but is more often seen as a spiritual representation of nature's power. The Thunderbird can be benevolent—protecting Native Americans from monsters and evil spirits, and providing rain for crops—or malevolent—preying on people and animals, and destroying the land with hail storms and floods.

Below **Ghost Dance shirt with Thunderbird design, Plains culture.** The result of a vision beheld by Wovoka, a Paiute man, the Ghost Dance was said to bring peace, hope, and prosperity to the native peoples. The Thunderbird design may have symbolized protection for the owner of this shirt.

In the morning there was great joy in the camp. The rod was not pointing in any direction. It only faced straight up. But before they could settle in they knew that they must first honor their ancestors. A grand ceremony was performed and the tribe buried their ancestors' bones in a special mound.

But soon after making their home in this new land it was apparent that even this place could not support everyone. But the people did not want to leave the mound where they had buried their ancestors. It was decided that one of the brothers would lead half the tribe north to settle. In time it was reported that the people found prosperous land in the north and they became a tribe of their own. Even today one can find the northern tribe thriving. And one can find the southern tribe still alive and well, living close to the sacred mound where their ancestors remain.

SKY MYSTERIES: STORIES OF THE WORLD ABOVE

The world above has always enchanted and mystified Native Americans. Just about every star has been named, and there are a great many myths inspired by the celestial realm. Many tribal myths tell of great journeys across the skies to uncover hidden secrets of life below, above, and beyond. Some of the most sacred ceremonies and dances of Native American tribes have come to the peoples from the skies. But the world above is not an entirely safe place. For every kind spirit there is always a violent one eager to ambush any would-be sojourner.

Flying Sky Spirits
SEMINOLE PEOPLE

There once were five young men who were far too curious for their own good. They had many questions about their world that no one in the village could answer.

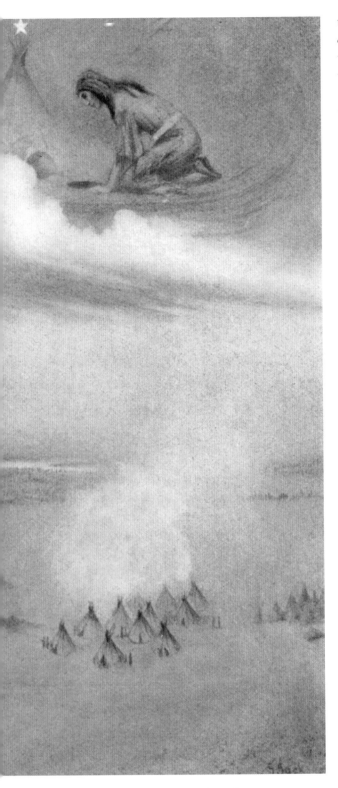

Often they were seen doing nothing but staring into the sky, talking among themselves.

One day a question about flying sky spirits came up among the men. One of them suggested that the only way to get an answer was to travel to the sky and meet the Great Spirit.

The men packed their bags and started the long journey to the edge of the land, with hopes of learning about all the mysteries from the Great Spirit itself. When they reached the land's end they stared into the expansive sky. They decided that to be sure about

their own safety they would throw their bags over the edge to see if they could float. Much to their surprise the bags floated in the wind. The men did not hesitate in jumping over the edge.

And so they made their way across the sky for many days, looking for the Great Spirit. Finally they came upon an old woman living in a tiny lodge, who asked them why they had come there.

They told her of their journey to see the Great Spirit, and of their question about flying sky spirits, then asked her which way they must go.

The old woman answered that they could not see the Great Spirit at this time, and instructed them to stay with her for a few days.

During the first evening the curiosity of the men was too great. They did not want to wait with the old woman. The men decided to leave the lodge and continue on with their journey.

Not far from the old woman's lodge they came upon a band of angels. The angels were playing a game that the men used to play back in their village. The angels invited the men to join them. After the game, two of the men decided they wanted to become angels. Suddenly the Great Spirit appeared and promised to grant the men their wish.

A kettle of water was placed upon a fire. When the water began to boil, the Great Spirit placed the two men in the pot. They were boiled down to their bones. The Great Spirit removed the bones from the kettle and put them back together. The bones suddenly turned into angels dressed in white. The other men were in such awe, their strong curiosity about life's mysteries seemed fulfilled.

"What other mysteries would you like to know?" the Great Spirit asked.

The men looked at each other and could think of no other questions about life's mysteries for the Great Spirit. Instead they asked if they could return to their world. The Great Spirit instructed the men to sleep, and when they awoke they would find themselves back in their village. And indeed the Great Spirit's words proved true, for when the men opened their eyes after a deep sleep they were back in their village. The chief of the village was relieved when the men announced that they no longer wanted to know the secrets of the great mysteries.

Left *Feather-woman Gazes Down From Sky Country* by James Jack. In this Blackfeet legend, Feather-woman marries a star-man and lives in the sky with him. He tells her of a place where she can dig up turnips, but warns her not to dig up the big turnip. One day, full of curiosity about the big turnip, Feather-woman digs it up—only to discover she has made a hole in the clouds, through which she can see her people down on earth. On seeing the Blackfeet camp, Feather-woman becomes sad.

Below **Buckskin chart of the night sky, Pawnee people.** The stars were held in great reverence by the Pawnee people, as they saw the stars as benevolent gods responsible for providing them with sacred ceremonial bundles. There were numerous rituals devoted to the stars, and homes were often laid out in the shape of important constellations.

Above **Cave painting of the sun, Chumash people.** According to Chumash mythology, the sun lights the world by carrying a flaming bark torch across the sky. At the end of his long journey he causes the torch to throw many sparks up into the sky, which become the stars.

Sun's Daughter

CHEROKEE PEOPLE

While visiting her daughter and brother moon one afternoon, the sun complained about the people below. She did not care for the way they always squinted their eyes at her. Brother moon said he liked the people, as they always smiled at him. This, of course, made the sun jealous, and she decided to send a burning fever down to the people.

The sun made good on her promise. A terrible fever spread throughout the land below. Many people grew very sick and quite a few died. The people were bewildered as to why the sun was causing such sickness among their own. Those

*There is no death.
Only a change of worlds.*

CHIEF SEATTLE (SEATHL),
DUWAMISH (1786–1866)

who were strong enough decided they needed to kill the sun if their people were to live.

It was decided that someone would need to use a bit of magic to turn into a snake. He would wait at the door of the sun's daughter's house, and when the sun visited he would bite the sun. Special magic was prepared and a volunteer offered to have a spell cast on him that would turn him into a snake. Once he was changed into a snake the volunteer went to the daughter's house and waited.

But during the wait the snake was startled when the daughter opened the front door. He accidentally bit her instead. The daughter fell dead, and the snake quickly returned to earth.

When the sun found her dead daughter she was distraught. She hid herself behind the clouds and grieved. This, of course, put an end to the fever, but also made the world turn cold and dark. The people feared the sun would never stop grieving and that eventually they would all freeze. They decided they needed to bring the sun's daughter back from the land of dancing ghosts.

The sun promised that if the people brought her daughter back, she would come out from behind the clouds and would not send another fever among them. And so seven people were selected for the mission of bringing the daughter back. It was a short journey, and they spotted the daughter right away. She was dancing with the other ghosts.

They made a plan to catch her off guard. Two men would strike her over the head with clubs, two would keep watch, and the rest of them would be prepared to place her in a box.

Once the men accomplished their goal of knocking the sun's daughter out and placing her in the box, they quickly made their way toward home. But along the way the daughter complained loudly that she was not able to breathe in the box. She wanted the men to open the lid a little.

But just as they opened the box's lid the daughter turned into a bird and flew out of the box and back to the land of ghosts. The men surmised that she had loved dancing more than life.

The men debated a long time about what to tell the sun. They feared greatly that the sun would never return upon hearing about their failure to rescue her daughter. But as the days passed the sun realized that the men had failed. She began to cry, which caused a great flood on the earth. The people were so desperate

NATIVE AMERICAN DANCE

Native American dance has many functions, including the expression of emotion, the promotion of cultural identity, the healing of ills, the influencing of nature, and the honoring of gods. Dances are thought to have been given to the tribes by the Great Spirit, animal friends, or even vanquished monsters, to be passed on from generation to generation to ensure the ongoing preservation of ancient beliefs and ways of living.

Many Native American dances are performed in a circular pattern, symbolizing the never-ending circle of life. Although the dances can be accompanied by a range of instruments—from rattles and whistles to rhythm sticks—the base drum beat is at the center of the dance and represents the beating heart of nature personified, Mother Earth.

Some of the most well-known Native American dances include the Ute Bear Dance, the Hopi Snake Dance, and the Sun Dance and Ghost Dance performed by many of the Plains peoples.

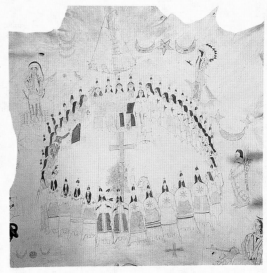

Below **Hide painting showing Sun Dance, Sioux people.** The Sun Dance was held only once a year, at the time of the summer solstice. It brought the whole tribe together for a sacred ceremony celebrating renewal and regeneration, which lasted four to eight days.

they told the sun that all they could offer her was her daughter's special dance. When the sun saw how the people danced like her daughter she was immensely relieved. From that day forward each time the sun felt sad and began to cry—causing rain to fall—the people would dance like her daughter. And that would ease the sun's grief for her daughter.

TRIBAL PASSAGES: LOVE, DEATH, AND THE COMING OF AGE

Tribal myths were critical for keeping a sense of harmony and balance among the villagers. Roles were always made clear. Whether it was hunting or cooking, each person in the tribe contributed to this balance by fulfilling their designated role. And while having to leave the mother's bosom to cross into the difficult world of adulthood came with its share of trauma, and the sudden death of a loved one was not always immediately accepted, the recognition of natural and spiritual passages among community members was always steadfast. It was through hearing the traditional tribal myths that the villagers found their life's calling and the courage to face such necessary tribal passages.

Left **Pot decorated with images of severed hands, Hopewell people.** Used to hold funerary offerings, special mortuary pots were placed beside the deceased. The body and its grave goods were then buried under enormous amounts of earth—these earth mounds sometimes took the shape of animals such as snakes or alligators.

The Rattlesnake's Wife

POMO PEOPLE

When the clover was just right to eat, little girls loved to go into the fields and pluck it. Often they would pass by secret pits of rattlesnakes that lived in the rocks. The snakes kept to themselves because they feared the humans. Little did they know that the humans feared them as well.

One bright and breezy afternoon a rattlesnake happened to be slithering along through the grass when he noticed a little girl picking some of the clover. More than curious, the snake watched the young girl, noticing how beautiful she looked.

When the girl was finished picking the clover she started for home, and the snake followed her. Just as they neared her home he turned himself into a human, for he was overcome with desire. When he came to the door the family was surprised to see him, for they had never seen him before. The girl's village was very small and everyone knew everyone.

The rattlesnake told the girl's father that he had seen his beautiful daughter out in the fields, and wished to marry her. Not prepared to say yes or no, the family invited the stranger to stay the night. In the early morning he turned back into a snake. He realized he needed to leave before the family saw him. But upon arriving back among the other rattlesnakes his desire for the young girl grew. He went back to her home and just before he reached her door he turned back into a human.

Above **Carved coiled serpent with incised diamond pattern.** A pre-Columbian artifact from an unknown Californian tribe, this carving probably represents a western diamondback rattlesnake, which is found throughout southwestern U.S.A. This particular snake features in the art and mythology of the region as a symbol of power and sexual potency.

Right *The Monster Rattlesnake* by James Jack. In a Sioux myth, a war party is confronted by a monster rattlesnake, who rears up as if to strike. The men are afraid, but the chief bravely aims his arrow at the monster rattlesnake and kills it with one shot.

The family invited him to stay again for they still had not made up their minds. But in the morning he again turned back into a rattlesnake. This went on for four days straight. And, like the snake's desire for the girl, the little girl's affection for the stranger grew as well.

Finally on the fifth day the snake decided that he was not going to wait anymore. Should he stay a fifth night he would not leave in the morning. Sure enough, he was asked to stay the night and in the morning, as expected, he turned back into a rattlesnake. Instead of leaving he waited until the family awakened.

Once again he asked for the girl's hand in marriage. The mother of the girl looked around the room, not knowing where the voice came from. Then she looked on the ground and saw the rattlesnake beside her. She was terrified and ran out of the house. But the girl did not. She found the snake even more appealing, and agreed to become his wife.

The girl returned with the snake to his home in the rocks. They lived very well together for many years. The girl even bore four boys. As the children grew older they realized that their mother did not look very much like their father. Their mother explained that she was a human, not a rattlesnake like their father. She warned them that if they saw any humans they must not bite them, for they were their relatives.

She decided that she would let the snakes crawl all over her body to see that humans were not their enemies. The snakes slithered across her frame and were satisfied. They vowed that they would never strike out against the humans if they should ever meet them in the fields.

One day the woman realized that she needed to return home to tell her parents what had happened to her. And though her family was happy to see her again, they were equally sad to learn that she was going back to the rattlesnakes. It was the last time her family ever saw her again.

Dark Wind

MENOMINEE PEOPLE

In the thick woods surrounding the Great Waters there lived a little girl with her mother in their hut covered with birch bark. The girl's father was away on a hunt along the northern shore and would not return until autumn. For the women, summer was a time of gathering berries and herbs while the men hunted deer and other larger animals. This was a time to store up for the long, cold winter that would come upon the thick woods in just a few months.

Left **Native American Woman and Child, 1758.** In a Menominee myth, the dark southern sky signaled danger. However, in general the Menominee people saw the upper world as a good place ruled by the sun, a place that was separated from the evil lower realm by an island of earth inhabited by humans.

Below **Anthropomorphic bowl, Coast Salish people.** Bowls featuring seated human figures were used by shamans in the purification rites associated with the onset of female puberty. The figures often have a rattlesnake carved down the back, which is a symbol of fertility.

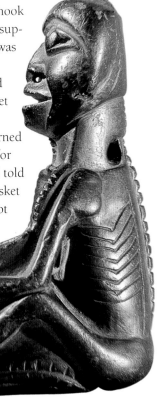

But one morning the mother decided her little girl would have to stay home because the southern sky was the darkest it had been all year. The girl watched her mother staring at the black clouds, then begged to be allowed to go with her mother.

The mother just looked at her daughter and shook her head. She told the girl she would be back by suppertime, and instructed her to make sure the fire was started by the time she returned.

The little girl stood in front of her mother and stomped her bare feet into the grass, refusing to let her mother leave without her.

But the mother would not be swayed. She warned her daughter of the dark wind that was coming for her, the wind that comes for all girls her age, and told her to go inside. The girl clung to her mother's basket and burst into tears, as she was afraid and did not want to be left alone.

At that her mother relented. But before allowing the girl to gather food with her, the mother made her promise that she would never look at the southern sky until nightfall. The girl promised that she would keep her eyes on her work and not the sky.

Right **Fetish bowl, Zuni people.** Fetishes were animal or nature spirits carved from stone, which offered the owner luck, protection, fertility, and more when they were looked after properly. The fetish was kept in a special decorated bowl, and was "fed" through a hole in the side of the pottery piece.

Later that afternoon as the entire sky began to darken, the mother grew very tired and said she needed to rest against a large pine tree. She warned her daughter again about not looking at the southern sky. But as soon as her mother fell into a deep sleep the little girl raced to the edge of the forest so she could get a clear view of the sky.

Suddenly the day turned to night. A huge wind came screaming out of the southern sky. It whipped around the girl, sweeping her off the ground, up into the clouds. But as quickly as she was swept up she came down again, landing softly on a bush of blackberries. She quickly got up and ran to her mother, who was still sleeping. Fearing that she would get in trouble for looking at the southern sky, the little girl did not tell her mother what had happened.

Later that night the mother awoke to the screams of her daughter. She held the girl in her arms, wiping the cold sweat from her forehead. Before she could say anything her little girl began to give birth to three children—Nanabozho, Brother Wolf, and a sharp stone. It was then the mother realized that her young daughter had looked into the darkness of the southern sky. Before she could scold the girl she saw that the

sharp edges of the stone had pierced her daughter's womb. The mother tried to stop the bleeding, but the girl had lost too much blood. By morning her daughter was dead.

The mother cared for Nanabozho and Brother Wolf as her own children. When the two had grown up she placed the stone in her small pouch and led everyone to the edge of the forest. She watched as Nanabozho and Brother Wolf ran off to live on their own. The mother looked at the southern sky, which was bright blue. She reached into her pouch and held the sharp stone in her hand. Then she flung it toward the sky, and it never returned.

The Red Feather

ZUNI PEOPLE

It was the most unexpected thing to happen to any young man. One day, after returning from a long and tiring journey, he found his wife's body in her bed, icy cold with death.

He pleaded with his dead wife to come back from the spirit world and comfort him. That night she appeared to him, and told him she must go on a journey. She added that if he followed her he would have the chance to bring her back into the world of the living.

Then the wife reached for a bright red eagle feather and raised it slowly to her head. As she tied it to her long hair she told her husband that the feather would be his guiding light because spirits become invisible in the other world.

Eager to have his wife back, the man followed her. For many days he trailed, trying to keep up. Then one day they reached a deep ravine. But while she easily moved down the ravine without effort, the husband began to slip, almost falling to certain death. But a nearby squirrel called out to the man, and pointed out the safest passage to take. The man was grateful to the squirrel, as he managed to safely reach the bottom of the ravine.

Once at the bottom he followed his wife to a dark lake. She dove into the water, sinking beneath the

THE MAGNIFICENT EAGLE

Respected for its special strength and skill, and revered as sacred, the eagle played a prominent role in the lives of most Native American peoples. Many saw the eagle as a messenger, carrying prayers to the gods and conveying visions to the warriors and holy men. Their talons were considered powerful talismans that protected the owner from harm, and medicine men used the tubelike bones from the wings to extract the spirit of disease from the body.

But perhaps the most valued part of the eagle was its feathers. They represented the eagle's courage, power, and intelligence, and the special few who bore the feathers on their headdresses or weapons were thought to be imbued with those much-venerated characteristics.

There are many myths related to the eagle. Hopi people believed that the dead were transformed into clouds in the sky, where the eagle was the ruler, while the Delaware people tell the story of the chief who was able to lead his people safely through enemy territory with the help of an eagle's feather.

Below **Eagle wing fan, Crow people.** The feathered wing of the sacred eagle was used by the shaman of the Crow tribe during curing rituals, as the eagle was seen as a powerful medicine.

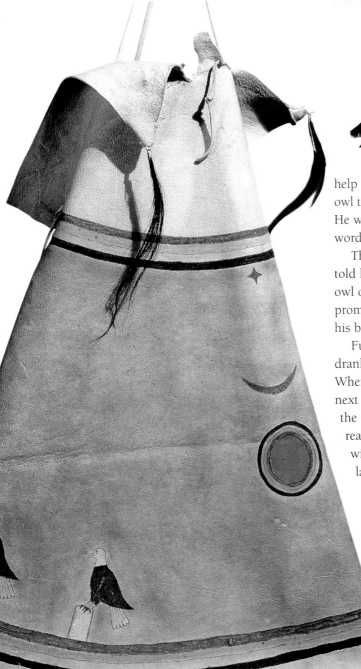

surface. Fearing he would drown if he pursued her, the man sat on the shore in despair. But then an owl noticed the man and felt sorry for him. He offered to help the man find his wife. The man had to follow the owl to his people's cave and listen to their instructions. He warned the man that if he did not listen to their words he would lose his wife forever.

The man promised he would do whatever the owls told him to do. As soon as they reached the cave, the owl offered some sleeping medicine to the man. He promised that when the man awoke, he would find his bride at his side.

Fully trusting the group of wise owls, the man drank the medicine. In minutes he was fast asleep. When he awoke he was overjoyed to see his wife next to him. But when he reached for her, one of the owls told him not to touch her until the couple reached the man's village. If the man touched his wife before then, she would be returned to the land of the dead forever.

The man believed the owl's words, and he fought the temptation to embrace his wife on their journey home. Just as they were nearing the outskirts of their village she grew very tired and begged her husband to let her take a short nap. While she slept the man was so taken by her beauty that he reached out and touched her brow. Suddenly she turned invisible, leaving the red feather in her place on the ground.

Left **Model of a medicine tipi, Cheyenne people.** Medicine tipis were usually erected for ceremonial purposes, and the exterior decoration came from a vision or dream. This tipi bears images of the sun, moon, and a star, as well as eagles ready to carry the owner's prayers from earth to the spirits in the sky.

INUIT MYTHOLOGY

As with the Native American cultures discussed elsewhere in this volume, Inuit peoples from the North American Arctic (which include peoples from Canada, Alaska, and Greenland) have had to adapt to the changes brought by European colonization of North America. These changes have affected their cultures, including their religions and mythology. However, the timing and the degree of change introduced in these cultures and their myths differ from region to region. For instance, Danish explorers, traders, and missionaries landed in Greenland over 300 years ago, causing great changes in religious practices. In contrast, although Russians first visited western Alaska in the mid- to late 1700s, it was not until the 1890s that a sustained U.S. presence, in the form of missionary-teachers and Revenue Cutter servicemen, forced great changes in Yup'ik and Inupiaq religions. In Canada, government educational and settlement programs were not instituted among the Inuit until the 1930s. This difference in timing has affected how many and what kind of traditional myths are still told in Inuit communities today.

Presenting traditional Inuit myths in published form has many inherent difficulties. The preferred method for retelling the stories is to refrain from editing them, in order to allow readers to hear the indigenous Inuit voices. In addition, contemporary folklore scholarship frowns upon retelling myths that mix several versions from different places and different storytellers. Such retellings would not allow readers to know which words came from the scholar and which from the storyteller, or where the myth or story originated. Contemporary folklore scholars also frown upon retelling myths that the scholar did not personally record, and if one does, proper attribution must be given. Finally, contemporary scholars now recognize indigenous intellectual property rights, so that, ethically speaking, scholars should always obtain permission from the native people before telling a particular story from that tribe or clan. The myths retold in this chapter are widely known, and fall under three themes important to Inuit peoples: creation, relationships, and animals. Where possible, all sources of information have been provided.

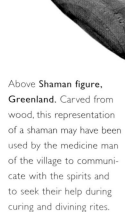

Above **Shaman figure, Greenland.** Carved from wood, this representation of a shaman may have been used by the medicine man of the village to communicate with the spirits and to seek their help during curing and divining rites.

THE "REAL PEOPLE"

In the North American Arctic (including Greenland), "Inuit" is the general term used for all Eskimoan peoples and is the preferred term for those peoples living in Canada. "Inuit" means "people" and is the plural form of the word "inuk," or "person." However, in Alaska, the indigenous peoples prefer their own name. The people in southwestern Alaska are "Yup'ik," which means "real people." The native people of northwestern and northern Alaska prefer the term "Inupiaq," again meaning "real people." The Inuit people of Greenland prefer "Greenlanders," or "Kalaallit" in their language.

Right **Female fertility figurine known as the "Okvik Madonna."** Produced during the Okvik period of indigenous Alaskan history—which occurred around 2,000 years ago—this simple sculpture was carved from the ivory of a walrus.

CREATION

The following three myths recount the origins of various things in Inuit cosmology. The first two stories reveal the origin of two of the three principal powers in Inuit thought. The first tale is based upon a myth found in Knud Rasmussen's *Report of the Fifth Thule Expedition* and tells the origin of the female sea spirit known as "Sedna." The second myth tells the origin of

Above **Walrus figurine, Ipiutak people, Alaska.** Marine mammals such as walruses and whales feature prominently in the myths of the Inuit peoples, especially those from seaside areas such as the Ipiutak culture (A.D. 1–800), which existed close to the Bering Strait.

the sun and moon (and thus, the "moon man," one of the principal spiritual powers) and is based upon tales found in Hinrich Rink's *Tales and Traditions of the Eskimo*, Lawrence Hennigh's "Control of Incest in Eskimo Folktales," and Knud Rasmussen's *The People of the Polar North*. The third myth tells the story of how the crane got blue eyes, and is a well-known tale from the Yup'ik people. The version included here is based upon a myth found in Lorraine Donoghue Koranda's *Alaskan Eskimo Songs and Stories*.

The Girl Who Would Not Marry

INUIT PEOPLE, POVUNGNITUK (QUEBEC)

There once was a girl who refused to take a husband, and in time her father grew angry and gave her to his dog. The dog took her for his wife and the girl soon became pregnant. The father left the girl on a small island and the dog joined her. From time to time, the dog would leave and come back with meat. The girl bore many children—some were in the form of dogs, and others in the form of humans.

After a while, the father felt sorry for his daughter. He took the dog, loaded him with stones and sand, and let him drown. After that, the father brought meat to the island to feed his daughter and grandchildren. However, the girl was angry with him, so she asked her children to attack him. The father escaped and decided not to come back to the island. Because they were hungry on the island, the girl put her dog-children into a boot sole and they drifted to land to become the ancestors of the white men. The human-children went into another boot sole and they became the ancestors of the Inuit peoples. Then the daughter returned home to live with her parents.

One day, while her father was hunting, a hunter in a kayak appeared at their house. The girl agreed to marry him because he seemed like a fine large man, but she eventually discovered that he was actually a very small bird with ugly eyes. They lived together and had a child. One day the girl's father set out in a boat to find her, and arrived while the girl's husband was out hunting. He took her away in his boat. The husband discovered them and caused a storm that almost capsized the boat. In fear, the father threw his daughter overboard, but she clung to the gunwale. He chopped off her first finger joints and they became seals. He chopped off her second finger joints and they became bearded seals. He chopped off the last joints and they became walruses. The girl then sank into the water and became Sedna, the mother spirit of the sea beasts.

Below **Seal-shaped snuff box, Inuit culture, Canada.** According to a popular Inuit myth, seals were created from the fingers of Sedna, the goddess of the sea. Sedna was also known as Arnarquagsag by indigenous Greenland people and Nerivik by native Alaskan cultures.

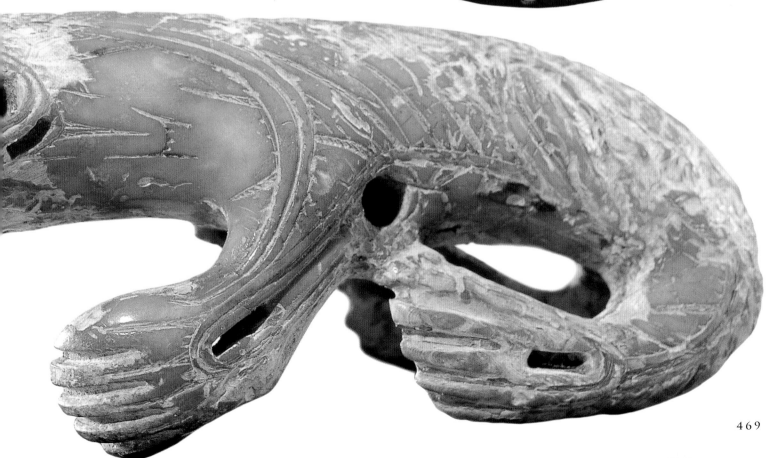

Right **Serving bowl, Eskimo culture, Alaska.** Decorated with a strange mythological creature, this bowl has been painted red and has had the rim steamed and bent into a rounded shape. Bowls like this were used by indigenous women to bring food to the men in their special house, known as a *kashim*.

The Sun and the Moon
INUPIAQ PEOPLE, ALASKA

Two orphans, a sister and a brother, lived together, although the brother always slept in the men's house. The sister did not want to get married. Many young men asked for her hand in marriage, but she refused. Her brother urged her to marry, but she still refused. One night, someone visited her in bed. She was very scared, but she let him go to bed with her. He left the room before daylight. This occurred for several nights. Finally, she decided to find out who it was. When the man next slipped into bed with her, she put soot on her hand from the lamp and marked the man on his cheek.

In the morning, the sister went to the men's house and looked through the skylight. She looked from face to face to see who her visitor might be. Finally, she looked at her brother and he had a soot mark on his cheek. She was surprised by this and went home. She took her *ulu* (women's knife) and a big wooden bowl. She cut off both of her breasts and put them in the bowl. Then she went back to the men's house without putting her parka on, and a great deal of deep red blood marked her tracks. When she got to the men's house, she went in and gave the bowl to her brother, stating that if he wanted her so badly, he could have her breasts. She turned and ran out of the men's house, and her brother chased her around the building. Presently, both of them rose higher and higher into the air. The girl kept running and became the sun. The brother became the moon.

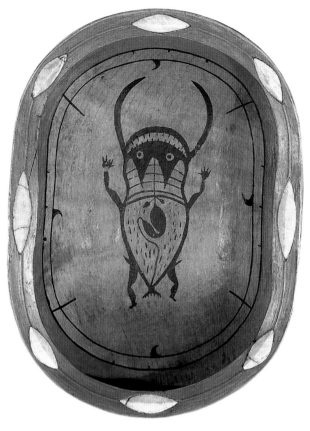

How Crane Got Blue Eyes
YUP'IK PEOPLE, ALASKA

One day, as Crane was walking along, he decided to eat some berries. So he took his eyes off and put them on a stump. He told his eyes that if they saw someone, to yell and let him know. Crane started eating berries. Presently, his eyes shouted out that somebody was coming and they were going to take the eyes away. Crane went to his eyes, put them back on, and looked around. He told his eyes that it was only a piece of wood drifting in the river. He put his eyes back on the stump and told them not to tell him any more stories. He began eating berries again.

A few minutes later, his eyes yelled that somebody was coming and they were going to take the eyes away. Crane put his eyes back on and said that it was only a leaf floating to the ground. He took his eyes off again and continued to eat berries. He told his eyes not to tell any more stories. A few minutes later, the eyes started yelling that somebody was coming and they were going to take the eyes away. Crane ignored the eyes this time and soon the eyes' cries came from farther and farther away.

After he finished eating, Crane discovered that someone had stolen the eyes. So he decided to use cranberries for his eyes instead, and he put them in— but everything was much too red. He then put in blackberries for his eyes, but everything was much too dark. So he found some nice blueberries and put them in, and everything was just perfect. And, ever since then, the crane has had blue eyes.

Below **Mask of the moon spirit, Eskimo culture, western Alaska.** The moon "face" is surrounded by a painted white board that symbolizes the air, circular hoops that reflect the levels found in the cosmos, and a number of feathers that represent the stars.

RELATIONSHIPS

In the Arctic, immediate family and extended family relationships are very important. The following story relates the happy fate of family members who help each other and the terrible outcome for those that do not. Versions of this myth are told throughout the North American Arctic from Alaska to Greenland. This retelling is based upon the myth found in Howard Norman's *Northern Tales*, Edwin S. Hall's *The Eskimo Storyteller: Folktales from Noatak, Alaska,* Hinrich Rink's *Tales and Traditions of the Eskimo,* and Zebedee Nungak and Eugene Arima's *Eskimo Stories from Povungnituk, Quebec.*

The Blind Boy and the Loon
KALAALLIT (GREENLANDER) PEOPLE

There once was a boy who lived with his grandmother and sister. The boy was quite a good hunter, always bringing home plenty of game that his grandmother had to clean and prepare. Eventually the grandmother began to resent all the work that she had to do when the boy came back from hunting. Using magic, she took the boy's snow goggles and put them over a fire. When the boy next used his goggles, he slowly began to lose his sight. Soon he was no longer able to hunt, and he had to stay in the igloo.

By winter, the grandmother, brother, and sister were going hungry. One day, a bear started to eat their skin windowpane. The women were scared, but the boy asked his sister for his bow and arrow and then asked her to aim for him. He shot his arrow and killed the bear. However, the grandmother lied to him and told him that the arrow had missed the bear entirely. The sister whispered to her brother that he did indeed kill the bear. The grandmother butchered the bear and shared the meat with the sister, but only gave broth to the boy.

As spring approached, the boy asked his sister to take him outside. He decided to lie down and rest next to a lake while she continued gathering fuel. Loons noticed the blind boy by the lake. One of them flew to the boy and told him to climb on its head. The loon then dove into the lake several times.

Afterwards, the boy was able to see again, and when the sister arrived, they returned home.

Several days later, as they camped near the sea, they saw beluga whales offshore. The boy prepared to harpoon them and tied the end of his harpoon line to his sister so she could help haul in the heavy whale. He aimed and killed a small whale and they hauled it in. The grandmother then asked him to tie her to his harpoon line. He did so, but this time, he aimed for a much larger whale. This big whale was only wounded, and it began swimming far from shore, taking the grandmother with him. The grandmother was dragged underwater and her long, white hair became coiled into a thick braid. The whale pulled her down to the bottom of the sea and she became the black narwhal with a long, twisted, white tusk emerging from the top part of its mouth.

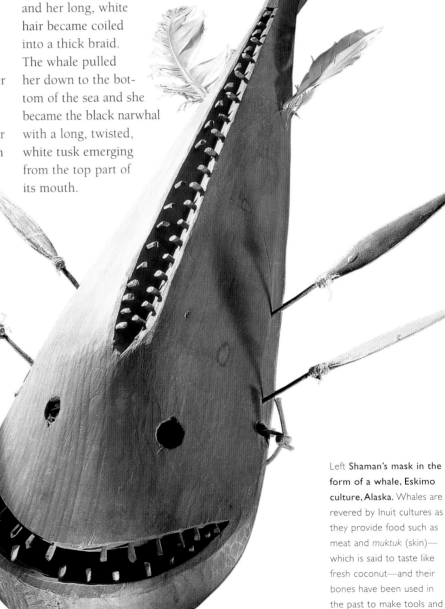

Left **Snow goggles, Eskimo culture, Alaska.** Carved from a piece of wood or bone, snow goggles were worn by people of the Arctic region to reduce the glare of the sun off the snow and avoid snow blindness. Unfortunately for the boy in the Kalaallit myth, his grandmother placed a spell on his snow goggles which made him lose his sight.

Left **Shaman's mask in the form of a whale, Eskimo culture, Alaska.** Whales are revered by Inuit cultures as they provide food such as meat and *muktuk* (skin)—which is said to taste like fresh coconut—and their bones have been used in the past to make tools and hunting implements.

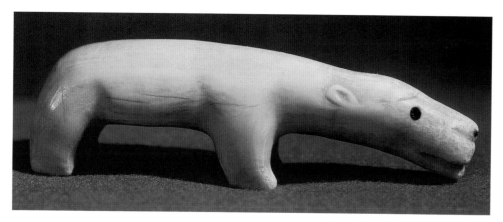

Above **Polar bear, Eskimo culture, Alaska.** The sheer size and power of the polar bear has made it the "king" of the Arctic animals. Called *nanuq* or *nanuk* by the Inuit peoples, legend has it that there was a race of polar-bear men that hunted in their white fur coats during the day, but returned to their igloos at night where they took their coats off.

ANIMALS

In the following myth, the origins of merrymaking and war are told. The story is the basis for Wolf Dance performances, which the King Island Inupiaq of Bering Strait performed in 1982 and in 1991. One of the central themes of Inuit cosmology—namely reciprocal relationships with animals—is prominent in this myth, in which a hunter and the eagles engage in several exchanges. This version of the myth was first recorded in 1924 by Knud Rasmussen, from a King Islander in Nome, Alaska.

We felt that all things were like us people, down to small animals like the mouse, and the things like wood. The wood is glad to the person who is using it, and the person is glad to the wood for being there to be used.

JOE FRIDAY, YUP'IK PEOPLE

The Eagle-Wolf Dance

INUPIAQ PEOPLE, KING ISLAND (ALASKA)

A hunter named Marten killed a giant eagle and distributed the meat to others in his community. He then dried the skin and put offerings of meat into its claws, after which he became a better hunter. Some time later, he went hunting again and met two fox-men, who took him to a strange land. They flew swiftly through the air, going further and further into the country until the hunter heard a loud throbbing sound, which the fox-men said was the heart beat of the mother of the eagle that Marten had killed. He was frightened because he thought the mother eagle would hurt him in revenge for killing her son. Instead, the eagles greeted him kindly and held a feast for him outside the house— Marten had never seen such feasting before.

He then went into the house, where the eagle mother told him that she appreciated the care he gave her son's skin. She also told him she wanted to exchange gifts with him. He told her he wanted to return home and the eagle mother requested plaited sinew in exchange. Marten removed the plaited sinew from his arrow and gave it to the eagle mother, who was pleased. After another feast inside, she asked him to hold a great feast for her son's skin, for which he would need to send messengers to a neighboring village. The eagle mother also taught the hunter how to sing and dance and make merry, and in return for his feast, Marten would have to make a drum that sounded like her heart. The hunter

REINCARNATION AND RECIPROCITY

Inuit people believe that both human and animal souls are reincarnated after death. Death is not feared, necessarily, but is accepted as part of the ongoing cycle of life. In addition, humans and animals exist in equal and reciprocal relationships with each other. Animals are thought to be another class of people, as capable of intelligence and free will as humans, but wearing different "clothes" (their animal skins).

Animals are also believed to have special powers of observation, which they use to keep an eye on human beings. In other words, animals watch hunters and their wives and reward those people that are generous and industrious by allowing the hunter to kill them. In return, hunters have to perform certain rituals that return the spirits of dead animals to their world so they can be reborn. Animals do not give

themselves to hunters that do not follow proper rules for behavior.

Below **Arrow straightener in the shape of a caribou, Eskimo culture, Alaska.** This was an important tool for the Inuit hunter, as it both straightened the shaft of his arrows and served to soothe the souls of the caribou that he shot—ensuring that he would have continued hunting success.

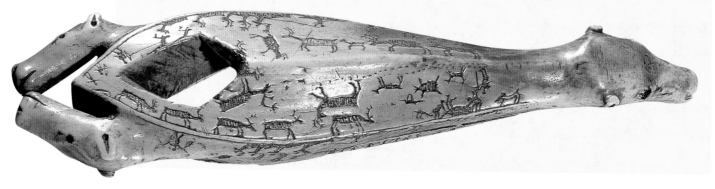

promised, and the eagle mother gave him two caribou heart sacks filled with the ear tips of caribou, wolverine, and wolf. She told him not to lay these down on the ground. The fox-men then returned Marten some distance from his home.

When Marten came to a river, he stopped to have a drink of water. In front of him, Marten saw a steep slope filled with holes. Suddenly, a flock of swallows disappeared into the holes. Then the heads of wolves peered out and began dancing. He was so surprised that he dropped his gifts. He heard a thunderous noise and all the ear tips were suddenly transformed into caribou skins, dried meat, and wolf and wolverine furs. He brought his bundle of gifts home and began preparations for a feast. He taught the other people how to sing and dance. Then Marten sent out messengers. To imitate the sound of the eagle mother's heart, he created a drum from a wooden box topped with sawlike teeth that represented the eagle's home.

He also created a large platform with holes in it to represent the vision of the swallows and wolves that he saw by the river bank. During the dancing at the feast, the dancers would slip into the holes and come out as dancing wolves.

Marten then went hunting for more food. He shot an arrow at a caribou but his arrow flew too high, and he soon discovered that he had accidentally killed one of his special messengers. He became sad and confused. He did not want to stop his festival, so he took the messenger's body home and dried it. Some days later, the guests arrived. After being entertained outside the feast hall, they all went inside. Marten brought in the dried body of the messenger. Songs and dances were performed, but without enthusiasm because of the corpse. When the festival was over, the other messengers decided to kill Marten, but he killed them first. Thus it is always so that merry-making and war go hand in hand.

Above *A Young Indian and his Totem Spirit* by James Jack. Falling exhausted to the ground, the northern Inuit man asks for help from his tribe's guardian or totem spirit, the she-wolf Utonagan. These days the name "Utonagan" has been applied to a breed of dog that closely resembles its ancestor, the wolf.

MESOAMERICAN MYTHOLOGY

Mesoamerica is a geographical and cultural region that takes in present-day Mexico, Guatemala, Honduras, Costa Rica, Belize, and El Salvador. It is thought that the first people arrived in this area about 15,000 years ago, having crossed the land bridge across the Bering Strait between what is now Russia and Alaska, and then moving south.

From about 2500 B.C. until the Spanish invasion in A.D. 1519, Mesoamerica was the center of several civilizations that were highly developed in terms of language, writing, art, architecture, mathematics, astronomy, and agriculture. Basically, these civilizations were known as Olmec (2000 B.C.–A.D. 250), Maya (A.D. 250–900), and Toltec and Aztec (A.D. 900–1500). There was no central or united government, but rather the area was separated into various individual city-states that were often at war with each other.

Right Huehueteotl, god of fire, late Olmec culture. This ceramic representation of Huehueteotl was used during religious ceremonies, when incense was burned in the brazier above the god's head. The Olmec people are considered the "mother culture" of Mesoamerica, as many of their gods and rituals were absorbed by later cultures.

ART AND ARCHITECTURE

The Mesoamerican societies were highly skilled in arts and crafts, and much of the knowledge that we have of their culture and spirituality has been gleaned from their murals, pottery, and sculpture.

Jewelry, masks, and carvings were beautifully crafted in gold, turquoise, obsidian, or jade. Brightly colored feathers, particularly the vivid green feathers of the quetzal bird, were used to decorate clothing and military uniforms.

The Spanish conquerors of the sixteenth century were amazed at the artistic accomplishments of these people. But they were even more astonished at the grandeur and sophistication of their cities, the most important of these being the Mayan cities of Palenque, Tikal, and Chichén Itzá, and the Aztec cities of Teotihuacan and Tenochtitlan.

The palace at Palenque took over two centuries to construct, and is an architectural masterpiece. The chambers in Palenque's Temple of Inscriptions were said to lead to the Underworld. Tikal, meaning "the place where the spirit voices are heard," was a great metropolis built in the center of the jungle. Chichén Itzá features the magnificent pyramid known as the Temple of the Warriors, the largest ball court in Central America, and the sacred well where sacrificial victims were offered to the rain god Chaac.

Teotihuacan was an Aztec place of pilgrimage and an extremely significant sacred site, especially revered for the Pyramids of the Sun and the Moon. Tenochtitlan, the Aztec political and spiritual center, was built in A.D. 1325 on an island in Lake Texcoco ("the lake of the moon") and is now buried under the present-day Mexican capital, Mexico City. The Aztec city was built with the divine inspiration and guidance of the war deity Huitzilopochtli.

PEOPLE OF MAIZE

The economies of Mesoamerica were based chiefly on farming, especially of maize (also known as corn). The crops were grown by means of the slash-and-burn technique in the rain forests, in irrigated fields, or in the ingenious floating gardens known as *chinampas*. Beans, chilies, and squash—as well as cocoa pods, which were gathered in the wild—were also considered valuable crops for the people of Mesoamerica.

Due to the large-scale growing of maize, the Mesoamerican people evolved from a hunter-gather culture to a settled, agrarian society; this resulted in a population increase and development of larger villages and towns.

The success of the maize crop was so essential to physical and financial well-being that it permeated many Mesoamerican myths, symbols, and rituals. The Mayan creation story tells that

MAYAN AND AZTEC DEITIES

DEITY	MAYAN	AZTEC
SUPREME GOD	HUNAB KU, ITZAMNA	OMETEOTL
MOON GODDESS	IXCHEL	XOCHIQUETZAL
SUN GOD	KINICH AHAU	TONATIUH
WIND GOD	GUCUMATZ (KUKULCAN)	QUETZALCOATL (EHECATL)
RAIN GOD	CHAAC	TLALOC
MAIZE OR FERTILITY GOD	YUM KAAX, HUN HUNAHPU	XIPE TOTEC, CENTEOTL
FERTILITY GODDESS	AKHUSHTAL	COATLICUE
DEATH GOD	AH PUCH	MICTLANTECUHTLI

the first human beings were made from maize kernels that had been ground into meal. In an Aztec legend, the plumed serpent deity Quetzalcoatl changed himself into an ant to gather the seeds of what would become the first maize field.

Prayer, ritual, and sacrifice were performed for the deities of fertility, sun, and rain, in the hope that by appeasing the gods the Mesoamericans would in return receive a fruitful harvest.

SACRIFICE AND WAR

The belief in sacrificial offerings—of gold, flowers, and animals, but, most importantly, of human life—was an intrinsic part of Mesoamerican religion. The people thought that if they kept the gods well supplied with blood, the gods would then reward them with a good balance of sun and rain.

But there were deeper, existential reasons for these sacrifices. For the most part, the gods and goddesses were demanding and unpredictable. Both Mayan and Aztec creation myths explain how the world and the people in it could be annihilated on a divine whim, and it was the duty of the people to please the gods so fully that the world would not be destroyed again. The gods would suitably reward victims of sacrifice (especially self-sacrifice, or suicide) with an exalted place in the heavens.

The Maya, and particularly the Aztec, were militaristic nations, and prisoners of war provided a convenient supply of sacrificial victims. The main form of sacrifice was having one's heart cut out; beheading and being skinned (flayed) alive were also commonly practiced. Human sacrifice was also an important element of *pokatok*, the ritual ball game.

WHAT HAS REMAINED

The Spanish conquerors of Mesoamerica, led by Hernando Cortés in 1519, were to eventually abolish human sacrifice, but they practiced different forms of cruelty. They took over the farmlands and forced people into slavery. Many temples and pyramids were destroyed and, as a result, so were their histories and sacred texts. Thousands of Mayan codices were lost, and only a scant few (including the valuable *Popol Vuh*) survived.

Some visionary Spanish monks, such as Bernardino de Sahagún, felt it was important to preserve the ancient Mesoamerican manuscripts. The *Florentine Codex*, transcribed by de Sahagún, is the result of many years' work, and tells us a great deal about the Aztec worldview.

Today, despite centuries of Christianity, some of the old beliefs and ceremonies continue, often creatively blended with Catholic rituals. The surviving literature, art, and architecture are testament to these proud, fascinating, and complex people.

Above **Aztec human sacrifice.** It has been estimated that up to 250,000 people were sacrificed every year during the fifteenth century, when the Aztec civilization was at its most powerful.

Left **Cuauhxicalli, Aztec culture.** Elaborately carved from stone, the cuauhxicalli (or "eagle bowl") was an important vessel used by the Aztecs to store the hearts of human sacrifices.

MAYAN MYTHOLOGY

In what is now Guatemala, Honduras, and the Yucatan Peninsula of Mexico, the Mayan civilization reached its peak between A.D. 250 and A.D. 900. It was a highly organized, sophisticated society, as evidenced at the sites of Palenque and Chichén Itzá on the Yucatan Peninsula, and Tikal in Guatemala.

Most of what we know about the spiritual life of the Mayan people comes from the few books (known as codices) that were not destroyed by the Spanish conquerors, and the *Popol Vuh*, the major sacred text of the Maya. The Maya believed in unseen powers that were present in all of nature, the balance between darkness and light, and the eternal cycle of death and regeneration.

Going to your sacrifice as the winning stroke of your life is the essence of the early sacrificial ideal.

JOSEPH CAMPBELL (1904–1987)

MAYAN COSMOLOGY

The Mayan universe consisted of three parts: heaven (the Overworld), earth (the Middleworld), and the Underworld, and each of these parts was connected to the others by the World Tree.

The Overworld

Unlike the afterlife of many belief systems, the Mayan Overworld was not a heavenly reward for being virtuous. The only way one could gain entry to the Overworld paradise was through a violent death. The most exalted levels were reserved for sacrifice victims. Then there were levels for those who died in battle, those who died in childbirth, and those who died in fire or flood. Those who took their own life were sent to a heavenly realm ruled by Ixtab, the suicide goddess, who is often depicted as having a noose around her neck.

The Middleworld

It was thought that the Middleworld came into existence when the gods spoke the word "earth," and it arose gently, like a mist out of the ocean.

Below **Mayan sacrifice.** This carved stone relief from the ball court at El Tajin, Veracruz, depicts the ritualistic sacrifice of the losing ball-game competitors. According to Mayan cosmology, victims of sacrifice would occupy their own special level of the Overworld.

After the earth was created, it was organized in the same way as the Mayans arranged their maize fields, with the process being described in the Mayan book of creation, *Popol Vuh,* as "the fourfold siding, fourfold cornering, measuring, fourfold staking … of the earth, the four sides, the four corners."

The Underworld

The Underworld was known as Xibalba ("The Place of Fright"), and, like the Overworld, it also had many levels; it was the place where everyone went unless they experienced a violent death. The only way out of Xibalba was by passing a series of grueling tests in which mortals matched wits against the many Underworld inhabitants (as seen in the *Popol Vuh* story of the Hero Twins).

Artists' interpretations about Xibalba vary. Some depict it as being underground; others portray it as being underwater. The demons of the Underworld are shown to be hideous, foul, and grotesque, and are quite often adorned with necklaces made of human eyeballs.

THE BOOK OF MAYAN CREATION

The ancient hieroglyphic *Popol Vuh* (meaning "Book of Counsel") is the creation story of the Guatemalan Quiche Maya people.

Through their complex mathematical calculations, the Mayans concluded that the earth (Middleworld) came into being in 3114 B.C. (on August 13, to be exact). The beginning of the *Popol Vuh* sounds remarkably like the Bible's Book of Genesis, possibly because the original sacred text was transcribed by Spanish monks, who saw the value in preserving the manuscript but could not escape their religious background:

> There was nothing standing; only the calm water, the placid sea, alone and tranquil … then came the word.

Together, the gods Gucumatz and Hurakan uttered the word "earth," and the world came into being, rising up from the sea.

Although the two gods were happy with what they had created, the earth seemed very empty and quiet. So they filled it with animals—birds, reptiles, mammals, and fish—in the hope that these creatures would sing their praises. But when Gucumatz and Hurakan instructed the animals to speak, the gods were horrified at the crude and sacrilegious sounds that the animals emitted. "We shall fashion other creatures to obey us. Accept your lot. Your flesh shall be torn apart."

The First Humans

Disappointed at the animals' lack of eloquence, the gods set about trying to come up with a being who would support them by worship and sacrifice. But unlike the animals, trees, waterways, and landforms—which came into existence merely by thought and word—the gods realized that these special human beings would have to come from the solid substance of the earth itself.

In their first attempt to make a person, the gods used mud and clay. However, these creatures either fell apart because they were so soft, or hardened into useless rocks with human shapes. The gods then decided to enlist the help of the grandfather god Xpiyacoc and the grandmother goddess Xmucane. These wise elders suggested that wood might be a more suitable material. The wooden mannequins—made from the coral tree and the fiber from the bulrush—were certainly an improvement over the ones made from mud. But they lacked the intelligence and refinement necessary to appease the gods. In a fit of rage, Hurakan sent a wild storm to destroy the wooden creatures.

Finally, they found some yellow, white, black, and red maize kernels. Xmucane ground the kernels into a meal that she mixed with water, and the resulting dough formed the first human beings (four men and four women), in whom the gods were satisfied. Their main flaw was that they were too intelligent and curious—so the gods caused a cloud to form over their vision and perception, so that they would never have perfect knowledge, and would always be dependent on the deities to help them solve life's mysteries.

Above *The Creation of the Earth* by Diego Rivera (1886–1957). According to the *Popol Vuh*, the sacred text of the Maya, in the beginning there was only water. When the gods Gucumatz and Hurakan spoke the word "earth" the waters receded, revealing the world.

THE WORLD TREE

Central to the Mayan belief system is the World Tree *(Wakah-chan)*, which literally means "raised-up sky." The tree joins the Overworld, Middleworld, and Underworld into a unified cosmic whole.

The World Tree (whose color is green) is the central axis of the universe, along which souls of the dead migrate. Its roots reach down to the depths of the Underworld, and its crown extends to the top of the heavenly realms. It was believed that the souls of

people who committed suicide were sent to rest in the shade of the World Tree under the protection of the goddess Ixtab.

Four special trees in the Middleworld correspond to the four directions, and each has a different color: north (white), south (yellow), east (red), and west (black). Each direction has symbolic birds and animals of the same colors. White, yellow, red, and black are also the colors of the maize kernels that were used to create the first humans.

THE HERO TWINS

As well as the story of creation, the *Popol Vuh* includes many tales of the exploits of the Hero Twins, the most well-known of all the Meso-american mythological figures.

The First Hero Twins: One Hunahpu and Seven Hunahpu

Xpiyacoc and Xmucane, the god and goddess who were later instrumental in creating the first human beings out of corn, had twin sons known as One Hunahpu and Seven Hunahpu.

The twins loved to play *pokatok*, a popular ball game that was very swift and often violent, and that became a ritual central to Mesoamerican culture. The object of the game was to get a solid rubber ball into a stone ring at the end of a special court, using only knees, elbows, or hips. It happened that their stone ball court was just above the entry to Xibalba, the Under-world. Not only were the Underworld lords annoyed by the loud noises that accompanied the ball games, but they were also extremely envious of the twins' awesome athletic prowess. Two of the lords, One Death and Seven Death, summoned the twins to the Underworld to play ball, with the view to killing them and stealing their play-ing court. The twins' mother, Xmucane, suspected foul play and tried to persuade them not to go, but they disregarded her warnings.

To get to Xibalba the twins succeeding in crossing three loathsome and dangerous rivers: the first was full of blood, the second was full of pus, and the third was full of sharp spikes. After a series of arduous and humiliating tasks that they were tricked into failing, the brothers were sacrificed, their bodies buried under the ball court, and the head of One Hunahpu hung in a calabash tree. (Some versions of the story say that the head was transformed into a gourd, and it was forbidden for anyone to look at the tree or eat of its fruit.) The lords sent back the twins' ball-playing equipment, which Xmucane sadly hid away in the rafters of her house.

One day a young Underworld maiden by the name of Xquic ("Blood Moon") stopped to look at the tree. The head of One Hunahpu, or gourd, spat in her hand, and she became pregnant. Banished by her father, she retreated to the Overworld to the home of Xmucane to give birth to the next generation of Hero Twins.

The Second Hero Twins: Hunahpu and Xbalanque

When the twins Hunahpu and Xbalanque were born, Xmucane took them into her family, which included the first sons of One Hunahpu: One Monkey and One Artisan.

Like their father and uncle, Hunahpu and Xbalanque were bright and adventurous. They were also expert hunters and had magical powers. Because they were so handsome and clever, they aroused the jealousy of their half brothers, who would steal their food and try to get them into all kinds of trouble. Although One Monkey and One Artisan could be bad-tempered and lazy, they were also highly artistic and musical. Eventually Hunahpu and Xbalanque had enough of their brothers' tormenting, and they trapped them in a tree and changed them into monkeys.

The Ordeals of Hunahpu and Xbalanque

One day when the Hero Twins were out hunting, they caught a rat. They were just about to throw it into a fire, when the rat told them what had happened to their father and uncle in Xibalba. He also told them about the ball-game equipment (including helmets, belts, wrist-guards, and knee-guards) that was stored in their grandmother's house.

The second generation of twins loved the ball game, just as One Hunahpu and Seven Hunahpu had done. And they resolved that as soon as they could, they would avenge their father's death. Before long, the noise of their constant playing began to anger the Xibalba lords, and they summoned the twins to the Underworld.

Like their father and uncle before them, the brothers traversed the three dreaded rivers, and once they reached the Underworld, a series of tests awaited them. They bravely survived the dangers of each successive night in the House of Gloom, the Razor House, the Jaguar House, the House of Cold, and the House of Fire, outwitting the dark lords' traps and trickery. Their last—and hardest—night was to be spent in the House of Bats. The most vicious bat bit off Hunahpu's head, and, to add insult to injury, the lords forced Xbalanque to play a game of *pokatok* using his brother's head as a ball. Xbalanque was quick-witted, however; he found a rabbit to impersonate the ball, and quickly retrieved Hunahpu's head and attached it to his brother's body.

After all that, the Hero Twins allowed themselves to be sacrificed by fire, but several days later they emerged from a river as fishlike beings. They traveled throughout the Underworld, entertaining people with their songs, dances, and magic. Eventually the twins were summoned to a command performance by the two most powerful dark rulers, and were ordered to sacrifice themselves yet again. They obeyed the order, and instantly came back to life. The lords wanted the twins to perform the same magic on them, which they did, but they did not reverse the spell to bring the lords back to life. Xibalba became merely a shadow of its former self, and the victorious Hero Twins ascended into the heavens, eventually becoming the sun and moon.

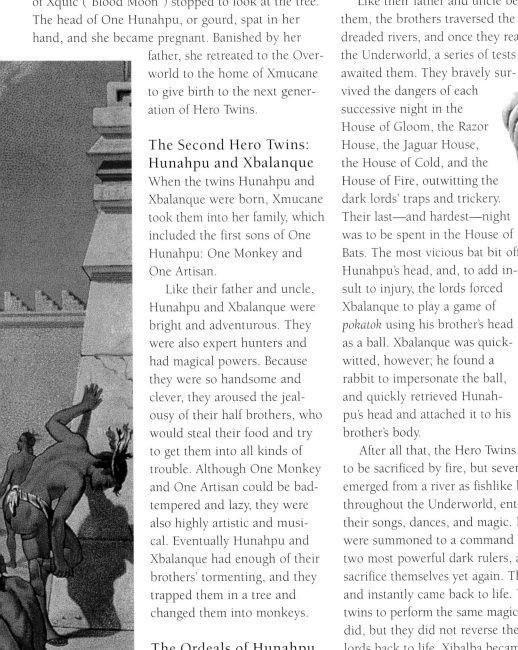

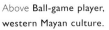

Above **Ball-game player, western Mayan culture.** *Pokatok* players could not use their hands or feet to touch the ball, but they could employ the yokes and *palmas* (stone accessories) they wore, or stone *manoplas* (hand-held objects), to hit the ball. The first team to score was usually declared the winner—and the losing team were almost always sacrificed by decapitation.

4

MAYAN DEITIES

The Maya had approximately 170 gods and goddesses in their pantheon, whose presence permeated every part of their daily lives. There were gods for all aspects of nature—animals, earth, wind, rain, sun, and moon—who required continuous homage and frequent offerings (which occasionally took the form of bloodletting or human sacrifice).

Hunab Ku: the God Behind the Gods

Meaning "only spirit" or "the single god," Hunab Ku is unusual in that he is the only Mayan god that is totally abstract and invisible. Some believe him to be the creator of the gods, earth, and sky. He is the father of Itzamna, the supreme god.

There is another version of the Mayan creation story that goes like this: Hunab Ku first created a world that he populated with little people, and then destroyed by flood, assisted by a great serpent who spewed forth the raging waters from his mouth. He then created a world inhabited by a strange race of people known as the Dzolob, which was destroyed by flood as well. But the third time Hunab Ku created the world, he filled it with the Mayan people, in whom he was very pleased.

Itzamna: the Supreme God

Itzamna, some believe, is the visible manifestation of Hunab Ku, and he is certainly a multitalented and multifunctional deity. Firstly, he is the moon god, husband of the moon goddess Ixchel, and the patron

Below Head of Itzamna by Frederick Catherwood (1799–1854). Originally located at Izamal in Mexico, this stucco stone head no longer exists. But it was described by John Lloyd Stephens, during his 1841 expedition to the Yucatan region with Catherwood, as having a "stone one foot six inches long [that] protrudes from the chin, intended, perhaps, for burning copal on, as a sort of altar."

god of royalty. Itzamna loved his people, and bestowed on them the gifts of books, writing, calendars, and medicine. His name means "Iguana House" or "Lizard House," reflecting the Mayan view that the framework of the earth was formed by the bodies of lizards.

Itzamna is a benign patriarch, often pictured as an elderly man with square eyes, a prominent jaw, and a hawklike nose. The ceremonies of the Mayan New Year honor Itzamna, as does the Temple of the Cross located at Palenque.

Ixchel: the Moon Goddess

Ixchel is a formidable goddess, associated with the moon, tides, and floods. In some accounts she is the wife of the supreme god Itzamna, whereas other stories have her married to the sun god Kinich Ahau (her husbands may even be considered to be two aspects of the one deity).

As a young wife, Ixchel was very unhappy because she was barren—in fact, she had no reproductive organs whatsoever. One day a deer came and stepped on her abdomen, thus enabling her to bear children, who were known as the Bacabs.

Ixchel is capricious and, like the moon, she is also ever-changing. She is the benevolent rainbow mother

or Ah Hoya ("he who urinates"), Chaac was essentially a benevolent god, but one whose continued goodness depended on regular rituals and sacrifices. He sometimes instructed his people to abstain from either food or sex, but when he was in a harsher mood, he could order them to be tied up and thrown into the sacred well at Chichén Itzá.

Chaac appears in many faces and guises. Some images show him with a curled, snoutlike nose, and sometimes he is seen with scales or catfish whiskers, or with tears flowing from his eyes. Often he is seen painted blue and wielding an axe, which he uses to create lightning and thunder. Chaac is closely aligned with the maize god Yum Kaax, and still features prominently in the ceremonial life of the people living in the Yucatan region today, especially at the coming of the important wet season. When a frog croaks, signifying the onset of rain, it is thought to be the voice of Chaac.

Left **Mask of the Mayan rain god Chaac.** The Codz Poop building at Kabah in the Yucatan region of Mexico features 250 masks of Chaac. One of the many beliefs about Chaac is that he uses his hooked nose to penetrate the clouds, causing rain to fall.

patron goddess of both childbirth and weaving. But she is also depicted as a fierce hag, her helmet and skirt adorned with snakes (very much like the Aztec goddess Coatlicue). She holds a jug of water that she could either sprinkle kindly on the crops, or pour down in a devastating flood.

The Bacabs

Itzamna the supreme god and Ixchel the moon goddess had four sons, collectively known as the Bacabs. Coming from such exalted parents, the Bacabs were indeed very important deities. Because the earth was thought to be flat, the Bacabs' function was to stand at each corner of the earth and hold up the thirteen layers of the sky like a canopy; they are often seen depicted with upraised arms, and are sometimes represented as jaguars. The Bacabs are associated with the four directions, as illustrated in the Mayan World Tree: north (white), south (yellow), east (red), and west (black). The most well-known of the Bacabs is the rain god Chaac (in fact, some academics believe that the four Bacabs are simply four aspects of the one god—Chaac).

Chaac: the Rain God

Because life cannot exist without water, Chaac (or Chac) the rain god is the most revered of all the Mayan deities—his Aztec counterpart is Tlaloc. Also known as Ah Tzenul ("he who gives food to others")

THE MAIZE GOD

Maize, or corn, was the Mayan staple crop, and was grown not only in fields, but in valleys and on rocky hillsides. It was prepared and consumed in a variety of ways, such as tortillas, tamales, and atole, a hot beverage. Because maize was so essential to the Mayans' very survival, it featured prominently in their mythological, religious, and ceremonial life.

The Mayan creation myth tells how the first human beings were fashioned out of ground maize meal. And one of the most revered deities was the maize god, who was called by many names: Hun Hunahpu, Ah Mun, or Yum Kaax (Lord of the Forest). This was a benign, passive god often portrayed as a young man with a ripe ear of maize sprouting from his head. Rituals and offerings to the maize god were of great importance and were performed regularly.

Right **Mayan maize god.** So popular was the maize god that it is believed the Maya performed cranial deformation on infants so that their head grew elongated like the shape of an ear of maize.

Gucumatz: the Feathered Serpent

Like his Aztec counterpart Quetzalcoatl, Gucumatz (also known as Kukulcan or Kukulkan) is the god of wind and is thought to have come from the west, bringing with him all the secrets of the universe. Sometimes he is pictured as moving through the water, and he may be yet another manifestation of the supreme god Itzamna.

At Chichén Itzá there is a magnificent temple dedicated to Gucumatz. At both the spring equinox and autumn equinox, Gucumatz appears as a large, serpent-shaped shadow across the steps of the temple.

Below **Mayan stone sculpture of Gucumatz.** In association with Hurakan, Gucumatz was responsible for the creation of the Mayan world and human beings. He taught the people about civilization and agriculture, and is often portrayed as a snake.

Hurakan: the Storm God

According to the Mayan book of creation, *Popol Vuh,* the god Hurakan collaborated with Gucumatz in creating the Earth, and fashioning the first humans out of mud and wood.

Hurakan was a harsh god. Displeased because he found the wooden folk so dull and witless, he destroyed them in a flood. However some survived, and those that did were tormented mercilessly. Hurakan employed wild dogs and violent monsters with names like "Gouger of Faces" and "Crunching Jaguar" to terrify and mutilate his poor wretched mistakes. Most of the wooden people were destroyed, but some fled into caves, never to be seen again.

Kinich Ahau: the Sun God

Having both a light and a dark aspect, Kinich Ahau is the sun by day, but at night he becomes the jaguar lord Balam, prowling the lower regions of the Underworld. Kinich Ahau is protector of the city of Izamal, and, in the name of Ah Xoc Kin, the sun god is also the patron of poetry and music.

Left **Terracotta relief of the Mayan sun god.** Situated on a temple wall at Campeche in Mexico, this decorative relief of Kinich Ahau shows the sun god in his rising and setting forms. As patron of Izamal, he was believed to visit the people of the city at noon every day in the guise of a macaw.

Ixtab and Ah Puch: the Deities of Death

Only people who have died a violent or suicidal death can enter the heavenly realms. Ixtab, the goddess of suicide, escorts into paradise the souls of people who have died by their own hand, and serves them food and drink in the shade of the World Tree. Ixtab is portrayed as rather a fearsome creature hanging from a noose.

As a beautiful young goddess Ixtab took great delight in luring men into the forest, seducing and bewitching them, and then vanishing. Some men stayed lost in the forest, and those who found their way home went insane, forever longing for her love.

Ah Puch (or Yum Cimil), the lord of death, is the ruler of the lowest level of the Underworld and takes many different forms: as a skeleton, as a distended gangrenous corpse, or as an owl.

AZTEC MYTHOLOGY

The Aztec civilization of Mexico existed between A.D. 1325 and A.D. 1521. It was a militaristic empire, whose spiritual belief system encompassed over 1,000 deities. The Aztec universe was multilayered, and its creation stories complex. Many of the ancient texts were destroyed by the Spanish, and much of our knowledge of Aztec religion comes from the *Florentine Codex*, transcribed by Franciscan monk Bernardino de Sahagún.

A THREE-PART UNIVERSE

In the Aztec belief system, the universe was tripartite, or composed of three parts: Earth, Heaven, and the Underworld.

Earth

At the center of the Aztec universe—the meeting place of Heaven, Earth, and the Underworld—was the capital city of Tenochtitlan. According to legend, the local people were known as the Tenochca, but the war god Huitzilopochtli renamed them the Mexica, and instructed them to build their capital on an island in the middle of Lake Texcoco. At the heart of the city stood the magnificent Great Temple, which was dedicated to both Huitzilopochtli and the Aztec rain god, known as Tlaloc.

Heaven

Heaven was a huge dome comprising 13 levels that reached upward from the surface of the Earth. In the highest of the heavens lived Ometeotl, the Supreme Being and the god of duality—no other god or mortal could enter this exalted realm.

Then there were the afterlife levels, which varied according to the status of one's spiritual life at the time of physical death. The House of the Sun in the east was the ultimate reward—souls could stay there forever and would never have to return to Earth. In the west was a peaceful afterlife reserved for those who died in battle or during childbirth. Other good souls could end up in remarkable places such as the Land of Clouds, the Land of the Fleshless, or the Land of Water and Mist.

The Underworld

Only those who died in battle or during childbirth could go straight to Heaven. Everyone else had to first go to the Underworld known as Mictlan, which means "that which is below us." The fearsome lord of the Underworld, Mictlantecuhtli, is often portrayed as a squatting, skeletonlike creature with a pointed hat and rather large, bulging eyes.

When a soul reached the Underworld, they were met by Black Tezcatlipoca, who sent them on their journey through Mictlan's nine levels. The soul would have to complete a series of challenging tests within a period of four years, traversing a frightening landscape of quaking mountains and treacherous rivers. If they passed, the souls were allowed into one of the heavenly realms, but if they failed, they had to stay in the lowest level for eternity.

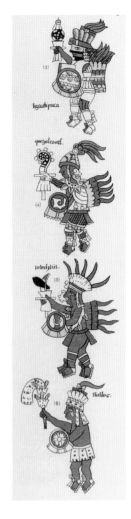

Above **Aztec gods from the *Florentine Codex*.** Produced by Bernardino de Sahagún (c.1500–1590) in the 1570s, the *Florentine Codex* contains encyclopedic information and 1,846 illustrations that reveal the beliefs, rituals, and lifestyle of the Aztecs.

Left **Mictecacihuatl, Aztec goddess of the dead.** Known as the "Lady of the Dead," Mictecacihuatl is the wife of Mictlantecuhtli, lord of the Underworld. Mictecacihuatl presides over the Dia de los Muertos (Day of the Dead) festival, when the souls of ancestors are thought to return to visit their families.

CREATION OF THE FOUR DIRECTIONS

The Supreme God Ometeotl went by many epithets: Tloque Nahuaque, God above All, the Lord of Two, Lord of Duality, and Lord of the Ring. Although sometimes referred to as "lord," Ometeotl actually had both masculine and feminine attributes, and encompassed both good and evil. As a male he was known as Ometecuhtli, and as a female, Omecihuatl.

From the timeless void, Ometeotl created him/herself, and then gave birth to four sons, who went forth to create the universe at the four points of the compass. These four sons (who are often compared to the Bacabs in Mayan mythology) were different aspects of the god Tezcatlipoca.

East

The direction associated with the rising sun was created by Red Tezcatlipoca, who was also known as Xipe Totec, the much-revered god of agriculture and fertility, as well as regeneration.

North

The North was ruled by Black Tezcatlipoca, generally known as Tezcatlipoca, or "Smoking Mirror," the Lord of the Night Sky. He had a rather malevolent nature and could be capricious and manipulative.

West

Quetzalcoatl, the "Plumed Serpent," is White Tezcatlipoca, and connected with the west and the setting sun. He was the best-known and most-loved deity in the Aztec pantheon, and chief rival of his brother Tezcatlipoca.

South

There seems to be more than one Blue Tezcatlipoca. Some sources say that the South was created by Tlaloc, the rain god. Others attribute this direction to Huitzilopochtli, the god of war. Both of these deities were highly revered by the Aztecs.

CREATION OF THE FIVE SUNS

We have seen how the world was created by four gods at the four sacred directions. There is another Aztec story of creation, which focuses on the five successive ages, or "suns." But it is a story of destruction as well as creation: the Aztecs believed that the world was created and destroyed four times, and each age was ruled by a particular deity and its corresponding element.

The Sun of Earth

The First Sun was known as the Sun of Earth, whose creator and ruler was Tezcatlipoca. This age was inhabited by mighty giants. However, Tezcatlipoca's brother, Quetzalcoatl, was displeased with the giants, and he sent jaguars down to annihilate all of the giants and the earth itself.

Above **Ehecatl, Aztec god of the wind.** One of the many manifestations of the god Quetzalcoatl, Ehecatl is often shown with a mouth in the form of a bird's beak. As god of the wind, his breath is said to move the sun and bring rain clouds.

Right **Tonatiuh, Aztec god of the sun.** In this detailed illustration from the *Codex Vaticanus*, Tonatiuh watches over a priest who is burning incense. Tonatiuh rules the Fifth Sun—or present era—and the Aztecs believed that any weakness in him would lead to the end of the world. So sacrifices and offerings were regularly made to keep the sun god happy and strong.

The Sun of Air

After the First Sun was destroyed and Tezcatlipoca returned to the sky to become the constellation Ursa Major, the world was re-created by Quetzalcoatl, in one of his many aspects—the wind god Ehecatl. Many years passed, and the gods felt that the people were too sinful and needed to be destroyed yet again. Tezcatlipoca came to Earth, sending a violent wind, and those who survived were changed into monkeys.

The Sun of Rain

Tlaloc, the rain god, presided over this Third Sun. Quetzalcoatl eventually punished the people for not fulfilling their sacrificial duties by sending a rain of ash. The survivors of this fiery storm became birds.

The Sun of Water

The Fourth Sun—the Sun of Water—was both created and destroyed by the powerful water and fertility goddess Coatlicue (or Chalchiuhtlicue), sister of the rain god Tlaloc. Those who came through the flood were turned into fishes.

THE CALENDAR STONE

The Aztecs placed great value on the study of mathematics and astronomy, and developed complex timekeeping systems. Their concept of time was cyclical rather than linear; it was dependent on and controlled by divine forces. The Aztecs had two concurrent calendars: one of 260 days running clockwise (coinciding with the human gestation period), and one of 365 days, running counterclockwise.

Constructed in the fifteenth century, the famous Calendar Stone (also known as the Sun Stone) was discovered in 1790 at the Aztec capital of Tenochtitlan, now Mexico City. The stone is 12 ft (3.5 m) in diameter, weighs 25 tons (25.5 tonnes), and is elaborately carved out of basalt.

At the center of the Calendar Stone is the recognizable face of the sun god Tonatiuh, creator of the Fifth Sun. The four squares that surround Tonatiuh depict the four previous ages (or "suns") that were destroyed by either animals, wind, fire, or water. At the outer edge of the stone are two sacred serpents, which symbolize both the cyclical and spiraling nature of the dance of life.

Below **Aztec Calendar Stone.** Now the centerpiece of Mexico's National Museum of Anthropology, the Calendar Stone was commissioned by the Aztec ruler Axayacatl in 1469. There are indications that the basalt surface was originally painted.

The Fifth Sun

The Fifth Sun is the present era, and the Aztecs believed it to be the final sun. After the sky had collapsed, the four sons of Ometeotl—Xipe Totec, Tezcatlipoca, Quetzalcoatl, and Tlaloc—were transformed into trees, and in a spirit of cooperation, they raised the sky once again. The fifth age is ruled by the sun god Tonatiuh.

It was thought that after each cataclysm the world progressed to a higher level of spirituality, and the Fifth Sun is the most highly evolved era so far. However, the Aztecs believed that unless mortals worked in harmony with the gods, through worship and sacrifice, the Fifth Sun would eventually be devastated, never to be created again.

QUETZALCOATL: THE PLUMED SERPENT

Quetzalcoatl has many different aspects—both human and divine—and he has been likened to both King Arthur and Jesus Christ. His name is derived from the two words: *quetzal*, a beautiful green-feathered bird from the mountains of Central America, and *coatl*, meaning snake. He is most often portrayed as "the plumed serpent," a creature that links Earth with the heavens. The temple of Quetzalcoatl is one of the most magnificent architectural features of the ancient city of Teotihuacan. Quetzalcoatl's symbol is the conch shell, which has associations with both the wind and the sea.

Thought to be a reincarnation of an older Toltec deity, Quetzalcoatl is also linked to the Mayan god of wind, Gucumatz (Kukulcan) and the Aztec wind god Ehecatl. He is also White Tezcatlipoca, creator and ruler of the Second Sun, the Sun of Air. Legend even weaves the Quetzalcoatl figure into a real-life historical personage, Topiltzin, a visionary and compassionate tenth-century Toltec ruler who abolished the ritual of human sacrifice.

The following two stories demonstrate the nurturing, life-affirming qualities of Quetzalcoatl.

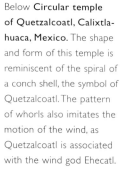

Below **Circular temple of Quetzalcoatl, Calixtlahuaca, Mexico.** The shape and form of this temple is reminiscent of the spiral of a conch shell, the symbol of Quetzalcoatl. The pattern of whorls also imitates the motion of the wind, as Quetzalcoatl is associated with the wind god Ehecatl.

The Compassionate Creator

After the Fourth Sun was destroyed, it was Quetzalcoatl's responsibility to create a new race of human beings. Accompanied by Xolotl, his dog-headed twin brother, Quetzalcoatl made the journey down to Mictlan, the Underworld, and gathered the bones of the people who had been drowned in the flood.

Right **Quetzalcoatl, the feathered serpent.** This modern representation of the wind god as a man reflects the legend of Topiltzin, the fair-skinned Toltec ruler who was said to be the wise and peaceful earthly incarnation of Quetzalcoatl.

The Lord of the Underworld, Mictlantecuhtli, was not pleased—he wanted to keep the bones to himself, so he sent his nasty pet quails to chase Quetzalcoatl and Xolotl away. When Quetzalcoatl dropped the bones, breaking them into many pieces, he was disheartened. But the old snake goddess, Cihuacoatl, came to his aid. She gathered the broken bones and ground them up in a jade bowl. Quetzalcoatl mixed his blood with the ground bones to form the first human beings of the Fifth Sun.

The human population eventually grew so large that their food supply dwindled. Quetzalcoatl needed to come up with a clever plan to feed them. One day he happened to be watching an ant coming out from a rock, carrying a kernel of maize. Quetzalcoatl had never seen maize before, and when he tasted it, he realized that it would be the perfect food for his people. He soon discovered that there were quite a lot of maize kernels under the rock, so he transformed himself into an ant, and moved a great many kernels—enough to fill a whole bag—which would be planted to become the first maize field.

Quetzalcoatl was also instrumental in developing the intoxicating drink from the maguey cactus known as pulque, which he thought would bring much pleasure to the world. But in a strange irony, the alcoholic beverage that was meant to be enjoyed by his people would also lead to his undoing.

Descent and Ascension

Because of Quetzalcoatl's many great achievements and contributions, he had become the most popular Aztec deity. His brother Tezcatlipoca was extremely jealous of Quetzalcoatl, and he conspired with Tlazolteotl, the wicked goddess of lust and intoxication, to get rid of him. She prepared a special brew for Quetzalcoatl and his sister and got them both drunk—so drunk, in fact, that they ended up sleeping together.

*Quetzalcoatl!
Who knows what he meant
to the dead Aztecs, and to the older
Indians, who knew him before the
Aztecs raised their deity to the heights
of horror and vindictiveness?*

D.H. LAWRENCE (1885–1930),
THE PLUMED SERPENT

Tezcatlipoca and Tlazolteotl told all the other gods what had happened. Quetzalcoatl was so mortified by what he had done that he sailed off to the east on a raft made of serpents, promising one day to return to his people. Eventually the other gods realized that Quetzalcoatl had been tricked, but by then it was too late—he was gone.

It was prophesied that Quetzalcoatl would return in the year Ce-Acatl, or 1519 in the Christian calendar. As it turned out, that was the year that Hernando Cortés arrived in Mexico. Because Cortés was such an imposing presence, many of the Aztecs thought that he was Quetzalcoatl, and due to that strange coincidence, the Spanish were quite easily able to conquer the Mexicans.

Another version of the Quetzalcoatl legend says that he burned himself on a funeral pyre, and his ashes flew up to the sky as rare and colorful birds, which then became the planet Venus.

Above **The birth of Quetzalcoatl.** Stories of this remarkable event vary. Topiltzin–Quetzalcoatl was born to Chimalman after a spear-throwing competition made her pregnant. The god Quetzalcoatl–Ehecatl is believed to have been fathered by the supreme Aztec god Ometeotl (also known as Tonacatecuhtli).

back of his head that he used as a tool of divination, with which he could predict events of the future, and tell what was in people's souls.

Tezcatlipoca also has one foot made of obsidian, and stories vary as to how he lost his real foot. One version tells how he fell in love with Xochiquetzal, the moon and flower goddess and wife of Tlaloc, the rain god. When Tezcatlipoca tried to seduce the goddess, her enraged husband threw him off their heavenly mountaintop and Tezcatlipoca's foot came right off. Tezcatlipoca replaced the foot with an obsidian mirror.

Another version tells how Tezcatlipoca and his brother Quetzalcoatl were sent to Earth to fight Cipactli, the crocodilelike Earth Monster who lived under the water. Tezcatlipoca stuck his foot into the water, trying to lure the monster out, and as he did so, Cipactli bit his foot off.

Above **Mixcoatl, Aztec god of hunting.** The husband of Coatlicue, Mixcoatl is called the cloud serpent as he symbolizes the nebulous Milky Way. He is the god of hunting, war, and the North Star, and was responsible for creating fire by spinning the heavens around a central point.

Right **The dismemberment of Coyolxauhqui.** This stone monolith, measuring 10 ft (3 m) across, shows Coatlicue's daughter Coyolxauhqui after the fight with her half-brother Huitzilopochtli. Coyolxauhqui was decapitated and torn limb from limb during the battle.

TEZCATLIPOCA: LORD OF THE NIGHT SKY

Sometimes compared to Jupiter and Lucifer, as well as to the Mayan god Hurakan, Tezcatlipoca is perhaps the most enigmatic and impressive of all the Aztec deities. As the son of Ometeotl, the Supreme Being, he is one of the four creators of the universe and the ruler of the First Sun (the Sun of Earth) and destroyer of the Second Sun (the Sun of Air).

The animal associated with Tezcatlipoca is the mighty jaguar. The Aztecs thought that the pattern of the jaguar skin resembled the night sky, and pictures of Tezcatlipoca usually show him wearing the animal's skin.

So vast is Tezcatlipoca's importance and influence that he is the patron of royalty, sorcerers, and criminals, and is a prototype for other war deities such as Huitzilopochtli. And, like Huitzilopochtli, he advocated and encouraged human sacrifice.

The Smoking Mirror

As well as the jaguar, Tezcatlipoca is inextricably linked with his "smoking mirror" of obsidian, a cloudy black stone. In fact, the Aztec word for obsidian is "tezcat." Tezcatlipoca had a mirror attached to the

Rival of Quetzalcoatl

Although not as popular as his brother Quetzalcoatl, some consider Tezcatlipoca to be second in greatness only to their father Ometeotl, with Quetzalcoatl venerated more as an Aztec cultural hero.

The brothers had always been rivals, and would demolish each other's creations. One day, in a fit of jealousy, Tezcatlipoca got his brother drunk and then tricked him into sleeping with their sister, an event that led to Quetzalcoatl's dramatic fall from grace.

Tezcatlipoca and Quetzalcoatl represent the dualities of the universe—night and day, light and dark, good and evil, creation and destruction— the opposing forces that are necessary for regeneration and the maintenance of cosmic balance.

COATLICUE AND HUITZILOPOCHTLI: GREAT MOTHER AND WARRIOR SON

The foremost Aztec female deity, Coatlicue (also known as Chalchiuhtlicue), was both the creator and the destroyer of the Fourth Sun (the Sun of Water). As well as being a fertility goddess, she is also the patron of all bodies of water including oceans, rivers, lakes, and waterfalls.

From all accounts, Coatlicue has an awesome presence: her face is bloody and fleshless, she has clawlike hands and feet, her breasts are wrinkled and pendulous, and she wears a necklace formed from human body parts (a reminder of the necessity of sacrifice). Her skirt is made of live snakes, from which she gets the names "She of the Jade Skirt" and "She of the Serpent Skirt."

How Coatlicue Became Pregnant

Coatlicue had borne 400 children and, understandably, she did not want any more, so she ceased having sexual relations with her husband Mixcoatl, the cloud serpent. One day as Coatlicue was sweeping, a colorful feather ball fell out of the sky, which she caught and placed inside her blouse. After her work was finished she decided to have another look at the ball, but it had disappeared.

Months passed, and Coatlicue discovered she was with child. She was mystified, since she hadn't slept with her husband, or anyone else for that matter, for quite some time; she reasoned that it must have been the ball that made her pregnant. When her body could not keep the pregnancy a secret any longer, her children were disgraced, since they knew Mixcoatl could not have been this baby's father. One of Coatlicue's daughters, Coyolxauhqui ("Golden Bells"), arranged with her siblings to kill their mother and her unborn child, to save face and retain their supremacy.

Birth of Huitzilopochtli

Just as all 400 of Coatlicue's offspring gathered to attack her, an amazing thing happened. The child—Huitzilopochtli—emerged forth from the womb, fully grown and fully clothed, with leather sandals on his feet and carrying a spear and shield.

He killed most of his brothers and sisters, including Coyolxauhqui, their mother's favorite, who he beheaded and dismembered. Huitzilopochtli then threw Coyolxauhqui's head up into the sky, which became the moon.

Blue Hummingbird on the Left

As a result of his bold and bloody massacre, Huitzilopochtli gained the respect of all—including his surviving siblings—and he became the god of war. He also became the revered national deity of the Aztec people.

His name means "Blue Hummingbird on the Left" (left was thought to be south), since Huitzilopochtli guided the exodus of the Aztecs south from Atzlan to establish the capital at Tenochtitlan. Hummingbirds are particularly significant, since it was believed that they carried the souls of dead warriors. A temple was built in Huitzilopochtli's honor at Tenochtitlan, where many human hearts were offered to appease the deity.

Below **Coatlicue, Aztec goddess of fertility.** At over 8 ft (2.4 m) in height, this imposing statue of Coatlicue is one of the most famous sculptures from the Aztec era. It clearly shows Coatlicue's skirt of writhing snakes, which were popular Aztec symbols of fertility.

Right **Tlaloc, the Aztec rain god, on the lid of a painted vessel.** The importance of life-giving water meant that appeasing the rain god was essential for the Aztecs. Human sacrifices were performed, and offerings of flowers and songs were made during the festival of Tozoztontli.

Below **Gold pectoral with the face of Xipe Totec.** As the god of spring, Xipe Totec allowed his skin to be flayed to represent the shedding of the outer part of the maize seed. After being flayed he became a golden god, and hence was the patron of goldsmiths.

DEITIES OF FERTILITY, WATER, AND WINE

The Aztecs worshipped well over 1,000 gods and goddesses, who watched over and participated in every aspect of their lives. Here are a few of the most revered and feared.

Xipe Totec: the Flayed Earth God

Associated with the young shoots of spring maize, Xipe Totec is the god of fertility and regeneration.

Because maize was the staple crop of the Aztecs and essential to life, many people were sacrificed to Xipe Totec and other deities so that the gods would ensure a good crop. One of the favored forms of sacrifice was being flayed (skinned alive). The captors of the victims, as well as the priests, sometimes wore the skins over their naked bodies to symbolize the maize seeds, which lose their outer covering when the new growth appears.

Xipe Totec is often pictured as wearing a flayed human skin. It is also believed that he allowed his own skin to be peeled off to set an example to his people, and as a sign of renewal and regeneration.

Tlaloc: the Rain God

As creator of the Sun of Rain, the Third Sun, Tlaloc is one of the most important deities in the Aztec pantheon, and corresponds to the Mayan rain god Chaac. He is sometimes said to be the brother-consort of Coatlicue ("She of the Jade Skirt").

Tlaloc has four jugs, from which he pours down rain onto the Earth; some rain is benign and helpful for crops, and some is destructive. He is assisted by a sky serpent, which holds a vast amount of water inside its huge belly.

Sometimes pictured as a fierce creature with tusks and circles around his eyes, Tlaloc is a demanding god, requiring many sacrificial victims. In times of drought, people would sacrifice their babies, whose tears were said to help the rain fall. The rituals to appease Tlaloc often necessitated that the priests eat the flesh of the victims.

Anyone who was struck by lightning, or died by drowning or infectious disease, was welcomed into a paradise known as Tlalocan ("Place of Tlaloc").

Xochiquetzal: "Feather Flower"

Xochiquetzal also goes by the name of "Richly Plumed Flower," and is depicted as being adorned in quetzal feathers. She is a versatile deity, being the goddess of the moon, flowers, marriage, and children, and is patron of artists and weavers. Xochiquetzal is renowned for her beauty, youth, and sex appeal, but is also a great upholder of family values. When she was married to Tlaloc the rain god, Tezcatlipoca desired her so greatly that he ended up losing his foot when fighting for her affections.

Tlazolteotl: Goddess of Filth and Excrement

Presenting another side of female sexuality, Tlazolteotl is an important deity. She is the goddess of fertility, lust, and intoxication—of human abasement and the darker side of human sexuality—and encourages and pardons infidelities. Sometimes pictured as having

spindles in her hair, she is the patron of spinners, as well as of witchcraft and even steam baths.

When the jealous Tezcatlipoca got Quetzalcoatl drunk and tricked him into sleeping with his sister, he had enlisted the help of Tlazolteotl.

Whereas the flower goddess Xochiquetzal never ages, and is only ever portrayed as a beautiful young woman, Tlazolteotl is often depicted as an old crone in a squatting position.

Mayahuel: Goddess of Pulque

Pulque is the alcoholic drink made from the maguey cactus. After he created the first humans, Quetzalcoatl felt that they were too serious, and that they needed something to bring them cheer.

Quetzalcoatl traveled up to the heavens to persuade the virgin goddess Mayahuel to come to Earth and help him create a pleasurable substance. When they arrived on Earth, the god and goddess transformed themselves into a tree, the branches entwined in a lovers' embrace.

Mayahuel's enraged grandmother Tzitzimitl swooped down to Earth and tore the tree apart, feeding the pieces of what was Mayahuel to her entourage of star demons. Quetzalcoatl buried the fragments that were left, and from that planting sprouted the splendid maguey cactus.

Above **Tlalocan, paradise of Tlaloc.** Souls who came here were looked after by Tlaloc's servants, the Tlaloques. After four years the souls were reincarnated as human beings again.

THE SHAMAN

In ancient Mexico, the shaman was considered a highly respected member of the community, and served a vital function as an intermediary between the spirit world and the natural world.

Shamans did not choose their career—they were either born into it, or were called through special dreams and visions. An important part of the Aztec belief system was the interconnectedness of all things—living and dead—and it was the role of the shaman to work with the energy of the world beyond everyday perception.

Pulque, an alcoholic drink made from the maguey cactus, was widely used in ceremonies, as were hallucinogens such as peyote and datura. Masks, chanting, drums, rattles, and other instruments were also employed to help the shaman reach an altered state of consciousness.

The modern-day shaman practices within the ancient cultural tradition, invoking the myths and deities of old. They may prescribe herbal medicines, retrieve lost souls, read the future, or perform cleansings on a home or individual who has been bewitched.

SOUTH AMERICAN MYTHOLOGY

The ancient civilizations of South America thrived in diverse landscapes of intense natural beauty, encompassing the towering Andes Mountains, the surrounding plains and valleys, and the magnificent Amazon rain forest.

It is thought that the first people traveled to this continent from Siberia between 9000 and 5000 B.C. The earliest Andean culture—the Chavín—is estimated to have thrived between 900 and 200 B.C., and for centuries civilizations changed and progressed, culminating in the Inca empire.

The Inca ruled from A.D. 1400 to 1532, and were a highly organized, disciplined, and stratified society. They made great advances in both agriculture and building construction, and had a sophisticated network of roads and communication.

Most of our knowledge of Andean civilizations comes from archaeological evidence, as they had no writing systems. The Inca had a record-keeping system known as *quipu*, involving knotted string. Myths were held by the *quipucamayoqs* (the knot makers), as well as the *amautas* (the court poets), and the *mamacunas* (the virgins of the sun temples). As the Inca took over other civilizations, they adopted their deities, sacred sites, and legends.

The people of the Amazon had a purely oral tradition. Their myths varied from tribe to tribe, focusing on the natural world and the balance of power within human relationships and between humanity and nature. Most of what we know of the Amazonian myths is due to the work of anthropologists.

COMMON THREADS

Several common themes recur in the myths and histories of the South Americans, and the stories generally fall into the following categories: the origin of the world, the great flood, the creation of human beings, the cultural hero, and the animal story.

All of the civilizations tell of a belief in a creator deity, and in many cases there is an endless cycle of creation and destruction. This is seen very clearly in the Inca concept of *pachacuti*.

The Andean cultures tried to make sense of the cosmos, setting up astronomical observation posts so that they could study the celestial bodies. The sun, moon, and often the stars were deified, and were inextricably linked to the agricultural and ceremonial life of the people.

Human sacrifice (especially of young children) was deemed to be a necessary part of religious life, especially in times of adversity. Artwork of the Moche people graphically depicts ritual scenes of strangling and beheading, and the great sun gods of the Inca and Chibcha—Inti and Bochica respectively—were especially demanding of human blood.

Naturally occurring drugs such as coca and the hallucinogenic *ayahuasca* were regularly used in rituals and ceremonies to enable the priests and shamans to communicate with the spirits. During festivals and other important events the people of the Andes enjoyed drinking *chicha*, an alcoholic beverage made from maize fermented with human saliva.

Cultural heroes featured prominently in all the mythologies. Sometimes semi-divine, they were traveling teachers who brought civilization, law, living skills, and morals to less advanced people.

Right **Sun god mask, La Tolita culture.** Well-known for working with gold, the people of Ecuador's La Tolita culture (which existed from 500 B.C. to A.D. 500) created masks for special occasions. The wearer of the mask was said to take on the power of the deity represented by the mask—in this case the sun god.

Right **Detail from an eighteenth-century carpet showing an Incan person with flora and fauna.** The indigenous South Americans lived in harmony with their natural environment, and treated the animals and plants with respect. There are many myths involving native creatures such as llamas, jaguars, and anacondas, which reveal the importance of these animals in everyday life.

THE NATURAL WORLD

The people of the Andes and the Amazon lived closely with the natural world, and their myths are dominated by flora, fauna, and natural disasters.

In South America, the jaguar was considered the king of beasts, and was thought to once control the earth. The city of Cuzco was designed in the shape of a puma. Llamas were revered for their many practical uses, and they were also believed to have the gift of prophecy. In the Andean view of the universe, the souls of the dead were reincarnated as llamas, and the serpent ruled the underworld, the puma was the lord of the middleworld, and the condor presided over the upperworld.

Natural disasters such as floods and earthquakes occurred regularly throughout history and mythology, and were thought to be acts of the gods: either as punishment, or for purification and renewal.

SACRED PLACES

There are several places throughout South America that are considered by the native inhabitants to be very sacred, and some of them are connected with the stories of creation and human origin.

Tiahuanaco in the Bolivian Andes was a major pilgrimage center, and the highest city in the ancient world. Pachacamac was another revered pilgrimage site in central Peru, an amazing place with a temple built on an artificial hill. According to Inca legend, the first humans emerged from Lake Titicaca; within the lake lie the Island of the Sun and the Island of the Moon. Machu Picchu was a beautifully designed city set high in the Andes, and was used as a spiritual retreat for the royal family. Cuzco, the Inca capital, was considered to be the navel of the world, and the meeting place of the earth and sky. The focal point of Cuzco was the complex of temples at Coricancha.

ANCESTOR WORSHIP

Throughout the South American continent, people honored the spirits of their ancestors in various ways. Human bodies were preserved as mummies, and were brought out to worship during ceremonial occasions. There were certain features in the landscape (such as rocks, caves, and hills) that had special significance because it was believed that the souls of the ancestors departed the earthly realm from these places, and left a small part of their spirit behind. These places were called *paccariscas*. Some tribes of the Amazon rain forest practiced cannibalism to preserve the revered qualities of their forebears.

SOUTH AMERICA

SPANISH CONQUEST

Francisco Pizarro arrived in South America in 1532, and in just 20 years the entire continent was under Spanish control. They came in search of gold, and even tried to drain Lake Guatavita in Colombia where the myth of El Dorado originated.

The Catholic priests were often relentless in their zeal to convert the natives. They took over or demolished temples; destroyed idols, mummies, and *quipus*; and abolished rituals and festivals. One priest, Francisco de Avila, made a thorough inquiry into the old religious practices to prove their inferiority. These chronicles were known as *Idolatrias*, and record many of the beliefs and legends of the conquered people.

Many of the old ways have become amalgamated within the Catholic tradition. In addition, many Westerners are now making pilgrimages to places such as Machu Picchu, and traveling to the Amazon to learn the wisdom of the shamans.

EARLY PRE-INCA ANDEAN CULTURES

Several civilizations thrived in the Andes region for many centuries prior to the emergence of the Inca empire. These include the ancient Chavín, Paracas, Moche (Mohica), and Nazca cultures.

Chavín

The Chavín culture existed during the Early Horizon Period (900–200 B.C.) in present-day north-central Peru. It has been described as the "mother culture" of the Andes, and was named after the site where the culture was first discovered, the religious center of Chavín de Huántar in the Ancash highlands.

The temple is the oldest and, some say, the most beautiful in South America. It was believed to be the center of the cosmos, and features a carved stone monolith known as the Lanzon, a half-human/half-monster oracle figure. Many images of the Staff Deity also endure from this period: a fertility god/goddess with birdlike, snakelike, or catlike characteristics (often with fangs), holding a staff in each hand.

Paracas

Also from the Early Horizon Period, the Paracas culture occurred along the southern coast of Peru. The Paracas people created some superbly colored textiles made from llama wool and cotton, and were pioneers in the art of mummification. Archaeologists have noted from studying their textiles and other craftwork that the Paracas people worshipped a deity who has become known in modern times as the Oculate Being because of its large, penetrating eyes. The Oculate Being incorporates features of several different creatures: feline, bird, killer whale, and fox.

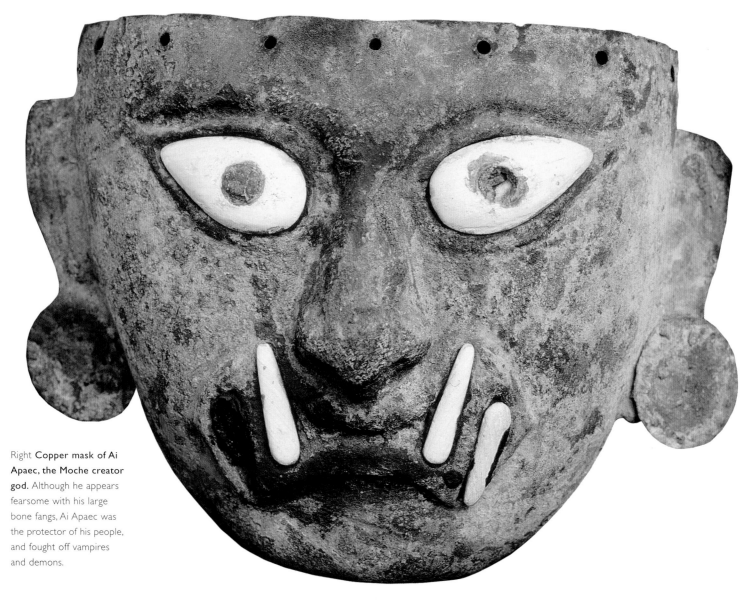

Right **Copper mask of Ai Apaec, the Moche creator god.** Although he appears fearsome with his large bone fangs, Ai Apaec was the protector of his people, and fought off vampires and demons.

Moche

The Moche (or Mohica) culture existed between A.D. 1 and 700 (in the Intermediate Period) throughout the coastal valleys of northern Peru. As their artifacts clearly demonstrate, the Moche people were both skilled and prolific artisans in a variety of mediums: ceramic pottery, metalwork, gold and silver jewelry, textiles, murals, and friezes.

Moche artwork indicates that they were a warlike people, and that the wars were often motivated by the need for sacrifice victims to appease the gods. The Moche experienced floods and earthquakes, signs of the gods' displeasure, and the more violent the weather conditions, the greater the need for sacrifice.

The most favored form of sacrifice was slitting the throat, and then presenting the victim's body and blood to the deities. There is a terrifying statue that shows a rather Satan-like figure (perhaps a deity or an executioner) pulling a man's hair, preparing to cut his throat. Ritual burial sites have revealed the skeletons of young girls who had been beaten on the head by clubs, and then had their legs pulled off.

Ai Apaec, the god of creation, is one of the most important deities in the Moche pantheon, and the precursor to the Inca god Viracocha. He is a distant and impersonal god of the sky and mountains, and features prominently in Moche iconography. Ai Apaec is often pictured in fearsome warrior mode, with slanted eyes, a fanged mouth, and a belt and head-dress made of snakes.

Si is the Moche word for moon, and is the name of the unisex moon deity, who was also in charge of fertility, rain, and the sea. Unlike Ai Apaec, who was

fairly remote, Si seemed to be more involved in the activities of mortals. The Huaca de la Luna (Temple of the Moon) was built in honor of Si.

In Moche culture, the moon was more important than the sun. The harsh desert sun was seen more as an enemy than a friend, and many of their religious ceremonies were performed at night.

The most feared and bloodthirsty Moche deity goes by the name of Decapitator God. He is portrayed as half-human and half-spider, or half-human and half-jaguar, and his likeness is seen on every type of art-work, especially around ritual sites. He has four sharp fangs protruding from a contorted mouth, piercing eyes, and a beard.

Unfortunately, no myths or stories seem to have survived from this interesting era.

Nazca

The Nazca culture also flourished during the Intermediate Period (from 200 B.C. to A.D. 500) in Peru's southern coastal desert valleys. This culture developed a sophisticated underground irrigation system, and had excellent textiles and ceramics. But the Nazca culture is most well known for the incredible system of geoglyphs (symbols scored into the earth) known as the Nazca Lines, which cover a total area of 190 sq miles (500 sq km) and have been carbon-dated to A.D. 350.

NAZCA LINES

The Nazca Lines are South America's greatest mystery. They are a complex of close to 300 geoglyphs that are found mainly in the Pampa de Ingenio desert of Peru.

As well as lines and geometric shapes, the images also include humanlike figures, flowers, fish, insects, and various animals and birds. They were made by etching, or scraping, the surface pebbles of the desert floor so that the lighter rock underneath could show through. Some of the drawings on hillsides can be seen from the plains below, but most can only be viewed from the air.

There are several theories about the origins of the Nazca Lines. Some think that they were of astronomical and astrological significance. Others believe that they were used for ritual walks. According to Erich von Daniken in his 1970 book, *Chariots of the Gods*, the lines were the work of UFOs. It is also possible that the drawings were a form of visual prayer to the sky and mountain deities in the hope that they would bestow rain on the arid desert landscape.

Left **The Oculate Being, Paracas culture.** Made from alpaca wool, this fine example of a Paracas textile shows the Oculate Being in human form. He is wearing a golden diadem (ornamental headband) and holding a snake. A snakelike creature also hovers above his head.

Above **Shaman on painted vessel, Nazca culture.** As with most South American cultures, the shaman played an important role in the lives of the Nazca people. It has been suggested that the spirits of the shamans were able to soar above the landscape and direct the people to create the immense Nazca Lines for religious purposes.

LATE PRE-INCA ANDEAN CULTURES

The centuries leading up to the Inca empire were known as the Middle Horizon Period (A.D. 500–1000) and the Late Intermediate Period (A.D. 1000–1400). During the Middle Horizon Period, the major political, cultural, and religious centers were Huarí in the Peruvian highlands, Pachacamac on the coast, and Tiahuanaco in the Lake Titicaca Basin. Chan Chan was the capital of the Kingdom of Chimor (or Chimu) during the Late Intermediate Period, in the area previously ruled by the Moche (or Mochica) people in the north Peruvian coastal valleys.

Below **Passage of Fish and Birds, Chan Chan.** The extensive ruins of Chan Chan are located near the present-day Peruvian town of Trujillo. Many of the adobe brick walls still show the fascination of the original inhabitants with the fauna of the region, and the designs may have had both a religious and an aesthetic function.

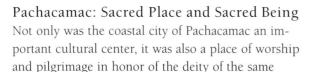

[They] commonly acknowledge a supreme lord and author of all things, which they of Peru called ... Pachacamac, or Pachayachachic, which is the creator of heaven and earth ...

JOSÉ DE ACOSTA (1540–1600), JESUIT MISSIONARY

Pachacamac: Sacred Place and Sacred Being

Not only was the coastal city of Pachacamac an important cultural center, it was also a place of worship and pilgrimage in honor of the deity of the same

name, which means "earth-maker" or "the one who animates the world."

The complex of temples and pyramids at Pachacamac (near present-day Lima) was an awe-inspiring sight, built on top of an artificial hill made of adobe bricks. These buildings were adorned with beautiful murals and frescoes and held many treasures. The major focus of the sacred site was the oracle of Pachacamac, as represented by a wooden idol. Priests that had been specially ordained would act as mediums between the pilgrim and the oracle—as no ordinary human being was deemed worthy of direct contact—and even the priest was not able to gaze at the idol uncovered.

When the Incas later took over Pachacamac, they were so impressed with the temple's grandeur that the only change they made was to add a chapel in honor of their sun god, Inti.

Pachacamac, the creator deity, was the son of the sun and moon, and the god of earthquakes and fire, and he was worshipped by the people of the Andes for close to 1,000 years. There are several myths illustrating just what a harsh and mighty deity Pachacamac could be.

Before Pachacamac existed, he had a half-brother named Con, who was also the son of the sun, and an imposing deity in his own right. Con arrived from the north, and as he traveled the land, he would move mountains or fill up valleys to make his journey easier. He designed a beautiful fertile land, but became lonely, so he decided to create some people to share the land and its bounty with him. Con soon became displeased with the people he created, thinking them lazy and ungrateful. He turned their lush farmlands into barren rocky ground, thus making life much harder for them.

One day Pachacamac appeared, and decided he wanted his brother's creation all to himself. He challenged and defeated Con, and changed the people into monkeys. All the crops withered away and died. Pachacamac then set about creating people of his own—one man and one woman. But because he neglected to provide food for them, the man died, and the woman knew that she would soon die herself if she did not get help. So she approached the sun for assistance, and the sun obliged her by making her pregnant through the force of his rays. After her son was born, Pachacamac became extremely jealous. He killed the boy, then chopped the body up and scattered the pieces. The boy's teeth became maize

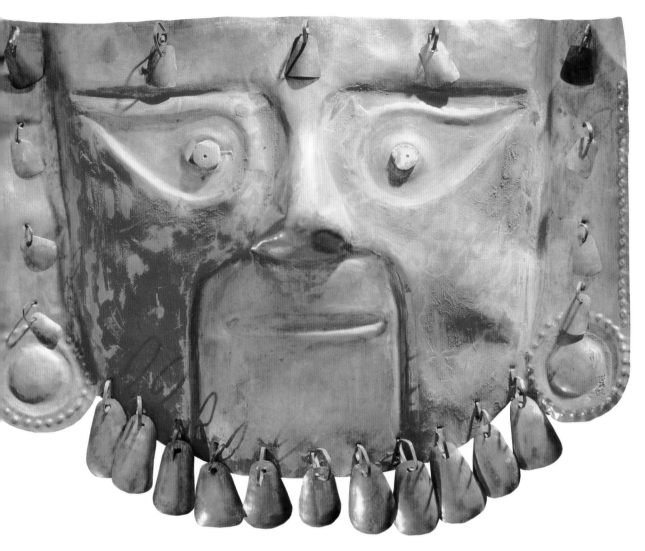

and his bones became the yucca plant. This story seems to be a parable about the importance of human sacrifice (especially the sacrifice of children) to ensure a bountiful harvest.

The *Huarochirí Manuscript*

This seventeenth-century text was written in the Quechua language under the direction of Spanish priest Francisco de Avila. It has been likened to the Mayan *Popol Vuh*, and details the myths, culture, and beliefs of the Huarochirí (or Warachirí) people of the western Andes. The purpose of the manuscript was to compare the indigenous beliefs with Christianity—rather unfavorably, one would think, judging from the manuscript's original title: *A Narrative of the Errors, False Gods, and Other Superstitions and Diabolical Rites of the Indians* (1608).

PARIACACA AND HUALLALLO CARUINCHO

One of the many stories of the *Huarochirí Manuscript* tells of the rain god Pariacaca, who was an important deity of the region. During a flood, five eggs were found on Mount Condor Coto. Falcons emerged from these five eggs, flying in all directions, and transforming themselves into men, who became the five aspects of the divine Pariacaca.

The most powerful deity of the Huarochirí people was Huallallo Caruincho, known as the "Man Eater." He was the god of fire and volcanoes, and was very demanding and autocratic. Huallallo Caruincho had a rule that there could only be two children per family, and one child had to be eaten by the god.

Pariacaca decided that he wanted to challenge the vile supremacy of this tyrannical god. His weapon would be water and Huallallo Caruincho's would be fire. A long battle ensued. Because Pariacaca was a multiple deity, he could attack Huallallo Caruincho from five different directions at once. Although he was a formidable opponent, Huallallo Caruincho eventually surrendered, fleeing toward the jungles of the Amazon.

Above **Stele (sculpted upright slab) of pre-Incan god Coniraya Viracocha.** Dating from the period A.D. 600–1200, this simple stone sculpture of the creator deity was found at the ruins of Tiahuanaco in Bolivia. Coniraya Viracocha's influence was such that the Incas absorbed the myths and characteristics of the deity into their own creator god, Viracocha.

a kindly woman brought him a cup of maize beer and some food. After he was refreshed, he told the woman to take her family and leave the village, because something terrible was going to happen in five days. And he warned her not to tell anyone else, or she would be destroyed too. The woman followed Pariacaca's instructions. Five days later, Pariacaca caused torrential rain to fall from the mountain, which washed everyone in the village out to sea.

CONIRAYA VIRACOCHA

The second chapter of the *Huarochirí Manuscript* contains the story of Coniraya Viracocha, a pre-Inca deity who was later taken up by the Incas and incorporated into their creator, Viracocha. This chapter details the exploits of Coniraya Viracocha as he journeyed throughout the universe on foot, dressed as a penniless beggar.

While visiting a village by the sea, Coniraya Viracocha fell in love with a beautiful virgin named Cavillaca, but she was not interested in him because he was old and poor. But Coniraya Viracocha was mad with desire, and he shapeshifted himself into a bird so he could follow her around and watch her without being noticed.

One day as Cavillaca was weaving a tapestry underneath the shade of her favorite lucuma tree, Coniraya Viracocha flew to the tree and ejaculated some sperm into one of the orange fruits, causing the fruit to drop to the ground. Cavillaca saw how lovely and ripe the fruit was, so she picked it up and ate it.

Because she was a virgin, Cavillaca was absolutely horrified to find herself pregnant—especially as she did not have a clue as to who the father could possibly be—and in due course she gave birth to a son. When the baby was about six months old Cavillaca was determined to learn the identity of the father. She gathered together all the men of the village, and

Another version of the story tells that while he was on his journey to fight Huallallo Caruincho, Pariacaca stopped at a village during a festival, and sat down at a banquet table. Because of Pariacaca's bedraggled, road-weary appearance, nobody offered him anything ⸱at or drink. Pariacaca was outraged—didn't these ⸱⸱ realize who he was? Finally, after many hours,

For when the Indians worshipped it they said, "Coniraya Viracocha ... thou art Lord of all ...

TRANSLATED FROM THE *HUAROCHIRÍ MANUSCRIPT* BY CLEMENTS R. MARKHAM (1830–1916)

MUMMIES

The practice of preserving bodies as mummies (mallquis) was carried out from the very earliest Andean civilizations, and was a very important aspect of ancestor worship.

The mummy bundles were wrapped in alternating layers of cloth and sand, and then tied up with fiber rope. Sometimes clothes, jewelry, or other personal belongings were wrapped in the bundle. Often a mask or head was added, made from wood or copper, and decorated with feathers, shells, or fabric. The mummies were not actually buried, but were stored in special buildings or caves, and became preserved by the hot, dry, desert atmosphere.

At mallqui rituals, the mummies were brought out of storage, put on display, and given offerings of food and chicha (maize beer). During the ceremonies, the people would relate myths about the history of the clan, and share their knowledge. These rituals were thought to please the gods, and bring prosperity and spiritual merit.

Above right **Death mask from a Chimor (Chimu) mummy bundle.** In the Chimor (Chimu) culture, the deceased were placed in a sitting position before being wrapped in layers of cloth. The mask was placed over the head area of the bundle.

her baby reached the ocean near Pachacamac, they were turned into stones. Not one to give up easily, Coniraya Viracocha traveled on, asking each and every creature he passed along the way if they had seen his beloved.

Now you can choose the ending to this story, depending on how cynical or how romantic you are. In one version, when Coniraya Viracocha reached the coastal city of Pachacamac he came across two beautiful daughters of the god Pachacamac. Being the lustful god that he was, Coniraya Viracocha seduced one of the goddesses and wanted to bed her younger sister as well, but she became a bird and flew away from the god. The other ending tells that Coniraya Viracocha was so heartbroken not to have found his beloved Cavillaca and his son, that he made a raft out of his golden cloak and, like the Mesoamerican deity Quetzalcoatl, sailed away to the horizon, promising one day to return.

Below **Human head effigy, Inca culture.** Carved from wood, with startling eyes made from inlaid shell, this head was probably part of a mummy bundle. Placing the realistic head near the cloth-wrapped mummy ensured that the deceased retained human form in the afterlife.

asked whoever was responsible for making her pregnant to come forth and admit their cruel deed. Quite a few young men were eager to accept the responsibility for her baby, just so they could marry the gorgeous Cavillaca.

But Cavillaca was confused. How could so many men be this baby's father? So she decided to let her son choose. She placed him on the ground and told him to crawl to the man who was his true biological father. He was a bright little lad, and she trusted that he would know what to do. As it turned out, Coniraya Viracocha, dressed in his beggar's garb, was hanging around on the sidelines. Without any hesitation, the baby crawled right up to Coniraya Viracocha, and put his arms around the deity's leg.

Disgusted at the prospect of marrying this filthy itinerant, Cavillaca snatched the baby away and ran as fast as she could toward the sea. She did not look back to see Coniraya Viracocha remove his shabby gray cloak and transform himself into a handsome young god in golden finery. When Cavillaca and

Right **Pachacuti Inca Yupanqui, eighteenth-century Cuzco School painting.** The ninth emperor of the Incas officially ruled from 1438 to 1471, but legend has it that he became the sovereign of the Incas at age 22, and ruled his people for 103 years.

Below *Inca Sun Worship* by Bernard Picart (1673–1733). The Incas believed they were descendants of the sun god, Inti, and many temples and other sacred sites were devoted to worshipping the sun. A rock on Lake Titicaca's Island of the Sun is said to be the birthplace of the sun.

THE INCAS

By the time the Spanish arrived in South America in the sixteenth century, the Inca empire was the size of the Roman empire, extending 2,600 miles (4,186 km) throughout the Andes and beyond. The guiding force of this highly organized society was the ruler Pachacuti Inca Yupanqui.

Inca means "people of the sun," and the major deity of the Inca people was the sun god Inti. However, their belief system also absorbed the deities of the people whom they conquered.

The spirituality of the Incas had much in common with that of the Mesoamerican peoples in that it was focused on fertility and agriculture, especially the growing of maize (also known as corn). As in Mesoamerica, human sacrifice was practiced, but not on such a grand scale. The Inca people also believed in honoring and worshipping their ancestors.

INCA COSMOLOGY

Similar to the Aztec worldview, the Incas believed in cycles of creation and destruction. Each "age" or "sun" lasted 1,000 years, and was known as a *pachacuti,* named for the ruler Pachacuti Inca Yupanqui. *Pachacuti* virtually means the turning over of time and space. Each cycle was thought to be the reversal of the previous one, and the Inca civilization was in the cycle of the Fifth Sun, which ended at the time of European invasion.

Linked to the concept of *pachacuti* is the belief that the Spanish would one day be conquered and the Inca would rise again. Legend has it that the last Inca emperor, Atahualpa, was beheaded by the Spanish conqueror Francisco Pizarro, and that his head was buried at Cuzco. But the head never died, and over the years a body has been growing. When Atahualpa becomes a complete person again, he will rise from the earth and restore the ancient empire to its former glory.

Peruvian shamans have prophesied that in the twenty-first century a new *pachacuti* will evolve in which order will emerge out of chaos and peace will come from turmoil. In this golden age, the indigenous people of the world will take their rightful place, and the Eagle of the North will fly with the Condor of the South.

Heaven, Earth, and Underworld

The Inca believed that all of nature was permeated with a divine force, and that there were three levels of existence: the upperworld, *Hanaq Pacha,* which was inhabited by the gods and goddesses; *Kay Pacha,* the earth plane; and *Ukhu Pacha,* the land of the dead.

Inti, the sun god and father of the Inca emperors, was the most powerful deity. It was to Inti that most of the sacrifices, offerings, and rituals were performed. The Inca believed that if they led a virtuous life, they would join the sun god in the heavens.

Mama Quilla (or Mama Kilya), the moon goddess and wife of Inti, was also revered, and there is a temple at Cuzco in her honor.

As well as the sun and moon, the stars also had special significance. The Inca used the Milky Way to help them devise their calendar system and predict seasonal and weather changes. The stars in the Milky Way (or Mayu, the celestial river) were afforded the status of minor deities. The Pleiades, for instance, was the celestial patron of agriculture.

The earthly plane, too, was full of sacred meaning. There were supernatural forces associated with rocks, mountains, lakes, rivers, and trees. These forces were known as *huacas,* and the places they inhabited inspired great reverence.

People also had their own little *huacas* that they carried around with them. These could be stones or pebbles, or perhaps pieces of wood or stone carved

INTI RAYMI

Inti Raymi is the Inca festival of the winter solstice (which is in June in the Southern Hemisphere). It is held at Cuzco to honor the sun god, Inti, and celebrates the resurrection of the sun. Traditionally people fasted and abstained from sex for three days before the festival, and the proceedings lasted for nine days. A black llama was sacrificed, and the celebratory feast included cornmeal *(zancu),* round bread, and maize beer *(chicha).*

The essence of Inti Raymi is expressed in this prayer: "Oh creator and Sun and Thunder, be forever copious, do not make us old, let all things be at peace, multiply the people and let there be food, and let all things be fruitful."

After the Spanish conquest, the old rituals were considered sacrilegious and abolished, but Inti Raymi was revived in 1944, and moved to June 24 to coincide with the feast of St John the Baptist.

Today Inti Raymi attracts thousands of people from all over the world. It is a blend of reverence and revelry—a colorful carnival of singing and dancing in traditional costume.

Left **Gold llama, Inca culture.** Llamas were important to the Incas, and were often sacrificed during religious festivals. At other times they were used as sure-footed pack animals.

into the shape of a person, animal, or plant. A special type of *huaca* would be placed in a maize field or irrigation canal to ensure a good harvest. Many of these agricultural *huacas* were destroyed by the Spanish conquerors.

Paccariscas were not unlike *huacas,* and were generally found near natural formations like caves, rocks, mountains, and springs. But *paccariscas* were considered even more important because the people believed that it was at these sacred places that their ancestors departed for the spirit world, and where a bit of their soul was left behind. When people arrived at the *paccarisca,* they would utter the prayer: "Thou art my birthplace, thou art my lifespring. Guard me from evil. O Paccarisca!"

The Inca underworld was a cold and inhospitable place where immoral people went after death. It was ruled by Supay (or Cupay), a demonlike being.

INCA MYTHS OF ORIGIN

Pachacuti Inca Yupanqui, who reigned between A.D. 1438 and 1471, led the Inca empire into a golden age of prosperity and expansion. Among his many achievements were a national taxation system and a sophisticated road and communications network.

As a result of a spiritual experience, Pachacuti believed that he was the child of the sun god, Inti, and set about reorganizing the religious structure of the empire. Religious unification meant political unification, and the myths that were created served to support and reinforce Inca supremacy.

Major Inca Deities

Pachacuti's improvements extended to the Coricancha, the magnificent center of the capital city of Cuzco and one of the major sacred sites of the Inca empire. He dedicated special areas to each of the most important deities within the extensive Inca pantheon, including Viracocha, Inti, and Mama Quilla.

Right **Viracocha Inca, eighteenth-century Cuzco School painting.** The father of Pachacuti Inca Yupanqui, Viracocha Inca was the eighth ruler of the Incas. On his enthronement he was given the name Viracocha due to a vision of the supreme deity he beheld when still a prince.

IMPORTANT INCA DEITIES

NAME	REALM
APO	GOD OF THE MOUNTAINS
APOCATEQUIL	GOD OF LIGHTNING
APU ILLAPU	GOD OF THUNDER
CHANTICO	GODDESS OF GOLD
CHASCA	GODDESS OF VENUS
CHASCA COYLLUR	GOD OF FLOWERS
COCOMAMA	GODDESS OF HEALTH
CONIRAYA	GOD OF THE MOON
COPACATI	GODDESS OF THE LAKES
EKKEKO	GOD OF PROSPERITY
EPUNAMUN	GOD OF WAR
ILYAP'A	GOD OF THE WEATHER
INTI	GOD OF THE SUN
KA-ATA-KILLA	GODDESS OF THE MOON
KON	GOD OF THE RAIN AND THE SOUTH WIND
MAMA ALLPA	GODDESS OF THE HARVEST
MAMA COCHA	GODDESS OF THE SEA
MAMA OCLLO	GODDESS OF SPINNING
MAMA QUILLA	GODDESS OF THE MOON
MANCO CAPAC	GOD OF FIRE
PACHACAMAC	GOD OF THE EARTH
PACHAMAMA	GODDESS OF PLANTS AND ANIMALS
SUPAY	GOD OF DEATH AND THE UNDERWORLD
URCAGUARY	GOD OF BURIED TREASURE
URPIHUA-CHAC	GODDESS OF FISH AND FISHING
VIRACOCHA	SUPREME DEITY, THE CREATOR
ZARAMAMA	GODDESS OF MAIZE

VIRACOCHA: CREATOR AND SUPREME GOD

This remote, impersonal, and invisible deity was called by many names, corresponding to the many roles he played in the cycle of creation. Some of his epithets were Callya ("the ever-present one"), Pachayachachic ("world teacher"), Illa ("Light"), and Tici ("the beginning"). It was believed that he rose from Lake Titicaca to create the sun, moon, and stars.

There is a stone statue at the sacred site of Tiahuanaco in which he is represented as a weeping god. When someone died, special prayers were offered to Viracocha so that the soul would find a peaceful resting place. Small children were sacrificed to Viracocha at his temple in Cuzco and in places high in the mountains in the hope that the Inca people would be victorious in war.

In certain myths, Viracocha appears in various disguises—often as a pale-skinned man with a beard. In this human aspect he is both a teacher and a cultural hero.

INTI: THE SUN GOD

Although Viracocha was the highest-ranking god, Inti was the most popular deity, and was believed to be the ancestor of the royal family and the father of the Inca race. It was through Inti that the Inca received their name "people of the sun."

Inti was a benevolent god, and is honored at his own special temple in Coricancha at Cuzco, and at the "hitching post of the sun" at Machu Picchu, among other sacred places. The ancient festivals of the winter solstice (Inti Raymi) and summer solstice (Capac Raymi) pay homage to Inti and are popular celebrations with South Americans even today.

The Inca believed that if they lived a virtuous life, their spirits would join with the sun god in

the heavens. Inti is associated with the element of gold, and he is often represented as a large golden mask with a humanlike face.

MAMA QUILLA: THE MOON GODDESS

Mama Quilla, or Mama Kilya, is the highest-ranking female deity, the mother of the Incas, and protector of women. As the moon goddess, she governs the calendar and the passing of time. Originally she shone brighter than the sun, so the jealous Inti threw ashes in her face so he would be the more luminous.

Mama Quilla is associated with the element of silver, and there is a temple in her honor at Coricancha in Cuzco as well as at Machu Picchu. Because she is the wife, as well as sister, of the sun god Inti, this relationship set a precedent for brother-sister marriages within the royal family.

How Viracocha Created the World

One of the myths of creation that may even pre-date the Inca period centers on Viracocha, the supreme god. Viracocha and his wife Mama Cocha (goddess of the sea) lived in the sacred lake, Titicaca. One day Viracocha took mud from the bottom of the lake and created all the formations of the earth: the valleys, fields, and mountains.

Although he was pleased with his achievement, Viracocha felt that the earth needed people who could worship him, so he took blocks of stone and sculpted them into human beings. But he was unhappy with his first attempt: he had created ugly, shapeless giants who were stupid and disobedient, so he immediately destroyed them with a torrent of water.

Viracocha decided that before he endeavored to make any more people, he would create the Island of the Sun and the Island of the Moon within the lake itself; the sun and moon rose up from these islands, and Viracocha set them on their celestial course. Now that the sun was in the sky, Viracocha could actually see what he was doing.

Feeling more confident now, Viracocha then set about finding some clay from which to fashion a new group of humans. He shaped them into male and female, child and adult, and painted on clothes and hair. Viracocha was happy with these new folk, and led them underground where they were dispersed throughout a labyrinth of caves. The creator breathed into them his life force, and they went forth into the world to people the land.

Above **Silver maize plant, Inca culture.** Silver was associated with the moon goddess Mama Quilla (also known as Mama Kilya), as the color of the metal is similar to the glow of the full moon. This silver maize cob may well have been created specifically as a symbolic offering of food to the moon goddess.

Left **Inca temple of the sun god, Island of the Sun, Bolivia.** The Island of the Sun (also known as the Isla del Sol) sits amid the cool, blue waters of Lake Titicaca, the highest navigable lake in the world. Even today the indigenous population believes that the lake collects water sent by the nearby mountain deities, and offerings are made to ensure good fishing and safe sailing.

Below *Cuzco, Peru* by Georgius Braun (1541–1622). The great Inca capital, Cuzco was founded in the twelfth century by Manco Capac, son of the sun god Inti. From the majestic temple dedicated to Inti—the Coricancha—41 imaginary lines radiated outward, linking a number of shrines, small temples, and other sacred places.

Several ye.. .ssed, and Viracocha couldn't help but wonder what had become of his creatures on earth. So he took on human form, dressed as an old beggar, and wandered the countryside near Lake Titicaca, searching for his people. When Viracocha arrived at the first village, the people were intimidated by this wandering stranger, and tried to kill him. Viracocha was so angry that he took a thunderbolt from his bag and threw it into the forest, causing all the trees to catch on fire. The villagers realized that this man who could make fire was a powerful being indeed, and they got on their knees and begged for

mercy. Because Viracocha was compassionate, he forgave the people and called rain down from the heavens to quell the flames.

When he came to the next town, the people there recognized Viracocha for the divine presence that he was, and offered to build a golden throne for him to sit on whenever he passed through. Viracocha was delighted by this reception, and bestowed upon the people many blessings.

And so Viracocha traveled from place to place, rewarding the people who recognized him and paid homage, and punishing all those who ignored or

mistreated him. He finally arrived in Cuzco, which at that time was just a humble village. But the people were so industrious and hospitable that Viracocha told them he would send a great ruler, and their city would be known far and wide as the wondrous capital of the Inca empire.

The People of the Sun

There are several versions of this story, which tells of Manco Capac, the founder of the Inca dynasty, and the origins of the capital, Cuzco. The myth serves to clearly illustrate the divine origin and superiority of the Inca people, and outlines their basic social order.

After the first people were created by Viracocha, they were pretty much left to fend for themselves. They lived like beasts in caves: going naked or wearing animal skins, mating indiscriminately, and having no religion or education. For sustenance they ate game, grasses, roots, or wild berries, and when times were hard, they would be forced to eat each other.

Inti the sun god looked down from the heavens and despaired at the wretched state of humankind. So he sent his four sons and four daughters, collectively known as the Ayars, to travel the countryside and teach the people to be civilized. The sons' names were Ayar Manco Capac, Ayar Auca, Ayar Cachi, and Ayar Uchu, and the daughters Mama Ocllo, Mama Huaco, Mama Cura, and Mama Raua. Like Inti and Mama Quilla the moon goddess, these brothers and sisters were allowed to marry each other.

The Ayars entered the world through a heavenly window in Mount Tambo Toco near Lake Titicaca. However, not long after they began their journey, Ayar Cachi began to annoy everyone with his pride and destructiveness. His siblings lured him into a cave, and then pushed rocks against the opening so that he could not escape. Then Ayar Auca and Ayar Uchu displeased the gods with their disobedience, and were turned to stone.

Inti had given the leader, Ayar Manco Capac, a rod made of gold, and told him to plunge the rod into the earth wherever they stopped to rest. The place where the rod disappeared into the ground in one thrust was where they were instructed to settle. Trying several spots, eventually the rod disappeared

into the earth at a place that they ⌐ Cuzco, which literally means "the navel of the world."

Following Inti's strict instructions, the remaining Ayars stayed in Cuzco to begin their ministry. The people had never seen anyone like Manco Capac and his sisters before. They were beautiful beyond words, and wore shining golden cloaks and large gold discs in their ears. They were so wonderful that the local people wanted to emulate these children of the sun. Manco Capac taught the men how to plant seeds, till the soil, irrigate the fields, and make and use weapons. Mama Ocllo and her sisters taught the women how to spin and weave cotton and wool, and how to cook and sew. And as the people learned new ways and prospered, they went out and taught others. That is how the Inca empire began.

Left **Mama Ocllo, eighteenth-century Cuzco School painting.** Sometimes known as Mama Coya, Mama Ocllo was the sister–consort of Manco Capac, and was responsible for teaching women how to spin fiber, cook, sew, and weave. In one myth, Inti sent his children Mama Ocllo and Manco Capac to earth to civilize the people, while in another story the moon goddess Mama Quilla allowed her daughter Mama Ocllo to become Manco Capac's bride.

KNOTS OF HISTORY

Although the Incas had no system of writing as we know it, they had an efficient system of record-keeping known as *quipu*, which is the Quechua word for "knot."

Quipus were knotted strings made of cotton (or occasionally wool) which Inca rulers used to monitor taxes, population, military action, and the economy. As well as statistical information, *quipus* were also devices for keeping the stories, myths, poems, and history of the Incas. The people responsible for both encoding and decoding the information were known as *quipucamayoqs* ("knot makers"), and teams of messengers would swiftly transport the *quipus* from one city to another, covering as many as 150 miles (240 km) in one day.

Color, type of knot, and placement of knots on the string were all significant factors in interpreting the messages. For example, red would refer to the army, and white indicated peace. Only a handful of *quipus* survived the Spanish conquest, because the Catholic priests thought them to be the devil's handiwork.

Below **Quipus, Inca culture.** The information contained in *quipus* was lost to the modern world until Leland Locke deciphered their meaning in the early 1920s.

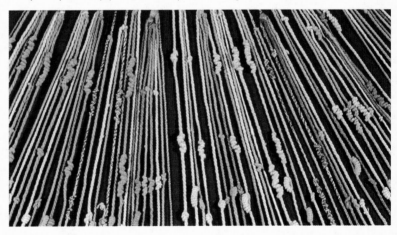

Above *Acllahuasi,* Machu Picchu, Peru. Over 80 percent of the mummies from Machu Picchu are female, leading archaeologists to believe that one of the prime purposes of this sacred city, at least in its later years, was as a training ground for the *acllas,* or "chosen women."

Right *Inca Sun Virgin* by Jan de la Cruz. The *acllas,* or Inca Sun Virgins, took a vow of chastity to honor the sun god, Inti. As they were considered "pure," they were responsible for preparing food for religious rituals and for weaving the cloth for garments worn by priests and the nobility.

WOMEN OF THE SUN

The major Inca centers such as Cuzco, Lake Titicaca, Pachacamac, and Machu Picchu all had temples dedicated to the sun god, Inti. Each of these temples contained a cloistered section known as an *acllahuasi,* the "house of the chosen women."

These "chosen women," or *acllas,* were young girls selected by a special committee that traveled throughout the empire searching for the most beautiful and unblemished eight-year-olds, preferably with pure Incan lineage. If a girl became an *aclla,* it was considered a great honor for her family and indeed for her entire village.

Acllas performed various duties, but their primary purpose was to be of service to the sun god. The highest class of *aclla,* known as the *mamacunas,* had to be of the purest bloodline, and were widely revered as saints. *Mamacunas* lived in celibacy their entire lives, and were thought to be able to communicate directly with the gods. They were responsible for looking after the temple, tending the sacred fires, and assisting the priests in their rituals (including sacrifices), and were the custodians of Inca history.

The young *acllas* learned how to weave, how to make the ceremonial *chicha* (maize beer) and *canca* (maize pudding), and how to care for mummies. When a girl reached the age of fourteen, the committee decided if she would return home or if she would proceed to the next stage. Some girls would be trained to look after the principal and secondary idols, and some would become the servants of the nobility and the priesthood. Others were earmarked as sacrificial offerings to the sun god, which was considered to be a great privilege. The girls of the lowest class, the *Pampa Aclla Conas,* either became concubines of the nobility and high-ranking military officers, or were given away in marriage for political purposes.

The Virgin and the Shepherd

There was once a virgin named Chuquillanto who lived at the *acllahuasi* in Cuzco. All the maidens there were selected for their impeccable beauty, but Chuquillanto was the most special, because her hair was the color of the sun.

The virgins had to follow a strict set of rules, including a rigorous regimen of personal hygiene. However, in the afternoon, once the work had been done and the bathing ritual completed, the girls were free to wander outside of the cloister, as long as they traveled in pairs.

One fine summer's day Chuquillanto and her friend were walking in a meadow, and were enchanted by sweet music that they could hear in the distance. They kept following the music, and finally arrived at the source of the sound—a handsome young shepherd named Acoynapa, playing the flute to his herd of llamas. When the shepherd laid eyes on Chuquillanto, he thought she must have been a goddess. Never before had he seen a girl whose hair was the color of gold, or who smelled as fresh as flowers. And never before had she heard such wondrous music.

That night, neither Chuquillanto nor Acoynapa could sleep a wink; both of them were burning with desire. But they knew what the punishment would be if Chuquillanto were to lose her virginity—she would be buried alive, and her partner would hanged by his feet. Days passed, and Acoynapa could not eat, sleep, or even play his flute—he was languishing for love. His mother, who was a skilled sorceress and clairvoyant, realized what was going on, and knew she had to do something or Acoynapa would die.

Chuquillanto could bear it no longer—she had to see her beloved again—and once more she took her friend along to Acoynapa's farm. Acoynapa's mother told the girl and her companion that her son was dead, but gave her his staff to remember him by. That night, Chuquillanto took the gift to bed with her, and was amazed when Acoynapa emerged from the staff; he was not dead at all, but placed in the enchanted staff by his mother. Thus hidden, Acoynapa stayed in the cloister, and the couple spent several nights together in blissful love.

But disaster soon struck—a plague of smallpox descended upon the land, and the priests decreed that the golden-haired virgin was to be sacrificed to Inti. How could Chuquillanto offer herself to Inti now

that she had been deflowered? If she told the truth, Acoynapa would be hanged. But if she let herself be sacrificed, Inti would be so displeased that he would bestow even further misery to the people. Chuquillanto and Acoynapa decided to run away to the jungle. They arrived at the border, and just when Chuquillanto and Acoynapa thought they were safe, they were suddenly turned into stone pillars, which will remain there for all eternity.

MACHU PICCHU

Situated high in the Andes, Machu Picchu (meaning "manly peak") was a royal estate and center of spiritual retreat thought to have been built by Emperor Pachacuti Inca Yupanqui in A.D. 1470.

Hiram Bingham of Yale University accidentally discovered the site in 1911, and when all the vegetation was cleared away, a magnificent city was revealed. Archaeologists discovered many bodies of young women there, leading them to believe that the settlement contained an *acllahuasi* ("house of the chosen women").

Machu Picchu was laid out in what we would call today an "eco-friendly" design, as

the 200 stone buildings blend harmoniously into the features of the environment. Because of its cultural and natural significance, Machu Picchu was awarded World Heritage status in 1983 and has since become a major tourist destination within South America.

Below **Machu Picchu, Peru.** Two of the main features of Machu Picchu are the Temple of the Three Windows and the "hitching post of the sun" (*intihuatana*). Comprising a pillar of stone set in a stone base, the *intihuatana* was used by Inca priests to "tie" the sun down as the winter solstice approached and the hours of daylight shortened.

THE CHIBCHA OF COLOMBIA

The Chibcha people (who are also known as the Muisca people) lived in the central highlands of present-day Colombia between A.D 900 and 1450. Their civilization was basically contemporary with the Inca, and comprised three tribes: the Iraca, the Zaque, and the Zipa.

Both the lifestyle and the economy of the Chibcha people revolved around metallurgy: copper, silver, and especially gold. To the Chibcha, gold was imbued with mystical qualities, and this is exemplified in the story of the gilded man, who later became known by the Spanish—and the rest of the world—as El Dorado.

El Dorado

The well-known legend of El Dorado was based on a Chibcha ritual that was performed when a new chieftain was appointed.

Prior to the inauguration ceremony, the prospective chieftain spent several days in fasting and contemplation. Thus purified, he traveled to Lake Guatavita. At the sacred lake, he removed all of his clothing, and his attendants painted his body with an adhesive resin, and then sprinkled gold dust all over his body.

The appointed ruler stepped onto a raft, which was heaped with treasures made of gold and other precious materials. The raft drifted across the lake amid music and fanfare. When it reached the center of the lake, everyone became silent as the chieftain and his entourage each tossed the objects into the water as offerings to the gods. Another version of the story tells that as well as throwing valuable objects into the lake, the chieftain dove into the lake and washed the gold dust from his body as a further gift to the gods.

As well as this special ritual, the Chibcha people would regularly throw valuables into Lake Iguaque as part of their devotional practices to honor the goddess Bachue. When the Spaniards heard these stories, they thought that they must have entered a land of unlimited wealth, and their lust for

gold was heightened even further. The name El Dorado has since become synonymous with a utopian fantasy of riches and power.

The Creation of the World

Chiminigagua was the supreme being and creator deity. The Chibcha believed that before creation, the universe was in total darkness. Chiminigagua, who held all the light of the world within him, decided to unleash it. He transformed himself into a flock of black birds which dispensed light from their beaks as they flew over the mountain peaks. After the world was illuminated, Chiminigagua then created the sun and moon to brighten the sky.

Although Chiminigagua was the all-powerful creator, he was not revered as highly as other deities such as Bachue, the mother of the Chibcha race, or Bochica, the bringer of civilization.

Bachue: the Mother Goddess

Bachue ("she of the large breasts") was the goddess of fertility, water, and agriculture. She was also known as Furachogue ("beneficent woman"). One day she appeared as if by magic from Lake Iguaque, carrying her little son. When the boy reached puberty, Bachue began to mate with him, and they produced many children. Bachue was so prolific that most of her pregnancies resulted in multiple births.

Bachue and her partner lived in the village of Iguaque long enough to see their great-grandchildren. But the time came when they had to return to the lake, their spiritual home. So they gathered their tribe together and urged them to lead a good life and perform their religious duties.

They transformed themselves into snakes, and went back to the sacred lake from whence they came.

The Chibcha loved the goddess Bachue so much that they would make pilgrimages to Lake Iguaque and make offerings of gold and precious jewels to her. Occasionally, devotees would be rewarded with dreams and visions of the divine serpents.

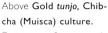

Above **Gold *tunjo*, Chibcha (Muisca) culture.** *Tunjos* were figures used as religious or votive offerings by the Chibcha people. They were mostly anthropomorphic (in human form), and may have represented past rulers of the civilization. Other *tunjos* portrayed animals, or depicted scenes of political or social significance.

> *He [the chieftain] went about all covered with powdered gold, as casually as if it were powdered salt. For it seemed to him that to wear any other finery was less beautiful ...*
>
> GONZALO FERNÁNDEZ DE OVIEDO (1478–1557), SPANISH HISTORIAN

Bochica: the Bringer of Civilization

Bochica is sometimes designated as the Chibcha sun god, but he is more often thought of as a cultural hero who brought living skills and high moral standards to the Chibcha. Like other cultural heroes of mythology, Bochica was portrayed as a wise old bearded man. He traveled around the country, teaching the grateful people metalwork, weaving, building, and how to use a calendar.

Bochica was married to Huitaca (or Chia), the moon goddess. While Bochica advocated sobriety and fidelity, Huitaca promoted drunkenness and promiscuity, so naturally, many people were eager to follow her example. This caused Bochica great heartache, after all his hard work in trying to bring laws and refinement to his people.

Huitaca used her powers of enchantment to help Bochica's main rival, Chibchacum, to flood the plains of Teguendama. Bochica became so enraged that he turned his wife into an owl, condemning her to live forever as a nocturnal creature. He then changed himself into the sun to evaporate the water. With his magic staff he created channels in the rocks into which the water could drain— these are known as the Teguendama waterfalls.

As punishment for causing the flood, Bochica sent Chibchacum down into the bowels of the earth and forced him to carry the world on his shoulders. When Chibchacum moves the world from one shoulder to the other, an earthquake occurs.

Above **Gold model of the raft used in the Lake Guatavita ceremony.** The raft used by the Chibchas in the ritual that formed the basis of the El Dorado legend was made from local rushes. It was richly decorated and carried four braziers that burned highly perfumed incense.

Left *El Dorado, the Golden Man* by Theodore de Bry (1528–1598). As part of the ritual to make him the chieftain, the naked Chibcha man would be covered in a sticky resin and then have fine gold dust blown over his body. He would then sail out onto Lake Guatavita, to make offerings of gold to the god who lived at the bottom of the lake. In another myth, the offerings were made to a monster who was holding the spirit of an earlier chieftain's wife captive in the depths of the lake.

509

MYTHS OF THE RIVERS AND RAIN FORESTS

The Amazon region of South America features the largest rain forest—and one of the largest rivers—on the planet. For thousands of years, the people of this region have lived intimately with nature in small tribal communities.

The myths of the Amazon are localized, and focus on plants and animals, the river, the daily activities of the people (such as hunting and cooking), and their rituals and ceremonies. Shamans feature prominently in the myths, and in many cases are the myth-keepers of their tribes.

Shamanism is not a religion, per-se, it is a set of techniques, and the principal technique is the use of psychedelic plants.

TERENCE MCKENNA
(1946–2000), AUTHOR

Uaica and the Sleep Tree

From the late nineteenth century to well into the twentieth century, teams of anthropologists lived among the people of the Xingu River region of Brazil and recorded their myths. Here is just one of the many fascinating Xingu River stories.

Uaica was a hunter from the Juruna tribe. One day while exploring in the rain forest he came across a gigantic tree, the like of which he'd never seen before, and he was awe-struck by its unique beauty, immense age, and majestic grandeur.

Uaica also noticed something very peculiar—a pile of animals lying motionless beneath the tree. At first Uaica thought the animals were asleep, but when he looked more closely, he realized they were dead. He began to feel dizzy and drowsy and feared he might have been bewitched and would meet the same fate as the animals, but no matter how hard he tried he could not stay awake.

Sinaa, the jaguar ancestor of the Juruna people, appeared to Uaica in a dream, and taught him the secrets of healing and divination. Uaica awoke feeling blissful and refreshed, and returned to the tree many times, to enter the dreaming trance and to receive the jaguar's teachings. But one day Sinaa instructed Uaica that never again should he return to the tree, although he told Uaica that he could take away some of the bark.

When Uaica returned home to his village, he discovered that by brewing a tea from the sacred bark

Below **Dance festival of an Amazonian tribe.** Deep within the Amazon rain forest, tribespeople used the sound and movement associated with age-old sacred dances to worship their deities, to empower warriors, and to honor the spirits of their ancestors.

and drinking it, he could re-enter the dreaming state and communicate with Sinaa once more. He also learned that the special tea had curative properties, and he soon became known throughout the land as a great healer and cultural hero.

The villagers had great love and respect for Uaica, and thought he should be married. Someone so good and wise should have a child, so that his knowledge would be passed down. However, Uaica was not so wise in choosing a wife. They were not married very long when Uaica's wife became unfaithful, and she and her lover plotted to kill Uaica.

One night the lover snuck up behind Uaica and attempted to strike him on the head with a club. But because Uaica had the spirit of the jaguar ancestor within him, he had eyes in the back of his head, and was able to get out of the way of the club. However, the club left a huge hole in the ground, and Uaica fell into it, disappearing down into the center of the earth, never to be seen again.

How the Jaguar Lost His Fire

This engaging myth, from the Kayapo tribe of tropical Brazil, tells of how mankind acquired fire.

A young boy named Botoque was out hunting for birds with his older brother when they spotted a large macaw nest at the top of a cliff. The older brother soon persuaded Botoque to climb up a pole and steal the eggs from the nest.

Botoque was quite jubilant when he found two eggs, which he promptly threw down to his brother. However, as the eggs fell downward, they turned into stones and broke the brother's hand as he tried to catch them. The older boy was so furious that he stormed off, deliberately knocking the pole down to the ground and leaving Botoque stranded up on the cliff for two days without any food or water.

Poor Botoque began to despair when, from his clifftop, he saw an amazing sight. It was a jaguar, walking upright on two legs, carrying a bow and arrow and a big basket of freshly killed meat. The jaguar spotted Botoque, and with a deep and kindly voice, asked the boy if he would like some help. Botoque was terrified and shook his head, but the jaguar replaced the pole and eventually Botoque slid down.

The jaguar sensed that Botoque hadn't eaten for days, and invited him home for a meal of roasted meat. Botoque did not know what roasted meat was (they ate raw meat in his village), but he was so cold and hungry that he accepted the invitation. When they arrived home, the jaguar's wife was roasting meat over an open fire and Botoque was amazed—he had never seen fire before, or felt such incredible warmth. And he had never tasted anything as wonderful as the tender roasted boar meat.

Botoque stayed with the jaguar for many days, and the jaguar treated him like his own son. He taught him how to use the bow and arrow, and how to build fires and cook food. Botoque would have been happy staying with the jaguar, except for one thing: the jaguar's wife. She was jealous of Botoque, and was cruel to him at every opportunity.

Because of this harsh treatment, Botoque soon became very homesick—he was even starting to miss his older brother—and told the jaguar that he needed to return to his village. Wiping a tear from his eye, the jaguar said farewell to Botoque, and gave him a basket of cooked meat. Then he very sternly told Botoque that under no circumstances should he let his tribespeople know about fire.

Botoque's mother was thrilled to have her son home again and invited her neighbors around for

Left **Funerary urn, Marajo Island, Brazil.** Marajo Island is located in the mouth of the Amazon and Tocantins Rivers, and the ceramics from this area date back over 1,600 years. This red, black, and white funerary urn depicts a crouching female fertility deity with large eyes and a protruding tongue. The bones of the ancestors were kept in urns so the spirits of the deceased remained close to the family.

Below **Gold feline figure, Chavín culture, Peru.** Felines played an important role in the mythology of many South American peoples. Cults devoted to the jaguar existed in Peru, while Amazonian peoples believed in the jaguar spirit—a powerful symbol of strength, athleticism, and dark magic.

SPIRITS AND VISIONS

To the people of the Amazon region, the spiritual world was just as real as the physical world around them. In fact, the features of the natural world—such as the rivers, plants, stones, birds, and animals—were all believed to contain their own unique spirit essence.

Shamans are the intermediary between the earthly and the divine realms. Often with the assistance of a mind-altering substance such as *ayahuasca* (a native plant), they would enter a trance and would be able to see and communicate with the gods, the ancestors, as well as the spirits that move through all things. In their altered state, they could shape-shift into the body of another creature, such as a snake or jaguar.

To this day, shamans are respected members of their Amazon communities. They diagnose and cure illnesses, exorcise demons, see into the future, and help dying people make the transition into the next life.

Left **Gold Darien pectoral representing a shaman, Colombia.** The Tukano people of Colombia's Amazon region believe shamans cause lightning to streak across the sky when they throw special crystals at their foes.

a feast of the delicious roasted meat. They were all extremely curious about how the meat was cooked, and eventually Botoque broke his promise to the jaguar and told them about fire, and what a wonderful thing it was. The next day Botoque brought two tribesmen to the jaguar's cottage when he was out hunting, and they were so impressed with the marvelous fire that they decided to take away all the logs that were burning in the jaguar's hearth.

When the jaguar returned from hunting, he was angry and disappointed that Botoque had betrayed him. From that time on, the jaguar became a wild and vicious creature, as he was forced by Botoque's treachery to live in the cold and dark, to hunt with his teeth and claws, and to eat his meat raw. Botoque became a cultural hero, having gained supremacy over the animal kingdom and brought the bow and arrow and the knowledge of fire to his people.

Below *Making Curare in the Brazilian Forest* by François-Auguste Biard (1798–1882). Curare, a deadly poison used for hunting, was carefully prepared by the shaman of the tribe.

RECOMMENDED READING

The Classical Era

Aeschylus. *The Oresteia: Agamemnon; The Libation Bearers; Eumenides* (translated by R. Fagles). Penguin: London, 1977.

Apollonius. *The Voyage of Argo* (translated by E.V. Rieu). Penguin: London, 1975.

Bremmer, Jan and Nicholas Horsfall. *Roman Myth and Mythography.* University of London: London, 1987.

Bulfinch, Thomas. *The Illustrated Age of Fable.* Harper Collins Publishers: London, 1998.

Carpenter, T. *Art and Myth in Ancient Greece.* Thames & Hudson: London, 1991.

Euripides. *The Bacchae and Other Plays: Ion; The Women of Troy; Helen; The Bacchae* (translated by P. Vellacott). Penguin: London, 1973.

Graf, F. *Greek Mythology.* John Hopkins University Press: Baltimore, 1993.

Graves, Robert. *The Greek Myths.* Penguin: London, 1960.

Hesiod. *The Work and Days/Theogony/The Shield of Herakles* (translated by R. Lattimore). University of Michigan Press: Ann Arbor, 1991.

Homer. *The Iliad* (translated by E.V. Rieu). Penguin: London, 2003.

Homer. *The Odyssey* (translated by E.V. Rieu). Penguin: London, 2003.

Hughes, Ted. *Tales from Ovid.* Faber & Faber: London, 1997.

Kamara, Peter. *Ancient Roman Mythology.* Promotional Reprint Company Ltd.: London, 1996.

Kerenyi, C. *The Heroes of the Greeks.* Thames & Hudson: London, 1997.

Lefkowitz, K. *Women in Greek Mythology.* Duckworth: London, 1986.

Ogilvie, R.M. *The Romans and their Gods.* Chatto & Windus Ltd.: London, 1969.

Ovid. *Metamorphoses* (translated by M. Innes). Penguin: London, 1973.

Scullard, H.H. *Festivals and Ceremonies of the Roman Republic.* Thames & Hudson: London, 1981.

Sophocles. *The Three Theban Plays: Antigone; Oedipus the King; Oedipus at Colonus* (translated by R. Fagles). Penguin: London, 1984.

Virgil. *The Aeneid* (translated by D. West). Penguin: London, 2003.

European Mythology

Berresford-Ellis, Peter. *A Dictionary of Celtic Mythology.* Oxford University Press: Oxford, 1992.

Berresford-Ellis, Peter. *A Dictionary of Irish Mythology.* Oxford University Press: Oxford, 1987.

Burgess, Glyn S. (translator). *The Lais of Marie de France.* Penguin USA: New York, 1986.

Crossley-Holland, Kevin (ed.). *Norse Myths.* Random House: London, 1981.

Cunliffe, Barry. *The Ancient Celts.* Penguin: London, 1999.

Davidson, H.R. Ellis. *Gods and Myths of Northern Europe.* Viking Press: New York, 1990.

Davies, John. *The Celts.* Cassell: London, 2000.

Gantz, Jeffrey (ed.). *The Mabinogion.* Penguin: Harmondsworth, 1976.

Green, Miranda J. *Celtic Myths.* British Museum Press: London, 1993.

Jones, Gwyn and Thomas Jones (eds.). *The Mabinogion.* Everyman Library: London, 1949.

Larrington, Carolyne (translator). *The Poetic Edda.* Oxford University Press: Oxford, 1997.

Lönnrot, Elias. *The Kalevala (World's Classics,* edited by Keith Bosley). Oxford University Press: Oxford, 1989.

MacCana, Proinsias. *Celtic Mythology.* Hamlyn: London, 1970.

Malory, Sir Thomas. *Le Morte d'Arthur* (edited by R.M. Lumiansky). Collier Books: New York, 1986.

Matthews, Caitlín. *Mabon and the Mysteries of Britain.* Arkana: London, 1987.

Spirin, Genaddy. *The Tale of the Firebird* (translated by Tatiana Popova). Philomel Books: New York, 2002.

Sturluson, Snorri. *Edda* (translated by Anthony Faulkes). Everyman Library: London, 1995.

Tennyson, Alfred. *Idylls of the King (Penguin Classics,* edited by J.M. Gray). Penguin USA: New York, 1989.

Tolkien, J.R.R. and E.V. Gordon (eds.). *Sir Gawain and the Green Knight.* Oxford University Press: Oxford, 1967.

de Troyes, Chrétien. *Arthurian Romances (Penguin Classics,* translated by Carleton W. Carroll). Penguin USA: New York, 1991.

Virtanen, Leea and Thomas Dubois. *Finnish Folklore.* University of Washington Press: Seattle, 2001.

Egyptian and African Mythology

Bartels, L. *Oromo Religions: Myths and Rites of the Western Oromo of Ethiopia—an Attempt to Understand.* Reiner: Berlin, 1983.

Courlander, Harold. *A Treasury of African Folklore.* Marlowe & Company: New York, 1996.

Hart, G. *Egyptian Myths.* British Museum Press: London, 1990.

Idowu, E.B. *Olodumare—God in Yoruba Belief.* Longmans: London, 1962.

Itayemi, P. and P. Gurrey. *Folk Tales and Fables (Africa* series). Penguin: Harmondsworth, 1953.

Kenyatta, Jomo. *Facing Mount Kenya: The Tribal Life of the Gikuyu.* Martin, Secker, & Warburg: London, 1938.

Knappert, Jan. *An Encyclopedia of Myth and Legend: African Mythology.* Diamond Books: London, 1995.

Lurker, M. *The Gods and Symbols of Ancient Egypt.* Thames & Hudson: London, 1980.

Mahfouz, Naguib. *Voices from the Other World: Ancient Egyptian Tales* (translated by Raymond Stock). American University: Cairo, 2003.

Omer-Cooper, John. *History of Southern Africa (Second Edition).* James Currey: London, 1994.

Parrinder, E.G. *African Mythology.* Paul Hamlyn: Feltham, 1968.

Parrinder, E.G. *West African Religions.* Epworth Press: London, 1949.

Pelton, R. *The Trickster in West Africa.* University of California Press: Berkeley, 1980.

Shaw, Ian (ed.). *The Oxford History of Ancient Egypt.* Oxford University Press: Oxford, 2002.

Spence, Lewis. *Ancient Egyptian Myths and Legends.* Dover Publications: New York, 1991.

Storm, Rachel. *Egyptian Mythology: Myths and Legends of Egypt, Persia, Asia Minor, Sumer and Babylon.* Lorenz Books: London, 2000.

Middle East and Asian Mythology

Aston, W.G. (translator). *Nihongi: Chronicles of Japan from the Earliest Times to A.D. 697.* Tuttle: Rutland and Tokyo, 1972.

Birrell, Anne. *Chinese Mythology: An Introduction.* John Hopkins University Press: Baltimore, 1993.

Black, Jeremy and Anthony Green. *Gods, Demons and Symbols of Ancient Mesopotamia: An Illustrated Dictionary.* University of Texas Press: Austin, 1992.

Blacker, Carmen. *The Catalpa Bow: A Study of Shamanistic Practices in Japan.* Allen & Unwin: London, 1975.

Ching, Julia. *Mysticism and Sacred Kingship in China: The Heart of Chinese Wisdom,* Cambridge University Press: Cambridge, 1997.

Christie, Anthony. *Chinese Mythology.* Paul Hamlyn: London, 1968.

513

Crawford, Harriet E.W. *Sumer and the Sumerians.* Cambridge University Press: Cambridge, 1991.

Curtis, Vesta Sarkhosh. *Persian Myths.* British Museum Press: London, 1993.

Dalley, Stephanie (translator). *Myths from Mesopotamia: Creation, the Flood, Gilgamesh, and Others.* Oxford University Press: Oxford, 1991.

Danielou, A. *Hindu Polytheism.* Routledge and K. Paul: London, 1964.

Dawood, N.J. (translator). *Aladdin and Other Tales from The Thousand and One Nights.* Penguin Books: Harmondsworth, 1957.

Dimmitt, C. and J.A.B. van Buitenen. *Classical Hindu Mythology: A Reader in the Sanskrit Puranas.* Temple University Press: Philadelphia, 1978.

George, Andrew (translator). *The Epic of Gilgamesh: The Babylonian Epic Poem and Other Texts in Akkadian and Sumerian.* Penguin USA: New York, 2000.

Girardot, N.J. *Myth and Meaning in Early Taoism.* University of California Press: Berkeley, 1983.

Kitagawa, J.M. *Religion in Japanese History.* Columbia University Press: New York, 1966.

Knappert, Jan. *Islamic Legends: Histories of the Heroes, Saints, and Prophets of Islam.* E.J. Brill: Leiden, 1985.

Norbu, Namkhai. *Drung, Deu and Bön: Narrations, Symbolic Languages and the Bön Tradition in Ancient Tibet.* Library of Tibetan Works and Archives: Dharamsala, 1995.

O'Flaherty, W. *Hindu Myths.* Penguin: Harmondsworth, 1975.

Rappoport, Angelo Solomon. *Myth and Legend of Ancient Israel.* Ktav: New York, 1966.

Samuel, Geoffrey, Hamish Gregor and Elisabeth Stutchbury (eds.). *Tantra and Popular Religion in Tibet.* International Academy of Indian Culture: New Delhi, 1994.

Thomsen, H. *The New Religions of Japan.* Tuttle: Rutland, 1963.

Mythology of Oceania

Beckwith, M. *Hawaiian Mythology.* Bishop Museum: Honolulu, 1940.

Berndt, Ronald and Catherine Berndt. *Man, Land and Myth in North Australia. The Gunwinggu People.* Ure Smith: Sydney, 1970.

Best, E. *The Astronomical Knowledge of the Maori.* Government Printer: Wellington, 1925.

Best, E. *Maori Religion and Mythology, Volumes 1 and 2.* Government Printer: Wellington, 1925.

Buck, P. *The Coming of the Maori.* Polynesian Society: Wellington, 1949.

Charlesworth, Max, Howard Morphy, Diane Bell, and Kenneth Maddock (eds.). *Religion in Aboriginal Australia: An Anthology.* University of Queensland Press: St. Lucia, 1984.

Davis, Stephen. *Man of all Seasons: An Aboriginal Perspective of the Natural Environment.* Angus & Robertson: Sydney, 1989.

Handy, E.S.C. *Polynesian Religion.* Bishop Museum: Honolulu, 1927.

Hemming, Steven and Philip Jones, with Philip Clarke. *Ngurunderi: An Aboriginal Dreaming.* South Australian Museum: Adelaide, 1989.

Hiatt, Lester (ed.). *Australian Aboriginal Mythology: Essays in Honour of W.E.H. Stanner.* Australian Institute of Aboriginal Studies: Canberra, 1975.

Holden, Robert. *Bunyips: Australia's Folklore of Fear.* National Library of Australia: Canberra, 2001.

Isaacs, Jennifer. *Australian Dreaming: 40,000 Years of Aboriginal History.* Lansdowne Press: Sydney, 1980.

Keen, Ian. *Knowledge and Secrecy in an Aboriginal Religion: Yolngu of North-east Arnhem Land.* Oxford University Press: Melbourne, 1994.

Mowaljarlai, David and Jutta Malnic. *Yorro Yorro, Aboriginal Creation and the Renewal of Nature: Rock Paintings and Stories from the Australian Kimberley.* Inner Traditions: Rochester, Vermont, 1993.

Orbell, M. *The Illustrated Encyclopedia of Maori Myth and Legend.* Canterbury University Press: Christchurch, 1995.

Smith, Heide. *Tiwi: The Life and Art of Australia's Tiwi People.* Angus & Robertson: Sydney, 1990.

Tregear E. *The Maori–Polynesian Comparative Dictionary.* Lyon and Blair: Wellington, 1891.

Tunbridge, Dorothy. *Flinders Ranges Dreaming.* Aboriginal Studies Press: Canberra, 1988.

Walker, R. *Ka Whawhai Tonu Matou: Struggle Without End.* Penguin: Auckland, 1990.

White, J. *Ancient History of the Maori, Vols. 1–6.* Government Printer: Wellington, 1887–1890.

Mythology of the Americas

Bierhorst, J. *The Mythology of North America.* William Morrow: New York, 1985.

Burrin, Kathleen (ed.). *The Spirit of Ancient Peru.* Thames & Hudson: New York, 1997.

Fagan, B. *Ancient North America.* Thames & Hudson: London and New York, 1995.

Hall, Jr., Edwin S. *The Eskimo Storyteller: Folktales from Noatak, Alaska.* The University of Tennessee Press: Knoxville, 1975.

Hardin, T. (ed.). *Legends and Lore of the American Indians.* Barnes and Noble Inc.: New York, 1993.

Hennigh, Lawrence. "Control of Incest in Eskimo Folktales." *Journal of American Folklore 79 (312):* pp356–369.

Jones, David M. and Brian L. Molyneaux. *The Mythology of the Americas.* Lorenz Books: London, 2001.

Josephy, Jr., Alvin M. *500 Nations: An Illustrated History of North American Indians.* Hutchinson/Pimlico: London, 1995

Koranda, Lorraine Donoghue. *Alaskan Eskimo Songs and Stories.* University of Washington Press: Seattle, 1972.

Laughton, Timothy. *The Maya: Life, Myth, and Art.* Duncan Baird Publishers: London, 1998.

Nicholson, Irene. *Mexican and Central American Mythology.* Paul Hamlyn: New York, 1967.

Norman, Howard (ed.). *Northern Tales: Traditional Stories of Eskimo and Indian Peoples.* Pantheon Books: New York, 1990.

Nungak, Zebedee and Eugene Arima. *Eskimo Stories from Povungnituk, Quebec.* The Queen's Printer: Ottawa, 1969.

Osborne, Harold. *South American Mythology.* Hamlyn: London, 1968.

Rasmussen, Knud. *The Alaskan Eskimos. Report of the Fifth Thule Expedition 1921–1924 10(3).* Gyldendalske Boghandel, Nordisk Forlag: Copenhagen, 1952.

Rasmussen, Knud. *Intellectual Culture of the Iglulik Eskimos. Report of the Fifth Thule Expedition 1921–1924, 7(1).* Gyldendalske Boghandel, Nordisk Forlag: Copenhagen, 1929.

Rasmussen, Knud. *The Netsilik Eskimos: Social Life and Spiritual Culture. Report of the Fifth Thule Expedition 1921–1924, 8(1-2).* Gyldendalske Boghandel, Nordisk Forlag: Copenhagen, 1931.

Rasmussen, Knud. *The People of the Polar North: A Record.* Kegan Paul, Trench, Trubner & Co. Ltd: London, 1908.

Rink, Hinrich. *Tales and Traditions of the Eskimo.* Dover Publications, Inc: Mineola, New York, 1997.

Roberts, Timothy R. *Gods of the Maya, Aztecs, and Incas.* Friedman/Fairfax Publishers: New York, 1996.

INDEX

Plain numbers indicate references in text. *Italicized* numbers indicate references in image captions or maps, while **bold** numbers indicate references in break-out boxes or family trees.

Picture Credits

The Publisher would like to thank the following picture libraries and other copyright owners for permission to reproduce their images. Every attempt has been made to obtain permission for use of all images from the copyright owners, however, if any errors or omissions have occurred Global Book Publishing would be pleased to hear from copyright owners.

Key: (t) top of page; (b) bottom of page; (l) left side of page; (r) right side of page; (c) center of page.

The Art Archive, London: 13(c), 68(t), 187(b), 230(t), 271, 274(t), 331(b), 384(b), 402(b), 417(t), 438(c), 452(b), 483(t), 509(b); Accademia Venice/Dagli Orti (A): 96; Album/Joseph Martin: 482(b); Antenna Gallery Dakar Senegal/Dagli Orti: 12(c), 310(b), 311; Antochiw Collection Mexico/Mireille Vautier: 478(b); Archaeological Museum Aleppo Syria/Dagli Orti: 325(t), 326; Archaeological Museum Baghdad/Dagli Orti: 322(b), 324(b); Archaeological Museum Delphi/Dagli Orti: 45(b), 48(l), 48(r), 174(t); Archaeological Museum Florence/Dagli Orti: 114(t); Archaeological Museum Lima/Dagli Orti: 495(c); Archaeological Museum Lima/Mireille Vautier: 501(c), 505(b); Archaeological Museum Mykonos/Dagli Orti: 181(b); Archaeological Museum Naples: 164(t), 242(b); Archaeological Museum Naples/Dagli Orti (A): 43(b), 49(t), 79(t), 91(t), 95(t), 169(tl), 173(t), 185(b), 189; Archaeological Museum Nauplia Nafplion/Dagli Orti: 177(t); Archaeological Museum Paestum/Dagli Orti: 18(t); Archaeological Museum Palermo/Dagli Orti: 111(t), 190(b); Archaeological Museum Piraeus/Dagli Orti: 42–43(t), 166; Archaeological Museum Sousse Tunisia/Dagli Orti: 94; Archaeological Museum Sparta/Dagli Orti: 169(b); Archaeological Museum Syracuse/Dagli Orti: 117(t), 132(b), 180(b); Archaeological Museum Thasos: 117(b); Archaeological Museum Tikal Guatemala/Dagli Orti: 490(t); Archaeological Museum Timgad Algeria/Dagli Orti: 33; Archaeological Museum Tipasa Algeria/Dagli Orti: 164(b); Archaeological Museum Venice/Dagli Orti (A): 57(t), 95(b); Ateneum Helsinki/Dagli Orti: 251; Bardo Museum Tunis/Dagli Orti: 192; Bargello Museum Florence/Dagli Orti: 75(b), 108(b); Basilique Saint Denis Paris/Dagli Orti: 168; Biblioteca Apostolica Vaticana: 193(t); Biblioteca Estense Modena/Dagli Orti: cover (inset picture 4), 264(t), 264(r), 299(b); Biblioteca

Estense Modena/Dagli Orti (A): 58(t), 124(t); Biblioteca Nacional Madrid/Dagli Orti: 11(c), 504; Biblioteca Nacional Mexico/Dagli Orti: 480(b); Biblioteca Nazionale Marciana Venice/Dagli Orti: 13(b), 265(b), 270(b); Biblioteca Nazionale Turin/Dagli Orti: 273(t), 280(b); Bibliothèque des Arts Décoratifs Paris/Dagli Orti: 80(t), 90(t), 126(t), 132–133(t), 172(t), 207(b), 287(t), 372–373; Bibliothèque des Arts Décoratifs Paris/Dagli Orti (A): 506(b); Bibliothèque Inguimbertine Carpentras/Dagli Orti: 98(t); Bibliothèque Municipale Dijon/Dagli Orti: cover (inset picture 6), 85(t); Bill Manns: 442, 454–455(t); Bodleian Library Oxford: 218, 268(t), 270(t), 337(b) [Ouseley Add 24 folio 127v]; Bodleian Library Oxford/The Bodleian Library: 10(c), 83(t) [Douce 135 folio 35v], 330(b) [Ouseley Add 176 folio 311v], 333 [Bodley Or 133 folio 33v], 338 [Pers b1 folio 15a], 349(t) [Douce OR.a1 folio 44r]; British Library: 210–211, 230(b), 265(t), 273(b), 280(t), 340(t), 341, 344, 345(t), 348; British Museum: 351, 356, 357(t); British Museum/Dagli Orti: 320(t), 327(b); British Museum/Eileen Tweedy: 228, 420–421, 481(b); British Museum/Jacqueline Hyde: 295; Cabinet des Estampes Strasbourg/Dagli Orti: 281; Cathedral Museum Ferrara/Dagli Orti (A): 201(t); Cathedral of Santiago de Compostela/Dagli Orti: 266(l); Cathedral Treasury Aachen/Dagli Orti: 266(b); Château d'Ancy-le-Franc/Dagli Orti: 44; Château de Blois/Dagli Orti: 60; Château de Chambord/Dagli Orti: 194(t), 197(b); Château de Dampierre/Dagli Orti: 196(b); Château de Gue-Pean/Dagli Orti: 171(b); Christie's/Eileen Tweedy: 324(t); City Archaeological Coll Milan: 120; Civiche Racc d'Arte Pavia, Italy: 197(t); Civiche Racc d'Arte Pavia, Italy/Dagli Orti: 16; Collection Antonovich/Dagli Orti: 285(b), 294(b); Conseil Général Saint Brieuc/Dagli Orti: 212(b); Cyprus Museum Nicosia/Dagli Orti: 32(b); Dagli Orti: cover (inset picture 1), 2–3, 221, 239(t), 245(t), 282–283, 284(b), 288, 291(t), 292(l), 296, 297(t), 322(t), 327(t), 392(b), 486, 491, 496, 503(b), 506(t), 507; Dagli Orti (A): 31(t), 45(b), 109, 135, 157, 186, 187(t), 191, 209(t), 300, 399(t), 510; Egyptian Museum Cairo/Dagli Orti: 10(b), 103, 291(b); Eileen Tweedy: 234(b); Ephesus Museum Turkey/Dagli Orti (A): 184(t); Fitzwilliam Museum Cambridge/Dagli Orti (A): 63(t); Freer Gallery of Art: 352(b); Galleria d'Arte Moderna Rome/Dagli Orti (A): 161(t); Galleria d'Arte Moderna Udine Italy/Dagli Orti (A): 11(t); Galleria Borghese Rome/Dagli

Orti (A): 47, 61(b), 68(b), 82, 198(b); Galleria Nazionale Parma/Dagli Orti (A): 177(b); Gustavium Garden Uppsala/Dagli Orti: 237(b); Harper Collins Publishers: 79(b); Heraklion Museum/Dagli Orti: 183(b); Hermitage Museum Saint Petersburg/Dagli Orti: 256(t); Historiska Muséet Stockholm/Dagli Orti: 237(t), 241(t), 245(b); Horniman Museum/Eileen Tweedy: 7; Jan Vinchon Numismatist Paris/Dagli Orti: 39(t); JFB: 266(t); La Rocca Sanvitale Fontanellato/Dagli Orti: 65; Lucien Biton Collection Paris/Dagli Orti: 4, 358(b), 367(b); Mesa Verde National Park Museum/Mireille Vautier: 425; Mexican National Library/Mireille Vautier: cover (inset picture 2), 484–485(b), 488(t); Mireille Vautier: 434; Moor Park Golf Club/Eileen Tweedy: 34, 36(b); Musée Alésia Alise Sainte Reine France/Dagli Orti: 214, 216(b), 229(t); Musée des Arts Africains et Océaniens/Dagli Orti: 308(r) 391(t); Musée des Arts Africains et Océaniens/Dagli Orti (A): 302, 387(t), 388(r), 390(b), 391(b), 395(t); Musée des Arts Décoratifs Paris/Dagli Orti (A): 195; Musée des Beaux Arts Orléans/Dagli Orti (A): 104; Musée des Beaux Arts Rouen/Dagli Orti: 127; Musée des Beaux Arts Tours/Dagli Orti: 278(t); Musée de la Civilisation Gallo-Romaine Lyons/Dagli Orti: 91(b); Musée Condé Chantilly/Dagli Orti: 215(t), 215(b), 267(b), 272, 276(t), 331(t); Musée Guimet Paris: 371; Musée Guimet Paris/Dagli Orti: 368(t); Musée du Louvre Paris: 119, 198–199(t); Musée du Louvre Paris/Dagli Orti: cover (main picture), 14–15, 17, 27(b), 29(t), 39(b), 49(b), 51(b), 55(t), 61(t), 64(t), 66(t), 72(t), 84(b), 87(t), 88, 100, 107(b), 112, 114(b), 123(t), 126(b), 134(b), 139(r), 144(t), 149(t), 163(b), 169(r), 174(b), 188(t), 203(b), 286(b), 287(b), 289(t), 290, 293(t), 297(b), 320(b), 323(t), 325(b), 328, 332(t); Musée de la Marine Paris/Dagli Orti: 381; Musée du Nouveau Monde La Rochelle/Dagli Orti: 500(b), 512(b); Musée Thomas Dobrée Nantes/Dagli Orti: 62; Museo de Arte Colonial de Santa Catalina Cuzco/Dagli Orti: 492(b); Museo Banco Central de Quito Ecuador/Dagli Orti: 492(t); Museo Capitolino Rome/Dagli Orti (A): 203(t), 204(b); Museo di Capodimonte, Naples/Dagli Orti (A): 196(t); Museo di Castelvecchio Verona/Dagli Orti (A): 90(b); Museo Catedrálicio Zamora Spain/Dagli Orti: 167; Museo Ciudad Mexico/Dagli Orti (A): 475(t), 487(t); Museo Civico Alessandria, Italy/Dagli Orti (A): 51(t); Museo Civico Padua/Dagli Orti: 138–139(c); Museo Civico Treviso/Dagli Orti: 269; Museo della Civilta Romana Rome/Dagli Orti: 199(b); Museo Correr Venice: 55(b); Museo del Duomo Friuli/Dagli Orti: 240;

Museo Larco Herrera Lima/Album/J. Enrique Molina: 494(b); Museo Nazionale d'Arte Orientale Rome/Dagli Orti: 370(b); Museo Nazionale Reggio Calabria/Dagli Orti: 41(b), 176(b), 205(bl), 205(br); Museo Nazionale Taranto/Dagli Orti: 20, 26–27(t), 46(b), 102(t), 158, 179(b); Museo Nazionale Terme Rome/Dagli Orti: 150(t); Museo dell'Opera del Duomo Florence/Dagli Orti: 102(b); Museo del Oro Bogota: 509(t); Museo del Oro Bogota/Dagli Orti: 508; Museo del Oro Lima/Dagli Orti: 497(t), 511(b); Museo Pedro de Osma Lima/Mireille Vautier: 500(t), 502(t), 505(t); Museo del Prado Madrid: 134(t), 144(b); Museo del Prado Madrid/Album/Joseph Martin: 84(t); Museo del Prado Madrid/Dagli Orti (A): 8–9, 35(b), 113; Museo Regional de Oaxaca Mexico/Dagli Orti: 490(b); Museo del Templo Mayor Mexico/Dagli Orti: 488(c); Museo di Villa Giulia Rome/Dagli Orti: 111(b); Museum of Anatolian Civilisations Ankara/Dagli Orti: 332(b); Museum of Carthage/Dagli Orti: 69; Muzeul de Constantza Romania/Dagli Orti: 121(t); National Anthropological Museum Mexico/Dagli Orti: 1, 474, 475(b), 479(c), 480–481(t), 483(b), 484(t), 485(c), 487(c), 489; National Archaeological Museum Athens/Dagli Orti: 21(c), 30(t), 137, 156(b), 185(t), 193(b), 209(b); National Army Museum London: 315(t); National Bank of Mexico/Dagli Orti (A): 334; National Gallery Budapest/Dagli Orti (A): 212(t); National Gallery London/Eileen Tweedy: 38, 56, 58(b), 93, 201(b); National Museum Bucharest/Dagli Orti: 258(b), 262(b); National Museum of Prague/Dagli Orti: 219(b), 258(t); National Palace Museum Taiwan: 353; Nationalmuseet Copenhagen Denmark/Dagli Orti: 216(t); Neuschwanstein Castle Germany/Dagli Orti: 279; Nicolas Sapieha: 476, 482(t); Oriental Art Museum Genoa/Dagli Orti (A): 359, 362(t), 366(t); Palazzo Arco Mantua Italy: 115, 122; Palazzo Barberini Rome/Dagli Orti (A): 172(b), 205(t); Palazzo Pitti Florence/Dagli Orti (A): 23; Palazzo Reale Madrid/Dagli Orti: 40; Palazzo Reale Milan/Dagli Orti: 194(b); Palazzo del Te Mantua/Dagli Orti (A): 24; Palazzo Vecchio Florence: 156(t); Prehistoric Museum Møesgard Hojbjerg Denmark/Dagli Orti: 242(t); Private Collection/Dagli Orti: 285(t), 292(r), 337(t); Private Collection/Dagli Orti (A): 298(b); Private Collection Paris/Dagli Orti: 12–13(t), 250(l), 347(t), 367(t), 369, 472(t); Ragab Papyrus Institute Cairo/Dagli Orti: 5; Richard Wagner Museum Bayreuth/Dagli Orti: 232; Salamanca University/Dagli Orti (A): 28; San Clemente Basilica Rome/Dagli Orti: 257; San Zeno Maggiore Verona, Italy/Dagli Orti (A): 25(t), 335(b); Sibelius Museum Turku Finland/Dagli Orti (A): 253(b);